The American Indian

Also by Roger L. Nichols

General Henry Atkinson: A Western Military Career (Norman, 1965)

(ed.) *The Missouri Expedition, 1818–1820: The Journal of Surgeon John Gale* (Norman, 1969)

(ed. with George R. Adams) *The American Indian: Past and Present* (Waltham, Mass., 1971)

(with Leonard Dinnerstein and David M. Reimers) *Natives and Strangers: Ethnic Groups and the Building of America* (New York, 1979)

(with Patrick L. Halley) *Stephen Long and American Frontier Exploration* (Newark, Del., 1980)

(ed.) *Arizona Directory of Historians and Historical Organizations* (Tucson, 1985)

(ed.) *American Frontier and Western Issues: A Historiographical Review* (Westport, Conn., 1986)

Black Hawk and the Warrior's Path (Arlington Heights, Ill., 1992)

Indians in the United States and Canada: A Comparative History (Lincoln, Neb., 1998)

(ed.) *Black Hawk's Autobiography* (Ames, Iowa, 1999)

American Indians in U.S. History (Norman, 2003)

The American Indian

Past and Present

Sixth Edition

EDITED BY ROGER L. NICHOLS

University of Oklahoma Press : Norman

Library of Congress Cataloging-in-Publication Data

The American Indian : past and present / edited by Roger L. Nichols.—6th ed.
    p. cm.
ISBN 978-0-8061-3856-5 (pbk. : alk. paper)
1. Indians of North America.
I. Nichols, Roger L.
E77.2.A47 2008
970.004′97—dc22

2007043867

The paper in this book meets the guidelines for permanence
and durability of the Committee on Production Guidelines for
Book Longevity of the Council on Library Resources, Inc. ∞

1 2 3 4 5 6 7 8 9 10

To Marilyn Nichols
Thanks for every day!

Contents

Maps

Acknowledgments

Many people helped with the planning and preparation of this new edition, and they all deserve thanks. Ten unnamed scholars at other colleges and universities read one or another version of the proposal and offered suggestions concerning the focus, organization, and contents of the book.

Professors Katherine Osburn and John Wunder provided specific suggestions. Marcus Burtner and Katrina Jagodinsky, students in a recent graduate course of mine, also made valuable recommendations.

This was my first experience producing an electronic version of the anthology in preparation for publication, and it proved substantially more difficult than the "photocopy and submit" method of the earlier editions. Young-Gie Min, Senior Support Systems Analyst at the University of Arizona Social and Behavioral Sciences Research Institute, helped to "tame" the scanner for me. Lucas Guthrie, Support Systems Analyst for the History Department, spent nearly as much time on the project as I did. Without the help these two able men provided, this edition would never have been completed.

Thanks are also due to Alessandra Jacobi Tamulevich, acquisitions editor for American Indian and Latin American studies, Jay Dew, associate editor, and the editorial, production, and promotion staff at the University of Oklahoma Press.

Introduction

As a minority group within this society, American Indians have always attracted more attention than their numbers might seem to deserve. The U.S. Census Bureau's 2000 figures show the American Indian and Alaska Native population at 2,475,965, or 0.9 percent of the total counted that year, a modest sized group. If one chooses to add those individuals who combined some other ancestry with American Indian and Alaska Native categories, that figure increases to 4,119,301, or 1.5 percent of the 281 million people counted by the census takers. Whichever of these two figures one uses, the total is but a tiny sliver of our society. An obvious question, then, emerges: "Why has this small group received far more attention than its size might warrant when compared to most other larger ethnic, racial, or immigrant groups?"

The answers to that question are complex, and it is not my purpose to offer any lengthy discussion of them here. Nevertheless, Indians differ from others in our society because their ancestors lived in America for millennia. Unlike immigrants, Indians experienced invasion, warfare, disease, and the loss of their lands and resources. In addition, by choosing to remain outside the general society in order to retain their various cultures and identities, they often set themselves apart from others. This frustrated and angered both officials and social reformers, leading to a continuing set of laws and other demands that tribal groups change almost everything about their lives to become "real" Americans. From the sixteenth century to the present, some tribal people have resisted, struggling to retain their specific cultures, and, to some extent, to remain at least partly outside the mainstream national society.

The story of their experiences during the past four hundred and fifty years continues to fascinate others. The survival of at least 570 federally recognized tribes and another forty-five groups that have achieved recognition by individual states suggests a determination and staying power never anticipated by anyone. Their presence on and off reservations across the country provides the impetus for the many college and university courses in American Indian history or Native American studies. These readings are designed for instructors and students in such classes. They include essays that cover the entire chronology of American history, providing examples of central issues faced by the tribes and the rest of society, and illustrating how these issues played out in each region of the country. It quickly becomes clear that the experiences of tribal groups changed repeatedly and that variety is the most accurate way to label their individual histories.

During the first decade of the twenty-first century, long-standing difficulties continue to receive analysis while new issues also emerge. Disputes within and among Indian groups remain. For example, tribal members who live in the cities often tend to see issues differently from those who remain on reservations. Some tribes are not enthusiastic about accepting other newly acknowledged groups as truly "Indian." These differences are only a part of the disputes that divide tribal societies, to say nothing about Indians' problems with the majority population and the various governmental agencies they encounter frequently.

As the face of Indian country has changed over the generations, scholarship on American Indian related questions has shifted as well. Governmental, policy, and legal issues related to tribal affairs remain, but the focus continues to re-adjust. Rarely today do scholars employ ideas that present Indians as victims of history. Indeed, much of the current scholarship tries to look at issues from a tribal perspective within various social science frameworks. While race and gender continue to serve as useful analytical tools, studies of imperialism, colonialism, and racism all have brought changes to the field. In addition to their continued focusing on long-standing issues, increasingly scholars have turned their attention to twentieth-century events and questions. They have focused on topics such as urbanization, increasing political participation, labor, health, and education, all within a framework of tribal self-determination and striving for local sovereignty. Many of these issues received some thought in the past, but now they stand in the forefront of scholarship on Indians.

While not ignoring subjects of continuing interest such as government relations, military actions, and some biographical focus, this edition seeks to make students aware of the new varieties of literature concerning Indians in American society. The essays included here trace the ever-changing situations of Indians as tribes and as individuals. Beginning with the subject of early contacts with invading Europeans, the readings bring the reader through Native experiences of military defeat, relocations to reservations, programs of mandatory acculturation, and militant national protests to the present when at times it is difficult to tell just who is an Indian.

Those seeking Indian wars or famous massacres will have to stretch their historical understanding of past ideas and events. The older "boots and saddles" approach gets only modest attention these days. Certainly such things happened, but usually they proved to be the symptoms of failure and not central to national policy or tribal desires. As such they offer few clues to help understand past ideas or events. These readings bring together essays written over the last thirty years, most published in the last decade. They represent some of the best new scholarship. The organizational format is offered with the hope that it will provide a modest framework, but not one that ties the chapters so tightly together that they cannot be fit into other valid patterns that instructors use.

In choosing the essays for this anthology, every effort was made to find items by competent scholars. Numerous other items could have been included, but those chosen represent a broad cross section of topics and authors. Each article appears in full with no deletions from the authors' original texts, except for the omission of scholarly notes. Each of the six sections offer a brief discussion to introduce the themes represented by the essays. A brief headnote then introduces each reading. Suggestions for further reading and a few study questions provide help for students interested in learning still more.

Important Events in Native American History

1535	Jacques Cartier lands in St. Lawrence Valley
1539–43	De Soto invades the southeastern United States
1540–42	Coronado invades New Mexico and the Southwest
1565	St. Augustine, Florida founded by Spain
1584–90	English Roanoke Island, North Carolina colony fails
1598	Oñate brings settlers into New Mexico
1607	English found Jamestown, Virginia settlement
1608	French found Quebec settlement
	French and Hurons begin Iroquois Wars
1609–14	First Anglo-Powhatan War in Virginia
1616–19	Epidemics sweep through coastal tribes of New England
1620	Pilgrims found Plymouth Colony
1621	Massasoit and Pilgrims sign a long-lasting treaty
1622	Opechancanough leads major Indian attack on Virginia
1637	English launch the Pequot War in New England
1642–43	Dutch defeat Hudson River Valley Tribes in New Amsterdam
1644–46	Opechancanough defeated and killed in last Powhatan resistance
1649	Iroquois begin destruction of Hurons
1661	Franciscans raid Pueblo kivas to destroy Indian religious items
1675–76	Metacom's (King Philip's) War in New England
	Bacon's Rebellion and war with Virginia tribes
1680	Pueblo Revolt drives Spanish from Southwest
1691	Spanish reconquer New Mexico
1701	Iroquois Confederacy makes peace with France and Great Britain
1703–1704	Slave raids against Apalachees in northern Florida
1711–13	Tuscarora War in Carolina
1712–50	Mesquakie Wars with French
1715–16	Yamassee War in Carolina
1722	Abenaki War in Maine
	Tuscaroras join Iroquois Confederacy in New York
1729–31	French destroy Natchez Tribe in Mississippi
1751	Pima Revolt drives Spain out of Arizona
1763	Royal Proclamation Line tries to separate tribes and pioneers
	Pontiac leads a multitribal rebellion against the British
1769	Spanish begin settlement of California

1871	Congress ends the treaty system
1872–73	Modoc War in Oregon
1874	Red River War in Texas
1875–77	Great Sioux War; Custer defeated in 1876
1877	Nez Perce War
1878	Funds appropriated for Indian police forces on the reservations
1879	National Indian Association founded
	Richard Pratt founds Carlisle Indian School
1881	Sun Dance outlawed, tribal medicine men arrested
1882	Indian Rights Association founded
1883	Lake Mohonk Conferences begin
	Courts of Indian Offenses established
1884	Beginning of modern peyotism rites
1885	Helen Hunt Jackson publishes *A Century of Dishonor*
1886	Geronimo's surrender ends the Apache Wars
1887	Dawes Severalty Act (General Allotment Act) passed
1889	Wovoka spreads his Ghost Dance teachings
1890	Massacre of Sioux at Wounded Knee, South Dakota
1896	Office of Indian Affairs orders adult males to have hair cut
1903	*Lone Wolf v. Hitchcock* decision
1907	Burke Act amends the Dawes Act
1911	Society of American Indians founded
1917–18	Eight thousand Indians serve in World War I
1918	Native American Church incorporated in Oklahoma
1923	Committee of One Hundred investigation of Indian affairs
1924	American Indian Citizenship Act
1926	National Council of American Indians founded
1928	Meriam Report published
1934	Indian Reorganization Act passed
1935	Indian Arts and Crafts Board established
1941–45	Twenty-five thousand Indians serve in World War II
1944	National Congress of American Indians founded
1946	Indian Claims Commission established
1952	Public Law 280
1953	House Concurrent Resolution 108
	Congress revises liquor regulations for Indians
1957	Reservation industries program begins
1961	American Indian Chicago Conference demands self-determination
	National Indian Youth Council founded
1964	Institute of American Indian Arts founded at Santa Fe
1966	Navajo found Rough Rock Demonstration School
1968	Congress passes the Indian Bill of Rights
	American Indian Movement (AIM) founded

1969	N. Scott Momaday (Kiowa) wins Pulitzer Prize for *House Made of Dawn*
	Indians occupy Alcatraz Island
1970	Taos Pueblo regains Blue Lake
1971	Alaska Native Claims Settlement Act
1972	Trail of Broken Treaties and occupation of BIA office in Washington, D.C.
1973	Sixty-seven day confrontation at Wounded Knee
1974	*United States v. State of Washington*—Boldt decision
1975	Indian Self-Determination and Educational Assistance Act
1978	American Indian Religious Freedom Act
	Tribally Controlled Community College Act
	Federal Tribal Acknowledgement Program established
1980	Penobscot/Passamaquoddy claims settled
1988	Indian Gaming Regulatory Act
1990	Native American Grave Protection and Repatriation Act
	Employment Division v. Smith decision
1991	Custer Battlefield National Monument renamed Little Bighorn Battlefield National Monument
1992	Mashantucket Pequots begin work on Foxwoods Casino in Connecticut
1994	George Gustav Heye Center of the National Museum of the American Indian opened in New York City
1996	Kennewick Man discovered
	Winona LaDuke Green Party vice presidential candidate
1998	Thirty-one tribal colleges in operation
2000	U.S. Census lists 4,119,301 Indian people
	Winona LaDuke's second Green Party vice presidential candidacy
2004	National Museum of the American Indian opened
2006	274 Indian casinos in twenty-eight states
	Over 580 tribes recognized by U.S.
	Forty-five tribes recognized by particular states

The American Indian

PART ONE

Invasions and Colonialism

Europeans viewed their early sixteenth-century landings on the shores of North America as discoveries, but in some sense they brought discoveries with them as well. Precontact America certainly had its share of competition, trade, diplomatic wrangling, and even slavery and warfare. Yet the arrival of the newcomers introduced new ideas and practices, and before long the presence of the invaders had changed the aboriginal world forever. In doing so the actions and presence of the newcomers had both positive and negative results. For example, highly intolerant priests and other clergy forced their versions of Christianity on tribal peoples who already had ancient and solid religions of their own. The essay on Spanish missions and the Pueblo Revolt analyzes one result. Microbes from Europe introduced new diseases and produced devastating epidemics that swept through the native populations. Alcohol and firearms also took their toll. In addition, the European eagerness to possess the land, harvest its resources, and dominate tribal peoples led to much higher levels of violence and destruction than archaeologists have located for the precontact era.

Despite the devastation invading Europeans brought with them, occasionally their actions proved somewhat positive. Traders' goods, often not much different but usually more specialized than similar items the Indians produced themselves, made life for tribal dwellers more comfortable than it had been. When it suited their needs, colonial leaders sought to prevent intertribal warfare or at least turn it to their own benefit. In their eyes the newcomers viewed their efforts to bring Indians into the developing international colonial systems as positive steps in a movement toward civilization.

At the same time, Native people perceived the Europeans in a variety of ways. As dangerous adversaries, armor-clad soldiers bearing firearms and often on horseback represented both a military and cultural threat to tribal societies. Not all attacks on the Native people were military. Virginia DeJohn Anderson illustrates how the European introduction of domestic livestock disrupted the local Indian hunting, gathering, and farming practices. Yet many villagers began keeping domestic animals to fill the gaps in their diets when wild animals disappeared. Meanwhile the invaders brought manufactured goods including firearms, metal tools, and textiles to trade, and these items could make Native life more comfortable that it had been. The essays in this section illustrate how tribal people and Europeans dealt with each other during an era of immense stress and change.

CHAPTER ONE

How Indians Got Red

Nancy Shoemaker

Recently a group of Pakistani students reminded me of something that most Americans either never knew or have forgotten. That is, people in many parts of the world still call the members of North American Native groups Red Indians. Today this is to differentiate them from the citizens of India, but that was not always the case. Looking at the development of early modern ideas about race in this essay, Nancy Shoemaker traces early uses of *red* as a descriptive label by colonists and Indians alike. For at least the first century of contact, early Europeans commented that Eastern tribal people looked "tawny" or brown. While noting that occasionally they painted their faces or parts of their bodies red, commentators rarely used color in referring to the tribal groups. Despite this, by the 1720s some Indians had begun identifying themselves as red men or red people. The narrative traces how both colonists and Native people gradually began to use red and white as a way to characterize the two societies. It examines Indian ideas about colors as symbols for peace and war and as a means to differentiate between themselves and the newcomers. It also traces the Europeans' increasing use of red and white to distinguish Native people from themselves.

Scholars working on the history of race as an idea assume that Europeans were the sole inventors of it. Undeniably, race (the belief that people can be categorized by observable physical differences such as skin color) flourished with the early modern European slave trade. Sometime in the eighteenth century, race outpaced the older categories of Christian and pagan to become the primary justification for expropriating the land and labor of others. As a system of categorizing people, race fulfilled Europe's ideological needs by creating the illusion that human difference was biologically ordained. But, as Europeans spun their web of racial hierarchies, what were non-Europeans thinking about race? His-

"How Indians Got Red" appeared in *The American Historical Review* 102, no. 3 (June 1997): 624–44.

torians have yet to tackle this question in depth, instead focusing on how whites constructed images of others. This approach to the historical emergence of race as a system for categorizing people replicates what it purports to critique, since the emphasis on European image-making consigns American Indians and other non-white peoples to a passive role in the construction of knowledge. They exist only as the objects of white observation, and the power to label or name resides with Europeans.

One example of this tendency is the standard explanation for how Indians got to be "red": European explorers saw that Indians wore red paint and so called them "red." In "From White Man to Redskin: Changing Anglo-American Perceptions of the American Indian," Alden Vaughan moved toward correcting this misconception when he instead credited the Swedish naturalist Carolus Linnaeus with making "red" a racial category in his 1740 edition of *Systema Naturae*. How Linnaeus arrived at "red" remains a small mystery. He may have heard of red-painted Indians, but the Greek physician Galen's medical philosophy of the four humors must also have served as inspiration, for in the 1758 edition of *Systema Naturae*, Linnaeus attached telltale descriptive labels to each color of people: red people were choleric, white sanguine, yellow melancholic, and black phlegmatic. Thus Linnaeus adapted an existing system of color-based categories to account for differences between the world's peoples.

However, giving Linnaeus sole credit perpetuates another misconception. Linnaeus chose "red" as a category for Indians, but he was not the first person to do so. More than a decade before the 1740 edition of *Systema Naturae*, American Indians, particularly Indians in the Southeast, were calling themselves "red." This article discusses when, how, and why southeastern Indians introduced the term "red people," or "red men," into the language of Indian-European contact. It then explores what "red" meant to one southeastern Indian group, the Cherokees, in their initial encounters with English colonists and in their later encounters with Americans. While Linnaeus groped toward an explanation of difference embedded in the human body, eighteenth-century southeastern Indians, in dialogue with Europeans, drew on their own color symbolism to develop categories that could account for biological, cultural, and political differences.

By the mid-1720s, from Louisiana to South Carolina, Indians were claiming the category "red" for themselves in the arena of Indian-European diplomacy. In 1725, the French asked a group of Indians in council at Mobile whether they would like to become Christian and recorded a Taensas chief's response:

> Long ago . . . there were three men in a cave, one white, one red and one black. The white man went out first and he took the good road that led him into a fine hunting ground. . . . The red man who is the Indian, for they call themselves in their language "Red Men," went out of the cave second. He went astray from the good road and took another which led him into a country where the hunting was less abundant. The black man, who is the negro, having been the third to go out, got entirely lost in a very bad country in which he did not find

anything on which to live. Since that time the red man and the black man have been looking for the white man to restore them to the good road.

This Taensas chief divided humankind into three color-based categories. Moreover, his French audience understood "Red Men" to be an Indian contribution to the lexicon of French settlement in North America.

While this story was being told to the French near the Mississippi River, Indians further to the east were introducing the term "red people" into English-Indian diplomacy. In George Chicken's journal of a 1725 delegation to the Cherokees, several Chickasaws arrived at the council and said they wanted "peace with the White people and desire[d] to have their own way and to take revenge of the red people," by which they meant the Creek Indians. Throughout the journal, Chicken himself called Indians simply "Indians." A year later, the English in South Carolina negotiated a peace between the Creeks and Cherokees. Adhering to diplomatic custom, a Creek headman, Chigilee, offered a "large white Eagle's Wing" to the Cherokees and said he wanted peace with them. The Cherokee speaker responded, "I See Your white Wing there, but Shall not receive it till I find you'l be good to the white People, nor will I till you talke further; It is now come to this. We are the Red People now mett together. Our flesh is both alike, but we must have further Talke with you." Later in the council, the Creek-allied Cowetaw Warrior called the Cherokees "those Red People," and another Indian speaker remarked that "the greate men of the white & Red people are now friends, and it Shall never be my fault if this peace is broke." In the council transcript, the phrase "red people" appears only within the speeches of Indian delegates.

"Red" Indians quickly became standard usage in southeastern Indian diplomacy. By the 1730s, the French in Louisiana had incorporated "red men" into the language of French-Indian diplomacy and had adopted the term as a generic label for Indians in their own correspondence. And by the 1750s, the English in the Southeast addressed Indians as "red people," although the English used the term less often than Indian speakers and usually only in response to an Indian speech.

In every instance, "red men" and "red people" were forms of address unaccompanied by European descriptions of Indians. Antoine Simon Le Page du Pratt, a French farmer in Louisiana who later wrote a book about his experiences, called Indians "Hommes Rouges" but believed that they were born white and then "turn[ed] brown, as they are rubbed with bear's oil and exposed to the sun." Other Europeans also commented on how Indians looked and what color they were, either with paint or without paint, but rarely was that color red. Eighteenth-century accounts of Indians tended to follow the pattern set by the earliest European explorers of the Southeast, the Spanish, and described Indians as "brown of skin" but "painted and ochred, red, black, white, yellow and vermilion in stripes." The skin color Europeans most commonly attributed to Indians was "tawny." Thus ethnographic descriptions of Indians mentioned a multitude of colors; only in the language of eighteenth-century French-Indian and English-Indian diplomacy were Indians "red people."

There are two likely scenarios for why Indians began to identify themselves as "red." First, "red" may have been an Indian response to meeting strange new people who called themselves "white" to distinguish themselves from their "black" or "Negro" slaves. Second, some Indians may have considered themselves "red" or been called so by other Indians before the arrival of Europeans. Actually, these are not mutually exclusive scenarios but instead work in combination. In a variety of situations, "red" was a logical category for Indians to claim for themselves, and then, just as the Columbus misnomer "Indian" spread to people at great distances from Columbus, the Caribbean, and 1492, the process of Indian-European contact gradually made "red" a generic label for all Indians.

The first scenario suggests that a kind of dialectic took place: Europeans called themselves "white," and Indians responded with "red." The best evidence for this scenario is the rarity of "red" Indians in the Northeast in contrast to comparable records for the Southeast. Origin stories like the one the Taensas chief told the French must have circulated to some extent among northeastern Indians, for a baptized Delaware Indian in the Ohio area told a Jesuit in 1757 that the Trinity had created "men, as we find them upon earth, as red, black and white, and that they had destined one for praying, another for hunting, and another for war." Other rare uses of "Red Men" in the Northeast can be linked to Linnaeus. Pehr Kalm, a Swedish naturalist and Linnaeus protégé, mentioned "Red Men" several times in the journal of his trip from Delaware to Canada (1748–51). (Kalm's visits with Benjamin Franklin may have inspired Franklin's "Observations Concerning the Increase of Mankind" [1851], which "listed Indians among the world's "tawny" peoples but then ambiguously proposed "excluding all Blacks and Tawneys" from America so that "the lovely White and Red" could prevail.) Despite an occasional "red" in the historical record of the Northeast, when in council with the English, northeastern Indians did not call themselves "red" and were not called "red" by others. What had by mid-century become commonplace in the language of southeastern Indian diplomacy was still a novelty in the Northeast.

Indian languages provide further evidence that the idea of "red" Indians was indigenous to the Southeast. From the St. Lawrence to the Upper Mississippi, the word "Indian," when interpreted into native languages, usually came to be equated with the native word for "people," sometimes translated as "men," "real people," or "original people." The contemporary French historian Bacqueville de la Potherie observed this pattern in the Great Lakes region when he wrote of an Indian telling the fur trader Perrot "that when 'the men' arrived they would render him thanks; it is thus that all savages are designated among themselves, while they call the French, 'French,' and the [other] people from Europe by the names of their respective nations."

In contrast, in southeastern Indian languages, the word or phrase meaning "Indian" originates in the word for the color "red." A nineteenth-century glossary of Natchez words collected by anthropologist Daniel Brinton translates "Indian, red man" into *tvmh-pakup* (man-red). In Choctaw and Chickasaw, closely related Muskogean languages, the word for Indian is *hatak api homma,* a combination of *hatak* (man) and *homma* (red). And in R. M. Loughridge's dictionary of Muskogee (Creek), "Indian" is given as *este-cate,* man-red. Because Indian speeches made their way into the historical record only after being translated into a European language, it is difficult to know exactly what was said at these councils. There must have been instances when an Indian speaker said *hatak api homma* and the interpreter said in English "Indian." But when Englishmen said "Indian" and Frenchmen said *sauvage,* when and why did interpreters turn to the Choctaws or Chickasaws and say *hatak api homma*? At some point in the dialogue between Indians and Europeans, "Indians" came to mean "red men" or "red people" in the native languages of southeastern Indians.

The southeastern origins of "red" Indians is good evidence for the first scenario—that Indians called themselves "red" in response to meeting people who called themselves "white"—because Europeans settling the Southeast did indeed have a "white" identity. In the early 1700s, Carolina colonists, many of whom had emigrated from Barbados, already divided their world into "white, black, & Indians." The first English colony to develop a plantation economy dependent on slave labor, Barbados may also have been the first English colony to experience the transition in identity from "Christian" to "white." One mid-seventeenth-century visitor to Barbados, who wrote of "Negroes," "Indians" and "Christians," told an anecdote that may explain why "white" replaced "Christian." A slave wished to become Christian, but the slave's master responded that "we could not make a Christian a Slave . . . [nor] a Slave a Christian . . . [for] being once a Christian, he could no more account him a Slave, and so lose the hold they had of them as Slaves, by making them Christians." By the end of the seventeenth century, Barbadians who were neither black nor Indian were well on their way to becoming "white." When they left Barbados for Carolina, they brought "Negroe slaves" and an emerging "white" identity with them.

"Christians" in the Northeast lagged several decades behind their southern counterparts in self-identifying as "white." The Dutch in New Netherland called themselves "Christian" for the duration of their control over the colony, and the English continued with "Christian" until about the 1730s, when the term "white people" began to appear with more frequency. As in Barbados, black slavery seems to have caused the transition from "Christian" to "white." In the 1740s, Sir William Johnson, British superintendent of Indian Affairs in the Northeast, wrote most often about relations between "Christians and Indians." But when Johnson solicited an acquaintance to buy him some "Negroes," for Johnson did own black slaves, he also asked for an indentured servant, "a good Cliver lad of a white man."

When English settlers in Carolina first met Indians, they called themselves "white people," a term that could be literally translated into native languages. A different naming process must have occurred in the Northeast because "Christian" cannot be translated into native languages. Instead, the names Indians invented for Europeans predominated. The Iroquois, for example, called Europeans "hatchetmakers." In English translations of Indian speeches, Indian speakers seem to be using "Christian" in the seventeenth century and "white people" by the mid-eighteenth century, but probably it was the interpreters who changed, first interpreting the Iroquois word for "hatchetmakers" into "Christians" and later into "white people."

The Southeast also makes sense for the second component of the dialectic—why Indians responded with "red" instead of yellow, brown, or even tawny. Red and white symbols, articulating a dualism between war and peace, permeated southeastern Indian cultures. White was "their fixt emblem of peace, friendship, happiness, prosperity, purity, holiness, &C." The "white path" meant peaceful relations between towns or nations. The "red" or "bloody" path meant war. War chiefs "painted blood-red" and civil chiefs "painted milk white" shared political authority within towns, and towns themselves were designated "white" or "red" as a means to delegate intratribal responsibilities in times of peace and war. "Red" and "white" were, therefore, metaphors for moieties, or complementary divisions, within southeastern Indian societies. Although northern tribes such as the Iroquois understood red and white symbols to stand for war and peace, the juxtaposition of "red" and "white" rarely figured in the discourse and ritual of Iroquois diplomacy. For southeastern Indians, "red" would have been the logical rejoinder to "white." Indeed, at the 1725–26 councils with the English, mentioned earlier, Indians who spoke of bringing "red people" and "white people" together may have meant people who advocated war and people who advocated peace. The English did appear as peacemakers at these councils, and the Indians may have thought that was why they were calling themselves "white people." The English, meanwhile, probably understood the Indian phrase "red people" to be only a reference to complexion.

This first scenario for how Indians got to be "red" fits the English Southeast but less neatly explains why "red men" made its way into French-Indian diplomacy. The language evidence is the same. In the Mobilian trade jargon, the "vulgar tongue" in which the French and Indians communicated, the words for Indian, European, and African were rooted in words for the colors red, white, and black. And the French in Louisiana had "Negre" slaves and a "blanc" identity. Andre Penicaut, a member of Pierre Le Moyne d'Iberville's 1698 expedition to the Lower Mississippi, explained the Indians' curiosity about the French as caused by their being "astonished at seeing white-skinned people." Later, when offered "as many women as there were men in our party," Iberville held out his hand to the Indians and "made them understand that their skin—red and tanned—should not come close to that of the French, which was white." This is, incidentally, one of the few references to Indians having red skin; elsewhere in his account, Penicaut described Indians as having "very tawny skin."

In contrast to the English in Carolina, however, the French did not so persistently refer to themselves as "white people" but self-identified more often by nationality: "les Français." The transcripts of Indian-European councils reveal another difference. When in conversation with the English, Indians usually paired "red people" with "white people" as though they were thinking of complementary moieties. In the French records, "red men" appears alone, suggesting that "red" emerged independently from French claims to the category white."

The second scenario for the origins of "red" fits French-Indian relations better. Early in their explorations of the Mississippi, the French encountered several Indian groups who already had "red" identities. "Red men," once introduced into diplomatic discourse by one Indian tribe, might have spread geographically and become part of the language of people unfamiliar with its origin. The French planter Le Page du Pratz implied that this was the case. Although he sometimes called the Natchez "Hommes Rouges," he also wrote, "When the Natchez retired to this part of America, where I saw them, they there found several nations, or rather the remains of several nations, some on the east, others on the west of the Mississippi. These are the people who are distinguished among the natives by the name of Red Men; and their origin is so much the more obscure, as they have not so distinct a tradition, as the Natchez."

Undoubtedly, one such tribe was the Houmas, a Muskogean-speaking people in the Lower Mississippi Valley whose name translates into English as "red." Early French expeditions of the Southeast, headed by La Salle and Iberville in the 1680s and 1690s, encountered "Oumas" near the mouth of the Mississippi. But these exploring parties communicated with Indians largely by signs, and neither La Salle nor Iberville translated "Ouma" into "red" or seemed to be aware of what it meant. In early meetings with Indians along the Mississippi, as the French worked to acquire the rudiments of native languages, they may have inadvertently used native ways of speaking in such a way as to popularize "red men" as a catch phrase for all Indians.

How and when certain tribes came to be called "red" is unclear, but there seems to have been some connection between a "red" identity and origin stories. According to anthropologist John R. Swanton, the Houmas and the neighboring Chakchiumas owed their tribal names to the red crawfish that created the earth. Another "red" tribe whom the French encountered in explorations further to the north were the Mesquakies, or "red earths," whose origin story tells of how "the first men and the first women [were made] out of clay that was as red as the reddest blood." Origin stories such as these could also be adapted to account for differences between peoples. A twentieth-century folklorist recorded that "the Saukies (Saukieock, to speak the plural as they do) say jokingly that Geechee Manito-ah made the Saukie out of yellow clay and the Squakie out of red."

Just as some Indians used animals to create metaphorical social divisions, called totems or clans, southeastern Indians may have used their variegated landscape to explain differences between peoples. European explorers of the Southeast were especially struck by the colors of the land. One trader said of Chickasaw country, "The Land here is a thinn mold on Topp of a red stiff Clay and white Marle." Le Page du Pratz characterized lower Louisiana as abounding in red clay, although "the White Hill" near the Natchez had "several veins of an earth, that is white, greasy, and very fine, with which I have seen very good potters ware made. On the same hill there are veins of ochre, of which the Natchez had just taken some to stain their earthen ware, which looked well enough; when it was besmeared with ochre, it became red on burning." An Englishman described what was probably the same hill as being made of "White Clay streaked with Red & Yellow," and later in his journey he "Remark'd a Reddish soil somewhat like Red ocre, which the Indians use instead of Vermillion when they cannot get the latter."

Before European trade introduced vermillion, Indians made paint out of clay, and paint marked social positioning, whether one was for war or peace, for example. The colors of the land matched the color symbolism of southeastern Indians in other contexts. The Taensas, who were related to the Natchez and also lived near this white, red, and yellow clay cliff, replicated these colors in their temple, which a French Jesuit described as having on the outside "three figures of eagles made of wood, and painted red, yellow, and white." Inside the temple, shelves held baskets of "Idols," including "figures of men and women made of stone or baked clay." These "figures" might have been references to the Taensas origin story, if it resembled that of the Natchez. According to Le Page du Pratz, "The guardian of the [Natchez] temple having told me that God had made man with his own hands, I asked him if he knew how that was done. He answered, 'that God had kneaded some clay, such as that which potters use, and had made it into a little man; and that after examining it, and finding it well formed, he blew up his work, and forthwith that little man had life, grew, acted, walked, and found himself a man perfectly well shaped.'" Le Page du Pratz did not ask whether God used red, white, or yellow clay.

Not all Indians believed that people originated in clay. H. B. Cushman, writing in the nineteenth century, recorded that "in regard to the origin of man, the one [story] generally accepted among the Choctaws, as well as many other tribes was that man and all other forms of life had originated from the common mother earth through the agency of the Great Spirit; . . . that the human race sprang from many different primeval pairs created by the Great Spirit in various parts of the earth in which man was found; and according to the different natural features of the world in which man abode, so their views varied with regard to the substance of which man was created; [whether from the trees, from the rocks, or from the earth]."

The stories Le Page du Pratz and Cushman heard may have been the same stories told among the Natchez and Choctaws before the arrival of Europeans, new stories created for the benefit of European listeners, or old stories adjusted to account for the existence of Europeans. Origin stories in the historical record are naturally suspect. They often appear within the accounts of missionaries, who were eager to hear native explanations of how the world was created so that they could correct them and tell how the world was really created. Anticipating what missionaries wanted to hear, Indians who were already acquainted with the biblical account may have recycled some version of it for the missionaries' benefit. Curiously, at least one proselytizing Christian, Roger Williams of Rhode Island, faithfully translated the Hebrew word *adam,* which means red earth or soil, into an Algonquian language, consequently telling Indians that God had made the first man out of red earth. However, Williams's Indian acquaintances rejected his version, insisting that God carved the first people out of stone but, dissatisfied with the result, made them from a tree instead. Since seventeenth-century New England Indians were not thought of as "red," Williams's origin story lacked the political content it could have assumed in other times and places. And yet, if missionaries elsewhere followed Williams's example, some Indians might have found this origin story compatible with their own or a story worth appropriating.

Eighteenth-century Europeans were themselves engaged in a struggle to keep the truth of their origin story alive, despite the challenge to it incurred with the European "discovery" of the Americas. The rise of black slavery was just one cause behind the collapse of Christian and pagan as a system of categories and the emergence of new categories based on the science of race. A second reason for the shift to a new set of categories must have been the hard questions posed by the existence of Indians: Were Indians descended from Adam and Eve or were there separate creations? Were Indians the lost tribe of Israel? Were they on the ark with Noah? As Europeans debated how to fit Native Americans into the biblical account of human origins, Indians must also have been discussing how to fit the appearance of these new people, Europeans and Africans, into their stories of human creation. Like the Genesis story, the Natchez and Choctaw stories described the divine origins of humans but could also be adapted to explain or allow for differences among humans: Indians, Europeans, and Africans "came out of the ground" in different places and thus were different peoples.

But were they, then, of a different race? The first scenario for how Indians got to be "red"—"red" as a response to "white"—suggests that "red" and "white" were metaphors for assumed positions, like school colors today, and not racial categories rooted in biological difference. The second scenario, positing a precontact identity as "red" based on beliefs about origins, raises the possibility that Indians came to see "red" and "white" as designating innate, divinely ordained differences between peoples. Were "white" and "red" in European-Indian diplomacy intended as symbols that could be put on and taken off or did they refer to differences thought to be embedded in the body, in skin color? Unfortunately, there is no simple answer.

James Adair certainly thought that Indians had their own racial identity. A trader who lived for many years with the Cherokees and Chickasaws, Adair later tried to prove in his *History of the American Indians* that Indians descended from

Jews. Like many of his contemporaries, Adair believed that "the Indian colour is not natural" but came from their "method of living." However, he also wrote that Indians were "of a copper or red-clay colour" and "are so strongly attached to, and prejudiced in favour of, their own colour, that they think as meanly of the whites, as we possibly can do of them." His phrasing, "red-clay colour," is unusual and may have come from conversations with Indians, not from his own observation.

More suggestive of race were eighteenth-century Indians' efforts to determine social identity through empirical, biological criteria. A trader to the Cherokees told of how they had killed an enemy who "was by his Confession an Over the Lake Indian, and by his Whiteness they supposed him to be a whiteman's Son." Another trader described an incident in which Twightwee (Miami) Indians visiting the Shawnees "den[ied] they had brought either Scalps or Prisoners, the *Shawnanese* suspecting them, had the Curiosity. to search their Bags, and finding two Scalps in them, that by the Softness of the Hair did not feel like *Indian* Scalps, they wash'd them clean, and found them to be the Scalps of some Christians." As the science of race emerged in Europe, Indians were similarly reading meaning into observable bodily differences as a way to find order in an increasingly complicated world.

Another kind of racialism is evident outside of the Southeast in speeches made by Indians who, even though they did not call themselves "red people," challenged European claims to power by asserting a racial identity. In the 1740s, an Iroquois speaker in council with the English emphasized Iroquois independence by highlighting the racial divide between Europeans and Indians: "The World at the first was made on the other Side of the Great Water different from what it is on this Side, as may be known from the different Colours of our Skin, and of our Flesh, and that which you call Justice may not be so amongst us; you have your Laws and Customs, and so have we." And in the 1750s, Indians began promoting pan-Indian resistance by evoking racial ties, as when the Delawares and Shawnees appealed to the Iroquois to "take up the Hatchet against the White People, without distinction, for all their Skin was of one Colour and the Indians of a Nother and if the Six Nations wou'd strike the French, they wou'd strike the English." Northeastern Indians may have been incorporating a concept Europeans introduced to them—that skin color was significant—or they came to this idea on their own.

Thus eighteenth-century Indians did use biology either to reveal identity or to build a common identity. However, most often, Indians used "red" and "white" for their rhetorical power as metaphors intended to capture the essence of social relationships. Closer examination of three contexts in which the Cherokees placed themselves in a "red" category shows that the Cherokees adopted color-based categories as a strategy to inform the English about social obligations. Two of these examples come from the trader Alexander Longe's 1725 "Postscript." In this document, neither Longe nor the Cherokee conjuror he spoke to referred to Indians as "red" explicitly, but the Cherokees by implication fell into a "red" category. The third example comes from a 1730 Cherokee-English council held in London.

First, however, there is a complication that requires explanation. The Cherokee language has two red colors. *Agigage* is a bright red originating in the Cherokee word for blood. *Wodige,* which usually translates as "brown," is a red-brown color derived from the Cherokee word for red paint, *wadi,* which was made out of red clay before the Cherokees acquired vermillion in trade. Interpreters might have translated either word into English as "red." These two colors had strong associations because the Cherokees used red-brown face paint to evoke the blood-red natural powers of the body. Anthropologist Raymond Fogelson depicted this connection as gendered: the face paint worn by warriors and associated with death complemented the menstrual blood and life-giving powers of women. A mid-eighteenth-century dictionary, compiled by the German engineer of an English fort in Cherokee country, demonstrates the obscure boundary between *agigage* and *wodige,* between the social and the biological. "Indian" is given as "Wodikehe," suggesting that the "red people" in council transcripts came from *wodige,* but the dictionary then translates "Wodikehe" as "Indian, painted Man," not "red man." The following three Cherokee examples invoke both *agigage* and *wodige.*

In the same year as the Taensas chief told his story about the white, red, and black men emerging from a cave, Longe interviewed a Cherokee "prist," or conjuror, to gauge the Cherokees' receptivity to Christian missionaries. The conjuror answered Longe in much the same way as the Taensas chief, by telling an origin story. In the beginning, everything was water. The Great Man Above gave a crawfish some dirt to spread and then made the sun and moon. After he had made all living things, "he toke some white Clay and mead the white man and one white woman . . . and then he mead tow and Two of Evry nashun under the sone[,] woman and man[.] They have incrased Ever since but I think that The english are the first that he mead because he has Indued them with knowledge of meaking all things." Although it is left unsaid what color clay other nations were made from, Cherokee land, lying in what is now northeastern Georgia, eastern Tennessee, and the western Carolinas, is one of the regions in North America most noted for its extensive banks of red clay.

The conjuror told another story that positioned Indians as "red," but this time he linked skin color to the abstractly colored gods of the four directions. The god in the north was a black god colored like the negro and he is verrie cross. . . . [T]hat in the Est is the couler of us Indians and hee is something beter than the other [other sources call this god in the east *red/agigage*]. . . . [H]e that is in the south is a verrie good one and white as row Inglish are, and soe mild that we love him out of mesh or . . . [Y]ow are whiter Then all other nashons or people under the sun[.] [T]he grate king of heaven has given row the knowledge of all things[.] Shurely he has a grater love for row then us and for us then The negrows." It was not until Longe pressed him for more information on the fourth god that the conjuror found a color for him. He was "the Colour of the spanards." In other accounts of the gods of the four directions, his color would have been "blue," but "blue" men had no parallel in the nascent racial categories of the Southeast.

The conjuror's reluctance to take the story to its implausible conclusion, blue Spaniards, reveals the reason for his storytelling. Longe thought he was gathering information on Cherokee religious beliefs, but the conjuror was tailoring his story for his audience. The origin story was probably a fabrication, too, a familiar plot with additional expository details, most notably the idea that whites were created first. In both stories, the conjuror flattered Longe with deference to white superiority, but, when asked directly about whether the Cherokees would like missionaries to come among them, he expressed doubts about their efficacy, for "these white men that Lives amonghts us a traiding are more deboched and more wicked Then the beatest of our young felows[.] is itt nott a shame for Them that has such good prists and such knowledge as they have To be worse then the Indians that are In a maner but like wolves." With these narratives, the conjuror intended to instruct Longe in how white people *should* behave.

In the third example, the 1730 treaty signing in London, the Cherokee speaker claimed the category "red" in yet another context. This treaty originated in the bizarre ambitions of an English eccentric, Sir Alexander Cuming, who on his own initiative visited the Cherokees and invited seven of them to London to meet the king. When they got there, the seven Cherokees found themselves part of treaty negotiations in which the English speaker said that, since the Cherokees were "now the children of the Great King of Great Britain and he their father," they "must be always ready at the Governor's command to fight against any Nation whether they be white men or Indians who shall dare to molest or hurt the English." The English also sought good trading relations, the return of escaped slaves, and legal jurisdiction in murders between Cherokees and colonists. To seal the terms of the treaty, the English distributed presents of guns, knives, kettles, wampum belts, and "a piece of Red Cloth." The Cherokee speaker, overcome by the "glittering show of the courtiers," acceded to these demands and said, "We look upon the Great King George as the Sun and as our Father and upon ourselves as his children[.] For tho' we are red and you white yet our hands and hearts are join'd together. We came hither naked and poor, as the Worm of the Earth, but you have everything: and we that have nothing must love you."

In asserting a "red" identity, the Indian speaker at the 1730 London council treated "red" and "white" as moieties tying the Cherokees and English to an alliance in which each had a distinct, complementary role to play. During the ensuing decades, the Cherokees recalled the London treaty often to remind the English of the bargain they had made. As one Cherokee said at a 1757 council, "I remember my Father, King George, said, That the White People and we were equally his Children, And that both had an equal Right to the Land. Our Brothers, the White People, understanding making of Cloaths and other Necessaries for us, And we understood fighting; so if your People will furnish Cloaths and other Necessaries for us, We will assist you in defending the Country."

If the Cherokees were extending their conception of town politics to explain each other's role in the alliance, the English were metaphorically to assume the role of the civil or "white" chief and the Cherokees were to be the head warrior or "red" chief. A "white" chief of a Cherokee town did not actually clothe his townspeople, but he did oversee communal resources and was responsible for the welfare of guests and town residents unable to fend for themselves. "White" chiefs also mediated and advocated peace. Although not truly seeking peace but control over who fought with whom, the English would have appeared on the ritual stage of diplomacy to be taking on the role of peacemakers. Simultaneously, the Cherokees derided the English ability to make war. These metaphorical positions of English/white/peace and Cherokee/red/war found confirmation in the kin terms used to explain the Cherokee-English alliance. The Cherokees willingly became "younger brothers" to English colonial governors and "children" of the English king. Within Cherokee society, "white" already had associations with old and "red" with young, as in the age structure of Cherokee politics: civil chiefs were usually a generation older than war chiefs.

The variety of contexts in which the Cherokees situated themselves as "red" shows that "red" did not have a definite, fixed meaning. In one context, it meant the war moiety, in another there was a hint of origins in red clay, and in a third situation, the "red" god of the east was ranked second but otherwise lacked characteristics. Whether the Cherokees meant "red people" *or* "painted people" is equally ambiguous. The war moiety involved both red colors. (*Wodige* paint symbolized *agigage* activities.) The god of the east was the color *of agigage,* while origins in red clay would make one the color of *wodige.* If the Cherokees had a "red" identity in 1725–30, it was just emerging.

Most significant, these three examples show that the Cherokees became "red" as a consequence of trying to define "whiteness." In contrast to the vagueness and contextuality of what it meant to be "red," all three examples give the same understanding of "white." In the two stories told by the Cherokee conjuror, whites were ranked first because they had the "knowledge of meaking all things." Indians were ranked second. The Cherokees also accepted this ranking at the London treaty council when they allied with the English in exchange for trade goods. Superior wealth and technology justified European claims to the high-status category of "white." Presumably, it was blacks' status as slaves that relegated them to the lowest rank. The Taensas story about the three races leaving the cave used the same ranking based on wealth (the white man "took the good road that led him into a fine hunting ground") and similarly grounded this ranking in an age hierarchy: the white man was the first to leave the cave. This deference to white superiority was a diplomatic pose, for among themselves the Cherokees said very different things about white people, calling them "the white nothings," "the ugly white people," and "white dung-hill fowls."

Thus, in the early eighteenth century, the Cherokees elaborated on their own color symbolism to create a set of categories to stand for their diplomatic relationship with the English. The rhetorical purpose of color-based categories became even more transparent after the Revolutionary War, when the Cherokees rejected the former meanings of "red" and "white" and attempted to negotiate new meanings to counter American assumptions of conquest. As in the early eighteenth century, Cherokee speakers used their origin story as a base to explain social positioning, but they recast the origin story to assert precedence. At the 1785 treaty council at Hopewell, Cherokee chief Old Tassel said, "I am made of this earth, on which the great man above placed me, to possess it. . . . You must know the red people are the aborigines of this land, and that it is but a few years since the white people found it out. I am of the first stock, as the commissioners know, and a native of this land; and the white people are now living on it as our friends."

Old Tassel's reminder to U.S. treaty commissioners that the "red people" were the original occupants of the land constituted a Cherokee challenge to U.S. hegemony that endured into the 1790s and early 1800s. After complaining in 1792 that "we are bound up all round with white people, that we have not room to hunt," the Little Nephew said, "though we are red, you must know one person made us both. The red people were made first. . . . Our great father above made us both; and, if he was to take it into his head that the whites had injured the reds, he would certainly punish them for it." In the 1790s, another Cherokee told some missionaries, "The Great Father of all breathing things, in the beginning created all men, the white, the red and the black . . . The whites are now called the older brothers and the red the younger. I do not object to this and will call them so though really the naming should have been reversed, for the red people dwelt here first." And in the 1830s, a Cherokee man told of how God had made the first man out of red clay. Because Indians were red, they had obviously been made first: "The Red people therefore are the real people, as their name *yuwiya*, indicates." Thus, after the revolution, the Cherokees abandoned the mutually agreed-upon racial hierarchy that had granted whites a higher status in exchange for trade goods. Emphasizing their age and precedence as a people, they defined "red" differently to neutralize the hierarchy Americans thought they had inherited from Britain.

Cherokee insistence that the red people were made first was partly a response to how whites regarded them. At Hopewell, U.S. treaty commissioners claimed that they only wanted to make the Cherokees happy, "regardless of any distinction of color, or of any difference in our customs, our manners, or particular situation." The Cherokees were skeptical. One Cherokee complained to Moravian missionaries in the 1790s, "but many people think that we Indians are too evil and bad to become good people, and that we are too unclean and brown [probably *wodige*]." The Cherokees saw that skin-color categories had become the predominant indicator of status in the American South, and "black" labor and "red" land the two most marketable commodities. English trade goods justified the Cherokees' deference in the early eighteenth century, but now they were unlikely to gain anything in a racial hierarchy that was pushing the category "red" closer to the category "black."

The wordplay and invention surrounding Cherokee uses of "red" and "white" give the illusion of complete plasticity, but it was only the meanings of "red" and "white" that changed with the situation. The Cherokees never claimed to be any other color than "red," and the English, even when being insulted, were always "white." By the end of the century, the color-based categories that grew out of Cherokee color symbolism had become racial categories because the Cherokees described the origins of difference as being innate, the product of separate creations, and they spoke of skin color as if it were a meaningful index of difference. But they persistently molded what race meant to fit particular contexts.

Eighteenth-century Indians and Europeans were engaged in the same mental processes. They experimented with notions of biological difference in an attempt to develop methods for discerning individual allegiances. They adapted origin beliefs to come up with divine explanations for political, cultural, and social divisions. They dealt with the sudden diversity of people by creating new knowledge out of old knowledge, new color-based categories derived from their traditional color symbolism. Thus the Cherokee conjuror in Longe's account and Linnaeus were compatriots in the same intellectual enterprise. The two groups also spent most of the eighteenth century expressing confusion and disagreement about the origins of human difference, the significance of bodily variation, and how and why God, or the Great Man Above, had created such different people. It would take another century for the science of race to reach its full height and then one more century for the idea of race to be seriously questioned. Perhaps we are now at the brink of the apocalypse, when the idea of race will be abandoned entirely and another system of categories will emerge to take its place.

In the meantime, "red" continues to be contested. Indians may have named themselves "red," but they could not prevent whites from making it a derogatory term. By the nineteenth century, whites had appropriated "red man" and put it to their own uses. Appearing in the novels of James Fenimore Cooper, captivity narratives, and dime novels, ultimately to be taken up by tobacco advertisers and national sports teams, the noble "Red Man" and the brutal "Redskin" evolved into demeaning and dehumanizing racial epithets. But, at the same time, Indians could always use "red" to claim a positive identity and to make a statement about difference, to build pan-Indian alliances as in the native women's organization Women of All Red Nations, or to articulate American Indian grievances as in Vine Deloria, Jr.'s critique of Euroamerican ethnocentrism, *God Is Red* (1973).

The adaptability of racial categories to fit particular political and social alignments illuminates critical features of the idea of race in general. People do not believe in race abstractly but instead manipulate racial categories to suit contextualized objectives. Yet scholars seeking to understand race as a cultural construction should exercise care not to dismiss physical differences between peoples as pure figments of imagination. Why did Indians begin to see in skin color the potential for categorizing themselves, Europeans, and Africans but not use skin color to distinguish among Indians? Is it because there was indeed greater observable, biological difference between the peoples of Europe, Africa, and America than among them? There are physical differences; our collective imaginations organize these differences to make meaning of them and are constantly at work altering those meanings.

Suggested Reading

There are two items worth noting that touch on issues raised by Shoemaker's essay: Neal Salisbury, "The Indians' Old World: Native Americans and the Coming of the Europeans," *William and Mary Quarterly* 53 (July 1996): 435–58; and Everett L. York, "Ethnocentricity or Racism: Some Thoughts on the Nature of Early Indian-White Relations," *American Indian Quarterly* 1 (Winter 1974–75): 281–91. For a broader range of issues, see Peter H. Wood, Gregory A. Waselkov, and M. Thomas Hatley, eds., *Powhatan's Mantle: Indians in the Colonial Southeast* (Lincoln: University of Nebraska Press, 1989).

CHAPTER TWO

Spanish Missions, Cultural Conflict, and the Pueblo Revolt of 1680

HENRY WARNER BOWDEN

When Europeans reached North America during the sixteenth century, their presence and actions changed the lives of Native people forever. Military men claimed vast regions for their sovereigns while seeking riches and honor for themselves. Often accompanied by farmers, artisans, and clergy, they penetrated the continent from every direction and met dozens of Indian groups. Although the encounters between Natives and newcomers proved to be as varied as the languages the invaders spoke, a frequent pattern of violence marked the interracial encounters. Determined to dominate each local situation, often the Europeans used military force to gain economic and social control. When the Indians' passive resistance or diplomacy failed, they launched raids or even full-scale war to drive out their tormentors. The Pueblo Revolt was one such movement to reassert Indian independence during the colonial era. This essay presents a variety of causes for the incident and traces the role played by the shaman Popé in helping create the movement to drive out the hated Spanish. Recent scholarship suggests that another leader may have played important roles as well.

Historians who try to understand encounters between red men and white men in the seventeenth century are immediately confronted with a problem: Indians were not literate, and they left no records of the sort we are accustomed to studying. For centuries the only information about aboriginal populations in the Americas was derived from European narratives, conditioned by viewpoints that harbored an outsider's values. Archaeology added some indigenous references, but the evidence has usually been too meager for adequate generalization. Historians have pursued the goal of avoiding white men's biases and viewing Indian

"Spanish Missions, Cultural Conflict, and the Pueblo Revolt of 1680" appeared in *Church History* 44, no. 2 (March 1975): 217–28.

cultures as having an integrity all their own; but that goal has remained an ideal, causing more despair than hope of eventual success. As far as the history of early New Mexico is concerned, the situation is worsened by the fact that most church and government archives were burned during the fighting of 1680–96.

In the twentieth century contributions of anthropological field workers have provided a wealth of new learning about Indian life. This scientific information is less distorted by culturally conditioned biases, and its disclosures are not tied to European source materials. Our modern data afford independent perspectives, new sources of information and opportunities for revising historical knowledge. A discriminating use of anthropological materials can free us from the narrow vision of a single cultural viewpoint and allow us more adequately to interpret past events that involved separate cultural units. Students of history now have the opportunity to work with new tools and ask new questions in addition to applying familiar methods to fresh data.

From an anthropologist's perspective, we can utilize a more comprehensive definition of religion and study its functional qualities in a particular cultural setting. That kind of inquiry makes it possible to understand the content of any people's world view, the unifying and normative place which religion has in the society's ethos and, most important, those aspects posing fundamental contrasts to alien cultures. The selection of Spanish missionary efforts in seventeenth-century New Mexico may be especially fruitful for a new interpretation of certain historical events because it provides a context in which the religious focus was apparent and significant for both cultures. The Rio Grande Pueblos organized most of their activities around a well-articulated system of religious symbols and practices; the Spaniards had long been conscious of religious motives behind many of their heroic efforts. An analysis of what was really at issue between Spanish and Pueblo cultures on the religious level can shed light on their similarities, antipathies and reasons for armed conflict between them.

Of course anthropological information is not a panacea to be used uncritically, and one must confront the difficulties involved in a study that proceeds from present observations back into the past. It may be that contemporary reports of Pueblo rituals, calendar cycles, social structure and so forth, represent patterns that did not exist in the same configurations during the 1600s. It is also possible that an analysis of conflicts between the religions of Indian and Spaniard could highlight tensions disproportionately. Points of conflict in a specific context will indicate what was cherished enough at that time to defend against external pressures for change. But such conflicts do not show us the relative value of those cultural elements in a setting where they were unchallenged and allowed to seek their own level. The best we can hope for in studying two cultures is to identify their salient features in the limited context of their confronting each other. One should not conclude from comparative study that the controverted issues were categories of major significance within a society, relative to their own hierarchies of values. Another pitfall to avoid is that of attributing awareness or deliberate motives to people when they may not have been conscious of the issues in the way we describe them. Historical events must be interpreted with ideas based on as much information as relevant sources provide, but we can never go on to say that those specific categories and definitions were in the minds of the protagonists at the time. Despite these difficulties, it is still fair to say that facts and insights from anthropologists provide new avenues in the historian's search for an adequate understanding of red-white contact and the role religions played in the process. What follows is an attempt to demonstrate the results of such a study conducted within a limited area.

In 1598 the upper Rio Grande valley was viewed as an outpost of Spanish civilization, an opportunity for colonizing, mining and missionary exploits. By that time it had been the home of Keresan- and Tanoan-speaking Indians for over three hundred years. Under the leadership of Juan de Oñate an initial force of 400 persons, including 10 Franciscan friars, made their way upriver to the territory where approximately 30 to 40 thousand Pueblos inhabited an estimated 75 to 80 permanent towns. The first decade was a time of mismanagement and unsteady beginnings for both churchmen and civilians, but in 1609 the crown stabilized the colony with strong financial and administrative support, largely for the sake of its missionary enterprise. With Santo Domingo and Santa Fe established as bases of operations for church and state respectively, the prospects for growth were bright.

Missionary work among the Indians seemed to go well from the outset. As village leaders of the six tribal groups became acquainted with the friars and their message, they are reported to have welcomed them, expressed polite interest in their ideas and asked to know more. The district was soon divided into mission stations, and though the manpower shortage spread them thinly, priests were assigned to cover each area. Congregations were formed; catechetical instruction was begun; slowly a number of churches and chapels were built adjacent to the major pueblos. Various statistical reports of this period are not very reliable, but a realistic estimation is that an average of less than thirty Franciscans labored among colonists and natives during the seventeenth century and ministered to a baptized population of approximately 20,000 Pueblos.

One cannot discern a pattern of constantly increasing growth. There was a great deal of internecine strife between ecclesiastical and governmental authorities, and missionary efforts seem to have been hampered as a result. By 1630 the missions had spread numerically and geographically as far as they could in view of their problems with secular opposition, replacement difficulties and delays in supply and communication. After that, their history is one of trying to maintain the level of achievement rather than pursuing larger and more ambitious objectives.

Converting more people to Christian practices was, nevertheless, the reason for New Mexico's existence, and the friars performed their tasks with singleness of purpose. That zeal led them to concentrate on restricting Indian religious activities, especially during the 1670s. There had been some conflict between native and Spanish priests from the start, and sporadic outbursts of hostility had occurred at intervals; but in 1675 the clash of cultures became more pronounced on each side with resentment and bitterness increasing proportionately. Native ceremonies and liturgical articles had long been outlawed by Spanish officials, but those injunctions were suddenly enforced with renewed vigor. Essential ceremonial chambers *(kivas)* and many altars were seized, dances were strictly forbidden, masks and prayer sticks were destroyed, priests and medicinemen were imprisoned, flogged or hanged. Throughout the decade there was a determined action by both arms of Spanish culture to eradicate every vestige of Indian life, world view as well as ethos.

In August 1680 a general uprising of native peoples put a stop to those repressive measures. Every pueblo from Acoma to Pecos, from Taos to lsleta rose to destroy the Spanish presence north of EI Paso. Of the 2,500 colonists approximately 380 were killed, including 21 of the 33 resident friars. All survivors were forced to retreat south, taking what few possessions they could carry while fleeing for safety. The successful Indians methodically rid themselves of every reminder of Spanish intrusion. They destroyed a great deal of property, including churches with their records, images and ceremonial paraphernalia. Renouncing the alien faith, Pueblos bathed to cleanse themselves from the effects of baptism. They abandoned foreign dress, stopped using Spanish names and left their Christian wives. Their rejection of Hispanic cultural patterns and the restoration of revitalized native ways was as thorough as the united efforts of chiefs and people could make them.

Why did the revolt occur? What were the primary factors leading to bloodshed at that particular time, and what can account for its deliberately anti-ecclesiastical character? Ranches and government buildings were also hit, but almost every church in the territory was demolished. Colonists of all types were killed when unfortunate enough to be caught in vulnerable positions, but the clergy were usually the first to die in every pueblo. Why did the spokesmen and symbols of Christianity receive the concentrated fury of Pueblo vengeance? The answer to these questions can be sought in a study of religions, their nature and place in the two cultures whose conflict rose to such an overt level. Religion was a factor at the core of each way of life, and if we can understand what contrasted at the center, we will be in a better position to interpret conflicts in the wider circles of cultural interaction, even to the point of seeing reasons for war.

During the initial stages of red-white contact there were enough similarities between their religions to allow for a degree of mutual understanding. On the tangible level, each side used altars, religious calendars, aids for prayer (feathered sticks or rosary beads), luxurious costumes for a distinct priesthood which presided over regularly appointed ceremonies, ritual chants in languages somewhat removed from everyday usage. Christian baptism corresponded easily to the Pueblo practice of head washing and the giving of a new name when one was initiated into special organizations. Catholic saints elevated from the ranks of men and women formed a parallel with Pueblo hero[e]s who once lived among the people in human shape, now petitioned as powerful spirits. Spaniards were wont to experience visions, demonic as well as beatific, and this too provided a link with a people who saw horned snakes, cloud people (*shiwanna*) and witches. The use of incense and holy water was close to Pueblo priests who made "clouds" with yucca suds for rain or sprayed consecrated water on an ailing patient. Kissing the hand of a friar was likened to the practice of "drawing in the breath" of a native priest or a loved one.

More intangibly, each religious system was based on beliefs that the world was ordered according to divine sanctions. The wills and wisdom of dominions beyond human making were thought by adherents of both cultures to be actively engaged in directing the weather, fortunes of war, personal fate and national destiny. Conversely both interpreted disease, drought and famine as either the result of malevolent spirits or the displeasure of gods who would not overlook human frailty. Within these positive and negative emphases it would be difficult to say whether the love of good or fear of evil predominated in the day-to-day actions of either people. But each religion in its own way emphasized divine power as that which gave order and meaning to their adherents' identity and mode of life.

These similarities were not appreciated by the Franciscans in New Mexico as an avenue for introducing their mission program. Unlike the Jesuits in Arizona and northwestern Mexico, they did not begin by utilizing aspects of existing religion and move from them to Christian formulations. Instead they were convinced either that the Indians possessed no religion at all or that they had been lured by the Devil into a repugnant congeries of idol worship and superstition. These spiritual conquerors matched their military counterparts in holding that the natives were barbarians who lacked any civilized notion of law or legitimate authority. Indian settlements were not viewed as properly organized communities; their forms of body covering were not considered true clothing; their sexual practices were judged to be disgracefully unregulated. So from the outset the friars set themselves the goal of stamping out every particle of native religion and substituting Catholic doctrines and practices, using force if necessary.

In keeping with these attitudes the Franciscans' behavior toward the Pueblos' religion conflicted sharply with tangible aspects of local custom. Almost without exception they did not try to master native languages or translate Christian ideas into them. They insisted that Indians learn Spanish. To supplant misguided native beliefs and ceremonial patterns, the missionaries operated on a policy of compulsory attendance at mass—for all baptized Indians but not all Spaniards. They made native officials (*fiscals*) punish their own people for failure to conform to this rule. With the aid of governors and soldiers they raided ancient ceremonial chambers and tried to prevent their future use. Masks and ritual paraphernalia of all kinds were periodically confiscated and burned. Traditional leaders who persisted in continuing the old rituals were arrested, and the gentle sons of St. Francis directed that they be whipped or executed as a menace to this life and an obstacle to the next.

These areas of tension in physical confrontations were symptoms of more fundamental conflicts that lay beneath the surface. No one at that time seemed to realize how different their cultural orientations were, but modern anthropology has helped us see that there were serious contradictions between Pueblo and Spaniard in the categories of world view, personal identity and moral obligation.

Pueblo views of the world were diametrically opposed to western European ones. The underworld rather than heaven or the sky was their locus for sources of life. There was no reference to a primal god, an *ex nihilo* creation of matter, or any transcendental direction over the affairs of the natural world. Gods, men, animals and plants emerged through an opening in the underworld's roof (seen as a navel or *shipapu* from earth, the middle stratum of the cosmos), and all of them came from below to dwell on the surface of this world. In the time of beginnings many gods or *katsina* had lived with the people and taught them how to cope with their new environment. Patterns and procedures thought to stem from that time and from those sources carried the sanction of ultimate authority:

> Thus the Indians got their culture—their houses, weapons, tools, and cultivated plants, their clans, priests and societies, their songs, prayers, ceremonies and paraphernalia. That is why they live, work and worship . . . as they do: because their ways of life were established by the gods long ago. . . . To ignore or violate, to lose the customs of the old days . . . [would be] to bring misfortune . . . even extinction, upon themselves.

Compared with the Spanish notion of a heavenly creator who guided his people from above, the Pueblo view derived strength from the opposite direction, and it was much more explicit about divinely instituted patterns of activity.

Instead of beginning with a belief that the natural world was the Lord's footstool and man's economic resource, Indians of the Rio Grande gave the earth a sacred status of its own. In comparison with Europeans who felt free to use natural materials for any secular purpose they fancied, Pueblos had a more profound respect for the basically sacred constitution of natural objects. Their place in this world was what really mattered to them, and sacred space radiated in concentric circles from the center, which was either the local village or a nearby place of emergence. Everything in the cosmos had its place by reference to this center. Everything from points on the compass to changing seasons was bounded and controllable because the earth was an orderly environment that circumscribed the harmony of all good things. Instead of wishing to escape this world or destroy it through exploitation, Pueblos affirmed their existence in it and husbanded their lives along with nature as parts of a single sanctified life system. It was a complete, substantial and satisfying world, and one could know enough about life, death and proper conduct to feel gratified by living in it according to established ways.

Another point at which the two cultures stood in striking contrast to each other had to do with personal identity; that is, their worlds were different, and they thought of the people in them differently too. The European view enhanced the role of the individual, his free choice and opportunities to distinguish himself from others. Whether by valor or charity, by deeds of might or sacrifice, personal merit was a virtue to be prized and cultivated. For Pueblos, however, personal identity was always defined by reference to the community, not at its expense. The self as any Spaniard would have defined it was submerged, and all of Indian society's values emphasized the well-being of the collectivity rather than that of the individual. Personal distinction was shunned, not sought; innovation was discouraged. Anyone who strove constantly to distinguish himself from his fellows was more likely to be ostracized and charged with witchcraft than to receive admiration from his townspeople.

The antithetical nature of this cultural trait is fairly easy to see when measured against Christian doctrines of salvation and the church. From its beginnings Christianity has almost always conveyed the assumption that its adherents were a separate people, sheep separated from the goats, wheat from the chaff, a faithful remnant saved from' destruction by a merciful God. This salvation of separate individuals has usually included some degree of voluntary belief and personal morality, a combination of faith and works in which the responsibility of the believer played an important role in securing the final result. In Pueblo life there were no such thoughts. Everyone belonged to the group, and everyone was certain to reach the afterworld (enter *shipapu*) regardless of his merits or demerits. The only qualification on this cultural universalism was the idea that those failing to lead a good life would have a more difficult time reaching the place of emergence/reentry. There was no place of reward for the good and another of retribution for those less virtuous. As one valuable description put it, "to die in a pueblo is not to become dead but to return to the only real life there is; one 'changes houses' and rejoins the ancestors. . . ." Just as there was no community-separating heaven and hell, there was no concept of atonement, no vicarious sacrifice, no redemption—none of these because there was no need.

Christianity came to the Pueblos preaching doctrine that required a psychological sense of separation from the aboriginal group. The missionaries saw the church as an institution composed of believers gathered in anticipation of ultimate rescue out of this life. The church thus embodied a community-dividing thrust. Not all members of society would be saved, only the baptized. Not all Indians or Spaniards were expected at mass (and incidentally punished for failure to attend), only those gathered into the communion of saints. The church cut through families and clans, through moieties and secret societies. Its contrast

with native religious forms was stark enough when it stood simply as a competitive institution; but its major threat to native life stemmed from a disruptive
capacity to offer salvation only to individuals.

Differing ideas of moral obligation comprised a third general category of
conflict. For Spanish preachers ethical guidelines were thought to derive from
biblical and theological traditions, sources transcending any particular cultural
group. Pueblos derived their sense of duty and propriety within an understanding of the community and its needs. The missionaries defined good and bad actions on a standard possessed by the church, seen as a divine institution that did
not, in ideal terms at least, coincide with the totality of any cultural unit or their
various civil offices. Natives based their model of ethical judgment on a standard
that comprehended all facets of their society and did not see any reason for going beyond them. Europeans thought that sanctions against improper conduct
would apply in the afterlife, usually in addition to, not in place of, temporal effects. Indians expected ultimate sanctions, like death for witchcraft, to apply in
this life with no rewards or punishments reserved for the future.

The more important differences between Indian and European emerged in
actually trying to live by these divergent views of right conduct while attempting
to convert one's opposite number. The friars stressed attendance at mass, morning and evening prayer, monogamy with no divorce and obedience to Spanish
magistrates as fundamental elements of moral life. Pueblo activities were aligned
with the order of nature and had been organized into an elaborate system of
societies which presided over a cycle of ritual ceremonies. The Indians' central
obligation was to participate in and to perpetuate those rites which insured a
well-ordered life for the pueblo and its circle of physical needs. Most village
adults belonged to at least one of many societies, usually from eight to twenty
in a pueblo that presided over vital functions like planting, irrigation or rain
making, hunting, harvesting, rules enforcement and curing physical ailments.
Existence itself, the very elements that gave meaning and structure to Indian life
as a cultural unit, depended on cycles of corporate activity grouped rationally
around an agrarian calendar year. Social structures conformed to the works necessary for cooperating with natural rhythms. Ritual activities were orchestrated
to facilitate these works; food, shelter and health followed as a result of attention
to ceremonial obligations. If this combination of activities and moral obligations
were ever suppressed to a serious degree, the threat to Pueblo existence would be
quite serious indeed.

None of the standard interpretations of Spanish activity and Pueblo resistance
in the seventeenth century have noticed the important role religion played in the
tensions between the two cultures. They have usually stressed disputes over land
and water rights, abuses in the *ecomienda* labor system or the obtrusive presence
of a military *entrada* in another nation's territory. The major theme in historical writing for well over a century now has been to interpret Indian rebellion as
an expression of economic and political self-determination. Discussions' of the

Pueblo Revolt of 1680 thus parallel other patriotic revolutions in the western hemisphere against a familiar archetype of tyranny and oppression.

But is this an adequate explanation? It does not account for why the uprising occurred when it did, that is, why the various nations were desperate enough at that particular time to combine their strength and cooperate as never before. It does not explain why a war ostensibly over land, labor and personal freedom should have taken such an overtly anti-Christian turn. It implies that Spanish civil and ecclesiastical authorities would have been successful if their means had been less harsh. It fails to realize how antithetical the two cultures really were in the seventeenth century and how deeply the Pueblos were committed to maintaining the integrity of their cultural system, one that grounded their existence in realities they knew always to have pertained. Interpretations of the conflict offered thus far have overemphasized the political and economic factors, leaving several important questions unanswered and omitting consideration of relevant information about the values and motivations of people actually confronting a rival culture.

Suggestions for a more adequate historical interpretation would build on the physical and non-material cultural differences already discussed and then concentrate on events beginning in 1667. From that year to 1672 there was an extended drought and crop failure. Most of the population, Indian and colonist alike, was reduced to eating "hides that they had and the straps of the carts, preparing them for food by soaking ... and roasting them in the fire with maize, and boiling them with herbs and roots." In 1671 a great pestilence carried off many people and livestock. By 1672 the nomadic Apaches and Navajos, also pinched by dwindling food supplies, increased their raids on the settled areas and brought more ruin. One of the Spaniards' feudal promises had always been to protect their charges from such raids; now that promise was seen for what it was worth. By 1675 at least six pueblos had been wiped out, and most others were in desperate straits.

In the light of such conditions it is not surprising to see that the Pueblos began to abandon Spanish habits and return to their folkways. In the past they had been willing to accept the advantages of Spanish technology and even the externals of the new religion, as long as imported items served material and social ends. When missionaries insisted that acceptance of Christianity forbade any retention of aboriginal beliefs and required denial of native rituals, there were probably some opportunists willing to go even that far. But when all of them realized that the new ways were no better than the old ones in bringing rain, curing disease or preventing invasions—indeed, when they seemed to be the cause of so much suffering—then a massive return to the more trusted patterns of ancient teaching was in the offing.

Ironically enough, at the same time Indian practices were being revitalized, the Spanish mounted an energetic campaign to extinguish them altogether. Relations between church and state had been stormy throughout most of the century, but in the person of Juan Francisco de Trevino, arriving as governor sometime after 1670, the missionaries finally found a civil magistrate willing to enforce their suppression of native religion with wholehearted cooperation. As the Indians were moving in one direction, Spanish forces tried with increasing brutality to move them toward the opposite pole. In 1675 forty-seven ceremonial leaders were arrested. Three were hanged, another committed suicide, and the others were released after being whipped only because the Indians made a show of force. Plans for a wider and more effective revolt were not long in forthcoming, and most of the central figures, including el Popé, came from among those leaders publicly humiliated.

The fighting of 1680 caught the Spanish by surprise, and their evacuation left the Indians free to follow precontact standards of conduct as they wished. There was an abortive attempt to reconquer the land in 1682, but for the *better* part of fifteen years the Pueblos had little molestation from soldiers or friars. New Mexico was conquered again by 1696, and Indian resistance took two new forms. Thousands moved west to live with a similar but more remote culture, the Hopi; those who stayed in the river valleys compartmentalized their lives into outward conformity to the dominant culture and inner loyalty to their own.

In piecing together the best possible historical interpretation of these events it is important to notice that political, economic and personal factors did play a role, but they do not tell the whole story. The cultural antagonism between Spaniard and Pueblo had fundamentally religious roots, and an adequate understanding of the 1680 hostilities must give them priority. In the last analysis the Indian war was an attempt to preserve the kind of life which they thought the gods had ordained and which aliens were obviously destroying. The tribes united voluntarily to expel the Spanish because their coercive tactics were preventing a life based on true beliefs and conduct—an ethos seen not only as proper, but as the one way to stave off the disease and famine confronting them. The Pueblo Revolt was an act of people determined to reject Christian civilization because it posed a direct threat to their culture and religion, to their integrated structures which embodied indispensable elements for Pueblo survival.

This study of a particular cultural conflict may be useful in shedding more light on one set of concrete historical circumstances and in providing a more comprehensive interpretation of all the factors that were in operation there. But it stands as only one case study in a field that needs a great deal of attention. Historians are now in a position to capitalize on sophisticated treatments of religion in cultural contexts and blend them with more standard surveys of missionary activity. The day has come when we can adjust one-sided interpretations of red-white relations, correcting them with a wealth of new material and a more comprehensive understanding of Indian life. This new awareness is the key to better history of hundreds of cultures whose integrity and richness we are just beginning to appreciate. Once this is under way, the scope and quality of Christian missions can be more realistically viewed within specific contexts.

Suggested Reading

This essay gives the traditional account of the rebellion. Bowden placed the Pueblo Revolt in the broad context of Christian missions during the colonial era in *American Indians and Christian Missions: Studies in Cultural Conflict* (Chicago: University of Chicago Press, 1981). A newer version of this incident, suggesting a broader leadership that worked with Pópe, is presented in Stefanie Beninato, "Pópe, Pose-yemu, and Naranjo: A New Look at Leadership in the Pueblo Revolt of 1680," *New Mexico Review* 65 (October 1990): 417–35. A book-length study of these events can be found in Andrew L. Knaut, *The Pueblo Revolt: Conquest and Resistance in Seventeenth Century New Mexico* (Norman: University of Oklahoma Press, 1995). For an overview of events in the colonial Southwest, see David J. Weber, *The Spanish Frontier in North America* (New Haven: Yale University Press, 1992).

CHAPTER THREE

King Philip's Herds

Indians, Colonists, and the Problem of Livestock in Early New England

VIRGINIA DeJOHN ANDERSON

While religious strife helped push Indians and Spanish into war in New Mexico, land grabbing and fur trade disputes brought conflict to Virginia. In New England by the mid-seventeenth century, land disputes and religious issues also led to conflict between colonists and tribal groups. Yet a new factor became central there. In this essay Virginia DeJohn Anderson analyzes some of the economic and cultural disputes resulting from British importation of domestic livestock into the region. Expecting to establish agricultural communities, the English brought cattle and hogs to the region from the beginning. The mere presence of the animals proved less important than the colonists' refusal to keep them behind fences. Unchecked, the animals repeatedly damaged or destroyed Indian crops and clam beds. When tribesmen shot cattle to protect their crops, they faced court sentences. After the Indian villagers began raising hogs themselves, the English objected to the competition and demanded that the Indians keep their animals fenced and out of the colonists' fields. The essay demonstrates how differing cultural and economic practices increased interracial tensions between New England Natives and newcomers.

One late spring day in 1669, the ambitious younger son of a prominent Rhode Island family received a letter from the town clerk of Portsmouth. Like many of his neighbors, the young man raised livestock and followed the common practice of placing his pigs on a nearby island where they could forage safe from predators. But that was what brought him to the attention of Portsmouth's inhabitants, who ordered the clerk to reprimand him for "intrudeinge on" the town's

"King Philip's Herds" appeared in *William and Mary Quarterly* 51, no. 4 (October 1994): 601–624.

rights when he ferried his beasts to "Hog-Island." The townsmen insisted that he remove "Such Swine or other Catle" as he had put there, on pain of legal action. They took the unusual step of instructing the clerk to make two copies of the letter and retain the duplicate—in effect preparing their legal case even before the recipient contested their action.

It was by no means unusual for seventeenth-century New Englanders to find themselves in trouble with local officials, particularly when their search for gain conflicted with the rights of the community. But this case was different. We can only wonder what Metacom, whom the English called King Philip, made of the peremptory directive from the Portsmouth town clerk—for indeed it was to him, son of Massasoit and now sachem of the Wampanoags himself, that the letter was addressed. Because the records (which directed no comparable order to any English swine owner) do not mention the outcome of the dispute, we may suppose that Philip complied with the town's demand. The episode was thus brief, but it was no less important for that, because it involved the man whose name would soon be associated with what was, in proportion to the populations involved, the most destructive war in American history.

For three centuries, historians have depicted Philip in many ways—as a savage chieftain, an implacable foe of innocent Christian settlers, and a doomed victim of European aggressors—but never as a keeper of swine. Although the Hog Island episode may seem unrelated to the subsequent horrors of King Philip's War, the two events were in fact linked. Philip resorted to violence in 1675 because of mounting frustrations with colonists, and no problem vexed relations between settlers and Indians more frequently in the years before the war than the control of livestock. English colonists imported thousands of cattle, swine, sheep, and horses (none of which is native to North America) because they considered livestock essential to their survival, never supposing that the beasts would become objectionable to the Indians. But the animals exacerbated a host of problems related to subsistence practices, land use, property rights and, ultimately, political authority. Throughout the 1660s, Philip found himself caught in the middle, trying to defend Indian rights even as he adapted to the English presence. The snub delivered by Portsmouth's inhabitants showed him the limits of English flexibility, indicating that the colonists ultimately valued their livestock more than good relations with his people. When Philip recognized that fact, he took a critical step on the path that led him from livestock keeper to war leader.

Successful colonization of New England depended heavily on domestic animals. Nowhere is this better seen than in the early history of Plymouth Colony. Not until 1624—four years after the *Mayflower's* arrival—did Edward Winslow bring from England "three heifers and a bull, the first beginning of any cattle of that kind in the land." This date, not coincidentally, marked the end of the Pilgrims' "starving times" as dairy products and meat began to supplement their diet. By 1627, natural increase and further importations brought the Plymouth herd to at least fifteen animals, whose muscle power increased agricultural productivity. The leaders of Massachusetts Bay Colony, perhaps learning from Plymouth's experience, brought animals from the start. John Winthrop regularly noted the arrival of settlers and livestock during the 1630s, often recording levels of shipboard mortality among animals as well as people. Edward Johnson estimated that participants in the Great Migration spent £12,000 to transport livestock across the ocean, not counting the original cost of the animals.

Early descriptions often focused on the land's ability to support livestock. John Smith noted that in New England there was "grasse plenty, though very long and thicke stalked, which being neither mowne nor eaten, is very ranke, yet all their cattell like and prosper well therewith." Francis Higginson informed English friends that the "fertility of the soil is to be admired at, as appeareth in the abundance of grass that groweth everywhere." "It is scarce to be believed," he added, "how our kine and goats, horses, and hogs do thrive and prosper here and like well of this country." Colonists preferred to settle in areas with ample natural forage. Salt marshes attracted settlers to Hampton, New Hampshire, and Sudbury's founders valued their town's riverside fresh meadow. Haverhill's settlers negotiated with the colony government for a large tract for their town in order to satisfy their "over-weaning desire . . . after Medow land." Most inland clearings bore mute witness to recent habitation by Indians, whose periodic burnings kept the areas from reverting to forest.

The size of a town's herds soon became an important measure of its prosperity. As early as 1634, William Wood noted that Dorchester, Roxbury, and Cambridge were particularly "well stored" with cattle. Other commentators added to the list of towns with burgeoning herds. In 1651, Edward Johnson tallied the human and livestock populations for several communities as a measure of divine favor. His enumeration revealed that towns with three or four dozen families also contained several hundred head of livestock. Like Old Testament patriarchs, New England farmers counted their blessings as they surveyed their herds.

Their interest in livestock grew in part from their English experience. Many settlers came from England's wood-pasture region, where they had engaged in a mixed husbandry of cattle and grain. In New England, the balance in that agrarian equation tipped toward livestock because the region's chronic labor shortage made raising cattle a particularly efficient use of resources: Selectmen usually hired one or two town herdsmen, freeing other livestock owners to clear fields, till crops, and construct buildings and fences. Until settlers managed to plant English hay, livestock foraged, on the abundant, though less nutritious, native grasses, converting otherwise worthless herbage into milk and meat for consumption and sale. Livestock were so important to survival that New Englanders reversed the usual English fencing practices. English law required farmers to protect their crops by confining livestock within fenced or hedged pastures, but New England farmers were enjoined to construct and maintain sufficiently sturdy fences around cornfields to keep their peripatetic beasts out.

Raising livestock had cultural as well as economic ramifications. For colonists, the absence of indigenous domestic animals underscored the region's essential wildness. "The country is yet raw," wrote Robert Cushman in 1621, "the land untilled; the cities not builded; the cattle not settled." The English saw a disturbing symmetry between the savagery of the land and its human and animal inhabitants. America, noted Cushman, "is spacious and void," and the Indians "do but run over the grass, as do also the foxes and wild beasts." Such evaluations ultimately fueled colonists' own claims to the land. The "savage people," argued John Winthrop, held no legitimate title "for they inclose no ground, neither have they cattell to maintayne it, but remove their dwellings as they have occasion." Winthrop's objection to the Indians' semi-nomadic habits stemmed from a cultural assumption that equated civilization with sedentary way of life that he linked to the keeping of domesticated animals. Drawing on biblical history, Winthrop argued that a "civil" right to the earth resulted when, "as men and cattell increased, they appropriated some parcells of ground by enclosing and peculiar manurance." Subduing—indeed, domesticating—the wilderness with English people and English beasts thus became a cultural imperative. New England could become a new Canaan, a land of milk and honey, only if, Thomas Morton wryly observed, "the Milke came by the industry" of its civilizing immigrants and their imported livestock.

Accordingly, only those Indians who submitted to "domestication" could live in the New England Canaan. They had to accept Christianity, of course; in addition, colonists insisted that they adopt English ways entirely, including the keeping of domestic animals. Roger Williams urged natives to move "from Barbarism to Civilitie, in forsaking their filthy nakednes, in keeping some kind of Cattell." John Eliot offered livestock, among other material incentives, to entice Indians to become civilized. He admonished one native audience: "if you were more wise to know God, and obey his Commands, you would work more then [sic] you do." Labor six days a week, as God commanded and the English did, and, Eliot promised, "you should have cloths, houses, cattle, riches as they have. God would give you them."

To assist Indians in making this transformation, Puritan officials established fourteen "praying towns" where they could proceed toward conversion as they earned the material rewards Providence would bestow. The inhabitants of these communities not only would learn to worship God as the English did but also would wear English clothes, live in English framed houses, and farm with English animals. Among the goods sent from England to support this civilizing program were seven bells for oxen, to be distributed to Indian farmers who exchanged their traditional hoe agriculture for the plow. Soon the increase in livestock became as much a hallmark of the success of the praying towns as it was of English communities. Daniel Gookin reported in 1674 that the praying town of Hassanamesitt (Grafton) was "an apt place for keeping of cattle and swine; in which respect this people are the best stored of any Indian town of their size." He went on to observe, however, that though these natives "do as well, or rather better, than any other Indians" in raising crops and animals, they "are very far short of the English both in diligence and providence."

Praying Indians raised livestock as participants in what may be called an experiment in acculturation. By moving to places such as Natick or Hassanamesitt, they announced their intention to follow English ways—including animal husbandry—in hopes of finding favor with the Christian God. But the praying towns never contained more than a tiny minority of the native population; most Indians rejected the invitation to exchange their ways for English ones. For the vast majority, the cattle and swine that served as emblems of the praying Indians' transformation had a very different meaning. They became instead a source of friction, revealing profound differences between Indians and colonists.

As Indians encountered these unfamiliar animals, they had to decide what to call them. Williams reported that the Narragansetts first looked for similarities in appearance and behavior between an indigenous animal and one of the new beasts and simply used the name of the known beast for both animals. Thus *ockqutchaun-nug,* the name of a "wild beast of a reddish haire about the bignesse of a Pig, and rooting like a Pig," was used for English swine. Finding no suitable parallels for most domestic animals, however, the Narragansetts resorted to neologisms such as "cowsnuck," "goatesuck," and eventually "hogsuck" *or* "pigsuck." The "termination *suck,* is common in their language," Williams explained, "and therefore they added it to our English Cattell, not else knowing what names to give them."

Giving these animals Indian names in no way implied that most Indians wanted to own livestock. In fact, contact with domestic animals initially produced the opposite reaction, because livestock husbandry did not fit easily with native practices. Indians could hardly undertake winter hunting expeditions accompanied by herds of cattle that required shelter and fodder to survive the cold weather. Swine would compete with their owners for nuts, berries, and roots, and the presence of livestock of any kind tended to drive away deer. Moreover, the Indians, for whom most beasts were literally fair game, struggled with the very notion of property in animals. They assumed that one could own only dead animals, which hunters shared with their families.

Further, the adoption of livestock would alter women's lives in crucial ways by affecting the traditional gender-based division of labor. Would women, who were mainly responsible for agricultural production, assume new duties of animal husbandry? If not, how would men's involvement with livestock rearing alter women's powerful role as the primary suppliers of food? Who would protect women's crops from the animals? How would the very different temporal cycle of livestock reproduction and care be reconciled with an Indian calendar that identified the months according to stages in the planting cycle?

Animal husbandry also challenged native spiritual beliefs and practices. Because their mental universe assumed no rigid distinction between human and animal beings, the Indians' hunting rituals aimed to appease the spirits of creatures that were not so much inferior to, as different from, their human killers. Such beliefs helped to make sense of a world in which animals were deemed equally rightful occupants of the forest and whose killing required an intimate knowledge of their habits. Would Indians be able to apply these ideas about animals as *manitous,* or other-than-human persons, to domestic beasts as well? Or would those beasts' English provenance and dependence on human owners prohibit their incorporation into the spiritual world with bears, deer, and beaver?

Finally, a decision to keep livestock ran counter to a powerful hostility toward domestic animals that dated from the earliest years of English settlement. Because colonists often established towns on the sites of former Indian villages depopulated by the epidemics that preceded their arrival, no line of demarcation separated English from Indian habitation. Native villages and colonial towns could be quite close together, and the accident of propinquity made for tense relations. At least at first, friction between these unlikely neighbors grew less from the very different ideas that informed Indian and English concepts of property than from the behavior of livestock. Let loose to forage in the woods, the animals wandered away from English towns into Indian cornfields, ate their fill, and moved on.

Indians, who had never had to build fences to protect their fields, were unprepared for the onslaught. Even their underground storage pits proved vulnerable, as swine "found a way to unhinge their barn doors and rob their garners," prompting native women to "implore their husbands' help to roll the bodies of trees" over the pits to prevent further damage. Hogs attacked another important food source when they "watch[ed] the low water (as the Indian women do)" along the shoreline and rooted for clams, making themselves "most hatefull to all Natives," who called them "filthy cut throats, &c." In Plymouth Colony, settlers in Rehoboth and their Indian neighbors engaged in a long-running dispute over damages from trespassing animals. At first, in 1653, the colonists claimed to "know nothing of" the Indian complaints. By 1656, settlers had erected a fence along the town boundary, but because a stream—across which livestock were "apte to swime"—also separated English and native lands, the animals still made their way into Indian cornfields. Four years later, Philip's older brother Wamsutta, known to the English as Alexander, was still bringing the Indians' complaints to the attention of Plymouth authorities.

English livestock also proved to be a nuisance as they roamed through the woods. Cattle and swine walked into deer traps, and the English held the Indians liable for any injuries they sustained. Similarly, in 1638, when William Hathorne of Salem found one of his cows stuck with an arrow, he insisted on restitution. Salem officials demanded the exorbitant sum of £100 from local Indians at a time when a cow was generally valued at about £20. Roger Williams pleaded the natives' case with John Winthrop, explaining that the colonists had charged the wrong Indians and that the sachems were outraged because the English held them personally responsible for the fine levied for their subjects' purported offense. "Nor doe they believe that the English Magistrates doe so practice," Williams reported, "and therefore they hope that what is Righteous amongst our Selves we will accept of from them."

Williams went on to observe that "the Busines is ravelld and needes a patient and gentle hand to rectifie Misunderstanding of Each other and misprisions." He foresaw that endless recriminations would flow from colonists' attempts to raise. livestock in the same space where Indians hunted. Native leaders, finding Williams a sympathetic listener, informed him of the "feares of their Men in hunting or travelling," for they had reason to believe they would be held responsible for every domestic animal found hurt or dead in the woods. Williams urged Winthrop to work with the Indians to contrive an equitable procedure to be followed in similar cases so that Indian hunters would not feel so much at risk from the rigors of a judicial system that appeared biased against them.

Instead of recognizing the fundamental incompatibility of English and Indian subsistence regimes, colonial authorities repeatedly permitted joint use of land. In so doing, they assumed that Indians would agree that the colonists' livestock had, in effect, use rights to the woods and fields too. Indians could hunt on lands claimed by the English only if they accepted certain restrictions on their activities. Indians who set traps within the town of Barnstable, for instance, had "fully and dilligenttly" to visit their traps daily to check for ensnared livestock and, if any were found, "thaye shall speedyli lett them out." The Connecticut government imposed stricter limits on Indian hunters when the town of Pequot was founded in 1649. Uncas, the Mohegan sachem, was instructed "that no trapps [should] bee sett by him or any of his men" within the town, although colonial officials saw no reason completely "to prohibitt and restraine Uncus and his men from hunting and fishing" unless they did so on the Sabbath. Connecticut authorities acquired meadow land from the Tunxis Indians in 1650 and similarly recognized native rights of hunting, fishing, and fowling on the property so long as such activities "be not dun to the breach of any orders in the country to hurt cattle." As late as 1676, in the aftermath of King Philip's War, Connecticut officials allowed "friendly" Indians "to hunt in the conquered lands in the Narrogancett Country, provided they sett not traps to prejudice English cattell."

Joint use was doomed to failure, not by Indian unwillingness to comply with English conditions, but by the insurmountable problems that arose from grazing livestock on hunting lands. Accidental injuries were bound to occur and to disturb colonists, while Indians resented the damage done by domestic animals wandering out of the woods and into their cornfields. The behavior of livestock—creatures as indispensable to the English as they were obnoxious to the Indians—undermined the efforts of each group to get along with the other. Attempts to resolve disputes stemming from trespassing livestock led only to mutual frustration.

The Indians were doubtless the first to recognize the difficulties inherent in the joint use of land and the unrestricted foraging of colonists' animals. One Connecticut sachem actually attempted to restrict the *settlers'* use of land that he was willing to grant them outright. When Pyarnikee, who lived near Stamford, negotiated with town officials, he tried to make the English agree not to put their livestock on the tract, for he knew that "the English hoggs would be ready to spoyle their [the Indians'] corne" in an adjacent field," and that "the cattell, in case they came over the said five mile river," would do likewise. But the colonists would only assure Pyarnikee that livestock would always travel under the supervision of a keeper.

In another case, in 1648 in Rhode Island, an unfortunate Shawomet Indian spent five days chasing swine from his cornfields, only to be confronted by an Englishman, armed with a cudgel, who "asked the Indian in a rage whie he drove out the Swine." When he replied, "because they dide eate the Corne," the Englishman "ran upon the indian," and a melee ensued among the disputants' companions. An attempt to adjudicate the case led to further complications, for the Englishmen involved were Rhode Islanders whereas the land where the incident occurred was claimed by Plymouth. Skeptical of his chances for a fair hearing in the Plymouth court, Pumham, a Shawomet sachem acting on behalf of the aggrieved Indians, asked to have the case tried in Massachusetts.

It might seem remarkable that Pumham trusted the English judicial system at all. Yet like Pumham, many Indians used colonial courts to seek redress for damage caused by trespassing livestock. English authorities, in turn, often recognized the legitimacy of such complaints and granted restitution, as in 1632 when the Massachusetts General Court ordered Sir Richard Saltonstall to "give Saggamore John a hogshead of corne for the hurt his cattell did him in his corne." Trespass complaints were so frequent, however, that colonial governments instructed individual towns to establish procedures for local arbitration lest the courts be overwhelmed. In Plymouth Colony, the task of reviewing such cases fell either to town selectmen or to ad hoc committees. If the livestock owner ignored their orders to pay damages, the aggrieved Indian could "repaire to some Majestrate for a warrant to recover such award by distraint." Massachusetts and Connecticut adopted similar measures.

But the colonists were less accommodating than they seemed. They insisted that Indians resort to an English court system that was foreign to them, the proceedings of which were conducted in an incomprehensible language necessitating the use of not always reliable translators. (In the case described above, one of Pumham's objections to using the Plymouth court was his mistrust of the court interpreters.) Moreover, the English soon required Indians to fence their cornfields before they could seek reparations. As early as 1632, Sagamore John, who received the award of damages from Saltonstall, had to promise "against the next yeare, & soe ever after" to fence his fields. In 1640 Massachusetts law required settlers to help their Indian neighbors "in felling of Trees, Ryving & sharpning railes, and holing of posts" for fences, but this friendly gesture was coupled with stern provisos. Any Indian who refused to fence his fields after such help was offered forfeited his right to sue for damages. In addition, Indian complainants had to identify which beasts had trampled their corn—an impossible task if the animals had come and gone before the damage was discovered. Beginning in the 1650s, Plymouth magistrates allowed Indians to impound offending beasts, but this meant either that they had to drive the animals to the nearest English pound or construct one on their own land and walk to the nearest town to give "speedy notice" of any animals so confined.

Even if they complied with English conditions, Indians could not depend on the equitable enforcement of animal trespass laws. The coercive power of colonial governments was limited—magistrates could hardly march off to view every downed fence and ruined field—and reliance on local adjudication meant that townsmen had to police themselves. New England colonists were notoriously litigious, but it was one thing to defend against the charges of an English neighbor and quite another to judge impartially an Indian's accusations of trespass. When problems arose near the centers of colonial government, Indians could generally get a fair hearing, as did Sagamore John near Boston. But the enforcement of animal trespass laws became more haphazard toward the edges of settlement. Indians in the praying town of Okommakamesit (Marlborough)—thirty miles from Boston—abandoned a 150-acre tract with an apple orchard for "it brings little or no profit to them, nor is ever like to do; because the Englishmen's cattle, &c. devour all in it, because it lies open and unfenced," and they clearly expected no redress. Along the disputed border between Rhode Island and Plymouth, settlers could scarcely agree among themselves who was in charge. Under such circumstances, as Pumham and his fellow Shawomets discovered, cudgel-wielding Englishmen all too easily took the law into their own hands. Farther away—in Maine, for example—even the pretense of due process could vanish. In 1636, Saco commissioners empowered one of their number to "excecut any Indians that ar proved to have killed any swyne of the Inglishe" and ordered all settlers summarily to "apprehend, execute or kill any Indian that hath binne known to murder any English, kill ther Cattell or any waie spoyle ther goods or doe them violence."

Given the deficiencies of the colonial legal system, it is not surprising that many Indians dealt with intrusive livestock according to their own notions of justice. Indians who stole or killed livestock probably committed such deeds less as acts of wanton mischief, as the English assumed, than in retribution for damages suffered. In their loosely knit village bands, Indians placed a premium on loyalty to kin rather than to the larger social group. The strength of these kinship bonds at once limited the authority of sachems (a point lost on the magistrates who had ordered sachems to pay for Hathorne's cow) and sanctioned acts of violence undertaken in revenge for wrongs done to family members. English authorities did not bother to inquire into Indian motives for theft and violence toward animals. But when, for instance, Pumham and other Shawomets—who had previously encountered irascible colonists and ineffective courts—were later charged with "killing cattle, and forceable entry" on settlers' lands, it takes little imagination to suspect that they were exacting their own retributive justice.

Once they took matters into their own hands, Indians could be charged with theft and destruction of property with the full force of English law turned against them. The penalties for such offenses further corroded relations between the groups. Unable to pay the requisite fines—often levied in English money—Indians found themselves imprisoned or sentenced to corporal punishment. Thus their options shrank even as livestock populations grew. Retaliation against the animals brought severe sanctions from the English, while efforts to accommodate the beasts on English terms required unacceptable alterations in Indian agriculture and the virtual abandonment of hunting. By the middle of the seventeenth century it was clear to the Indians that the English and their troublesome animals would not go away. The English, for their part, assumed that the solution was for Indians to abandon their ways and become livestock keepers themselves.

Some Indians—most notably King Philip—adopted livestock husbandry, though not in capitulation to English example and exhortation. Their adaptation was not a step, either intentional or inadvertent, toward acculturation, for they refused to make the complete transformation advocated by Englishmen who linked animal husbandry to the acquisition of civilized ways. The natives' decision instead fit into a broader pattern of intercultural borrowing that formed an important theme in Anglo-Indian relations during the first decades of contact. Much as settlers incorporated native crops and farming techniques into their agricultural system, Indians selected from an array of English manufactures such items as guns, cloth, and iron pots that were more efficient substitutes for bows and arrows, animal skins, and earthenware. Neither group forfeited its cultural identity in so doing, and when some Indians began to raise livestock—again largely for practical considerations—they deliberately selected the English beast that would least disrupt their accustomed routines.

Indians who raised livestock overwhelmingly preferred hogs. More than any other imported creatures, swine resembled dogs, the one domesticated animal that Indians already had. Both species scavenged for food and ate scraps from their owners' meals. Although hogs also competed with humans for wild plants and shellfish and could damage native cornfields, these disadvantages were offset by the meat they supplied and the fact that Indians could deal with their own swine however they wished. Like dogs, swine aggressively fended off predators, such as wolves. Roger Williams recorded an instance of "two English Swine, big with Pig," driving a wolf from a freshly killed deer and devouring the prey themselves. Hogs could also be trained like dogs to come when called, a useful trait in an animal that foraged for itself in the woods.

Swine keeping required relatively few adjustments to native subsistence routines—far fewer than cattle rearing would have involved. It made minimal demands on labor, rendering *moot* the issue of who—men or women—would bear primary responsibility for their care. Keeping cattle would have either dramatically increased women's work loads or involved men in new types of labor tying them more closely to the village site. Cattle needed nightly feeding, and cows had to be milked daily. Most male calves would have had to be castrated, and the few bulls required careful handling. Since cattle needed fodder and shelter during the winter, Indians would have had to gather and dry hay and build and clean barns—activities that infringed on their mobility during the hunting season. Some members of each village would have had to become herdsmen. Losing a cow in the woods was a more serious matter than losing a pig, for pigs had a far higher rate of reproduction.

In return for a limited investment in labor, native hog keepers acquired a year-round supply of protein that replaced the meat they could no longer get from a dwindling deer population. These Indians may in fact have enjoyed an improved diet, avoiding the seasonal malnutrition resulting from their former dependence on corn and game. Swine also provided products that replaced items formerly obtained from wild animals. Gookin noted in 1674 that Indians "used to oil their skins and hair with bear's grease heretofore, but now with swine's fat." And in at least one instance, Indians fashioned moccasins from "green hogs skinns" in place of deerskin. Settlers, in contrast, valued cattle for reasons that had little appeal for Indians. They plowed with oxen, but Indians who farmed with hoes did not need them. Colonists also prized the meat and dairy products supplied by their herds; although Indians would eat beef, most native adults were physiologically unable to digest lactose except in tiny amounts and would have learned to avoid milk products.

Settlers raised hogs and ate pork, but they did not share the Indians' preference for swine over cattle. Cattle were docile and, to the English mind, superior beasts. Swine, on the contrary, were slovenly creatures that wallowed in mud, gobbled up garbage, and were rumored to kill unwary children. Colonists named their cows Brindle and Sparke and Velvet; no one named pigs. The English kept swine as if on sufferance, tolerating their obnoxious behavior in order to eat salt pork, ham, and bacon. Most of all, swine keeping did not promote hard work and regular habits so well as cattle rearing did. Writers who extolled the civilizing benefits of livestock husbandry doubtless envisioned sedentary Indian farmers peacefully gathering hay and tending herds of cattle alongside their English neighbors, but the reality was hardly so bucolic.

Settlers instead encountered Indians who lived much as they always had, but who now had swine wandering across their lands—and occasionally into English cornfields. The colonists recognized only grudgingly the Indians' property in animals and usually assumed that the natives' hogs were stolen. In 1672, Bay Colony officials insisted that Indians pilfered swine although they acknowledged that "it be very difficult to proove" that they had done so. Other explanations—

that the Indians had captured feral animals or had purchased hogs from settlers—were seldom advanced. The fact that "the English, especially in the inland
plantations, loose many swine" and that Indians had hogs invited suspicion.

To discourage the theft of animals among themselves and to identify strays,
settlers used earmarks. Each owner had a distinctive mark that was entered in
the town records, to be checked when an animal was reported stolen or a stray
was found. The proliferation of town and colony orders requiring earmarks, as
well as the increasing intricacy of the marks themselves—a mixture of crops,
slits, "forks," "half-pennies," and so on—provides as good a measure as any of
the growing livestock population. The earmark itself became a form of property
handed down from one generation to the next. Instead of assigning earmarks to
native owners, however, magistrates ordered that "no Indians shall give any ear
mark to their Swine, upon the penalty of the forfeiture" of the animal. An Indian who wished to sell a hog had to bring it with its ears intact; if he sold pork,
he had to produce the unmarked ears from the carcass. This practice made native purchases of English hogs problematic, for the animals would already have
marked ears. Should the Indian subsequently desire to sell such an animal, he
could be required to "bring good Testimonies that he honestly obtained such
Swine so marked, of some English." Moreover, Indian owners were at the mercy
of unscrupulous settlers who might steal their animals and mark them as their
own. Colonists did not prohibit Indian ownership of swine, but they denied Indians the acknowledged symbol of legitimate possession.

The Indians' selective involvement with animal husbandry scarcely improved
relations between natives and colonists. To the previous list of problems new
and equally vexing issues were added, including trespasses by Indian animals,
theft, and difficulties with proving ownership of animal property. For settlers,
probably the least welcome change appeared when enterprising Indians started
selling swine and pork in competition with English producers of the same commodities. Many orders pertaining to earmarks begin with a preamble that assumes that native competition went hand in hand with native dishonesty. In the
Bay Colony, there was "ground to suspect that some of the Indians doe steale
& sell the English mens swine;" in Plymouth, settlers complained "of Indians
stealing of live Hogs from the English, and selling them." Thus magistrates urged
colonists to mark their animals to protect their property from native thieves. In
fact, the charges of theft were not substantiated; the real problem was commercial, not criminal. Earmark regulations aimed at least as much to make Indian
sales difficult as to make Indians honest.

Competition with Indians was more than colonists had bargained for. In
1669—just six years before the start of King Philip's War—the Plymouth General Court proposed to license certain colonists "to trade powder, shott, guns, and
mony (now under prohibition) with the Indians" as a means of discouraging the
local Indians' pork trade. The magistrates complained that "a greate parte of the
porke that is now carryed by the Indians to Boston" was "sold there at an under

rate," hurting Plymouth pork sellers. The court felt no need to make explicit connections between its proposal to sell arms and its complaint about competition, but the likeliest explanation is that Plymouth Indians were using the proceeds of their Boston pork sales to purchase guns from licensed Bay Colony sellers, tapping into an arms trade that the Massachusetts General Court had established in the previous year. If the Indians could obtain arms from Plymouth suppliers, they presumably would cede the Boston pork trade to Old Colony producers. The court expressed no particular interest in helping out Boston consumers who spurned the wares of their fellow Englishmen in order to buy cheaper meat; its explicit aim was to ensure that the pork trade would "fall into the hands of some of our people, and soe the prise may be kept up."

The Plymouth government's concern in this instance testifies to a remarkable set of native adaptations. If the Indians indeed brought pork and not live animals to the Bay Colony, they had learned to preserve meat in a way that appealed to English consumers. Some colonists, noting native ignorance of salting techniques, had assumed that Indians did not know how to preserve food. We do not know whether Plymouth Indians had learned to salt as well as to sell pork, but there is no doubt that they had identified Boston as New England's most lucrative food market. Almost from the start, Boston merchants and shopkeepers vied with farmers over the relatively scarce amount of land on the small peninsula occupied by the town. As early as 1636, officials prohibited families from grazing more than two cows on the peninsula itself, and in 1647, the town herd was fixed at seventy beasts. By 1658, swine had become such a public nuisance that Boston officials required owners to keep them "in their owne ground," effectively limiting the number of hogs each family could maintain. Given these restrictions, many Bostonians apparently gave up raising animals and bought meat from livestock producers in nearby towns, who were also raising stock for the West Indies market. Did the Plymouth Indians know this when they went to Boston? Their business acumen should not be underestimated. Although he did not refer specifically to the meat trade, Williams noticed that Indian traders "will beate all markets and try all places, and runne twenty thirty, yea forty mile, and more, and lodge in the Woods, to save six pence." Ironically, native enterprise met with suspicion rather than approbation from colonists who liked the Indians less the more like the English they became.

The extent of native livestock husbandry is difficult to measure because colonial records mainly preserve instances in which animals became a source of conflict. The evidence does suggest that Indians residing near English settlements had a greater tendency to raise domestic animals than did those farther away. The Wampanoags, living in the Mount Hope area between Plymouth Colony and Rhode Island, apparently began to raise hogs by the middle of the seventeenth century, after some thirty years of contact with English settlers. The location and timing of their adaptation were scarcely accidental.

The Wampanoags had close contact with settlers and, accordingly, a greater need for livestock than did native peoples living elsewhere. The ecological changes caused by English settlers steadily converting woodland into fenced fields and open meadows around Mount Hope reduced the deer population on which the Wampanoags depended; their swine keeping substituted one form of protein for another. Their trade in hogs and pork may also have been intended to offer a new commodity to settlers as other trade items disappeared or diminished in value. By the 1660s, the New England fur trade had ended with the virtual extinction of beaver. At the same time, English demand for wampum sharply declined as an improving overseas trade brought in more hard currency and colonies ceased accepting wampum as legal tender. But hogs and pork failed as substitutes for furs and wampum. Most colonists owned swine themselves and—as the response of the Plymouth magistrates in 1669 suggests—evidently preferred to limit the market in animals to English producers.

Wampanoag swine keeping also contributed to growing tensions with colonists over land, creating disputes that were even harder to resolve than those concerning trade. Land that diminished in usefulness to Indians as it ceased to support familiar subsistence activities regained value for raising hogs; indeed, such places as offshore islands held a special attraction to keepers of swine. The Wampanoags' desire to retain their land awakened precisely when settlers evinced an interest in acquiring it. By the 1660s, a younger generation of settlers had reached maturity and needed farms. In Plymouth Colony, bounded on the north by the more powerful Bay Colony and on the west by an obstreperous Rhode Island, aggressive settlers eyed the lands of their Wampanoag neighbors. During the 1660s, new villages were formed at Dartmouth, Swansea, and Middleborough, while established towns such as Rehoboth and Taunton enlarged their holdings—and in effect blockaded the Wampanoags on Mount Hope peninsula.

No man was harder pressed by these developments than King Philip. As sachem of the Wampanoags since 1662, he had tried to protect his people and preserve their independence in the face of English intrusion. Over time, his tasks became far more difficult. The number of occasions when the interests of Indians and settlers came into conflict grew as his ability to mediate diminished. Since Wampanoag land bordered on Massachusetts, Rhode Island, and Plymouth, Philip had to contend at various times with three, often competing, colonial governments. Even more problematic were his relations with neighboring towns, whose inhabitants pursued their economic advantage with little fear of intervention from any colony government and no regard for how their actions would affect Indian welfare.

Philip confronted the implications of New England localism most directly in cases of trespass. Colonial governments ordered towns to address Indian grievances but could not or would not enforce compliance. For six years, beginning in the mid-1650s, Rehoboth's inhabitants virtually ignored complaints from nearby Indians about damage from livestock, despite orders from the Plymouth court to solve the problem. In 1664, more than a decade after the issue first arose, Philip

himself appeared at court—this time to complain about Rehoboth men trespassing on Wampanoag land to cut timber—and even then he may have hoped
for a favorable outcome. But if he did, the court soon compounded his problems
by deciding to refer trespass cases to the selectmen of the towns involved. From
then on, Philip and his people would have to seek justice at the hands of the very
people who might well own the offending beasts.

The Wampanoag leader's problems in dealing with townsmen whose attitudes
ranged from unsympathetic to hostile worsened after the colony government
declared its hands-off policy on trespass and reached a low point in 1671, when
Plymouth officials charged Philip with stockpiling arms and conspiring with
other Indian groups to attack the colonists. He denied the charges and appealed
to Bay Colony magistrates to confirm his innocence. But Plymouth threatened
coercion if he did not submit to its authority, and Philip signed a compact that
further eroded his ability to safeguard Wampanoag interests. This agreement
compelled him to seek Plymouth's approval before he disposed of any native territory, but colony officials were not similarly constrained by the need for Philip's
permission before they approached Indians to purchase land. He also agreed
that differences between natives and settlers would be referred to the colony government for resolution, although the magistrates' record in dealing even with
straightforward cases of trespass gave little cause for optimism.

The Plymouth court intended to subvert Philip's authority over his people
in order to facilitate the acquisition of Wampanoag land by a new generation
of colonists who would, in turn, raise new generations of livestock. As early as
1632, William Bradford recognized that settlers who owned animals required
a lot of land to support their beasts. He complained when families abandoned
Plymouth to form new towns where meadow was available, but he could not
stop them. Instead, he could only lament that "no man now thought he could
live except he had cattle and a great deal of ground to keep them." Expansion
accelerated during the 1660s and early 1670s, once again fueled by a burgeoning
livestock population. During the two decades before King Philip's War, Plymouth officials approached local Indians at least twenty-three times to purchase
land, often mentioning a specific need for pasture. Sometimes they only wanted
"some small parcells"; on other occasions they desired "all such lands as the Indians can well spare."

The need to sustain their herds drove the English to seek Indian land, and their
expansionary moves collided with an urgent Wampanoag need to preserve what
remained of their territory. Joint use of land, although fraught with problems,
at least recognized mutual subsistence needs; by the 1660s, however, the practice
had greatly diminished.

Now the English not only wanted more land but demanded exclusive use of
it. They asserted their property rights even in situations when accommodating
Indian interests would have presented little threat. Allowing Philip to put his
swine on Hog Island probably would not have harmed Portsmouth's inhabitants

and might have improved relations between Indians and settlers. But what was Philip to think of the townsmen's summary refusal to share land, even when he proposed to use it for precisely the same purpose as they did? In that spring of 1669, Philip personally experienced the same English intransigence that he encountered as the representative of his people. After the Hog Island episode, and even more after his forced submission to Plymouth in 1671, he could not fail to see that while the colonists insisted that he yield to them, they would not yield in any way to him.

In an atmosphere of increasing tension, trespass assumed new significance. As colonists moved closer to native villages, the chances that livestock would stray onto Indian lands multiplied. With both groups competing for a limited supply of land, colonists did not restrain their animals from grazing wherever they could, while Indians grew ever more sensitive to such intrusions. Whenever livestock were concerned, the English ignored the Indians' property rights, while demanding that the natives recognize English rights. Indians resented encroachment by beasts that usually presaged the approach of Englishmen requesting formal ownership of land that their animals had already informally appropriated. Faced with the manifest inability—or unwillingness—of New England towns to solve the problem of trespass, and discouraged from seeking help from colony governments, Indians often resorted to their own means of animal control; they killed the offending beasts. This response would once have landed Indians in court, but by 1671 they faced far more serious consequences.

In that year, a group of angry colonists living near Natick very nearly attacked the Wampanoags of Mount Hope for killing livestock that had trespassed on Indian land. Interceding on behalf of the Indians, the Bay Colony's Indian commissioner, Daniel Gookin, begged for forbearance from the settlers, arguing that "it was not worth *fighting with Indians about horses and hogs,* as matters too low to shed blood." He urged the settlers to keep their animals on their own land; if any strayed into native territory and were killed, the owners should make a record of the fact, presumably to facilitate legal recovery. War was averted, but this incident nonetheless showed that tension over livestock had reached dangerously high levels.

Both sides now understood that disputes over trespassing animals epitomized differences so profound as to defy peaceful solution. Whenever Indians killed livestock that had damaged their cornfields, colonists denounced such acts as willful violations of English property rights—rights that some settlers wanted to defend by force of arms. For Indians, trespassing animals constituted an intolerable violation of *their* sovereign rights over their land. The problem intensified by the early 1670s, for the English were determined to deprive Philip of all means of ensuring the integrity of the shrinking tracts of Wampanoag land, even as they refused effectively to control their beasts. The issue of trespassing livestock generated such tension precisely because it could not be separated from fundamental questions of property rights and authority.

When war broke out in 1675, the Indians attacked first, but the underlying causes resembled those that had provoked English belligerence four years earlier. John Easton, a Rhode Island Quaker, sought out Philip early in the conflict to ask why he fought the colonists; Philip's response indicated that intermingled concerns about sovereignty, land, and animals had made war inevitable. He supplied Easton with a litany of grievances that recalled past confrontations with the English and particularly stressed intractable problems over land and animals. He complained that when Indian leaders agreed to sell land, "the English wold say it was more than thay agred to and a writing must be prove [proof] against all them." If any sachem opposed such sales, the English would "make a nother king that wold give or seell them there land, that now thay had no hopes left to kepe ani land." Even after they sold land, Indians suffered from English encroachments, for "the English Catell and horses still incresed that when thay removed 30 mill from wher English had anithing to do"—impossible for the native inhabitants of Mount Hope—"thay Could not kepe ther coren from being spoyled." The Indians had expected that "when the English boft [bought] land of them that thay wold have kept ther Catell upone ther owne land."

Because livestock had come to symbolize the relentless advance of English settlement, the animals were special targets of native enmity during the war. Colonel Benjamin Church, who led colonial forces in several campaigns, reported that Indians "began their hostilities with plundering and destroying cattle." In an attack near Brookfield, Indians burned dwellings and "made great spoyle of the cattel belonging to the inhabitants." At Rehoboth "they drove away many cattell & h[ors]es"; at Providence they "killd neer an hundered cattell"; in the Narragansett country they took away "at the least a thousand horses & it is like two thousan Cattell And many Sheep." As the human toll also mounted in the summer of 1675, English forces failed to stop Philip from slipping away from Mount Hope and only managed to capture "six, eight, or ten young Pigs of King Philip's Herds."

The livestock on which colonists depended exposed them to ambush. Early in the war, Indians attacked "five Men coming from Road-Island, to look up their Cattel upon Pocasset Neck." Settlers sought refuge in garrison houses and secured their cattle in palisaded yards but could not provide enough hay to sustain them for long. Sooner or later they had to drive the creatures out to pasture or bring in more hay. Philip and his forces—who had a keen understanding of the voraciousness of English livestock—would be waiting. Near Groton in March 1676 "a Parcel of Indians . . . laid an Ambush for two Carts, which went from the Garison to fetch in some Hay." At about the same time at Concord, "two men going for Hay, one of them was killed." Settlers counted themselves lucky when they escaped, even if their animals fell victim. When Hatfield inhabitants let their livestock out to graze in May 1676, they lost the entire herd of seventy cattle and horses to Indians who had anticipated the move.

The Indians seized and killed cattle mainly to deprive the colonists of food, but some of their depredations also suggest an intense animosity toward the animals themselves. One contemporary reported that "what cattle they took they seldom killed outright: or if they did, would eat but little of the flesh, but rather cut their bellies, and letting them go several days, trailing their guts after them, putting out their eyes, or cutting off one leg, &c." Increase Mather described an incident near Chelmsford when Indians "took a Cow, knocked off one of her horns, cut out her tongue, and so left the poor creature in great misery." Such mutilations recalled the tortures more often inflicted on human victims and perhaps similarly served a ritual purpose. Certainly when Indians—who found a use for nearly every scrap of dead game animals—killed cattle "& let them ly & did neither eat them nor carry them away," they did so deliberately to send a message of terror to their enemies.

Symbolic expressions of enmity, however, were a luxury that the Indians generally could not afford. As the war progressed, with cornfields ruined and hunting interrupted, Indians often needed captured livestock for food. When Church and his troops came upon an abandoned Indian encampment in an orchard, they found the apples gone and evidence of "the flesh of swine, which they had killed that day." At another site, colonial forces "found some of the English Beef boiling" in Indian kettles. In Maine, where fighting dragged on for months after Philip's death in August 1676, the "English took much Plunder from the Indians, about a thousand Weight of dried Beef, with other Things." Edward Randolph, sent by the crown to investigate New England affairs in the summer of 1676, reported to the Council of Trade on the devastation caused by the war. He estimated that the settlers had lost. "eight thousand head of Cattle great and small"—a tremendous reduction in the livestock population but not enough to starve the colonists into defeat or sustain the Indians to victory.

The presence of livestock in New England was not the sole cause of the deterioration in relations between Indians and settlers. But because of their ubiquity and steady increase, domestic animals played a critical role in the larger, tragic human drama. The settlers had never been able to live without livestock, but as the animal population grew, Indians found it increasingly difficult to live with them. Both sides threatened violence over the issue of livestock—the English in 1671 and the Indians, who made good on the threat, in 1675. The cultural divide separating Indians and colonists would have existed without the importation to America of domestic animals. But the presence of livestock brought differences into focus, created innumerable occasions for friction, tested the limits of cooperation—and led, in the end, to war.

Suggested Reading

Anderson explores the events and ideas considered in her essay more fully in *Creatures of Empire: How Domestic Animals Transformed Early America* (New York: Oxford University Press, 2004). In *Igniting King Philip's War: The John Sassamon Murder Trial* (Lawrence: University Press of Kansas, 2001), Yasuhide Kawashima highlights the impact of colonial authorities legal actions against the New England tribes. Daniel Richter's *Facing East from Indian Country: A Native History of Early America* (Cambridge, Mass.: Harvard University Press, 2001), gives an Indian perspective on many incidents during the colonial era. James D. Drake offers a new look at King Philip's War in his *King Philip's War: Civil War in New England, 1675–76* (Amherst: University of Massachusetts Press, 1999). Karen Ordahl Kupperman, *Indians and English: Facing Off in Early America* (Ithaca, N.Y.: Cornell University Press, 2000), examines contacts between Natives and newcomers in New England and south to the Chesapeake Bay.

PART TWO

Change and Continuity

The worst violence passed and relations between Indians and the Europeans gradually fell into distinct categories. Tribal people adopted and adapted new technologies, economic structures, and alliances to suit their own goals. For western groups on the fringes of the Great Plains, in particular, horses became an ever more important factor in their lives. Pekka Hämäläinen's discussion shows how these beasts changed the lives of buffalo hunters permanently. Without horses hunters could only attack animals that ventured into their immediate vicinity. Once mounted, however, hunters could follow vast herds for months. At the same time, their new mobility allowed plains people to expand their home territories, to seek new ones, or to raid their sedentary agricultural neighbors. Over time this increased the competition and conflict among Indian groups.

For tribes most directly in the path of intruding settlements, other factors proved important and often destructive. Epidemic diseases that had swept through Native societies upon first contact recurred for generations, reducing populations and disrupting social and economic practices. Coastal groups such as the Catawba suffered dramatic population losses that forced the survivors to join remnants of other tribes to create new village societies. Concurrently, repeated warfare between the international competitors as well as between whites and Indians continued to disrupt patterns of Native existence and reduce tribal populations.

During the seventeenth and eighteenth centuries, tribal numbers dropped while European colonies expanded their economies, territories, and populations. Gradually, as some Indian communities tried to untangle themselves from the thick Euro-American web, some Native leaders turned to religious and cultural solutions for their difficulties. On occasion they revived dormant ceremonies. More often, however, they sought to incorporate religious items into their teachings, much as they had adopted new technologies and goods into their economies. Alfred A. Cave chronicles how the Delaware shaman Neolin mixed some new ideas and practices with earlier ones as Indian and colonial peoples grappled with finding ways to deal with each other.

CHAPTER FOUR

The Rise and Fall of Plains Indian Horse Cultures

Pekka Hämäläinen

The most widespread popular image of American Indians depicts them as mounted buffalo hunters, bedecked with feathered headdresses and living in tepees. This essay examines the central element in that picture—the horse. These animals transformed almost every facet of plains life. They brought speed and mobility to people who had always walked everywhere. The horse allowed hunters to range farther from their camps and to bring home larger amounts of game than they had ever been able to hunt on foot. This freedom of movement enabled them to seek new lands, extend trade networks, and even carry out raiding and warfare against distant enemies. At the same time mounted warriors proved to be tough opponents as they defended their homelands with skill and tenacity. In analyzing these changes to village life, the author points out negative results of adopting the horse culture. Mobility increased levels of intertribal violence. It encouraged the destruction of the buffalo herds and even altered gender-based work within the villages. For the Plains Indians, horses brought fundamental and permanent changes to their lives and the plains environment.

After more than a century of intense academic scrutiny and popular fascination, the history of Plains Indians and horses has become a quintessential American epic. A sweeping story of cultural collision and fusion, it tells how the obscure foot nomads of the Great Plains encountered and embraced the peculiar Old World export and, by reinventing themselves as equestrian people, created one of history's most renowned horse cultures, personified in the iconic figure of the mounted warrior. Such romantic images may have lost much of their appeal for

"The Rise and Fall of Plains Indian Horse Cultures" appeared in *Journal of American History* 90, no. 3 (December 2003): 833–62.

modern historians, but recent academic trends have, rather curiously, only further glorified the history of Plains Indians and horses. As studies in Indian-European relations and environmental history have established the destructiveness of the Columbian exchange, it has become standard academic practice to set the splendor and prosperity of the mounted Plains Indians against the dark backdrop of death, disease, and despair that defines Europe's biological expansion to the Americas. In today's scholarship, the Plains Indian horse culture represents the ultimate anomaly—ecological imperialism working to Indians' advantage.

Taking a cue from that juxtaposition, virtually all modern histories portray the rise of the Plains Indian horse culture as a straightforward success story. According to this view, horses spread northward from the Spanish Southwest, repeatedly creating a frontier of fresh possibility, opening for each tribe in its path a new era of unforeseen wealth, power, and security. With the dispersal completed by the late eighteenth century, the entire Plains became the scene for an equestrian experiment that lifted the Indians, both materially and figuratively, to a new level of existence, while uniquely equipping them to resist future Euro-American invasions. Arguably, this view holds its appeal because it makes for a compelling and fundamentally uplifting story that is easy to incorporate into historical overviews and textbooks.

That success story has a bleak undercurrent that went largely unnoticed until recently, when ground-breaking studies shed light on the harmful effects of horses on Plains Indian socioeconomic systems and the environment. Horses did bring new possibilities, prosperity, and power to Plains Indians, but they also brought destabilization, dispossession, and destruction. The transformational power of horses was simply too vast. Although Plains Indians had experienced constant and profound culture changes before European contact, the sudden appearance of horses among dog-using pedestrian people set off changes that could spin out of control as easily as they could make life richer and more comfortable. Horses helped Indians do virtually everything—move, hunt, trade, and wage war—more effectively, but they also disrupted subsistence economies, wrecked grassland and bison ecologies, created new social inequalities, unhinged gender relations, undermined traditional political hierarchies, and intensified resource competition and warfare. The introduction of horses, then, was a decidedly mixed blessing. The horse era began for most Plains Indians with high expectations but soon collapsed into a series of unsolvable economic, social, political, and ecological contradictions.

The purpose of this essay is to trace those contradictions. Rather than merely listing the evils of equestrianism, it shows how both the drawbacks and the benefits of horse use shaped the history of Plains Indians. Indeed, conventional histories have not only underestimated the negative aspects of horse use; they may have even more glaringly underestimated some of its empowering effects. The history of Plains Indian equestrianism, in short, is a story of astounding successes and inevitable, daunting failures. Moreover, this essay argues, the patterns of success and failure took widely different forms in different parts of the Plains, giving rise to several distinctive horse cultures. Traditionally, scholars have recognized only two Plains horse cultures: the classic, flamboyant equestrian culture of the western Plains nomads and the less dynamic horse culture of the eastern Plains village farmers. Inherent in that model is a tendency to cast the villagers as cultural reactionaries who failed to embrace the liberating powers of equestrianism and, locked in space and time, were crushed by the double invasion of the aggressive nomads and the encroaching Americans.

The east-west, farmer-nomad dichotomy reflects both continuing academic efforts to categorize native societies into such artificial entities as culture areas and, more broadly, the long-standing scholarly conviction that North American history is best understood along longitudinal lines. In that view, the Mississippi watershed, the line of semiaridity along the ninety-eighth meridian, and the Rocky Mountains were and are great geographic barriers and ecological fault lines that have forced humans to make fundamental adjustments to their ways of life. The farmer-nomad paradigm of Plains Indian history and the very idea that there is a distinctive western history are expressions of the still prevalent east-west focus of our historical thinking. For scholars trying to understand the multifaceted history of Plains Indian equestrianism, however, the most revealing dynamics might be latitudinal rather than longitudinal. The central fact in the rise of Plains Indian horse cultures was the south-north orientation of the grasslands, which meant that the northward spreading horse frontier crossed several climatic belts. As a result, there were vast differences in the horse wealth of the tribes, particularly along the south-north axis, differences enough to generate contrasting patterns and distinctive histories. Moreover, all tribes—whether nomads or farmers, rich or poor in horses—faced difficulties in balancing horse numbers, ecological constraints, economic-military demands, and cultural imperatives, and the search for balance elicited a wide range of creative but variously successful equestrian adaptations that transcended the farmer-nomad dichotomy.

A comparative view that highlights variations in Plains Indian equestrianism also illuminates the history of Indian-Euro-American relations in the center of the continent. Reflecting their contrasting equestrian adaptations, Plains tribes adopted very different policies toward Euro-American colonists, policies that had deep and far-reaching effects and reverberated across a vast geographic expanse. At its height, the effective sphere of influence of the equestrian Plains Indians extended from northern Mexico into central Canada and from the Continental Divide to the Deep South. Finally, a comparative approach helps sharpen our understanding of the westward expansion of the United States. It explains, for example, why the U.S. Army waged long and costly wars against the Lakotas, while it managed to defeat the Comanches—in many ways the Lakotas' equals in power and influence in the early nineteenth century—with only a few decisive battles that, unlike Red Cloud's War or Little Bighorn, never made it into the lexicon of American history. More generally, the comparative approach shows that the oft-cited Lakota example represents the exception rather than the norm of Plains Indian equestrian experience.

Horses, Pastoralism, and Overabundance: The Southern Plains

Plains Indian horse cultures emerged from one of the great failures of Spanish colonialism. Spain's explosive expansion across the Americas was essentially equestrian. Horses—which had not lived in the Western Hemisphere since the Pleistocene extinctions—allowed the conquistadors to cover and claim vast areas and to shock and subjugate more numerous native forces. The Spanish preserved their military edge with relative ease in the tropical lowlands, where horses rarely became feral, but things became increasingly difficult in the late sixteenth century, when they approached the Great Plains. Discouraged by the vast, seemingly resource-devoid grasslands, the Spanish stopped in their tracks and built the colony of New Mexico. The horse frontier, however, kept moving on toward the Plains, hardly even losing momentum. The Jumanos, a multiethnic community of hunter-traders occupying the Texas Plains, may have obtained horses through their northern Mexican trade links even before the Spanish established colonial roots in New Mexico. The more northerly Apaches, the Jumanos' long-time rivals, received horses from Pueblo Indian apostates, who had run away from the missions in New Mexico. Instructed by the renegades, Apaches emerged as skillful riders and raiders by the 1650s.

The rapid shift to equestrianism was made possible by a nearly perfect fit between Spanish horses and the southern Plains environment. The region's long growing season guaranteed an ample supply of grass, and although the hot and dry summers exposed horses to ailments ranging from dehydration to starvation, those hazards did not thwart the proliferation of Spanish Barbs, descendants of hardy and heat-resilient North African stock. As Jumanos and Apaches traded for, and stole, horses from New Mexico and Texas, they experienced a profound techno-economic revolution. With horses, they could search for and kill bison with exhilarating ease and travel farther to trade, raid, and wage war. Horses also made nomadism infinitely more agreeable, especially for women, who were relieved of carrying belongings when moving camp. Most significant, horses opened a more direct way to tap energy. Dogs, Indians' only domesticated animals before horses, used the Plains' greatest energy source—the grasses— only indirectly, by consuming the meat of grass-eating animals their owners acquired for them, whereas horses drew their energy directly from grasses, bringing their masters one step closer to the ultimate energy source. Seizing the seemingly unlimited opportunities, Jumanos and Apaches built the first distinctive horse cultures of the Plains. Jumanos forged a long-distance trade network between New Mexico and the Caddo villages in eastern Texas, while Apaches integrated horses into their mixed hunting-farming economy, fashioning an intricate but dependable blend of part-time agriculture with seasonal mounted bison hunting and nomadism.

Despite their innovativeness and dynamism, the Jumano and Apache horse cultures would not last. Growing rapidly in numbers and eager to win a more secure outlet for their bison products in New Mexico, the Apaches destroyed the Jumanos as an ethnic group, annihilating some bands and absorbing others. By the early eighteenth century, Apaches dominated the entire southern Plains. But while they were still expanding their farming and hunting ranges to the east, north, and south, a different kind of mounted people, the Comanches, pushed down the Arkansas Valley from the southern Rocky Mountains, bringing with them the rudiments of a specialized mounted hunting system. That horse complex had been pioneered by the Rocky Mountain Utes, who had been experimenting with equestrianism since the mid-seventeenth century. Having migrated from the northern Plains to the southern Rockies in the late seventeenth century, Comanches simply borrowed the hunting culture of their Ute allies and transplanted it to the Plains. Other improbable promoters of Comanche equestrianism were the Pueblo Indians, who in 1680 drove the Spanish out of New Mexico, confiscated their horse herds, and embarked on a vigorous livestock trade with the Comanches and Utes. Supplied by Pueblo Indians and guided by Utes, Comanches moved rapidly into equestrianism. By the 1710s they had enough horses to invade the bison-rich grasslands.

At the heart of the ensuing Apache-Comanche wars was a collision between two highly contrasting horse cultures. Having become a remarkably adaptive society during their wide-ranging migrations, Comanches were able to transform themselves into a fully mounted society with astounding speed: Within a generation after their arrival on the southern Plains, they had mastered equestrian nomadism, hunting, and warfare and were able to challenge Apaches across the region. Moreover, Comanches' burgeoning horse wealth made the wars against Apaches not only possible but inevitable. To support their growing herds, Comanches needed reliable access to grass and water, which made it imperative for them to remove Apache gardens from the river valleys, the only spots on the grasslands where the crucial resources were available year-round. It was then, in competition with the fully equestrian Comanches, that Apaches found their mixed economy restraining and troublesome. Tied to their farms and only partially mounted, they were all but defenseless against the swift and unpredictable guerrilla attacks. By the early 1760s, Comanches had swept virtually all Apache bands from the southern Plains to their margins.

Comanche victory introduced the Plains to the era of full-blown equestrianism that was marked by highly efficient mounted bison chases, extensive reliance on bison for subsistence, and intensive nomadism. In fact, so complete was the equestrian shift that the Comanches can be viewed as pastoral people as well as hunters. The core of Comanche pastoralism was intensive trade in horses and mules, which was stimulated by a shifting political and economic geography. In

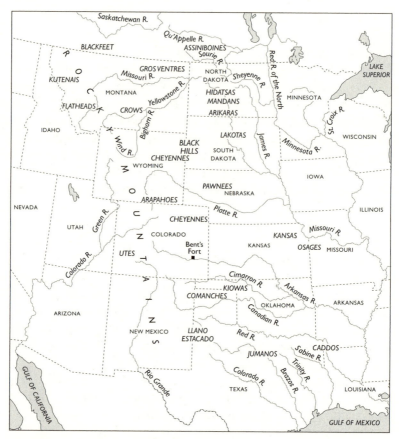

Plains Indians in the early nineteenth century. Over the preceding
century and a half, the use of horses had spread from south to north,
and different tribes had created very different horse cultures.

1750 the bulk of the horse wealth in the continent's center was still in the Southwest, a situation Spanish officials desperately tried to maintain by prohibiting all
livestock trade with Indians. Twenty-five years later, however, Comanche raiders
had transferred much of the New Mexican horse wealth into their own camps,
turning the Comanchería into the main livestock surplus area for three deficit
regions: the northern Plains, where climatic conditions kept the Indians chronically horse-poor; the southern prairies, where most tribes did not have a direct
access to Spanish ranches; and New Mexico, where the Comanches themselves
stimulated artificial demand through raiding.

Capitalizing on these imbalances, in the late eighteenth century Comanches
built a multifaceted trade empire that mantled the entire midcontinent. The
focal point of the trade system was the upper Arkansas basin, where western
Comanches ran a thriving seasonal trade center. In winter and summer, the

principal trading seasons, native and European trading parties traveled to western Comanche camps, where they purchased horses and mules with guns and other manufactured goods and then took the animals to the northern and eastern Plains, Mississippi Valley, and New Mexico. Another key trading sphere was on the northern part of the Llano Estacado, the vast flatlands of New Mexico and Texas, where Comanches did business with New Mexican traders known as comancheros, exchanging horses and bison products for metal goods, fabrics, flour, and corn. Farther east, along the middle Red and Brazos rivers, eastern Comanche bands operated a sprawling raiding-trading system. They plundered vast numbers of horses and mules during large-scale summer raids into Texas and then channeled the animals into New Mexico through the upper Arkansas trade center and to Louisiana through Wichita middlemen. In the early nineteenth century, after having ousted Wichitas from the trade chain, eastern Comanches controlled a bustling trade gateway, which funneled horses and mules to Americans, Osages, and the immigrant tribes of Indian Territory and absorbed guns and other manufactured goods. The volume of these eastern transactions could be staggering. In the late eighteenth and early nineteenth centuries, Comanches often sold hundreds of horses and mules to American trading parties, and in 1847, at a single trade fair, they reportedly sold fifteen hundred mules to Osages for seventy-five thousand dollars worth of manufactured goods. The ramifications of the trade were felt far beyond the Mississippi watershed, where Comanche horses and mules fueled the expansion of the American settlement frontier into Missouri and the opening of cotton lands in the South.

The effects extended to the north as well. The flourishing Comanche trade empire became a magnet for other nomads, who began to gravitate to the south and mimic the Comanche livestock economy. This changed the equestrian history of the western Plains. In the 1760s, soon after having acquired horses on the Black Hills, the Kiowas attached themselves to the Comanche trade network and began shuttling horses from the upper Arkansas center to the northern Plains. In the 1780s, drawn by warmer climates and greater horse wealth, Kiowas left their Black Hills homelands for good, pushed south of the Arkansas River, and, after a period of fighting, in 1806 made peace with the Comanches. Thereafter, the two tribes operated as close allies, sharing a similar horse culture. The next migration wave followed soon after. Enticed by the vacant niche in the trade chain, several Cheyenne and Arapaho bands migrated from the Black Hills to the central Plains, positioning themselves between the Arkansas center and the Mandan-Hidatsa trade nexus on the middle Missouri River. By this time, the Comanche and Kiowa livestock economy had reached such magnitude that Cheyennes and Arapahoes could become highly specialized intermediaries. Trade was disrupted briefly in the 1830s, when Cheyennes and Arapahoes made a bid to monopolize access to the newly established Bent's Fort on the Arkansas River, but commercial gravity soon pulled the tribes back together. The four tribes formed a peace in 1840, agreed on a joint occupancy of the Arkansas basin, and embarked on extensive livestock trade with Charles and William Bent, who in turn supplied the Santa Fe traders, overlanders, and the booming mule industry in Missouri.

The livestock trade made the Indians extraordinarily wealthy, but the new economy also required profound and often difficult adjustments. The southern Plains tribes were balancing between two economies—a trade economy demanding large numbers of surplus horses and a subsistence economy demanding large numbers of bison—and the balancing act created a perennial dilemma: they had to maintain much larger domestic herds than specialized bison hunters would have found optimal. In fact, the southern Plains pastoralists and horse traders kept two sets of animals that served different economic and cultural needs. The stolen horses and mules were reserved for trade and passed through the trade networks rapidly, whereas the animals they raised themselves were treated almost like family members. "Some men," Post Oak Jim, a Comanche, told an anthropologist in 1933, "loved their horses more than they loved their wives." In the 1850s, Sanaco, a Comanche chief, refused to sell his favorite horse to an American official, explaining that trading the animal "would prove a calamity to his whole band, as it often required all the speed of this animal to insure success in the buffalo chase . . . moreover, he said (patting his favorite on the neck), 'I love him very much.'"

Trying to meet their commercial, domestic, and cultural needs, the southern Plains pastoralists acquired and maintained vast herds. According to contemporary estimates, an average early-nineteenth-century Comanche or Kiowa family owned thirty-five horses and mules, five to six times more than basic hunting and transportation needs would have required. As middleman traders, Cheyennes and Arapahoes could get by with smaller herds, but they too had more horses than was needed for effective mounted nomadism. Their wealth did not come without complications. In a Cheyenne tradition, the All-Father Creator, Maheo, told Cheyenne priests, "You may have horses," but he warned them about the inevitable sacrifices: "If you have horses everything will be changed for you forever." He offered specifics. "You will have to move around a lot to find pasture for your horses. . . . You will have to have fights with other tribes, who will want your pasture land or the places you hunt. . . . Think, before you decide."

Like other southern Plains tribes, Cheyennes became hunter-pastoralists who lived on their horses' terms. They geared their movement patterns, annual cycle of subsistence activities, and labor organization—all long determined by the habits of the bison—around the foraging requirements of their horses. They spent winters in river bottoms, seeking shelter, water, and cottonwood for their animals and making only sporadic hunts. Winters were particularly onerous for women, whose responsibility it was to secure additional winter forage, such as cottonwood bark, for horses. In late spring the Indians returned to the open grasslands, where they broke into numerous small groups that migrated constantly, carefully coordinating their moves to guarantee a steady supply of grass and fresh, low-saline water for their herds. Hunting assumed a greater role, but since the horses demanded continuous management and protection, major hunting efforts had to be limited to a few concentrated sprees. The southern Plains Indians did most of their hunting in early summer, when their horses had recovered from the hardships of winter, and in late fall, when bison had completed mating and had grown their thick winter robes. Those brief, communitywide hunts were the only time when the scattered bands could come together and nourish a sense of tribal identity and communal solidarity. The southern Plains Indians were not full-fledged pastoralists in that they still relied on bison for the bulk of their dietary needs and used horseflesh only as an emergency food. By all other criteria, however, they had become pastoral people.

This pastoral shift also restructured foreign relations. In a process that mirrored the evolution of many other pastoral cultures, intensive livestock herding and trade entangled Plains pastoralists in almost constant raiding warfare with neighboring sedentary groups. Although ingrained in the male warrior cult, raiding was for Plains pastoralists primarily an act of resource extraction. Even though wild horses were readily available on the Texas Plains, the pastoralists always preferred to supplement their domestic production by raiding. There were compelling economic reasons for this. Raiding not only supplied domesticated, ready-to-sell horses but also allowed the Indians to capture mules that commanded high prices in eastern markets. Raiding also yielded an important by-product: slave labor. In the early nineteenth century, as Comanches and Kiowas extended their livestock raids toward the untapped ranches in Texas and northern Mexico, they also brought back hundreds of captives, emerging by the 1820s as large-scale slave owners. The captives formed the core labor force that allowed Comanches and Kiowas to elevate their livestock herding and trade into the largest industry in the midcontinent. Comanche and Kiowa raids had an enormous impact south of the Rio Grande, turning much of northern Mexico into an exploited and fragmented raiding hinterland. One observer wrote in 1846 that "scarcely has a hacienda or rancho on the frontier been unvisited, and every where the people have been killed or captured. The roads are impassable, all traffick is stopped, the ranchos barricaded, and the inhabitants afraid to venture out of their doors." The destruction proved critical during the Mexican-American War; through their power politics, Comanches and Kiowas had inadvertently paved the way for the United States' takeover of the Southwest.

Meanwhile, the Indians themselves were struggling to cope with the massive injection of privately owned human and horse wealth into their societies. By the early nineteenth century, marked status distinctions had emerged among Comanches and Kiowas. At the top of the hierarchy were the few men who had accumulated dozens or even hundreds of surplus horses that allowed them to dominate the wealth-generating livestock trade. By giving away valuable trade goods and horses, those men could acquire several wives and slaves, prestige, and political support. The most successful of them became band leaders and, if their diplomatic skills matched their business skills, divisional headmen. Kiowas called them *óngop* (the fine, distinguished, perfect, or best). The women of prominent families enjoyed extensive privileges as well. It was not uncommon for the *paraio* (chief wife) of a wealthy Comanche man to command several "chore wives" and captive boys who did most of the heavy work from hide dressing to daily horse herding.

The vast majority of people belonged to the second tier of middling sorts who owned ten to twenty horses—enough for comfortable nomadism but not for extensive livestock trade or a place among those considered well-off. Although the heads of such middling families sometimes built large herds as a result of gifts from wealthy relatives, their ascendancy to the highest social rank was blocked by their position at the receiving end of the status-producing generosity chains. Lacking access to large-scale captive labor, the women of the middling families spent more time herding horses than the women of the elite families. Kiowas called the middle-rank people *óndeigúp'a* (second best). At the bottom of the ladder were men with only a few or no horses, known simply as the *kóon* (poor) among Kiowas, who deemed it necessary to assert, "The poor are also allowed. They are our own people." The poor men had to borrow horses for hunting and serve as herders in return, but their anguish was more social than material in nature. Lacking horses, they also lacked the crucial social capital that opened access to marriage, the fundamental symbol of masculine honor, and in frustration often tried to steal the wives of higher-ranking men.

In the end, however, the greatest threats to native societies from pastoralism were ecological. The very strategies that had made possible the extraordinary florescence of the southern Plains horse culture also precipitated its collapse. Intense horse herding, growing domestic horse herds, and large-scale trade proved too heavy for the grassland ecology, triggering a steep decline in bison numbers. Large domestic herds competed with bison for the limited riverine resources, depriving bison of their means of winter survival and possibly transmitting deadly bovine diseases such as anthrax. Making matters worse, Comanches opened their hunting territories to foreign groups in exchange for trade privileges, and Cheyennes and Arapahoes embarked in the 1820s on intensive production of buffalo robes to fuel their trade with Americans. Pressured from all sides, bison herds became seriously depleted on the Texas Plains by the 1830s. By the 1850s, following a deep drought and the opening of several heavily trafficked overland trails across the central Plains, the bison herds were vanishing all across the western Plains below the Platte River, causing periodic famines.

As their subsistence economy crumbled with the dwindling bison herds, Comanches lost the ability to restore their numbers after disease epidemics. Their population fell from some 20,000 in the 1820s to fewer than 5,000 in the 1860s, forcing them to scale down their political and economic ambitions. They dismantled their trade empire, yielded large tracts to the Anglo-Texan ranching frontier, and, together with Kiowas, Cheyennes, and Arapahoes, concentrated on opportunistic raiding along the Santa Fe Trail. The decrease in the bison herds also fueled internal rivalry, splintering the Cheyennes and Arapahoes into bitter factions that struggled for the shrinking resources and for political power. Starving and desperate, the southern Plains tribes began to raise even more horses, which they increasingly used for food. With up to eighty horses per family in the 1850s and 1860s, they were in the process of becoming bona fide pastoralists who relied on domesticated animals for much of their food supply.

When the U.S. Army pushed to the southern and central Plains after the Civil War, the pastoral conversion was still incomplete. Fully aware that the Indians' greatest weakness lay in their shifting economy, the army launched a total war that combined cooperation with professional buffalo hunters, prolonged winter campaigns that disrupted the Indians' herding cycle, and systematic slaughtering of captured Indian horses. American hunters finished off the remaining bison from the central Plains by 1868, setting the stage for a brutal and decisive campaign against the Cheyennes and Arapahoes the following winter. The army then took the total warfare to Comanche and Kiowa territory, where American hunters, protected and supplied by army soldiers, virtually exterminated the bison herds by the fall of 1874. The following winter campaign, the so-called Red River War, was merely a stamping out of people who had lost their ability both to feed and to defend themselves.

A World Divided by Horses: The Northern Plains

During the seventeenth and early eighteenth centuries, when the southern and central Plains saw the rise and fall of several horse cultures, the northern Plains tribes continued their traditional pedestrian existence. For more than a century, the horse frontier remained locked in the south, its expansion curbed by an unfavorable commercial geography: horses remained scarce on the southern Plains before the Pueblo Revolt of 1680 unleashed large-scale diffusion, and the region's Indians preferred to trade their valuable animals to the wealthy farming villages in the east. In fact, the first horses spread to the north, not through the Plains, but via the ancient Rocky Mountain trade network, which connected the Rio Grande valley to the northern Rockies. This trade chain carried horses, along with the knowledge of how to use and train them, to Shoshones and Flatheads by 1700 and to Blackfeet and Crows by 1740. After this breakthrough, horses spread rapidly across the northern Plains, reaching the region's farthest corners by the 1750s.

An account of Saukamappee, an elderly Cree Indian who lived among the Blackfeet and related Blackfoot traditions to the English fur trader David Thompson in 1787, provides a window into the cultural dynamics of horse adoption on the northern Plains. In about 1730, Saukamappee joined several Blackfoot bands that planned to slip into Shoshone territory to hunt bison and deer and, they hoped, "to see a horse of which we had heard so much." Locating the mounted Shoshones proved difficult for the pedestrian Blackfeet, but finally, "as the leaves were falling," they heard of a horse that "was killed by an arrow shot into his belly." The Blackfeet gathered around the dead animal, trying to make sense of the singular encounter: "we all admired him, he put us in mind of a Stag that had lost his horns; and we did not know what name to give him. But as he was a slave to Man, like the dog, which carried our things; he was named the Big Dog." Saukamappee's account captures two important aspects of the equestrian shift. First, Indians' prior experience with dogs greatly facilitated the incorporation of horses: having turned dogs into their beasts of burden, they were culturally preadapted for the utilization and subjugation of horses as well. The close association between dogs and horses was universal on the northern Plains, as various tribal names for the horse indicate: big-dog (Blackfoot and Cree), great-dog (Assiniboine), seven dogs (Sarcee), and medicine-dog (Lakota). Second, the idea of horses as superior dogs reveals a central feature of Indians' expectations: with the shift from dog to horse power, a future of unforeseen material prosperity seemed to have opened for them.

But the elation faded almost immediately, dissolved by harsh ecological realities. Climatic conditions became increasingly unsuitable for horses above the Platte, turning outright hostile north of the Missouri, the ecological fault line of Plains Indian equestrianism. The long and cold winters reduced the quantity, quality, and availability of forage, exposing the animals to starvation and causing heavy winter losses. In the winter of 1773 on the Saskatchewan Plains, a camp of Hudson's Bay Company traders, Assiniboines, and Crees lost large numbers of horses, "which," the Indians noted matter-of-factly, "is the case at this season of the year." The average winters were demanding enough, but in vicious ones, with deep snows and prolonged cold spells, the consequences could be catastrophic. In 1801–1802, for example, Blackfeet and Gros Ventres suffered heavy losses during an uncommonly severe winter; the latter lost between 80 and 100 horses to the cold (as well as more than 100 to enemy raiders), which left them virtually horseless. Such difficulties kept most northern Plains tribes chronically horse-poor. The household average varied between one and five, and many families had no horses at all. Only the southernmost of the three Blackfoot tribes, the Piegans, were relatively wealthy, possessing approximately ten horses per family. Piegans' success in herding was made possible by two ecological advantages: they had access to the protective Marias River valley, a superb winter sanctuary for horses, and their home territory was in the chinook belt along the eastern slopes of the Rocky Mountains, where warm dry winds made winters tolerable.

Their poverty in horses prevented most northern Plains tribes from making a complete shift to mounted nomadism. To do so, they would have needed at least six horses per family—one for hunting, two for riding, and three for dragging the lodge poles and carrying the tipi cover and other possessions. On the northern Plains only a few families managed to acquire enough horses for the nomadic takeoff. Most families relied heavily on dog transportation, which in turn kept them poor by general Plains standards: their tipis were small and crowded, they had few belongings beyond necessities, they walked when camps were moved, and they continued the pre-horse practices of abandoning the sick and disabled.

The scarcity of horses also precluded the shift to effective mounted hunting; with the exception of the Piegan Blackfeet, all northern tribes continued to make extensive use of the traditional pounding method. Pounding did not require as many horses as the mounted chase, but it was very labor intensive, involving the construction of extensive funnels and elaborate log and stone corrals into which the bison were driven. Pounding was also unpredictable. In mounted chases hunters went to the bison, but in pounding bison had to be brought to hunters—a complicated task that could fail in several ways: the bison could bolt prematurely, the flanks could fail to contain the frightened animals, or the corral could break under the mass of the frenzied herd. All in all, the great increases in material wealth, comfort, security, and spare time that became the standard for most southern and central Plains tribes remained unattainable for most northern Indians.

An even more fundamental difference between the southern and northern Plains equestrian societies was their relationship to Euro-American markets. The horse-rich southern tribes built an elaborate livestock trade system, which allowed them not only to remain independent of Euro-American markets but also to exploit the Spanish and Mexican settlements through horse and slave raiding. In the north, by contrast, the introduction of horses paved the way for Euro-American-driven fur trade and capitalist penetration.

Since the late seventeenth century the fur companies had tried to expand into the northern Plains, but they were invariably rebuffed by the Indians, who were unwilling to engage in laborious beaver trapping. That changed dramatically in the mid-eighteenth century when the Shoshones and Flatheads acquired horses and began to push into the hunting ranges of the pedestrian Blackfeet and Gros Ventres. Desperate to acquire firearms to block this equestrian onslaught, Blackfeet and Gros Ventres established close ties with Assiniboines and Crees, who in turn began an active gun trade with British and French traders on the Plains-woodlands border. The effectiveness of armed warfare—the Shoshone-Flathead coalition was in full retreat by the 1770s—only increased the demand for guns. Seizing the opportunity, the Hudson's Bay and North West companies built several trading posts among Assiniboines and Crees in the 1780s, turning the far northern Plains into a major fur trade district. Instead of beaver pelts, the companies now asked the Indians to produce buffalo robes and pemmican, a concentrated high-calorie mix of dried, pounded buffalo meat, fat, and berries, which they used to supply their extended trading post chains across central Canada.

The escalating fur trade brought military security to northern Plains Indians, but it also entangled them in a global capitalist economy that was, at least initially, largely beyond their control and comprehension. The fur trade exposed them to market fluctuations and alcohol and threatened to reduce them to debt and dependency. Yet the northern Plains tribes proved remarkably capable of absorbing such threats. They accepted European goods selectively, played off competing fur companies for steady profits, and incorporated alcohol into their ritual life to offset its corrupting effects. The real threat of market penetration was at once subtler and more profound: the fur trade helped change the relatively egalitarian tribes into highly stratified rank societies. But the fur trade alone did not trigger the process. The fur trade acted as a catalytic agent of social change on the northern Plains because the region's native societies had already been exposed to the disruptive effects of another alien element—the horse.

From the beginning, horse use undermined the egalitarian ethos of the northern Plains societies. Since horses were both extremely valuable and scarce, even the slightest differences in their ownership had far-reaching social repercussions. The owners of several horses not only enjoyed an above-average standard of living but also dominated the fur trade. Hunting on horseback, they could procure meat and robes much more easily than those who still relied on the laborious and uncertain pounding method. The polarization became even more pronounced after 1830, when American merchants entered the upper Missouri and the demand shifted from provisions to bison robes. Since preparing marketable robes was extremely laborious, it placed greater demands on female labor, and only a man with several wives could procure significant numbers of robes to trade. However, because bride-price was now often paid in horses, only the owners of several horses could arrange multiple marriages. Under such conditions, the concentration of wealth, status, and power could be astounding. As one visitor noted at mid-century: "It is a fine sight to see one of those big men among the Blackfeet, who has two or three lodges, five or six wives, twenty or thirty children, and fifty to a hundred head of horses; for his trade amounts to upward of $2,000 a year."

A personal trade of such magnitude translated into stacks of guns, blankets, and tools, but its significance was more than material. By redistributing their wealth in lavish giveaways, the rich could gain status, secure support in councils, and monopolize leadership positions. Such success made the other emerging elite, trading post agents, eager to attach themselves to high-ranking native men by marrying their daughters. Those marriages created the tight web of kinship relations and cultural compromises between native societies and trading posts characteristic of the middle ground, but they also solidified high-ranking families' privileged access to markets and prestige goods. Most important, the rich could use their horses to rig the production system to their own advantage. For example, the wealthy Blackfeet routinely lent their horses to the poor for hunting, collected between 50 and 100 percent robes as payment, and then sold the surplus at trading posts. Among the Crees, the poor and orphans often joined a high-ranking man's camp and became *otockinikima* (laborers) who worked as herders, skinners, and processors in exchange for food and clothes. Although such practices established a safety net for horse-poor families, they also disproportionately benefited the horse-rich men who for all practical purposes had become protocapitalists: they hired people for wages, avoided manual labor, and extracted wealth through their privileged access to the means of production and global markets. At the other end of the scale, people with few or no horses were becoming increasingly marginalized. If they did not attach themselves to privileged members of their bands, they often sold their labor directly to trading posts, working as herders, hunters, messengers, and guides, usually for paltry pay. In either case, they were serving elite people, who harvested great profits from their labor,

It has been argued that rigid rank distinctions did not emerge among the horse-rich southern Plains tribes because preexisting reciprocity obligations turned horses into a fluid form of property and prevented the wealthy families from denying non owners' access to their horses. In the north, however, a crucial difference emerged: horses were less often included in the property pool that circulated through the tribal reciprocity networks. The rich always redistributed trade goods and food—often lavishly—to meet their generosity obligations and solidify their social standing, but they generally only lent horses and, as noted, usually in exchange for extensive labor services. Horses circulated freely only within the immediate kinship network, giving rise to rigid and hereditary wealth and status distinctions: Blackfeet called the sons of the very rich *minipoka* (children of plenty). The elite also dominated the horse-raiding industry by manipulating the distribution of spoils so that men with weaker connections were often left with few or no horses. Finally, wealthy horse owners managed to protect their herds against the principal external threats, weather and enemy raids. According to oral tradition, Buffalo Back Fat, a rich Blackfoot chief of the early nineteenth century, advised his family members to diversify their wealth: "Don't put all your wealth in horses. If all your horses are taken from you one night by the enemy, they won't come back to you. You will be destitute. So be prepared. Build up supplies of fine, clean clothing, good weapons, sacred bundles and other valuable goods. Then, if some enemy takes all your horses, you can use your other possessions to obtain the horses you need."

The end result was a relatively rigid rank society in which exchange and social relations of production benefited a selected few at the expense of the vast majority. The concentration of wealth and power in the hands of a few had a particularly strong impact on the lives of women who married into large polygynous households; Blackfeet used the term "slave wife" to refer to any additional wife beyond a man's first three. Such women worked hard feeding and watering horses, scraping and tanning hides, and cutting and drying meat, and yet, unlike women in general, often had subordinate positions in the households. They had few personal possessions, wore inferior clothes, and were frequently abused by their husbands, who relied on violence to control their growing labor pool. Many of them also married very young, bore children when still in early puberty, and consequently ran a high risk of losing their lives while giving birth. Exploited, controlled, and hoarded by the male elite, the extra wives were considered less companions than instruments of production.

The most serious threat facing all northern Plains Indians in the equestrian period was the constant warfare that stemmed from the chronic scarcity of horses and the relentless Euro-American economic expansion. Between 1795 and 1802 the competing Hudson's Bay and North West companies built several trading posts deep on the Plains, providing the Blackfeet with a direct access to manufactured goods. No longer dependent on their Assiniboine and Cree allies for guns, Blackfeet cut off their horse trade and focused on building up their own herds. It was a devastating blow to Assiniboines and Crees. Discouraged by the harsh climate and the heavy labor investments required by winter herding, both had come to detest systematic winter care of horses as a waste of energy. They often cut their herds loose in forested areas at the beginning of winter and collected the survivors in the spring, when, as one observer put it, the "poor brutes" were "in a shocking condition." They accepted high winter losses as an inevitable part of equestrianism and relied on outside sources to restock their herds. Thus when Blackfeet ended their horse trade, they in effect destroyed the foundation of Assiniboines' and Crees' equestrian existence.

Assiniboines and Crees tried to compensate by using manufactured goods to purchase horses from the Mandan and Hidatsa villages, but they were soon edged out again, this time by American traders who ascended the Missouri River after 1804 and provided Mandans and Hidatsas with a steady access to eastern markets. Twice marginalized by Euro-American markets, Assiniboines and Crees saw their horse herds quickly disappearing and, facing collapse as equestrian peoples, turned to the only available option: they began raiding the neighboring Mandans, Hidatsas, Blackfeet, and Gros Ventres for horses. Inevitably, the wars spilled over to the bordering regions. Desperate to find additional supplies of horses, Assiniboines and Crees began to trade guns to Kutenais and Flatheads, thus making it possible for those mountain tribes to renew their expansion into Blackfoot and Gros Ventre lands. Losing horses to the north and west, Blackfeet and Gros Ventres in turn launched ferocious raids into Crow country to the south. Although the primary causes for the wars were the chronic scarcity of horses and their unequal distribution among different tribes, the warfare also reflected internal social conditions. This is illustrated by a Cree tale of a well-off man who instructed his son not to participate in horse raiding: "Here, my son, dress yourself. . . . Poor men are they who go on the warpath . . . for they hope to steal horses; but you, your horse is handsome; he is fleet of foot. And you yourself are handsome; you are not poor."

Punctuated only by short truces, the horse wars raged for over half a century, corroding the northern Plains horse culture from within. Although in theory the raids focused on property, in practice they led to frequent and bloody clashes, which sparked deadly counterattacks as the relatives tried to avenge their dead. It was estimated that women constituted between 65 and 75 percent of the total population of many northern Plains societies, a disparity that speaks volumes about the lethal nature of the horse wars. The endemic warfare also generated acute economic insecurity; dozens of animals were often taken in a single raid, which could leave already-poor bands virtually horseless. Finally, warfare was critical to the decline of bison herds. By fueling a fierce arms race, constant fighting compelled the tribes to maintain high-level production of buffalo robes for markets and to discard traditional checks against overhunting. In the 1840s bison herds were declining on both sides of the upper Missouri River, causing widespread starvation. So intense was the rivalry that it did not have the usual effect of creating buffer zones, neutral lands where game animals could find respite from human predation. On the contrary, the wars over buffalo-hunting ranges pitted even the oldest partners, Blackfeet and their Gros Ventre allies and Assiniboines and their Cree allies, against one another, critically weakening all sides. That made Euro-American military takeover virtually effortless. Exhausted by starvation, disease, and decades of fighting, the northern tribes could rally only weak resistance against the encroaching Americans and Canadians. By 1877, after only a few fights with the U.S. Army, all northern tribes were confined on reservations on both sides of the forty-ninth parallel.

Among the northern tribes the horse wars were especially detrimental to the Crows, who thus far had largely escaped the negative aspects of equestrianism. An offshoot of the Hidatsa nation, the Crows migrated in the seventeenth century to the Yellowstone River, where they cleared small gardens. Soon after, they obtained horses and, like the other northern tribes, found mounted life both liberating and troubling. Encouraged by the possibilities of equestrian hunting, they cut off their farming activities—only gradually to realize that horse herding was complicated in the northern climate. However, in their quest to make equestrianism work in the harsh latitudes, Crows had a crucial advantage: they had access to the Rocky Mountain foothills and, through South Pass, to the Wind River basin. Fashioning an elaborate system of transhumance, they moved their herds each winter to the protective mountain canyons, where the growing season was longer and where their animals could escape the elements on the Plains. Migrations to the highland pastures not only minimized winter losses but also allowed Crows to meet Shoshone traders at regular fairs and tap into the Rocky Mountain horse reservoir.

The famed Crow chief Arapooish, speaking around 1830, told a visitor that the Great Spirit had put Crow country "exactly in the right place," emphasizing winter conditions: "To the north it is cold; the winters are long and bitter, with no grass; you cannot keep horses there, but must travel with dogs." In Crow country, by contrast, winters were much more tolerable: "when winter comes on, you can take shelter in the woody bottoms along the rivers; there you will find buffalo meat for yourselves, and cotton-wood bark for your horses: or you may winter in the Wind River valley, where there is salt weed in abundance." Making the most of the favorable geography, the Crows built sizable herds. The household average varied between 15 and 22 horses, many families owned between 30 and 60, and the accepted poverty limit for a family was between 10 and 20—more than the tribal average of most northern Plains groups. Such wealth allowed Crows to become successful middleman traders who channeled large numbers of horses from the Shoshone rendezvous to the Mandan and Hidatsa villages, where they routinely marked up their prices by 100 percent. They were known across the Plains for their trading savvy, large stocks of manufactured goods, and fierce independence of Euro-American markets.

That very prosperity was the Crows' undoing. The hard-pressed Blackfeet and Gros Ventres made raiding in the horse-rich Crow country a destructive routine by the 1820s. Desperate to obtain guns to block these incursions, Crows opened their lands to American fur traders and, inevitably, to the traders' microbes. Already reeling from war and disease, Crows suffered another blow in the 1830s when the Lakotas reached the Black Hills, where they were within striking distance of Crow horse herds. Caught between two aggressive fronts, Crows faced a rapid decline. One observer noted in the 1850s that they lived "in the hourly expectation of losing all their horses" and predicted that they "cannot long exist as a nation." Crows tried to escape annihilation by forging a series of desperate alliances, first with the much-weakened Assiniboines and Gros Ventres, then with the Americans, who recruited them as army scouts while driving them onto ever-smaller reservations.

The Incompatible Element:
The Horse among the Eastern Plains Villagers

As troubled as equestrian history was among the southern and northern Plains nomads, the complexities and contradictions of horse use were even more tangible among the eastern Plains village farmers. But at first horses seemed to offer only advantages and spread rapidly to the east; supplied by Jumano and Comanche traders, all villagers had horses by 1750. Even the Cheyennes, who had left the upper Mississippi Valley under Chippewa pressure, encountered the horse frontier on the Sheyehne River in the 1750s. Thus equipped, they began a grand migration that would take them across the eastern, northern, and central Plains and through almost every equestrian adaptation of the Plains. Two decades later, they had moved to the Missouri River, where they built farming villages near the Arikaras and gained a secure access to horses.

As elsewhere on the Plains, the benefits of equestrianism were immediate and irresistible. All villagers incorporated the horse into the hunt and began to make extended biannual forays to the bison-rich western Plains. Most villagers also added a new dimension to their traditional food trade by becoming middlemen between western horse nomads and Euro-American colonists in the Mississippi Valley. But horses simultaneously placed unprecedented pressure on village life.

If not carefully watched, horses destroyed cornfields with their voracious appetites and sharp hooves, and horse pastures competed with farms for the limited tracts of arable bottomland. In winter, when grass was in short supply, horses consumed enormous amounts of cottonwood bark, depleting the scarce timber resources. The villagers' privileged access to the colonial markets also invited attacks from the neighboring nomads, which forced the less mobile villagers to acquire even more horses and thus to place even greater pressure on local environments.

Previous scholarship has documented the inbuilt contradictions and mounting external threats. What has been less clear is the diversity of the villagers' responses to those equestrian dilemmas. The late-eighteenth- and early-nineteenth-century eastern Plains saw the emergence of several distinctive horse cultures, which all exhibited remarkable cultural flexibility and creativity in the face of overwhelming odds.

The Mandans, Hidatsas, and Arikaras chose to continue intensive agriculture and to suppress nomadic tendencies. Although they channeled massive numbers of horses through their villages, a typical household kept only one or two animals—far from enough for successful mounted hunts. In 1797 a visitor remarked that "even for the sole purpose of hunting their Horses are too few." All groups preferred small-scale hunts that seldom took more than a few days. Indeed, instead of leaving the Missouri Valley to chase bison on the Plains, Mandans, Hidatsas, and Arikaras let the river bring resources to them. Each spring and early summer, they collected huge numbers of drowned buffaloes floating past their villages and in time grew to favor the meat "to any other kind of food." "The stench is absolutely intolerable," an observer noted, "yet the soup made from it which is bottle green is reckoned delicious."

Those strategies had immediate rewards. The small herds did not compete with farms for the floodplain acreage, and the livestock trade allowed the villagers to trade away extra horses before the herds became ecologically unmanageable. As a result, their farming economy remained strong and crops voluminous. Given the northern climate, crop failures were strikingly rare, and their large fields yielded enough corn for their own use, trade, and even for their horses. Besides helping stabilize the farming economy, the livestock trade also brought handsome profits to Mandans and Hidatsas, who became the main horse suppliers to the vast deficit region north of the Missouri.

The sedentary and trade-oriented way of life followed economic incentives, but it also exposed Mandans, Hidatsas, and Arikaras to fatal external threats. Essentially garrison communities, they were relatively safe against frontal assaults but vulnerable to siege tactics. The Lakotas—who had reached the Missouri by 1800—frequently besieged the towns for weeks and forced the villagers to pay corn as tribute or, alternatively, interrupted the villagers' farming and hunting cycle and then sold them overpriced meat and robes. When Meriwether Lewis and William Clark probed the region, they dubbed the Arikaras "tenants at will," people who were at once exploited by and dependent upon the Lakotas. More destructive still, the villagers had become prime targets for epidemic diseases. Trade brought in deadly microbes that thrived in the crowded towns, while the small domestic herds and fear of Lakota attacks prevented the villagers from escaping the epidemics to the Plains. Huddled in their villages with "2, 3 & 4 families in a Cabin, their horses & Dogs in the Same hut," as Lewis and Clark reported, Mandans, Hidatsas, and Arikaras were struck repeatedly by devastating smallpox, measles, and influenza epidemics in the late eighteenth and early nineteenth centuries. The final blow came with the smallpox epidemic of 1837–38, which killed a third of the Hidatsas, half of the Arikaras, and nearly all the Mandans.

Meanwhile, the more southern villagers—Pawnees, Omahas, Poncas, Otoe-Missourias, Kansas, Osages, and Wichitas—chose a different strategy. They acquired large horse herds, put more emphasis on hunting, and became increasingly nomadic. By 1800 all those groups were spending up to seven months a year on the Plains and relying on bison meat rather than corn as their main source of food. The Cheyennes not only traveled to the west to hunt but stayed there permanently. Fleeing Lakota attacks and disease, they abandoned their Missouri villages in the 1780s and migrated two hundred miles west to the Black Hills. There, in the unique wet microclimate created by the mountain range, they continued to cultivate small plots while gradually gearing their society and economy toward intensive bison hunting and mounted nomadism.

On the surface, the nomadic shift seemed a success. Large horse herds gave protection against the western nomads, the hunts yielded robes that could be traded for guns at American posts along the Missouri, and the prolonged absences from villages reduced exposure to diseases. The hunts also doubled as an ecological safety valve by providing forage for horses and time for the overtaxed home environs to recuperate and for the farming system to operate. Combined, these factors made possible a relatively stable demographic development and the preservation of military power. The most numerous groups, Pawnees and Osages, were still major players in the complex borderland rivalries and negotiations among the Spanish, Americans, and Indians in the 1800s and 1810s. In the long run, however, nomadism created more problems than it solved. The extended hunts resulted in tangled and overlapping claims over hunting ranges, turning the eastern Plains into a viciously contested war zone where even the oldest allies often clashed violently. Worse still, the intensified hunting pressure depleted bison at an alarming rate, nearly exterminating the herds from the eastern Plains by 1825. Facing starvation, the villagers had to push even deeper into the western Plains, where good hunts were still possible. However, these hunting excursions elicited an ultra-aggressive reaction among the western nomads, who saw the hunts as an invasion of their homelands.

The rising level of warfare was evident in the southern section of the villager-nomad front in the 1820s, when Comanches were continually attacking Wichitas and sending two thousand-strong war parties against Osages. The attacks locked Osages to the east just when their homelands were becoming flooded with eastern immigrant Indians and infested with disease. Having ceded most of their lands north of the Red River by 1825, the increasingly nomadic Osages pushed aggressively southward, forcing the Wichitas to cluster in small fortified villages along the Brazos and Trinity rivers, where they soon fell under the shadow of the Texas republic. Some Wichitas even joined Comanche bands and, in effect, became naturalized Comanches.

The warfare was even more intense in the north, where Lakotas confronted the westward-pushing Omahas, Poncas, Otoe-Missourias, and Pawnees. The villagers' weakness in those wars stemmed from a typical equestrian paradox: their shift toward nomadism had put them on a collision course with Lakotas, yet they were not nomadic and mobile enough to defend themselves successfully in the ensuing wars. When they moved to the Plains to hunt, the villagers clung to their traditional social structure and moved in large units. Such mass parties were relatively protected against full-scale assaults yet easy to detect and vulnerable to hit-and-run attacks. By the 1830s the hunts had become a high-risk venture that produced little meat and high death tolls. While some Lakota bands thwarted eastern tribes' hunts in the west, others spread even greater destruction in the near-empty villages, stealing horses, burning houses, pillaging and destroying food caches, and killing the old and sick who had been left behind. The motive for such destruction was obvious: to eliminate the villagers' subsistence base and undermine their ability to compete for bison.

The Plains villagers' predicament during the equestrian period was thus both simple and daunting: the new era favored specialization and intensive nomadism, not their adaptive diversity. In hindsight, there seems to have been only one feasible solution—become fully nomadic and face the western tribes on more equal military terms. But such a transition could not be reduced to a simple cost-benefit calculation. Traditional leaders resisted nomadism, as they would lose their central roles as the controllers and redistributors of the agricultural surplus, and strong historical and spiritual ties connected the villagers to their ancestral lands, making the transition unthinkable for many and difficult for all. Moreover, to the villagers farming was more than a source of sustenance; it represented the very foundation and continuity of the universe. In Pawnee folklore, for example, corn and life were inseparable—"the voice of Mother Corn," renewed each year by painting a mouth and windpipe on a cob stem, "was the 'breath of life.'" As a result, most eastern tribes remained attached to their villages even when it had become clear that balancing between nomadism and farming would only weaken their chances of military survival. Only few experimented with nomadism. Facing assaults, disease, and death in their villages, Omahas, Poncas, and Arikaras deserted their homes and fields several times in the early nineteenth century for desperate attempts at life on the western Plains, but each time brutal Lakota attacks pushed them back. By 1850 the three groups had returned to their villages, where they were soon engulfed by the American settlement frontier.

Only one village group, Cheyennes, made a successful transition to nomadism. They had found nearly perfect conditions for this demanding shift in the Black Hills. Soon after their arrival in the early 1790s, they formed an enduring alliance with Arapahoes, longtime residents of the area, and opened a trade relationship with Lakotas. According to Cheyennes' oral history, their generosity with horses was the basis of the Lakota treaty. "The Sioux . . . only had dogs. . . . The Cheyennes gave them horses and other gifts. That practice is still in vogue." The Lakota accord resulted in a generation of relative peace during which Cheyennes gradually gave up farming and shifted to full-scale nomadism. With the conversion completed by 1810, their options seemed wide open. Some Cheyenne and Arapaho bands migrated to the central Plains, where they experienced a rapid rise and an equally rapid fall as horse traders and pastoralists. The remaining bands stayed in the north and forged an alliance with the expanding Lakotas. In doing so, they became participants in the only true success story of Plains Indian equestrianism.

Balance and Power: The Lakota Expansion

The remarkable ascendancy and staying power of Lakotas, their aggressive westward invasion and their ability to resist Americans well into the 1870s, have traditionally been explained by volume and organizational capability: they had more people, more horses, and more guns, and they possessed a more efficient military organization than their Indian and American rivals. But sheer volume and military efficiency is only half the explanation. Lakotas also became so dominant because they succeeded where almost all other Plains tribes had failed— finding a functional equilibrium among horse numbers, ecological constraints, and economic, cultural, and military imperatives.

Seen from one angle, large horse herds were the foundation of Lakotas' power: there was a direct correlation between their growing horse wealth and their ability to conquer. In the mid-eighteenth century, when horses were still a rarity among them, Lakotas were neither expanding nor domineering. In fact, they were facing a deepening crisis. Still largely untouched by European diseases, they were growing rapidly in numbers, and their homelands between the Mississippi and Missouri rivers were becoming depleted of bison and beaver. To the west, across the Missouri, stretched the vast bison-rich grasslands, but the pedestrian Lakotas were unable to penetrate the barrier of the populous and horse-using Mandans, Hidatsas, and Arikaras. So firm was the villagers' blockade that some Lakota bands settled down near the Arikaras to cultivate small fields, apparently abandoning their expansionist ambitions. The balance of power did not shift until the 1780s, when Lakotas managed to buy and steal enough horses from Arikaras to employ effective mounted tactics. At the same time, between 1780 and 1795 smallpox outbreaks ravaged the Missouri Valley, inflicting much higher casualties among the villagers than among the mobile Lakotas. After the epidemic outburst had exhausted itself, the dozens of villages that had lined the Missouri Valley had been reduced to a scattered few. By the mid-1790s, mounted Lakota war parties had driven the Arikaras upriver, thus opening a wide entranceway across the Missouri.

Once established on the west side of the Missouri, Lakotas had better access to horses and were soon ready to invade the prime buffalo range between the Missouri and Platte rivers. The expansion took place largely beyond Euro-American observation, but the Lakota calendars, or winter counts, hide paintings that recorded the most important or memorable events a group experienced in a year, suggest a close link between horse raiding and conquest. Many early nineteenth-century Oglala Lakota winter counts note massive horse raids and military victories. The terse but telling accounts also capture the thrill of discovering the abounding equestrian possibilities that existed on the western Plains. Many winters were remembered for equestrian breakthroughs, such as catching "many wild horses south of the Platte River" or bringing "home iron shod (horses)," "curley-haired horses," and "decorated tails." While committing themselves to nomadism and full-time hunting in the West, the increasingly mobile Lakotas regularly returned to the middle Missouri to raid the Arikaras for corn. They also prevented American attempts to mediate an accord between Mandans and Arikaras that might strengthen the latter, "because," as one observer put it, "they would lose, in the Ricaras, a certain kind of serf, who cultivates for them and who, as they say, takes, for them, the place of women."

By the 1830s Lakotas had seized the coveted Black Hills and forged an alliance with northern Cheyennes and Arapahoes, who were absorbed into the Lakota military-economic complex. However, those critical triumphs did not abate their expansion, which took on an added dimension: The Lakotas started to transform themselves into a hegemonic power. Once again, equestrian power played a crucial role. Moving in wide ranging parties, they raided Crows for horses in the west, captured large numbers of wild horses along the North Platte River, and then used their cavalry power to drive the Pawnees to the south and east and to plunder and collect tribute at the middle Missouri villages. By weakening the eastern tribes, the Lakotas could also dominate the burgeoning American fur trade along the Missouri. By 1850 they controlled a vast region between the Platte and upper Missouri rivers. Late converts to equestrianism, they had mastered mounted hunting and built an awe-inspiring military-economic complex that allowed them to become the dominant power of the northern Plains.

The extraordinary expansion and endurance of the Lakotas stemmed from a mixture of adaptive genius, favorable circumstances, and historical contingency. They were a populous nation with strong allies, a steady access to American markets, and a flexible political system that allowed the autonomous bands to take periodic unified action. They were also surrounded by weakened native groups, Crows, Pawnees, and Arikaras, and they largely escaped the deleterious effects of the changes sapping the strength of many Plains nomads after 1830—the removal of eastern Indians to Indian Territory, the opening of overland trails, and the consequent invasion of deadly microbes. But a comparative view shows that the Lakota success story had a paradoxical ecological component—relatively small horse herds. Although Lakota territory was more suitable for horse herding than the far northern Plains, it was nevertheless a region of harsh winters and a rather short growing season. Such conditions placed strict limitations on horse use and posed serious dangers to animal husbandry. Lakotas often found their horses too weak for hunting even during regular winters, while deep snows and severe colds could leave entire bands horseless. Such disasters, coupled with the exigencies of winter care, encouraged Lakotas to keep the herds comparatively small. Several contemporaries estimated that they were about as wealthy as Crows, which would put them in the twenty-horses-per-household range. Such herds were sufficient for mounted hunting and warfare but paled in comparison to the enormous wealth of the southern nomads.

This at least partially imposed management of herd size was a blessing in disguise; moderate in size, Lakota herds never became a serious threat to the riverine ecosystems and bison herds. Although Lakotas became much more heavily involved in the fur trade than the southern nomads—from the early 1830s on, they produced tens of thousands of robes for eastern markets each year—the bison ecology in their homelands remained relatively stable. Bison herds did not weaken noticeably until the mid-1840s, and even then the decline was less drastic than in the south. In the 1850s and 1860s, Lakotas were still enjoying good hunts, especially in the western ranges they had seized from the weakened Crows. Meanwhile, the southern Plains bison herds had been shrinking since the turn of the century, compromising the tribes' ability to rebuild their populations after epidemic outbreaks.

These contrasting ecological and demographic trajectories sent Lakotas and Comanches, who in the 1840s had shared between them the greater part of the western Plains, into sharply contrasting political trajectories. In the 1820s, both had numbered more than 20,000; by the early 1870s, however, the total Comanche population had dropped below 4,000, whereas the Lakotas still had more than 11,000 people living outside the agencies. Those 11,000, together with their Cheyenne and Arapaho allies, forced the United States into prolonged wars and delivered two stinging defeats—in 1868 and 1876—to the emerging world power. The only truly functioning equestrian culture of the Plains, the Lakotas, northern Cheyennes, and northern Arapahoes were also the last to be defeated.

For decades the Lakota experience has dominated our views of Plains Indians: it has become the model for all Plains nomads and their histories. The Lakota exodus from the Mississippi Valley into the heart of the northern Plains has become the metanarrative of the eighteenth- and nineteenth-century Plains, a story that supposedly encapsulates the full spectrum of Plains Indian experience from the adoption of horses to the exhilarating affluence of the buffalo days and from the fierce resistance against the American empire to the final, dreadful defeat. The Lakota story has also become the centerpiece of the corrective histories that have challenged the ethnocentric interpretations of colonial history in general and Plains history in particular. As Richard White has shown, the power struggles on the nineteenth-century northern Plains were not simply native resistance to overwhelming Euro-American onslaught, but rather a collision between two expansive powers, the United States and the Lakotas. White's celebrated essay revealed how the pivotal chapter in the continent's past, the westward expansion of the United States, appeared from the Lakota perspective, a point of view that has tended to dominate our perception of that history ever since.

Yet, for all its compelling, universal features, the Lakota experience was in many ways anomalous. The traditional interpretation emphasizes horses and equestrian warfare as the critical factors behind Plains Indians' exceptional ability to resist and postpone the American takeover. This view has been strongly influenced by the history of Lakotas and, as it turns out, really applies only to them. Viewed broadly, the history of Plains horse cultures was a promising experiment that eventually became marred by in-built contradictions that compromised the power of most tribes well before their first confrontation with the U.S. Army. The Lakotas became the most enduring native power of the equestrian Plains by default: they escaped the adaptive complications of the eastern Plains, the overabundance and ecological instability of the southern Plains, and the destructive divisiveness and social and military volatility of the northern Plains.

The overemphasis on the Lakotas in historical overviews is problematic on an even more fundamental level: it creates distorting historical shortsightedness. The rise of Lakotas' equestrian culture on the Plains was a late phenomenon that existed only in the nineteenth century, and the excessive focus on that brief, glorified period conceals the deep, multidimensional, and often troubled equestrian history that shaped the story of the continental center for almost three centuries.

Suggested Reading

Scholars have considered Spain's reintroduction of the horse to North America to have been one of the most significant events of the colonial era. Gary Clayton Anderson, *The Indian Southwest, 1580–1830: Ethnogenesis and Reinvention* (Norman: University of Oklahoma Press, 1999) provides a regional context for this reading. Hämäläinen relates the impact of the horse on the southern plains trading system in "The Western Comanche Trade Center: Rethinking the Plains Indian Trade System," *Western Historical Quarterly* 29 (Winter 1998): 485–513. For an understanding of similar events on the northern plains, see Richard White, "The Winning of the West: The Expansion of the Western Sioux in the Eighteenth and Nineteenth Centuries," *Journal of American History* 65 (September 1978): 319–43.

CHAPTER FIVE

The Indians' New World

The Catawba Experience

JAMES H. MERRELL

While the horse changed Indian life in the Southwest and on the plains, Europeans in other regions introduced ideas, technologies, and trade practices that had major impacts on Native life. In fact, as the author demonstrates, the mere presence of European neighbors altered nearly every facet of tribal society. This analysis examines the social, economic, and political bases of eastern coastal groups for nearly two centuries. It demonstrates how the growing presence of colonists changed tribal life so completely that the author seems justified in labeling the result a "New World" for the Indians. European diseases first swept through Native villages, killing thousands. Then kinship systems broke down, languages disappeared, and political leadership shifted as even the basics of everyday life needed restructuring. With a keen eye for detail, the author shows how and why these things occurred. His discussion places the Indian experiences at the center of Native and newcomer exchanges. By the end of the essay, he has illustrated the variety of methods Indians developed to ensure their own survival through peaceful relations with their white neighbors.

In August 1608 John Smith and his band of explorers captured an Indian named Amoroleck during a skirmish along the Rappahannock River. Asked why his men—a hunting party from towns upstream—had attacked the English, Amoroleck replied that they had heard the strangers "were a people come from under the world, to take their world from them." Smith's prisoner grasped a simple yet important truth that students of colonial America have overlooked: After 1492 Native Americans lived in a world every bit as new as that confronting transplanted Africans or Europeans.

"The Indians' New World" appeared in *William and Mary Quarterly* 41, no. 4 (October 1984): 537–65.

The failure to explore the Indians' new world helps explain why, despite many excellent studies of the Native American past, colonial history often remains, "a history of those men and women—English, European, and African—who transformed America from a geographical expression into a new nation." One reason Indians generally are left out may be the apparent inability to fit them into the new-world theme, a theme that exerts a powerful hold on our historical imagination and runs throughout our efforts to interpret American development. From Frederick Jackson Turner to David Grayson Allen, from Melville J. Herskovits to Daniel C. Littlefield, scholars have analyzed encounters between peoples from the Old World and conditions in the New, studying the complex interplay between Europeans or African cultural patterns and the American environment. Indians crossed no ocean, peopled no faraway land. It might seem logical to exclude them.

The natives' segregation persists, in no small degree, because historians still tend to think only of the new world as the New World, a geographic entity bounded by the Atlantic Ocean on the one side and the Pacific on the other. Recent research suggests that process was as important as place. Many settlers in New England recreated familiar forms with such success that they did not really face an alien environment until long after their arrival. Africans, on the other hand, were struck by the shock of the new at the moment of their enslavement well before they stepped on board ship or set foot on American soil. If the Atlantic was not a barrier between one world and another, if what happened to people was more a matter of subtle cultural processes than mere physical displacements, perhaps we should set aside the maps and think instead of a "world" as the physical and cultural milieu within which people live and a "new world" as a dramatically different milieu demanding basic changes in ways of life. Considered in these terms, the experience of natives was more closely akin to that of immigrants and slaves, and the idea of an encounter between worlds can—indeed, must—include the aboriginal inhabitants of America.

For American Indians a new order arrived in three distinct yet overlapping stages. First, alien microbes killed vast numbers of natives, sometimes before the victims had seen a white or black face. Next came traders who exchanged European technology for Indian products and brought natives into the developing world market. In time traders gave way to settlers eager to develop the land according to their own lights. These three intrusions combined to transform native existence, disrupting established cultural habits and requiring creative responses to drastically altered conditions. Like their new neighbors, then, Indians were forced to blend old and new in ways that would permit them to survive in the present without forsaking their past. By the close of the colonial era Native Americans as well as whites and blacks had created new societies, each similar to, yet very different from, its parent culture.

The range of native societies produced by this mingling of ingredients probably exceeded the variety of social forms Europeans and Africans developed. Rather than survey the broad spectrum of Indian adaptations, this article considers in some depth the response of natives in one area, the southern piedmont. Avoiding extinction and eschewing retreat, the Indians of the piedmont have been in continuous contact with the invaders from across the sea almost since the beginning of the colonial period, thus permitting a thorough analysis of cultural intercourse. Moreover, a regional approach embracing groups from South Carolina to Virginia can transcend narrow (and still poorly understood) ethnic or "tribal" boundaries without sacrificing the richness of detail a focused study provides.

Indeed, piedmont peoples had so much in common that a regional perspective is almost imperative. No formal political ties bound them at the onset of European contact, but a similar environment shaped their lives, and their adjustment to this environment fostered cultural uniformity. Perhaps even more important, these groups shared a single history once Europeans and Africans arrived on the scene. Drawn together by their cultural affinities and their common plight, after 1700 they migrated to the Catawba Nation, a cluster of villages along the border between the Carolinas that became the focus of native life in the region. Tracing the experience of these upland communities both before and after they joined the Catawbas can illustrate the consequences of contact and illuminate the process by which natives learned to survive in their own new world.

For centuries ancestors of the Catawbas had lived astride important aboriginal trade routes and straddled the boundary between two cultural traditions, a position that involved them in a far-flung network of contacts and affected everything from potting techniques to burial practices. Nonetheless, Africans and Europeans were utterly unlike any earlier foreign visitors to the piedmont. Their arrival meant more than merely another encounter with outsiders; it marked an important turning point in Indian history. Once these newcomers disembarked and began to feel their way across the continent, they forever altered the course and pace of native development.

Bacteria brought the most profound disturbances to upcountry villages. When Hernando de Soto led the first Europeans into the area in 1540, he found large towns already "grown up in grass" because "there had been a pest in the land" two years before, a malady probably brought inland by natives who had visited distant Spanish posts. The sources are silent about other "pests" over the next century, but soon after the English began colonizing Carolina in 1670 the disease pattern became all too clear. Major epidemics struck the region at least once every generation—in 1698, 1718, 1738, and 1759—and a variety of less virulent illnesses almost never left native settlements.

Indians were not the only inhabitants of colonial America living—and dying—in a new disease environment. The swamps and lowlands of the Chesapeake were a deathtrap for Europeans, and sickness obliged colonists to discard or rearrange many of the social forms brought from England. Among native peoples long isolated from the rest of the world and therefore lacking immunity to pathogens introduced by the intruders, the devastation was even more severe. John Lawson, who visited the Carolina upcountry in 1701, when perhaps ten thousand Indians were still there, estimated that "there is not the sixth Savage living within two hundred Miles of all our Settlements, as there were fifty Years ago." The recent smallpox epidemic "destroy'd whole Towns," he remarked, "without leaving one Indian alive in the Village." Resistance to disease developed with painful slowness; colonists reported that the outbreak of smallpox in 1759 wiped out 60 percent of the natives, and, according to one source, "the woods were offensive with the dead bodies of the Indians; and dogs, wolves, and vultures were . . . busy for months in banqueting on them."

Survivors of these horrors were thrust into a situation no less alien than what European immigrants and African slaves found. The collected wisdom of generations could vanish in a matter of days if sickness struck older members of a community who kept sacred traditions and taught special skills. When many of the elders succumbed at once, the deep pools of collective memory grew shallow and some dried up altogether. In 1710 Indians near Charleston told a settler that "they have forgot most of their traditions since the Establishment of this Colony, they keep their Festivals and can tell but little of the reasons: their Old Men are dead." Impoverishment of a rich cultural heritage followed the spread of disease. Nearly a century later a South Carolinian exaggerated but captured the general trend when he noted that Catawbas "have forgotten their ancient rites, ceremonies, and manufactures."

The same diseases that robbed a piedmont town of some of its most precious resources also stripped it of the population necessary to maintain an independent existence. In order to survive, groups were compelled to construct new societies from the splintered remnants of the old. The result was a kaleidoscopic array of migrations from ancient territories and mergers with nearby peoples. While such behavior was not unheard of in aboriginal times, population levels fell so precipitously after contact that survivors endured disruptions unlike anything previously known.

The dislocations of the Saponi Indians illustrate the common course of events. In 1670 they lived on the Staunton River in Virginia and were closely affiliated with a group called Nahyssans. A decade later Saponis moved toward the coast and built a town near the Occaneechees. When John Lawson came upon them along the Yadkin River in 1701, they were on the verge of banding together in a single village with Tutelos and Keyauwees. Soon thereafter Saponis applied to Virginia officials for permission to move to the Meherrin River, where Occaneechees, Tutelos, and others joined them. In 1714, at the urging of Virginia's Lt. Gov. Alexander Spotswood, these groups settled at Fort Christanna farther up the Meherrin. Their friendship with Virginia soured during the 1720s, and most of the "Christanna Indians" moved to the Catawba Nation. For some reason this arrangement did not satisfy them, and many returned to Virginia in 1732, remaining there for a decade before choosing to migrate north and accept the protection of the Iroquois.

Saponis were unusual only in their decision to leave the Catawbas. Enos, Oc-caneechees, Waterees, Keyauwees, Cheraws, and others have their own stories to tell, similar in outline if not in detail. With the exception of the towns near the confluence of Sugar Creek and the Catawba River that composed the heart of the Catawba Nation, piedmont communities decimated by disease lived through a common round of catastrophes, shifting from place to place and group to group in search of a safe haven. Most eventually ended up in the Nation, and during the opening decades of the eighteenth century the villages scattered across the southern upcountry were abandoned as people drifted into the Catawba orbit.

No mere catalog of migrations and mergers can begin to convey how pro-foundly unsettling this experience was for those swept up in it. While upcountry Indians did not sail away to some distant land, they, too, were among the up-rooted, leaving their ancestral homes to try to make a new life elsewhere. The peripatetic existence of Saponis and others proved deeply disruptive. A village and its surrounding territory were important elements of personal and collective identity, physical links in a chain binding a group to its past and making a local-ity sacred. Colonists, convinced that Indians were by Nature "a shifting, wan-dring People," were oblivious to this, but Lawson offered a glimpse of the reasons for native attachment to a particular locale. "In our way," he wrote on leaving an Eno-Shakori town in 1701, "there stood a great Stone about the Size of a large Oven, and hollow; this the Indians took great Notice of, putting some Tobacco into the Concavity, and spitting after it. I ask'd them the Reason of their so doing, but they made me no Answer." Natives throughout the interior honored similar places—graves of ancestors, monuments of stones commemorating important events—that could not be left behind without some cost.

The toll could be physical as well as spiritual, for even the most uneventful of moves interrupted the established cycle of subsistence. Belongings had to be packed and unpacked, dwellings constructed, palisades raised. Once migrants had completed the business of settling in, the still more arduous task of exploit-ing new terrain awaited them. Living in one place year after year endowed a people with intimate knowledge of the area. The richest soils, the best hunting grounds, the choicest sites for gathering nuts or berries—none could be learned without years of experience, tested by time and passed down from one genera-tion to the next. Small wonder that Carolina Indians worried about being "driven to some unknown Country, to live, hunt, and get our Bread in."

Some displaced groups tried to leave "unknown Country" behind and make their way back home. In 1716 Enos asked Virginia's permission to settle at "Enoe Town" on the North Carolina frontier, their location in Lawson's day. Seven-teen years later William Byrd II came upon an abandoned Cheraw village on a tributary of the upper Roanoke River and remarked how "it must have been a great misfortune to them to be obliged to abandon so beautiful a dwelling." The Indians apparently agreed: In 1717 the Virginia Council received "Divers appli-cations" from the Cheraws (now living along the Pee Dee River) "for Liberty to

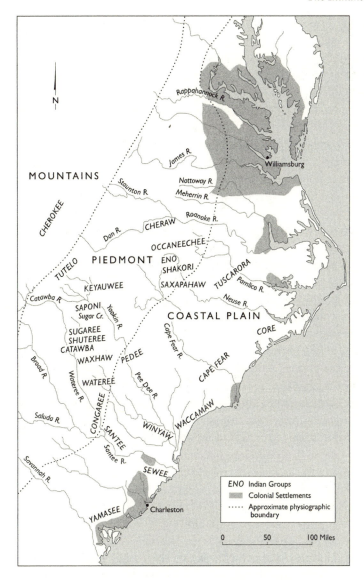

The Carolinas
and Virginia,
ca. 1700. Based
on a map by
Linda Merrell.

Seat themselves on the head of Roanoke River." Few natives managed to return
permanently to their homelands. But their efforts to retrace their steps hint at a
profound sense of loss and testify to the powerful hold of ancient sites.

Compounding the trauma of leaving familiar territories was the necessity of
abandoning customary relationships. Casting their lot with others traditionally considered foreign compelled Indians to rearrange basic ways of ordering
their existence. Despite frequent contacts among peoples, native life had always
centered in kin and town. The consequences of this deep seated localism were
evident even to a newcomer like John Lawson, who in 1701 found striking dif-

ferences in language, dress, and physical appearance among Carolina Indians living only a few miles apart. Rules governing behavior also drew sharp distinctions between outsiders and one's own "Country-Folks." Indians were "very kind, and charitable to one another," Lawson reported, "but more especially to those of their own Nation." A visitor desiring a liaison with a local woman was required to approach her relatives and the village headman. On the other hand, "if it be an Indian of their own Town or Neighbourhood, that wants a Mistress, he comes to none but the Girl." Lawson seemed unperturbed by this barrier until he discovered that a "Thief [is] held in Disgrace, that steals from any of his Country-Folks," "but to steal from the English [or any other foreigners] they reckon no Harm."

Communities unable to continue on their own had to revise these rules and reweave the social fabric into new designs. What language would be spoken? How would fields be laid out, hunting territories divided, houses built? How would decisions be reached, offenders punished, ceremonies performed? When Lawson remarked that "nowadays" the Indians must seek mates "amongst Strangers," he unwittingly characterized life in native Carolina. Those who managed to withstand the ravages of disease had to redefine the meaning of the term stranger and transform outsiders into insiders.

The need to harmonize discordant peoples, an unpleasant fact of life for all Native Americans, was no less common among black and white inhabitants of America during these years. Africans from a host of different groups were thrown into slavery together and forced to seek some common cultural ground, to blend or set aside clashing habits and beliefs. Europeans who came to America also met unexpected and unwelcome ethnic, religious, and linguistic diversity. The roots of the problem were quite different; the problem itself was much the same. In each case people from different backgrounds had to forge a common culture and a common future.

Indians in the southern uplands customarily combined with others like themselves in an attempt to solve the dilemma. Following the "principle of least effort," shattered communities cushioned the blows inflicted by disease and depopulation by joining a kindred society known through generations of trade and alliances. Thus, Saponis coalesced with Occaneechees and Tutelos—nearby groups "speaking much the same language"—and Catawbas became a sanctuary for culturally related refugees from throughout the region. Even after moving in with friends and neighbors, however, natives tended to cling to ethnic boundaries in order to ease the transition. In 1715 Spotswood noticed that the Saponis and others gathered at Fort Christanna were "confederated together, tho' still preserving their different Rules." Indians entering the Catawba Nation were equally conservative. As late as 1743 a visitor could hear more than twenty dialects spoken by peoples living there, and some bands continued to reside in separate towns under their own leaders.

Time inevitably sapped the strength of ethnic feeling, allowing a more unified Nation to emerge from the collection of Indian communities that occupied the valleys of the Catawba River and its tributaries. By the mid-eighteenth century, the authority of village headmen was waning and leaders from the host population had begun to take responsibility for the actions of constituent groups. The babel of different tongues fell silent as "Katahba," the Nation's "standard, or court-dialect," slowly drowned out all others. Eventually entire peoples followed their languages and their leaders into oblivion, leaving only personal names like Santee Jemmy, Cheraw George, Congaree Jamie, Saponey Johnny, and Eno Jemmy as reminders of the Nation's diverse heritage.

No European observer recorded the means by which nations became mere names and a congeries of groups forged itself into one people. No doubt the colonists' habit of ignoring ethnic distinctions and lumping confederated entities together under the Catawba rubric encouraged amalgamation. But Anglo-American efforts to create a society by proclamation were invariably unsuccessful; consolidation had to come from within. In the absence of evidence, it seems reasonable to conclude that years of contacts paved the way for a closer relationship. Once a group moved to the Nation, intermarriages blurred ancient kinship networks, joint war parties or hunting expeditions brought young men together, and elders met in a council that gave everyone some say by including "all the Indian Chiefs or Head Men of that [Catawba] Nation and the several Tribes amongst them together." The concentration of settlements within a day's walk of one another facilitated contact and communication. From their close proximity, common experience, and shared concerns, people developed ceremonies and myths that compensated for those lost to disease and gave the Nation a stronger collective consciousness. Associations evolved that balanced traditional narrow ethnic allegiance with a new, broader, "national" identity, a balance that tilted steadily toward the latter. Ethnic differences died hard, but the peoples of the Catawba Nation learned to speak with a single voice.

Muskets and kettles came to the piedmont more slowly than smallpox and measles. Spanish explorers distributed a few gifts to local headmen, but inhabitants of the interior did not enjoy their first real taste of the fruits of European technology until Englishmen began venturing inland after 1650. Indians these traders met in upcountry towns were glad to barter for the more efficient tools, more lethal weapons, and more durable clothing that colonists offered. Spurred on by eager natives, men from Virginia and Carolina quickly flooded the region with the material trappings of European culture. In 1701 John Lawson considered the Wateree Chickanees "very poor in English Effects" because a few of them lacked muskets.

Slower to arrive, trade goods were also less obvious agents of change. The Indians' ability to absorb foreign artifacts into established modes of existence hid the revolutionary consequences of trade for some time. Natives leaped the technological gulf with ease in part because they were discriminating shoppers. If hoes were too small, beads too large, or cloth the wrong color, Indian traders refused them. Items they did select fit smoothly into existing ways. Waxhaws tied horse bells around their ankles at ceremonial dances, and some of the traditional stone pipes passed among the spectators at these dances had been shaped by metal files. Those who could not afford a European weapon fashioned arrows from broken glass. Those who could went to great lengths to "set [a new musket] streight, sometimes shooting away above 100 Loads of Ammunition, before they bring the Gun to shoot according to their Mind."

Not every piece of merchandise hauled into the upcountry on a trader's pack-horse could be "set streight" so easily. Liquor, for example, proved both impossible to resist and extraordinarily destructive. Indians "have no Power to refrain this Enemy," Lawson observed, "though sensible how many of them (are by it) hurry'd into the other World before their Time." And yet even here, natives aware of the risks sought to control alcohol by incorporating it into their ceremonial life as a device for achieving a different level of consciousness. Consumption was usually restricted to men, who "go as solemnly about it, as if it were part of their Religion," preferring to drink only at night and only in quantities sufficient to stupefy them. When ritual could not confine liquor to safe channels, Indians went still further and excused the excesses of overindulgence by refusing to hold an intoxicated person responsible for his actions. "They never call any Man to account for what he did, when he was drunk," wrote Lawson, "but say, it was the Drink that caused his Misbehaviour, therefore he ought to be forgiven."

Working to absorb even the most dangerous commodities acquired from their new neighbors, aboriginal inhabitants of the uplands, like African slaves in the lowlands, made themselves at home in a different technological environment. Indians became convinced that "Guns, and Ammunition, besides a great many other Necessaries . . . are helpful to Man" and eagerly searched for the key that would unlock the secret of their production. At first many were confident that the "Quera, or good Spirit," would teach them to make these commodities "when that good Spirit sees fit." Later they decided to help their deity along by approaching the colonists. In 1757 Catawbas asked Gov. Arthur Dobbs of North Carolina "to send us Smiths and other Tradesmen to teach our Children."

It was not the new products themselves but the Indians' failure to learn the mysteries of manufacture from either Dobbs or the Quera that marked the real revolution wrought by trade. During the seventeenth and eighteenth centuries everyone in eastern North America—masters and slaves, farmers near the coast and Indians near the mountains—became producers of raw materials for foreign markets and found themselves caught up in an international economic network. Piedmont natives were part of this larger process, but their adjustment was more difficult because the contrast with previous ways was so pronounced. Before European contact, the localism characteristic of life in the uplands had been sustained by a remarkable degree of self-sufficiency. Trade among peoples, while common, was conducted primarily in commodities such as copper, mica, and shells, items that, exchanged with the appropriate ceremony, initiated or confirmed friendships among groups. Few, if any, villages relied on outsiders for goods essential to daily life.

Intercultural exchange eroded this traditional independence and entangled natives in a web of commercial relations few of them understood and none controlled. In 1670 the explorer John Lederer observed a striking disparity in the trading habits of Indians living near Virginia and those deep in the interior. The "remoter Indians," still operating within a precontact framework, were content with ornamental items such as mirrors, beads, "and all manner of gaudy toys and knacks for children." "Neighbour-Indians," on the other hand, habitually traded with colonists for cloth, metal tools, and weapons. Before long, towns near and far were demanding the entire range of European wares and were growing accustomed—even addicted—to them. "They say we English are fools for . . . not always going with a gun," one Virginia colonist familiar with piedmont Indians wrote in the early 1690s, "for they think themselves undrest and not fit to walk abroad, unless they have their gun on their shoulder, and their shot-bag by their side." Such an enthusiastic conversion to the new technology eroded ancient craft skills and hastened complete dependence on substitutes only colonists could supply.

By forcing Indians to look beyond their own territories for certain indispensable products, Anglo-American traders inserted new variables into the aboriginal equation of exchange. Colonists sought two commodities from Indians—human beings and deerskins—and both undermined established relationships among native groups. While the demand for slaves encouraged piedmont peoples to expand their traditional warfare, the demand for peltry may have fostered conflicts over hunting territories. Those who did not fight each other for slaves or deerskins fought each other for the European products these could bring. As firearms, cloth, and other items became increasingly important to native existence, competition replaced comity at the foundation of trade encounters as villages scrambled for the cargoes of merchandise. Some were in a better position to profit than others. In the early 1670s Occaneechees living on an island in the Roanoke River enjoyed power out of all proportion to their numbers because they controlled an important ford on the trading path from Virginia to the interior, and they resorted to threats, and even to force, to retain their advantage. In Lawson's day Tuscaroras did the same, "hating that any of these Westward Indians should have any Commerce with the English, which would prove a Hinderance to their Gains."

Competition among native groups was only the beginning of the transformation brought about by new forms of exchange. Inhabitants of the piedmont might bypass the native middleman, but they could not break free from a perilous dependence on colonial sources of supply. The danger may not have been immediately apparent to Indians caught up in the excitement of acquiring new and wonderful things. For years they managed to dictate the terms of trade, compelling visitors from Carolina and Virginia to abide by aboriginal codes of conduct and playing one colony's traders against the other to ensure an abundance of goods at favorable rates. But the natives' influence over the protocol of exchange combined with their skill at incorporating alien products to mask a loss of control over their own destiny. The mask came off when, in 1715, the traders—and the trade goods—suddenly disappeared during the Yamassee War.

The conflict's origins lay in a growing colonial awareness of the Indians' need for regular supplies of European merchandise. In 1701 Lawson pronounced the Santees "very tractable" because of their close connections with South Carolina. Eight years later he was convinced that the colonial officials in Charleston "are absolute Masters over the Indians . . . within the Circle of their Trade." Carolina traders who shared this conviction quite naturally felt less and less constrained to obey native rules governing proper behavior. Abuses against Indians mounted until some men were literally getting away with murder. When repeated appeals to colonial officials failed, natives throughout Carolina began to consider war. Persuaded by Yamassee ambassadors that the conspiracy was widespread, and convinced by years of ruthless commercial competition between Virginia and Carolina that an attack on one colony would not affect relations with the other, in the spring of 1715 Catawbas and their neighbors joined the invasion of South Carolina.

The decision to fight was disastrous. Colonists everywhere shut off the flow of goods to the interior, and after some initial successes Carolina's native enemies soon plumbed the depths of their dependence. In a matter of months refugees holed up in Charleston noticed that "the Indians want ammunition and are not able to mend their Arms." The peace negotiations that ensued revealed a desperate thirst for fresh supplies of European wares. Ambassadors from piedmont towns invariably spoke in a single breath of restoring "a Peace and a free Trade," and one delegation even admitted that its people "cannot live without the assistance of the English."

Natives unable to live without the English henceforth tried to live with them. No upcountry group mounted a direct challenge to Anglo-America after 1715. Trade quickly resumed, and the piedmont Indians, now concentrated almost exclusively in the Catawba valley, briefly enjoyed a regular supply of necessary products sold by men willing once again to deal according to the old rules. By mid-century, however, deer were scarce and fresh sources of slaves almost impossible to find. Anglo-American traders took their business elsewhere, leaving inhabitants of the Nation with another material crisis of different but equally dangerous dimensions.

Indians casting about for an alternative means of procuring the commodities they craved looked to imperial officials. During the 1740s and 1750s native dependence shifted from colonial traders to colonial authorities as Catawba leaders repeatedly visited provincial capitals to request goods. These delegations came not to beg but to bargain. Catawbas were still of enormous value to the English as allies and frontier guards, especially at a time when Anglo-America felt threatened by the French and their Indian auxiliaries. The Nation's position within reach of Virginia and both Carolinas enhanced its value by enabling headmen to approach all three colonies and offer their people's services to the highest bidder.

The strategy yielded Indians an arsenal of ammunition and a variety of other merchandise that helped offset the declining trade. Crown officials were especially generous when the Nation managed to play one colony off against another. In 1746 a rumor that the Catawbas were about to move to Virginia was enough to garner them a large shipment of powder and lead from officials in Charleston concerned about losing this "valuable people." A decade later, while the two Carolinas fought for the honor of constructing a fort in the Nation, the Indians encouraged (and received) gifts symbolizing good will from both colonies without reaching an agreement with either. Surveying the tangled thicket of promises and presents, the Crown's superintendent of Indian affairs, Edmond Atkin, ruefully admitted that "the People of both Provinces . . . have I beleive [sic] tampered too much on both sides with those Indians, who seem to understand well how to make their Advantage of it."

By the end of the colonial period delicate negotiations across cultural boundaries were as familiar to Catawbas as the strouds they wore and the muskets they carried. But no matter how shrewdly the headmen loosened provincial purse strings to extract vital merchandise, they could not escape the simple fact that they no longer held the purse containing everything needed for their daily existence. In the space of a century the Indians had become thoroughly embedded in an alien economy, denizens of a new material world. The ancient self-sufficiency was only a dim memory in the minds of the Nation's elders.

The Catawba peoples were veterans of countless campaigns against disease and masters of the arts of trade long before the third major element of their new world, white planters, became an integral part of their life. Settlement of the Carolina uplands did not begin until the 1730s, but once underway it spread with frightening speed. In November 1752 concerned Catawbas reminded South Carolina governor James Glen how they had "complained already . . . that the white People were settled too near us." Two years later five hundred families lived within thirty miles of the Nation and surveyors were running their lines into the middle of native towns. "[T]hose Indians are now in a fair way to be surrounded by White People," one observer concluded.

Settlers' attitudes were as alarming as their numbers. Unlike traders who profited from them or colonial officials who deployed them as allies, ordinary colonists had little use for Indians. Natives made poor servants and worse slaves; they obstructed settlement; they attracted enemy warriors to the area. Even men who respected Indians and earned a living by trading with them admitted that they made unpleasant neighbors. "We may observe of them as of the fire," wrote the South Carolina trader James Adair after considering the Catawbas' situation on the eve of the American Revolution, "it is safe and useful, cherished at proper distance; but if too near us, it becomes dangerous, and will scorch if not consume us."

A common fondness for alcohol increased the likelihood of intercultural hostilities. Catawba leaders acknowledged that the Indians "get very Drunk with [liquor] this is the Very Cause that they oftentimes Commit those Crimes that is offencive to You and us." Colonists were equally prone to bouts of drunkenness. In the 1760s the itinerant Anglican minister, Charles Woodmason, was shocked to find the citizens of one South Carolina upcountry community "continually drunk." More appalling still, after attending church services "one half of them got drunk before they went home." Indians sometimes suffered at the hands of intoxicated farmers. In 1760 a Catawba woman was murdered when she happened by a tavern shortly after four of its patrons "swore they would kill the first Indian they should meet with."

Even when sober, natives and newcomers found many reasons to quarrel. Catawbas were outraged if colonists built farms on the Indians' doorstep or tramped across ancient burial grounds. Planters, ignorant of (or indifferent to) native rules of hospitality, considered Indians who requested food nothing more than beggars and angrily drove them away. Other disputes arose when the Nation's young men went looking for trouble. As hunting, warfare, and other traditional avenues for achieving status narrowed, Catawba youths transferred older patterns of behavior into a new arena by raiding nearby farms and hunting cattle or horses.

Contrasting images of the piedmont landscape quite unintentionally generated still more friction. Colonists determined to tame what they considered a wilderness were in fact erasing a native signature on the land and scrawling their own. Bridges, buildings, fences, roads, crops, and other "improvements" made the area comfortable and familiar to colonists but uncomfortable and unfamiliar to Indians. "The Country side wear[s] a New face," proclaimed Woodmason proudly; to the original inhabitants, it was a grim face indeed. "His Land was spoiled," one Catawba headman told British officials in 1763. "They have spoiled him 100 Miles every way." Under these circumstances, even a settler with no wish to fight Indians met opposition to his fences, his outbuildings, his very presence. Similarly, a Catawba on a routine foray into traditional hunting territories had his weapon destroyed, his goods confiscated, his life threatened by men with different notions of the proper use of the land.

To make matters worse, the importance both cultures attached to personal independence hampered efforts by authorities on either side to resolve conflicts. Piedmont settlers along the border between the Carolinas were "people of desperate fortune," a frightened North Carolina official reported after visiting the area. "[N]o officer of Justice from either Province dare meddle with them." Woodmason, who spent even more time in the region, came to the same conclusion. "We are without any Law, or Order," he complained; the inhabitants' "Impudence is so very high, as to be past bearing." Catawba leaders could have sympathized. Headmen informed colonists that the Nation's people "are oftentimes Cautioned from . . . ill Doings altho' to no purpose for we Cannot be present at all times to Look after them." "What they have done I could not prevent," one chief explained.

Unruly, angry, intoxicated Catawbas and Carolinians were constantly at odds during the middle decades of the eighteenth century. Planters who considered Indians "proud and deveilish" were themselves accused by natives of being "very bad and quarrelsome." Warriors made a habit of "going into the Settlements, robbing and stealing where ever they get an Oppertunity." Complaints generally brought no satisfaction— "they laugh and makes their Game of it, and says it is what they will"—leading some settlers to "whip [Indians] about the head, beat and abuse them." "The white People . . . and the Cuttahbaws, are Continually at varience," a visitor to the Nation fretted in June 1759, "and Dayly New Animositys Doth a rise Between them which In my Humble oppion will be of Bad Consequence In a Short time, Both Partys Being obstinate."

The litany of intercultural crimes committed by each side disguised a fundamental shift in the balance of physical and cultural power. In the early years of colonization of the interior the least disturbance by Indians sent scattered planters into a panic. Soon, however, Catawbas were few, colonists many, and it was the natives who now lived in fear. "[T]he white men [who] Lives Near the Neation is Contenuely asembleing and goes In the [Indian] towns In Bodys . . . ," worried another observer during the tense summer of 1759. "[T]he[y] tretton the[y] will Kill all the Cattabues."

The Indians would have to find some way to get along with these unpleasant neighbors if the Nation was to survive. As Catawba population fell below five hundred after the smallpox epidemic of 1759 and the number of colonists continued to climb, natives gradually came to recognize the futility of violent resistance. During the last decades of the eighteenth century they drew on years of experience in dealing with Europeans at a distance and sought to overturn the common conviction that Indian neighbors were frightening and useless.

This process was not the result of some clever plan; Catawbas had no strategy for survival. A headman could warn them that "the White people were now seated all round them and by that means had them entirely in their power." He could not command them to submit peacefully to the invasion of their homeland. The Nation's continued existence required countless individual decisions, made in a host of diverse circumstances, to complain rather than retaliate, to accept a subordinate place in a land that once was theirs. Few of the choices made survive in the record. But it is clear that, like the response to disease and to technology, the adaptation to white settlement was both painful and prolonged.

Catawbas took one of the first steps along the road to accommodation in the early 1760s, when they used their influence with colonial officials to acquire a reservation encompassing the heart of their ancient territories. This grant gave the Indians a land base, grounded in Anglo-American law, that prevented farmers from shouldering them aside. Equally important, Catawbas now had a commodity to exchange with nearby settlers. These men wanted land, the natives had plenty, and shortly before the Revolution the Nation was renting tracts to planters for cash, livestock, and manufactured goods.

Important as it was, land was not the only item Catawbas began trading to their neighbors. Some Indians put their skills as hunters and woodsmen to a different use, picking up stray horses and escaped slaves for a reward. Others bartered their pottery, baskets, and table mats. Still others traveled through the upcountry, demonstrating their prowess with the bow and arrow before appreciative audiences. The exchange of these goods and services for European merchandise marked an important adjustment to the settlers' arrival. In the past, natives had acquired essential items by trading peltry and slaves or requesting gifts from representatives of the Crown. But piedmont planters frowned on hunting and warfare, while provincial authorities—finding Catawbas less useful as the Nation's population declined and the French threat disappeared—discouraged formal visits and handed out fewer presents. Hence the Indians had to develop new avenues of exchange that would enable them to obtain goods in ways less objectionable to their neighbors. Pots, baskets, and acres proved harmless substitutes for earlier methods of earning an income.

Quite apart from its economic benefits, trade had a profound impact on the character of Catawba-settler relations. Through countless repetitions of the same simple procedure at homesteads scattered across the Carolinas, a new form of intercourse arose, based not on suspicion and an expectation of conflict but on trust and a measure of friendship. When a farmer looked out his window and saw Indians approaching, his reaction more commonly became to pick up money or a jug of whiskey rather than a musket or an axe. The natives now appeared, the settler knew, not to plunder or kill, but to peddle their wares or collect their rents.

The development of new trade forms could not bury all of the differences between Catawba and colonist overnight. But in the latter half of the eighteenth century the beleaguered Indians learned to rely on peaceful means of resolving intercultural conflicts that did arise. Drawing a sharp distinction between "the good men that have rented Lands from us" and "the bad People [who] has frequently imposed upon us," Catawbas called on the former to protect the Nation from the latter. In 1771 they met with the prominent Camden storekeeper, Joseph Kershaw, to request that he "represent us when [we are] a grieved." After the Revolution the position became more formal. Catawbas informed the South Carolina government that, being "destitute of a man to take care of, and assist us in our affairs," they had chosen one Robert Patten "to take charge of our affairs, and to act and do for us."

Neither Patten nor any other intermediary could have protected the Nation had it not joined the patriot side during the Revolutionary War. Though one scholar has termed the Indians' contribution to the cause "rather negligible," they fought in battles throughout the southeast and supplied rebel forces with food from time to time. These actions made the Catawbas heroes and laid the foundation for their popular renown as staunch patriots. In 1781 their old friend Kershaw told Catawba leaders how he welcomed the end of "this Long and Bloody War, in which You have taken so Noble a part and have fought and Bled with your white Brothers of America." Grateful Carolinians would not soon forget the Nation's service. Shortly after the Civil War an elderly settler whose father had served with the Indians in the Revolution echoed Kershaw's sentiments, recalling that "his father never communicated much to him [about the Catawbas], except that all the tribe . . . served the entire war . . . and fought most heroically."

Catawbas rose even higher in their neighbors' esteem when they began calling their chiefs "General" instead of "King" and stressed that these men were elected by the people. The change reflected little if any real shift in the Nation's political forms, but it delighted the victorious Revolutionaries. In 1794 the Charleston City Gazette reported that during the war "King" Frow had abdicated and the Indians chose "General" New River in his stead. "What a pity," the paper concluded, "certain people on a certain island have not as good optics as the Catawbas!" In the same year, the citizens of Camden celebrated the anniversary of the fall of the Bastille by raising their glasses to toast "King Prow[sic]—may all kings who will not follow his example follow that of Louis XVI." Like tales of Indian patriots, the story proved durable. Nearly a century after the Revolution one nearby planter wrote that "the Catawbas, emulating the examples of their white brethren, threw off regal government."

The Indians' new image as republicans and patriots, added to their trade with whites and their willingness to resolve conflicts peacefully, brought settlers to view Catawbas in a different light. By 1800 the natives were no longer violent and dangerous strangers but what one visitor termed an "inoffensive" people and one group of planters called "harmless and friendly" neighbors. They had become traders of pottery but not deerskins, experts with a bow and arrow but not hunters, ferocious warriors against runaway slaves or tories but not against settlers. In these ways Catawbas could be distinctively Indian yet reassuringly harmless at the same time.

The Nation's separate identity rested on such obvious aboriginal traits. But its survival ultimately depended on a more general conformity with the surrounding society. During the nineteenth century both settlers and Indians owned or rented land. Both spoke proudly of their Revolutionary heritage and their republican forms of government. Both drank to excess. Even the fact that Catawbas were not Christians failed to differentiate them sharply from nearby white settlements, where, one visitor noted in 1822, "little attention is paid to the sabbath, or religeon."

In retrospect it is clear that these similarities were as superficial as they were essential. For all the changes generated by contacts with vital Euro-American and Afro-American cultures, the Nation was never torn loose from its cultural moorings. Well after the Revolution Indians maintained a distinctive way of life rich in tradition and meaningful to those it embraced. Ceremonies conducted by headmen and folk tales told by relatives continued to transmit traditional values and skills from one generation to the next. Catawba children grew up speaking

the native language, making bows and arrows or pottery, and otherwise following patterns of belief and behavior derived from the past. The Indians' physical
appearance and the meandering paths that set Catawba settlements off from
neighboring communities served to reinforce this cultural isolation.

The natives' utter indifference to missionary efforts after 1800 testified to the
enduring power of established ways. Several clergymen stopped at the reservation in the first years of the nineteenth century; some stayed a year or two; none
enjoyed any success. As one white South Carolinian noted in 1826, Catawbas
were "Indians still." Outward conformity made it easier for them to blend into
the changed landscape. Beneath the surface lay a more complex story.

Those few outsiders who tried to piece together that story generally found it
difficult to learn much from the Indians. A people shrewd enough to discard the
title of "King" was shrewd enough to understand that some things were better
left unsaid and unseen. Catawbas kept their Indian names, and sometimes their
language, a secret from prying visitors. They echoed the racist attitudes of their
white neighbors and even owned a few slaves, all the time trading with blacks
and hiring them to work in the Nation, where the laborers "enjoyed considerable freedom" among the natives. Like Afro-Americans on the plantation who
adopted a happy, childlike demeanor to placate suspicious whites, Indians on
the reservation learned that a "harmless and friendly" posture revealing little
of life in the Nation was best suited to conditions in post-Revolutionary South
Carolina.

Success in clinging to their cultural identity and at least a fraction of their ancient lands cannot obscure the cost Catawba peoples paid. From the time the first
European arrived, the deck was stacked against them. They played the hand dealt
them well enough to survive, but they could never win. An incident that took
place at the end of the eighteenth century helps shed light on the consequences
of compromise. When the Catawba headman, General New River, accidentally
injured the horse he had borrowed from a nearby planter named Thomas Spratt,
Spratt responded by "banging old New River with a pole allover the yard." This
episode provided the settler with a colorful tale for his grandchildren; its effect
on New River and his descendants can only be imagined. Catawbas did succeed in the sense that they adjusted to a hostile and different world, becoming
trusted friends instead of feared enemies. Had they been any less successful, they
would not have survived the eighteenth century. But poverty and oppression
have plagued the Nation from New River's day to our own. For a people who had
once been proprietors of the piedmont, the pain of learning new rules was very
great, the price of success very high.

On that August day in 1608 when Amoroleck feared the loss of his world,
John Smith assured him that the English "came to them in peace, and to seeke
their loves." Events soon proved Amoroleck right and his captor wrong. Over the
course of the next three centuries not only Amoroleck and other piedmont Indians but natives throughout North America had their world stolen and another

put in its place. Though this occurred at different times and in different ways, no Indians escaped the explosive mixture of deadly bacteria, material riches, and alien peoples that was the invasion of America. Those in the southern piedmont who survived the onslaught were ensconced in their new world by the end of the eighteenth century. Population levels stabilized as the Catawba peoples developed immunities to once-lethal diseases. Rents, sales of pottery, and other economic activities proved adequate to support the Nation at a stable (if low) level of material life. Finally, the Indians' image as "inoffensive" neighbors gave them a place in South Carolina society and continues to sustain them today.

Vast differences separated Catawbas and other natives from their colonial contemporaries. Europeans were the colonizers, Africans the enslaved, Indians the dispossessed: From these distinct positions came distinct histories. Yet once we acknowledge the differences, instructive similarities remain that help to integrate natives more thoroughly into the story of early America. By carving a niche for themselves in response to drastically different conditions, the peoples who composed the Catawba Nation shared in the most fundamental of American experiences. Like Afro-Americans, these Indians were compelled to accept a subordinate position in American life yet did not altogether lose their cultural integrity. Like settlers of the Chesapeake, aboriginal inhabitants of the uplands adjusted to appalling mortality rates and wrestled with the difficult task of "living with death." Like inhabitants of the Middle Colonies, piedmont groups learned to cope with unprecedented ethnic diversity by balancing the pull of traditional loyalties with the demands of a new social order. Like Puritans in New England, Catawbas found that a new world did not arrive all at once and that localism, self-sufficiency, and the power of old ways were only gradually eroded by conditions in colonial America. More hints of a comparable heritage could be added to this list, but by now it should be clear that Indians belong on the colonial stage as important actors in the unfolding American drama rather than bit players, props, or spectators. For they, too, lived in a new world.

Suggested Reading

Merrell gives a fuller analysis of issues raised here in his *The Indians' New World: Catawbas and Their Neighbors from European Contact through the Era of Removal* (Chapel Hill: University of North Carolina Press, 1989). Helen C. Rountree, *Pocahontas's People: The Powhatan Indians of Virginia through Four Centuries* (Norman: University of Oklahoma Press, 1990), examines how the coastal people in Virginia faced similar problems. Farther south, in Carolina, the English colonial invasion brought warfare and slavery to that region. This story is presented in Alan Gallay, *The Indian Slave Trade: The Rise of the English Empire in the American South* (New Haven: Yale University Press, 2002).

CHAPTER SIX

The Delaware Prophet Neolin

A Reappraisal

ALFRED A. CAVE

Once Europeans arrived in North America, the resident tribal societies suffered military defeats, epidemic diseases, land losses, and devastating social and cultural disruptions. Responding to these disasters and hoping to make sense out of their new circumstances, many Indians turned to their traditional religious ceremonies and beliefs. Village shamans usually directed this process as they sought to explain the changes in their local circumstances. Scholars studying these "tribal revitalization movements" often analyze the beliefs of a particular religious spokesman, seeking both the motivations and the sources of his teachings. Neolin, a Delaware shaman, is one of the earliest to attract this attention.

Living in the 1750s, nearly a century and a half after the European invaders arrived, Neolin witnessed the disruption of Indian life resulting from the Anglo-American victory in the French and Indian War. His teachings added elements of Christianity to traditional Native beliefs, in particular the concept of the Great Spirit who punished evildoers, and provided a religious base that the Ottawa Chieftain Pontiac used in his 1763 effort to unify some tribal resistance to the British authorities.

In challenging European colonial expansionism and cultural hegemony, Third World nativist revitalization movements have commonly used ideas borrowed from the dominant power. Students of those movements disagree as to whether the key to understanding revitalization ideology is to be found in their appropriation of Judeo-Christian concepts of providence and divine judgment or in their reaffirmation of indigenous beliefs and practices. It is thus not surprising that while some analyses of the Delaware (Lenape) prophets of the eighteenth century portray them as traditionalists who incorporated some borrowed ideas

"The Delaware Prophet Neolin" appeared in *Ethnohistory* 46, no. 2 (Spring 1999): 265–90.

into an inherited body of beliefs and practices, others argue the prophets were radical innovators whose core message was grounded in concepts of sin and redemption borrowed from Christian missionaries. A classic and extreme example of the latter interpretation is found in a 1971 study of the Delaware prophets which concluded that "by the mid-eighteenth century, the Delaware had internalized white culture to the extent that they could no longer distinguish it from their own." Accordingly, the Delaware nativist revival could not have been "an outgrowth of indigenous tradition," but rather must be seen "as a basically European innovation expressed in native idiom."

This article seeks to demonstrate, through a reexamination of their teachings, that those who have portrayed the religious innovations of the Delaware prophets as essentially nonindigenous not only overstate their case but also misconstrue the basic nature of the prophets' appeal. Admittedly, the prophets made use of certain ideas about God and the Devil and about heaven and hell that were not only borrowed from Christianity but that, on the surface, appear to have few if any counterparts in traditional beliefs. In calling for certain changes in religious practice they also sometimes echoed Christian missionaries in condemning their traditionalist rivals as witches and devil worshippers. But preoccupation with their indebtedness to Christian teachings can too easily divert us from the more important task of placing their prophetic messages within their proper cultural context. If we are to understand these nativist revitalization movements, we must also seek to explain, as one recent writer points out, "why the prophetic response seemed a natural and rational one to the prophets and their followers." A vital key to the prophets' appeal is to be found in their invocation of the familiar, and in their skill in incorporating borrowed concepts within a nativist framework. We must therefore focus our attention on their "ability to tap all of the ambiguous power of enduring symbol and myth and ritual" by blending elements that drew on "age-old patterns" as well as those that were clearly "innovative."

We cannot, of course, deny the influence of Christian teachings on the Delaware prophets. The issue is one of emphasis and balance. The syncretic religious movements led by postcontact revitalization prophets blended traditional and borrowed concepts and were neither purely indigenous nor "basically European" in origin. Nativist revitalization leaders, to cite Anthony F. C. Wallace's classic definition, clearly sought "the elimination of alien persons, customs, values, and/or materials from the mazeway." But they also sought to identify and excise elements in the traditional culture which they regarded as sources of corruption, weakness, and failure, with particular attention to transgressions resulting in the presumed forfeiture of the favor of supernatural beings whose good will and benevolent intervention was so essential to individual and collective well-being. In their identification of those transgressions, the prophets often invoked religious concepts and values borrowed from the same alien culture whose influence they sought to neutralize. The prophets' power came from the relevance of their teachings to the particular circumstances of their followers. The interplay of indigenous and alien elements in the prophetic message reflected very specific social needs and historical circumstances.

With those considerations in mind, let us assess the role played by both indigenous and borrowed concepts in the teachings of the Delaware prophets, with particular attention to the work of Neolin. Neolin was not the first of the so-called Delaware prophets. But the reports we have of the teachings of his predecessors are terse and vague. Prior to Neolin, white observers paid little attention to Indian "prophets." But Neolin's claim that he had spoken to the creator himself, and had received instruction on the means to be employed "to drive the white people out of their country" came to the attention of the English at a time of extreme tension on the western frontier! Neolin's teachings were quoted extensively by the war leader Pontiac and provided spiritual support to the nativist uprisings of 1763–64. Neolin and his disciples had extensive contact with whites, and were far less secretive about their beliefs than were their predecessors. Hence, reports of his teachings provide us with the only reasonably comprehensive view we have of an eighteenth-century Native American prophetic movement.

The Delaware prophets were the product of a century of upheaval and dislocation. Although recognized as a distinct group by both the Dutch and the English, the Delaware, more properly referred to as the Lenape or Lenni Lenape, spoke several dialects of two distinctive eastern Algonquian languages, Munsee and Unami. At the time of first contact with Europeans, they possessed no cohesive tribal institutions and were not entirely uniform in culture. Prior to the mid-eighteenth century, they had no real identity as a "tribe" or "nation." The center of Lenape life was the village, generally inhabited by a few hundred members. Some villages were loosely linked in transitory alliances generally formed to counter an external threat, but for the most part local autonomy prevailed. The villages were "virtually autonomous settlements probably composed of lineages and clans" which "dealt effectively with most social problems, both economic and governmental. above the clan level there were but few poorly developed institutions."

The Lenape homelands in the early seventeenth century were located in the Delaware Valley of New Jersey, in eastern Pennsylvania, and in southeastern New York. Pressure from both Europeans and Indian rivals forced the Delaware westward. They suffered severe attrition from both infectious European diseases, to which they had no immunity, and from the intensified intergroup warfare that followed soon after trade with Europeans began. Within a few decades, alcohol also took its toll. Contemporary accounts spoke of both depopulation and demoralization as basic realities of Lenape life in the European colonial era. The process of western migration was marked by severe disruptions in established social patterns. As one authority notes, "geographical displacement" of the various Lenape communities occurred unevenly "as small groups sold their land or were forced from it at various times. The scattered, decimated, and unorganized bands . . . soon gathered, or were gathered, as they had never been in pre-European times. The 'towns' that grew up in the river valleys of Pennsylvania in the early decades of the eighteenth century were not formed from homogeneous cultural units." The prophetic movement had its origins in those refugees' villages whose inhabitants, of diverse background but with a common sense of loss, were receptive to a call to renewal. The process of dispossession and removal continued throughout the first half of the eighteenth century, as the Lenape bands in Pennsylvania lost land and were forced westward in the notorious "Walking Purchase of 1737" and the Albany Purchase of 1754. Many found refuge in new communities in the upper Ohio Valley.

It is in this period of dispossession and migration that we encounter the first evidence of nativist prophetic activity among the Delaware and their Indian neighbors. In 1737, Conrad Weiser learned of the teachings of a "seer" at Otseningo on the Susquehanna River who had told the wretched Shawnee and Onondaga refugees assembled there that their hunger and misery were punishments for their involvement in trade with Europeans and for their addiction to European rum. The Great Spirit, angered by their drunkenness, had driven away the game, and would "wipe them from the earth" if they did not forsake their evil collusion with aliens. Several years later the Moravian missionary Frederick Post learned of two other prophets in the Susquehanna Valley. A Munsee holy man named Papoonan called for peaceful resistance to European expansionism through the abandonment of trade with whites and the revival of "the ancient Customs & Manners" of Native Americans. Papoonan taught that God was angry with Indians for becoming as greedy and materialistic as the European intruders.

At a neighboring village upriver on the Susquehanna, Wangomend, the Assinisink prophet, using a chart that demonstrated that rum drinkers went to hell, preached a more militant resistance to Europeans and their ways. Post reported that Wangomend's followers assembled in emotionally charged mass meetings where they spoke tearfully of the "Dreams and Revelations" that had given them power and sought catharsis in frantic dancing and singing. The prophet declared himself the enemy of those who sought to teach Christian doctrine in the native American villages on the frontier. Salvation from "perdition," Wangomend declared, could come only from adherence to the "great and good spirit" who had called on Indians to renounce all innovations of European origin. Wangomend told Post's fellow Moravian missionary John Heckewelder that the Great Spirit had allowed him "to take a peep into the heavens, of which there were three, one for the Indians, one for the Negroes, and another for the white people. That of the Indians he observed to be the happiest of the three, and that of the whites the unhappiest; for they were under chastisement for their ill treatment of the Indians, and for possessing themselves of the land which God had given to them. They were also punished for making beasts of the Negroes, by selling them as the Indians do their horses and dogs, and beating them unmercifully, although God had created them as well as the rest of mankind."

The prophetic message spread throughout the Native American communities in Pennsylvania and the Ohio country. The Presbyterian missionary John Brainerd, seeking to convert the Lenape and their neighbors to the religion of Christ, complained in 1751 that the villagers now boldly asserted that God had created Indians, Negroes, and whites separately, and favored people of color. The supreme being, they argued, had "given the white man a book and told him that he must worship by that," but "placed no such restriction on others." Christianity was therefore a religion for whites only, containing nothing of value for God's other peoples. Not only were whites not superior to Indians, they were morally suspect, as they had enslaved the Negroes and now plotted to take the Indians' lands "and make slaves of them and their children." Unable to win his informants' trust, Brainerd could learn little about the activities of the nativist prophets who were so effectively undermining his efforts. He did hear rumors about "a revelation lately made by a young squaw in a trance," rumors that suggested opposition to the local, accomodationist Delaware leadership.

The reports of Weiser, Post, Heckewelder, and Brainerd not only bear witness to growing nativist anger against whites but also suggest that Native American religious innovators were now using, for their own purposes, new concepts of a supreme, omnipotent, and judgmental creator deity, and of heaven and hell, modeled after missionary accounts of the Christian God, concepts which they blended with traditionalist beliefs about both the efficacy of ritual ("frantic dances and singing") and of individual vision quests ("Dreams and Revelations.")

Out of the turmoil of Delaware dispossession and migration emerged new political leaders who, perhaps inspired by the prophets, forged a new sense of ethnic identity and independence in the refugee villages of the west. Driven from many of those areas in Pennsylvania where they had earlier resettled, a majority of the Lenape found refuge in the Ohio country in the 1750s. While the Delaware were still resident in the east, the Iroquois, with English encouragement and mixed results, had attempted to deny Delaware self-determination, designating a "Half King" to supervise their affairs and hold them in a subordinate status. Iroquois intervention as enforcers for white land claimants had contributed to Delaware dispossession, but their control over their presumed Lenape subjects was never as complete as colonial pretense and later historical myth maintained. In the Ohio country, as Newcomb notes, the Delaware rose "Phoenix-like, from the ashes of their subjugation and removal and . . . forged themselves into a tribe that was able to defy the Six Nations and the Europeans." Scarooyaday, an Oneida appointed to act as the Six Nations' "viceroy over the Ohio Delawares," had little real authority and served more as a negotiator than as a proconsul. The British soon recognized that the Iroquois had no effective control in the west. In their efforts to shore up their own influence in the Ohio country, they asked the Iroquois to designate a "King of the Delawares" with whom they might deal. Bowing to necessity, the Iroquois recognized the authority of Shingas, a Delaware sachem who had won the respect of his compatriots as a strong and independent leader. Colonial authorities came to regret the choice, for Shingas, no puppet, would soon send war parties in support of French efforts to exclude the British from the trans-Appalachian west. Some Delaware bands remaining in the Susquehanna Valley would also, for a time, give support to the French in the so-called French and Indian War.

The bungling of the British major general Edward Braddock helped precipitate Delaware belligerency during that conflict. When the western Delaware chief Shingas sought guarantees of Indian rights in the Ohio country, Braddock replied that "no savage should inherit land." The general also haughtily declined Delaware and Shawnee offers to accompany his troops on their march against Fort Duquesne, a blunder that contributed to, if it did not cause, his disastrous defeat and death at the forks of the Ohio. The British humiliation at Fort Duquesne inspired not only Delaware and Shawnee but also some Seneca and Cayuga from the Iroquois confederation to join the French. However, French failure to provide adequate support for their Native American allies impelled both the western and eastern Delaware, and other Indian belligerents, to make peace with the British before the war's end.

Soon after the French capitulation, the overbearing behavior of the British victors triggered renewed Indian insurgency. Despite the warnings of seasoned Indian agents and traders such as Sir William Johnson and George Croghan, the British commander Lord Amherst ended the policy of reaffirming kinship ties with Indian allies through gift giving, condoned price increases in the Indian trade, and seized lands rightfully belonging to the Iroquois to reward some of his officers. The underlying cause of Native American unrest was, of course, the perception, reinforced by Amherst's bungling, that the British intended to deprive them of both their land and their dignity. Early efforts by an anti-British Seneca faction to organize a pan-Indian uprising failed. The Ottawa war leader Pontiac, along with other less celebrated insurgents, were more successful. The teachings of the Delaware prophet Neolin played an important role in that success.

The prophet resided in Tuscarawas Town in the Ohio country during the years when Delaware refugees in the west forged a new tribal identity. Neolin's message, first reported in 1762, drew upon but greatly amplified the teachings of the earlier Delaware prophets. It reflected both an intensified anger against whites, particularly the British, and a commitment, perhaps not present in earlier prophetic messages, to a new concept of Indian solidarity that unified old antagonists and created a new racial identity.

The fullest account we have of Neolin's message is contained in a report, written by a French resident of Detroit, of a story told by Pontiac to his followers during the siege of 1763. The story described Neolin's journey to heaven, his meeting with the creator of the universe (the Master of Life), and the message which the creator instructed him to carry back to his people. Neolin had learned in a dream that he must visit this supreme being. He accordingly set off equipped for "a hunting journey," carrying "provisions, and ammunition, and a big kettle."

After walking eight days toward the celestial realm, "he halted at sunset, as usual, at the opening of a little prairie upon the bank of a stream that seemed to him a suitable camping place. As he was preparing his shelter he beheld at the other end of the prairie where he camped, three roads, wide, and plainly marked." Although somewhat surprised, Neolin "went on working on his shelter, so as to be protected from the weather, and made a fire." As he cooked his meal in the gathering twilight, he was astounded to see that "the three roads became all the brighter the darker it grew, a thing that surprised him to the point of fear." But as he reflected on that strange apparition, he came to realize that one of those roads must lead to the Master of Life, the object of his quest.

The next morning he set out upon the broadest of the roads. Pausing to catch his breath after half a day of walking, Neolin "suddenly saw a great fire coming out of the earth." As he approached, the flames soared higher. Terrified, he retraced his route and, back at the prairie, "took another road which was narrower than the first one." But after a few hours' travel he once again encountered an inferno and, trembling, made his way back to the beginning. Setting out on the third and narrowest trail, he journeyed for a day without encountering anything of note. But "suddenly he saw before him what appeared to be a mountain of marvelous whiteness, and he stopped, overcome with astonishment."

Approaching the mountain, Neolin "could no longer see any road and was sad." Looking around, he finally beheld a woman "of radiant beauty, whose garments dimmed the whiteness of the snow. She was seated." As he gazed upon that apparition, she spoke to him in his own dialect, and explained that to approach the Master of Life he must first disrobe, leave all his possessions behind, and go bathe in a nearby river. Neolin followed her instructions and, naked, then tried to climb the mountain. But it was "perpendicular, pathless, and smooth as ice." Unable to make any headway, he appealed to the woman in white. She told him that he must use only "his left hand and his left foot" in the ascent. The climb was difficult, but Neolin somehow made it to the top "by dint of effort." At the summit, the woman disappeared. He was now without a guide. He saw to his right three villages. "He did not know them for they seemed of different construction from is own, prettier and more orderly in appearance."

After some reflection, Neolin walked toward the most attractive village but halfway there remembered that he was naked and stopped, confused and uncertain as to what to do next. Then "he heard a voice telling him to continue and that he ought not to fear, because, having bathed as he had, he could go on in assurance." At the gate to the village, he was greeted by "a handsome man, all dressed in white," who promised to take him to the Master of Life. Coming to "a place of surpassing beauty," Neolin encountered a figure "who took him by the hand and gave him a hat all bordered with gold to sit down upon." He was reluctant, "for fear of spoiling the hat, but he was ordered to do so, and obeyed without reply."

Neolin was now in the presence of the Master of Life, who declared: "I am He who hath created the heavens and the earth, the trees, lakes, rivers, all men, and all thou seest and hath seen upon the earth. Because I love you, ye must do what I say and love, and not do what I hate." He learned that the creator was displeased with his Indian children, and that the sufferings which had plagued them were the results of their transgressions. The Master of Life denounced their addiction to the white man's alcohol, and deplored Indian polygamy, sexual promiscuity, witchcraft, and strife. But their gravest offense was toleration of European intruders. "This land where ye dwell I have made for you and not for others," Neolin was told. "Whence comes it that ye permit the Whites upon your lands? Can ye not live without them? I know that those whom ye call the children of the Great Father supply your needs, but if ye were not evil as ye are, ye could surely do without them. Ye could live as ye did live before knowing them, before those whom ye call your brothers had come upon the land. Did ye not live by bows and arrows? Ye had no need of gun or powder, or anything else, and nevertheless ye caught animals to live upon and to dress yourselves with their skins. But when I saw that ye were given up to evil, I led the wild animals to the depths of the forests so that ye had to depend upon your brothers [the whites] to feed and shelter you. Ye have only to become good again and do what I wish, and I will send back the animals for your food."

The Master of Life then declared that to regain his favor and restore the game animals that once sustained his people, the Indians must resist further European incursions. "As to those who come to trouble your lands,—drive them out, make war upon them. I do not love them at all; they know me not, and are my enemies. . . . Send them back to the lands which I have created and let them stay there." Indians must also pray only to the Master of Life, using a set prayer he had given Neolin, and abandon their practice of calling upon other deities and spirit protectors, "because in 'making medicine' one talks with the evil spirit." Finally, the creator called for Indian unity and assured his children that "when ye shall have need of anything, address yourselves to me; and as to your brothers, I shall give it to you as to them; do not sell to your brothers what I have put on earth for food. In short, be good and ye shall receive your needs. When ye meet one another exchange greetings and proffer the left hand which is nearest the heart." On his return from his journey to heaven, Neolin announced that God had promised that, if his commandments were kept, he would restore the good life his people had enjoyed before the European invasion of the continent.

Other sources confirm the accuracy of Pontiac's account of Neolin's message. The Moravian missionary John Heckewelder learned from Indian informants that the prophet claimed that the Master of Life had demanded that they "put off entirely . . . the customs which you have adopted since the white people came among us; you are to return to that former happy state, in which we loved in peace and plenty, before these strangers came to disturb us." They were not to tolerate white incursions on the lands God had given them. Above all, however, Indians must now engage in the pure worship of the creator and pray only to the Master of Life, using a set prayer he had given Neolin. They must repudiate their shamans and the forces those shamans invoked. If those instructions were obeyed, Neolin promised that "the great Spirit [will] give success to our arms . . . . He will give us strength to conquer our enemies." Similar accounts are to be found in the journal of the Quaker trader James Kenny and in the captivity narrative of John M'Culloch.

Neolin's description of his journey to heaven drew upon powerful and ubiquitous themes in traditional Native American spiritual lore. The prophet's quest was undertaken in response to a dream. As one recent authority notes, "the most vital and intimate phase of Delaware religion was a belief in dreams and visions, and in the existence of personal guardian spirits. The vision was the point of contact, a line of communication between the supernatural world and the sphere of everyday life." Equally familiar was the idea of a sky journey culminating in a religious revelation. Dowd has noted that "throughout the Eastern Woodlands, Native Americans commonly believed that their rituals and ceremonies had once been gifts, donated by benevolent forces. According to some myths, culture heroes had received these ceremonies after crossing into other dimensions of the universe. Such crossings were always dangerous and themselves required ritual. . . . Successful passage to and from the upper world . . . required supernatural aid and ceremony. Such travel entailed risks but could bring great rewards." Neolin's description of an encounter, on the road to heaven, with a flaming inferno drew upon that traditional belief in the exceptional difficulty and danger of such travel. The figure of the woman in white who taught Neolin the means of ascending the crystal mountain of heaven and the man in white who led him into the presence of God were immediately recognizable, for it was understood that sky journeys were not possible without a spirit guide. The strange method employed to climb the mountain suggests use of a ritual to gain access to the higher realm. Finally, Neolin's revelation of commandments that, if observed, would bring about the restoration of game and the defeat of the invader, was comprehensible within a tradition that held that the acquisition of power was the prime purpose of a spiritual quest.

But it does not follow that we can explain Neolin's prophecy as an outgrowth of indigenous beliefs. Although his trip to heaven in the particulars outlined above resembled a shamanic sky journey, other aspects of his message are clearly alien to Delaware tradition. Despite their opposition to cultural accommodation with Europeans, Neolin and other nativist preachers of revitalization were not calling for a strict return to traditional spiritual practices. Their invocation of an omnipotent, omnipresent Jehovah-like supreme deity, who had presumably punished his Indian children for their adherence to certain well-established traditional practices, such as polygamy and the "medicine dance," represented a radical new development in Native American religious thought. In order to understand this revitalization movement, we must digress and reflect upon traditional Native American concepts of the holy, for only then can we place Neolin and his contemporaries in their proper context. Belief in an all-powerful creator god, omnipotent, omnipresent, and in firm control of historical processes, was not a characteristic of precontact Native American religions. As numerous authorities have noted, prior to the European invasion, Indians in North America had no concept of an anthropomorphic male creator god as "a ruling deity" personally governing the universe and intervening in the daily lives of human beings. While they had various conceptions of a creator, ranging all the way from a highly abstract Great Holy Flame of Life to a Great Condor, Indians usually regarded that deity as a distant and austere figure, neither omnipresent nor omnipotent in human affairs. Their conceptions of the supreme being were far more complex and sophisticated than early European observers realized. As one authority notes, those ideas of the deity included the Pawnee Tirawa, "a mighty power in human form," who could be "seen or heard or felt" by human beings only "through sixteen lesser powers, especially Wind, Cloud, Lightning, and Thunder," as well as the Sioux Wakan Tanka, also knowable only through sixteen manifestations. "In his person as Wakinyan Tanka, the Thunder Being and giver of revelation," the Sioux supreme being "is shapeless but winged, headless but beaked; all of his young come from a single egg, and when he devours them they become his many selves." Among the Beaver of the Pacific Northwest we encounter Yagasati, "who is both male and female, motionless but the creator of all motion." The Zuni deity Poshayaank'i lives in mist, has an almost human shape, but "looks like fire." The Winnebago Ma'ura made man in his image, "but appears only as a voice and a ray of light." These diverse supreme beings and/or creator gods (the creator was not always the supreme being) were seldom objects of direct human supplication, nor were they represented as jealous gods who punished those humans who had recourse to other spirits. Instead, sacred power was most often sought through the intercession of lesser spirit beings, and was believed to be immanent in many objects both animate and inanimate in the physical world.

Like other Eastern Woodland Indians, Neolin's people, the Lenape, were a deeply religious folk who regularly sought guidance and assistance from the spirit world. But, as noted above, the spiritual power that was so important both to the individual's well-being, and to the community, did not usually come directly from a supreme being. Their conceptions of the creator's nature and role were varied. Lenape stories of the creation, as recorded by European traders and missionaries in the early contact period, were not consistent. Some spoke of the present world as the handiwork of a tortoise who carried the island humans would later occupy on his back and lifted land out of the primal waters that covered the universe. In that version, the first men and women sprouted from the root of a tree that grew in the middle of earth. Other early Delaware informants related that the world was created by a pregnant woman who fell from the sky at the dawn of time. In eighteenth-century sources we encounter Kishelemukong, a male sky god "who creates us by his thoughts." It is likely that earlier European commentators mistook stories about the creation event for accounts of the ultimate creator himself.

It is not to be assumed that Kishelemukong was a postcontact innovation. This creator deity was not, however, the omnipresent, omnipotent, and judgmental god Neolin would later call "the Master of Life." The Delaware creator contemplated his creation, but he did not rule it directly. A Delaware informant told C. C. Trowbridge in 1823 that while the creator remained on earth for a short time after the creation, and exercised "moral superintendency of all affairs therein," he soon departed and never returned. The Moravian missionary Heckewelder related that the Delaware believed that they must look to "the subordinate spirits . . . between God and man" for help and protection, for the creator had turned the world over to those spirits. Direct access to the creator was achieved only during the Big House (Gamwing) ceremony. As Miller notes, in this ceremony, celebrated in "a special building symbolic of the universe," the Delaware renewed "their spiritual ties with all creation." In that renewal, "the entire congregation symbolically rose each night through one of the twelve layers between earth and heaven, finally reaching the abode of the Creator ('the one who thought us into being') on the last night." But in their everyday life, the Delaware addressed their supplications to the "agents to whom he [the creator] has given charge of the elements, and with whom the people feel they have a close personal relation, as their actions are seen in every sunrise and thunderstorm, and felt in every wind that blows across woodland and prairie."

Individual access to the sacred was fundamental to traditional Delaware religious practice. Through vision quests in adolescence, Delaware males commonly obtained protection and gained power from various spirit beings. An early European observer of the Lenape, writing in 1656, reported that their young men generally made contact with an "idol" at age fifteen. In the following century the Moravian missionary David Zeisberger reported that young Delaware males undertook their vision quests between the ages of twelve and fourteen. Contact with the supernatural through the vision quest was essential to the Delaware, as it brought success to the hunter and prowess to the warrior. For that reason, parents sometimes drove their teenaged sons from their homes and forced them to take refuge in wilderness areas believed to be frequented by spirits. Those few Delaware males whose vision quests failed to obtain the guidance of a spirit were regarded as marginal people, devoid of power, deficient in manhood. Zeisberger found that the Delaware claimed to receive spirit power from a great variety of entities, ranging from celestial objects to insects. He was surprised to learn that some Lenapes received visions from such "ridiculously insignificant creatures as ants." Although the form they assumed might on occasion strike Europeans as bizarre, the role these entities played in Delaware life cannot be overstated. Those whose vision quests were successful fabricated small representations of their guardians, which they wore on a chain around the neck. They believed, as Zeisberger related, that they were now able, through spirit power, to "perform extraordinary exploits."

Shamans enjoyed an access to the spirit world of an exceptional order that emanated from "the extraordinary potency" of their particular visions. Through those visions, they were able to personally manifest "the holiness of the other world," expressed through remarkable physical transformations in which they sometimes turned into animals and at other times left their bodies altogether to embark on sky journeys to the spirit realm. Rituals conducted by shamans played a vital role in the life of the community, for through them the people collectively received "vital energy" from the spirit world. "The dramatic actions, the emotional chants, the terrifying masks, and the elaborate dances all bring about contact with a spiritual energy that sustains society." Shamanic power was utilized in other ways as well. Among the Delaware, some shamans specialized in divination and in rain making. Others made love potions, or prepared "medicine" to assist hunters in locating and killing game. Many were devoted to the curing of illness, perhaps the shamans' most important function. Delaware women as well as men served as shamans. They tended to be elderly, and were well paid for their services in wampum, peltry, tobacco, and other valued substances.

Despite the crucial role of the shamans, they possessed no monopoly on supernatural power, which in the Lenape world was open to all through dreams and visions. As one authority notes, "An individual who received his guardian spirit in a vision could appeal to this spirit as his own special protector for aid and comfort in times of trouble, and sometimes to foretell coming events. The guardian spirit, usually an animal or bird, took a personal interest in his affairs, whereas the creator and the subordinate Manetuwak were so busy controlling other natural forces that they might not be able to concern themselves with the affairs of one individual."

The Manetuwak were four spirits, located at each of the cardinal directions, to whom the creator had assigned responsibility for the world's natural forces. The Delaware addressed these Manetuwak as grandparents. Three grandfathers presided over the north, the west, and the east. Koo-hum-mun-nah, "Our Grandmother," was the guardian of the south. These powerful deities, aided by the sun and the moon, whom the Delaware venerated as Elder Brothers, controlled the weather, and were objects of human supplication. In the great semiannual communal rituals of the Delaware, the Green Corn Ceremony and the Big House Ceremony, the creator and the four great Manetuwak played a prominent part. They were invoked in the chants that accompanied the intense drumming and dancing, and were also mentioned in individual prayers during communal ceremonies. But in their descriptions of the spirits that influenced their lives, the Delaware spoke often of lesser spirits. Among them were Thunderbeings, described as "huge birds with human heads whose duty it was to water the earth." They were manifested in thunder and lightning, and were said to protect the world from the Great Horned Serpent, an evil reptile who once lived in the sea. Spirit protectors had killed the Great Horned Serpent, but the pieces of its flesh that were preserved in medicine bundles were said to possess great power. Also of great importance were the Masked Being, sometimes described as the Keeper of Animals, a spirit being who controlled the activities of game; the Earth Mother, "whose duty it is to carry and nourish the people and the animals"; and "Mother Corn, who has dominion over all vegetation and is envisioned as an elderly woman who resides in the far heavens." Communal well-being depended on the favor of those spirits, and also on neutralizing the power of various malevolent beings. Delaware songs, dances, and sacrifices of "burnt meat, tobacco, cedar and other substances," were all intended to gain the assistance of nature spirits. In these observances those spirits, not the creator directly, offered protection to those who successfully invoked their power. The public recitation of visions obtained from such guardian spirits was a highlight of major Delaware religious ceremonials.

The cataloging of religious ideas, practices, and rituals commonly found in most scholarly accounts of the Delaware does not capture the underlying unifying principles that infused their spiritual life with coherence and meaning. Jay Miller, however, has endeavored to probe "the internal logical consistency that serves to integrate, maintain, and reinterpret" Delaware culture. He finds that "Delaware culture derives from the basic equation of Woman and Man, mediated by Mind. . . . In terms of expression, Woman is constrained, specific, limited, segregating, masked, and exclusive; Man is unconstrained, generic, unlimited, integrating, unmarked, and inclusive. Mind is open, permeating, limitless, congregating, and inclusive." Delaware ritual, in Miller's analysis, was grounded in the culture's interplay of gender and mind, "expressing community identity and cosmic harmony," and affirming both "responsibility and revelation."

Assuming that Miller's analysis is valid, how does Neolin relate to that traditional Delaware cosmology? While there is some evidence that the prophet encouraged the Big House rite as "a means of proclaiming Delaware identity," his own teachings about the nature of the supreme deity as a jealous, male sky god is not consistent with the subtle, intricately balanced interplay between a creator who "functions through thought" and the gendered spirit beings who are his agents that lies at the heart of traditional Delaware belief. Reliance on the help of lesser spirits, as we have noted, was an essential element of Delaware spirituality, observed even in the one rite (the Big House) wherein the people approached the creator directly. How are we to interpret Neolin's insistence that the creator abominated the practice of calling upon lesser deities? You will recall that in Neolin's sky journey revelation, the Master of Life warned that when "ye conjure and resort to the medicine dance, believing that ye speak to me; ye are mistaken,—it is to the Manitou that ye speak, an evil spirit who prompts you to nothing but wrong, and who listens to you out of ignorance of me." At one level, Neolin's condemnation of certain shamanic practices made eminent good sense to traditionalists who believed that shamanic power, being morally neutral, and subject to manipulation, could be used malevolently. Neolin lived in a time of heightened witchcraft anxiety within Native American communities. Those anxieties were the product of the deprivation and demoralization that followed in the wake of epidemics, military defeats, loss of land, and forced migrations. But Neolin departs from the traditional understanding of witchcraft. He does not denounce medicine men for their abuse of their power; he charges that they are in collusion with the "Evil One." We have here a vision of a dualistic spirit world with the Master of Life in opposition to a hated "evil spirit."

Who was Neolin's "Evil One"? The prophet may have been influenced to some degree by traditional Lenape stories about the Mahtanu, a trickster figure who spoiled the creator's perfect work by such malicious acts as adding thorns to berry bushes and creating stinging insects and poisonous reptiles. But the Mahtanu did not play the commanding role that Neolin assigned to the Evil One, who on closer analysis resembles the Christian Devil. The Moravian missionary George Loskiel noted that the Lenape had "no idea of the Devil, as the Prince of Darkness, before Europeans came into the county." In his warnings against the "Medicine Dance," Neolin in effect portrayed a form of Devil worship. That idea is one that he probably picked up from contact with Christian missionaries. His "Evil One" has no real counterpart in the traditional Lenape pantheon.

Neolin also spoke of hell. While an earlier Delaware religious teacher had assured the Presbyterian missionary David Brainerd that belief in a place of eternal torment in the afterlife was a Christian superstition that had no counterpart in Native American lore, Neolin threatened those who failed to heed his message with hellfire. The prophet and his followers, M'Culloch reported, relied upon a diagram of the afterlife that portrayed a heaven and hell corresponding not to Native American conceptions but to Christian teachings. In his drawing, Neolin included one area where the fortunate "went immediately after death to heaven" and another, populated by the "abandonedly wicked" who were dispatched "immediately on the road that leads to hell." There were other areas, reminiscent of the Catholic Purgatory, "where the wicked have to undergo a certain degree of punishment, before they are admitted into heaven." Between heaven and that place of temporary affliction lie "a pure spring of water, where those who have been punished . . . stop to quench their thirsts, after they have undergone purgation by fire."

John Heckewelder, who also had seen a copy of Neolin's map of heaven and hell, learned that when explaining the meaning of the design, the prophet claimed that Indians could no longer enter paradise through the usual, broad avenue, as it was "now in the possession of the white people." Instead, they were forced to traverse a narrow and treacherous pathway, which was "both difficult and dangerous for them to enter, there being many impediments in their way, besides a large ditch leading to a gulf below, over which they had to leap." The evil spirit laid in wait at the ditch, seized Indians who faltered, and carried them away to a parched and hungry wasteland where he sometimes "transformed men into horses to be ridden at his pleasure." As Heckewelder recounted Neolin's message, the prophet charged that Indian appeasement of whites had resulted not only in misery in this life but in torment in the life to come. Pointing to the lost avenue to paradise, Neolin would exclaim:

Look here! See what we have lost by neglect and disobedience; by being remiss in the expression of our gratitude to the great Spirit, for what he has bestowed on us; by neglecting to make to him sufficient sacrifices; by looking upon a people of a different color from our own, who had come across a great lake, as if they were part of ourselves, by suffering to sit down by our side, and looking at them with indifference, when they were not only taking our country from us, but this (pointing to the spot), this, our own avenue, leading into those beautiful regions which were destined for us. Such is the sad condition to which we are reduced.

The argument, advanced by some scholars, that Neolin replaced taboo with a new sense of sin borrowed from Euro-American Christians, while not invalid, to some extent oversimplifies and overstates the case. While many of the commandments of Neolin's Master of Life are reminiscent of those of the Judeo-Christian God, and no doubt reflect missionary influence, the new ritual observances Neolin sought to establish do not quite fit the pattern of a religion grounded in concepts of guilt, repentance, and atonement. While he denounced certain traditional shamanic rituals, the prophet instituted numerous new ritual practices that reflected a Native American, not a Euro-American understanding of the relationship of human beings and spiritual forces. He required his followers to buy, and use twice a day, a prayer stick on which had been carved the prayer given him by the Master of Life. He also required that they purchase from him a parchment which he called "the Great Book or Writing." But this was not a scripture. It was rather a map that charted the route to heaven. Neolin initiated a ritual handshake and rites of purification involving both sexual abstinence and use of an emetic probably derived from the Black Drink of the southeast. Finally, he placed a prohibition on the use of flint and steel in making fires, and of firearms in hunting game, and called for the elimination of foodstuffs of European origin from the Native American diet. Observance of these rituals and prohibitions, Neolin declared, would give to his followers that infusion of sacred power essential to ridding the land of the corrupting presence of the white man. The concept of ritual observance as the gateway to the attainment of supernatural power was not borrowed from Christians; it was fundamental to Native American spirituality. Here again we find in Neolin's teachings an interweaving of traditional and syncretic elements.

It is not sufficient, however, to note that the Delaware Prophet invoked both traditional and borrowed ideas about God, the Devil, and witches in his call for a reformation in Native American religious practices. Neolin's message must be placed within its historical context. It came at a time when the Lenape and other dispossessed and threatened peoples were not only angry about past losses, but desperately worried about the future. Neolin provided an ideological basis for resistance and hope by proclaiming that unity against the intruders would be rewarded by the favor and protection of the creator. His revelation that the Delaware were enduring privations because of their transgressions drew in part on the commonplace Native American assumption that grave misfortunes would befall those who offended the spirits. An example is the belief, noted earlier, that offenses against the Master of Animals would be punished by the disappearance of game. But Neolin added a new element into the customary explanations of worldly misfortune by his emphasis on moral, as opposed to ritual, offenses, by his identification of the source of wrath as the creator himself, and by his extension of punishment into the world to come. Those aspects of his doctrine appear on the surface to be purely Christian in origin and therefore alien. But in fact they were well suited to the changed circumstances of Delaware life.

Emphasis on divine providence and on salvation, both communal and individual, served immediate and pressing needs. By replacing, or at least supplementing, the traditional vision quests, healing ceremonies, and communal rituals of renewal with a religion of moral commandments reinforced by the promise of heaven for the righteous and hellfire for the disobedient, the prophet armed his followers with a powerful means of shoring up the discipline their beleaguered and divided communities needed if they were to resist further white incursions. The idea of a historic divine providence, inexorable and just, reinforced that discipline and added a badly needed measure of hope for this world. Even the new emphasis on moral guilt, seemingly alien to a people accustomed to relating to spirit beings in terms of ritual and taboo, was empowering, for, as Richard White notes, "the great advantage of accepting guilt is that it restores power to the guilty party. To take the blame is, in a sense, to take control." The nativist doctrines which condemned Indians for their compromises with whites and threatened utter catastrophe if emulation of European ways did not cease complemented borrowed concepts about God and divine providence nicely, as together they affirmed that through reformation the future would indeed belong to the Great Spirit's chosen people. Neolin's denunciations of both those who engaged in the "Medicine Dance" and those who compromised with Europeans reflected and served the political needs, for traditionalist village leaders were an impediment to tribal and pan-Indian unification, and accomodationist leaders had accepted dispossession and exile. Receptivity to Neolin's teachings was an outgrowth of disaffection with leaders who had either failed to protect or who had sold out.

The prophet's teachings spread throughout the Delaware bands. On March 1, 1763 the trader James Kenny noted in his journal that he had learned from a Delaware informant that their "Whole Nation" had agreed to follow Neolin. They were training boys "to the use of the bow and arrow," and hoped, after a seven-year transitional period, to "Clothe themselves with Skins" and eat only traditional foods obtained in the old way. They would then "quit all commerce with the White People." The movement, Kenny reported, was restricted to the Delaware, as "none of the other Nations" had accepted "the Scheme."

Kenny was mistaken in his assumption that the prophetic movement was limited to the Delaware. Neolin's preaching helped provide the spiritual foundation not only of Delaware unity but also of a nascent pan-Indian resistance movement. Within the year, the message had reached demoralized and disaffected tribes as far west as the Illinois country. It played a major role in the resistance movement mounted by Pontiac and other war leaders who sought to mobilize a pan-Indian uprising against British occupation of the trans-Allegheny regions. The Delaware prophets' call for Native American unity, their assertion of a divinely sanctioned Indian racial identity, as Dowd reminds us, represented a dramatic departure from "the heritage of Indian diversity and of highly localized, familial, and ethnically oriented government. . . . In reaching beyond both the boundaries of clan or village and the less easily defined boundaries of people, chiefdom, nation or confederacy to include all Native Americans, the seekers of Indian unity threatened to subvert both the authority of clan or village leaders and the concentrating authority of those whom the Anglo-Americans called 'tribal' chiefs." The popular appeal of Neolin's message of hope and of resistance in Native American communities inhabited by dispossessed refugees and by indigenous peoples fearful of loss of power and autonomy is understandable. Old leadership sustained by the old religion of the medicine man–shaman had failed to protect against disease, hunger, and defeat. To many Native Americans who pondered the meaning of recent events, the old way now seemed to be devoid of power. The new religion of Christ, which had seemingly empowered the white man, seemed to many Indians a strange and alien faith, identified with the invader and not suited to the Indian way. But the message of the prophets brought word from a powerful deity, the creator himself, who promised salvation to the Indian both in this world and the next. The revitalization gospel offered both an explanation of suffering and defeat, and a promise of victory and restoration. It brought hope to those who had despaired.

Recent reassessments of Pontiac have suggested that while earlier historians often exaggerated his personal role in the uprisings of 1763–64, the overall accomplishments of the Native American resistance with which he was associated generally have been underestimated. Although Pontiac's warriors were not successful in expelling the British from Detroit or Pittsburgh, neither were they decisively defeated by their European adversaries, as earlier insurgents had been. As one recent scholar notes, "an unprecedented balance of power had been achieved, the war had become a stalemate; and the peace was an accommodation." The movement's success was made possible by intertribal cooperation. While Pontiac and others failed to unite all of the tribes, the coalitions they did forge were fairly formidable. Our information on the means used to achieve that measure of unity is scanty, but the reports we do have reveal that Pontiac, in his pan-Indian appeal, referred constantly to the revelations of Neolin and invoked the power and authority of Neolin's new God. The religion of the Delaware prophet, as we have seen, was grounded in a new belief that all Indians were God's chosen people, that whites were children of an evil spirit, and that the road to salvation lay in Indian unity and in the reclamation of Indian ways. It was, quite simply, the religion of an incipient pan-Indian movement that, had objective circumstances been more favorable, might well have paved the way to the emergence of Native American nationalism and a Native American state. Pontiac, of course, adapted Neolin's teachings to his own needs. He exempted the French, whose military assistance he hoped to receive, from condemnation as enemies of the Master of Life. His version of the prophet's teachings placed somewhat more emphasis on armed resistance, and less on cultural renewal, than we find in other accounts. But it cannot be said that he misrepresented Neolin's basic message. The important point is that Neolin's proclamation that the creator himself favored Indians and regarded whites as intruders provided powerful spiritual support for the leaders of armed resistance. It is no coincidence that when Tecumseh, half a century after the death of Pontiac, revived the call for a pan-Indian uprising he claimed the sanction of a body of religious teachings promulgated by his brother, Tenskwatawa, the Shawnee prophet, that were in most particulars virtually identical to the revelations of Neolin. In 1764 the vision of an Indian nation sustained by the favor of the Great Spirit could not be realized, for the centrifugal tendencies of Native American societies prevailed over the call to unity and resistance. But the armed uprisings the prophets did help inspire and rationalize remind us anew of both the crucial role of ideology in shaping human responses to historic change and of the ingenuity of indigenous peoples in appropriating alien ideas to serve as weapons in their struggles to reassert their cultural integrity.

The most significant contribution of Neolin and other eighteenth- and early-nineteenth-century revitalization prophets to Native American life is to be found in their appropriation of Judeo-Christian ideas about a creator god in control of historical processes and their recasting of that deity as the Great Spirit. They did not simply borrow those ideas wholesale, but rather reinterpreted teachings of Christian missionaries by drawing upon fundamental and underlying Native American concepts about their relationships to the created world and the spiritual forces that animate it. Hence, the high God they envisioned was not the Christian God who required that all peoples submit to the religion of Christ and embrace European values and customs. He was instead a deity who smiled upon the Indian way, who was angered by their compromises with the intruders, and who promised that repudiation of Europeans and all their works would lead to the restoration of the good world that Indians enjoyed before their corruption. Revelations about the creator's plan for mankind constituted the most significant and radical aspect of the prophetic message, for the dreams and visions which were customary in spiritual Lenape life were not ordinarily cast in such a grandiose communal/historical mode. The Great Spirit, like the Judeo-Christian God, had a grand historical design, one ideally suited to emergent insurgent movements.

The new doctrine of the Great Spirit as ruler and judge of mankind offered powerful ideological support to advocates of armed resistance such as Neolin and the later Shawnee prophet Tenskwatawa. But belief in obedience to the will of the creator was also a vital part of the message of later revitalization prophets, such as Handsome Lake and the Kickapoo prophet Kenekuk, who rejected violence and preached coexistence. As they called upon their people to embrace those cultural changes deemed vital to their survival and, at the same time, reminded whites of their obligations to respect treaty obligations and Native rights, these visionaries often warned, in the words of Kenekuk, that "everything belongs to the Great Spirit. If he chooses to make the earth shake, or turn it over, ... [no one] can stop it." That sense of historical providence linked to a concept of supernatural intervention to assure the ultimate triumph of divine justice, so fundamental to later Native American religious movements such as the Ghost Dance, had its roots in the teachings of Neolin and his contemporaries. While their appropriation of certain Judeo-Christian ideas is undeniable, undue emphasis upon the nonindigenous aspects of their prophecies obscures both the creativity and the significance of their work.

Suggested Reading

The Prophet Neolin's religious experiences and actions give an early example of how some Indian shamans used religious teachings to help their fellow tribal members deal with the turmoil the European invasions brought. Gregory Evans Dowd, *A Spirited Resistance: The North American Indian Struggle for Unity, 1745–1815* (Baltimore: Johns Hopkins University Press, 1992), examines these issues carefully. His more recent *War Under Heaven: Pontiac, the Indian Nations, and the British Empire* (Baltimore: Johns Hopkins University Press, 2002), considers other elements in the colonial situation. Michael N. McConnell, in *A Country Between: The Upper Ohio Valley and Its People, 1724–1774* (Lincoln: University of Nebraska Press, 1992), provides a broader regional context for some of the events in Neolin's life.

PART THREE

Facing the United States

When the United States became independent, its population and government sought to push Indians aside as they moved west. The new nation used treaties and warfare to acquire tribal lands. For their part, tribal leaders sought help from Britain in the North, Spain in the South, and from other tribes as well. These actions by both sides led to frequent negotiations, sporadic warfare, and migrations that took people away from the pioneers and occasionally even beyond American borders.

From independence to the end of the War of 1812, warfare among Indians and whites occurred in almost all of the states between the Appalachian Mountains and the Mississippi River. Hordes of pioneers swept onto tribal lands as beleaguered villagers sought to retain their homes and customs. Colin Calloway depicts how Shawnee efforts to stem the tide of settlers found little success. By the 1820s fighting spread west to the upper Missouri Valley. There, however, neither the U.S. government nor settlers seeking land triggered the first conflict in the region. Rather, the Arikara War of 1823 resulted from economic competition among St. Louis fur traders and also from Indian versus Indian issues that grew out of Sioux efforts to dominate their agricultural village neighbors in the region.

By the 1820s, the early hopes of many tribal groups to continue living as neighbors with the aggressive Americans had been dashed. Federal officials shared this pessimism and soon developed a plan to force the tribes west beyond the Mississippi. This process of Removal, begun during Thomas Jefferson's administration, continued well into the 1840s and pushed most eastern tribes out of their ancestral homelands. Much of the general literature on this topic focuses on the Cherokee "Trail of Tears." Donna L. Akers reminds us that many other tribes faced similar experiences and presents their side of the story effectively.

During the middle decades of the nineteenth century, the international fur trade became an increasingly important factor for Indians in the Missouri Valley, the northern plains, and the Rocky Mountains. Whether the French from Montreal, the British from Hudson's Bay, the Americans from St. Louis, or the Mexicans from Taos, the intruders brought manufactured goods and epidemic disease to the western tribes. They built trading posts deep in Indian country and supplied them with steamboats. As front men for an expanding nation, traders frequently intermarried with villagers along the Missouri River. These individuals, their Indian partners, or their children often served as translators during the treaty negotiating sessions through which Raymond J. DeMallie says the U.S. hoped to control the Western scene.

CHAPTER SEVEN

"We Have Always Been the Frontier"

The American Revolution in Shawnee Country

COLIN G. CALLOWAY

This essay uses the Ohio Shawnee tribe to examine the impact the American Revolution had on Indians living west of the Appalachian Mountains. Their experiences suggest that conflict between tribal people and the advancing pioneers—and the governments representing them—went far beyond the 1775–83 era. The author depicts the American War for Independence not as a central but rather as the latest incident in a long chain of events that brought interracial conflict to the region.

Calloway demonstrates the variety of tactics that tribal leaders used in an attempt to stay out of the conflict. He then examines the failure of those tactics and the emergence of divisions within the tribe and its leaders. Finally, he considers the motivations behind tribal policies toward the United States. At first they sought peace and hoped to remain neutral. That failed because neighboring tribes and the British pressured them to fight and American attacks enraged many leaders. Clearly seeking to retain their ancestral lands, they negotiated, fled, or fought, but all in vain. In 1795, weakened and divided, they surrendered much of their territory to the victorious Americans.

Despite the central importance of the American Revolution in American history and historiography, the full story of all the participants has yet to be told. Indian experiences continue to receive one-dimensional treatment in most studies of the American Revolution, and historians of the era still suffer from the "Drums Along the Mohawk" syndrome where Indians are concerned. The Indians' *role* in the war still attracts far more attention than does the impact of the war on their

"'We Have Always Been the Frontier'" appeared in *American Indian Quarterly* 16, no. 1 (Winter 1992): 39–51.

home front; tribes feature as military and political units, but their experiences as human communities are neglected. With few exceptions, the Indian story in the Revolution remains relegated to secondary importance and easy explanation: The Indians chose the wrong side and lost. To better understand the reality of the Revolution for American Indians, we need to shift our focus to Indian country and to Indian communities.

The Shawnees exemplify the inadequacy of standard portrayals of Indian experiences during the Revolution. To suggest that for the Shawnees the American Revolution began in 1775 is rather like telling Poland that World War II began with Pearl Harbor. Shawnees were fighting for their freedom long before Lexington and, as for many Indian peoples, the Revolution renewed and intensified familiar pressures on their lands and culture. Nor did the Shawnees' Revolution end in 1783; it was one phase in a Twenty Years War that continued until at least the Treaty of Greenville in 1795. During this war the Shawnees occupied the front lines in the fight for the Ohio River. As village chiefs from Chillicothe told the British in 1779, "We have always been the Frontier." For twenty years, the American Revolution translated into a story of political fragmentation and burning villages in Shawnee country. It was also a story of change and endurance in Shawnee communities.

The Shawnees traditionally comprised five divisions, each with specific responsibilities. The Chillicothe and Thawekila divisions took care of political concerns that affected the whole tribe and generally supplied tribal political leaders. The Maquachakes were concerned with health and medicine and provided healers and counselors. The Piquas were responsible for matters of religion and ritual, and the Kispokis generally took the lead in preparing and training for war and supplying war chiefs. Before the Revolution these divisions seem to have functioned as semi-autonomous political units, occupied particular towns, and possessed their own sacred bundles.

In 1673 Marquette described the Ohio Valley as the place "where dwell the people called Chaouanons in so great numbers that in one district there are as many as twenty-three villages, and fifteen in another quite near one another." But Iroquois pressure drove these people out, and war, migrations, political fragmentation, disease, economic disruption, and cultural changes had already taken their toll by the time the Shawnee tribes reassembled in southeastern Ohio by the middle of the eighteenth century, settling on lands set aside for them by the Wyandots.

The Shawnees' long struggle to defend their homelands against encroachment from Virginia intensified after the Iroquois sold their lands out from under them at the Treaty of Fort Stanwix in 1768. Two years later the Shawnees were working to form a confederacy of tribes in opposition to the Stanwix cession. Tensions exploded after a series of petty frontier skirmishes in Dunmore's War in 1774. The British Indian Department effectively isolated the Shawnees, and when the Shawnees sent a war belt soliciting Iroquois assistance, the Onondagas threw it back at them. After the Battle of Point Pleasant and the destruction of their towns on the Muskingum River, some Shawnees became reconciled to the loss of their lands south of the Ohio as the price of the peace negotiated with Lord Dunmore at Camp Charlotte; others never accepted the situation as one war merged into another.

When the Revolution broke out, most Shawnees endeavored to remain neutral, and several towns moved away from the Scioto to the Miami River and its tributaries. But American encroachments persisted, and Shawnee chiefs told the Virginians in July 1775, "We are often inclined to believe there is no resting place for us and that your Intentions were [sic] to deprive us entirely of our whole Country." American commissioners traveling through Indian country in the summer of 1775 found the Shawnees "Constantly Counseling" and "the Women all seemed very uneasy in Expectation that there would be War." A Maquachake woman told commissioner Richard Butler that the Shawnees were divided, with the Chillicothe and Piqua divisions of the tribe displaying growing militancy. The Shawnees who showed up at the Treaty of Fort Pitt that fall confirmed the Ohio River as the boundary of Indian and white lands, a line the Shawnees fought to hold for the next twenty years.

When Indian agent Matthew Elliott visited Kispoke Shawnee towns in the summer of 1776, he feared a general Indian war. Shawnee emissaries carried a nine-foot war belt to the Cherokees, igniting bloody warfare on the borders of Virginia and the Carolinas. Nevertheless, that fall Shawnee peace advocates attended another multi-tribal treaty council at Fort Pitt, which the American agent George Morgan misread as a broader commitment to neutrality by the tribes. Disease may have added to the disruption in Shawnee villages that year.

The Shawnees occupied a crucial yet precarious position between the frontiers of Virginia and Kentucky and the hostile Mingo bands at Pluggy's Town and elsewhere closer to Detroit. Tribes already allied to the British threatened the Shawnees with attack if they contemplated peace with the Virginians, and they became embroiled in the escalating conflict. But participation was never total. Different groups and individuals interpreted things differently and came to different conclusions about the best course to pursue in tumultuous times. Chief Cornstalk and other peace advocates kept the Americans informed about developments in Indian country and within their own tribe. In late February 1777, Cornstalk, Kishanosity, Molontha, the war chief Oweeconne, and other Maquachake head chiefs sent messengers to George Morgan, assuring him of their desire for peace and blaming the Mingoes for corrupting their young warriors. Cornstalk had little authority beyond his own Maquachake division by this time, and he warned that he could neither restrain his warriors nor stop the drift to war. The chiefs said they intended to separate from those who wanted war and to build a new town. In March, the Delaware Council reminded the Shawnees of what had befallen them three years earlier and invited them to settle at the Delaware capital, Coshocton. Cornstalk planned to move his people closer to the Delawares where, he said, they would be safer from Mingo threats. But the war party was gaining in strength in Shawnee villages, and that same year Shawnee warriors accepted a war belt from Governor Henry Hamilton at Detroit and joined the Mingoes in raiding the American frontier. George Morgan and Edward Hand reported in July that two tribes of the Shawnees had "become unmanageable," while two others remained in the American sphere. The oldest Shawnees early in the next century could not remember an occasion when "more than one-half of the nation have been at war at the same time."

Cornstalk's murder by American militia in 1777 drove many Shawnees into the arms of the British. As General Hand recognized, "If we had anything to expect from that Nation it is now Vanished." Black Fish invaded Kentucky in the winter of 1777–78, capturing Daniel Boone and twenty-six companions in a snowstorm. But revenge was not the only motor driving the Shawnees: Cornstalk's Maquachakes remained predominantly neutral. White Eyes, the pro-American leader of the Delaware Turtle clan, said the Maquachakes took "hold to the Chain of Friendship & mind nothing else." Seventeen Maquachake families under Kishanosity, Oweeconne, and Nimwha, Cornstalk's brother, moved to Coshocton and, in White Eyes' words, "became the same people. The Maquachake division remained the most inclined to peace throughout the war. Cornstalk's sister, the "Grenadier Squaw," consistently supported the American cause. But as concern over American encroachments grew, more Shawnees accepted Hamilton's war belt in the spring of 1778.

The nation divided over the question of continued and perhaps endless resistance to the Americans. Many Maquachakes and Kispokis wanted peace, but most Chillicothes and Piquas remained cool to the Americans and favored joining the Mingoes. Kikusgawlowa (Kishkalwa) had led part of the Thawekilas south into Creek country in 1774, brought them back to the Ohio years later, and then moved west of the Mississippi. Also by early 1774, 170 families had "packed up everything" and removed from the Scioto, rather than "be Hemmed in on all Sides by the White People, and then be at their mercy." Others followed suit, and by 1779 or 1780 some 1,200 Shawnees, primarily from the Thawekila, Piqua, and Kispoki divisions, led by Yellow Hawk and Black Stump, had begun to leave their Ohio homelands and migrated west to Missouri, where they took up lands near Cape Girardeau under the auspices of the Spanish government. Long-distance migration was nothing new: Shawnee traditions say they began to cross the Mississippi as early as 1763, and Missouri Indians killed a Shawnee chief in the west in 1773. But no early migrations split the nation like this one. Shawnee movements in the west continued, and Shawnee history after the Revolution has to be traced in Missouri, Kansas, Texas, and Oklahoma, as well as in Ohio and Indiana.

The Shawnees who remained in Ohio were mainly Chillicothes and Maqua–chakes, with an amalgam of members from other divisions who refused to leave their homelands. The Maquachakes may have continued to hope for accommodation with the Americans, but when Daniel Brodhead sent the Shawnees a speech in 1779 advising them to listen to the peace-minded Delawares and ignore British agents who had come 3,000 miles "only to Rob & Steal," the warriors burned it in defiance. Shawnee emissaries carried the war hatchet south to Creek country. Thomas Jefferson wanted to see the Ohio Shawnees exterminated or driven from their lands, and he advocated turning other tribes against them. American invasions of Shawnee country became almost an annual event, and the Shawnees' Revolution became a story of "Drums Along the Miami," as American troops burned crops and villages, while American forts on the perimeters of their country kept Shawnee communities on a war footing.

In 1779, with the Shawnees badly weakened by recent out-migrations, John Bowman led an inglorious campaign from Kentucky against the principal town of Chillicothe. A handful of warriors repelled and harassed the attackers, but Chief Black Fish suffered a mortal wound. A severe winter followed, and Shawnee emissaries urged the British to provide the support they had promised. Nevertheless, Shawnees were active on the frontiers the following spring: The British at Detroit reported that the Shawnees and their allies were bringing in scalps every day, "having at present a great field to act upon."

In 1780, the Shawnees burned Chillicothe themselves rather than let it fall to George Rogers Clark. Luring the Americans on to ground of their own choosing, they fought a full-scale battle at Piqua on the Mad River, until Clark turned his artillery on the village council house where many of the people had taken refuge. Clark described the town as "composed of well built cabins located along the river, each surrounded by a strip of corn," and his men spent two days burning cornfields and plundering Shawnee graves for burial goods and scalps. The inhabitants of Piqua withdrew and rebuilt their town on the Great Miami River. Shawnee losses were slight, but the destruction of their corn hit them hard "on account of our Women and Children who are left now destitute of Shelter in the Woods or Food to subsist upon." Captive Mary Erskine said the Shawnees lived the whole winter on meat, and refugees filtered into Detroit in search of food and shelter from the British, just as Iroquois refugees fled to Niagara after Sullivan's expedition. In council at Detroit the following spring, Wry Neck urged the British to gather their soldiers and muster the Lake tribes to support the Shawnee war effort. "We see ourselves weak and our arms feeble to the force of the enemy," said the Shawnee chief. "'Tis now upwards of Twenty Years since we have been alone engaged against the Virginians."

Clark was back in Shawnee country in the fall of 1782. According to Daniel Boone, who accompanied the expedition, Clark burned five villages, "entirely destroyed their corn and other fruits, and spread desolation through their country." Most of the warriors were absent when Clark attacked, and reports of atrocities by the "white Savages Virginians" flew through Indian country. But the Shawnees refused to be drawn into open battle and evidently suffered minimal losses.

American strikes continued after the Revolution, with Kentucky militia staging regular incursions across the Ohio. The Maquachakes returned their war-belts to the British in 1784, signifying their intention to remain at peace, and their chief Molontha was the voice of accommodation at the Treaty of Fort Finney in January 1786. But months later Benjamin Logan's Kentucky militia conducted "a wild scampering foray" into Shawnee country. They burned Maquachake villages, killed some women and children, and hatcheted Molontha to death under his American flag. "Logan found none but old men, women and children in the towns," said Ebenezer Denny: "They made no resistance; the men were literally murdered." In 1787 Robert Todd burned the old Chillicothe town on Paint Creek and killed a handful of Indians. General Josiah Harmar burned more villages and crops in 1790. Chillicothe was attacked four times between 1779 and 1790, but the Shawnees kept rebuilding it with the same name in different locations.

Even when not subjected to direct assault on their villages, the Shawnees suffered heavily. Recurrent invasion and forced migration no doubt disrupted the Shawnee ceremonial calendar, which, for instance, observed the Green Corn Festival during the summer months when the Americans targeted their attacks on Shawnee villages. As among the Iroquois, continual fighting and the loss of men who knew the ceremonies meant that traditional rituals of preparing and going to war became neglected, disrupted, or imperfectly performed.

Warriors could not provide for their families when away on campaign, and loss of vital crops of squash, corn, and beans meant increased reliance on hunting at a time when hunters were not available. Similar dietary imbalance among the Mohawks produced widespread sickness. Already dependent on outsiders for firearms and manufactured goods, Shawnees now looked to the British for food and other necessities. But the British, stretched to the limit, discouraged them from congregating at Detroit and sent out war parties as a means of relieving the pressure on the king's stores.

The war altered the location and composition of Shawnee communities. Indian villages were not exclusive ethnic units, but in the chaos of the Revolution, Shawnee communities splintered and restructured. Each American invasion caused a renewed shift to the northwest until the Shawnee population became congregated in new towns on the Auglaize and Maumee rivers. While some families migrated west or took up residence with the Delawares, others moved south to Cherokee and Creek country, where they joined southern warriors in their fight, and by 1791 there were four Shawnee towns on the Tallapoosee River. Physical movement was a relatively simple operation for the Shawnees, as their lodges "could be built easily in a few days, and were abandoned with little concern," but leaving familiar sites doubtless took an economic and emotional toll. Moreover, transportation of a division's sacred bundle was of primary concern in such movements, since desecration courted disaster, and splinter groups who remained behind or moved away from the rest of the division presumably found themselves without the protection of a sacred bundle.

Meanwhile, Mingoes, Senecas, and Cherokees joined Shawnee communities to continue the war effort. Moravian missionary Reverend John Heckewelder reported, "The Shawnees lost many of their men during these contests; but they were in a manner replaced by individuals of other nations joining them," and he noted that about one hundred "turbulent Cherokees" came over to the Shawnees. Shawnee towns took on the appearance of renegade strongholds in American eyes. The distinctions and particular responsibilities of the five ancient Shawnee divisions seem to have become blurred as some groups migrated west of the Mississippi and, by the war's end, Shawnee families from the several divisions crowded into the towns not destroyed by Clark. After the war, Shawnee towns on the Glaize became part of a multitribal community.

The Revolution also intensified shifts in leadership. The principal war chief, Kishanosity, was discredited after Dunmore's War "on which acct. the Shawanese have thrown him down and have taken all his Power out of his Hands." Henceforth Kishanosity took a peaceful stance, along with Wryneck, Nimwha, and Cornstalk. The latter's murder left a void among the Maquachakes, as did the death of Black Fish at Chillicothe in 1779. Black Snake handed over leadership of the Kispokis to Yellow Hawk when he chose to remain in Ohio. Nimwha died in 1780. Molontha was killed in 1786. Black Hoof did not attain prominence until after the Revolution.

Traditionally, Shawnee chiefs were expected to be peaceful. Village chiefs took precedence over war chiefs in council, and war chiefs assumed only temporary responsibility for the conduct of expeditions after obtaining the advice of the council. But endemic warfare enhanced the prestige of war leaders. With communities on a permanent war footing, the traditional surrender of power by the village chiefs became unnecessary, and the normally temporary authority of war leaders assumed permanent status. As early as 1774, Shawnees reported, "Our People at the lower Towns have no Chiefs amongst them but all are Warriors," and in 1777 chiefs were unable to control warriors who had fallen under the influence of the bellicose Mingoes: "When I speak to them they will attend for a Moment & sit still whilst they are within my Sight . . . at night they steal their Blankets & run off to where the evil Spirit leads them." Virginia's Indian commissioners reckoned that of all tribes Shawnee chiefs had least control over their warriors. The presence of members of other tribes in their villages further limited the chiefs' authority. Maquachake and Kispoki delegates in 1778 attributed all the trouble to Mingoes "who live among us and will not listen to us."

The authority of the elder chiefs was further undermined by a new generation of warriors who came of age during the Twenty Years War. At the Treaty of Fort Finney in January 1786, Richard Butler found "that many of the young fellows which have grown up through the course of the war, and trained like young hounds to blood, have a great attachment to the British; . . . the chiefs of any repute are and have been averse to the war, but their influence is not of sufficient weight to prevent them from committing mischief, which they regret very much." Six years later, in meetings held at the Glaize, Shawnee war leaders sat in front of civil chiefs at the councils, contrary to traditionally accepted seating arrangements. This new generation of warriors carried the fight into the next century and new leaders like Tecumseh attracted followings that cut across traditional patterns, or, as Americans saw things, were outlaws from other tribes.

While traditional leaders struggled with the new times, outsiders exerted increasing influence in Shawnee councils. Allies dispensed guns and support via client chiefs. Indian agents like James and Simon Girty, Matthew Elliott, and Alexander McKee acted as vital intermediaries between the Shawnees and their British allies, and served as conduits through which supplies and gifts flowed to Shawnee villages. McKee, Elliott, and James Girty had Shawnee wives and extensive kinship ties in Shawnee villages. They accompanied Shawnee warriors into battle, enjoyed standing in Shawnee councils, and perhaps even influenced the relocation of Shawnee towns. British observers agreed on McKee's remarkable influence over the Shawnees, while Daniel Brodhead, offering rewards for McKee and the Girty brothers, voiced the American line that "the Shawanese would not have been so foolish if it was not put into their heads by some bad people who live with them & are paid by the English to tell them lyes."

By 1782, the Revolution had become a total war for the Shawnees. When Clark invaded their country that year, boys, old men, and women marched out to fight, together with "every man . . . who was able to crawl." Traditionally, Shawnees had often adopted captives to help maintain population levels, but now, with the war taking its toll, captives were painted black and marked for death with increasing frequency. Even so, the Shawnees still held in "mild captivity" the prisoners they had formerly taken; only those recently captured who had threatened their extermination were put to death. Shawnee warriors carried the war to the Americans, participated in the rout of the Kentuckians at Blue Licks, and assisted in the defeat of William Crawford's expedition in 1782.

Then, just as it seemed the Shawnees were winning their war, Britain snatched them from the jaws of victory. British officers and agents were suddenly urging the chiefs to restrain their warriors and tried to sell them the Peace of Paris as offering a new era of peace with the Americans. When hunters from Chillicothe lost stock to American horse thieves in the summer of 1783, Major DePeyster at Detroit regretted their loss but pointed out "the times are very Critical . . . the World wants to be at Peace & its time they should be so." If the Shawnees took action, "it must be an affair of your own, as your Father can take no part in it."

This was the real disaster of the Revolution for the Shawnees. Independence unleashed a flood of settlers and speculators. Between 1775 and 1790, some 80,000 non-Indians poured into Shawnee country. With Simon Girty interpreting, Captain Johnny told the Americans in 1785, "you are drawing so close to us that we can almost hear the noise of your axes felling our Trees and settling our Country," and warned that if settlers crossed the Ohio "we shall take up a

Rod and whip them back to your side." Disgruntled Shawnees met the American commissioners Richard Butler and George Rogers Clark at Fort Finney in 1786, "complaining that we were putting them to live on ponds, and leaving them no land to live or raise corn on." Despite a defiant speech by the head warrior Kekewepelethe, the Shawnees ceded tribal lands east of the Great Miami, warning the Americans, "this is not the way to make a good or lasting Peace to take our Chiefs Prisoners and come with Soldiers at your Backs." More Shawnees migrated across the Mississippi—some two hundred Shawnees and Delawares left their villages on the Miami in the summer of 1787 and settled in the west—but British predictions that the Shawnees' fight for their lands would continue proved accurate.

Burned villages and crops, murdered chiefs, divided councils, economic disruption, migrations, losses in battle, and betrayal to their enemies all made the Revolution one of the darkest periods in Shawnee history. In reading the reports of American commanders, it is easy to assume that their expeditions into Shawnee country administered knockout blows. The strategy of burning crops and villages late in the season certainly produced terrible suffering, but burning villages and killing noncombatants do not necessarily destroy a people's capacity for resistance or their will to win. The Shawnees pulled back as American armies advanced into their country, watched as the troops torched villages and cornfields, and then returned or rebuilt new homes in safer locations after the enemy departed. Shawnee communities survived the destruction of their villages, albeit often in altered form. Untouched food sources beyond the reach of American strikes, and British supplies at Detroit, sustained the Shawnee war effort into the 1790s. George Rogers Clark recognized the futility of destroying Indian towns "when they can get four fold what they lose from the English," and Alexander McKee agreed. Not until 1794 did the Americans get at the extensive cornfields on the Auglaize and Maumee rivers, which Anthony Wayne described as "the grand emporium of the hostile Indians of the West."

For a time during the Revolution, many Shawnees came to identify Britain's cause as their own, and the dwindling of British support hit them hard. But the struggle that terminated for redcoats and patriots in 1783 did not end for the Shawnees. The Shawnees carried on the fight for another dozen years and took a leading role in an emerging multitribal confederacy. By 1795 the war for Ohio was lost, the old chiefs sought accommodation with the Americans, and the people underwent further migrations. Defeat, loss of land, and continued disruption of traditional ways generated further upheaval and despair in Shawnee communities. But out of chaos came renewed hope, as the Shawnee Prophet preached moral and religious reform and Tecumseh led a pan-Indian defense of remaining tribal lands. As a new century got under way, Shawnees once again found themselves at the frontier of resistance to American expansion.

Suggested Reading

Calloway provides an extended discussion of these topics in *The American Revolution in Indian Country: Crisis and Diversity in Native American Communities* (New York: Cambridge University Press, 1995). John Sugden, *Blue Jacket: Warrior of the Shawnees* (Lincoln: University of Nebraska Press, 2000) covers the resistance to American advances into the Ohio Valley through the 1790s, when U.S. forces defeated the Shawnees and their allies to take most of present-day Ohio. Colin G. Calloway, *Crown and Calumet: British-Indian Relations, 1783–1815* (Norman: University of Oklahoma Press, 1987) shows the continuing role of British agents among the tribes of the Old Northwest in the generation after American independence.

CHAPTER EIGHT

Removing the Heart of the Choctaw People

Indian Removal from a Native Perspective

Donna L. Akers

This essay opens with an acknowledgment that many scholars have analyzed the Indian Removal policy implemented during the 1830s. The author notes that politics, economics, nationalism, and imperialism have received attention in studies seeking to explain why the United States turned to Removal of tribal people. She finds that all of these policy studies lack the same crucial element. They ignore or do not fully use traditional Native sources because most of those sources are oral and viewed by many scholars with suspicion. As a result, almost none of the existing scholarship comes to grips with what the forced migrations meant to the Indians themselves.

To remedy this the author presents a traditional Choctaw account of early tribal migrations and their arrival in Mississippi. She asserts that fundamental religious beliefs about the proper treatment of ancestors' bones provide an insight into the Indians' refusal to consider selling their traditional land. Those same traditions also help to explain why many Choctaws were willing to die rather than acquiesce to the move west.

In 1830, the United States Congress passed the Indian Removal Act, effectively authorizing President Andrew Jackson to dispossess and forcibly remove thousands of Native people from their homelands in the American Southeast to lands west of the Mississippi River. The Removal Era has been explored by American historians over the years using classic historical methods and sources. They have recorded and analyzed the usual political and economic happenings and the prominent men with which these events are associated. White America's philosophical and cultural beliefs have been examined in an effort to understand the

"Removing the Heart of the Choctaw People" appeared in *American Indian Culture and Research Journal* 23, no. 3 (1999): 63–76.

underpinnings of Manifest Destiny and America's insatiable drive for land and dominance. Various racial and political attitudes have been studied, along with economic factors such as the price of cotton on the world market. What has rarely been examined, however, is what Removal meant to Native people, from a Native point of view.

The archives and other written sources that are usually mined by modem scholars are almost exclusively written by non-Native people. Government and military records and accounts, even personal journals and diaries, reflect white authorship. Some of these sources include transcriptions of the speeches and other oral communications made by Native people. But these are, almost without exception, orations that were crafted and intended for white audiences— usually government personnel or national legislatures—and therefore conform to the Native perception of what would be important or meaningful to the larger American culture.

Sources that Native people trust to relate their experiences sometimes differ markedly from those considered valid or reliable by mainstream white historians. Most Native groups passed cultural and historical knowledge from generation to generation not through written records but through oral accounts. Some mainstream scholars distrust oral sources, so often the information available from these records is omitted from the historical record, leaving a one-sided version of American history. Oral narratives contain an illimitable opportunity for Native cultural understanding and knowledge. Although they may evolve over the years, this makes them not less reliable than written records, but more so—if one is seeking information regarding the Native perception of events within their cultural context. To understand the historical experience of the Choctaws, it is essential to enter their world to the greatest extent possible. Without an understanding of the Choctaw world, historians only relate the experience of white America.

Sources written in Native languages also are largely excluded from the historical record—usually because of pedestrian difficulties inherent in translation. In addition, however, this is due to the racialist/colonialist thinking of the dominant majority, which discounts the value of Native sources. It would be unthinkable for a French historian not to have a working knowledge of the French language. Why is it acceptable for students of Native people not to be familiar with, or knowledgeable about, the language(s) of the people they are researching? To get at the historical experiences and perspectives of all participants during the Removal Era, therefore, it is necessary to consult the oral as well as the written record—and to examine records written in Native languages as well as European.

In 1830 the Choctaw Nation occupied some of the most fertile lands in North America. In the heart of what would become the Cotton Kingdom, the Choctaws' lands encompassed most of the Mississippi delta lands of Mississippi, as well as regions of Alabama and Louisiana. According to Choctaw traditions, these lands had been Choctaw lands forever, given to them by the Great Spirit, Chitokaka.

The Choctaws resided in villages along rivers and streams, where they followed a primarily agricultural and sedentary lifestyle.

Choctaw society was based on matrilineal kinship. Clans provided the fundamental Choctaw identity, and heritage was reckoned through the mother's line. During the late eighteenth century, a few white men moved among the Choctaws as traders, adventurers, or outcasts of their own European or American homelands. Some married Choctaw women and spent their lives enveloped in Choctaw society. Since matrilineal kinship provided Choctaw identity, their offspring were fully accepted and reared as Choctaws. The children's first language was Choctaw, and their social training and identity was that of Choctaw children. Their paternal heritage sometimes contributed a rudimentary knowledge of the English language. Their father's occasional Euramerican visitors, as well as the tribe's participation in commerce among the white traders, brought exposure to the distant world of Americans on the east coast. But for the most part these influences were limited, and most of the so-called mixed-blood families lived lives dominated, on a day-to-day basis, by the Choctaw world.

In the early nineteenth century the Choctaws sought to appease American demands by ceding sections of land that, at first, seemed of negligible necessity to the Choctaws. However, the demands for land cessions continued and escalated, until during the mid-1810s, Choctaws leaders saw that they must halt further cessions altogether. Choctaw participation in the world market was limited primarily to trading deer hides in exchange for guns, ammunition, metal tools, and utensils. A few among the Choctaw had begun to sell crops and cattle to nearby Native or white communities, but as their land base shrank from cessions to the United States, so did the game supply within Choctaw territories. The Choctaw economy had incorporated the fur trade and the resulting acquisition of European manufactured goods into the core of Choctaw life. The sudden contraction of this market and the increased difficulty in obtaining European trade goods created a violent disruption and rapid disintegration of Choctaw society. Simultaneously, white traders smuggled enormous quantities of illegal liquor into the Choctaw Nation, promoting its consumption and hence the erosion of Choctaw life ways. Real deprivation and economic hardship struck with a vengeance, as a whirlwind of change battered the Choctaws from every direction.

In order to understand the enormous psychological impact the Removal Era had on the Choctaws, one must examine the range of relationships between themselves and non-Choctaws. Relations with outsiders were a fundamental facet of Choctaw being. Reciprocity was at the heart of all relations, including those formed by kinship or clan. Relations with outsiders followed the precepts of kinship, and to Choctaws, these relations were not a parody of kinship relations, but were, in fact, actual kinship realized. White Americans and Europeans had long observed these facets of diplomacy and ritual friendship among the Choctaws and other Native peoples. However, they understood only vaguely that these rituals encompassed a fundamental concept central to Native belief systems.

To the Choctaw, fictive kinship relations with outsiders were essential to human coexistence and could not be avoided. The Choctaw Nation defined outsiders as either kin or foe. They believed that everything in life—the physical, mental, abstract, and concrete—was of one functional whole, one system that tied every being together in permanent yet ever dynamic relationships. If all were partners in an interconnected system, one could not act without affecting all others. Therefore, harmonious relationships with animal spirits, inanimate objects, and other human beings were essential. In this worldview, balance and harmony were fundamental to the community's and the individual's existence and well-being. If balance or harmonic relations were disturbed, dire consequences would follow, causing all to suffer.

In their earliest relations with the United States, the Choctaw Nation came from a powerful position. Allied with the Americans during the War of 1812, they provided essential assistance during the Battle of New Orleans, fighting under Andrew Jackson. Subsequently, they assisted Jackson in his assault on the Red Sticks, tipping the balance to the Americans during the Battle of Horseshoe Bend. Intense loyalty and fidelity to one's allies and kin permeated these relations. In the second decade of the nineteenth century, even as the relative balance of power shifted and Choctaws became weaker than the ever-strengthening Americans, the Choctaws believed that their relationship with the Americans would continue unchanged. Since all were part of a non-hierarchical system in the Choctaw worldview, each group would continue to recognize and act upon the bonds of kinship, even though their relative power or strength might change.

However, the American government conceptualized its relationship with the Choctaw within a hierarchical framework based on relative power. To Americans, it was natural for Choctaws to assume an inferior role. All their dealings with the Choctaws reflect an arrogance founded on their unquestioning belief in their own cultural superiority. Prior to 1800, and perhaps in the first decade of that century, the United States recognized the strength and military prowess of the Choctaws and sought to engage in a diplomatic relationship between equals. In the next two decades, however, Choctaw power declined precipitously, relative to that of the American nation. As a result, Americans began to view their relations with the Choctaws as one of superior to inferior in both the military and political sense. Having always had a persistent belief in their unquestionable moral and cultural superiority, Americans married the changing relationship of power to their philosophical belief in their inherent superiority, creating a monster that consumed the lands and lives of thousands of Native people without compunction.

The 1820s saw the rise of Andrew Jackson to national prominence. He was extremely popular in the backwoods areas of the American South, where he consistently called for the expulsion of the resident Native nations. The momentum of expansionism escalated exponentially during this decade, as whites poured into the western reaches of the American South hungering for cheap land, and the constituents of American politicians demanded the expulsion, by force if necessary, of the Indians occupying lands they coveted. Whites began invading and squatting on Choctaw soil. The Choctaws thought that surely their "Father" in Washington would evict these interlopers, as promised in the treaties. The reciprocal relationships long recognized between the Choctaws and the American government demanded this much. The Choctaws were confident, because of their traditional expectations of the behavior of allies and friends, that the American government would stem the incursions into their lands, and would guarantee, as promised, their continued sovereignty and territorial integrity. Despite Jackson's long personal history with the Choctaws, however, he now formed the core of those calling for their dispossession and exile. This betrayal was met with disbelief and shock. As a traditional people, the Choctaws found the pace of events and the sudden shift in American policy from assimilation to dispossession incomprehensible. Even the most biculturally adapted Choctaws never believed that betrayal on such a scale actually would occur. The treachery of their old ally, Jackson, and his sponsorship of their expulsion and exile created a tremendous reaction among the Choctaws. But before we explore their reaction to this betrayal, one must examine what dispossession and exile meant to the Choctaw people.

Indian Removal, as the whites termed it, created moral and spiritual crises intimately linked to fundamental Choctaw beliefs about place, origin, and identity. Choctaws had a deep spiritual and physical attachment to the earth. The earth was the source of all power, a "numinous presence of the divine, the sacred, the truly real by reference to which everything else found its orientation." Most Native people, including Choctaws, vested the earth with an overriding maternal quality: the earth mother gave life and sustained all living things. As siblings, all humans and animals intimately were connected, kindred in a literal sense. All had spirits and destinies irrevocably intertwined with the destiny of humankind.

Many traditional Choctaws believed that humans sprang from the earth from many primeval pairs scattered over the regions of the earth. They were each created separately from the different natural features and substances found in the region of the earth in which each people lived. For example, in a land of forests, the original humans came from the trees; in rugged, mountainous areas, they came from the rocks; on the plains, people emerged from the soil. "Mother earth" gave birth literally as well as spiritually to the Choctaw people.

After their arrival in the American Southeast, sometime back in the ancient mists of time, the Choctaws began to inter their dead in a great mound, built to honor the spirits of the dead. Taking three generations to construct, this sacred mound was called Nanih Waiya, known also as Ishki Chito, "the Great Mother." This pyramidal mound was located in the southern part of what is now Winston County, Mississippi. Years passed in peace, and then a devastating epidemic struck the people. Everyone died but the headman, who was immortal. When all but this one had perished, the great mound opened and swallowed him.

After the passage of many years, the Great Spirit created four infants, two of each sex, out of the ashes of the dead at the foot of Nanih Waiya. They were suckled by a panther, and when they were older and strong enough to leave, the prophet emerged from the Mother and gave them bows, arrows, and an earthen pot. Stretching out his arms, he said, "I give you these hunting grounds for your homes. When you leave them you die." With these words, he stamped his foot; Nanih Waiya opened, and, holding his arms above his head, he disappeared forever.

All Choctaw children learned these stories in childhood. They were taught as moral and historical lessons, intertwining the spiritual and literal as did the Choctaws in all areas of their lives. Through the oral traditions, Choctaws learned that they not only were part of the Earth, but also part of a specific region of the earth. The gift of the Great Spirit was this land. They were never to leave it, or the nation would die.

The original migration tradition of the Choctaw people emphasizes their attachment to this particular spot of earth (a sacred reciprocal agreement with the dead also is tied to this specific place). This tradition relates how the Choctaw people traveled for forty-three years, everyone carrying the bones of their ancestors. Many of the people carried so many bones that they were unable to carry anything else. Some were so overloaded that they would carry one load forward a half day's journey, deposit it, and then return for the remainder, which they then would carry forward the next day. This task was considered a sacred duty. According to the spiritual teachers, the spirits of the dead "hovered around their bones to see that they were respectfully cared for, and that they would be offended and punished with bad luck, sickness, or even death for indignities, or neglect of their bones."

Each day, at the end of their travels, the people's leader—the Isht Ahullo—would plant the Sacred Pole in the ground. At dawn, the leader would rise and see the direction in which the Sacred Pole was leaning—the direction in which the people were to travel that day. One morning at dawn, the leader observed that the Pole "danced and punched itself deeper into the ground; and after some time settled in a perpendicular position, without having nodded or bowed in any direction." The Choctaws' long journey was at last at an end. The Choctaws arrived at the leaning hill—known to the people later as Nanih Waiya—in a "plentiful, fruitful land of tall trees and running waters" envisioned by the great Choctaw chiefs in a vision forty-three years before.

At the end of this journey, some of the younger Choctaws did not understand their sacred duty to the dead bones of their deceased kinsmen. The Isht Ahullo explained that the people always must take care of "the precious remains of the fathers and mothers," for the Choctaw people were charged by the spirits, who are hovering thick around us now, to take care of them; and carry them whithersoever the nation moves. And this we must not, we dare not fail to do. Were we to cast away the bones of our fathers, mothers, brothers, sisters, for the wild dogs to gnaw in the wilderness, our hunters could kill no more meat; hunger and disease would follow; then confusion and death would come; and the wild dogs would become fat on the unscaffolded carcasses of this unfeeling nation of forgetful people. The vengeance of the offended spirits would be poured out upon this foolish nation.

In historical times, the Choctaws continued to take their responsibility to the spirits of the dead very seriously. Every time they moved their villages, they transported the remains of those who had died. This duty was considered a sacred pact with the dead. In return for honoring the remains of the dead, living Choctaws would be watched over by the spirits of their ancestors. The spirit spoke to the living through dreams and visions, guiding and assisting the Choctaws in all things.

Traditional Choctaws literally believed that they emerged from the Great Mother Mound. In the mid-nineteenth century, the elderly Choctaws, when asked their place of birth, insisted that they emerged from Nanih Waiya. Thus, the forced exile from Mississippi separated the Choctaw people from their own mother. They had been warned by the prophets that the people would all die if they ever left their lands.

The Choctaws tried to convey the imperative reasons that they remained in the lands of their ancestors to the U.S. agents and government. They could not understand the whites' assertion that they took the Choctaws' well-being to heart as they forced them away from that which gave them life. One old man haltingly attempted to impart some understanding of their dilemma to an American agent. He said, "We wish to remain here where we have grown up as the herbs of the woods, and do not wish to be transplanted into another soil." The Choctaws saw themselves as part of the soil, an integral element of the ecosystem, tied inextricably to this specific part of the earth. Their world was a vast, complex system of life and spirits, all comprising an indivisible whole. Like the old man's herbs, the Choctaws believed they could not be separated from their mother, the land of which they were a part. The Choctaws could no more be separated from these lands and survive than could the pine forests of the Southeast be uprooted and transplanted hundreds of miles to the West. The Choctaws were part of their homelands. Separation from it meant their death.

Compounding the enormity of the thought of separation from their homelands was the Choctaw understanding of the west as the direction of death. West, both a direction and a place, held special meaning in Choctaw cosmology. The Choctaw afterworld was located on earth, somewhere in the west. According to Choctaw traditions, the *shilup*, or inside shadow, one of the two spirits that every person has, left the body after death and traveled low over the earth to the west, the Land of Death. Choctaw mortuary rituals had to be performed properly or the *shilup* could not make the journey to the afterworld and instead would hover about the place of death, punishing the living kin who had failed him.

Once the *shilup* arrived in the west, it went to a place of happiness and delight, *shilup I yokni.* However, murderers were excluded from this happy ending. They were unable to find the path leading to the land of happiness and instead remained in view of, but unable to reach, that destination. This place of the murderous spirits was called *atuklant illi,* the Second Death. The horror this place conjured up in the minds of Choctaws cannot be overestimated. It was the land of the living dead, the place where the most horrible spirits roamed in unending despair and hopelessness. It was said that in this place, "the trees are all dead, and the waters are full of toads and lizards, and snakes—where the dead are always hungry, and have nothing to eat—are always sick and never die—where the sun never shines; and where the spirits climb up by the thousands on the sides of a high rock from which they can overlook the beautiful country of the good hunting-grounds but never can reach it." This was the destination the Americans reserved for the Choctaw people.

To the Choctaw, the west, then, was the Land of the Dead; it was the location of the Second Death, where spirits unable to reach the afterworld roamed forever. The west was the direction from which their ancestors fled in ancient times out of dire necessity. Leaving their homelands in the east meant breaking the covenant with the spirits of the ancestors. In the Choctaw worldview, the act of leaving would mean the nation's death. If they left behind the remains of the dead and abandoned their sacred duty, they would commit the most heinous crime in Choctaw cosmology.

The American arrangements for their physical removal left the Choctaws no choice. They had to abandon the bones of the dead. Under the best of circumstances, there was no way for them physically to disinter all the remains and transport them. In fact, the Choctaws had to abandon most of their material possessions since the United States government provided few conveyances for people, much less baggage. Most necessities remained behind, such as the hominy mortars which the women considered their most essential tool for food preparation.

Abandoning the bones of the dead was unthinkable to most Choctaws. Even the more acculturated Choctaws of mixed Native and white heritage found themselves unable to reconcile themselves to such an act. Many Choctaws, therefore, refused to leave. The Choctaws believed that every human had two souls. The *shilup* left the body and traveled west to the Land of Death. The *shilombish,* however, remained at the site of death guarding the remains of the body and its treatment by living Choctaws. One elderly Choctaw man explained this to the American agents: "In those pines you hear the ghosts of the departed. Their ashes are here, and we have been left to protect them. Our warriors are nearly all gone to the far country west but here are our dead. Shall we go, too, and give their "bones to the wolves?" Women especially were reluctant to leave. Many families were split apart, as mothers and grandmothers adamantly refused to abandon the bones of their dead children and their *shilombish*, the outside shadow.

The Treaty of Dancing Rabbit Creek was the instrument used by the United States government to force the Choctaws from their homes. Under the guise of legality, this treaty was procured in 1830 by fraud and deception, against the consent of almost the entire Choctaw Nation. Over the subsequent protests of thousands of Native people and white missionaries, the U.S. Senate ratified the treaty, and the government informed the Choctaws that they had three years in which to leave.

This news produced the most profound reactions among the Choctaw. Chaos was the immediate result. The people quit planting crops, many simply gave up. The months of summer passed without a harvest, and when the winter came, the people began to starve. Alcoholic bingeing became the norm, and the children suffered. Drinking led to violence, as hopelessness engulfed the nation. Thirteen Choctaws died from alcohol poisoning in one month. One missionary reported that the entire nation was in utter disarray. The men stopped hunting, the women stopped planting, starvation and disease followed. Children wailed all night from hunger and inattention. Missionary Cyrus Kingsbury reported that the consequences of the treaty "almost beggars description. Loud exclamations are heard against the treaty in almost every part of the nation. The nation is literally in mourning. Multitudes are so distressed with their prospects as to sit down in a kind of sullen despair. They know not what to do."

In 1831 the first parties were assembled to leave at certain appointed gathering places throughout the nation. The night before one party departed, the women covered their heads with their skirts, keening the death songs all night long. The Warriors sat stoically; facing away from the fires, into the woods. In the morning, as the soldiers stirred the reluctant Choctaws, men and women lovingly touched the leaves and branches of the trees as they departed. They left in autumn, as one of the worst winters in memory struck throughout the South. When they reached the Mississippi River, they were stopped indefinitely by ice floes obstructing passage. The ferries and steamboats stopped running, forcing parties of Choctaws to camp out night after night in freezing rain. The Choctaws seemed unsurprised by the suffering; they were forewarned by the oral prophecies.

The journey to the West was characterized by American ineptitude, incompetence, and mud. Many Choctaws died or became seriously ill due to exposure, disease, and inhumane arrangements for their journey. Most of the nation was forced to walk the entire journey, which was more than five hundred miles. They traveled in kinship groups. Stories are still related of the suffering and death inflicted on the Choctaw people. One large group of emigrants was lost in a Mississippi swamp. The men, women, children, and elderly walked in chest deep swamp water for thirty miles. They went without food for nearly six days, and many began dying from exposure and starvation. They had given up and were singing their death songs when a rescue party reached them. One witness reported that among the bodies of the dead Choctaws were one hundred horses standing up in the mud, stiff from death. The survivors were so disoriented that their rescuers had to lead them out of the swamp by their hands, like little children.

A Memphis citizen observed a group of exiled Choctaws on the road, completely unprepared for the harsh winter weather. They had no tents—nothing with which to shelter themselves. Not one in ten had even a moccasin on their feet and the great majority of them walked. This same man witnessed the travails of another Choctaw party who camped in the woods near his home. One night a hail storm began, followed by two days of heavy snowfall. The Choctaw party was stranded in the coldest winter weather the region ever had experienced. He reported that they lay in their camp for more than two weeks without shelter of any kind and with very few supplies. The second week, the weather averaged twelve degrees Fahrenheit. The abrupt departure left many with little or no time to prepare or pack necessities, which they were told would be supplied by the United States government. The government failed to do so. Only one blanket was issued per family—and most families averaged six members. Yet another party traveled through sleet and snow for twenty-four hours, most barefoot and nearly naked, in order to reach Vicksburg without exhausting their inadequate supplies. The disgusted U.S. Army captain who was their official escort, reported that "If I could have done it with propriety I would have given them shoes. I distributed all the tents and this party are entirely without." He complained about the inadequate provisions made for the Choctaws, and said that the sight of these people and their suffering would convince anyone of the need for an additional allowance for transportation.

As if the weather were not enough, the Choctaws were dogged by sickness on their exile west. Cholera, the most dreaded scourge of the times, struck again and again. A report of its presence in Memphis caused all the wagon drivers hired by the U.S. government to abandon their teams, leaving 150 wagons for the sick and aged standing with full teams of horses. Agent William Armstrong reported that these Choctaws had suffered dreadfully from cholera, stating, "The woods are filled with the graves of the victims. Death was hourly among us and road lined with the sick."

The Choctaws were forced to abandon traditional mourning rituals on the journey west. The bodies of the dead were not scaffolded. Typically lasting more than three months, the rituals were viewed as superstitious and heathen by the United States agents. The Choctaws sought to take their dead with them to the new lands, but the U.S. agents did not allow them to do so. One group's U.S. agent forced the Choctaws to bury their dead the morning after their death, according to Euroamerican tradition. He expressed his satisfaction in his report to his superiors in Washington that the dead had been "decently interred." The Choctaws, of course, understood that the *shilup* of these people were unable to travel to the land of death without the proper ritual of scaffolding and funeral cries. They would be forced to wander the earth, and would punish those who had thus abandoned their sacred duty.

Nearly one-third of the Choctaw Nation died on the march west. Many of these were young children and elderly tribespeople, who disproportionately suffered from exposure, hunger, and disease. The enormous death toll produced social and political chaos. The council of elders that governed each town no longer existed when the Choctaws tried to rebuild in the West. The clans could not survive the death of so many of the elders. The elders were the leaders of each clan—they made the important clan decisions, and all those affecting the smaller kinship units. Since clans traveled together, some suffered death disproportionately, thus upsetting the checks and balances of power so carefully constructed over the centuries by the Choctaw. Their deaths also severely impacted the transmission and survival of cultural knowledge and ritual.

Place always had played an important part in the identity of the Choctaw people. Red and white towns informed the martial or civil responsibilities and emphases of the townsmen. The dispersion of representatives of all clans throughout towns in the nation formed an essential network of unity and cohesiveness, and mitigated conflict among men. The deaths of so many of their people prevented the Choctaws from replicating the physical organization essential to their identity in the new lands of the West. This severe blow to kinship and identity rent the Nation and exacerbated the confusion and depression they suffered after their arrival.

The Choctaws always have been survivors, and have shown themselves adept at meeting the challenges of a changing environment. Within a few years the majority had found kinsmen, erected shelters, and cleared fields. As early as 1833, several hundred Choctaw families had settled on the banks of the Arkansas River, planting crops in anticipation of the arrival later of many more emigrants, for whom they planned to provide corn. Perhaps these folks thought they had escaped the worst, for the spring planting had gone well and most of the people who survived the march were recovering. However, some saw the anger of the spirits raining down on the nation when in June 1833 the Arkansas River overflowed its banks in the greatest flood in its history. In astonishment at the damage done by the raging waters, the United States agent wrote that the Choctaw houses and fields were completely washed away, as though they had never existed. The cattle and horses some Choctaws had managed to bring with them drowned. Incessant rains continued all spring, flooding the entire river network in the new Choctaw Nation. Since the agrarian Choctaws always lived near rivers and streams, many, if not most, were ruined that year. Some families were completely stranded by the high waters, and many began to starve.

Terrible sickness followed the floods. Carcasses of dead animals lined the riverbanks and floated in the waters, making it unfit for human consumption. The U.S. agent wrote that many were starving—"more than they ever suffered before from hunger." He reported many came to him begging for food, having had nothing to eat "for 10, 12, 15 days." The children cried continuously from hunger, and many died. "Within the hearing of a gun from this spot," he wrote, "100 Choctaws had died within the past week." He reported that of the entire number of emigrants, one-fifth died from the floods, disease, and starvation. Many Choctaws were "even reduced to eating the flesh of animals found dead in the woods and on the wayside," reported the agent. He appealed to a nearby army unit for food for the Choctaws. The provisioning officer sent them fifty barrels of bad pork which had putrefied and spoiled. Earlier in the year, the Choctaws had refused to accept his proffer of these provisions, but now, the officer reported to his superior, "he was happy to inform General Gibson that since they were reduced to starvation, they would doubtless be glad to get it."

In fulfillment of the prophecies, the nation was dying. As soon as they departed from their beloved homelands in the east, the Choctaws succumbed to exposure, illness, accidents, depression, misery, and death. No one was left unscathed. Even the U.S. agents were appalled at the suffering of the Choctaw people. The official U.S. government reports indicated that some 20 percent of the Choctaw people had died on the journey, and a great number more—perhaps another 20 percent—died soon after their arrival. The elders died disproportionately, making reestablishment of social and political institutions problematic. Old living patterns, important to the cohesion of the nation, proved impossible to duplicate in the West. Many survivors of the journey did not move from their point of entry into the new lands. According to American observers, they were so depressed, they simply stayed put where they landed and did nothing. Some did not even build shelters or make any effort at all to clear fields or plant crops. Suicide became commonplace, whereas it was almost unknown in prior times.

Word traveled to and from the old nation in the Southeast and the new lands in the years of the Removal. Choctaw families in the West reported the great tragedy befalling the nation. Some of the newly arrived émigrés turned around and started back. Others wrote kin that they should not come west. Those who stayed behind in Mississippi, intending to come later, now decided not to make the journey at all. These people became the prey of invading whites, many of whom were unscrupulous and had no compassion for Native people in distress. The thousands of Choctaws still in Mississippi were forced off their lands and into the remote and worthless swamplands. From there they sometimes would return to look upon their former bountiful homes and farms, all now in the hands of white men.

The new lands of the Choctaws in the West became known among the Choctaw as the Land of Death. The misfortunes continued. On November 13, 1833, the Choctaws experienced a terrible omen. That night, an extraordinary meteor shower lit up the night sky as bright as day "with myriads of meteors darting about in the sky." Some of the women and children screamed and cried in terror, while others hid. All night long, the showers continued. The terror was not limited to the Choctaws. The Kiowas recorded this event, too, finding it so important that they named the season "the Winter that the Stars Fell." The Choctaws knew that the Great Spirit spoke through natural events such as this and that the unnatural event portended great misfortune. This celestial event coincided with the U.S. announcement that no more provisions would be provided for the people. The period covered by the treaty for their emigration had expired. And despite the terrible floods and illness and death suffered in the past two years, the United States intended to do nothing more to assist the exiles.

The suffering of the Choctaw people intensified with the horror of a smallpox pandemic that struck Native people throughout the West from 1836 to 1840. More than 10,000 Native people died in the northern plains alone. Newly arrived emigrants in the Choctaw Nation brought the disease with them. More than 1,000 Choctaws died, including their renowned and beloved leader, Mingo Mushulatubbee. Some families were destroyed completely, all members succumbing within days of each other. Whooping cough decimated the population of babies and toddlers among the Choctaws. One observer reported that all of the small children for miles were killed by one whooping cough epidemic in the nations.

As the decade of the 1840s began, the Choctaw people struggled to survive and rebuild in their new lands. The nation had been decimated by Indian Removal. Some estimate that more than one-third of the nation died as a result of their forced exile west and as many as 4,000 Choctaws remained behind in the Southeast, to be dispossessed from their homes and relegated to wandering in the swamplands, working occasionally as stoop laborers on lands that had been their own. The social and political organization of the nation was in shambles. The clans so central to Choctaw identity and community barely survived the exile. Despite the terrors of the 1830s, however, the nation refused to die. The Choctaws began to rebuild, and in an uneven fashion social and political institutions began once again to function.

The story of the American policy of Indian Removal must be reexamined and retold. It was not merely an official, dry, legal instrument as it often is portrayed. Removal, as experienced by Native people, was an official U.S. policy of death and destruction that created untold human pain and misery. It was unjust, inhumane, and a product of the worst impulses of Western society. Indian Removal cannot be separated from the human suffering it evoked—from the toll on the human spirit of the Native people. It cannot be remembered by Americans as merely an official U.S. policy, but must be understood in terms of the human suffering it caused, and the thousands of deaths and lives it destroyed.

Suggested Reading

In her book, *Living in the Land of Death: The Choctaw Nation, 1830–1860* (East Lansing: Michigan State University Press, 2004), Akers expands on the ideas from her essay and demonstrates the importance of tribal beliefs in the decades after Removal. The policy of Removal is most clearly presented in Ronald Satz, *American Indian Policy in the Jackso-*

nian Era (Lincoln: University of Nebraska Press, 1975). Richard White shows that not all Choctaws responded as Akers suggests in *The Roots of Dependency: Subsistence, Environment, and Social Change Among the Choctaws, Pawnees, and Navajos* (Lincoln: University of Nebraska Press, 1983). William McLaughlin, *Cherokee Renascence in the New Republic* (New Haven: Yale University Press, 1986), examines social changes in a neighboring tribe just before Removal.

CHAPTER NINE

Backdrop for Disaster

Causes of the Arikara War of 1823

ROGER L. NICHOLS

Frequent wars between the United States and various groups of Indians punctuate the narrative of American history. These varied widely from local, minor clashes to major campaigns with hundreds of casualties and deaths. Conflicts between the Arikara villagers and other Americans in South Dakota led to the nation's first Indian war beyond the Mississippi River. The clash did not occur because of land-hungry pioneers or ham-handed federal negotiators. Rather it illustrates the multilayered complexity of dealing with Native people and suggests that intruding whites had little interest or skill in understanding Indian motivations.

This essay notes that long-term demographic trends, the introduction of epidemic disease, disruptions in the physical environment, and social and economic shifts growing out of the fur trade all had impacts on Arikara life and society. Yet when violence erupted, the Missouri River traders had no clear understanding of its causes. Rather than seeking out the roots of Arikara discontent, they merely labeled these Indians as dangerous and unpredictable. The war, therefore, found traders and U.S. officials unprepared for conflict.

Rays from the setting sun illuminated the Saint Louis waterfront as the keelboats *Rocky Mountains* and *Yellowstone Packet* pulled away from shore and headed north into the Mississippi River current. With sails in place, flags flying, and hired musicians serenading spectators who lined the riverbank, William Ashley's party of seventy mountain men began its journey on 10 March 1823, heading north and west toward the Rocky Mountains. Weeks passed uneventfully as they

"Backdrop for Disaster" appeared in *South Dakota History* 14, no. 2 (Summer 1984): 93–113. Reprinted from *South Dakota History* © 1984 by the South Dakota State Historical Society.

toiled up the Missouri River. By late May, they were traveling through present-day South Dakota where events shattered their comfortable routine. Stopping briefly to trade for horses, the whites provoked a fight with the unpredictable Arikara Indians, who were then occupying two villages along the Missouri near the mouth of the Grand River. This incident, labeled "the worst disaster in western fur trade history," coupled with the retaliatory expedition against the villagers led by Col. Henry Leavenworth later that summer, came to be known as the Arikara War.

The conflict paralleled many early nineteenth century Indian wars in which, for what at the time seemed unclear reasons, Indian Americans attacked intruding white Americans. With surprise on their side, the Indians won the initial skirmish, driving the trappers from the scene. Once the frontiersmen recovered from their shock, however, an overwhelming force invaded the Indian country to punish the tribesmen. This counterattack succeeded. The Arikara fled, leaving the enraged whites to burn their abandoned villages.

Students of South Dakota history undoubtedly recall these events well. Nevertheless, a few details of the incident may clarify the situation and help to explain how and why this war occurred. Hurrying up the Missouri toward the Rockies, Ashley had not expected to visit the Arikara. In fact, reports of their hostility that spring convinced him that they should be avoided. Just south of the Indian towns, however, he learned that his partners in the mountains needed another forty or fifty horses for use that coming season. Thus, despite misgivings, and with little advance thought, Ashley decided to halt. He hoped that the ninety-man party of trappers and boatmen was large enough to persuade the Indians to trade rather than fight. After a short parley on 30 May, the chiefs agreed to trade the next morning. On 31 May, the trappers and Indians began their barter, but with limited success. Far from other sources of horses, the Arikara demanded top prices for their animals. Since Ashley had not anticipated this trading session, his stock of trade items may not have been adequate. When the trading ended that day, the whites had only nineteen horses, and the Indians had balked at the amount and quality of the whites' trade goods.

Continuing signs of Indian discontent convinced Ashley that he should move quickly upriver with the few horses he had obtained. Unfortunately, bad weather made it impossible to travel the next morning. The whites were forced to remain, some guarding the animals on the beach while the rest huddled aboard the boats waiting for the storm to pass. At dawn the following day, 2 June, the Arikara warriors attacked. In a few minutes, their musket balls and arrows destroyed the horses and killed or wounded most of the trappers on the beach. Caught by surprise and defeated soundly, Ashley's remaining men scrambled aboard the keelboats and fled downstream.

News of the Arikara attack reached Fort Atkinson, just north of present-day Omaha, Nebraska, and set into motion a combination rescue effort and retaliatory expedition. Col. Henry Leavenworth rushed six companies of United States infantrymen upriver, while Saint Louis trader Joshua Pilcher joined the troops with a force of nearly sixty trappers and fur company employees. Along the way, this so-called Missouri Legion recruited a force of nearly seven hundred fifty Sioux allies. By early August 1823, the mixed group of soldiers, trappers, and Indians arrived at the Arikara villages, where the mounted Sioux auxiliaries swept ahead of the foot soldiers and launched a preliminary attack on their long-time foes. A stream of Arikara warriors poured out of the villages to meet them. After spirited fighting, the Arikara saw the regular troops moving up and fled back behind the village palisades.

The next morning, 10 August, Colonel Leavenworth ordered his artillery to shell the villages, but, through ineptitude or carelessness, the soldiers sent most of their shots whistling harmlessly overhead. Seeing this, the colonel ordered an infantry attack on the upper village. Although the soldiers fought bravely, the Indian defenders refused to budge. At that point, fearing both a possible heavy loss of his men and perhaps even the total destruction of the Indian towns, Leavenworth chose to negotiate an end to the fighting. Late that afternoon, the whites persuaded several Arikara chiefs to join them for peace talks. Although divided and bickering acrimoniously among themselves, the invading forces concluded a treaty with the Indians the next day, but the wary Arikara abandoned their villages during the following night. On 15 August, Leavenworth led his force back down the river to Fort Atkinson. No sooner had the soldiers left, than several fur company employees burned the villages to the ground. As a result of this campaign, the Arikara scattered. Many of them moved away from their traditional home for more than a decade.

There is little dispute about these events. Yet, both Indian and white motivations remain murky. To reach an understanding of the forces that led to the Arikara War, several factors have to be considered. The nature of Arikara village life and society provides one clue to the reasons behind the Arikaras' actions. The villagers' pattern of dealing with other American Indian groups in the Missouri Valley likewise offers some insights into their behavior toward all outsiders. Obviously, these Indians had developed a bitter hostility toward the white traders or they would not have risked an all-out war with them, and the growth of anti-white attitudes needs to be examined. At the same time, white ideas about the Arikara and the traders' responses to the villagers provide the other necessary threads in the pattern. When taken together, the Indian and white motivations offer the basis for a clear perception of the conflict. Historical accounts of Indian wars often focus chiefly on white actions. In this circumstance, however, the Indian motivations, attitudes, and actions proved more important than those of the whites in shaping the course of events. The following discussion, therefore, focuses more attention on Arikara actions than on those of Ashley or the Leavenworth Expedition.

Among the developments that propelled the Arikara toward their 1823 encounter with Ashley's trappers were several long term trends within the villagers' society that played increasingly important roles. A Caddoan people related to, or perhaps part of, the Skidi Pawnee, the Arikara lived in nearly permanent towns on the banks of the Missouri River throughout most of the eighteenth century. There, between the White and Cheyenne rivers in central South Dakota, they fished in the Missouri, farmed its banks and bottom lands, hunted on the nearby plains to the west, and participated in the existing Indian trade network. The most important long-term trends in their society resulted from their growing role as traders. In that capacity, they increased their corn production and exchanged their surplus harvest with the nearby hunting peoples for meat, hides, and leather goods. This activity tied the villagers into trade patterns that connected aboriginal peoples from central Canada to the borders of Mexico, and from the Rocky Mountains to the Mississippi River and beyond.

In the mid-eighteenth century, or earlier, the Arikara traders added European goods to their traditional wares. People from the southern plains offered horses to the Missouri Valley dwellers, while manufactured goods and guns filtered south and west from Canada. Before long, European traders followed their goods into the Indian towns, forever altering aboriginal life. As the century drew to a close, the Arikara economy had undergone fundamental changes. Their earlier trade had been a matter of choice, an exchange of surplus goods with other tribal people. Now, they shaped their economy to reflect their dependence on trading. True, they still hunted, but in most years their catch did not provide enough meat or hides to meet their needs. Nor did exchange of their surplus corn by itself supply these necessities any longer. Increasingly, their aboriginal customers demanded guns, ammunition, and manufactured goods in addition to foodstuffs. By accident or design, the villagers became ever more dependent on their white trading partners for survival.

Within most Indian communities, "trade was embedded in a network of social relations" so that few individuals gained new status because of it. Direct trade with Europeans, however, brought opportunities for increased wealth within many tribes and bands. Before the fur-and-hide trade, clan chiefs and other village leaders maintained a superior status because of their social functions. Direct trading with whites meant that individual hunters might acquire more wealth than was possible under the aboriginal system. Chiefs might still take a share of this new wealth, but a growing individual participation in the trade with the whites produced new economic pressures within many Indian societies. There is little direct evidence that this pattern was of major importance in the Arikara villages, but the lack of evidence may reflect the inability of white traders, who provided the early accounts of the Arikara, to perceive their own impact on the villagers. This pattern seems to have occurred repeatedly among other aboriginal groups, and there is little reason to dismiss it as a factor among the Arikara.

While such changes reshaped the villagers' economic life, even more disruptive events rent the fabric of Arikara society. Soon after the first meetings between European traders and the Arikara, a series of major smallpox epidemics swept across the Missouri Valley and out onto the northern plains. Although the chronology and severity of these epidemics remain shrouded in antiquity, the combined results unquestionably proved disastrous. Modern scholars and eighteenth-century observers agree that the epidemics destroyed nearly three-quarters of all the Indians in South Dakota. The disease struck the Arikara and other sedentary agricultural tribes a devastating blow, one from which they never fully recovered. As the pox swept through their villages, it killed or terrorized most of the inhabitants. Village, band, clan, and even family organization crumbled as aboriginal healers failed to halt the plagues. The result was catastrophic, and by 1795, most of the Indians had died. In that year, a resident trader reported: "In ancient times the Ricara nation was very large; it counted thirty-two populous villages, now depopulated and almost entirely destroyed by the smallpox A few families only, from each of the villages, escaped; these united and formed the two villages now here." When Lewis and Clark visited the tribe in late 1804, they learned that the existing three villages, located near the mouth of the Grand River, included the survivors of some eighteen earlier towns along both sides of the Missouri.

While the smallpox epidemics killed most of the Indians and disrupted or destroyed their social cohesion, the consolidation of survivors in two or three villages also brought unforeseen and continuing problems. Individuals from at least ten distinct bands, each with different leaders and varying customs, as well as major linguistic differences, huddled together in their new settlements. A higher percentage of band leaders and chiefs survived than did the population as a whole. Pierre-Antoine Tabeau reported that there were more than forty-two chiefs living in the three villages in 1804. Each of the many chiefs, Tabeau noted, "wishes at least to have followers and tolerates no form of dependence" on others. This situation brought nearly incessant wrangling among contending leaders as their factions disrupted village life with "internal and destructive quarrels."

Such pressures on the Arikara not only affected the nature and operation of their society, but they also had direct impact on their dealings with other Indians. In particular, their divided and quarreling leadership caused problems and made other situations worse than they needed to be, especially in relationships with the neighboring Mandan, Hidatsa, and Sioux. The Sioux, largest of these Indian groups, threatened all three agricultural village tribes. Although the Mandan, Hidatsa, and Arikara shared a similar function as middlemen in the area trade network and suffered alike at the hands of Sioux raiders, they quarreled and even fought with one another rather than presenting a united front in response to Sioux aggression. Not only did the Sioux "pursue a system of preventing trade to all [Indian] nations up the Upper Missouri," but they also raided the villagers' crops and horse herds repeatedly.

In the Arikaras' case, the lack of clear leadership in their fractured society made it difficult for them to pursue any consistent policy toward their neighbors. In fact, it created an instability that caused other groups to see the tribe as dangerous and unpredictable. The Frenchman Tabeau complained that the splintered nature of Arikara village leadership led to endless conflicts as the chiefs and their followers robbed each other and threatened to fight others in their own communities. What was worse, in his opinion, was the Arikaras' continuing inability to settle disputes with the Mandan and Hidatsa so that the three agricultural tribes could unite to defend themselves against the Sioux. Tabeau felt certain that Arikara leaders realized that it was imperative to ally themselves with the Mandans; yet they could not do so. He noted that all their efforts to make peace with that tribe failed because of "individual jealousy" within the villages. Divided leadership or a lack of unity, then, destroyed "all the plans which tend to bring about peace" with their natural allies.

The situation also made their response to direct Sioux aggression ineffective much of the time. All the roots of the conflict between these two tribes are not clear, but certainly the Sioux looked down upon their sedentary neighbors, treating the Arikara as inferior beings who farmed and did other such women's chores for their benefit. Sioux arrogance grew steadily more intolerable, and by the early nineteenth century, they acted as if they were the masters rather than the equals of their trading partners. When they came to trade, Sioux visitors did little bargaining over prices. Instead, they took what they wanted and gave the villagers whatever amount of skins and meat they deemed adequate. To amuse themselves and show disdain for the Arikara, they often pillaged and trampled gardens, beat and insulted Arikara women, and ran off the villagers' horses. Outnumbered, divided, and often leaderless, the Arikara seemed unable to respond effectively to Sioux assaults.

Customs related to wealth and status among the upper Missouri Valley tribes also kept their intertribal relationships in turmoil. For young men, status within the village resulted from acts of bravery. Usually, such acts included either stealing horses or fighting men from the surrounding tribes. Once a raid took place, the victims often retaliated, and a cycle of violent competition and warfare continued for generations. The warriors had strong social and economic motivations for their actions, and with village controls weakened among the Arikara, there were few restraints to curb raids against erstwhile allies or friends. Not only did these attacks and counterattacks prevent any lasting peace, but practices related to success and failure on these expeditions also worsened the situation further. If raiders returned home without success, the warriors would "'cast their robes' . . . and vow to kill the first person they meet, provided he be not of their own nation." This custom explains many incidents that otherwise make little sense—particularly when the Indians visited their wrath on white traders passing through their country. Thus, the situation among the tribes of the upper Missouri region by 1800 was one of uneasy peace and bitter economic rivalry, punctuated by recurring raids and warfare.

As long as the Missouri Valley Indians dealt only with each other, matters remained relatively simple, but once white traders and trappers entered the scene, the situation became more complicated. Prior to the 1790s, the Arikara had encountered few whites, but the next several decades brought increasing numbers of Euro-Americans into the region. The presence of white traders aggravated existing stresses and violence among the Indians by accident, and perhaps by design as well. For example, the incident in which Teton Sioux threatened Lewis and Clark during the summer of 1804 resulted directly from the efforts of those Indians to close the upper Missouri to white traders. The Sioux assumed that the explorers carried commercial goods and that the village people would get some of those trade items. In a series of stalling actions and near skirmishes, they tried to prevent the whites from traveling further upstream. At the same time, the Arikara, Mandan, and Hidatsa lived in fear that their downriver rivals would restrict their sources of manufactured goods. Therefore, the village tribes did whatever they could to keep their trade channels open and reacted violently when they thought the whites had cooperated with their enemies or had pursued policies that might hurt them. These intertribal rivalries became so bitter that often the warriors' treatment of whites depended upon whether or not the traders had dealt with their Indian competitors.

Examples of this attitude abound. After Lewis and Clark ran the Sioux blockade of the Missouri in 1804, the Arikara welcomed them enthusiastically. The explorers spent five pleasant days among the villagers and reported that these people "were all friendly & Glad to See US." Nevertheless, the explorers' actions while they were with the Arikara triggered a major incident a few years later. Following their orders, Lewis and Clark persuaded Arikara leader Ankedoucharo to join a delegation of Missouri Valley chiefs going east to Washington, D.C. The Indians reached the capital in 1806, and while there, Ankedoucharo and several other chiefs died. It took until the spring of 1807 for the government to inform the uneasy villagers of their chief's death. The Indians had no way of knowing what had happened and suspected the whites of having killed their chief.

Angered by what they saw as American treachery, the villagers turned violently against the whites along the Missouri in 1807. Saint Louis trader Manuel Lisa encountered their hostility first in late summer, when several hundred armed warriors confronted his party near the villages. The Indians fired a few shots over the boats and ordered the whites ashore, but Lisa relieved the tension and escaped without a fight. At this point, the United States government blundered onto the scene in its efforts to return the Mandan chief Shahaka to his North Dakota home. Shahaka had been among the group of Indian leaders taken east a year earlier, and in May 1807, Ensign Nathaniel Pryor started up the Missouri to escort him home. After an uneventful trip, the whites reached the Arikara towns in September, completely unaware of the Indians' anger or the earlier incident with Lisa's party. Pryor found the Arikara sullen and angry. At the upper village, warriors attacked, and after a brief exchange of shots, the unprepared whites retreated downstream. The government officials who dispatched the escort assumed that the Arikara had received news of their own chiefs death peacefully, and they ignored or failed to realize that the Arikara and Mandan were at war with each other that summer.

It is not surprising that the Arikara met the whites with hostility. The government had only recently notified them of Ankedoucharo's death, and the Americans now arrived escorting an enemy chief past their towns. The Arikara's hostile response gave them an early reputation as a dangerous and unpredictable people. They were, after all, the only regional tribe to fight with United States troops up to that time. Their attack persuaded federal officials that they needed a strong force when they next tried to return the Mandan chief to his home village. Two years later, an escort of militiamen under the command of Pierre Chouteau awed the Arikara enough that they apologized and promised to remain at peace.

Although no other major incidents occurred during the next few years, little happened to change American ideas about the Arikara either. Most traders treated them gingerly, remembering the attack on Pryor and his men. In 1811, however, the villagers appeared as protectors, not attackers, of two large expeditions of whites traveling through their country. That summer, groups of traders led by Wilson P. Hunt and Manuel Lisa raced each other up the Missouri, both hoping to avoid the hostile Sioux. Neither succeeded, but both got past them without bloodshed. Less than a week later, the traders met a combined Arikara, Mandan, and Hidatsa war party of nearly three hundred men. At first, the whites feared that the Indians would attack, but, to their relief, the warriors escorted them north toward their home villages.

Once again, the bitter rivalries between the agricultural trading villagers and the Sioux hunters explain much of this apparent dramatic shift in behavior. For a change, the Arikara and their northern neighbors had put aside their differences to form a defensive alliance against the Sioux. They welcomed the traders because the whites carried a crucial supply of manufactured trade items, especially weapons and ammunition. The Indians seemed apprehensive that without the safety their escort offered, the traders might be frightened enough to turn back downstream, as the Crooks and McClellan party had done just two years earlier after an encounter with the Sioux. Arikara actions in this incident reflected their determination to protect their economic status through continued trade with the whites. Their actions may also have indicated a growing Indian awareness of their dependence on the whites for the manufactured goods that had come to play such an important role in the upper Missouri trade patterns.

Bitter rivalries and divisions among the chiefs, however, continued to disrupt the Arikara towns and often kept visiting whites uncertain how to approach these people. In August 1812, for example, Manuel Lisa again had trouble with them. A few days before Lisa and his men reached the Arikara settlements, Le Gauche, "The Left-Handed," a hereditary chief, met them near the river. He visited for a short time—just long enough for Lisa to give him a few small gifts before returning to the village. Lisa's presents to Le Gauche infuriated rival chiefs, and when the whites arrived at the village, they encountered silence and obvious anger. Lisa demanded to know what had happened. Once the disgruntled chiefs explained, he offered enough presents to soothe their hurt feelings. While this incident illustrated the continuing importance of internal village divisions in shaping Indian responses to outsiders, the Arikaras' lack of violence in this case showed something else. By this time, they seem to have realized that because they had few furs or hides to offer the whites, they had to remain on their best behavior in order to retain a local trading post. Without such a post, they had no reliable source of white goods.

During the War of 1812 and the confused years after that conflict, few Americans penetrated the upper Missouri region. In fact, before 1818, there seems to have been little regular commerce between the villagers and the Saint Louis merchants. From 1820 on, relations between Americans and the Arikara deteriorated steadily. Time and lack of documentation shroud many of the circumstances, and Indian motivations during that era must remain uncertain. Nevertheless, some patterns continued. By 1820, the Saint Louis traders had moved north to the Big Bend of the Missouri, where they had established a trading post among the Sioux, about one hundred fifty miles south of the Arikara towns. From that location, the whites provided arms, munitions, and other trade items to the hunting bands of the region. The Arikara responded to the new trading activity with violence. In 1820, a large war party attacked and robbed two trading posts along the Missouri. Here, one must assume that the villagers struck the whites out of frustration and jealousy. They had no dependable source of manufactured goods, while their Sioux enemies had several.

By the early 1820s, even the most obtuse company trader should have been able to discern the relationships among the Arikara, their Indian competitors, and the white traders. The villagers' actions toward the Americans varied from vicious attacks, through strained relations, to enthusiastic friendship, depending on the internal social pressures on the tribe and the success or failure of their dealings with the Sioux. Instead of acknowledging these pressures, the traders seemed both uninformed and uncaring. Either attitude seems strange because their livelihood and their lives depended upon their ability to understand the situation clearly. Without any firm basis for their picture of the Arikara, most traders seem to have accepted the negative descriptions current about these Indians. Certainly, intermittent violence by the tribesmen colored the whites' perceptions of them, but it seems likely that the negative reports of their customs and appearance fed the traders' fear and loathing of these people. Revulsion at their practice of incest and high incidence of venereal disease, grumbling about the expense of having to maintain an unprofitable trading post in their vicinity, and the confusion and violence resulting from their shattered village society all helped to persuade the traders that the Arikara were indeed troublesome and dangerous. Before the 1823 incidents, they had acquired a reputation as the most unpredictable and hostile tribe along the Missouri.

It is only with this understanding of the Indian situation and actions that the

Arikara War of 1823 can be understood. The local, or short-range, causes of that conflict began in 1822, when William Ashley and Andrew Henry led a group of white trappers into the northern Rocky Mountains. There, they went into direct competition with both Indian trappers and traders, a move guaranteed to disrupt earlier patterns of Indian trade. The logical result would be that white traders and trappers would supplant Indians in those activities. In the fall of 1822, however, that possibility remained in the future. Ashley's expedition stopped at the Arikara villages in early September to trade for horses. The chiefs welcomed the white men and probably made their usual request that a trading post be established for them. Ashley, of course, had little interest in beginning an unprofitable trading post, for he planned to avoid stationary trading facilities and, by bringing his men directly to the mountains, to bypass Indian hunters altogether. Nevertheless, as part of his effort to tell the Missouri Valley tribes whatever he "thought most likely to secure and continue their friendship," he promised to supply the goods they wanted from Saint Louis the next spring. Ashley failed to recognize the significance of his promise to the village leaders and would pay dearly for breaking it. When no trader moved into their vicinity the next year, the Arikara must have realized that the whites had not meant what they said.

Had that been the only issue between the village chiefs and Ashley, the 1823 violence might have been avoided. Other problems existed, however. A major cause for Arikara hostility in the summer of 1823 grew out of an incident with some Missouri Fur Company employees. In March of that year, a group of Arikara hunters had met some of these traders riding near Cedar Fort, a trading post established for the Sioux near the Big Bend of the Missouri. The traders were carrying hides to the nearby post, and the Arikara demanded that the whites surrender the goods to them, but the traders refused. Outraged, the Arikara robbed and beat them. Their anger grew out of seeing the traders helping the hated Sioux rather than from any general anti-white feelings. The assault may also have resulted from Arikara frustration over their continuing inability to persuade the whites to keep a permanent trading post open near their villages, an ongoing source of friction between the Arikara and Saint Louis merchants.

Only a few days after the fight with the traders, another and larger party of Arikara unsuccessfully attacked Cedar Fort, the Missouri Fur Company post. This time, two of the Indians died and several others were wounded. One of those killed was the son of Grey Eyes, a prominent Arikara chief. Reports of the incident indicated that the Indians' failure to defeat the traders and plunder their goods had infuriated and humiliated the warriors, and that they were not likely to be discriminating in their vengeance against whites. Unfortunately for Ashley's men, they ventured up the Missouri just in time to bear the brunt of this anger and frustration.

Ashley's actions toward the villagers almost certainly played some part in bringing about the Indian attack as well. As mentioned earlier, he had, in 1822, pledged to give the Arikara what they wanted most from the whites—undoubtedly a resident trader and thus a dependable supply of manufactured goods. Clearly, he had little intention of keeping his promise. At the same time, he had tried to assure them that his own trappers posed no competitive threat to their efforts as Indian traders. The mountain men would gather and transport the furs themselves, but because the villagers usually traded buffalo hides rather than the pelts of smaller, fur-bearing animals, he hoped that no problems would result.

Before his ninety trappers and boatmen reached the Arikara towns in late May of 1823, Ashley had learned of the Indians' attack on Cedar Fort, and he reported taking "all the precaution in my power for some days before I reached their towns." Once there, he anchored the keelboats in midstream and rowed ashore in a small skiff to meet Indian leaders and get their assurances of . . . peaceful trade. Dissension between the two villages and among Arikara leaders was apparent as the village leaders came down to the shore, for they agreed to talk only "after a long consultation among themselves." The trader invited two chiefs, Little Soldier and Grey Eyes, aboard his skiff, and, to his surprise, the latter agreed. Grey Eyes was reputed to be the most anti-white of the Arikara leaders and had also lost a son in the abortive raid at Cedar Fort that spring. His cooperation calmed Ashley's fears somewhat. The Indian leaders returned to their villages, and later that evening, Grey Eyes reported that the Indians would be ready to open trade in the morning.

On 31 May, the barter began, with the Indians bringing horses and buffalo robes to exchange for guns, ammunition, and other trade items. Business moved slowly, and when the whites had nineteen of the forty horses they needed, a dispute arose. Some Indians objected to the number and kinds of guns and the limited amount of powder the whites displayed. It is unclear whether they thought that Ashley's party offered too little for the horses or whether the Arikara merely wanted more guns and powder to use in their own trade with the plains tribes. In either case, barter ceased for the day, and Ashley decided to take the animals they had already acquired and leave the next morning. Bad weather prevented this plan, and the mountain men had little choice but to remain. They could not move upstream against the strong wind and current, and to retreat downstream would only postpone the need to pass the villages. While they waited for the storm to pass, Chief Bear of the upper village invited Ashley to his lodge. The Indians assured the visitors of their friendship, and Little Soldier even warned of a possible attack by other elements in the tribe. His warning proved to be correct. At sunrise on 2 June, a hail of arrows and musket balls drove the trappers back downstream.

Clearly, divided leadership and conflicting desires within the Indian towns contributed to the attack. By this time, no formal Arikara tribe existed. The villages consisted of survivors of many earlier communities, and the Indians had never managed to restructure their society so that it functioned in an integrated manner. Ashley and his party noted confusion among the Indians over whether to trade or fight, but the traders seemed ignorant of how splintered Arikara society had become or how much danger this represented for them. The chiefs Grey Eyes, Little Soldier, and Bear all reacted differently to the whites' presence. The first was friendly and then became hostile. The second was aloof but later warned of danger, while the third remained friendly throughout the visit. The attitude of each town toward its guests was also different. The murder of one of Ashley's men took place in the lower village, and it was from there that Grey Eyes and his followers launched their dawn attack on the trappers. In the upper village, however, Bear and his followers vehemently denied responsibility for the fighting. Later that summer, Colonel Leavenworth reported that "the people of the upper village would not give up their horses to pay for the mischief which the Chief Grey Eyes of the lower village had done."

The Leavenworth Expedition later in the summer failed to defeat the Arikara. but it ushered in a period of difficulty for the Indians. Once the invading white army left, the bands separated. Some fled north up the Missouri. A few people remained near the now burned villages and gradually resettled there. Others moved south and west into Nebraska to live with the Pawnee for a time. One band even traveled to eastern Wyoming. In 1837, after more than a decade, the bands reunited on the Missouri, just in time to be further decimated by the smallpox epidemic that swept up the valley that summer. Thus, these people, who had survived continuing warfare with Indian neighbors and sporadic fighting with the whites, succumbed instead to disease.

Many accounts of their role in the early history of South Dakota and the fur trade stress the Arikaras' treacherous nature and the danger they posed to peacefully inclined traders. Certainly, they killed and robbed enough white trappers and traders along the Missouri and on the nearby plains during the first third of the nineteenth century to deserve the negative reputation they acquired among whites. Yet, except for the two famous attacks—the first against Ensign Pryor in 1807 and the second against Ashley's men in 1823—their record appears to be little more violent or unpredictable than that of the Pawnee, Sioux, or Blackfeet during the same decades. In the Arikaras' case, a bitter newspaper war of charges and countercharges between Henry Leavenworth and Joshua Pilcher, growing out of the 1823 campaign, helped spread the denunciations of the tribe. In the 1830s, travelers, artists, and traders continued to add to the list of negative images fastened on the Arikara.

When all is said and done, however, the Arikara appear to have had some clear motivations for their actions. They remained friendly and at peace as long as the whites traded fairly and until they finally perceived the fur companies to be a major threat to their own economic well-being. They responded violently when whites aided their enemies, either their sometimes competitors the Mandans or their bitter foes the Sioux. The villagers assumed that it hurt them when the whites traded with their enemies. It is not surprising, then, that white traders were often in danger of retaliation. The Arikara strove repeatedly to keep a resident trader at or near their villages. When whites promised to locate a trader or post in their vicinity and then failed to do so, the Indians interpreted this failure as an unfriendly act and sometimes responded violently. It is also possible, of course, that certain Arikara chiefs used the divisions and confusions within their society for selfish purposes, or even that evil men fomented trouble for narrow local reasons. Whether this happened or not, the Arikara War of 1823 was not unique. It resembled other Indian wars and incidents in many ways. It was unplanned, unnecessary, and a disaster for the tribal people. There were no heroes, stirring slogans, or major accomplishments. Instead, the survivors of a once powerful tribe struck out at their perceived enemies and suffered adverse consequences. Their actions, whether we of the modern world believe them to be rational or not, made at least some sense to them at the time. In the long run, the white man's diseases, not his guns, resolved the issue. The survivors of the smallpox epidemic of 1837 eventually settled among the Mandan and Hidatsa in North Dakota, where most of their descendants remain today.

Suggested Reading

This little-known conflict included many elements that led to later conflicts between whites and Indians in the West. William R. Nester, *The Arikara War: The First Plains Indians War, 1823* (Missoula, Mont.: Mountain Press, 2001), provides only a modest analysis of the complicated reasons for this violence. The villagers' circumstances are best portrayed in Roy W. Meyer, *The Village Indians of the Upper Missouri: The Mandans, Hidatsas, and Arikaras* (Lincoln: University of Nebraska Press, 1977). The roles played by contending groups of St. Louis fur traders is explored in Richard M. Clokey, *William H. Ashley: Enterprise and Politics in the Trans-Mississippi West* (Norman: University of Oklahoma Press, 1980). For insight into the friction between frontier army officers and the fur traders, see John E. Sunder, *Joshua Pilcher: Fur Trader and Indian Agent* (Norman: University of Oklahoma Press, 1968).

CHAPTER TEN

Plains Indian Women and Interracial Marriage in the Upper Missouri Trade, 1804–1868

Michael Lansing

The preceding essay presented the Missouri River fur trade as a negative and destructive force in village life. This contribution recognizes the benefits Indians earned through the fur trade, but at the same time acknowledges that interracial economic and social actions created many problems. In addition, unlike much Indian history to date, this essay incorporates the roles played by women in the economy rather than merely overlooking their contributions. The author presents women as central to successful trading during the nineteenth-century Missouri River fur trade.

Much of the discussion focuses on the wives of local traders. In this position, women served as a bridge between Native village societies and intruding white men. Membership in leading tribal families made it possible for trader husbands to enter into existing economic patterns that might otherwise have been closed to them without the presence of their wives. The author also shows how Indian women themselves benefited from personal connections with whites without the loss of identity or social standing in Native society.

On 15 July 1835, as usual, Francis Chardon, bourgeois of Fort Clark, recorded the day's events in his personal journal. The numerous activities connected with the Indian trade on the Upper Missouri—stories of the local Mandan villagers, hunting, and the ups and downs of the hide trade—were unimportant that day. Instead, he noted "a Whipping" received from his Native wife, Tchon-su-mons-ka, for his "bad behavior" at a Mandan medicine dance that evening. A little over a year later, when Chardon "committed [fornication]," Tchon-su-mons-ka whipped him again. This Lakota woman, barely mentioned elsewhere in Chardon's journal, had the right, the will, and the ability to punish her white spouse for his indiscretions. These surprising accounts of an Indian woman whipping a white man provide valuable insight into the complex role of Plains women in interracial relationships, which originated in the Missouri Valley fur trade. Suggesting that Native women involved in these unions were both active and strong-willed, the stories illustrate the power of Indian women to assert themselves. Influenced by the fluid social dynamics of trade, the nature of relationships between Native women and Euro-American men on the Upper Missouri varied widely. Through their roles as mediators, economic informants, cultural transmitters, companions, producers, and consumers—all in the context of liaisons and intermarriage—Native women gained status in Indian and white eyes. As these women recouped and redefined older positions of power on a margin defined by Indian-white contact, collusion, and exchange, they acted as agents of change in their Plains societies. Eventually, changes introduced and sustained by these Native women helped reshape the tribal worlds from which they came.

Euro-American traders entered the Northern Plains world in the 1730s and 1740s. Moving west from the Great Lakes, French traders such as Pierre Gaultier de Varennes, the Sieur de la Verendrye, built a series of fur posts south of Winnipeg. Taken over by the Hudson's Bay Company and the North West Company in the 1780s, these forts kept up a brisk trade with the Mandan, Hidatsa, and Arikara while new posts further west incorporated Assiniboines, Gros Ventres, Blackfeet, Crows, and Lakotas into the exchange. Spanish and American firms, such as the Missouri Fur Company (1794), the Columbia Fur Company (1821), and the eventually dominant American Fur Company (1826), moved into the Upper Missouri region from the south and east.

By 1830, the British and Americans had fur posts scattered throughout the Upper Missouri drainage. Smaller "opposition" companies came and went as larger companies erected forts across the Northern Plains, bringing more whites into contact with Plains tribes and Plains women than ever before. Natives traded furs and buffalo hides in these fixed posts. As small communities, the forts attracted permanent Indian residents, including Native women, and quickly became the nuclei of a distinct fur trade society.

This interracial trade, an outgrowth of precontact intertribal exchange, involved Plains women on every level. Long before whites entered the Upper Missouri country, Missouri River villagers offered corn, squash, beans, and pumpkins—all grown by women—for the dried buffalo meat, dressed hides, and clothing—items processed or made by women of the nomadic tribes. Because Indian women produced and distributed items on both sides, they were the principal traders at trading fairs, controlling the supply and exchange of goods between groups. Men less frequently traded items with men from other tribes, and their barter usually involved ceremonial, instead of functional, objects. With Native women at its center, the precontact exchange proved a useful secondary source of food and goods supplementing the hunting, gathering, and agriculture of Northern Plains bands.

Indirect contact with whites altered that balance, elevating men's roles in intertribal exchange and making horses a particularly valuable trade item. Horses, owned and traded by men, supplanted food and clothing as the primary object of trade as they became a central element of Plains Indian cultures. While Indian women traded as they always had, their exchange assumed a secondary role. Seeing their roles limited by the new male-dominated horse exchange, Indian women expanded on an already important role for themselves in kinship relations. Marriages or liaisons symbolically and tangibly united different groups and prepared the way for vigorous trading sessions. Whether fictive or real, kinship ties were essential for positive trade relations and gradually created a role for women as intertribal go-betweens.

By the time John Bradbury, American scientist and adventurer, journeyed up the Missouri in 1811, Native women acting as cultural and physical intermediaries rewove themselves into the fabric of trade. Whenever he entered a lodge in the Arikara village he visited, Bradbury was met by a woman who

> examined my dress, and my mockasons: if any repair was wanting, she brought a small leather bag, in which she kept her awls and split sinew, and put it to rights. After conversing as well as we could by signs, if it was near night, I was made to understand that a bed was at my service; and in general this offer was accompanied by that of a bedfellow.

Shaped by the protocontact horse trade, services like these were refined and even institutionalized when Indian-white trading reached peak levels in the 1830s. Using their labor and sexuality to ensure good relations with outsiders, Plains women put intertribal and interracial relationships at the center of the exchange that lasted into the 1860s.

Relationships between Native women and Euro-American men operated within this arena alongside other gender dynamics. White traders brought their preconceptions of Indian women—most notably, the "squaw drudge" image—to these relationships even as Plains women initially defined the Euro-American men's appearance, actions, and ideologies, as "other." On this gender frontier, each became more familiar with the other over time, creating new gender identities and roles that induced broader ramifications for Indians and whites alike along the Upper Missouri.

Different levels of intimacy between Native women and fur traders formed the context in which both lived. When Manuel Lisa's keelboat landed near an Arikara village in 1807, "the women . . . appeared with bags of corn with which to open trade," just as they might have greeted Lakota or Assiniboine women in earlier decades. Fur traders represented a new market for these women who, over 40 years later, still traded with company employees. Edwin Denig, bourgeois at Fort Union, declared that the Arikara exchange with that post was carried on by their women who bring the corn by pansful or the squashes in strings, and supply themselves by the exchange with knives, hoes, combs, beads, paints, etc. . . . It may also be observed that though the women do all the labour of tilling they are amply compensated by having their full share of the profits.

Exchanging goods with men, rather than women (as they had in the precontact era), placed Plains women in the same economic arena as their male kin. Using money or credit earned in this manner, Native women became an important market for traders and the fur companies.

Besides meeting during trading sessions, Plains women and Euro-American men interacted in a fur trade society that encompassed a broad range of social encounters. In 1830 at Fort Tecumseh, some of the traders "played at cross-ball" with the local Lakota and Yanktonai women, raising the stakes of the match by betting "moccasins against beads." The men, in the end, "came off victorious."

Native women often loitered at the fur posts. On 24 February 1839, in a letter to Jacob Halsey, trader Honore Picotte complained that some old Indian women were hanging around his trading house "like as many rats knawing and scratching." More formal opportunities for mingling came at the occasional elaborate balls at the forts, such as the one John Audubon attended at Fort Union in 1843. "[I]n a short time [we] were amid the *beau monde* of these parts. Several squaws, attired in their best, were present, with all the guests, engages, clerks, etc." Numerous occasions for mixing across the entire social spectrum—from informal games to formal dances—resulted in many Indian women–fur employee unions, temporary or otherwise. Like Audubon, most Upper Missouri travelers duly noted that "every clerk and agent" working for the companies had "a wife."

The fur companies unofficially embraced liaisons between their Euro-American employees and Native women. Creating an atmosphere conducive to interracial relationships, trading firms wished to reap the economic benefits of Indian-white romance. In June 1835, Kenneth McKenzie wrote from Fort Union to William Laidlaw, the bourgeois at Fort Pierre, directing him to "give . . . board and lodging" to the Native wife of an American Fur Company (AFC) employee upon her arrival at the downriver post. Freely accepting and supporting such relationships, the companies exploited intimate bonds to gain economic leverage in the trade. They made Plains women extractive instruments of a worldwide economic system.

In a broad sense, the fur companies manipulated the romantic and sexual activity of some Indian women to further their own agenda. But the firms could not control these women's romances. Plains women governed their own sexual destinies. Visiting Arikara villages in 1809, Pierre Tabeau reported that "the husbands . . . paid no attention" to the relations between their white companions and the Native women. In fact, he noted that the women usually gave the traders the opportunity to take "romance by the tail." Indian and white men possessed little power over women's sexual activities so long as women stayed within their established role of creating bonds through sex to secure and ensure good trade with Native and Euro-American outsiders alike.

During the earliest years of the Indian-white exchange on the Upper Missouri, Native women saw Euro-American traders as powerful entities because of their technological know-how and material wealth. Indian women sexually sought them out for their knowledge, skills, and strength. Passing along the power of white men to Indian men through intercourse secured status for Plains women and made liaisons and intermarriage commonplace. But more was at stake in these unions than sexual companionship. Native women and fur employees sought each other out because of economic and social considerations born of trade.

Indian women who married white traders could expect immediate gains in material wealth. Soon after marriage they were "covered with mantles of blue and scarlet cloth—with beads and trinkets, and ribbons, in which they flounce and flirt about, the envied and tinselled belles of every tribe." Native women's families also reaped the material and political benefits of these relationships. Sharing and gift giving among relatives were expected behaviors in Plains communities, and Euro-American traders quickly learned that they had responsibilities to their new Indian kin as well as to their new Indian wives.

Kinship bonds with Euro-American traders gave a Native family status within Plains villages and camps. Tabeau recorded the efforts of one family to win the loyalty of a white trader through marriage to their daughter. The man's "reason, prudence, and economy" forced him to decline her hand, "not that delicacy was offended by this refusal . . . but the hope of rolling in the wealth of the son-in-law was frustrated." This trader, planning only a temporary stay in the river villages, realized that in his case, the costs of the Native bonds he would accrue in marriage outweighed any benefits. Thus he thwarted the efforts of both the woman and her family.

Many Euro-American traders felt that women who married them and lived in fur posts had easier lives than their counterparts who continued to marry inside the tribes. Philippe Regis de Trobriand, an army officer at Fort Berthold, claimed in 1867 that the "great ambition of a young 'squaw' is to be the wife of a white man, for . . . she is not subjected to exhausting work. . . . With a white man, they are better dressed, better cared for, better fed." White life at a fort was slightly more comfortable and more secure than life in a typical Plains camp or village, Trobriand's claim reflected an Euro-American bias that downplayed the status Native women derived from their work in the fields, gathering, and tanning skins, as well as other attractions of interracial marriage. Most traders failed to see beyond economics in their assessments of Indian women's desire for white spouses. Rudolph Kurz, Fort Union employee, went so far as to declare that "an Indian woman loves her white husband only for what he possesses."

Surely the economic attractions of interracial marriages influenced Native women's marital choice. Yet in terms of cultural identity, the distinct "otherness" of Euro-American fur employees may have been a more important attraction for Indian women. Faced with the drastic cultural and racial otherness of traders who reshaped their lives—and the lives of their Native kin—some Plains women wanted to better understand Euro-American culture and come to terms with it through its representatives. Matrimony provided a perfect opportunity to do so. For these women, cross-cultural marriage was an intimate and logical way to begin comprehending the cultural origins of non-Native dynamics at work in Plains communities.

These factors prompted Indian women on the Plains to actively pursue marriage with fur company employees. Soon after he arrived at Fort Atkinson in 1858, trader Henry Boller received two "offers of marriage" from the local Mandan women. When he refused both, one "lingered about the Fort for several days after, looking very disconsolable, and then disappeared." The other attempted to "prove how valuable she was" by "carrying firewood to the village" while passing in front of the "fort gates, that I might see her." Although both these women were rejected, Native women's marriage offers were just as often accepted. Like the Arikara women who told Tabeau in 1809 that "if enough whites came, the Ricaras would have no women," Plains women had numerous motivations to marry Euro-American employees.

Traders too, were inclined to marry Indian women for social and economic reasons. Many saw Native women as overworked, unrewarded, and abused by Native men acting according to Plains cultural norms. Some of the more self-serving traders viewed themselves as deliverers of these women, saving them from what they saw to be a hard existence and elevating them through interracial marriage to more "civilized" lives. The absence of Euro-American women on the Upper Missouri throughout the fur trade period moved fur employees to actively seek out Indian women for sexual and romantic companionship. They soon found that their amorous interests fit into Plains conventions involving women, sex, kinship, and trade.

Political considerations also motivated fur traders in these marriages—just as they had motivated Native women. In 1848, Edwin Denig, the bourgeois at Fort Union, told Kurz:

> adherents, their patronage is expanded, and they make correspondingly larger profits. Their Indian relatives remain loyal and trade with no other company.

Indian wives not only fostered and supported positive trade relations, but also increased the status of the Euro-American spouse in the wife's tribe. Marrying Plains women proved so popular that in 1811 an Arikara leader questioned Henry Brackenridge as to "whether you white people have any women amongst you." When Brackenridge replied with a yes, the man then asked, "Why is it that your people are so fond of our women, one might suppose they had never seen any before?"

Despite the attractions of interracial unions, fur employees often found themselves in matrimonial competition with Native men. Though Trobriand declared in 1867 that Indian women "would hardly risk losing the advantages of married life with a trader" and that leaving such bonds for Indian men "would be a real comedown from any point of view," Plains women periodically did just that. Chardon recorded the plight of a fellow AFC employee at Fort Clark who could not "for his life leave his squaw—for fear of someone running away with her." Later, he spoke of an Indian women he married after Tchon-su-mons-ka's death, declaring that "we agree very well together. I suppose on account of haveing no young Bucks near the Fort. However, spring is advancing and Numbers will flock in before long and then, Poor White Man, take care of your Ribs!" For some women, such as the Crow wife of a Fort Sarpy employee who in 1855 decided she liked "Indians better than whites," the cultural tensions inherent to interracial marriage simply could not compare to the familiarity of customary Plains marital bonds.

Marriage within Plains communities had long involved both informal and formal arrangements. Indian men sometimes eloped with or "stole" Native women from their husbands or families. Formal Plains marriages, on the other hand, involved an exchange of gifts between families. Polygamy, which came to prominence with the transforming effects of horses and the buffalo hide trade, was also a significant, though far from universal, facet of Plains matrimony. Indian-white unions associated with exchange mirrored customary Plains practices in numerous ways. But the fluid social dynamics of the Upper Missouri fur trade society—born of regular geographic movement, racial and cultural differences, and opposing economic agendas—produced interracial marriages that fit few fixed patterns.

Some marriages reflected stability and lasted until one partner's death. Edwin Denig remained married to his Assiniboine wife, Hai-kees-kak-wee-yah, until his death in 1858. His will, in which he left everything to her and their Metis children, aptly illustrates the strong romantic bonds interracial unions could produce. Alexander Culbertson and his Blackfeet wife, Natawista, united in an Indian camp outside Fort Union in 1840, remained married through good times and bad for nearly thirty years.

But fur trade marriages were just as often temporary affairs, ended by either the Native woman or the white trader. At the same post in 1851, an AFC employee married a Metis woman and then canceled the union when winter came, sending her on her way with "a good horse . . . abundant apparel," and "provisions." Plains women, too, could choose to leave Euro-American husbands. In 1839, Chardon reported that one of the "wives of the fort," a "young Ree [Arikara] damsel of 16," had eloped, leaving behind her white husband. Both traders and Native women actively deserted their spouses, though Indians and whites alike saw the desertion of Euro-American men as particularly corrupt. During his stay on the Upper Missouri, Maximilian, Prince of Wied, reported that "the Company maintains a number of agents at these different stations; during their stay they marry Indian women, but leave them, without scruple, when they are removed to another station, or are recalled to the United States." Many traders did end their relationships with Indian women when they left their wife's place of origin, or the trade altogether.

Sometimes, however, Native fur wives returned east with their husbands upon the men's departure from the trade. In 1851, Charles Larpenteur, longtime trader and clerk at Fort Union, took his Assiniboine wife to a farm in Harrison County, Iowa, with the intention to settle permanently. Soon after the move she was killed by a passing band of Omaha men who regarded her as a Lakota, since "she spoke that language." William Laidlaw, the bourgeois of Fort Tecumseh and later Fort Pierre, married a Lakota woman in 1826 and eventually moved to land near liberty, Missouri, where both died in the 1850s. In the settlements, the Indian wives of men formerly involved in the fur trade dealt with people who did not share their cultural conventions. Adapting to ideologies introduced by their white husbands at trading posts along the Upper Missouri, these Plains women survived and sometimes prospered in a non-Native world even as they retained much of their Plains heritage. During the summers of the 1850s, Natawista dressed in Blackfeet clothing and lived in a Blackfeet tipi erected in front of the family home outside Peoria, Illinois. Clearly, these women did not necessarily fully abandon their Indianness or fully adopt or accept Euro-American ways.

It may have been more comfortable for interracial couples to stay on the Plains, even after the Upper Missouri trade ended in the wake of Indian-white conflict in the late 1860s. Many remained in the region, rearing their families alongside Native communities. AFC clerk Malcolm Clark and his Metis wife left the trade and started a ranch on the main road between Fort Benton and Helena, Montana. James Chambers, clerk at Fort Sarpy, lived with his Gros Ventre wife along the Missouri River after leaving the AFC. These men, more often employees of a lower socioeconomic class than the clerks and bourgeois, had few reasons to leave the Upper Missouri, while their Native wives had none at all. Moving their families east was beyond their financial and social reach. Most fur trader–Indian woman unions, unconsecrated by Christian missionaries and priests and reflective of cultural collusion, were considered illegitimate in the settlements. The actual formality of these marriages varied according to the expectations of the people involved.

Euro-American men's behavior often mirrored that of Indian men, with the contributing factor of relaxed mores at the isolated fur posts. In November 1838, Chardon admitted to "being united to one, that I stole from my Friend . . . on my visit to Fort Pierre last summer." He also recorded the informal marriage ceremony of the fur posts, known as a *chariveree*, which accompanied the union of 80-year-old Toussaint Charbonneau to an Assiniboine woman at Fort Clark. The event, put on by "the young men of the Fort and two Rees," included "Drums, pans, kittles . . . beating," and "guns firing." More substantial nuptials involved a customary Plains marital exchange of gifts, such as the one accompanying Alexander Culbertson's marriage to Natawista in 1840. The clerk "sent nine horses" to the woman's Blackfeet family who reciprocated, formalizing the union in Native eyes.

Regardless of formality, fur trade marriages periodically involved polygyny. Once again Euro-American fur employees' behavior mirrored their Indian counterparts. For a time, Denig was married to two Assiniboine women, providing as an excuse "his kind feeling" towards the oldest "and of keeping her . . . as a companion" for his younger wife, Hai-kees-kak-wee-yah. According to Trobriand, the Native women in these marriages usually got on well. He claimed that the households of traders who took "a second companion . . . younger than the first" operated as they always had, with "no internal discord to disturb the customary peace."

A few clerks and bourgeois had families in both the settlements and the fur posts. In 1846, Kurz reported that the longtime AFC bourgeois James Kipp, "living here [Fort Clark] with [Mandan] squaw and children, had a white family in the states." AFC bourgeois Honore Picotte married a French woman in St. Louis in 1831, though he was also wed to two different Native women during the same period. At Fort Pierre in 1848, another fur employee was warned that

> Mrs. Picotte & Mrs. Kipp [the white wives of Joseph Picotte and Kipp] have the . . . intention of Coming up in the Steambt. I have no doubt that your Lady, when she hears it, will also wish to Come, and as there is every Probability of her doing so, would it not be well for you to dispense with the Society of at least some of your present Companions.

Polygyny involving Indian and white women, though accepted, was limited to those men who could afford to support two widely separated families.

Economic status proved one of the most important factors in any fur trade marriage. The ranks of the fur companies were organized along hierarchical lines. Well paid bourgeois and clerks filled the top ranks, while interpreters and tradesmen occupied positions in the middle of this hierarchy. Engages, laborers, and voyageurs, making up 81 percent of the average company workforce, occupied the lowest rung on the economic ladder. Although cost rarely prevented any employee from marrying a Plains woman, common laborers found it difficult to afford certain Native women. In 1849, Kurz declared that "a woman of rank" was too "expensive" for the common man to afford. Expensive or not, Indian women benefited from a Euro-American spouse's position in the posts. Such was the status of a trader at Fort Sarpy who by 1855 "had grown to be such a consequential person that his squaw could not go to the river for water."

Indian women from families defined in Native terms to be of lower status tended to marry engages and other lower-class employees, while Native and Metis women from leading families typically married clerks and bourgeois. Apparently, much depended on whether "a girl's parents" were from a "good family." Plains women who married laborers were usually "not valued at the purchase price of a horse," while the women who married men at the top of fur company hierarchies tended to be "the Daughters of chieves or of Descent indian families." Leading women and the female relations of prominent Native families more typically married conspicuous clerks than common employees.

Both the economic position of company men and Plains women and the cross-cultural unions they created intertwined with race. In 1855, the dissatisfied Native wife of an African American employee at Fort Sarpy left her husband for a better match among some "Young Crow Bucks." The heartbroken black man captured the racial dynamics at work in these marriages when he complained that the "White folks" at the post had "no feelings" for him because they suggested that "his color" failed to suit the Crow woman. Hispanic fur employees also found prominent Native women more interested in marrying white men, and as a result, usually married women from socially modest backgrounds at best. Leading Indian women looked down on Metis men, feeling that "all such no-color fellows" were lazy. Prominent Indian women, learning the racism of white traders and taking into consideration social and economic status, tended to frown on the lower positions and racial backgrounds of African American, Hispanic, and Metis employees.

Women, as well as men, were shunned for racial reasons. Jacob Halsey, AFC clerk, married a Metis woman because "as the gentleman of rather a refined taste he selected a half-breed which is one step more towards civilization." Though some traders continued to marry Native women from influential families, just as many looked to marry more socially acceptable Metis women instead, especially as the Upper Missouri Metis population grew with the passing years.

Race, economics, and gender worked in all of these interracial marriages to produce intricate power relationships between Plains women and Euro-American men. Typical of most fur employees, Chardon periodically whipped his Native wives, just as Tchon-su-mons-ka had whipped him, for offenses such as "not mending" his moccasins. Kurz decided that "several sound lashings or other rough treatment" were essential to "keep alive" an Indian woman's "respect and affection." Native men had for years tried to hold sway over Plains women by cutting off the hair or even the noses of unfaithful wives, and some fur company men adapted these practices. During his stay at Fort McKenzie in 1833, Maximilian reported that "the Whites had punished their Indian wives in the same way."

Even as they attempted to control these women, traders constantly complained about and resented Plains women's action—revealing other dynamics at work in cross-cultural unions. James Chambers recounted the embarrassment of an independent-minded Crow woman who in the process of showing off her dancing ability—and her status—at Fort Sarpy in 1855, "placed her divine foot in something of a dark brown substance that emitted an odor like anything but . . . roses. May blushed . . . the Squaws sighed the Bucks laughed & Big Six Shame on him, bellowed out May tramped on a green tird [sic]." Chardon recorded the swift return of a fellow employee's Native wife to her village after his death in 1837 even more sarcastically: "What affectionate Wives we all have in this Country!"

Plains women made their power and independence evident before, during, and after marriage. Chambers, who held a grudge against nearly every Indian woman he encountered, gave a Crow woman a "private . . . kicking" for calling "the Other men in the Fort . . . her slaves." In 1812 at Fort Manuel, "Garrows Wife, a Ree . . . came . . . this Morning she was going to sho[o]t her husband, she came here with that Intention." In 1858, Henry Boller saw the Native wife of John McBride, Fort Atkinson's bourgeois, attempt to knife her husband for an alleged infidelity, leading Boller to declare that "the devil has been getting into the women up here."

Adding to Boller's consternation was the fact that "M'Eldeys squaw" had run off "for 3 or 4 days." Indian women dissatisfied with their fur trader husbands resorted to violence, or, more often, simply left their spouses. In 1851, Kurz voiced a common complaint when he declared that Native wives "were difficult to keep." On 22 September 1834, Charbonneau left Fort Clark "in quest of one of his runaway wives." On 2 July 1836, "Newmas wife" had "run off" from the same post, so the trader "went to the Village" and "had a talk when she concluded to stay at least one night more." But the next day, his wife "left him positively," leaving the man to conclude that "marrying here is not the thing it is cracked up to be." Chardon sympathized with his coworker, moaning that he had "only [been] married 15 days and his wife deserted him."

Though the flight of unhappy Native wives caused fur traders to feel deserted and cheated, most did not attempt to forcibly return their runaway spouses. Their reluctance stemmed from the fact that "little Whites" were "entirely in the power of the Indians, and the relations of their wives," and thus were "obliged to submit." Frustrated by both the flight of Plains women from the fur posts and the support of such actions by their Indian kin, the abandoned husbands rationalized their inability to do anything in these situations by deciding that "if an Indian woman runs away, one is not to pay the least attention to her . . . one is to forget her. To go after her, to beg her to return . . . is not . . . considered worth while." Euro-American fur employees failed to recognize that, depending on their tribal identity, Plains women in interracial marriages could have more enduring and significant relationships with Native mothers, sisters, fathers, brothers, cousins, or grandparents than with their foreign husbands. Unable to balance conflicting loyalties and cultural imperatives, women who left their spouses opted out of cross-cultural unions.

Regardless of their outcome, interracial fur trade marriages generally signified the ultimate collusion of Plains and Euro-American peoples. The cultural synthesis propagated by these unions on the Upper Missouri presented a tangible symbol—namely, the rise of a sizable Northern Plains Metis population. Chardon, who on 6 May 1835 found his "family increased to one more Boy," was one of many white traders who discovered himself a new father. These progeny of interracial marriage, the most concrete legacy of Indian women involved in exchange, signified the complex relationships between Native Women and Euro-American men. Altered by these relationships, the world in which the Upper Missouri Metis lived their lives reflected new dynamics generated by Plains women and intermarriage in the fur trade.

The new dynamics created by social interplay and cross-cultural marriage involved Indian women on every level. Giving their husbands the "advantage of being constantly informed through their association . . . as to the demands of trade and the village or even the tent where they can immediately find buffalo robes stored away," the role of Native women as economic brokers grew with the Indian-white trade. Possessing inside information, fur trade wives also provided spouses with strong trading bonds to particular Native families. Between November 1854 and March 1856, Imitaikoan, the Blackfeet cousin of Alexander Culbertson's wife, visited Fort Benton four times to trade robes and horses—twice as often as any other Native trader. Trading with the Indian kin of Plains wives often served as the backbone of a fur post's annual intake. The powerful position of these Native women commanded the respect of most traders.

Simultaneously, Indian women living in the forts gave their Native relatives updates on the latest goods, company policies, and spousal trading plans. As the only Natives allowed to live at the posts, many of these women gained privileged station in Plains communities. Boasting full-time access to trade goods and information, Plains women circulated goods on both sides of the cultural divide. Giving and selling to fur employees Indian wares such as clothing, moccasins, bullboats, and other Native technologies essential for Plains survival, these fur trade wives were just as often the first to introduce and distribute commercial dyes, paints, trade cloth, and metal tools and utensils to Indian villages and camps. In doing so, they earned new respect in the eyes of their Native kin.

Bridging economics and culture, new opportunities for Plains women's religious groups also arose in the Upper Missouri fur trade society. The groups, such as the Mandan White Buffalo Cow society, were ritually responsible for ensuring good hunts or plentiful harvests. Sometimes the women of these societies entertained fur post employees with ceremonial dances and earned "small presents" in the process. Apparently the traders appreciated these dances, since they were performed often. Employees usually gave the dancers gifts. Adding a material aspect to women's cultural ceremonies, participation in religious dances at forts provided some Indian women with another way to acquire desired trade goods.

Euro-American interpreters, meeting the demands spawned by multicultural and multilingual trade, learned languages from their Indian wives and profited from the trade's dependency on numerous languages and the corresponding demand for knowledgeable intermediaries. Conversely, in a description of a social visit by Metis women to Fort Union in 1843, Audubon reported that "[Natawista] went out to meet them covered with a fine shawl, and the visitors followed her to her own room. These ladies spoke both the French and Cree languages." Since Natawista certainly knew Blackfeet, and possibly learned English from her husband, life at a fur post gave her working knowledge of no less than four languages and status in an exchange society hinging on cross-cultural communication. Utilizing whichever paradigm or method (or in this case, language) proved most useful for the situation at hand, Native women, along with white traders and Indian relatives, created a new social context specific to the Upper Missouri trade that reflected aspects of both cultures.

The fur posts themselves introduced new uses of space to Plains societies in general and Native women in particular. Indian women in every Plains tribe constructed and owned either tipis or earthlodges, housing six to ten people, all of whom had special spaces—accorded by gender and age—which only they occupied. In tipis, women slept on the south side, men on the north, with sacred items placed on tripods near the center or hung on the outside cover. Earthlodges boasted a shrine for the storage of religious objects, a central firepit for cooking, and often a corral for the family horses.

In contrast, fur post rooms shared by Native wives and their Euro-American husbands were usually no larger than eight to ten feet wide and ten to twelve feet long. Most had a fireplace and a bed or two. Unlike the Native residents of relatively comfortable tipis or earthlodges, white traders and travelers complained of heat, cold, and general discomfort when staying in post employees' quarters.

Traders frequently took Indian women into account when they planned post layouts. On 17 September 1834, James Hamilton wrote to fellow trader Jacob Halsey, telling him that an engage "paid me a visit a few days since, he says that he has built a very neat snug fort 100 feet square," with "plenty of accommodation for Robes and wives." But for Native women, the crowded square rooms contrasted with the circular lodges or tipis that symbolized Plains cosmologies familiar to them. Traders and their guests slept wherever there was room, stashing belongings wherever there was extra space. If of a religious mind, a trader might have a crucifix on a wall or a bible by his bed, but the rooms contained no specific sacred space. Traders failed to recognize that their use of space represented cultural bedlam to their Native wives.

Geographic bedlam also entangled Indian wives. The fluid nature of the Upper Missouri trade meant that movement, particularly up and down the river, was a constant companion of fur trade life. Before long, the speedy and convenient transportation utilized by Native fur trade wives—keelboats and steamboats—gave rise to the darker side of Indian-white contact. In the summer of 1837, a devastating smallpox epidemic spread to the Upper Missouri via the AFC-owned steamboat *St. Peter's*. Native women of nearly every Plains tribe were at the center of both the spread of and attempts to control the deadly outbreak, becoming ecological as well as economic and cultural intermediaries.

Among the passengers the *St. Peter's* dropped off at Fort Clark (and the nearby Mandan villages) on 19 June 1837, were three Arikara women returning from a downstream visit with the Pawnees. Boarding the steamboat at Council Bluffs in early May, they came into contact with a pox-infected deckhand. The women reeled from the effects of the deadly disease by the time the boat dropped off passengers at the Sioux Agency on 5 June. After exposing the Yanktonai population to the disease there, the *St. Peter's* continued upriver to Fort Pierre, where it picked up Jacob Halsey, and then headed for Fort Union.

Upon arriving at Fort Clark twelve days later, the three Arikara women—recovering but still infectious—left the boat to visit relatives and attend "a Frolicking" dance put on to celebrate the steamboat's coming. There, and over the next four days, they unknowingly spread the disease to the vulnerable Mandans. Because the women had moved into a nonsymptomatic stage of the illness, the *St. Peter's*, with Halsey—who manifested the disease soon after leaving Fort Clark—continued on its way the morning after the dance. Reaching Fort Union on 24 June, the boat, with a visibly ill Halsey who brought any celebration over their arrival to a speedy end, docked, and unloaded Halsey, his pregnant Metis wife, other passengers, and that season's trade goods.

Halsey, vaccinated in the settlements, soon recovered from his illness, but his wife "had a lying in and brought forth a female child to the wourld [sic] and was immediately taken by the smallpox. During her agonies in her illness, she fell out of bed [and] broke one of her blood vessels and bled to death." Despite fort employees' attempts to avoid contact with local Assiniboines, the disease quickly struck that tribe as well. In an attempt to block the spread of the pox, Charles Larpenteur and the other traders decided to inoculate the post's residents

> with the smallpox itself; and after the systems of those who were to be inoculated had been prepared according to Dr. Thomas' medical book, the operation was performed upon about 30 Indian squaws and a few white men . . . unfortunately . . . the operation proved fatal to most of our patients . . . days afterward there was such a stench in the fort that it could be smelt at the distance of 300 yards . . . some went crazy, and others were half eaten up by maggots before they died.

In the wake of this failure, Halsey estimated that at least 800 Assiniboines and 700 Blackfeet died in the area within two months.

The smallpox soon reached Fort McKenzie, spread by a Native man who hitched a ride on a keelboat from Fort Union. Alexander Culbertson, post bourgeois, heard of the coming disease and halted the boat at the mouth of the Judith River. The Blackfeet, however, eager to open the season's trade, pressured Culbertson to let the boat come to the post. After arriving, two passengers died. Once again, the Indian women of the post were gathered for inoculation. And once again, the effort failed—of the 27 Native women residing at the fort, 26 died. Ten days later, the epidemic scythed its way through the local Blackfeet camps, killing 6,000 men and women before abating.

Indian fur trade wives found themselves in the midst of epidemic disease on this and other occasions. Unwittingly, their association with traders spread undiagnosed but deadly sicknesses that drastically reduced Plains populations in the

1830s and 1840s. Although company inoculations eventually reduced mortality rates, these ecological invaders proved a fresh challenge to Indian women and Indian peoples.

By the 18505 and 1860s, Plains women faced white invaders. In 1853, Isaac Stevens, the new territorial governor of Washington, was appointed by Congress to chart a railroad route from St. Paul, Minnesota, to Puget Sound. Knowing he would pass through Blackfeet territory, Stevens selected longtime AFC bourgeois and shareholder Alexander Culbertson as special agent to the tribe, since "he had married a full-blood Blackfeet woman [Natawista]." When Culbertson attempted to leave her at Fort Union because of the dangerous nature of the journey, Natawista declared:

> My people are a good people, but they are jealous and vindictive. I am afraid that they and the whites will not understand each other; but my husband, if I go I may be able to explain things to them. I know there is anger, but, my husband where you go I will go, and where you die, I will die.

Despite obvious conflicts of loyalty and emotion, this Blackfeet woman decided that her knowledge of both Native and Euro-American culture could shape future relations between whites and her people.

When the American expedition and Blackfeet delegation met at Fort Benton, Stevens quickly "perceived the advantage derived from Mrs. Culbertson's presence. . . . In constant intercourse with the Indians," the governor happily reported, Natawista "inspired them with perfect confidence." Blackfeet men and women gathered around Natawista to hear stories about the white settlements. One evening, Stevens learned that "Mrs. Culbertson was telling stories . . . to her Indian friends of what she saw at St. Louis. As she described a fat woman whom she had seen exhibited, and sketched with great humor the ladies of St. Louis, it was pleasant to see the delight that beamed" from the Blackfeet around her. But Natawista did more than allay her people's concerns with stories that humanized and demystified whites. Using her influential position, she convinced her cousin Imitaikoan, a prominent Blackfeet leader, to allow the railroad to pass through tribal lands.

Realizing that her prominence as the daughter of a chief and wife of an important fur trader would give her the leverage she needed to convince her people to assist the Americans, Natawista played on Euro-American characterizations of her as "the most striking illustration of the high civilization which these tribes of the interior are capable of attaining," to gain the trust of the whites. Trusted by both sides, she diffused conflict between Blackfeet and Euro-Americans. Successful use of this mutual trust added to Natawista's already considerable status in Plains communities and in the trade, as well as from whites.

Wambdi Autepewin, born in a Lakota camp along the Missouri River in 1820, was another Native women whose experiences as a fur trade wife led to a later role as cultural and political broker. She married Honore Picotte, the general agent for the AFC's Upper Missouri Outfit, in 1838. With two children, the couple lived at Fort Pierre until Picotte retired from the trade—and probably Autepewin—in 1848. By 1850, the enterprising Lakota woman married Charles Galpin, another trader at the post. When he became bourgeois later that year, Autepewin found herself thrust into the upper levels of fur trade society. Described by one traveler as "bright minded," she quickly learned English and familiarized herself with Euro-American culture.

In September 1866, General Alfred Sully asked Wambdi Autepewin and her spouse to visit Yanktonai and Oglala camps along the Little Missouri River. Sully opened treaty negotiations with those bands at Fort Rice. Traveling alone, the couple reached the Indian camp and in a series of councils Autepewin convinced the bands to negotiate a peace. By late October, the two groups signed a treaty with Sully. Though peace was shortlived, the Lakota woman temporarily diffused Indian-white tensions in the region.

Autepewin gained a reputation for her particular abilities as a cultural and political intermediary. Father Pierre DeSmet himself a seasoned broker, enlisted her aid for important peace talks with the Lakota in 1868 at Fort Laramie. DeSmet declared that "Mrs. Galpin, being of Sioux birth and a near relation to several war chiefs," exercised "great influence among her people," and would be an invaluable mediating partner at the Native councils. When DeSmet's party arrived at the Lakota camp, this became abundantly clear. Protected by one of Wambdi Autepewin's nephews, the peace party overcame threats of violence. Convincing the Natives to hold a council, DeSmet and Autepewin's party met with Sitting Bull and Gall the next day. Trying "in every way that she could devise, to get them to come in and settle upon the Reservation," the Lakota woman implored her kin to make peace. Eventually, most of the Lakota bands signed the treaty, which established the Great Sioux Reservation.

Women such as Natawista and Wambdi Autepewin used wisdom gleaned in the Plains fur trade to become cultural and political mediators and add to the considerable station they already possessed. But the fur trade dynamics that gave them the tools to increase their personal status and improve their lives simultaneously created new personal tensions and undercut Plains societies. In fact, the lives of most Native women involved in the Upper Missouri trade were changed by its accompanying dynamics to the point where they themselves acted as agents of change. Indian women, attracted to the socioeconomic status gained through involvement in the trade, improved their position even as their acceptance and support of trade-related dynamics created conflicting loyalties and inadvertently contributed to the breakdown of Native traditions. Quite simply, the actions of Plains women involved in exchange helped to slowly transform Plains societies from within.

In her attempts to assuage both Blackfeet and Americans in the 1850s, Natawista paved the way for the ultimate symbol of Euro-American expansion and conquest—the railroad. Though Wambdi Autepewin found acceptance in

Native and white societies for her attempts at peaceful compromise during the 1860s, her acquiescence to Native removal improved her rank but eventually constrained the Lakota to reservations.

Indian women did not have to be as prominent as Natawista or Wambdi Autepewin to be an important agent of change on the Northern Plains. Admittedly, few Native women possessed the authority and power of these two influential brokers. Yet every Indian woman on the Upper Missouri affected and was affected by the results of involvement in the dynamic exchange environment. Tchon-su-mons-ka's experiences, for example, are as useful as Autepewin's Natawista's experiences in understanding Plains women and fur trade marriage in the Upper Missouri trade.

And so the story returns to where it began—to Fort Clark on a bluff overlooking the Missouri River and to a Lakota woman and her Euro-American husband. Tchon-su-mons-ka aptly demonstrated the independence and status gained by Native women involved in trade by whipping her white spouse for his breaches of conduct. She actively improved her social and economic position in both Indian and fur trade societies through the most intimate trade connection possible—marriage to a trader. Her Metis children, like those of other Plains women, were a significant legacy. In the end, however, this Lakota woman died of a disease brought to the region by men like her husband. The microscopic partners of fur traders proved to be as subtle and destructive as their macroscopic counterparts—namely, the trade-related changes that gradually transformed Native women and the Northern Plains. Though multicultural exchange on the Upper Missouri gave Tchon-su-mons-ka and Indian women like her the opportunity to improve their condition by bridging dissimilar worlds, the undermining effects of the changes on the Native peoples of the Plains wrought by these women eventually proved both calamitous and inescapable.

Suggested Reading

Although its focus ends several decades before Lansing's article, the best analysis of the Missouri Valley and Rocky Mountain fur trade is David Wishart, *The Fur Trade of the American West, 1807–1840* (Lincoln: University of Nebraska Press, 1979). Lucy E. Murphy, *A Gathering of Rivers: Indians, Métis, and Mining in the Western Great Lakes, 1737–1832* (Lincoln: University of Nebraska Press, 2000), considers the changing roles of Native women in the economy of the upper Mississippi Valley. There they functioned in similar ways to the Missouri River village women. Jacqueline Peterson and Jennifer S. H. Brown, eds., *The New Peoples: Being and Becoming Métis in North America* (Lincoln: University of Nebraska Press, 1985), analyze the actions of mixed-race families who lived north and west of the Great Lakes during the nineteenth century.

CHAPTER ELEVEN

Touching the Pen

Plains Indian Treaty Councils in Ethnohistorical Perspective

RAYMOND J. DeMALLIE

Until 1871 the treaty council provided an often-used arena for serious discussion between tribal representatives and U.S. officials. For the preceding several centuries, Indians had forced invading Europeans to follow Native practices for trade or negotiations. After independence these early patterns remained in use with little change at most of the nineteenth century councils. In fact, for the United States government, written treaties were the only form of agreement that had any legal standing. As a result, the author considers the records of treaty discussions as valuable sources for understanding basic differences between Native and United States diplomats.

He argues that the interpreters who helped guide these meetings were the best available and that their renditions of the speeches do not prevent an understanding of both the political objectives and cultural values represented by the speakers. The negotiations leading to the 1851 Treaty of Fort Laramie provide a case study of ritual practices, a list of demands, and the giving of presents to seal the agreement. The author examines Indian tactics and places treaty councils within the context of Plains Indians diplomacy as he uncovers the tribal bases for their words and actions at these meetings.

When Europeans met American Indians in the New World, the clash of human populations resulted in epidemics of disease; social, economic, and political pressures; religious conflict; and sometimes war. All such intercultural conflict takes place in two very different contexts, that of each of the cultures involved. Each culture constitutes a separate and distinctive idea system symbolizing the world, everything in it, and the relationship of all the parts. Culture as a symbol system

"Touching the Pen" appeared in Frederick C. Luebke, ed., *Ethnicity on the Great Plains* (Lincoln: University of Nebraska Press, 1980), 38–53.

provides the framework in which human behavior is motivated, perceived, and understood. Abstractly, the clash of two peoples may be viewed as the clash of two idea systems.

But culture contact is not abstract; it is in reality acted out through individual human beings. The historical record documents their behavior and motives and draws out of the accumulation of many individuals' actions a general understanding of larger events. It is rarely possible to separate human behavior from the motivating ideas of the cultures in which the behavior occurs. The clash of ideas cannot be observed as easily or in the same manner as conflict between individuals. However, an understanding of the fundamental conflicting ideas is essential to illuminate historians' accounts of the past by placing individual action within the ideological context out of which it arose.

The large body of transcripts of formal council proceedings between representatives of the United States government and representatives of American Indian tribes provides a unique opportunity to observe the clash of idea systems. Reduced to rhetoric, physical weapons laid aside, the opponents faced each other as representatives of their own societies and cultures and attempted to win tactical battles by the manipulation of concepts. Both white Americans and Indians alike attempted to use all of their intellectual skills, as well as the oratorical and persuasive devices of their cultures, to sway the council in their own interest. The verbatim records of the proceedings are therefore primary sources for analyzing cultural concepts self consciously utilized to gain diplomatic advantage. They are primary documents for the ethnohistorian, whose research combines historical methodology with the comparative and theoretical insights of anthropology.

One objection to the use of this material for historical or anthropological study is that it was inadequately or falsely interpreted from the original Indian languages. However, this is a futile objection. The interpreters were almost always named in the documents; most were mixed-bloods or non-Indian men married into an Indian tribe. They were the only interpreters the Indians had and their translations are as accurate as any ever obtained at that time. Significantly, after reading through a good number of the transcripts it is possible to pick out Indian idioms that are difficult to translate and that were therefore expressed in various ways in English, as well as standard words and phrases that were consistently translated in the same way but whose English glosses obviously did not accurately express the original idea in the Indian language. In many of these cases it is possible to postulate with a fair degree of certainty what the actual words were in the Indian original. Such difficulties in translation do not make the task of reconstructing ideological systems impossible; in fact, they make it easier, for it is in these areas where translation was difficult that differences in ideological systems are most clearly pointed up.

Solemn councils between representatives of both sides were the only acceptable means recognized by both Indians and whites for establishing formal relations between two peoples. For the Indians the council was the traditional way of making peace or negotiating with another people. For the white Americans it had been the custom, since the days of Jamestown, to counsel with the Indians. Under United States law, written treaties, signed by representatives of both sides, were the only legal means for dealing with Indian tribes, and councils evolved as the forum where treaties were presented to Indians and they were persuaded to sign them.

But if the council as a diplomatic forum was commonly understood by both whites and Indians, the concept of the treaty was not. For plains Indians, the council was an end in itself. What was important was the coming together in peace, smoking the pipe in common to pledge the truthfulness of all statements made, and the exchange of opinions. Plains Indian political systems did not use voting as the mechanism for settling issues; consensus politics was the rule. Issues had to be discussed from all points of view until a clear consensus was reached. Until that occurred, no decision was made, and once it was reached, no vote was necessary. Thus, from the Indians' point of view, the council was the agreement.

For white Americans, the council with its associated feasts and gift giving was only a preliminary to the real agreement, which was embodied in written form. The success of the council depended not on what was said, but on whether or not the necessary leaders, or later, the requisite percentage of the male population, could be induced to sign the document.

"Touching the pen," the action of the Indian in touching the end of the pen while the scribe marked an X after his name, was frequently objected to by Indian leaders. They did not understand the process, were suspicious of it, and felt it unnecessary. Whites, on the other hand, considered it to be essential. For individual Indian leaders, touching the pen apparently signified that they were validating all they had said at a council; in many cases the record of the treaty proceedings makes it clear that the Indian leaders did not realize their signatures committed them to only those statements written in the treaty. Sometimes, it is equally clear, treaty commissioners played on this to trick Indians into signing documents containing provisions to which they had not agreed.

The predominant historical view of treaty making is that Indians were taken advantage of by whites, who usually presented them with documents prepared in advance which they were persuaded, bribed, or threatened into signing. There is a great deal of truth to this view, but it ignores an important aspect. American Indian leaders were not mere pawns of the U.S. government. They did use political strategies to combat whites on their own ground and sometimes they were able to gain important concessions. They were at other times unsuccessful, and frequently their techniques were too subtle even to be understood by the commissioners. But analysis of some of these means provides important insights into plains Indian diplomacy and opens new dimensions for understanding the fundamental conflicts between Indians and whites on the western frontier.

This paper draws upon examples of treaty making among the Sioux, Kiowas, Comanches, Cheyennes, and Arapahoes from 1851 to 1892. First the 1851 Fort

Laramie treaty council is examined as representative of plains treaty councils and as illustrating the symbolic perspective in ethnohistory. Then various examples of Indian diplomacy are presented to illustrate the range of strategies that can be abstracted from the verbatim proceedings and to demonstrate the value of this approach.

The 1851 Treaty Council

The 1851 treaty council held near Fort Laramie may be taken as a model of plains treaty councils. It was on a larger scale than most since an estimated ten thousand Indians were present representing ten bands of Sioux as well as Cheyennes, Assiniboins, Shoshones, Arikaras, Gros Ventres (Hidatsas), Mandans, Arapahoes, and Crows. The encampment lasted nearly three weeks, from September 1 to September 21. During this period the commissioners met the Indians in council only about eight days. The rest of the time was occupied with the Indians counseling among themselves while the commissioners drew up a map of tribal territories, in Sunday recesses, and in waiting for the wagon train that was bringing the presents to be distributed after the treaty was signed.

Three general features of the council suggest a minimal model for plains treaty councils. The first is the ritual aspects, as practiced by both Indians and whites; the second is the recitation of both sides' demands and requests; and the third is the distribution of presents.

Ritual aspects. The ritual aspects of this council are fairly well recorded and are extremely significant for reconstructing the event in its fullest context. The Sioux and Cheyennes made the first gesture by erecting a large council lodge composed of several tipis to form a kind of amphitheater. This was the usual form for the council lodge when various bands came together and so was the culturally prescribed stage for serious deliberations. The U.S. commissioners took the next step by erecting a large tripod on which to hoist the American flag.

Preparations for the council were completed on a Saturday, but the commissioners announced that since the next day was "the white man's Medicine Day," no business could be transacted. The council began on Monday. Only headmen were allowed to enter the council lodge, and the order of their seating, by tribe, was arbitrarily decided by the commissioners. The council was called to order each day by the firing of the cannon and raising of the flag. The council began and ended with the smoking of the pipe by all the Indians and the commissioners. Colonel D. D. Mitchell, the chief commissioner, made an opening speech to set the moral tone of the meetings:

> I am sent here to transact business with you. Before commencing that I propose to smoke all around with you. The ceremony of smoking I regard as an important and solemn one, and I believe you all so regard it. When white men meet to transact important business, and they desire to test their truth and sincerity, they lay their hands on the Bible, the Book of the Great Spirit—their Great Medicine—and take an oath. When the red man intends to tell the truth,

and faithfully fulfill his promises, he takes an oath by smoking to the Great Spirit. The Great Spirit sees it all and knows it. Now I do not wish any Indian to smoke with me that has any deceit or lies in his heart—or has two hearts—or whose ears are not bored to hear what his Great Father at Washington has to propose, and perform whatever is agreed upon. All such will let the pipe pass. I don't want them to touch it.

At least three important points about this speech should be noted. First, the commissioner attempted to speak to the Indians in terms they would understand. The reporter who covered the council remarked on this aspect as follows: "His [Mitchell's] expressions were short, in simple language, such as they could readily understand, in many cases adopting various forms, and employing their own hyperbolical mode of thought. Between sentences he paused to see that the interpreters understood him correctly, and to allow time for them to communicate it to their respective tribes." Second, the commissioner made it clear that he considered the Indian form of oath by smoking the pipe to be a legitimate one, comparable to the white man's swearing on the Bible. Third, the use of the term Great Father at Washington must be considered to have been at least ambivalent. To some Indians it may have seemed a white man's claim that the Great Spirit lived in Washington, a boast that the whites enjoyed a closer relationship to God than did the Indians.

The smoking of the pipe by the commissioners was a self-conscious bow to Indian custom. In return the commissioners demanded at the end of the council that the Indians defer to the white man's custom of touching the pen to the treaty paper. Since they had already sworn themselves to truth, signing the treaty was redundant for the Indians, but they clearly understood it as an important ritual for the white men.

The other impressive bit of ceremony on the part of the whites was the celebration on the second Sunday of a Roman Catholic mass. In a large tipi in the half-breed camp, Father P. J. DeSmet said mass and preached to the assemblage in French. The pomp and ceremony of the event was as impressive to the St. Louis newspaper reporter who accompanied the treaty commission as it was to the Indians. Of DeSmet the newspaper man wrote: "The Indians regard him as a Great Medicine man, and always regard him with marked respect and kindness."

Throughout the council the Indians reciprocated rituals by holding dog feasts, warrior society dances, and displays of horsemanship.

Demands and requests. The second aspect of the council, the exchange of demands and requests, was done in the usual formal manner. On the first day Colonel Mitchell delivered a speech outlining the commission's intentions in visiting the Indians and enumerating the points of the proposed treaty. On ensuing days the Indian chiefs were allowed to give their responses. These were not spontaneous speeches, but were developed out of council meetings in the various tribal camps, and were essentially tribal or band position statements. Toward the end of the meeting the commissioners read the treaty, article by article, and the Indians were asked to sign. The only contribution that the Indians had been allowed to make to the actual content of the document was in terms of tribal boundaries. At this treaty council there was no real negotiation, in part because the Indians were not being asked to give up any land.

The Arapaho and Sioux responses to the 1851 treaty council are representative of two distinct strategies used by plains tribes to attempt to win favor and gain concessions from the United States. The Arapaho attitude may be characterized as conciliatory and the Sioux attitude as defiant. It must be clearly understood that these are descriptive of diplomatic strategies, not of individual emotions.

The Arapaho chiefs decided to go along with the whites in their various demands. They expressed particular gratitude that there would be an end to all warfare. Addressing Mitchell, Cut Nose, an Arapaho chief, stated: "You, Grandfather, are doing well for your children in coming so far and taking so much trouble about them. I think you will do us all much good; I will go home satisfied. I will sleep sound, and not have to watch my horses in the night, or be afraid for my squaws and children."

The oldest of the Arapaho chiefs, Authon-ish-ah, in a speech addressed to the Arapahoes themselves, seemed to take the tack that the chiefs alone could no longer take full care of the people, and that they would have to rely on the whites. He said: "Fathers and children, we give you all up to our white brethren, and now we shall have peace, the pleasantest thing in the world. The whites are friends to us, and they will be good to us if we don't lie to them. . . . The whites want to be good to us; let us not be fools, and refuse what they ask."

The Arapahoes agreed to appoint Little Owl as head chief of the tribe, and through him to transact all business with the whites. Cut Nose addressed Mitchell as follows: "We have chosen our chief as you requested us to do, Father. Whatever he does, we will support him in it, and we expect, Father, that the whites will support him." The Arapahoes clearly pointed out the reciprocal nature of the agreement as they understood it. Cut Nose requested that the whites pick out a country for themselves to live in, and not trespass into Arapaho hunting grounds. He also suggested that the whites "should give us game for what they drive off."

The Arapaho position, then, established rigid reciprocity between whites and Indians, the Arapahoes symbolically acknowledging the white men's power and binding them through the treaty to support the Indians. From the Arapaho viewpoint, the treaty worked to their advantage.

The Sioux attitude was very different. From the beginning they refused to cooperate in the matter of choosing a head chief. Blue Earth, the old Brule chief, told Mitchell: "We have decided differently from you, Father, about this chief for the Nation. We want a chief for each band, and if you will make one or two chiefs for each band, it will be much better for you and the whites. Then we will make soldiers of our young men, and we will make them good men to the whites and other Indians. But Father, we can't make one chief."

However, Mitchell was unyielding. He demanded that the Sioux bands all come together and unite as a single nation. Regarding bands he said: "Your Great Father will not recognize any such divisions." In the end Mitchell had to select representatives from each of the ten bands to be chiefs, and then select one of them to be head chief. His candidate, Frightening Bear, was then duly elected to the office by all of the band chiefs. The new head chief was not eager for the position. He said: "Father, I am a young man and have no experience. I do not desire to be chief of the Dahcotahs. . . . If you, Father, and our Great Father, require that I shall be chief, I will take this office." It is very clear that the whites had imposed a new political office on Sioux society, one unlike any they had ever had before. Since it potentially entailed great power, Frightening Bear publicly spoke of his worry that he would be assassinated out of jealousy. Certainly the Sioux did not accept the idea of having a head chief.

The Sioux also objected strenuously to drawing boundaries around tribal territories. Blue Earth said, "We claim half of all the country; but, we don't care for that, for we can hunt anywhere." Black Hawk, an Oglala, told the council:

> You have split the country and I don't like it. What we live upon we hunt for, and we hunt from the Platte to the Arkansas, and from here up to the Red But[t]e and the Sweet Water. . . . These lands once belonged to the Kiowas and Crows, but we [the Oglalas, Cheyennes, and Arapahoes] whipped these nations out of them, and in this we do what the white men do when they want the lands of the Indians.

Mitchell explained that the boundaries were not intended to limit the tribes in any way, so long as they remained at peace. Nonetheless, the Sioux never accepted the boundaries.

The Sioux presented the council with a number of demands of their own. Big Yancton asked for horses, cattle, and fowl to make reparation for damages done to the Indians. A chief of the Blackfoot Sioux asked for a hundred wagonloads of goods each year, and asked that they be sent more buffalo as well. The latter request may have represented a challenge to the white men's claim to have been sent to the Sioux by the "Great Father."

Painted Bear, a Yankton Sioux, may well have summarized the dominant Sioux attitude of the time in the following words: "Father, this is the third time I have met the whites. We don't understand their manners, nor their words. We know it is all very good, and for our own good, but we don't understand it all. We suppose the half breeds understand it, and we leave them to speak for us."

Many of the Sioux did not want to have any dealings with the United States. Their chiefs continually expressed their inability to understand the whites as well as their reliance on the mixed-bloods for advice. Unlike the Arapahoes, they refused to put trust in the whites and continued to pressure them for specific demands and concessions.

Distribution of presents. The third aspect of the council was the distribution of presents. Token presents were given in advance to the headmen of each tribe to redistribute to their followers. This served to validate their status in the tribe by giving tangible proof of the esteem in which they were held by the whites. At the end of the council, after the treaty was signed, the wagon train came up and the bulk of the presents were distributed. This was the most significant part of the council for most of the Indians present. The event is memorialized in Sioux winter counts as "The winter of the big distribution." The whites at the council clearly understood the importance of the gift-giving aspects of the event. The reporter wrote: "It is a standing rule with all Indians, that whenever they meet, especially upon occasions of this character, they must have presents of some kind or other. . . . Without these no man living—not even the President of the United States—would have any influence with them, nor could he get them into council, or keep them together a day.

Plains Indian Diplomacy

This general model of treaty making—ritual, counseling, and gift giving—holds from the earliest plains treaty councils with the Lewis and Clark expedition down through the various commissions that negotiated with the tribes beginning in the 1880s for the breakup of reservations by agreeing to the allotment of lands in severalty and the sale of "surplus" land for white settlement. The elaborateness of gift giving and ritual decreased, on the whole, through time, and the extent of negotiation somewhat increased, but the treaty council remained a relatively stable institution throughout the period.

Perhaps the single most frustrating aspect of the entire history of treaty making was the inability of the two sides to communicate with one another meaningfully. Both whites and Indians used the councils to deliver speeches composed in advance. Specific objections or questions by Indians were rarely answered when they were raised, but were answered a day or more later in the course of lengthy speeches. Many questions went unanswered, and many objections were simply ignored. Treaty commissioners frequently excused this practice by saying that the Indians' speeches were being recorded to be taken back to Washington. The commissioners told the Sioux in 1865, "We will take back all your words, and the Great Father will read all you have said." But in reality neither the Great Father nor anyone else ever read them. Most remain unpublished or generally unavailable.

Examination of these documents solely from the perspective of reconstructing chronological history is quite disappointing. Usable historical data often seem to be altogether lacking in the speeches, replaced instead by rhetorical devices. Rarely do the speeches, white or Indian, rely on logic. These are not intellectual debates about matters that can easily be discussed. They are the records of more dramatic conflict between mutually exclusive ways of life.

Study of Indian diplomatic techniques provides a wealth of data on tribal cultures. Some trends may be seen over time that are suggestive of deeper changes in Indian cultures. One such trend involves the expressed attitude toward land. At the 1851 treaty council there seems to have been, from the white man's point of view, a rather practical attitude put forward by the Indians. They were capable and eager to discuss boundary issues. In the quote from Black Hawk given earlier, the idea of landownership by right of conquest is clearly articulated. Later, when the whites returned to ask the Sioux for more land for roads, they refused. At an 1865 council Lame Deer, a Miniconjou chief, stripped off his clothes and said to the commissioners: "I stand here naked and this is my condition. Why will you trouble me for my land, my brothers? You told me you would not ask me for anything." Other leaders tried other strategies. Some claimed the land because they were born on it, because the bones of their forefathers lay in it, or because it had been given to them by God. One That Killed the White Buffalo Cow, a Lower Brule chief, told the commissioners in 1865: "Who does all this country here belong to? It is ours. It belonged to our fathers and our fathers' fathers." Yet at the same time, Iron Nation, another Lower Brule chief, said of his people, "The older ones came from Minnesota. There we were born."

The council proceedings suggest that Indians thought about land according to its utility; it was not measured or conceived of in the white man's way. When the 1865 commission asked Lone Horn, the Miniconjou chief, if he would like to live on the Missouri River, he answered simply, "When the buffalo comes close to the river, we come close to it. When the buffaloes go off, we go off after them." The same commission asked the Indians where Frog, the Lower Brule chief, lived. Iron Nation answered, "Everywhere; where he is." The attitude expressed seems to suggest that land was not seen as the constant—people and animals were the constant features. Hence the justification for Indian ownership of land tended to be expressed in terms of people and buffalo.

Later, when the Indians' land base was already severely eroded and tribes became more specifically tied to land in the form of reservations, purely religious reasons tended to be adduced to argue for retaining that land which was left. A typical example is the statement of Iseo, a Kiowa leader, in 1892: "Mother earth is something that we Indians love. . . . We do not know what to do about selling our mother to the government." Another example is this statement by Spotted Horse, a Cheyenne, in 1890: "We look upon this land as a home and as our mother and we don't expect to sell it." Old Crow, another Cheyenne, told the same commission: "The Great Spirit gave the Indians all this country and never tell them that they should sell it. . . . If you have had any such word from the Great Spirit that gave them this land I would like to hear it." The point here is to suggest that detailed study of the treaty council proceedings may provide more data than might at first glance be expected on such complex and abstract issues as changing attitudes toward land.

Tactics

A survey of Indian diplomatic tactics that repeatedly occur in treaty council records reveals an interesting variety as well as significant differences among tribes. A few examples will be discussed here to illustrate the variety and nature of these tactics, as well as the value of such data to an understanding of Indian cultures.

Sometimes religious and moral justifications were presented by Indian orators to treaty commissioners in order to explain the Indians' perspective on the white man. An excellent example of this type of diplomacy is provided by a council in November 1866, held in Kansas at the Big Bend of the Arkansas River. Commissioners were investigating the Indian situation on the southern plains and preparing for a great council that would be held the following year at Medicine Lodge Creek. The commissioners counseled with Lone Wolf, head chief of the Kiowas, and a delegation of headmen in order to discover information about past hostilities and to impress on the Indians the necessity of peace.

> Colonel J. H. Leavenworth told the Kiowas: The Great Chief at Washington has heard some bad news about you and he has sent out two of his chiefs to see if they are true. . . . The names of those that have acted badly we have put on a piece of paper, and we shall tell the Great Chief what we know about them and he will decide whether they live or die. If any of your people go to Texas or Old or New Mexico and commit depredations the Great Chief will not forget it, but he will send an army of his men and exterminate you.

These threats were not well received by the Kiowas. They had long heard whites boast of the power of the Great Chief or the Great Father in Washington, but they had never experienced it themselves. They were skeptical and they were angered to be ordered not to raid the whites to the south since it was economically important to them and also provided them with the regular means by which young men gained status to raise themselves in the social hierarchy.

Rather than take a stance blatantly antagonistic to that of the commissioners, Lone Wolf allowed White Bird, an old medicine man, to make the first speech in reply to the whites. The record of the proceedings reads as follows:

> The Indians then laid two circular pieces of paper on the floor; one blue and one white. Otank or White-bird, an old Indian then went through a form of prayer and spoke as follows to Lone Wolf in Kiowa, who repeated it to the Interpreter in Comanche.
>
>> LONE WOLF—That piece of paper (pointing to the white) represents the earth. There is a big water all around the earth. The circular blue paper is the sky. The sun goes around the earth. The sun is our father. All the red men in this country, all the Buffalo are all his (old man's). Our Great Father the sun told us that the white man would kill all of them, there is

no place for us to hide because the water is all around the earth. When my time comes to die I intend to die and not wait to be killed by the white men. I want you to write to the Great Chief and tell him that I understand my Great Father the sun, that my Great Father the sun sent me a message, that I went around the prairie poor and crying and the Great Father the sun sent me a message that I can read. A long time ago when I was little I began to study medicine and when we make a treaty with the white man I see it and know whether it is good or not. I am the man that makes it rain, I talk to the Great Father. If I have any difficulty with anyone and wish them to perish with thirst I stop the rain and if I wish them well I cause it to rain so that the corn can grow. My Great Father the sun told me that fire and water were alike, that we cannot live without either of them. This is all the old man's talk, he wishes to go to Washington.

He (Lone Wolf) then said that he wished to talk for himself. I do not know what the Great Chief at Washington will think of the old man's talk.

CAPT. BOGY—We have similar men among us who converse with the Great Spirit.

White Bird's speech is significant in several ways. It lays out an entire cosmology and belief system which is in direct contradiction to that of the whites. It puts the Great Chief in Washington into perspective under the power of the true Great Father, the sun. White Bird claims an especially close relationship to the sun, manifested in his power to control rain. Implied in his speech is his own belief that he is closer to the Great Spirit than is the white man's Great Chief. His desire to go to Washington was very likely motivated by a feeling that if he could but meet this Great Chief face to face he could best him with his power, matching him trick for trick.

Diplomatically, this speech was a good choice because it led into the refusal by the Kiowas, at least for the moment, to commit themselves to follow the will of the president, and provided moral and ethical grounds on which to do so. Unfortunately, it was probably ineffective. Bogy's comment relegates the speech to mere mysticism. Doubtless the commissioners simply missed the point. But the speech provides a good model of the Kiowa world as they presented it to oppose the view of the world propounded by the whites.

The use of kinship terms was another diplomatic tactic manipulated by Indians and whites alike. The 1865 treaty commissioners told the Miniconjou Sioux: "Your Great Father, the President, has selected us to come out to this country to visit his red children, the Dahcotahs. . . . The President, your Great Father, has not sent us to make peace because he is weak. . . . On the contrary, he pities his red children."

Lone Horn, the Miniconjou head chief, seems to have felt the need to maneuver around the father-child relationship established by the commissioners, clearly limiting the father role to the president and excluding the commissioners from it. He therefore addressed the commissioners as follows: "My friends, I will begin my speech with claiming relationship to all of you. I will call you my brothers." This is significant since the relationship between brothers in Lakota society was the closest of all family relationships; one could not refuse anything to a brother without giving mortal offense. The Sioux in particular, reflecting the great emphasis placed in their culture on kinship, were adept at manipulating kinship metaphors in order to attempt to jockey whites into positions where they would be forced to make concessions. Later in his speech Lone Horn chided the commissioners: "It is good that you, my friends, my brothers, make peace with me, but it seems to me you are holding back, and do not like to make peace freely." Unfortunately, the whites probably never understood the kinship strategy. Even in the example discussed here the commissioners failed to pick up on the significance of Lone Horn's statement and did not reciprocate by calling him brother. If they had, they would have placed themselves in the reciprocal brother relationship and would have improved their own bargaining position as well.

Government commissioners frequently used the expression "our red children" to put Indians into a subordinate position. Just as frequently, Indian orators exploited the father-children metaphor to ask for favors. In plains Indian cultures this relationship was a very important one in which the father gave freely to his children. At a Sioux treaty council in 1856, Bear Rib addressed General W. S. Harney as father: "My Father! What is there better to wish for than a father." Much later, in 1892, Lone Wolf, the Kiowa chief, used the metaphor ironically to make his point that Indians should be protected from land allotment. He said to the commissioners: "You will believe me when I say we were like babies not knowing how to get up and take care of ourselves."

Kinship terms used at treaty councils are significant symbols. They functioned as diplomatic devices that must be explored in order to understand the dynamics of the event. They are not merely paternalistic, racist, or subservient designations to be ignored in favor of what was really being said. Especially from the Indians' point of view, the use of kin terms was not a mere token, but embodied the real message of what was being communicated.

Another diplomatic tactic frequently used was to set up an equivalence between Indians and whites to provide a moral basis from which to ask that Indians be treated the same as whites. Eagle Drinking, a Comanche, told a commission in 1865: "I bear in my mind and heart the same feelings as the Great Father at Washington. I speak to my people as the Great Father at Washington does to his." In 1867 the Comanche chief Ten Bears told the commissioners: "My Great Father at Washington has the same heart that I have although I live on the prairies." In the same year the Comanche chief Rising Sun told the commissioners: "The Great Father is warm hearted, so am I."

It would be easy to proliferate examples, but the tactic was the same. By establishing the common humanity of whites and Indians, a moral base was established from which to negotiate for concessions. Many other tactical devices were also frequently manipulated for diplomatic advantage, among them the use of writing, factionalism, dependence on the government, shaming the government for broken promises, and emphasizing tribal differences.

Treaty council proceedings are valuable documents for reconstructing the symbolic expressions of Indian cultures as Indian orators attempted to use their skill to best the white man at diplomacy. These documents are major resources for the study of plains Indians, reflecting cultural changes through time. The publication of treaty council proceedings and thorough studies of them will vastly enrich our understanding of native American cultures on the plains and allow some reconstruction of the Indians' points of view as they were threatened with cultural extinction in the face of white American expansion.

Suggested Reading

This is one of the few accounts to give some insights into the Indian side of Western treaty making. Most discussions of the topic are in books that analyze formal American policy toward the tribes. These include Robert A. Trennert Jr., *Alternative to Extinction: Federal Indian Policy and the Beginnings of the Reservation System* (Philadelphia: Temple University Press, 1975); Francis Paul Prucha, *American Indian Treaties: The History of a Political Anomaly* (Berkeley: University of California Press, 1994); and Robert M. Utley, *The Indian Frontier of the American West, 1846–1890* (Albuquerque: University of New Mexico Press, 1984). The histories of particular tribes offer local examples of the treaty system in operation.

PART FOUR

Reservations, Resistance, and Renewal

By the 1860s federal authorities began to force most western tribal groups onto reservations. Sometimes they achieved this through treaty negotiations, promising a steady supply of food and other personal necessities. In other cases military pressure, mining rushes, and the continuing stream of settlers into their homelands persuaded Indians to accept white demands that they "settle down." As reservations developed during the last third of the nineteenth century, variety and innovation marked the tribal responses to their new circumstances. Scattered groups of tribal people in Washington and Oregon rejected the reservations, as Andrew Fisher shows, to create their own independent identity.

All groups faced continuing efforts to remake their societies through education, religion, and economic change. Indian initiatives and responses to moves for increased acculturation appeared in many forms. Some tribal people used the new locations as a base from which they could hunt, engage in multiband ceremonies, or merely to visit friends and relatives living elsewhere. As they came to understand governmental policies and structures, others strove to create at least partially new practices and identities. Rarely did they cooperate wholeheartedly with reservation agents or their programs.

Although some village children moved to distant boarding schools designed to destroy their Native cultures, most encountered the new "culture" at local day schools. Thomas Andrews analyzes how the Lakota people used the day schools to help achieve their own goals and thwart the plans of reservation officials. Adults, too old for the schools, tried to ignore or escape from efforts to cut the men's hair, dress everyone in western clothing, and force them to accept agriculture as their livelihood. Facing continuing pressures to accept acculturation, Indians worked to develop new and more knowledgeable leaders and learn how to manipulate local officials and their policies in ways to achieve tribal goals. The implementation of the General Allotment Act during the early 1890s brought reservation dwellers face to face with federal efforts to use agriculture and small-scale ranching to break up tribal communal landholding patterns. Elizabeth James illustrates how local whites, reservation dwellers, and the federal government sought to benefit from the new land system and how none of them achieved their goals entirely.

CHAPTER TWELVE

"They Mean to be Indians Always"

The Origins of the Columbia River Indian Identity, 1860–1885

ANDREW H. FISHER

When American pioneers reached the Pacific Northwest by the 1850s, they found dozens of small Indian groups scattered throughout the entire region. In the mid-1850s federal negotiator Isaac Stevens, seeking to clear land for settlers, negotiated treaties that established reservations for many of the local tribes. The specific locations of Indian lands and the demands that some Native groups settle alongside traditional rivals, even longtime enemies, made implementing the treaties difficult at best. Whatever else these agreements may have accomplished, they clearly disrupted many aspects of Indian life.

This essay examines the variety of tribal and individual responses to the American demands. While regional histories trace a number of Indian wars, most villages lacked the size and cohesion necessary for violent action. Native resistance to being forced out of their homelands instead followed other paths. Like reservation dwellers throughout the West, people slipped away from their new homes for religious ceremonies, to hunt or fish, or even to accept day labor jobs among the whites. This analysis shows how porous reservation boundaries were and the ways in which Native people retained their identity and personal independence in spite of them.

In November of 1878, as the Bannock War raged in eastern Oregon and Idaho, a small band of John Day Indians under military escort straggled onto the Warm Springs reservation. These so-called renegades had taken no part in the hostilities; in fact, they had fled the Umatilla reservation to escape the bloodshed there and had tried to warn white settlers of the danger. Nevertheless, agent

Copyright by the Western History Association. Reprinted by permission. The article first appeared as "'They Mean to be Indians Always': The Origins of Columbia River Indian Identity, 1860–85," *Western Historical Quarterly* 32, no. 4 (Winter 2001): 468–92.

John Smith regarded them as troublemakers and did not welcome their arrival at Warm Springs. Except for a handful, he protested, "[t]hese Indians do not belong to this reservation, having never been compelled to move onto it until this time. They are said to be very destitute, and it is evident some provision must be made for them." Smith would let them stay if they agreed to start farms and conform to agency rules. But he had no faith in their leader, Hehaney, who followed the teachings of Smohalla and refused to abandon the "savage" pursuits of his ancestors. "I put him in irons four different times," complained Smith, "and he always made fair promises when he was set free. . . . I am almost in hopes he will be sent to the Indian Territory. If sent here he must obey or be sent off." He did not obey. In the spring of 1879, Smith reported that Hehaney had left without permission, "taking most of the John Day's and some of the Warm Springs with him," and he had crossed the Columbia River for the ostensible purpose of making a home on the Yakama Reservation. He never reached the agency at Fort Simcoe, and the agent there later identified him among a group of non-reservation Natives who refused to provide any information for the tribal census. "He means to be an Indian always," huffed Smith, "in the fullest sense of the character attached to that name."

Hehaney and his followers represented a larger class of mid-Columbia Indians who denied belonging to any single reservation or recognized tribe. Between 1860 and 1885, federal officials constantly complained that many of the people assigned to the Umatilla, Warm Springs, and Yakama agencies remained at large on the public domain. Despite petitions from white settlers and threats of forced removal, these renegades refused to abandon their traditional village sites, cemeteries, and fishing stations along the Columbia River. Reservation residents often shared the same practical concerns, cultural commitments, and spiritual beliefs that prevented others from settling in the tribal homelands. Yet, the Office of Indian Affairs (OIA) increasingly viewed non-reservation Natives as a coherent group bent on undermining federal authority and corrupting their reservation kin. By the 1880s, the government had labeled them "Columbia River Indians," a term describing both an official category for renegades and a potential tribal identity. While ties of kinship and exchange continued to bind reservation and non-reservation Natives, each group began to develop a sense of difference from the other. Seeing themselves as more authentically Indian than reservation dwellers, "River People" purposefully stayed outside the lines that demarcated tribal territory and defined tribal identity under the emerging colonial order.

The story of Columbia River Indian resistance highlights two important but underdeveloped themes in Native American history. First, it demonstrates the porous nature of reservation boundaries and the persistence of Indian communities in off-reservation settings. As Brad Asher and Alexandra Harmon have shown in recent studies, many Indians in the Far West never moved to reservations, or they resided there only seasonally. Contrary to traditional histories, which emphasize the isolation and segregation of whole "tribes," newer works

Locations of mid-Columbia Indian reservations. Based on a map by Michael Darling, Portland Area Office, U.S. Bureau of Indian Affairs.

acknowledge that Native Americans frequently defied both geographical confinement and political classification. The Columbia River Indian example helps explain this larger pattern while also illustrating the particular ways in which one group coped with changing conditions, challenged federal authority, and altered the outcomes of national policy.

Second, the history of the River People adds to a growing body of literature on the construction of ethnic categories in the United States. Taking their cue from scholars in other fields, Indian historians have begun to treat tribal identity as a dynamic, historical process rather than a fixed, timeless essence. State power still shapes the discussion, but scholars now recognize that Native Americans have frequently contested the government's racial and tribal designations. "Within the framework of laws and federal policies," noted Alexandra Harmon, "various descendants of aboriginal people have taken the initiative to define themselves, trying to fashion identities that make sense to them." These identities generally have multiple dimensions or positions that shift depending on the social and political context. Sometimes complementing but often conflicting with other tribal designations, "Columbia River Indian" originated as a federal category for people who refused to adopt the residences and roles prescribed in the treaties. Through a process of negotiation with other Indians, as well as with the government, this category slowly evolved into a new ethnic consciousness. The story told here, then, is merely the first chapter of a longer, continuing history. In time, Columbia River Indians would build their own identity upon the foundation laid during the reservation period.

The treaties that placed Native Americans on reservations and assigned them to particular "tribes" clashed with the complex reality of aboriginal relations on the Columbia Plateau. Today, most River People trace their ancestry to one of the Sahaptin or Upper Chinookan villages that once lined the Columbia River from the Cascades to Priest Rapids. Prior to Euro-American contact, these independent communities typically formed the largest political units in a regional social network linked by shared territory, cultural affinity, economic exchange, and extensive intermarriage. Family ties crisscrossed the Columbia Basin, bridging both geographic barriers and linguistic boundaries, and people moved in and out of different social groupings throughout the seasonal round. In the spring and summer months, villages broke into small kin groups, which intermingled at important fishing and gathering sites such as Celilo Falls and Camas Prairie. During the winter, families often traveled to neighboring villages to participate in a regional complex of ceremonial dances and shamanistic performances. Consequently, individual Indians had multiple associations and multifaceted identities that would greatly complicate future attempts at categorization.

"Tribes," in the modern sense of the word, developed on the Columbia Plateau through a process of creative misunderstanding. As anthropologist Verne F. Ray noted in 1939, "Early settlers, traders, missionaries, and government officials carried with them from the east the notion that all Indian groups were of necessity organized along tribal lines. Upon learning a village name from a Native the whites immediately and indiscriminately applied it to all Indians of the vicinity." Some labels represented self designations, but others came from neighboring peoples with different languages or dialects. Few Native names survived transliteration without some degree of corruption and transcriptional variation. The Upper Chinookan–speaking Wascos, for example, had at least nineteen synonyms for their name in early Euro-American writings. Therefore, using such labels requires the caveat that they are historical creations with changing forms and ambiguous definitions.

From the government's perspective, tribal designations became fixed during treaty negotiations. In 1855, federal officials divided mid-Columbia River Indians into several discrete "tribes" and "bands" for the purposes of gaining title to their land and removing them to reservations. This process, driven more by political expediency than by aboriginal reality, entailed the arbitrary division of traditional social networks. Using pieces of the aboriginal pattern, now badly tattered by imported disease, federal officials partitioned the Columbia Plateau into ceded areas and lumped each area's inhabitants into one of several confederated tribes. Most of those living north of the Columbia River ostensibly became members of the Yakama Indian Nation, while those living south of it merged into either the Confederated Tribes of Warm Springs or the Confederated Tribes of the Umatilla Indian Reservation. At least on paper, the treaty commissioners divided kinship networks, reassigned political loyalties, and restructured group rights. In this way, the government attempted to create a system it could comprehend and control. Mid-Columbia Indians understood the treaties quite differently, however, and they did not instantly behave as unified tribes.

Nor did they readily accept geographical confinement. All of the Columbia Plateau treaties contained clauses guaranteeing the Indians' rights to harvest traditional foods at "usual and accustomed places" both on and off the reservations. Noting these provisions and the difficulty of accurate translation at the councils, ethnographer Eugene Hunn has argued that "the treaties were not understood as prohibiting continued residence at or adjacent to [the] Columbia River fisheries." Some families historically remained on the river year-round, fishing and trading with visitors, and they believed that the treaties allowed them to continue this lifestyle. According to Johnny Jackson, a current member of the Council of Columbia River Indian Chiefs: "We never moved because when the treaties were signed by chief Slockish at Walla Walla we reserved the right to live at our usual and accustomed sites along the river. These sites were reserved because they hold all of our religious sacred sites, cemeteries, gathering sites, fishing sites and where we have always maintained our livelihood." Despite persistent challenges from federal, state, and tribal authorities, this interpretation survived in Native oral traditions and inspired resistance to the reservation policy.

Many mid-Columbia Indians rejected the treaties outright because they had never agreed to them in the first place. Unwilling to surrender their traditional homelands, some Native leaders either withheld their presence from the treaty councils or withheld their signatures from the agreements. Wallachin, a Cascades headman, refused to sign the Treaty of Middle Oregon, "alleging as a reason that his people could not subsist away from the Columbia River, and declaring, 'I have said that I would not sell my country and I have but one talk.'" Other Indians never received notice of the councils and only learned of the treaties after the ink had dried. The fact that some groups therefore lacked direct representation did not overly concern either Governor Isaac I. Stevens or General Joel Palmer, the treaty commissioners for Washington Territory and Oregon, respectively. Ignoring the decentralized structure of Columbia Plateau politics, they accepted the marks of the designated "head chiefs" as binding upon all the tribal groups listed in the treaties. This practice expedited American diplomacy but infuriated the Indians who had not participated in the negotiations. According to Palmer, the

Klickitats in particular "were much enraged at the sale of their country without their knowledge or consent, and declared they would not abide by an agreement in which they had no voice." Indian anger erupted into armed confrontation during the so-called Yakama War of 1855–58, but violence ultimately proved less successful than other forms of resistance to federal policy.

After the war, which supposedly settled matters for good, the government expected all Indians to move to their designated agencies. Though many complied within the one-year deadline, many others over the next three decades stayed away or routinely crossed reservation boundaries. In 1881, roughly a third of the 3,400 Indians assigned to the Yakama agency either lived off the reservation entirely or resided there only in winter. Another third had permanent homes on the reservation but left each year during the fishing season. Similar conditions prevailed at the other agencies. In 1870, for example, Lieutenant W. H. Boyle noted that only 837 of the 1,622 Indians in his charge had relocated to the Umatilla reservation. When he visited the groups scattered along the Columbia River to demand their removal, they denied belonging to his agency and refused to recognize his authority. Such defiance demonstrated that federal policy had failed to erect impermeable racial barriers or fix the fluid tribal identities of mid-Columbia Indians.

Native mobility and autonomy frustrated efforts to restrict each tribe to its proper reservation. While the treaties produced new places of residence and new political affiliations, existing social ties remained intact, and Indians moved freely between communities where they had kin. The OIA struggled to conduct tribal censuses and to determine which Natives belonged where, as reservation populations fluctuated dramatically from season to season and from year to year. In 1873, Umatilla agent Narcisse A. Cornoyer stated that "a portion of the Indians belonging to these tribes still remain on the Columbia River, and some of these occasionally come on the reservation and profess to have come to remain; they will stay a short time and then leave again for the Columbia." Seven years later, Indian inspector William Pollock declared that only four of the fourteen tribes named in the Yakama treaty had any members on that reservation. Agent James Wilbur no longer bothered to enumerate the individual groups, yet Pollock thought it entirely possible to do so. By his estimate, 501 legitimate agency Indians mingled with some 300 to 850 others "near and remotely related to, and affiliating with, but not clearly traceable to any particular tribe." The current census, he said, "will show more than can properly be called Reservation Indians" after the "wandering vagrant Columbia River Indians are, by the rigors of winter, driven to the Reservation to subsist upon their more provident relatives."

Agents did not necessarily wish to claim these "vagrant" Natives, particularly if they appeared prone to cause problems or sap limited reservation resources. But the OIA could not easily distinguish between residents and renegades. Reservation Indians could become "vagabonds," or vice versa, in a matter of days. As Wilbur's successor, Robert H. Milroy, noted with obvious distaste:

> Nearly all [renegades] have relatives living here. When one of my Indians desires to free himself from the restraints of wholesome discipline, all he has to do is go to the Columbia River, join the Non Reservation Indians, and the agent's authority over him ceases, and he can gamble and get drunk as he likes.

While correctly noting the ease of the transformation, such descriptions distorted the reasons for interaction between renegades and reservation residents. Mid-Columbia Indians had always shared resources, and they continued to do so despite official displeasure with their "usual habit of roaming & visiting neighboring tribes." In the spring and summer, many reservation residents traveled to traditional fishing and gathering sites, where they mingled with renegades and often acquired that label. During the winter, renegades joined in ceremonial dances and feasts at the agencies. On such occasions, reservation residents could redistribute some of the government rations, agricultural produce, and livestock that confirmed their status as wealthy people. Thus, when agent Wilbur allocated treaty annuities in 1872, "runners were sent out in all directions and a grand rally made to gather in as many Indians as possible." To the disgust of inspector Pollock, "the agent's official accounts show that at that time he issued [treaty annuities] to only five hundred and twelve persons, *representatives* of seventeen hundred and eighteen (1718) Indians." The government had, in effect, sponsored a traditional Columbia Plateau "giveaway."

However, not even the lure of federal largesse could convince diehard renegades to affiliate with a single agency. Though some wintered on the reservations or sought refuge there in times of danger, they avoided claiming tribal membership for fear of jeopardizing their freedom. Hehaney and his people spent most of 1878 on the Umatilla reservation but kept their names from the agent to prevent being reported as permanent residents. Other renegades insisted that they had never set foot inside reservation lines or accepted any treaty benefits "for the reason that they believe by so doing they would admit the principle of having sold their right to occupy land." If they belonged to a particular agency, the OIA could demand their removal or compel their children to attend school. Distance and detachment partially relieved the pressures of forced assimilation, and some reservation residents used their renegade relations to foil federal policy. In 1884, for instance, agent Milroy staged a roundup of Native pupils only to discover that "all the school children of the Cotiahan [Kotiakan] band have been run off among the wild Indians along the Columbia River, some 90 miles distant, to pass out of the reach of my police."

Renegades knew enough about the federal bureaucracy—its limits and its internal divisions—to play different agencies and departments against each other. The rivalry between the Office of Indian Affairs and the Department of War furnished particularly fertile ground in which to sow discord. When agent Milroy sent his Indian police in pursuit of the renegades and their children, they immediately appealed to the military department of the Columbia. At a council with Captain F. K. Upham, several headmen "continued to insist upon a complaint against the reservation, with a request that the [department commander] might be informed." According to Upham:

> Buscappa [Pascappa], cheif [sic] of a small band living near Alder Creek, and Ko-tai-a-kon [Kotiakan] were particularly anxious that their grievances should be known; which were in effect, that while they, as a matter of principle, would not go to the reservation, and had never received any benefits or annuities therefrom, the agent at the Yakima reservation continued to send the Indian police after them, and particularly their children, insisting that they should be taught at the reservation schools, and [learn] the religion of the agency, and that their hair should be cut.

Milroy grudgingly complied with orders to confine his police to the reservation. His tirades against military interference irritated the U.S. Army, however, and local officers responded sympathetically to further complaints about his draconian policies. In 1885, the secretary of the interior requested Milroy's resignation, and the OIA forbade the use of agency police beyond reservation boundaries. The renegades and their reservation kin had won a small but significant victory over the agency that nominally controlled them.

High turnover within the OIA made it easier for Natives to manipulate the system, yet even experienced officials could be duped. A common ploy involved requesting permission to visit or transfer to a different agency, then failing to appear at the promised destination. In 1879, for example, the renegade leaders Stock (Suitz) and Pascappa asked to move their people from Umatilla to Fort Simcoe. Agent Cornoyer issued the requisite passes, along with instructions to proceed straight to the agency, but they ignored his directions and stayed on the Columbia River. Some Indians skipped the reservation regardless of whether they received official sanction. In 1870, the Tygh prophet Queahpahmah *dreamed that he was to leave Warm Springs* and demanded a pass, citing as reasons both his vision and the lack of good land on the reservation. When the agent refused, Queahpahmah "boldly announced to the Indians—though not to the Agent—that he was going and 'never would come back again.'" He returned eight years later, of his own accord, and assumed a position of leadership among the Warm Springs Indians. In the interim, however, he evaded capture and continued his "vagabond mode of life" from the relative safety of Priest Rapids.

Fugitives from the reservations blended smoothly into the more permanent renegade population along the Columbia River. The OIA did not systematically enumerate non-reservation Natives until the 1930s, but late nineteenth-century estimates pegged their numbers in the mid-Columbia region at roughly two thousand people. Sizeable villages persisted at Wishram and Celilo, and smaller settlements dotted tributaries from the Cascades to the Umatilla River. Farther upstream, renegades congregated near Wallula, Priest Rapids, and White Bluffs. Movement among these far-flung communities created new social networks embracing a wide range of Native ethnicities and tribal affiliations. The OIA recognized the polyglot composition of the renegade ranks but increasingly lumped them together as "Columbia River Indians." By the 1870s, this broad geographic label had become common in government correspondence and census reports, where it often appeared next to recognized tribal categories such as Umatilla, Wasco, and Yakama. It had also became virtually synonymous with the term "renegade." Not every renegade was a Columbia River Indian, but almost all Columbia River Indians were renegades in the eyes of federal officials.

Irate settlers generally associated renegades with the nearest agency and complained accordingly. Even though squatters and stockmen violated reservation boundaries throughout the late nineteenth century, the refusal of Indians to stay inside the lines infuriated their American neighbors. They vented their anger in letters, petitions, and editorials detailing the alleged abuses of the renegades and demanding immediate action from federal authorities. Perhaps the most impassioned plea came from E. S. Penham, a former Wasco County judge, who called attention to the Columbia River Indians living near The Dalles:

> Since you have declined to remove them they are worse than ever, and the result is they have burnt up my neighbor's grain stack, tools, etc. A poor man, illy able to sustain the loss. Beside are driving his wife, a sickly nervous woman, to the grave or insanity by her constant fears. In fact none of us in our neighborhood feel very safe. Our farms are in their line of travel from Dalles to Celilo and the fisheries, and they pass from town all times night and day in troops, and most of the time *crazy* drunk hollering and yelling as only drunken Indians can.

Later in the letter, he implored: "1 hope you will look into the matter at an early day, as we would like to realize [for] once the fact that we are not toiling for vagabond Indians."

Penham and his fellow petitioners played the role of injured innocents with great conviction, but their letters tell only a fraction of the story. Besides rustling Native stock and plying Indians with liquor, some settlers intentionally exaggerated the threat of Indian attack to encourage their removal and to advance their own claims to Native lands. 1n 1883, for example, two farmers in Klickitat County told agent Milroy that local whites had fled their homes in fear of an uprising by four hundred armed renegades. The Columbia River Indians in the area denied the allegations, declaring that "they never had a thought of going to war, that they are not fools and do not want to see their families scattered and themselves hanged." But Milroy had little interest in their version of events. "Whether these complaints are true or not," he informed the local military commander, "my duty to these Indians requires me to use all efforts to remove them from these constantly recurring disputes and troubles with white settlers." When Captain Thomas McGregor went to investigate, he concluded that the two white men had started the rumor in a bid to seize the Indians' land, and that "it [was] the wish of all the rest of the whites living in the vicinity of the Columbia River Indians that they be *let alone.*"

As this statement suggests, mutual fear and hostility masked a more complicated and conflicted relationship between Natives and newcomers. While some Americans anxiously avoided or greedily exploited their indigenous neighbors, others coexisted peacefully and even productively with local Indians. Faced with a shortage of potential spouses and sexual partners, white men looked to Native communities for female companions. The resulting relationships ran the gamut from rape and prostitution to marriage—a routine occurrence despite state and territorial statutes prohibiting interracial unions—and they produced a growing population of mixed-blood children. Other settlers turned to Native people for economic reasons. Unable to recruit adequate help from the small white population, Americans employed Indians as pack handlers, farm laborers, ranch hands, and domestic servants. By the mid-1880s, some Columbia River Indians had likewise hired immigrants to tend their crops and cattle. One government observer called these Native entrepreneurs "remarkable for their prompt cash payments for such labor." Many Indians shunned agriculture and wage work but readily traded horses or peddled fish, venison, and berries in American settlements. Whites often perceived these activities as a sign of Native dependency, but the existence of both a market and a marketable surplus suggests quite the opposite. Less self-reliant than they liked to believe, Americans confronted Indians who remained more self-sufficient and more hospitable to strangers than racial stereotypes allowed.

Economic cooperation and personal contact with Native neighbors gradually softened the attitudes of some immigrants. Lingering ambivalence easily flared into antagonism, yet many settlers tolerated or even defended the presence of Indians among them. Most did so out of self-interest. Farmers and fruit growers worried that overzealous agents would deprive them of the Indian labor that sustained their operations. In frontier towns such as Pendleton, Oregon, merchants eager for Native commerce argued that off-reservation transactions fell outside the federal trade and intercourse laws. Not all Americans had such mercenary motives, though, and a few went so far as to side with Indians against other whites. In 1884, when an aggressive settler chased Salmon Man and his family off their land along the Columbia River, their non-Indian neighbors testified that the Natives "were known to be honest, industrious and self-supporting, and that they had always occupied the site taken from them." A year earlier, during the scare in Klickitat County, white settlers had requested that Agent Milroy call off his police and leave the renegades alone. Though hardly starry-eyed idealists, these individuals set aside abstract notions of racial solidarity and tried to coexist with Columbia River Indians.

The OIA, rather than applauding such behavior, actively discouraged racial fraternization. In 1865, J. W. Perit Huntington, the Oregon superintendent of Indian affairs, warned that such interaction caused "the Indians [to] become an intolerable nuisance to the whites, and the effect upon themselves is most pernicious."

They are always drunken and debauched, their women become prostitute, and all soon become infected with loathsome diseases. There are found in every community a few [white] persons vile enough to associate with them and desire their presence. These persons naturally acquire the good will of the Indians and have much influence over them. By enticing them to leave the reservation, notifying them of the approach of the agent, and assisting them to conceal themselves from him, they often defeat the object of the government of keeping the white and red races apart. Another class of citizens, who are respectable, and do not furnish them whiskey or debauch their women, thoughtlessly encourage their presence to secure their services upon their farms or at other labor. But once away from the reservation, and beyond the control of the agent, they unavoidably come in contact with immoral influences, and the effect is the same as if the motive was bad.

To prevent these unwholesome effects, Huntington recommended punishing both the Indians who left the reservation without consent and the whites who abetted them. E. S. Penham, the county judge turned petitioner, would gladly have enforced such sanctions against his fellow citizens. In his opinion, "[t]he idea that these Indians are necessary to the convenience of the citizens of The Dalles is preposterous." The majority of the white population wanted the Indians removed, he insisted, "and they should not be permitted to roam at large . . . even if a few interested parties desire them to remain."

The majority of the white population, like Penham, ignored the fact that Indians had practical reasons for continuing to "roam at large." For one thing, they had to eat. Most Natives showed little interest in farming, and early agricultural ventures often failed due to inexperience, inadequate equipment, and poor growing conditions. Since the government could not feed them adequately, even staunch "progressives" had no choice but to harvest traditional foods. In 1869, for example, both the Warm Springs and Umatilla agents permitted Indians to leave the reservations because their crops had withered and they lacked sufficient rations. Two years later, a Wasco named Painost expressed frustration with the resulting contradiction:

> The Government has tried to do something for us, but the ground will not raise anything. So we must go outside and hunt deer on which to live. Then the news goes to the President that the Indians are wandering off their reservation troubling everybody. If we would live we must go outside, for the land is poor and will not raise anything.

Agents faced an equally impossible situation. Caught between hungry Natives, angry settlers, and impatient but parsimonious superiors, local officials struggled to reconcile national policy with the terms of the treaties and the demands of humanity. In 1878, when the OIA forbade Natives to leave their reservations without approval from Washington, D.C., agent John Smith respectfully disobeyed on the grounds that his charges "still need to go after their annual supplies of soft and dried salmon [and], in fact, by treaty stipulation they are entitled to permits to do so."

Even when reservation residents managed to raise a crop or amass a herd of cattle, they risked losing the fruits of their labor to "Snake" Indian raiders. Although intertribal warfare antedated the treaties, the struggling farmers on the Oregon reservations made attractive targets for marauding parties of Shoshones, Bannocks, and Northern Paiutes. In 1859, the Warm Springs agent reported that many Indians had deserted the reservation due to repeated depredations. Three years later, the local Indians were still "unwilling to remain on the reservation except in the immediate vicinity of the agency building, where they can be protected." Similar problems plagued the Umatilla agency, especially during the Bannock War of 1878. Fearing violence from avenging whites as well as from the "Snakes," Indians fled to the reservation only to discover that its lines offered little security. In fact, the agent reported, "Some of the most industrious and worthy Indians on the reservation have been reduced from comfortable circumstances to poverty by their losses." Many renegades, including Hehaney's band, preferred to take their chances on the public domain.

For those who stayed put, additional feelings of insecurity developed from the uncertain status of their new homes. Responding to pressure from American settlers, Congress and the OIA considered several proposals to abolish one or more of the Plateau reservations. As early as 1859, agent Andrew Cain recommended eliminating the Umatilla reservation and dispersing its residents to Warm Springs and Fort Simcoe. His proposal went nowhere, but Indian inspector Felix Brunot broached the subject again at an 1871 meeting with the confederated tribes. Their leaders unanimously rejected his proposition, so Brunot suggested eliminating the Warm Springs reservation instead. All but one of the tribal spokesmen there expressed vehement opposition at an 1876 council. Still, the government would not relent, and in 1885, Congress forced the reduction and allotment of Umatilla lands over tribal objections. Fearing a similar fate, Yakama leaders voiced "a strong desire that those living off the reservation be returned" to boost the tribal population. Agent Milroy encouraged such talk and advocated the use of military force to compel removal, yet few renegades heeded the call.

To many Native people, it must have seemed pointless to start a new life on a reservation that could soon disappear. Whites obviously could not make up their minds about where Indians belonged. Some settlers demanded the swift removal of renegades from the public domain; others clamored for the immediate dissolution of the reservation system. Meanwhile, ranchers and homesteaders ignored reservation lines that remained largely unsurveyed and unmarked in 1885. The resulting boundary disputes discouraged some Indians from settling in the tribal homelands—or at least gave them an excuse for not doing so. In 1889, inspector T. D. Marcum reported:

> There are about 100 Warm Springs Indians who now reside off the reserve along the Columbia River, who want to locate on that part of the reservation

now in controversy, but will not go upon the land until the north boundary line is definitely established, and will not do so if this land is cut off of the reserve.

The government seemed more concerned with keeping Indians on the reservation than with keeping whites off, and it had done little to make the reserves into hospitable homes. "I gave up [my lands] and moved and came here on this reservation," grumbled the Cayuse headman Howlishwampo. "I have been here 11 years and all that [Governor Stevens] promised I have not seen. I think it must be lost." Given the circumstances, mid-Columbia Indians had little faith in the "Great Father" and little incentive to make the reservation a permanent residence.

Even so, the passion with which tribal representatives defended their reservations demonstrated that some Indians had already come to value them as homelands. Faced with the prospect of removal to Fort Simcoe in 1876, the leading men of Warm Springs repeatedly stressed their attachment to the place set aside for them. "We gave up our country on the Columbia for this, and now that we have it we want to keep it," argued Tosymph of the Warm Springs people. "We were told that it was ours and no one should take it away from us." The Indians on the Umatilla and Yakama reservations expressed similar sentiments during their councils with Inspector Brunot. "I do not wish to sell any land or throw it away, as long as I live I will not sell it," declared Pierre (Meaniteat), an Umatilla treaty signer favored by the government. "[M]y heart will always be the same. That is all I want written. I am Indian." Howlishwampo of the Cayuses confirmed this sense of attachment to a clearly bounded Native space: "I am holding on to my land that I am living on. The country that is marked out for us we see with our hearts and with our eyes. . . . The land that we have here we hold with our bodies and our souls." Reservation Indians had planted crops and built homes. They had shed blood defending those homes against the "Snakes." They had buried their dead in reservation ground. Boundaries now mattered to these people, even if they frequently crossed them for economic and social reasons. They did not want the lines erased.

Differing attitudes toward the reservation gradually created divisions between residents and renegades. Fearful of losing their homes, some agency Indians criticized their kin for refusing to settle down on the lands set aside for them. Their continued presence on the public domain riled the settlers, making it harder to defend the reservations against claims that the Indians had broken the treaties or had kept too much land for themselves. Furthermore, reservation residents often shouldered the blame and suffered the consequences for problems caused by Columbia River Indians. "If the people were all good, white men would not trouble us," lamented White Swan (Joe Stwire), the head chief of the Yakama Nation. "Some of my people are wild and get into trouble with the whites. I am ashamed of them, because they are my people." An Indian named Frank, evidently feeling ashamed himself, confessed his sinful ways to inspector Brunot:

> I lived long ago at [Fort] Simcoe. My heart was, as it were, asleep. I used to hear good talk while I lived here. I was like a good man. Mr. Wilbur gave me good advice and I took it. Now it is like as if I had thrown away good things. I went away; I went away among those who did all that was wrong. My heart was sick. . . . When I see the white men, they are my friends. I don't steal white men's cattle. I don't want to steal; I want to do well, to farm; but I am away by myself among bad people.

Brunot obligingly pointed the way to salvation. To keep the reservations, he warned, "you must tell the absent [people] what is good, and get them to do what the President wants all to do. . . . You can make it sure that you will always live here by cultivating the land and getting others of your tribes to do so."

Tribal leaders tried to fulfill this mandate. Through formal requests and personal appeals, the residents of Warm Springs repeatedly urged the people at Celilo Falls "to come upon this reservation, take up land and make homes," but to no avail. After settling down himself, the former renegade Queahpahmah intervened to secure Hehaney's release from jail and return to the agency. Expressing regret at having "worked against the good" in the past, Queahpahmah assured agent Smith that Hehaney "will be a good man after he sees all the Indians are gathered up, for he will have no place to go, except here. If he comes back, we agree to see that he carries out his promises." Hehaney disagreed and soon embarrassed his former friend by bolting from the reservation. In 1883, he and five other Columbia River Indian headmen received a visit from Stick Joe, a Klickitat emissary sent to encourage their removal to Fort Simcoe. Acting on the orders of agent Milroy, "Joe suggested to them that it would be much better for them all to come to the Reservation, and locate themselves there." They preferred to remain on the river, near the fisheries and the graves of their ancestors, and Milroy's antics merely hardened their resolve. In 1885, during the showdown with his Indian police, the renegade chiefs vowed that they would never willingly go to the reservation. To do so, they believed, would compromise their very identity as Indians.

In contrast to Pierre, the Umatilla chief who insisted "I am Indian," renegades equated the reservations with assimilation and "whiteness." At first glance, this assessment seems correct, for many agency residents favored acculturation and celebrated the progress they had made since signing the treaties. "We know the President assigned us this country," stated Thomas Pearn, a Native preacher at Fort Simcoe. "We did as the agent said, and we received an education. I am a man. I have a new heart. The old heart we received from our fathers has passed away." "I believe we are prospering and advancing," agreed the Wasco headman Billy Chinook. "I would not for anything go back to what we were." In the same breath, however, he reiterated his tribe's commitment to retaining the reservation: "This is our home and it is as dear to us as anyone's home can be to them." The strength of this commitment confounded the OIA, which regarded the reservations as temporary nurseries of civilization. As soon as Native people outgrew their "Indian" traits and adopted those of the whites, the nurseries would be closed. Most reservation residents saw the future quite differently. In the words of Wenapsnoot, an Umatilla treaty signer, "I think now that we will raise our children together, we on the reservation and you outside."

Even when agency Indians spoke of becoming "like the whites," they did not necessarily intend to remove all the barriers separating them from American society. They wished to "improve" themselves, to achieve equality with whites, but they wished to do so in their own place. Sianooes, the head chief of the Wascos, articulated this position in an appeal to President Ulysses S. Grant:

> We are not going to abandon this reservation. It is first and last our home. We want farming utensils and we want schools and also a man to teach us in spiritual things. Then we want a good saw mill and cattle and sheep that we may manufacture to supply some of our necessities. I want you to be a safe shelter for my people on which they can rely for assistance. If you will give my people these things I will see that they improve them and we will be ready to listen to your instructions.

By following instructions and proving their good faith, Sianoose believed, his people would earn the right to remain at Warm Springs. They wanted to stay inside the lines, separate from American citizens, because they still considered themselves Indians.

Renegades wanted to stay outside the lines for the very same reason. As centers of federal power and control, reservations embodied the assault on Native culture and identity. Indian police and jails, Christian missionaries and churches, teachers and schools, agricultural instructors and farms—all of these things—placed reservation life in opposition to traditional "Indianness." Therefore, despite continuing interaction and intermarriage, many non-reservation Natives began to see themselves as more authentically Indian than reservation residents. "[Their leaders] profess to look with contempt on the reservation Indians, calling them whites and half-breeds," observed agent Cornoyer. "By thus appealing to the passions and pride of the Indians, they hold a control, not only on those living on the Columbia River, but on large numbers who reside upon the several reservations." Hoping to draw the John Day Indians away from Warm Springs, Hehaney derided his erstwhile ally Queahpahmah "for having given up his plurality of wives and Smohalla religion, telling him he might as well give up his food." Real Indians, he implied, subsisted on fish and the natural products of the earth; only white men lived by cultivation of the soil. Such criticism shows that Natives and agents alike made inflexible distinctions between "progressives" and "traditionals," between "civilized" reservation residents and "wild" renegades. While each group placed different values on these labels, both used them to define their identities and to shape their relationships with the federal government.

Stark contrasts made between renegades and residents concealed significant differences within each group. Among reservation Indians, in particular, varying degrees of acculturation generated friction along ethnic and religious lines. At Warm Springs, Wascos and Wishrams generally lived nearest the agency and expressed the greatest interest in learning white ways. Some became devout Christians and looked down on the "heathen" Sahaptins, who kept to the northern portion of the reservation and showed little inclination to farm or build homes. The Wascos opposed Hehaney's return in 1879, whereas the "Warm Springs" welcomed him with open arms. Meanwhile, on the Yakama reservation, Methodists and Catholics clashed with one another and with the traditionalist "Drummers and Dreamers." "This does not give us good hearts," explained George Paul, a Klickitat member of the Methodist congregation. "We do not all agree, and come to get good advice. . . . We would like the others to be separated from us, and those that are left would be as one." Similar splits developed on the Umatilla Reservation, where agent Cornoyer supported Catholic Indians against those who had joined Protestant churches or remained faithful to indigenous spirituality. Thanks to the early missionaries and the "Peace Policy" of the 1870s, which assigned each agency to a different denomination, Plateau Indians had learned to fight about God. Even though their agents often described them as a single group, reservation residents rarely displayed such harmony or homogeneity in their behavior.

Religion provided the ideological underpinning for renegade resistance and an incipient Columbia River Indian identity. Whereas many reservation residents had converted to Christianity, most non-reservation Indians followed the nativistic teachings of Smohalla and other "dreamer-prophets." Born around 1815 in a Wanapam village on the Columbia River, "the Priest" rose to prominence during the 1850s at the head of a powerful religious revitalization movement. His creed, called *waasaní* (Waashani, meaning "dancers" or "worship"), mingled indigenous spirituality with Christian concepts but explicitly renounced Euro-American culture. Claiming to have died twice and returned with instructions from the Creator, Smohalla declared that Indians must stop tilling the soil or face divine retribution. The Creator would reward obedience to this creed with world renewal. If Indians faithfully performed the *wáashat* (Washat, "dance"), the whites would die off or disappear, deceased relatives would return to life, and the land would revert to its pristine state. In the meantime, Smohalla declared, Indians must cast off white ways, reject the reservation system, and seek wisdom in dreams. Although he also preached nonviolence, his religion gave spiritual sanction to the defiance of federal authority.

To the government's dismay, the revitalized Waashani or "Dreamer" faith spread far beyond Smohalla's winter village at Priest Rapids. His vision appealed to Indian communities reeling from the impact of Euro-American diseases and settlement, and a host of disciples carried his creed up and down the Columbia River. Though some modified Waashani symbols and ceremonies, all retained the basic belief that Indians must remain free of white influences and return to traditional ways. "Their model of a man is an Indian," cursed one exasperated official. "They aspire to be Indian and nothing else." Accordingly, many Dreamers stayed off the reservations. The Umatilla prophets Wilatsi and Luls attracted followers to their camps along McKay Creek, near Pendleton. Another Umatilla Dreamer, Waltsac, roamed with Hehaney between the John Day River and Priest Rapids. Skamia held services near The Dalles and reputedly foretold the construction of the dam that would drown the fisheries and villages there. He ranked alongside Lishwailait, a Klickitat based on the White Salmon River, as one of Smohalla's greatest contemporaries and one of the OIA's principal nemeses. Together, these and other dreamer-prophets posed a significant challenge to the reservation policy.

Agents and missionaries, acting in concert with sympathetic Christian Natives, responded with a crusade to crush the Waashani faith. At the behest of Presbyterian Wascos, soldiers ordered Queahpahmah to stop performing the Washat ceremony. When he refused, they tossed his drum into the fire, then dragged him from a horse and threw him into jail. He continued to sing, even after they cut off one of his braids. Several years later, Homli complained that agent Cornoyer and the Roman Catholics at Umatilla persecuted his followers, "which makes their hearts sore, [and they] cannot stay on the reservation if they are not left alone, and allowed to worship God in their own way." Queahpahmah's traumatic experience clearly influenced his decision to leave Warm Springs in 1870. Fifteen years later, numerous Yakama families abandoned their reservation farms after agent Milroy clapped Kotiakan in irons and imprisoned him at hard labor for six weeks. "Runners have been going throughout the outlying country, and the Indians [are] generally very much excited," cautioned Captain James MacMurray. "Many advocate armed resistance and attack on the Klickitats who live near the agency and constitute the Indian police force." Far from suppressing the Waashani faith, coercion merely drove it underground or off the reservation, while also driving wedges between Columbia River Indians and their Christian kin.

The exodus of Dreamers to off-reservation sanctuaries confirmed fears that Smohalla and his disciples actively lured Indians away from the agencies. According to agent Cornoyer, the Priest "[had] emissaries constantly visiting the different reservations, corrupting the minds of the well-behaved and peaceable Indians and endeavoring to induce them to leave and go with him." Other dreamer-prophets followed his lead and aggressively proselytized their reservation relatives, thereby providing convenient scapegoats that beleaguered agents could blame for their troubles. "Until these Indians are placed under proper control," Cornoyer declared, "there will be no material improvement among the several reservations in eastern Oregon and Washington." Agent Smith concurred: "There should be something done to rid the community of this nuisance and the agents of the annoyance of having such a class [of Indians] in so close proximity to his own people, for the influences that come from there are all bad."

Frustrated with the limited reach of their authority, agents constantly urged the mobilization of military power to push renegades inside the lines. "It is useless to persuade this class of Indians to remove to reservations," snarled Cornoyer. "It has been tried again and again to no avail. The only way in my estimation to deal with them is to remove the principal medicine-men from their midst and compel the others to go on reservations and keep them there by force, if necessary, until they learn obedience." Inspector William Vandever, a former soldier himself, recommended giving the Columbia River Indians a choice between exile on the Colville reservation or banishment to the Indian Territory. The military district of the Columbia, however, rarely countenanced such drastic action except in times of war. The renegades remained peaceful enough, and their lands undesirable enough, that the Army saw little reason to incur the trouble and expense of rounding them up. Witness the sentiments of Colonel Charles Grover, the commanding officer at Fort Walla Walla:

> [T]hey are not in fact Reservation Indians, and never have been. They are a quiet peaceable people and have as good a natural right to their own homes as anybody else, and if they are unceremoniously expelled from them, it will probably result in an unnecessary and costly Indian War.

Even if the U.S. Army managed to remove them without provoking armed resistance, the Indians would not stay put unless constantly policed. Reservation boundaries remained too porous and other priorities too pressing. Hence, by the early 1880s, military officers had become leading advocates of allowing non-reservation Natives to select homesteads on the public domain.

Without firing a shot, Hehaney and his fellow Columbia River Indians had escaped the fate of more famous renegades such as Chief Joseph, Crazy Horse, and Geronimo. But they had also earned the lasting enmity of the OIA. No longer a neutral geographic designation, the term "Columbia River Indian" now connoted a negative attitude toward federal policy and the whole idea of "civilization." Agents stopped short of calling these people a tribe but described them as "a class, who were at heart hostile—refusing to live on the Reservation or to recognize the authority of the Agent, and rejecting all efforts to conciliate them." "All the small bands of Columbia River Indians are worthless vagabonds," fumed agent Cornoyer, "roaming from place to place, drinking, gambling, stealing horses, [etc.]." This poor reputation persisted for decades, coloring the renegades' relationship with federal officials and tribal authorities alike. Yet, non-reservation Natives took pride in their defiance, and many eventually adopted the label Columbia River Indian as an alternative tribal identity.

This identity emerged slowly and incompletely between 1860 and 1885. Aboriginal affiliations persisted both on and off the reservations, and most renegades did not yet call themselves Columbia River Indians. In fact, many identified with one or more of the confederated tribes and integrated the reservations into their seasonal round. Native identities remained complex and multifaceted. In the context of federal-tribal relations, a question about tribal membership could elicit the response, "I'm a Yakama," meaning an enrolled member of the Yakama

Nation. When speaking to another Indian, the same person might identify himself/herself by an aboriginal name such as "Wayam." The U.S. government merely added another dimension with the creation of a separate category for Columbia River Indians. Anxious to distinguish them from reservation residents, agents gave mid-Columbia renegades a group designation that underscored both their opposition to federal policy and their attachment to a particular place. This "label, like many tribal names devised by the government, suggested a level of organization and unity that did not exist at the time. However, for Natives who already called themselves *wana-hláma*, "people of the river," the term Columbia River Indian provided a natural fit.

Like the great river itself, depositing fresh layers of sediment on its bed, the passage of time added new layers to an evolving Columbia River Indian identity. From the 1880s to the 1920s, many non-reservation Natives secured land on the public domain through the Indian homestead laws and the Dawes Act. Intended to assimilate Native people into mainstream society, off reservation allotments and homesteads instead served an ironic and unexpected purpose. Shielded from the harsh winds of Americanization that buffeted reservation communities, Columbia River Indians retained much of their language and traditional culture, thereby reinforcing the belief that they were more "Indian" than their reservation kin. Isolation fostered a sense of independence and self-sufficiency, yet, government neglect also accentuated feelings of resentment towards the OIA and reservation residents. These contradictory sentiments added to the confusion created by shifting administrative jurisdictions and crisscrossing ties to the confederated tribes. Passed from agency to agency, non-reservation Natives began to feel that neither the Bureau of Indian Affairs (BIA) nor the tribal councils adequately represented their interests.

By the mid-twentieth century, many of these people had adopted the title of Columbia River Indian. Even as various push-pull forces compelled them to enroll in one of the confederated tribes, they retained a strong sense of difference. In 1942, Willie John Culpus, a member of the Yakama Nation, proudly informed federal officials that "he [did] not consider himself a true Yakima Indian even though his father and mother took allotments for themselves and himself on the Yakima Reservation . . . he follows the customs of the Columbia River Indian people." Echoing Culpus, traditional chiefs Tommy Thompson and William Yallup complained that "reservation Indians" had overrun the River People's fishing stations at Celilo Falls. Tensions between river-dwelling "home folk" and reservation "comers" mounted as salmon runs dwindled and dams caused the fisheries to become inundated. By the 1960s, treaty fishing rights had become the central marker of Columbia River Indian identity. While River People played a leading role in the struggle for those rights, the defiant stance of David Sohappy, Sr., and his supporters brought them into conflict with tribal governments. The Columbia River Indians became renegades once again, and many invoked that heritage in defending their right to fish free from state and tribal regulation.

Today, these people are generally proud members of their respective nations but retain strong roots on the river. As Yakama tribal member Mike George declared in 1993, "I prefer to call myself a Columbia River Indian. There were Indians that never wanted to go on the reservation, and we're some of them."

Suggested Reading

Few people outside of the Pacific Northwest even recognize the names of the major tribes in that region. Nevertheless, these tribes have received steadily increasing attention from scholars. Probably the best single study to examine the issues raised by this essay is Alexandra Harmon, *Indians in the Making: Ethnic Relations and Indian Identities around Puget Sound* (Berkeley: University of California Press, 1998). For an examination of how tribes in the area used religion to express their identity, see Robert H. Ruby and John H. Brown, *Dreamer-Prophets of the Columbia Plateau: Smohalla and Skolaskin* (Norman: University of Oklahoma Press, 1989). For an example of the single tribal histories for Northwestern tribes, see John Fahey, *The Kalispel Indians* (Norman: University of Oklahoma Press, 1986).

CHAPTER THIRTEEN

Turning the Tables on Assimilation

Oglala Lakotas and the Pine Ridge Day Schools, 1889–1920

THOMAS G. ANDREWS

Throughout American history, schools, churches, and farms have been the bases of nearly all government programs that attempted to bring Indians into American society. Based on the idea that Native people could and should be brought up to the level of other Americans, federal programs and social reformers alike assumed that education remained central and essential to achieving this goal. Once tribal people had been pushed onto reservations in the late nineteenth century, employees of the Office of Indian Affairs launched a full-fledged effort to assimilate their charges. Most scholars have examined the national system of boarding schools and how they operated. This essay looks at the local reservation day schools that dealt mostly with younger children.

The author analyzes the goals of reservation school teachers and how they were implemented. He also considers the tactics Indian children and their families developed to benefit from what the schools offered. While they objected to forced name, clothing and hair style changes, the Lakota sought to acquire particular skills from the schools to improve their lives while achieving their own goals, rather than those of the white man.

Ambitious, numerous, and controversial, boarding schools comprised the primary front in the federal government's campaign to assimilate Indian children into the American mainstream. Yet all too often, popular memory and historical scholarship alike have isolated residential schools from the larger educational context in which they operated. Boarding schools represented the largest and

Copyright by the Western History Association. Reprinted by permission. The article first appeared as "Turning the Tables on Assimilation: Oglala Lakotas and the Pine Ridge Day Schools, 1889–1920," *Western Historical Quarterly* 33, no. 4 (Winter 2002): 407–430.

most heavily publicized component of the government Indian school system, but they hardly comprised the sum total of government efforts to educate Native American children. Federal officials built more than a hundred day schools throughout the Indian reservations of the American West in the late nineteenth century. Moreover, in regulations first promulgated in 1894 and frequently reinforced in the following three decades, the Office of Indian Affairs carved out a crucial niche for day schools in the federal Indian education system. According to these rules, Indian children were to begin their formal education at local day schools, progress to reservation boarding schools around the age of ten, and leave their tribal homelands for further schooling only after they had exhausted their reservation's educational resources, usually around the age of sixteen. The scheme proved difficult to implement on many reservations; nonetheless, roughly 15–20 percent of the Indian children attending school in any given year between the late 1880s and the 1920s received their education not at residential institutions, but at local day schools. Just as importantly, at least as many more children likely arrived at boarding school only after years of day schooling.

Despite the appearance in recent years of dozens of fine monographs and articles on Indian education, the story of these important institutions nonetheless remains practically untold.

The history of the most extensive system of Indian day schools in the nation—the thirty or so little schoolhouses of southwestern South Dakota's Pine Ridge reservation—thus promises to provide an illuminating counterpoint to the better-known tale of deculturation, abuse, and resistance at residential institutions during the assimilation era. In this essay, I explore the important, but heretofore overlooked, story of the cultural contests that occurred at federal day schools on the homeland of the Oglala Lakota. I begin by examining the ideological lenses through which policymakers, teachers, and Oglalas conceptualized day schools. Then, I analyze how these agendas shaped academic instruction, manual training, and community work. In contrast to the fundamentally authoritarian nature of power at boarding schools, I find more dispersed power relations at play in the day schools. Neither policymakers, teachers, nor Oglalas could ever fully exercise their will upon each other. Thus, day schools became important sites of cultural contact and negotiation where Oglala people struggled to subvert and resist the federal project of destroying their culture and changing their life ways. Government officials envisioned day schools as weapons in their war against tribalism. The story of the Pine Ridge day schools, though, demonstrates that Oglalas managed to blunt the blow of assimilationist education. Moreover, it suggests how the people of Pine Ridge turned the tables on federal policy, refashioning day schools designed to eviscerate their culture into tools of individual and collective survival.

The day schools of Pine Ridge educated more Oglalas than any other component of the Indian school system. In many ways, these schools resembled little red school-houses elsewhere in rural America. Blackboards and portraits of

Washington and Lincoln graced the walls. Desks stood in neat rows. Windows offered distraction. Children of many ages crowded into single classrooms to recite readings from primers, master new lessons, play, and fight. Teachers maintained order, delighted at students' progress, and frowned upon their failings. But, in other ways, the Pine Ridge day schools represented another world altogether, because the men and women who created them endowed them with a singular purpose: to transform Indian children into Americans. Moreover, teachers at Indian day schools wrestled with unusual challenges. Finally, the Indian objects of the government's designs had notions of their own about schools and the role they could play in the tribe's future. Before we can understand what happened in the Pine Ridge day schools, then, we need to examine the varied and often conflicting agendas government bureaucrats, teachers, and Oglalas brought to the reservation's schoolhouses.

Literally and figuratively, policymakers, bureaucrats, and philanthropists were the architects of the day school system. They drafted plans for the schools, hired contractors to construct the buildings and instructors to teach in them, and supervised operations. A sense of mission guided them in all these arenas. An enlightened federal government, they believed, had to save Indians from extinction by dissolving tribal cultures and incorporating Indian individuals into the American nation. As Commissioner of Indian Affairs T. J. Morgan argued in 1889, the government had to liberate Indians from the ancient lifeways that would doom them "either to destruction or to hopeless degradation."

Allotment and education comprised dual fronts in this campaign to save individuals by destroying tribalism. Assimilationists intended the Dawes Act of 1887 to dismantle Indian patterns of communal land ownership in order to create a yeoman class tilling privately-owned lands. Removed from damaging tribal ties, made to embrace the plow instead of the gun, and rescued from dependence on government aid, individual Indians would become self-sufficient agriculturists, archetypal Jeffersonian citizens invigorating the nation instead of profligate wards enfeebling it.

Allotment would help assimilate Indians into the nation's economy and polity, while education would teach them how to speak, think, and work like other Americans. From the founding of the first Indian schools in the 1600s, Indian education lay within the bailiwick of Christian missionaries, but after the Civil War, the federal government increasingly assumed responsibility for educating Native children. In treaties signed with the Oglala and other Indian nations, the federal government promised to build schools for Indian children. These schools sought, as Morgan phrased it, "the disintegration of the tribes" and the instruction of Indian students "not as Indians, but as Americans."

The assault on tribalism began with moral training to inculcate mainstream American values, particularly Protestant Christianity, Anglo-Saxon civility, and republican virtue. Morgan urged that the whole course of study for the schools "should be fairly saturated with moral ideas, fear of God, and respect for the rights of others; love of truth and fidelity of duty; personal purity, philanthropy and patriotism." Moral training would teach students to respect the superiority of America's belief system and to disparage the hopeless primitivism of Indian cultures, supplanting the cultural norms of the tribe with those of the nation.

The academic portion of Indian instruction, meanwhile, focused on replacing supposedly doomed Native languages with English, the cornerstone of Anglo-Saxon civilization and the *lingua franca* of the American Melting Pot. To Richard Henry Pratt, founder of Carlisle Indian School and one of the most influential educators of the era, language constituted the "first great barrier to be thrown down in all work of assimilating and unifying our diverse population." Before students could progress to arithmetic, geography, history, or other subjects, they would first need to master English. The attack upon Native languages in Indian schools had broad cultural repercussions, for these languages were the creations and representations of Native epistemologies: they were the symbolic forms Indians used to conceptualize and communicate their ideas of the physical, social, and spiritual realms. By eradicating Indian languages, reformers hoped, they could begin to unravel what they considered the destructive bonds of culture that shackled Indian individuals to savage and doomed ways of life.

Equipped morally and linguistically to take their place in the mainstream of American society, Indian students were now ready, as Pratt put it, to be "wrought into shape and then sent to work on the great ocean of . . . industry and thrift." Eastern reformers and government officials alike argued that manual training would impart skills Indians would need to support themselves. Though Indian schools provided instruction in traditional trades as well as modern industrial occupations such as printing and machining, agriculture formed the core of the manual training curriculum. "The Indians' capital is very largely land," proclaimed Commissioner of Indian Affairs Francis Leupp, "and their environment and every natural circumstance make it peculiarly necessary that the great majority of them should become farmers and stock raisers." Yet the benefits of vocational instruction transcended mere economics. Superintendent of Indian Education W. Hailmann explained that so-called "industrial training" instilled "a keen sense of duty, self-control, persistence of will power, and all the other things that go to make up a strong, reliable character." Having acquired the virtues of honest industry, Indian scholars would graduate to positions as independent farmers or wage-earning laborers. In 1889, Treaty Commissioner William Warner advised the Oglalas that "the Great Spirit helps those who help themselves," and believed that if they followed his advice, Indians would stop draining the federal treasury, start producing wealth, and begin paying taxes.

The architects of assimilation were confident that this program of moral indoctrination, linguistic instruction, and manual training would turn Indians into Americans. Although assimilationists agreed on the message they wanted to impart, they argued strenuously about what medium would best convey "civilization" to the nation's Indian wards. Initially, most assimilationists felt that off-reservation boarding schools were best-suited for turning Indians into Americans. In the face of well-publicized reports that Indian boarding school graduates failed to flourish upon returning to their reservations, though, enthusiasm for off-reservation institutions began to wane by the early 1890s. Returned students had trouble conversing with relatives and neighbors who spoke only tribal languages, adjusting to tribal lifeways they had been taught to despise, and applying knowledge and skills learned in school to reservations blighted by poverty and underdevelopment. "Honest and truly," wrote one Sioux graduate, "I can't live among these Indians out here. Even I couldn't eat the food they cook." "I gave up trying to farm for myself," complained another, "for I didn't have the farm implements nor horses . . . [a] fellow can't get out and farm with nothing." As more returned students struggled to apply lessons imparted by Indian boarding schools, more educators began to sing the praises of on-reservation schools.

Reservation schools promised two benefits. First, reservation schools—particularly day schools—could accommodate more students for less money than off-reservation institutions. Secondly, reservation schools could spread the assimilationist gospel to entire Indian communities instead of reaching only the young. Off-reservation schools molded Indian children into American citizens much more quickly, Superintendent of Indian Education Daniel Dorchester admitted, but "simply educating a few pupils at the East" would do little to diffuse the "leaven of civilization" to "the dark haunts which we are most anxious to enlighten and transform." To destroy the tribe and assimilate the Indian, he argued, "the lever of uplift must be applied nearer to the base of Indian life—directly on the reservations." Dorchester and his allies believed that every reservation school would serve as a fulcrum for "lifting the whole reservations" to "avoid a large and irretrievable loss and furnish a ground of hope for the future of the Indian masses." Leupp later echoed Dorchester's argument. Residential institutions, he claimed, were "educational almshouses" that fostered dependence and laziness. Leupp advocated planting day schools on the reservations to "carry civilization to the Indian." Every school sown in Indian country would sprout into a "sphere of influence" that would indoctrinate Indian children in American ways and even "bring the older members of the race" into the national fold. From the day schools of the western reservations, the commissioner argued, "there should radiate into the Indian world all that is good and suitable for the Indians' advancement." Leupp, Dorchester, and their allies believed reservation schools would stretch tight federal dollars further and bridge the gap between school and reservation that returning students found so difficult to navigate.

Policymakers and reformers felt confident that academic, manual, and moral training in the Pine Ridge day schools would destroy the tribal bonds that held Oglala culture together and seamlessly transform Oglalas into Americans. Conceiving of Indian lifeways as time-trapped and monolithic, they assumed Lakotas would offer little resistance before capitulating and blending into the advancing tide of American progress. Subjected to the teachings of the most civilized and powerful nation in the world, how could the Oglalas fail to see the wisdom of abandoning their doomed ways of life and embracing the superior practices and beliefs America had to offer?

At each of the Pine Ridge day schools, the architects of assimilation entrusted a teacher and a housekeeper with educating the Oglalas. They preferred these emissaries of civilization to be white married couples, and they expected the men to teach and the women to keep house. Indian couples or pairs of white women ran a few schools, but most were headed by white couples from the states of the Old Northwest. A number of factors motivated couples to leave the comforts of home to teach on the reservation. Many "had come for a salary," claimed Luther Standing Bear. Others answered a humanitarian or missionary calling to guide the benighted Indians of the West towards the light of civilization. Though their motivations differed, most white teachers nonetheless shared the assimilationists' faith that the Oglalas' best chance in the future lay in English instruction, manual training, and moral indoctrination. But their assimilationist zeal soon evaporated as they discovered the isolation of their posts and their vulnerability as outsiders in Oglala settlements. In the cultural contests that pervaded the Pine Ridge day schools, white teachers could never forget that they were not on home ground.

Consider the story of Albert and Edith Kneale. In his 1950 memoir *Indian Agent*, Albert provides little sense of what led him and his wife to abandon a comfortable teaching post in upstate New York for the remote, hard living of Pine Ridge. The Indian Service held an exam in Rochester. Kneale took the test and a few months later accepted a teaching post on Pine Ridge. Never having ventured farther west than Buffalo, the young couple found the train ride to Pine Ridge "all new, all exciting, all most wonderful." As they encountered for the first time what Elaine Goodale Eastman eloquently termed the "strange, uncouth landscape" of the Great Plains, Albert noted in spare language how "the distances between towns and habitations" grew as the train traveled westward. "Trees and streams became more scarce. Fences disappeared. Occasionally we noted a strange structure of which we could make but little." At Rushville, Nebraska, the closest rail depot to the reservation, the Kneales disembarked and boarded a stage for the twenty-five mile drive to the agency through "utter desolation—no habitations, no trees . . . not a fence or stream." Frederick Jackson Turner famously declared that the American frontier had closed in 1890, but almost a decade later Pine Ridge remained a geographically and culturally isolated Oglala homeland, undeveloped and virtually unsettled by non-Natives.

Like most Anglo teachers, the Kneales had little or no personal experience with Native people. They were ecstatic when they reached the agency and got their first chance "to study at close range some of these wards of Uncle Sam," but the famous chief, Red Cloud, proved a disappointment. The Kneales expected Oglalas to act like the Indians they had encountered in captivity accounts, newspapers, and novels. "I had read Cooper's *Leatherstocking Tales*" lamented Kneale, "and had notions of how a chief should look." But Red Cloud "had none of these earmarks" and "looked much like the others." As Albert Kneale discovered, his preconceptions of Indians squared poorly with reservation reality.

The confused cultural encounters at the agency were but a prelude to the challenges that pervaded the Kneales' tenure at No. 10 Day School. Albert and Edith found their four-room cottage poorly built and sparsely furnished, while the shoddy school building next door contained a single room with windows on three sides. On the fourth wall hung a blackboard, a map of the United States, and a clock, which "served little purpose as there was seldom an opportunity to set it." The Kneales had crossed beyond the margins of an American society and economy inextricably dependent upon the minute division and measurement of time. "It was well nigh impossible to keep track of the days of the month," Albert lamented, "or even the week."

The isolation of their new post sank in even more deeply that afternoon when the Kneales' neighbors visited. Albert and Edith shook hands, looked around a roomful of Oglala faces, and smiled uncomfortably as their neighbors asked questions in a language they could not understand. The teachers became acutely aware of their status as the only white residents of a Lakota community. Like other Anglo teachers, they lived in isolation from other whites and depended on Oglala neighbors for assistance, companionship, and security. The architects of assimilation imagined that day schools would sow the seeds of civilization in the "dark haunts" of Indian Country, but day school teachers like Albert and Edith Kneale found themselves in no position to impose their worldview on their Indian neighbors. Teachers' weakness in the community counterbalanced their power in the classroom, while their success, as Albert Kneale discovered soon after arriving at No. 10, rested upon their ability and willingness to compromise.

One night, Kneale "was endeavoring to inveigle" an old Oglala man "into cutting his hair" to comply with American norms. After the teacher implored the Indian with every argument he could muster, the Oglala replied, "So it is not right for a man to wear his hair long?" Thinking the man had finally conceded his point, Kneale eagerly reaffirmed that men indeed should cut their hair short. But the teacher had stumbled into a trap the Oglala had sprung "with Socratic cleverness." Raising a finger to a portrait of Jesus upon the wall, the man asked mischievously "Whose picture is that?" Knowing he was "sunk," Kneale sullenly replied that it was Christ. "Well," replied the Indian, "Christ was a good man, so I have heard you say, and I note that he wore his hair long. I fear you are speaking lies, for either Christ was not a good man or else it is not wrong for a man to wear his hair long." Kneale could press the point no further, for his Lakota "vocabulary was not equal to the occasion." Not long after the incident, he and Edith "talked things over and decided we had better learn the Indian language." Tenacious and creative people who thrived on challenge, the Kneales stuck it out for three more years of such compromises and negotiations, but ultimately "the isolation was too great" and they transferred to a boarding school in Oklahoma. Most of their colleagues did not even last that long before the hardships of reservation life overwhelmed them. Like "Paph" Julian and his wife, many teachers "were not the least elated with" teaching on Pine Ridge, recalled Kneale. "The country itself frightened them, and the Indians terrorized them."

Though evidence is scarce, Oglalas clearly had their own ideas about education, and they invested schools like the one in which the Kneales taught with their own hopes and fears. The Oglala voices preserved in treaty minutes and letters to government officials express a shared belief that federal schools could provide the tribe's next generation with important skills that would protect the tribe's interests. Yet education, like most other thorny issues confronting the people of Pine Ridge during the reservation era, also exposed deep rifts within Oglala society.

Oglala children had attended federal schools for over a decade when a three-man commission arrived on Pine Ridge in the summer of 1889 seeking the tribe's consent to disband the Great Sioux Reservation. While many Lakota continued to harbor doubts about sending their children to school, Oglala leaders argued before the commission that children educated in American schools would serve as the tribe's best defense against the misunderstandings and errors of translation that had plagued the tribe in previous negotiations with the United States. High Wolf had "put [his] children out to different schools," but he knew "very well that they are not capable of doing any work for us yet." He wanted the commissioners to "wait until our children are advanced far enough and educated and return back home . . . and then we can speak about it and decide." White Cow Killer also saw Indian school graduates as protectors of tribal interests. He wanted to leave the crucial question of allotment "to the children that is [*sic*] off to school." The Oglalas, he claimed, had "lost a great deal and we are to blame for it, and I don't want to go ahead and lose anything more." These headmen may have simply been trying to delay unwelcome and divisive negotiations, yet their remarks indicate a sincere belief that schools would make young Oglalas conversant in English and familiarize them with American customs and culture. Thus trained, the next generation could counsel their people and pilot them through the shoals of the reservation era.

On an 1891 visit to Pine Ridge, Daniel Dorchester found "a great willingness" among "all classes of Indians . . . to have their children educated," and "even a demand for schools." But if Oglalas agreed that education would shield the tribe from further mistreatment, they disagreed bitterly over whether boarding or day schools would best meet the tribe's needs. Ho Flesh complained, "I don't care how many years those school-houses may be there and our children goes to school, they will never learn to read and write and talk English." Boarding school was the "only" place where his children could "learn anything." American Horse claimed that children learned more in four years of boarding school than in eight years of day school. He compared building day schools to "throwing money away for nothing."

While boarding school supporters stressed the superior education residential institutions provided, day school advocates emphasized the benefits of local schooling. "We can't send them here to this boarding-school," pleaded Little Wound at the 1889 negotiations. Because of the perils young children faced when they ran away from boarding school, he demanded "schools on the different creeks of the reservation." Oglalas such as Little Wound felt that day schools provided an antidote to the heartbreaking separation of parents and children that boarding entailed, not to mention immunity from the contagious diseases that brought many Oglala children home from distant institutions in caskets. As Red Cloud and Young Man Afraid of His Horses argued in an 1892 council with the Rosebud Sioux, their people did not want their children sent to schools in the East. "It does them more harm than good. The schools at the agencies are alright and they learn more."

Such disagreements over schooling reflected deeper conflicts between Oglalas about how best to cope with conquest and its legacies. American Horse and other so-called progressives felt that the Oglalas should change their ways and become more like other Americans. They advocated boarding schools because they wanted their children to learn the language, values, and technology of the dominant society as quickly as possible. "Traditionalists," on the other hand, tended to be cultural conservatives wary of sending their children away to be immersed in a foreign culture. Some tried to keep their children out of school altogether, but most preferred day schools. Compulsory attendance laws punished parents for keeping their children home. More importantly, many Oglalas realized the possibilities day schools provided. Not only did the little schoolhouses feed and clothe the impoverished people of Pine Ridge but they seemed to promise a middle path. By blending newly acquired skills from American culture with the influences of the family home and the Oglala community, many Oglalas hoped that day schools could give their children the best of both worlds.

Each fall when the school bells of Pine Ridge pealed out across the reservation, another cycle of negotiation began between the architects of assimilation, teachers, and Oglalas. Each brought their own hopes and fears to the day schools, and each tried to use the schools for their own purposes. Assimilationists divided the school day into three segments embodying their trinity of detribalization: morning academic instruction, afternoon industrial training, and evening moral edification and community work. They defined the shape of the school day, but they mostly left the daily operation of the schools to teachers. Teachers like the Kneales, meanwhile, felt like strangers within the borders of their own country, the sole white folks in communities where Lakota language and lifeways endured. The Oglalas, for their part, brought troubles of their own to the schools. They realized that education could safeguard their future, but it also threatened to further erode their cultural distinctiveness. Not everyone could have their way, and thus the school day became the venue for ongoing bargaining and subtle struggles.

Starting with two rituals that ushered in the school year, granting school names and remaking students' physical appearance, Oglala day school pupils learned to straddle two worlds: the schoolhouse community where they spent their mornings and afternoons and the Lakota community in which they spent their evenings and nights. Albert Kneale recalled how he excitedly prepared for the first day of school. He and Edith watched in their Sunday best as students arrived on horseback. After all the pupils had taken their seats, the New Yorker asked them to identify themselves. His repeated requests met with only blank stares and silence. Finally, Kneale "handed a paper and pencil to one of the larger boys and told him to write his name." The boy scribbled his name, then passed the paper on. After the sheet had traveled around the room, Kneale discovered that "[e]very child in the room, with the exception of the very smallest" had signed "his or her name in beautiful 'copybook' hand": Frank White Horse, Sarah Looks Twice, George Charging Bear, and others.

Kneale found the combination of Anglicized Lakota surnames with English Christian names intriguing, but he soon learned that these were just school names, "and no more than that." Kneale and his fellow teachers gave new names to Oglala children by compounding a popular American first name with a last name formed by Anglicizing the Lakota name of the child's father. Kneale claimed that children "were not known by these names to the Indians of the camp, nor even by their own parents." School names served as superficial markers of identity that most Oglala children left in the classroom at the end of the day. The ritual of naming, then, not only expressed the power teachers possessed; more importantly, it demonstrated how Oglala agency persistently circumscribed this power.

Names represented but the first form of Indian identity that day school teachers set out to change. After Kneale recorded the names he and his predecessor created, he began to transform the physical appearance of his pupils. The kids had been out of school for several months. The dust of summer covered their bodies, while lice riddled their long, unkempt hair. As Edith brought washtubs outside and told the girls to bathe, Albert handed clippers, shears, and combs to two of the "brightest-looking boys" and indicated that he wished them to go to work. When Kneale returned, he found the boys earnestly shearing other pupils' tresses. When one student pointed to the lice and nits infesting another child's hair, Kneale brought out kerosene and discovered to his delight that "the boys seemed to know what to do with" this common lice treatment. By the end of the day, Albert and Edith had made over the students at No. 10 to resemble poster children for the assimilationist cause: bodies scrubbed, scalps deloused, and hair cut to comply with the gendered norms of the dominant society. Like the famous before-and-after photos contrasting wild-haired braves in buckskins to immaculately groomed Victorians in starched collars and neat suits that Richard Henry Pratt used to illustrate the metamorphosis Carlisle Indian School effected, day school teachers sought to turn Oglalas into Americans by first making them look the part.

Though Kneale claimed that students acquiesced with these makeovers, his comments belie the trauma such physical transformations probably inflicted. Most Oglalas, for instance, considered long hair an important symbol of Indian masculinity, as Kneale learned in his Socratic dialogue with the old Indian not long after he arrived at No. 10. A few years later, the Oglala father Makes Enemy petitioned the commissioner of Indian affairs, asking permission for his son to wear long hair at school. "I have long since adopted the ways and customs of civilization in every particular," claimed the Oglala, "except that I have not yet cut off my hair." Makes Enemy did not understand why the way his son "[wore] his hair [would] have any thing to do with his learning, or living according to what they may teach at the school." Makes Enemy not only questioned the connection between physical appearance and education, but pointed out the hypocrisy of forcing Indian boys to wear their hair short. "I have been among the white people," he wrote, "and have seen that they are permitted to wear their hair as they choose, and have seen boys, and even men among the whites that wear their hair long. Cutting the hair does not make us Indians like they [*sic*] ways of the white man any better," concluded the defiant father, "and it does not keep us from being Indians."

Albert Kneale noted no rage or sadness as the boys' locks fell to the classroom floor, but perhaps his students shared Makes Enemy's view that short hair did not prevent them from "being Indians." Day school teachers imposed American names and American norms on their pupils, but these superficial modifications did little to alter what it meant to be Indian. From the first day of school, students became adept at adopting a dual identity. Externally, they took on school names, scrubbed skin, and short hair while internally resisting incursions into the deeper recesses of self-identity. The transformations day school teachers tried to enact at the beginning of the school year proved only skin deep.

Changing names and appearances proved but a prelude of things to come. Having renamed their pupils in the manner of American children and made them over to fit the part, teachers next endeavored to teach Oglala schoolchildren English and the manual skills they would need to succeed in the perilous currents of the American mainstream. Despite the designs of teachers and assimilationists, though, Oglalas managed to use morning classroom instruction and afternoon manual training in the day schools to navigate a route of their own.

The architects of assimilation devoted the morning academic program to teaching students English, but this often proved an agonizing process for the majority of Oglalas to whom it remained a foreign tongue. William Fire Thunder recalled that on his first day of school he knew exactly one word: "Yes"—one more word of English than any of his peers could speak! Like Calvin Jumping Bull, many students had only heard English spoken a few times before starting school, often by ranch hands or immigrant farmers who could not speak it "that well." Given students' lack of exposure to English, it took "[p]atient and laborious effort," to teach Oglala children the language, according to longtime day school teacher E. M. Keith. Having a sympathetic teacher helped. As his first year at No. 10 wore on, Kneale realized "that the children did understand a smattering of English." If he scorned or rushed them, they bit their tongues, but if he gave them time, "they could and would express themselves—however broken and faltering such expression might be." Pupils worried that they sounded silly, and teachers had to disarm these fears if they wanted their students to speak like Americans. Students always possessed considerable power—to refuse to articulate the English they already knew or to refuse to learn the language altogether. As Albert Kneale learned, most Lakota pupils could speak and understand English; "it just depended upon whether it was I that wanted something or *they.*"

The teacher-student dynamic changed significantly in classrooms led by Indians. Take the case of Clarence Three Stars, a voracious learner, superb teacher, and tireless advocate for his people whose remarkable teaching career spanned three decades. Though Three Stars began his formal schooling late and thus could not finish his studies at Carlisle, he compensated for his lack of training with boundless enthusiasm. "Always on the lookout for further advantages and improvement," he "always advised" other "returned students to subscribe for good papers and buy good books and read them over and over until they [had] acquired some knowledge." "Read! Read! Think! Think!," Three Stars exhorted, "and practice what you have learned, and add to it and be somebody! Be a man and stand your ground! Then you will be respected . . . by your friends and enemies." Improvement through education constituted Three Stars's "motto." Though a staunch advocate of learning about the wider world beyond the reservation, Three Stars championed the selective incorporation of those aspects of American culture that would ensure the Oglalas' individual and collective survival.

An accommodationist rather than an assimilationist, Three Stars performed a tightrope act throughout his twenty years of day school teaching. On the one hand, he had to convince his skeptical supervisors that an Oglala could succeed as a day school teacher. Early assimilationists emphasized the importance of training Indians to spread the gospel of civilization on their home reservations, but such sentiments foundered in the growing racism of the 1890s. To make matters worse, Pine Ridge officials enacted a general prohibition against Oglala teachers in 1896. "There is nothing of which I feel more certain," wrote the day school inspector, "than this[,] that Oglala teachers, full bloods, or nearly so, cannot make a success of Day School work." While Three Stars survived the inspector's purges to become the only Indian teacher on the reservation, the hostility of some agency personnel to Oglala instructors placed his job in constant jeopardy. In evaluations, reservation officials bemoaned that he "couldn't pass a civil service examination to save his neck" and backhandedly complemented him as "one of the most interesting of teachers, though taking it all around not the best." On the other hand, Three Stars felt compelled to use whatever methods he could to accomplish what he viewed as his most vital task: helping his students become proficient English speakers. In order to teach Oglalas to talk like Americans, however, Three Stars developed a uniquely Lakota approach, employing bilingual, bicultural techniques that contrasted radically with those of his non-Lakota colleagues. Instead of forcing English upon his students, Three Stars developed more nuanced techniques that drew from the local physical environment and traditional Lakota pedagogy. Given his tenuous position as an Oglala in the day school teaching corps, Three Stars risked his job by employing such methods, but supervisors could not quibble with his results. While other teachers had trouble getting beginning students to speak English at all, Three Stars had them "express[ing] themselves readily" in English before the onset of winter.

Three Stars believed that in order to learn English, students first had to learn how to connect objects with spoken words, then organize these words into narratives. He began by drawing stick figures on the blackboard to represent new vocabulary. Instead of deriving these words from the tales of cities and seashores that filled American primers, Three Stars taught words drawn from everyday life on Pine Ridge. Referring to a common teaching tool of the era, Three Stars admitted that it was "all right to have a sand table [similar to a sand box?] to describe and lay out invisible places and things that the pupils" had learned about from teachers and books, he conceded. He felt that it was much more effective pedagogy, though, to employ "the surroundings near the school and many many many real happenings occur daily." Teachers could use these objects and events "as original lessons in English." Students "could look out of the windows or go out and see the teams passing by" and make links between real objects and the words "hills, dam, bridge, cows, ditch, horses, chickens, garden, trees, etc." Three Stars believed Oglala children learned English more quickly when they could link words to their everyday experience. Students, he noted, seemed "to like more the real things than a table." Practical and relevant to reservation life, "real things" could move, collide, and interact to make stories on the ground and in students' minds.

Three Stars encouraged his pupils to craft stories out of new vocabulary words. "This is competition in talking," he explained, "it is comical sometimes how they wish to express themselves, they would try to imitate older pupils in language but I do not allow them, they must get the idea of thought themselves and express themselves, this, they do after a few lessons." Telling stories spurred pupils' imaginations and encouraged them to experiment with speaking English.

At the same time, making stories reinforced Oglala modes of thought in ways that helped students bridge Indian and American worlds. Once students had created a story, Three Stars asked them to illustrate it. Rose Catches, a former student of Three Stars, remembered: "If we had something in our mind, the meaning of the thoughts we had, we draw it on the paper. So we don't just scratch on the paper." In encouraging his students to read and write through drawings, Three Stars drew upon a long tradition of Oglala pictorial representation.

For centuries, each Oglala band had designated an artist/historian who recorded important events in tribal life by painting or drawing on hides, tipis, ledger sheets, and other media. "The picture," these men liked to say, "is the rope that ties memory solidly to the stake of truth." Though clearly inspired by Oglala traditions, Three Stars had students draw pictographic narratives in order to transcend language. Stories remained the same, after all, whether one used Lakota or English to narrate them. Three Stars staked his students' memories to a distinctly bicultural and bilingual "truth."

Three Stars incorporated other Lakota traditions into his teaching as well. Oglalas in the pre-reservation era used games to teach children hunting, housework, and other crucial skills. To help his students learn English, Three Stars altered the content of one such game, entitled The Bear and the Children, to provide continuity between past and present and smooth the gulf between the Lakota and English worlds. The game brought out "vividly to the childrens' [*sic*] minds that they would answer readily the questions: What do you see? *Taku wan-la-ka he?* What is this? *Le-taku-he?*" As in the pre-reservation days, such games taught children the skills they would need to cope in a difficult world. For Three Stars, speaking English had supplanted bison-hunting, hide-tanning, and Crow-fighting to become the new technology of survival.

White teachers tried to immerse their students in English. Three Stars, on the other hand, sought to build bridges between the Oglala and American tongues. Telling stories, drawing pictures, and playing games all helped students tie English to their own experience and make the language their own. Three Stars creatively drew upon the reservation environment and refashioned traditional pedagogical methods, but he also frequently taught in Lakota. "He gave us one day *wasicu* [English] lessons," Rose Catches remembered, "and the next day he turned around and he interpreted everything he teach us in *wasicu* way, in Indian." Three Stars "talked Indian" in the classroom and even taught the written Dakota language developed by American missionaries. He used "three kinds of books," Catches recalled. "One is drawing, one is Lakota language book. And one is *wasicu*." Three Stars designed remarkable teaching methods to prepare students for life in a dual society. In the home and tribal community, Lakota would remain dominant, but beyond Pine Ridge loomed another world that could no longer be ignored or wished away. Like the Oglala headmen who spoke at the 1889 negotiations, Three Stars saw speaking English as a critical weapon in the struggle against American encroachment.

Through his innovative teaching methods, Clarence Three Stars took English fluency, one of the central tenets of the assimilationist program, and recast it into a tool of Oglala survival. The architects of assimilation and most Anglo teachers envisioned linguistic instruction as a way to obliterate antiquated tribal languages and replace them with the keystone of Anglo-Saxon civilization. Three Stars, in contrast, and perhaps other Indian teachers, as well, imagined a bilingual future in which Lakota and English would coexist. They agreed that Oglala children needed to learn how to talk like Americans, but they turned assimilationist logic on its head: They emphasized English proficiency not because it allowed Indian children to be incorporated into the American mainstream, but because it gave them the strength to remain apart and persist as Oglalas in a nation controlled by whites. The school bell did not have to be the death knell of Oglala culture.

Few Anglo teachers could muster the energy, creativity, or dedication of Clarence Three Stars, nor could they have run a bilingual, bicultural classroom. Like Albert Kneale, many undoubtedly found the morning sessions frustrating, for "there seemed to be nothing gained through knowing that 'c-a-t' spells cat; arithmetic offered no attraction; not one was interested in knowing the name of the capital of New York, nor in the name of the stream into which the Missouri discharges its waters." At least the afternoons, Kneale consoled himself, "made up for" the humdrum mornings. Many pupils shared their teachers' relief at the end of the academic portion of the day, oral historian Jeanne Smith discovered. Outdoor chores provided "a break from the school routine, a chance to get outside, stretch their muscles and get away from the books for awhile." Calvin Jumping Bull explained that some students "really wanted to be out there because some of them were having a hard time with school."

Teachers and students alike craved a reprieve from the tensions and misunderstandings that pervaded day school mornings, but cultural contests often spilled over into the afternoon vocational lessons. The architects of assimilation included manual training in the Pine Ridge day school curriculum because they wanted to replace the nomadic hunting ways of the Lakotas with sedentary American agrarianism. But as in the remaking of student appearances and the teaching of English, Oglalas managed to selectively adapt only those aspects of the manual training curriculum that helped them meet the exigencies of reservation life. The case of school gardens suggests how the people of Pine Ridge picked and chose from what day schools had to offer, subverting assimilationist education and even recasting it into a means for cultural preservation.

Agriculture represented a central tenet of assimilation policy, yet environmental, economic, and cultural obstacles hampered teachers' efforts to convert Oglalas into farmers. Government parsimony denied schools the implements, draught animals, and seeds they needed to conduct agricultural programs. Student labor might have been plentiful, but the manual tasks necessary to support the school (cutting wood, cooking lunch, sewing clothes, and so forth) already consumed most pupils' afternoons. Moreover, Pine Ridge possessed poor soil and an extreme, unpredictable climate. Irrigation might have helped. Building dams and digging ditches required capital no Oglalas could muster, however, and federal water projects tended to benefit non-Indian farmers instead of tribal members. Most importantly, Oglalas knew farming would not work on their reservation, while the deep-seated prejudice of Oglala men that agriculture was an unmanly, un-Lakota pursuit compounded resistance.

Gardening, on the other hand, provoked no such qualms. The environmental constraints that crippled farming made gardening difficult, but the location of most reservation day schools near narrow, well-watered bottomlands easily accommodated small garden plots. Vegetables—particularly hardy root crops—fared much better in the harsh South Dakota climate than row crops like wheat and corn. Gardens required minimal capital, and though labor-intensive, schools could usually spare enough students to tend the plots. Most importantly, Oglalas embraced school gardens as fervently as they opposed farming. Their intimacy with the plains reassured them that produce could flourish in the fertile bottomlands along the reservation's creeks, while gardening seemed not to threaten their self-conception. And who could quibble with the results? Pupils, teachers, and parents alike eagerly anticipated harvest time. "When everything's good, nice and ripe," Rose Catches remembered, the Oglala community around No. 27 descended on the little school plot to help pick, clean, and can their share of the harvest. As the fruits of the day school gardens found their way into Oglala mouths via school lunches and home pantries, each crunch of carrot or bite of potato provided tangible, edible proof that the time and effort Oglala children put into the soil had been worthwhile. Gardens succeeded within the limits of the reservation environment and the bounds of Lakota identity. Just as importantly, they provided young Oglalas with a skill that supplemented and enlivened meager government rations. Inspired by the success of day school gardens, Oglalas soon started to raise vegetables of their own. So prolific had these plots become that a U.S. Department of the Interior official boasted in 1913 that "in the home of every child attending a day school at Pine Ridge Agency there is a garden of greater of [sic] less extent." Instead of American farmers, the children of Pine Ridge became Oglala gardeners.

When the day ended, the community of the schoolroom disbanded. Children buttoned their cumbersome government-issue coats, then melted back into the Oglala communities from which they had come. What had they learned that day, relatives might have asked. Not much, the children might have shrugged before enunciating a few English words and bragging about the seeds they had planted. As the days turned into weeks, months, and years, these small lessons accumulated, gained momentum, and rolled in surprising directions. The architects of assimilation expected that Indian children would abandon their ties to tribal cultures, learn to talk and work like Americans, and disappear into the mainstream. But this is not what happened on Pine Ridge. Instead, the people of the reservation engaged in an ongoing struggle to resist assimilationist schools and turn them into vehicles for cultural survival. Oglalas, they demonstrated, could talk and work like Americans without becoming American. In 1906, Makes Enemy had written that cutting the hair of Indian boys did not stop them from "being Indians." He could have said the same about speaking English or planting gardens. Knowing the language, Oglalas protected themselves against American encroachment. Growing their own food to supplement government rations, they ate better. Changing in small ways, the Oglala shielded themselves from the fundamental transformations assimilationists tried to enact.

After the pupils left, schoolhouses became, once again, two-person communities encircled by Lakota communities of hundreds. Though outnumbered and isolated, day school teachers nonetheless sought to meet assimilationist expectations by making their day schools "centers of usefulness" for the "advancement" of Lakotas young and old. Just as the Oglalas of Pine Ridge turned the tables on assimilationism within the school room, however, they adroitly blunted the cultural blow that assimilationists expected schools to administer during their evening community work. Instead of allowing the schoolhouses of the reservation to become the beacons of assimilation Leupp imagined radiating into every corner of the reservation, Oglalas transformed them into institutions that reinforced communal ties and eased the hardships of reservation life.

Day schools, for example, fortified bands or *tiyospaye,* helping these traditional band structures survive the transition to reservation life. Apart from the day schools at the agency, most schoolhouses stood in settlements of 100 to 300 Indians located along the creeks of Pine Ridge. Most of these communities developed when Oglalas slowly abandoned their nomadic ways to establish fixed communities with fellow band members. Kin ties remained so central in these settlements that Oglalas continued to call them simply *tiyospaye.* By keeping children within the *tiyospaye* instead of tearing them away, day schools strengthened the overlapping bonds of kinship and community. Rose Catches, for example, remembered that her mother told her to befriend her schoolmates, "but of course I knew most of them.... All these people along here used to be my relations from my mother's and my father's side." Rose found herself surrounded by cousins, "so we're all together all the time. Here, at home, or at school." Numerous interviews with Oglalas like Catches led Jeanne Smith to conclude that the day schools' compatibility "with traditional Oglala social organization" helped to make them "highly successful from a community standpoint."

Over time, the reservation's schoolhouses not only buttressed *tiyospaye* ties, they also became valuable community assets that Oglalas used to ameliorate the difficulties of reservation life. Day schools not only educated children, but fed, clothed, and cared for them as well. Adults benefited just as much. Many teachers kept their doors open after school, and Oglalas asked them for help without hesitation. As one instructor put it, Pine Ridge teachers possessed a "broad" job description, one that included the duties of "minister, farmer, gardener, cook, literary teacher, etc." Other teachers added "acting as nurse to sick Indians," "doing the janitor work," "trying to impress upon [the Indians] a higher standard of living," "home nursing, sanitation work," and "agricultural activities" to the list. Teaching on Pine Ridge, summarized another teacher, entailed an enormous amount of "general community work."

Oglalas pestered teachers constantly as they sought to employ day school instructors as cultural brokers who could help them make sense of the confusing complexities of the dominant society. A single doctor covered the entire reservation until the hiring of a second physician in 1906, and traditional healers were losing influence in the face of Euro-American diseases, so Oglalas often turned to teachers when *tiyospaye* members became ill. The local teacher, claimed E. C. Heckart, was "about the only friend the Indian has that he relys [*sic*] upon for help in sickness or other trouble." In the face of such virulent maladies as scrofula or tuberculosis, teachers could offer little but solace and comfort, but some did learn to treat broken bones, cuts, and colds, as well as to "administer simple remedies." American law and bureaucracy proved just as baffling as the diseases whites brought to Indian Country, and Oglalas frequently asked day school teachers for advice on topics ranging from settling estates to securing veterans' benefits. The people of Pine Ridge, in short, cultivated strategic alliances with day school teachers, relying upon them for help in their struggles with the medical, legal, and bureaucratic difficulties reservation life presented.

The architects of assimilation envisioned day schools as "spheres of influence" that would apply the "lever of uplift" to the "dark haunts" of Pine Ridge, but Oglalas had different plans. They did what they could to reshape day schools from agents of Americanization to bulwarks of Lakota community. Federal officials could craft blueprints for the Oglalas' future, but they could not keep the people of Pine Ridge from subvening these assimilationist designs and building histories of their own.

Why do Indian peoples and cultures, Indian lifeways and languages, Indian nations and worldviews survive and even thrive in the United States despite five centuries of deculturation, disease, and dispossession? No question is more central in understanding America's Native peoples and their complex histories. Yet given the number and diversity of Indian cultures, as well as the almost unfathomable variations in time, space, and culture that have shaped different pasts for different peoples, any attempt to address what Patricia Limerick has termed "the persistence of natives" in general or synthetic terms risks eliding more than it illuminates.

As scholars seek to solve this larger puzzle, the case of the Pine Ridge day schools provides small yet suggestive clues. In *Indian Agent,* day school teacher Albert Kneale tells a seemingly apocryphal tale that nonetheless provides an apt metaphor for the process of selective adaptation one important Indian group, the Oglalas of Pine Ridge, engaged in as they sought to rebuff American dominance. Approaching a tree-shrouded ford on Wounded Knee Creek with a new shotgun in hand and visions of roast duck in his mind, Kneale heard "a string of oaths that would do credit to the vocabulary of a seasoned mule skinner," the most notoriously foul-mouthed figure of the frontier. "Both surprised and interested," Kneale heard not the "broken, hesitating" English he usually heard in classroom and *tiyospaye,* but rather "clear and ringing and well enunciated" English. Convinced that no Oglala could speak the American tongue so adeptly, the young teacher wondered what could have brought a white man so far from home. But as he approached the crossing, Kneale discovered neither a mule skinner nor a wayward traveler, but rather an Indian whose stock had become mired in the mud.

Why did the young Indian speak such profane English so well? Having heard white men using the same language when their animals had foundered in a similar predicament, Kneale reasoned, the young Oglala must have figured "that these magical words added strength to the team." As he lashed his horses with whip and curses, then, the teacher thought the Oglala must have been deploying "the only English he knew" in order to free his horses from the creek's soggy grasp. Like most Oglalas, Kneale later discovered, the Indian "was familiar with every last bit of profanity to be found in the English language," though he "knew not another word of the tongue." The Oglalas had no idea what the foul words coming out of their mouths meant, Kneale claimed, yet they nonetheless "seemed to recognize the occasions that called for their use." In the vast majority of situations, Indians deployed the language they already had. Why say "horse" instead of "*tasunke*," or "white man" instead of "*wasicu*"? Sometimes, however, the occasion demanded something more, something different. So Oglalas made pragmatic additions to their vocabulary, incorporating into their lexicon the English expletives that Kneale delicately omitted from his account.

Whether the encounter Kneale relates ever occurred or not, the teacher's explanation of the incident nonetheless conveys a key insight about the Oglalas with whom Kneale worked and lived. In the period between the creation of the reservation and the wavering of assimilationist sentiment in the 1920s, the people of Pine Ridge acted not unlike the character in Albert Kneale's story. Like him, the Oglala children, parents, teachers, and community members who turned the tables on assimilationist education represented the continuation of an enduring theme in Oglala history: the integration of alien customs into Lakota lifeways. From embracing the horse and gun in the seventeenth and eighteenth centuries, to embarking on the great Teton migration westward in the eighteenth and nineteenth centuries, to adapting the day school curriculum to meet their own needs between 1889 and the 1920s, the Oglala people evinced a remarkable ability to incorporate new technologies and modes of thought. Indeed, this capacity had underpinned the tribe's survival for more than three turbulent centuries. In the end, then, the little schoolhouses that dotted the Pine Ridge Reservation presented what assimilationist educators might have called an object lesson: Not the lesson in detribalization and assimilation these architects of the day school system so earnestly desired, but rather a lesson in how native peoples have struggled to balance cultural change with cultural continuity in order to persist in the face of overwhelming odds, unconscionable violence, and heart-rending loss.

Suggested Reading

Scholars have focused primarily on late nineteenth-century boarding school Indian education so the reservation day schools have yet to receive a full account. Paul Robertson, *The Power of the Land: Identity, Ethnicity and Class Among the Oglala Sioux* (New York: Routledge, 2002), gives a broad analysis of events on the Sioux reservation. Frederick E. Hoxie, *Parading Through History, The Making of the Crow Nation in America, 1805–1935* (New York: Cambridge University Press, 1995), examines how another plains group dealt with similar issues. The most respected study of federal efforts to acculturate Native people through boarding schools is David Wallace Adams, *Education for Extinction: American Indians and the Boarding School Experience, 1875–1928* (Lawrence: University Press of Kansas, 1995). For an example of how individual boarding schools operated, see Tsianina Lomawaima, *They Called it Prairie Light: The Story of Chilocco Indian School* (Lincoln: University of Nebraska Press, 1994).

CHAPTER FOURTEEN

The Allotment Period on the Nez Perce Reservation

Encroachments, Obstacles, and Reactions

Elizabeth James

Throughout the nineteenth century American reformers thought that part of successful acculturation meant having Indians operate family farms. When it became clear that merely pushing the tribes onto reservations had failed to achieve that goal, Congress turned in 1887 to coercion and passed the General Allotment Act, also known as the Dawes Act. This legislation divided reservation lands into family farms and attempted to force individual families to take up the plow. Any "surplus" lands not assigned to Indians could then be sold to nearby whites for farming, ranching, or other businesses.

This essay shows how the Nez Perce tribe avoided some of the most destructive results of the policy because the person sent to oversee its implementation, Alice Fletcher, sought to enforce the regulations honestly. The author analyzes the efforts of local white farmers, area ranchers, and town residents to buy or lease Indian land during the years after allotment went into effect. Tribal members who actually tried to farm their own land faced difficult challenges. They lacked credit, the government provided too little equipment, seeds, or animals, and agriculture remained dependent on the ever unpredictable climate of the region.

The last years of the nineteenth century marked the beginning of a new era of Indian policy in the United States. Led by political and social reformers, the new philosophy sanctioned assimilation of Native Americans into the mainstream of Anglo-American society and culture. The General Allotment Act, passed by Congress in 1887, represented the crowning achievement for this group of re-

"The Allotment Period on the Nez Perce Reservation" appeared in *Idaho Yesterdays* 37, no. 1 (Spring 1993): 11–23. © 1993 Idaho State Historical Society.

formers. Also known as the Dawes Act or Severalty Act, it provided for the allotment of 160 acres of reservation lands to heads of households, and 80 acres per person to orphans and unmarried adults, who were enrolled members of Indian tribes. Remaining reservation lands would then be made available for Anglo agricultural settlement in tracts of not more than 160 acres.

A clear rationale lay behind the Dawes Act, which was to serve as a primary vehicle for assimilation. Proponents intended to transform Native Americans into Anglo-American farmers, changing not only their livelihood but their values and culture as well. Opening unallotted reservation lands to white settlement could, they believed, encourage the Indians toward that end as their new neighbors provided example and advice.

Like so many other plans to improve the lot of people, the provisions and intentions of the Severalty Act appeared at the time of its enactment to be both logical and possible. Instead the act worsened reservation conditions as many Native Americans began to feel cheated or discouraged. Many non-Indian people took advantage of opportunities created by changes in the Indian estate. Foremost among this group stood farmers and ranchers who generally cared little for the fate of Native Americans but coveted reservation lands.

Anthropologist Alice Fletcher contributed an active role in the drafting of and lobbying for passage of the Dawes Act. She believed that assimilation was the only hope for Native American survival and allotment was the best means of assimilation. Fletcher had previously spent some time with Native Americans and had allotted land on the Omaha and Winnebago reservations. With the change in federal policy, she held high hopes for the future of Native Americans. In 1889, she accepted a position as special agent in charge of allotment on the Nez Perce reservation in Idaho. When Fletcher arrived on May 28, she found a reservation surrounded by eager settlers, trespassers, and squatters.

Before and after the passage of the General Allotment Act, local newspapers avidly reported to residents in the nearby town of Lewiston the progress of the proposed policy and its implementation. Five years prior to the passage of the Dawes Act, the *Nez Perce News* had published an editorial recommending the use of the Nez Perce Reservation as an experiment in severalty and settlement—an arrangement that supposedly would benefit everyone concerned. When the government changed Indian policy as the paper urged, the Nez Perce could serve as a prototype of success in farming, education, and self-sufficiency. The editor's suggestion never materialized, but the coverage demonstrates Lewiston's early interest in the administration of reservation land.

Two days after Alice Fletcher's arrival in Idaho, the *Lewiston Teller* boldly announced: "Nez Perce Reservation to be Allotted at Once." The reports proclaimed the success of allotment on other reservations and praised Fletcher for her efficiency and reliability. The *Teller* predicted that the allotment process would be completed within fifteen months and expressed hope that Fletcher's efforts with the Nez Perce would result in the satisfaction of all concerned. No one could foresee the time and effort Alice Fletcher eventually expended in four tedious years of surveying land and tracing family relationships.

The *Lewiston Teller* most noticeably, but other newspapers such as the *Nez Perce News,* followed Fletcher's progress with care and reported every detail to the public. In November of 1891, another *Teller* headline proclaimed: "Nez Perce Reserve: It is Virtually Thrown open to Settlement and Cultivation." The newspaper reported that leasing could allow Anglos to farm land legally on the reservation and that thousands of acres would likely be available. In its continual advertising for more settlers, the paper also described Northwest Indian land as not only cheap but "far more desirable than the lands recently opened to settlement near Oklahoma." Concentrating on the amount of unallotted land, the newspaper illustrated the prevailing local attitude that Native Americans made no good use of the reservation: "the day is not far distant when actual settlers will be cultivating and rendering productive these broad acres so long locked up in the unused public domain." The *Teller* plainly reflected a significant amount of public interest in acquiring Nez Perce lands.

Another example of local attention took the form of an angry editorial written during or immediately after the negotiations for the sale of surplus lands. At first, enough Nez Perce objected to the cession of any land to block passage of an official agreement. The author referred to these Nez Perce leaders as "contemptable [*sic*] dogs" because they prevented the opening of the reservations to Anglo settlement. He claimed that "thousands of ready hands are now waiting for the privilege" of working Nez Perce lands. To gain the number of Nez Perce signatures needed, the editor advocated mass meetings that would force compliance. He then suggested that "a little rope" might be necessary to achieve their goal. If the editorial's tone indicated public sentiment, then settlers cared little for the concerns and desires of the Nez Perce. They believed that they had every legal and moral entitlement to reservation land.

Not satisfied to wait for the completed allotment process, local ranchers approached Alice Fletcher before she even entered the reservation. They demanded respect for their "rights" on the reservation. Fletcher's companion, Jane Gay, interpreted the situation as exactly what it represented, noting the cattlemen's ignorance of the intent of allotment. She wrote that they believed severalty "a skilful contrivance to disposess the aborigines and facilitate the opening up of their lands to squatter sovereignty." Fletcher defended the Nez Perce and her own integrity, patiently explaining to the cattlemen that her duty consisted of placing the Indians on the best lands. The Allotment Act was intended to benefit Native Americans, making them "self supporting and valuable citizens." Fletcher sometimes allowed people such as the cattlemen to believe that she possessed naive faculties. In this case she also did not discourage their assumption that because she was female, she therefore was apolitical and morally pure. Gay, who observed the whole proceeding, wrote that the men seemed baffled not only by Fletcher's words, but even more by the fact that a woman had spoken them. As they left, Gay overheard one grumble that a man would have been more easily intimidated.

While Fletcher did not let them intimidate her, the ranchers were equally determined to have their way. Other cattlemen approached her with the same intention and received the same polite response. The General Allotment Act authorized grazing lands to double the acreage of an allotment, and several people attempted to persuade Fletcher to give the Nez Perce less land by declaring it agricultural. If she did so, she increased the amount of land left over and therefore allowed more room for settlement. However, Alice Fletcher did not earn her exceptional position or fame through gullibility or ignorance. She knew only too well that thousands of non-Indian-owned cattle already grazed illegally on the reservation and prospective settlers surrounded the reservation in anticipation of its opening. Some had built houses inside the boundary, while other impatient squatters had already moved in to stake their claims.

Illegal entry on reservation lands was not new. Many cattle ranchers had simply ignored reservation boundaries and grazed their cattle on Nez Perce land throughout the later part of the nineteenth century. Agent George Norris first reported violations in his 1888 report. The year before, he had observed the reservation's excellent conditions for stock raising. He mentioned nothing of trespassing cattle, but he had held the office of agent for no more than a few weeks when he prepared the first report. By the time of his second report, the situation had become Norris' first order of business. Herds grazed freely on the reservation, and the settlers justified their use of the land by claiming the Nez Perce used none of it—and no fences existed to indicate that they did. The small reservation police force of five men could do little to remedy the situation. They patrolled 150 miles of boundary while remaining responsible for their other regular duties. They could drive trespassing stock off the reservation, but more often than not the same animals found their way back onto Nez Perce land. The crux of the matter, Norris noted, lay in the fact that local ranchers and farmers simply ignored the rights of the Nez Perce and the treaty obligations of the government to them.

Agent Warren Robbins also reported the presence of illegal stock in 1890. He conceded that they provided a "source of constant annoyance" but claimed "there are no great herds," only a few scattered about the reservation. A year previously, Jane Gay had dryly remarked: "We are told that there are approximately ten thousand head now eating the grass of the Indians." Robbins' next report expressed more concern over the matter. He complained that keeping trespassing cattle off the reservation constituted an impossible task. In 1890, Nez Perce–owned cattle totaled approximately 7,000 head. Few Nez Perce owned 100 or more head; the majority of stockmen raised small numbers of cattle. Statistics varied throughout the years, but at least as many Anglo-owned cattle grazed on the reservation as did Nez Perce–owned livestock.

Semiannual investigations by the Board of Indian Commissioners presented a more precise view of trespassing cattle. The earliest report of boundary violations came in 1884, from inspector W. A. Newell. He relayed complaints from the Nez Perce that not only did cattle invade their land, they lost approximately 500 head themselves when their own cattle wandered off the reservation and were branded by Anglo ranchers. Other complaints reached the Secretary of the Interior in 1887, and finally in 1889 inspector T. D. Marcum conducted an inquiry into the matter. Two men stood in the center of the controversy: Indian agent Charles Monteith and W. A. Caldwell. Other names surfaced in the testimony, but these two appeared repeatedly.

Caldwell had lived on the reservation since 1865, operating a mail station and raising stock. Other agency employees, such as blacksmith Thomas Barton, admitted to running cattle illegally on Nez Perce land with or without various agents' knowledge but claimed they were never ordered to stop. Several witnesses named Caldwell specifically as the most flagrant offender. Charles Fairfield, a reservation farmer, charged Monteith with having a financial interest in Caldwell's cattle business. Monteith and Caldwell denied the allegation, and it was never proven. Fairfield estimated Caldwell's herd at 500 to 600 cattle, but Caldwell claimed to have averaged only 100 head annually for the twenty years he resided on the reservation. Other witnesses supported Fairfield's statements.

Agency miller and sawyer W. W. Johnson testified that Nez Perce herds died of starvation because of the great amount of trespassing cattle. James Reuben, a respected tribal leader, spoke of Nez Perce–owned cattle bearing Caldwell's brand. Several other witnesses came forward to testify, including John P. Vollmer, president of the First National Bank of Lewiston. He reported that many Nez Perce objected to Monteith's second appointment as agent in 1889 and asked him to intercede on their behalf. While he declined to do so, Vollmer did tell Marcum that he believed local cattlemen supported Monteith's appointment because they felt he would allow them to graze their herds on the reservation "without hindrance."

No one presented proof supporting the allegations against Monteith, who seemed not to believe that a problem existed. He never addressed the issue of trespassing stock in any of his annual reports and only discussed it with representatives of the Indian Department when asked directly. He asserted that Nez Perce cattle grazed outside the reservation as well as inside and that he was too busy to deal with the issue, and he suggested that either the Indian Department charge a fee and permit the cattle on the reservation or the agency simply purchase trespassing cattle for a school herd. Monteith also claimed to have ordered Caldwell and others off the reservation, but no witness or statement confirmed that assertion. Obviously, Monteith's concerns differed significantly from those of the Nez Perce. Even if he did not personally profit through Caldwell's business, he failed to acknowledge how important the Nez Perce considered the issue of trespassing stock. Monteith often disagreed with Nez Perce about various reservation issues, and the tribe was concerned enough about his reappointment as agent in 1889 to dispatch James Reuben to Washington, D.C., to protest the department's decision.

The Nez Perce problem was not unique. Stock owners commonly encroached on Indian reservations throughout the Northwest during the latter part of the nineteenth century, when cattle ranching reached its peak in the region. The Klamath, Warm Springs, Malheur, Umatilla, Yakima, and Nez Perce reservations all suffered to some degree from illegal cattle grazing. A government order forced many stockmen off the Nez Perce reservation in 1890. The injunction was apparently not an agency ruling but may have resulted from Marcum's investigation in 1889. Whatever its source, many stock owners complied with the order. However, agent Robbins reported incidents again in 1891 and federal inspectors discovered additional violations in 1893.

Both lax Indian policy on the part of the federal government and the ruthlessness of stock owners share blame for excessive cattle trespassing. In the Nez Perce case, the cursory interest of agent Monteith also contributed to the problem. While people such as Alice Fletcher and several missionaries worked diligently to promote what they considered the Nez Perce's best interests, others such as Caldwell took advantage of every circumstance available. They profited at the expense of the Nez Perce and disregarded the effects their actions had on the Indians.

The opening of the reservation to settlement may itself have helped to end the problem. After 1890, agriculture, sheep breeding, and general overgrazing caused a rapid decline in the land available to run cattle. While other factors also affected the livestock industry's decline, allotment and settlement irreversibly divided up the reservation. Running large numbers of cattle eventually became more and more difficult for both Nez Perce and Anglos as the open range of the reservation gave way to agriculture. In 1905, Nez Perce agent F. G. Mattoon reported that the Nez Perce themselves collectively owned 3,000 head of cattle—an estimate less than half the 1890 figure.

The controversy over trespassing cattle peaked just before the opening of the reservation. With the implementation of the Allotment Act, other issues developed. The influx of settlers was perhaps the most obvious change. Many local whites settled on Nez Perce lands in 1895 and still others traveled specifically to Idaho to homestead on the reservation. Father Alexander Diomedi, long a missionary in the Northwest and a former priest in Lewiston, wrote a letter to a midwestern German settlement encouraging its residents to settle on the Idaho reservation. The recipients appointed a delegation to investigate the possibilities and its members reported favorably. Several families from the settlement thus moved to Idaho and purchased Nez Perce land. Still others discovered a new opportunity in the opening of Native American reservations after the depression of 1893, as surplus Native American lands provided a new start for many farmers who had lost everything they owned. Certainly a variety of settlers attempted farming on the reservation, all with their own stories. Their success with the opening of surplus land overshadowed any objection the Nez Perce might have had. After all (from the viewpoint of settlers), the government had passed a law and the Indians had agreed to sell their unallotted land.

A promoter for the Lewiston area justified allotment in the name of progress and development. A pamphlet entitled "Highlights in Lewiston History," published early in the twentieth century, included the 1895 opening. Lewiston, its author said, benefited from allotment because the reservation had previously "blocked entrance . . . to the whole inland country." The booklet continued by describing the aftermath of the opening as "red letter days for Lewiston" because of the influx of Anglo settlers, available land, and the money spent by both the new arrivals and the Nez Perce from their payments.

Surely the Nez Perce perceived the loss of their land as something less than a landmark event. A tribal history published in 1972 compared the opening of the Nez Perce reservation to the Oklahoma land rush of 1893. Indeed, the Meriam Report of 1928, which surveyed conditions on reservations across the country, revealed that by then the reservation as defined by the terms of the 1863 treaty contained only 1,300 Nez Perce residents—compared to 20,000 Anglos. Allotment terminated any concept of a physical area of land that might be considered "Nez Perce country," despite contrary views of mapmakers, agents, and lawyers. The Indians became "strangers on their own land."

The town of Orofino provided an example of the determination of Anglo settlers to establish their own communities. C. C. Fuller filed the original homestead claim on the site and took up residence on November 19, 1895, just one day after the official opening of the reservation. He first operated a trading post, while others established various businesses and enterprises. Determined to organize their new community, Fuller and others fought to acquire Nez Perce land titles, but the process was slow although few Nez Perce had the means to fight for their land in court, even if they desired to keep their allotment. Through settlers' perseverance and numerous litigations, Orofino finally became a town by the turn of the century.

As on many Native American reservations after allotment, few Nez Perce became Anglicized farmers as reformers and the federal government had intended. The twenty-five-year term of trust patents failed to provide a successful conversion period for two reasons: leasing and heirship problems. Many Nez Perce agreed to leases in which Anglo farmers worked the land and the owners lived off the rental money. Even if a Nez Perce farmed his or her own land, a death reduced any heirs' land base by at least half and usually more. The Nez Perce reservation gradually became more and more owned or operated by Anglos. As early as five months before the official opening of the reservation in 1895, inspector P. M. McCormick found "the greater portion" of Nez Perce renting their farms. Leasing became so prevalent nationwide that in 1906, the Burke Act eased federal restrictions on the practice. In June of the same year, Congress approved a special act specifically to allow Nez Perce the privilege of leasing.

Every annual report from the Nez Perce agency between 1895 and 1905 reported on leasing. In 1895, agent S. G. Fisher estimated that Anglo leasers had worked nine-tenths of the 10,000 acres in cultivation. The number increased annually, and by 1900 agent C. T. Stranahan admitted that most of the Nez Perce had become discouraged with farming. Two years later he asserted that the demand for leasing continued "unabated." In 1904, F. G. Mattoon, school superintendent in charge of the agency, acknowledged that the practice of leasing was subject to abuse. Leasing did not benefit the Nez Perce; in fact, it had the opposite effect. It made them dependent on lease income, a situation Mattoon compared to the old annuity and ration system. Indeed, the practice of leasing allotments undermined the very intentions of the Severalty Act. Native Americans no longer had to attempt to farm or develop their land. Nor did they have significant reasons to accept Anglo culture or society. They could live as they wanted, supported by the money from lease incomes.

Stranahan also complained of many Nez Perce negotiating their own leases. All contracts needed the approval of the agent as a representative of the Interior Department. Without his consent on the leases, Stranahan feared, agreements would cheat the Nez Perce. However, the agent refused to issue permits to some Nez Perce. If they did not want to farm, they then simply rented out the land with or without the agent's permission. Stranahan also pointed out the widespread disillusionment with farming but apparently did not connect the two situations.

Fractionated heirship contributed to the opposition of many Nez Perce to farming. A significant and widespread problem on most allotted reservations even to the present day, fractionated heirship results from nothing more than the death of an allottee. The heirs divide the land between themselves, the amount depending on that person's relationship to the deceased. As each of these heirs dies, the plot of land is further divided among next-generation heirs, and so on, until the acreage becomes incomprehensibly small fractions of a single allotment. As that occurs, each person takes less interest in the inheritance: the share of profit is simply too small to worry about. Often, heirs agree to lease or sell the allotment and divide the income. The problem of fractionated heirship developed almost from the start of allotment and obviously became more complicated with time.

Even with the best of all other conditions, one understands why the Nez Perce quickly became discouraged. As early as 1899, C. T. Stranahan noted the "quite perplexing" problem of distributing heirship allotments. He recommended that the government put forth a special effort to alleviate the already developing entanglements. His admonition went unnoticed and the problem became increasingly difficult to rectify. One particular allotment on the Nez Perce reservation eventually gained over sixty heirs with interests ranging from 10,800/103,680 to 90/103,680—a situation not particularly unusual for the Nez Perce or any other allotted reservation.

Even among those willing to attempt farming, such fractionated heirship discouraged their descendants. But ethnohistorical reasons also impeded the success of allotment in Idaho. Traditional Indian kinship patterns differed significantly from the Anglo-American ideals set forth by the Dawes Act. Prior to allotment, Nez Perce lived in extended family groups, but severalty required people to live with immediate family only and in isolated farmhouses. Traditional families consisted of several nuclear families, with no particular identifiable head of household. Continuing aboriginal family structures deterred the Nez Perce from segregating themselves on individual farms.

Writing in 1923, Oscar Lipps, superintendent of the Nez Perce Reservation, acknowledged problems stemming from allotment—particularly heirship and the disproportionate Anglo population. He noted that by then the Nez Perce held 100,000 acres of allotted and tribal lands, but Anglo settlers owned 650,000 acres. Almost every Nez Perce under the age of 27 owned land only through heirship, and often a dozen or more heirs received a tract of 80 acres to divide up among them. The only practicable solution, Lipps argued, consisted of selling the land and distributing the profit. Under existing conditions, the heirs could not even begin their own farms if they wanted to because all the productive land was gone.

The Nez Perce spent centuries adapting to new institutions and ideas, most evidently after white contact. Allotment presented special difficulties, however. Certainly few would have unconditionally accepted the Dawes Act, given a choice; but Native Americans were not given such a choice to accept or reject allotment, which in theory required them to throw away their entire culture and start anew. The government forced the Dawes Act on Native Americans. No question was raised about its ultimate goals, and no one offered the tribes an option. Ironically, on the Nez Perce reservation the height of Native American agricultural activity occurred before 1890. Nez Perce farming actually declined after allotment.

By 1911, many Nez Perce had lost land or money or both either directly or indirectly through severalty. The agency had cancelled over one hundred allotments and many more had been sold, leased, or erroneously awarded to the wrong heirs. The Nez Perce agent controlled the management, contracts, and legal decisions of many allotments. All lease payments went through his office, as did probate questions. At the direction of the Indian Office, the agent collected money and allowed each individual to withdraw only twenty-five dollars per month on his or her account. To further complicate matters, in 1909 the Commissioner of Indian Affairs prohibited merchants from issuing credit to Native Americans. Anyone who did so risked his license.

The Nez Perce considered that directive libelous in its suggestion of their untrustworthiness, and economically disastrous as well. They needed either credit or their full amounts of money. Twenty-five dollars a month scarcely allowed families to meet their needs, and it hindered them from making any major improvements on their land. The Nez Perce also had cause for complaint regarding treaty violations, unauthorized construction of roads and railroads through the reservation, and indiscriminate heirship rulings.

The Nez Perce asserted their rights as state and federal citizens. They sought access to the courts and other means of arbitration. Led by Starr J. Maxwell, Nez Perce tribal attorney, the Nez Perce presented their grievances to Congress. They introduced, via Idaho's senator William Borah, a document containing 131 exhibits, most of which were personal affidavits. The majority of witnesses specified the agent's control of their personal finances as a cause of hardship. Others reported their allotments diminished by roads and railroads built without permission or compensation. Still others objected to state hunting and fishing laws. Treaties had guaranteed fishing and hunting rights to the Nez Perce, but several tribal members had been arrested for violating game laws.

Many Nez Perce also complained about losing their first per-capita payments in 1895. Tom Williams' story echoed that of others. The agent induced him to deposit his money in the First National Bank at Moscow, Idaho. Shortly afterward, the bank failed. Charley Wat-to-lina, who also lost his deposits, estimated that the First National had accepted $200,000 to $300,000 from Nez Perce. Few, if any, received their money back.

The affidavits also documented some of the unfair heirship decisions. This problem affected many women, such as Mary Types, whose husbands had been previously married. When Types died, the superintendent awarded half of his allotment to their daughter and the other half to his first wife. Mary Types received nothing and wanted the case reviewed. He-yum-ka-yon-mi also requested an investigation into her claims. When her husband died, the agent awarded his allotment to his parents and she received nothing. In still another case, You-hoy-ta-mut-Kickt asked to recover her daughter's allotment. The agent had cancelled it because another woman by the same name as the daughter also owned an allotment. You-hoy-ta-mut-Kickt's daughter had died, but the other woman was still living.

In almost all the affidavits, the Nez Perce appear to have had legitimate concerns and objections. Severalty and the opening of the reservation created numerous difficulties. Even if federal policy failed to recognize the reality of allotment's impact until the 1930s, Native Americans did not. The Nez Perce memorial represented an effort to resolve their grievances within the legal framework of the government. The affidavits were not simply a list of complaints; individually they conveyed real problems, and collectively they showed a determination to be heard by Congress and the Indian Department.

Despite such problems, Superintendent Lipps believed wholly in the efficacy of the Dawes Act. Yet he realized how and why it created problems. He cited a new government study of Native American conditions, presumably the Meriam investigation, that offered a framework for ameliorating any negative situations for Native Americans. In his view, the Nez Perce lived better after allotment than they had in the eighteenth century. Before Lewis and Clark met the Nez Perce, in Lipps's view they were poverty stricken, leading a day-to-day existence in a futile search for food. At least after allotment, he suggested, few "blanket Indians" remained and most wore short hair. Lipps's faulty logic, ethnocentric interpretation, and vision of progress lack validity today, but he did recognize that allotment created drastic changes for Native Americans. While assimilation represented a primary goal of the legislation, short hair and Anglo clothing did little to help Native Americans become successful farmers. Lipps and many of his colleagues believed that these were signs of success for the Dawes Act and other measures aimed at assimilation. A contrasting Nez Perce view is that the Severalty Act attempted to prevent Native Americans "from being Indian."

In addition to agriculture, education was also an important aspect of the assimilation campaign. "Industrial training" prepared young Native Americans to take over their parents' allotments. Lapwai boasted its own government school, later moved to nearby Fort Lapwai. Its capacity held steady at about sixty pupils in industrial and academic training. The Catholic mission school at Slickpoo operated classes well into the twentieth century. Several Nez Perce also attended Carlisle in Pennsylvania and Chemewa in Oregon.

Lapwai Rural High School Number One became in 1909 the first white-Indian integrated school in the country. Mrs. John N. Alley, wife of the agency physician, initiated the plan. With the support of Presbyterian missionaries Kate McBeth and Mary Crawford, Alley served on the local board of education beginning in 1903. One of her first projects involved the construction of a new school building for Anglo children. Soon after its completion, she and others began planning a separate high school. They advocated an integrated school and held meetings with government officials and Nez Perce spokesmen. A local election in 1909 approved the plan, which included the use of already existing government school buildings and federal subsidies to the school system for Nez Perce students. By December of that year, approximately 300 students attended Lapwai Rural High School, 40 percent of whom were Nez Perce.

While education formed a major part of the assimilation campaign, as with severalty, reality differed significantly from the hopes and ideas of reformers. One of the major problems in Native American education during the allotment era was the lack of concern about it among land-seeking westerners who cared little for the fate or welfare of Native Americans. Their primary interest lay in freeing reservation land. These individuals considered any time, thought, or money spent on the matter wasted. On the Nez Perce reservation, school integration fell victim to this attitude; there was little concern on the part of non-Indian residents for equal opportunity in the district. Integrating the high school allowed government-salaried teachers to work there, but with minimal contributions from the school board. The district also benefited from subsidies and the use of government buildings. But local grammar schools remained segregated, and as a result the number of Nez Perce high school students gradually decreased. Consequently, the government teachers taught mostly Anglo students in government buildings at the expense of the Indian Office.

The assimilation program, as envisioned by proponents of allotment, failed on the Nez Perce reservation. Many Nez Perce resisted the government's efforts, and those who did not usually met with other obstacles. By the 1920s the Nez Perce took matters into their own hands, realizing the futility of relying on the federal government to aid their situation. Forming the Nez Perce Home and Farm Association (NPHFA) in 1923, they attempted to help each other collectively over a decade before the Indian Reorganization Act was passed to ameliorate reservation conditions.

The NPHFA could not give the Nez Perce direct self-government because of the federal government's custodianship policy. However, its formation expressed the tribe's desire for independence. The Indian office cooperated with their efforts and local newspapers and organizations also supported the venture. Corbett Lawyer drew up the NPHFA's five-year plan to improve Nez Perce education, health, and economy. Its goals met with limited success, but the Nez Perce had developed a prototype of Native American self-government.

In 1933, the United States Senate Subcommittee on Indian Affairs conducted hearings on the condition of Native Americans. The members visited almost every reservation in the country, including Lapwai. The investigation reflected the effects of the Great Depression by examining delinquent lease payments and the lack of available jobs. Notwithstanding the nation's economic problems, Chairman Burton K. Wheeler blamed Native Americans' problems almost exclusively on alcohol. If only they would all stop drinking, he believed, they could utilize their education, have good homes, and build themselves up.

The problem of Native American economic conditions went much beyond alcohol. Agency physician C. H. Koentz told of overcrowded conditions that contributed to the spread of tuberculosis and other diseases; he had once visited a two-person home and found ten people sleeping in one room. Racism also played a role. Caleb Carter argued with Wheeler over the existence of prejudice. Wheeler claimed none occurred in the Northwest, but Carter pointed out that Anglos often refused to work with Nez Perce. He knew of one particular farm where stacks of grain had stood since World War I because Anglo farmers refused to thresh for the owner. He also told of Lewiston businesses that refused to deal with Nez Perce, posting signs proclaiming "White trade only" to prohibit them from entering. Caleb Whitman then told of a job in which he had been hired as a clerk. Whitman had attended high school and taken a civil-service examination. However, when he reported for work, the foreman told him he had no jobs for Indians. In the end, Whitman swept and washed dishes.

Struggling against racism, disease, and the Great Depression, Native Americans found it almost impossible to succeed in the vision of the Dawes Act. Myopic views such as those of Wheeler and Oscar Lipps discouraged any serious consideration of Indian affairs even after the Meriam Commission published its findings. The realities of reservation life in the form of trespassers, squatters, leasing, fractionated heirship, and BIA policies would by themselves have prevented the success of allotment, and Native Americans did not want to become Anglo-Americans. Reformers had envisioned the complete disintegration of tribal relations, but their utopian plan failed almost as quickly as it was implemented. All of these factors made any attempt to farm a formidable undertaking.

Despite the failure of the specific goals of reformers and missionaries, the assimilation program did affect the Nez Perce. Albert Moore perhaps personified the amalgamation of Anglo-American and Nez Perce culture. Born in 1861, Moore lived until 1963—a member of one of the generations directly affected by the assimilation campaign. Moore became a Presbyterian minister in his younger years and remarked to missionary Mary Crawford how much he enjoyed teaching his people about Christ. He said it reminded him of *ipnu'tsililpt,* a native religious movement popular among the non-treaty Nez Perce. Crawford reprimanded him for comparing the two and told him his remark was "savage" and "foolishness." Moore quit the ministry at that moment and immediately moved away to another part of the reservation. A week later, Crawford apologized to him in a letter and asked him to return. Moore refused, and years later he said about the incident: "the missionaries never asked us how we believed. We believed in heaven, through dreams. We were Christians before the White man came."

Moore spoke of many changes that occurred on the Nez Perce reservation and lamented the fact that younger generations of Nez Perce no longer sought guardian spirits. He often thought of traditional practices in regard to the Anglo-American world around him. For instance, he enjoyed baseball, played the game himself, and regularly attended area minor-league and college games. Combining America's national pastime with his own cultural heritage, Moore suggested that baseball players take sweat baths for strength and endurance. The Nez Perce could not avoid exposure to Anglo-American institutions during the assimilation period. Albert Moore represents just one example of how many of them thought about and reacted to the changing world. Few either completely accepted or completely rejected the influence around them.

By the time John Collier became Commissioner of Indian Affairs and designed the Indian New Deal in 1934—signaling the end of the federal policy of allotment—the Nez Perce had developed a political system. They were organized enough to seriously consider, question, and debate the plan. A tribal business committee wrote to the Indian Department, presenting their specific questions and concerns. Upon receiving a reply, the Nez Perce held an election and voted to reject the Reorganization Act. They seemed already to be doing what Collier intended, so they did not believe it would particularly benefit them.

As one of the most important pieces of Indian legislation in United States history, the Dawes Act affected Native Americans across the country. With some slight adjustments, the policy remained in effect for over forty years. During that time, people of all backgrounds and philosophies touched the lives of Nez Perce. They ranged from pious missionaries to politicians to ruthless businessmen. Before the Indian Reorganization Act superseded the General Allotment Act, Native Americans faced a great deal of adversity in the form of incursions on their land and indifference to their welfare. The Dawes Act unfortunately gave these forces leverage to invade the Nez Perce reservation and take whatever personal profit was available. The Nez Perce collectively attempted to alleviate their difficulties through such methods as forming the NPHFA and presenting their concerns to Congress. Only years of work finally reestablished the Nez Perce Tribe politically and economically. Some problems, such as fractionated heirship and loss of large amounts of land, have continued into the present.

Suggested Reading

The federal government expected to achieve its goal of forcing the Indians to accept acculturation through the Dawes, or General Allotment, Act of 1887. As Elizabeth James has shown, this rarely happened. Other treatments of the policy appear in Janet A. McDonnell, *The Dispossession of the American Indian, 1887–1933* (Bloomington: Indiana University Press, 1991); Frederick E. Hoxie, *The Final Promise: The Campaign to Assimilate the Indians, 1888–1920* (Lincoln: University of Nebraska Press, 1984); and Melissa L. Meyer, *The White Earth Tragedy: Ethnicity and Dispossession at a Minnesota Anishinaabe Reservation* (Lincoln: University of Nebraska Press, 1994). Francis Paul Prucha, *American Indian Policy in Crisis: Christian Reformers and the Indians, 1865–1900* (Norman: University of Oklahoma Press, 1976), considers the roles that reformers outside the federal government played in American efforts to solve what they saw as the Indian "problem."

PART FIVE

Toward the Mainstream

By the early decades of the twentieth century, a combination of Indian decisions and federal activities on tribal reservations set into motion a gradual but wholesale shift in the lives of Native people. Throughout this process tribal members often subverted federal policies in order to achieve their own goals. For example, while bureaucrats expected to use reservations to further their social and economic programs, leading toward rapid acculturation, Indians used reservations as homelands and places of refuge where they could retain their culture. Some tribal members served as agency police or judges in the newly established Indian courts. Others worked to strengthen local tribal authority and to find ways of deflecting federal pressure to abandon their identity.

Reformers and bureaucrats considered education to be central in the process of stamping out "Indianness." Most children went to day schools on or next to their tribal homes, but by the late 1880s thousands of children attended distant boarding schools. Although boarding schools caused great confusion and misery for generations of children, they unwittingly helped create a pan-Indian movement that cut across band and tribal identities. As David Wallace Adams notes, schools such as Carlisle sometimes strengthened Indian self-awareness. The schools also accelerated the movement of tribal people away from the reservations, as did employment in several of the famous Wild West shows, traveling medicine shows, and military service in World War I. The war led to the legislation in 1924 granting American citizenship to any Indian peoples still lacking it.

By then many tribal members had left the reservations, hoping to find employment in nearby towns and cities. There tribal people encountered long-standing stereotypes about the "lazy" or "drunken Indian." In her essay on the Anishinaabeg of Minnesota, Kathryn Abbott posits that during the early twentieth century rural and small town inhabitants of all races shared drinking patterns. She also disputes the idea that Indians had some innate weakness concerning alcohol use. The Great Depression of the 1930s hit Indians hard because many tribal societies had only a precarious economic base to begin with. The 1934 Indian Reorganization Act sought to remedy this by encouraging cultural pride and providing economic assistance. While some groups benefited from this new approach through temporary employment and federal efforts to launch conservation programs, others received little help.

Paul C. Rosier discusses how the Blackfeet debated this legislation and their success in shaping it to accommodate their goals. Yet during the first decades of the twentieth century a continuing stream of people left the reservations, and their experiences away from home equipped them for closer contact with other Americans that increasingly characterized their situation.

CHAPTER FIFTEEN

More Than a Game

The Carlisle Indians Take to the Gridiron, 1893–1917

DAVID WALLACE ADAMS

By the late nineteenth century, newspaper headlines announcing messy Indian wars had become a thing of the past. Rather than fighting against the U.S. Army, young men from tribal reservations attended boarding schools scattered across the country. Founded by Richard Henry Pratt in 1879, the Carlisle Indian School in Pennsylvania stood as a model for others to imitate. Its superintendent spoke of having to "kill the Indian to save the man." By this he meant that the school curriculum should immerse its young learners in non-Indian things. While doing that, the school sought to strip away all of each student's Native past.

Many students gave in to such cultural battering, but as this essay shows, others used school activities to retain parts of their personal identity. In fact, athletes at Carlisle saw football as a way to compete and even defeat Ivy League teams representing white America. They received support from fans and even sports writers. Reporters described the games as modern versions of earlier wars and noted that Carlisle players proudly held their own against teams from far larger schools.

Sometime in 1893 more than three dozen young men crowded into the office of Richard Henry Pratt, superintendent of the Indian school at Carlisle, Pennsylvania, for the purpose of making an impassioned request: they wanted to play football. The background to the situation Pratt knew only too well. Once before he had sent an Indian team onto the gridiron, but when one of his players broke his leg, Pratt suspended the program. And now this new appeal. The group had selected their most eloquent spokesman to make their case. "While they stood around my desk, their black eyes intensely watching me," Pratt later remembered, "the orator gave practically all the arguments in favor of our contending in outside football . . . and ended by requesting the removal of the embargo." After listening to the group's plea, Pratt relented. He would allow a resumption of the football program, but only on two conditions: that the Indians always play fairly and never slug an opponent, and that they whip the best football teams in the country. The group readily agreed to both conditions. So began the Carlisle Indians' legendary 24-year-long struggle on the gridiron.

Pratt had his own reasons for supporting the delegation's appeal. As founder of Carlisle Indian School In 1879, Pratt was a central figure among the humanitarian reformers who sought to solve the "Indian problem" by a policy of forced acculturation, with schools playing a pivotal role in the process. Pratt's approach to the Indian question began with a simple proposition: culturally, Indians were savages, and as such, their days were numbered. The doctrine of civilized progress and the reality of white expansion and settlement meant that reservation Indians must either adopt the ways of whites or suffer eventual racial extinction. Pratt's special role in the reform cause was to demonstrate the potential of off-reservation schools as instruments for accomplishing the Indians' cultural transformation. Convinced that the source of Indian savagery was environmental rather than genetic, Pratt believed that the work of civilizing Indians could only be carried out if they were removed from the influences of reservation life for a period of five years or more. Pratt's philosophy would always be, "to civilize the Indian, get him into civilization. To keep him civilized, let him stay." Pratt believed that only through a regimented program of military discipline, academic instruction, industrial training, and civilized living conditions, could Indians internalize and appreciate the white man's civilization, and in the process shed their tribal heritage.

Sending Carlisle onto the gridiron, Pratt was now convinced, presented a wonderful opportunity to gain wider support for his ideas on Indian progress. The public, "dosed to the full" with Buffalo Bill Wild West Show exhibitions of Indian treachery and depictions of a race seemingly frozen in savagery, would now observe "show Indians" of a different sort—brainy, self-disciplined, gentlemanly athletes who could beat the white man at his own game. In the school newspaper, *Red Man*, Pratt declared: "The Indian is not dead yet, but alive and able to compete with the world, if allowed to use his God-given faculties. 'A fair field and no favor' is all he asks and he will render a good account of himself, whether in business, music, art, education or athletics." Altering the public's image of Indians would alter the opportunities afforded them. Celebrating a victory over Cornell in 1902, Pratt bellowed to a crowd of jubilant students just returned from parading through the nearby town of Carlisle: "Buffalo Bill travels allover the land parading what he intends the people to believe to be the particular qualities of the Indian. No man ever put a greater lie before the public than Buffalo Bill." In contradiction to the spectacle of the Wild West Show, Carlisle's victory over

Cornell demonstrated the potential of football to win white friends for the cause of full Indian acceptance into the American system. The proof was in the fact that local white citizens were telephoning by the score to congratulate Pratt on the great victory. Pratt reminded students how times had changed. Only a few decades before, if the townspeople of Carlisle had gotten word that Indians were coming into town, "they would have been badly scared: The women would have run down . . . and locked the cellar doors and the men would have got their guns ready to shoot." But now it was a different story altogether. "Our friends and neighbors, the white people, join in our rejoicing when we succeed even though those we overcome are their own race." Such was the promise of football.

By any measure, the gridiron record of the Carlisle Indians was remarkable. Between 1899 and 1914, years during which the team was primarily coached by Glenn "Pop" Warner, Carlisle dazzled the fans with their victories, defeating such football giants of the day as Harvard, Cornell, University of Pennsylvania, and Princeton. But what of Pratt's hope that his players' performance on the football field would project an image of the "new Indian"? As this essay will demonstrate, Pratt's expectations were to be only partially realized. And one reason his expectations were not met stems from an ironic miscalculation, the fact that in the minds of many observers the spectacle of Indian and white teams locked in violent struggle for territory could not help but evoke images of Fallen Timbers, Beecher's Island, and the Little Big Horn—images of what spectators considered red savages resisting the advance of white civilization.

This essay explores the complex and multiple meanings of Indian-white football, including its connection to the history of frontier conflict. First, it analyzes how the legacy of Indian wars shaped the response of both the popular press and white fans to the Indians' gridiron feats. In this regard, the paper conjoins two resonate narrative frameworks in turn-of-the-century America—the Frontier Myth and football. On the one hand, it assumes, like Richard Slotkin, that the Frontier Myth was at the heart of American identity, and that at the very heart of that myth was the heroic Indian war.

On the other hand, it takes seriously Clifford Geertz's idea of "deep play," the idea being that play—and by extension athletic contests such as football—is a "cultural text" that offers insights on society's values, longings, and conflictions. In drawing upon the Frontier Myth and football as cultural texts, this essay explores how the gridiron, in, say, a Harvard-Carlisle game, functioned as so much "mythic space" where the social drama of frontier conflict could be played out, experienced, and interpreted anew. Second, this essay examines the attitudes and motivations of the Indian players themselves. As subsequent discussion will reveal, while the symbolic and mythic dimensions of their gridiron wars were never far from players' consciousness, the various meanings they attached to the game went beyond this single association. But for all concerned—Pratt, the daily press, cheering white fans, and the players alike—Indian-white football was more that a game. It counted for something.

In turn-of-the-century America, making the connection between an Indian-white football contest and frontier war did not require a great leap of the imagination. Two factors, quite independent of the Carlisle story, could trigger the association. The first of these was the nature of the game itself. As both participants and observers of the game were quick to point out, football was strikingly similar to war. At its most fundamental level, football was a violent struggle between two armed camps for territory. As sports journalist Caspar Whitney observed in 1892, "The game is a mimic battlefield, on which the players must reconnoiter, skirmish, advance, attack, and retreat in good order." No one saw more clearly the parallels between war and football than Carlisle's coach, Glenn Warner. In 1912, at the height of Carlisle's glory years, Warner explained the connection with the precision of a military strategist:

> A football game is very similar, in many respects, to a war, and good generalship is as important in one as in the other. Each scrimmage represents a battle, in which the opposing forces are lined up opposite each other, one side defending itself against the attack of the other. The lines represent the infantry, and the backs can be likened to cavalry, quick moving, and able to charge the enemy at any spot, or rush to the support of any position attacked. The quarterback or the general of the side making the attack should study well the defense of the enemy, and decide whether to force through their center, turn their flank by a quick movement, deceive them with a fake movement in one direction while the real attack is made at another spot, or transfer the battle to a more favorable locality by a punt. In making this decision, he should take into consideration the condition of the field, the direction of the wind, and especially the position on the field, with reference to the goal or side lines, and the number of the down and the distance to be gained. If the wind is favorable, and the ball is near the goal line which his team is defending, the battle should by all means be transferred to the enemy's territory by a punt, reserving ammunition and strength for the attack when an opportunity is gained within striking distance of the enemy's goal.

It is impossible to imagine that Warner did not inject the war-football analogy into his locker room talks with his Indian players.

A second connection between football and frontier conflict can be found in those factors underlying the game's growing popularity in Victorian America. As John Higham has observed, it was in the 1890s that a "master impulse" transformed colleges into "theaters of organized physical combat." While the dramatic rise of football on college campuses cannot be reduced to a single factor, much of the game's appeal can be explained by what historians have come to call the "cult of manliness." As the argument goes, the growing industrialization and mechanization of turn-of-the-century America produced, particularly among the middle and upper classes, severe anxiety with respect to their loss of time-honored attributes of masculinity. In an older frontier America the opportunities for physical labor, wilderness adventure, and primitive expressions of violence, were not only available but frequently a precondition for survival. Denied these experiences, the rising generation of males were in danger of becoming over-civilized, if not feminized. Anemic replicas of their pioneer ancestors who had won a continent, the new generation was susceptible to a debilitating loss of "nerve force," hardly a recipe for long-term success in a world where only the fittest survived. It is this anxiety that in part explains the explosive popularity of exercise and organized sport, including football. "The first settlers in this country needed no sports for their training or for their diversion," remarked one enthusiast. "Building their own houses, there own roads and bridges, and defending the same from their savage neighbors, were enough." But in modern society, the "hardier virtues, which in the beginning made our forefathers capable of winning a place for us in the world," were at risk. Hence, "as wars become less frequent, gymnasiums and field sports increase in number and popularity." But football was not just any game and this explains its growing popularity on college campuses in late-nineteenth-century America. Football's special appeal was that it was simultaneously modern and anti-modern: modern in its emphasis on clock-like movement, hierarchical organization, disciplined cooperation, and technical efficiency; anti-modern in its reliance on ritualized violence, physical endurance, raw-boned courage, and football "instinct." Football was an ideal athletic forum for instructing a new generation in those manly virtues indigenous to the frontier experience, an ideal forum for creating the new American man—half Boone, half Rockefeller.

Part of football's appeal was in its capacity to tell stories, to convey meaning. But what stories? What meaning? As Michael Oriard has written, "Meaning resides not simply in texts but in the negotiations between texts and readers." In the instance of football this negotiation was especially complex by virtue of the fact that those involved in the construction of meaning came to the game from such varied vantage points: players, spectators, sports journalists, and readers of the daily newspaper. The role of newspapers, most of which employed sports editors by the 1890s, was seminal in this regard. In an effort to build and then hold their readership, newspaper coverage of the "big game" frequently included lengthy articles by sports writers, accompanied by sensational sketches, cartoons, diagrammatic reconstructions of game flow, and later, photographs. Situated between the game and their readers, sports journalists, as mediators of meaning, constantly struggled for ways to enhance their narratives. A Yale-Princeton football game was not just a game but a titanic struggle of historic significance, where players, like medieval knights or Roman gladiators, performed mythic feats of heroism. Interestingly, until the 1890s the latent narrative possibilities of football as a metaphor for frontier war remained unexploited.

But after the Indians took to the gridiron, sports writers immediately made the connection. Writing for the *New York Journal,* sportswriter Harry Beecher began his description of the 1900 Thanksgiving Day game between Carlisle and Columbia, in which the Indians were defeated by a score of 17 to 6, with the observation that the two races had a long history on the field of battle. "Now it is brawn, muscle and speed scrapping over a slippery football. Then it was toma-hawks and rifles with lives at stake. Of course, the redskins were beaten. They always were." When the Indians fell to Brown in 1897, readers of the *New York Herald* were told that it was the "victorious paleface who lured the wily redskin into the open, and there scalped him with his own tomahawk." No longer, the account continued, would the Carlisle Indian "leap forth from his well chosen ambuscade, and, with terror diffusing whoop, remove the cranial canopy from his . . . enemy." Vanquished on the gridiron, the Indian, "with disjointed whoop and blunted tomahawk, goes back to recuperate upon his reservation." Similarly, in 1896, an article in *New York World* (reprinted in *Red Man*), set the scene for the contest between Yale and Carlisle in 1896 this way: "On one side were the under-graduates of an old and great university. They represent, physically, the perfection of modern athletics, and intellectually, the culture and refinement of the best modern American life. On the other side was the aborigine, the real son of the forest and plain, the redskin of history, of story, of war, developed or veneered, as the case may be, by education." New Yorkers had their first oppor-tunity to see Carlisle players in 1895. The *New York Times* responded: "There was an uprising of Indians in the northern part of Manhattan Island yesterday after-noon. A band of eleven full-blooded warriors, with their war paint and feathers, attacked a band of men from the Young Men's Christian Association."

One is reminded at this point of James Oliver Robertson's assertion that Amer-ican football has been the least exportable of the nation's sports because "the en-tire game is built around the frontier, the line, the boundary. Football ritualizes the moving frontier, and the teamwork, cooperation, and individual heroism necessary to move that frontier; simultaneously, it also ritualizes the teamwork, cooperation, and individual heroism necessary to resist the moving frontier." Robertson continues to make his point: "Football players are pioneers and In-dians at the same time." This thesis is offered without any evidence whatsoever, and on the surface, may appear absurd. Even viewed through the lens of deep play it requires a considerable stretch of the imagination to believe that a foot-ball contest between two all-white teams spoke, consciously or unconsciously, to spectators' myth-ridden identities. On the other hand, watching all-Indian and all-white teams violently contesting turf required very little in the way of histori-cal imagination. The 1896 Harvard-Carlisle contest, for instance, was played just twenty years after Custer's defeat at the Little Bighorn, and just six years after Wounded Knee. When the two teams appeared on the field, the *Boston Globe* supposed:

> Never was there a spectacle so calculated to impress an imaginative mind. All the manifold interests of the present and the past, the near and far, were col-lected on the instant on Soldier's field. Over 500 years of education were rep-resented by the young palefaces in crimson, while centuries of fire and sun worship, medicine men incantations, ghost dances and mound building were

flashed before the inner vision by the appearances of the young men from Carlisle. Every glance at their swarthy faces and crow-black hair wafted the mind back to the days of Pontiac, King Philip, Samoset, the time of Hannah Dustin's escape, to Lovel's war and Marquette's trips of discovery in a fabric of birch bark.

For this writer, at least, Soldier's Field had assumed the attributes of mythic space where Indians and whites were reliving their dramatic, age-old encounters on the American landscape.

Nowhere is this connection clearer than in a *New York Herald* article on the Yale-Carlisle contest in 1897 in which Yale players were miraculously transformed into the "Leatherstockings" and the Carlisle players into Cooperesque versions of the noble savage. This imaginative journalist even manages to put words into the mouths of Indian players. "Ugh!" Carlisle's Thaddeus Redwater mutters before the game gets underway, "Pie Belt white man no good. Shoulders bend like willow tree." The Yale players, another Carlisle warrior pronounces, "dare not shut their eyes in the night. Their scalps will be so plenty that Indian [*sic*] shall burn them." For this journalist, the moment the Carlisle players stepped onto the gridiron dressed in their football "war paint"—nose guards, leg splints, and shoulder pads—they could not help but conjure up images of another time and place. Their long black hair and that "swinging trot peculiar to the North American savage" only enhanced the scene. The game began with the Indians intent on one objective: to place their "totem," the football, between the "twin saplings" of the white man. But as was so often the case in the history of the two races, the Leatherstockings proved to be a resourceful foe. "Like a herd of bisons came the sons of Yale. . . . The moving mass which the redskins saw presented an unbroken line. Every fierce eye of the oncoming host . . . was fixed upon the handful of savages who stood in the center of the prairie. The Indians faltered for a moment. They looked about them and saw no escape." The journalist went on to describe how like stampeding bison, like a prairie fire, the sons of Yale pushed the Indians back. "The Indians were thrown upon the earth and moccasined feet stamped upon their prostrate forms. . . . When the combatants rose to their feet after each encounter it seemed as though an Indian always lay helpless and writhing upon the ground." The Leatherstocking blend of civilized and primitive virtues was clearly too much for the Indians, and so on this day, Yale would defeat Carlisle by a score of 24 to 9, taking Indian "scalps" in the process. A battle-weary Redwater laments as he limps from the field, "The long-haired white men who dwell in the elbow of the river, could well sleep in the snow and feel no cold."

Newspaper cartoonists also let their imaginations run wild. In the same issue of a newspaper with a story describing Carlisle players as representative of the "new Indian," an illustrator depicted the players as nothing more than throwbacks of their "savage" ancestors. In an 1899 *Philadelphia Inquirer* cartoon a large, feather-bedecked Indian sits on a prostrate University of Pennsylvania player beside the comment "UGH! BIG INJUN." Slightly more creative is the *Minneapolis*

Tribune's depiction of a pipe-smoking Sitting Bull watching the University of Minnesota game. The old chief is seen to mutter: "In old days pale faces whip old Injuns heap. Now young Injuns lick pale faces." Twin-paneled "before" and "after" civilization illustrations worked especially well. In a *Boston Herald* cartoon over the caption "HOW INDIANS TOOK THE BALL IN 1699," an Indian warrior is seen taking a musket ball through the ribs, while a matching panel, "HOW THEY TAKE THE BALL TODAY," shows a Carlisle Indian tearing through Harvard's line. Similarly, in a *Minneapolis Journal* cartoon, over the words "SAME OLD SCARE" in the first panel "THE INDIANS ARE COMING—1848" the reader sees a buckskinned frontiersman being handed a musket; in the second "THE INDIANS ARE COMING—1908" a white football player is being handed his helmet. In 1896, a *Chicago Tribune* cartoonist depicted the Indian in the midst of cultural transformation in a single frame by showing a Carlisle player with long hair and feathers, but fully uniformed, throwing aside the tomahawk with one hand and raising a football to the heavens with the other. The caption read: "THE MODERN INDIAN DISCARDS THE TOMAHAWK FOR THE DEADLIER FOOTBALL AT THE CHICAGO COLISEUM."

Visual references to scalping was another common theme. "HOW AM I GOING TO GET THAT FELLOW'S SCALP?" a savage-looking Indian wonders as he confronts a helmeted University of Michigan player in 1901. After the Harvard victory over Carlisle in 1899, a much-relieved Harvard player clutches his head and remarks "I STILL HAVE MY SCALP." The situation is somewhat reversed in a closely-fought game between the University of Minnesota and Carlisle in 1907. In this instance, a Carlisle player's hair is literally exploding off his cranium, the caption reading, "WOW WHAT A SCARE! Well, if the Gopher didn't scalp Mr. Indian, he scared him bald-headed." Exploiting another familiar stereotype, a cartoonist for the *New York Journal* sketched a Carlisle player tipping a whiskey bottle over the caption, "An Appeal To The Great Spirit."

These illustrations and captions raise a question: Amid all such references to Indian savagery, just how successful was Pratt's grand vision of translating Carlisle's victories on the gridiron into greater public appreciation of the Indian's capacity for assimilation? The answer to this question is complex. Certainly, on one level, Pratt must have been disappointed. The objective of the football experiment was to awaken the public to the Indians' possibilities; it was not to provide an opportunity to revisit images of tomahawk-chopping, scalp-hungry savages. Still, Pratt's grand scheme was not altogether unsuccessful. The success of the Indians on the football field frequently prompted journalistic pronouncements that the old racial stereotypes were outdated and wrongheaded. After the Harvard-Carlisle game in 1896, the *New York Journal* juxtaposed the historic image of the Indian with that presented by the Carlisle players. "The Indians have invaded the East, and the people have not been scalped, burned alive or tomahawked," began the reporter's account. Quite the contrary, the Indians' skillful play and civilized bearing in a game that might have sparked evidence of latent savageness offered a strong counter argument to the oft-repeated sentiment that "the only good Indian is a dead one" and, in doing so, lent proof to Carlisle's philosophy that the race was fully capable of civilization. Similarly, the *New York Sun*, after noting spectators' support for the Indians in a contest with Yale, observed: "These young fellows, who would have been with Rain-in-the-Face and Sitting Bull at the Little Big Horn if they had been born thirty years before, were standing up nobly to the work of men who had five centuries the advantage of them in training and inheritance." Surely the immense sympathy of the crowd "signified the hearty welcome with which the redskins [were] received when they turn[ed] from the customs of savagery to the pursuits of civilization." After Carlisle's 1895 football season, a reporter for the *Cleveland Leader* wrote that the school's record on the football field demonstrated the players' fitness for the most modern achievements of American civilization." The Indians had performed magnificently against some of the finest universities in the country. It could no longer be assumed that the race was headed for "hopeless decline." Indeed, "in every sense, the Indian is a shining success as a football player. And if football is not the final test of the fitness of a race for the world's struggles and labors, things must be sadly askew, somewhere and somehow." Because the above accounts were also reprinted in *Red Man*, students as well as the general public were treated to these optimistic assessments of the Indians' future.

The Indians also scored big in their off-the-field appearances. Press accounts of the team's arrival, their pregame activities, and their attendance at various social events lent further support to the transformative influence of a Carlisle-like education. In city after city, journalists took note of the players' smart-looking uniforms and their thoroughly civilized demeanor. One reporter commented on the arrival of the Indians at a San Francisco hotel: "There is no loud talking, no smoking, no drinking, no profanity; there is not even slang in their conversation." This exemplary behavior was attributed to the school's emphasis on rules and military discipline. When the Indians strode into the lobby of Detroit's Hotel Cadillac in 1901, according to the *Detroit Free Press,* "there were no blood-curdling whoops, no war dances, no streaming ribbons." When the hotel clerk had the bad taste to ask a player in the process of signing the hotel register, "Where's your ribbons, and war whoops and—and tomahawks?" the Indian "just smiled and continued to write in a hand that would be a credit to a bank clerk." Prior to a game with the University of Denver, a reporter from the same city went out of his way to disabuse readers of old frontier stereotypes. Those who had shown up at the Brown Palace, one of Denver's finer hotels, expecting to see savage-looking Indians dressed in blankets and feathers went away sorely disappointed. The Carlisle players not only spoke perfect English, they would "stack up well with the white brother in point of intelligence, wit, and manly bearing."

Occasionally Pratt had his more articulate players address local gatherings. In 1896, after a disheartening game with Yale, Pratt and a dozen or so players attended Plymouth Congregational Church, the services conducted by the Reverend Lyman Abbott, one of the nation's leading advocates for Indian assimilation.

After disclaiming intimate knowledge of the intricacies of football, Abbott pronounced that the Carlisle players' skill and cool-headedness in the hard-fought contest with Yale surely proved that the Indian was capable of rising above "degradation and ignorance." The highlight of the occasion were the remarks of halfback Frank Cayou, an Omaha from Nebraska and one of Pratt's prize students. Cayou told the congregation how he had attended the World's Fair in Chicago three years before and how seeing the accomplishments of the white man had brought home to him the pitiful and degraded state of his race:

> Drunkenness and laziness is their curse. The white people keep the Indians on reservations. This degrades them. They are environed by civilization, but they are not of it. The Government sends my people money, and they drink it up. It was almost as bad to give them rations so freely, for they would eat in a short time what they had and go hungry without a thought for the morrow. I was that way, but I saw what the white people had done, and the desire possessed me—the ambition, I would say, to raise myself up and help my race. Their only hope is to live among the whites, be educated and adopt their ways.

The following year in Chicago, the day after a dramatic victory over the University of Illinois, the entire team attended a meeting of the Hyde Park YMCA. Once again, Cayou was the featured speaker. Some Americans might believe that the "only good Indian is a dead Indian," Cayou joked, but "there were no dead Indians at the Coliseum last night." The solution to the so-called Indian problem lay elsewhere, Cayou continued: "The greatest obstacle to the progress of the Indians is the reservation system. The Indians are penned up together and are not brought into contact with civilization. The environment is what makes men. Allow the Indian to mingle with civilized men and he will be civilized too."

One thing is clear. White football fans loved to cheer for the Indians. Indeed, when Carlisle played on neutral ground, crowd support was almost always on their side. In 1897, when Carlisle played Brown at the Polo Grounds, one sports correspondent reported how Brown supporters were "simply outdone by the opposition." In the game with Yale the same year, also at the Polo Grounds, the *New York Journal* reported that "the Red men were favorites from the kick-off." At one point in the game, when the Indians were plunging through Yale's line "like a drove of wild mustangs," the crowd "cheered and roared like a chained cyclone." Covering the same game, another reporter noted that in spite of the lusty cheers of four hundred Yale undergraduates, the crowd was "avowedly in sympathy with the 'underdog,' and cries of 'Carlisle' rang out throughout the contest." Even when the Indians played their games on the opposition's home turf, they were generously received. When the Indians played Harvard in 1900, "Those of the spectators who were not college men wanted the Indians at least to tie Harvard."

Why were white spectators so quick to root for the Indians? It is not easy to answer this question. The exercise of exploring the nature and meaning of fan psychology is a risky enterprise. Any such attempt must necessarily be based on limited and mostly circumstantial evidence; and must be framed in the context that Indian-white football, whether viewed as social drama or deep play, struck the psychological and mythic consciousness of fans at different levels. Carlisle's white fans, it turns out, had several reasons to cheer for the Indians. First, some found the Carlisle team living proof of the proposition espoused by Pratt and other reformers—namely, that Indians, while products of a savage heritage, were fully capable of making the transition to civilized life. Adherents of this view accepted, uncritically, the belief that policymakers' definition of the Indian problem had been accurate: savagism and civilization were irreconcilable states of existence in the progressive flow of historical time. Indians, fated for extinction as savages, might expect and surely deserved complete integration into the American polity once they were civilized. In a letter to the *New York Sun,* reprinted in *Red Man,* following Carlisle's game with Yale in 1896, one fan pointed out that the enthusiastic response of the 10,000 spectators seemed to signal a new day in Indian affairs: "It is safe to say that not one in one hundred of these ten thousand was not continuously, enthusiastically, and vociferously in sympathy with the Indians. It is the first time that this has been so. Never before has a great crowd of white Americans openly applauded the prowess and the deeds of a company of red Americans." The contest, the writer said, signified "a new appreciation of the possibilities of the red man, and it expressed, albeit without definite intention, a new hope for the Indian. Football is a scientific game, and the fact that these young red men have attained such proficiency in it demonstrates their capacity for the more useful and practical training which they receive at the Indian Industrial school."

A second reason for spectator support was the growing acceptance of the idea that Indians, while fated by historical circumstance to surrender their wilderness domain to a superior civilization, still had been terribly wronged, that the nation's original promise of "expansion with honor" had too often given way to betrayal and hypocrisy. If most fans had not read Helen Hunt Jackson's *A Century of Dishonor,* written just ten years before the Indians took to the gridiron, many embraced the sentiment of the book's title. "It is said that an Indian neither forgets nor forgives an injury," Clarke McAdams began his editorial following Carlisle's smashing victory over St. Louis University in 1908. The game's hero had been young Jim Thorpe. "Mr. Thorpe is a Sac and Fox. No Sac and Fox can either forget or forgive St. Louis. It was St. Louis that made the head men of the Sac and Fox nation drunk and induced them in this condition to sign away the tribal lands." Here, McAdams suggested, was the secret to Thorpe's stunning performance. And any fair-minded American should not begrudge the young Indian his moment of triumph. "No historian has ever attempted to defend the shameless manner in which St. Louis dealt with the Sac and Fox nation," McAdams continued. "Nor could any St. Louis football player hope to defend [the] goal against the young Sac and Fox impelled by a revenge that has waited for 75 years. Mr. Thorpe humiliated us nicely, which was just as it should have been. It was coming to us."

No situation was more guaranteed to awaken memories of historical mistreatment than the Yale-Carlisle contest in 1896. Played at Manhatten Field, the crowd was with the Indians from the game's start. Yale would win this particularly hard-fought contest, but only after a controversial ruling by referee Orrin Hickok, who, in the midst of a touchdown run by Carlisle's Jake Jamison, blew his whistle, declaring the ball dead. Hickok later admitted the mistake. As Jamison broke through Yale's line, Hickok thought the Carlisle player had been "downed," that is, the advance of the ball had been halted. Mistaken or not, the referee's ruling held, which sent both Carlisle players and their supporters in the grandstand into angry protest. For a minute, one reporter related, "everybody thought the Redmen would whip out their tomahawks and simply scalp the Sons of Eli in their tracks." The moment was indeed intense. As the crowd jeered, hissed, and howled their protest of the robbery, Carlisle players debated amongst themselves whether to return to the field. Finally, they did return and at the game's conclusion, against the background of a spirited ovation, were carried off the field on the shoulders of enthusiastic supporters. Spectators sympathetic to the Indian cause, saw the robbed touchdown as a metaphor for the nation's shabby treatment of its Indian "wards." The *New York Sun's* description of the episode reprinted in *Red Man,* viewed the unfortunate event as being "characteristic . . . of nearly all the crimes committed against the Indians by the whites, for it was accomplished by the man of all men who should have looked out for their interests and their rights." As referee, Hickok was responsible to see the game was played fairly. His role was reminiscent of that of the reservation agent, but the reporter continued "just as many an agent has proved false to his trust so this referee was to his." In another account of the episode, also reprinted in *Red Man,* a reporter for the *Rochester Advertiser* struck a more sarcastic note: "Now if we have a right to rob the Indian anywhere we certainly have a right to cheat him out of football games. . . . An Indian is an Indian just the same whether we find him on the buttes of the Dakotas or on Manhattan field, and the only strictly regular thing to do in either case is to hold him up and go through him."

A third explanation for spectator support is much more nuanced and takes us into a realm that may be described as deep play at its deepest. At the very heart of this explanation is the idea that many white spectators cheered for the Indians, not because they were civilized, nor because they had been wronged, but merely because they were Indians. Like the reporters who cast their stories of the racial clash on the gridiron as a metaphor for the real frontier Indian wars of the past, so too did Carlisle fans attribute to the spectacle a significance of mythic proportions. I am suggesting that at some level of consciousness, the thousands of white fans cheering for Carlisle must have realized that Indians and American identity were inextricably intertwined. But in this instance, the Frontier Myth told them they should root for the Indians. Without Indians there would have been no

Frontier Myth, or at least a myth stripped of much of its symbolic meaning. To imagine the American story without the Indian was, in effect, to imagine an America not worth imagining. In this sense, the villain in the American drama was as vital to the play as the hero. Then too, in post-frontier, industrial America, the "vanishing American" was increasingly becoming associated with the ideals and longings seemingly absent in the new social order—aboriginal freedom, primordial community, philosophical primitivism, mystical transcendence, connection to nature, and manly physicality. While some might applaud Carlisle players for their newly acquired civilized natures, others imagined nature's noblemen, innocent children of forest (and) plain, symbols of a lost Eden, what an earlier America had once known and must not forget. It was time to cheer for the Indians.

"And the spectators were with them," remarked a reporter for the *Boston Globe* covering the Carlisle-Harvard game in 1900, "the yodels of the crowd in the bleachers rising above the cheers." Similarly, in the *New York Sun's* 1896 account of the Carlisle-Yale contest, reprinted in *Red Man,* the reporter noted that every time the Indians made forward progress on the field their supporters "broke loose in a wild medley of sounds. Everybody seemed to have heard that the peculiar noise produced by rapidly and repeatedly clapping the hand over the mouth while in the act of shouting was a characteristic Indian way of yelling." During such times the exhilaration of the athletic contest meshed with the mythic space of the gridiron, transporting fans, if only for a fleeting moment, into the intoxicating and blurry world of "betwixt and betweeness" where the dichotomy of their white and Indian selves might be temporarily resolved, or at least transcended. In a sense, sending war whoops into the charged atmosphere of the grandstand was a kind of border-crossing, a diluted form of what Philip Deloria has characterized as "playing [I]ndian," a time-honored attempt of whites to ritualistically dissolve the "dialectical tensions at the heart of American identities." In the heat of battle, Carlisle fans might be transported to another time and space, they might even shed their civilized skins, embrace their Indian hearts, and enter a land where the deep-seated tensions—myth and history, civilization and savagism, Indian and white, memory and desire—were temporarily rendered extinct, or at least unproblematic. And at the game's close, if Carlisle should win the contest, what had been risked? Here was the beauty of it all: it was all just a game. However fans might play out their imaginations on the mythic space of the gridiron, real space—that is to say, the frontier—was safely in white hands. Clearly, it was a win-win situation.

Meanwhile, the Carlisle warriors tackled, bucked the line, and ate up the yards on the way to the "twin saplings." But what goal post? What meaning did Carlisle players read into the social drama of Indian-white football? Some reporters were quick to ascribe Indian enthusiasm on the gridiron to the natural desire of a vanquished people to settle an old score. Writing for the *New York Journal,* Stephen Crane surmised that players in the midst of game battle were thinking about how whites "have stolen a continent from us, a wide, wide continent which was ours, and lately they have stolen various touchdowns that were also ours. . . . It is too much. Let us, then, brothers, be revenged. Here is an opportunity. The white men line up in their pride. If sacrifice of bone and sinew can square the thing, let us sacrifice, and perhaps the smoke of our wigwam camp fire will blow softly against the dangling scalps of our enemies." In the 1895 game with Pennsylvania, a game in which "war waged fast, and war waged furious," an anonymous poet-reporter for the *Philadelphia Inquirer* imagined the inner thoughts of Carlisle's center as he spied the stalwart William Bull on the other side of the ball: "Oh, did I but have my long bow / Groaned the melancholy Lone Wolf / Then I'd do that sturdy man Bull / Do him up all right and proper / As my fathers did up Custer." Carlisle students must have found the reporter's poetic analysis, which was reprinted in *Red Man,* interesting. It is difficult to know what meaning Carlisle players gave to Indian-white football. Still, newspaper accounts and Carlisle school records on individual players, offer a fascinating glimpse into the players' attitudes. Two generalizations emerge from these sources: first, that Carlisle players read not a single but rather multiple meanings into their football accomplishments, and second, players viewed time spent on the gridiron as just one element in their overall Carlisle experience.

Some players simply loved the game itself, the exhilaration of performing heroic acts on the athletic field. Listen to Jim Thorpe recalling one of those special moments in the game with Harvard in 1911:

> As long as I live, I will never forget that moment. There I stood in the center of the field, the biggest crowd I had ever seen watching us, with the score tied and the game depending on the accuracy of my kick. I was tired enough so that all my muscles were relaxed. I had confidence, and I wasn't worried. The ball came back square and true, and I swung my leg with all the power and force that I had, and knew, as it left my toe, that it was headed straight for the crossbar and was sure to go over. . . . When the gun was fired and we knew that we had beated [sic] Harvard, the champions of the East, a feeling of pride that none of us has ever lost came over all of us, from Warner to the water-boy. As we meet now and then in our different fields of work, we no more than start to recall old times when the remembrance of that Harvard victory comes back and we smile again as we did on that day.

Some players clearly relished the public attention and material rewards that came with being a member of one of the nation's most distinctive football teams. In addition to being cheered by Indian and white fans, Carlisle players traveled the country and stayed in the finest hotels. Players also enjoyed a special status as one of the school's athletic elite, a status that manifested itself in a special "training table," separate living quarters, occasional gifts from the athletic fund, and being honored at the annual football banquet. The importance of these privileges is revealed in two letters team captain Pete Calac wrote to superintendent Oscar Lipps in the summer of 1915. Writing from Highland Park, Michigan, where Calac and several team members were gaining work experience with Ford Motor Company under the school's "outing" program, Carlisle's star running back expressed the team's concern and disappointment over rumors that Lipps was going to eliminate the special treatment that players had received in the past: "The training table and the building is the main talk among the boys here. They want a place where they can live and have the honor of living." Also of concern was the issue of whether the team could still have the privilege of wearing distinctive sweaters. "Say Mr. Lipps, I would like to ask if you could not get us some different varsity sweaters? I would like these sweaters with big necks. The neck part, being old gold and the body red, with end of the sleeves being old gold and edge of the sweater at the bottom also being old gold." Calac adds: "These other sweaters, it seems, everyone is wearing." As members of the school's warrior society, Calac seems to all but say, the footballers should be allowed to display their gridiron trophies.

Another factor that may have influenced players' attitudes relates to their degree of Indian ancestry. An examination of some 80 players' school files reveals that only 31, barely over one-third, were of full-Indian ancestry. Measured differently, 39 players, that is to say nearly half, were one-half or less Indian ancestry. The point here is that the blood quantum makeup of Carlisle football players told a different story of Indian-white contact from that propagated by sports journalists, which, at its very core, depicted frontier history as a protracted struggle across clearly defined racial and cultural boundaries. A majority of Carlisle players knew better. Their very bodies were physical testimony that the line separating Indians and whites on the frontier was rarely demarcated with the precision of chalk lines on a football field. Players' bodies told a story of blended identities and cultural exchange. Still, one must be careful about pushing this line of argument too far. Ethnic identity, historian Joanne Nagel reminds us, is a "dialectic between internal identification and external ascription." Levels of blood quantum can hardly be translated into equivalent measurements of ethnic identity. Indeed, there is good reason to suspect that the mixed-blood ancestry of Carlisle players was more than counterbalanced by the fact that to the wider world the Carlisle Indians were *Indians*. Moreover, when one considers the intertribal composition of the team, the fact that Choctaws, Senecas, Sioux, and Chippewas were a team—an association encouraged in part by the intensity and violence of the game—it seems reasonable to conclude that players, even more than other Carlisle students, were forging a new Pan-Indian ethnic identity. In that sense, the chalk lines on the gridiron still counted for something.

Another by-product of the football experience appears to have been a growing sense of ethnic pride. One manifestation of this can be seen in the efforts of several players to remove and replace Glenn Warner as the team's coach. The relationship between Carlisle players and Warner seems to have been a rocky one from the very first, stemming in large part from Warner's penchant for subjecting players to all manner of verbal abuse. "Having been coached by some rather hard-boiled gents during my years as a player," Warner later recounted, "I took a fairly extensive vocabulary with me to Carlisle, and made full use of it." As Warner goes on to relate, his use of rough language so inflamed team members' sensibilities that at one point several of his star players threatened to quit the team until he altered his ways. Realizing his mistake, Warner apologized "profoundly and profusely," and this ended the strike.

In fact, Warner's mistreatment of players would surface as one of the major themes in a special investigation of the school conducted by the Office of Indian Affairs in 1914. Particularly significant was the role played by football players in marshalling evidence against coach Warner. Several of the team's leading players—among them Gus Welsh, Elmer Bush, John Wallette, Edward Bracklin, Joe Guyon, and Pete Calac—submitted affidavits that Warner regularly mistreated players, heaping upon them not only verbal, but physical, abuse as well. Bush offered: "Mr. Warner is kind of rough to the football players, using profane language to them. I heard him curse a boy named William Hodge; called him a son of a bitch." Others testified that they had seen Warner strike or kick players on occasion. Inspector E. B. Linnen's description of Gus Welsh's complaints sounded a common theme in the charges: "He believes Mr. Warner is a good football coach, but a man with no principle; that he does not have the right influence over the student boys; that his is detrimental to their cause; that so long as he can use you he is all right with you; but the minute you voice your own sentiments and speak up for them he abuses you." The bottom line was that Warner no longer possessed the moral authority to coach the team and the players felt he should be removed—which subsequently occurred.

Who would replace him? And why shouldn't Indian players have an Indian coach? Actually, the latter question surfaced in a theoretical way at the 1898 football banquet when A. J. Standing, assistant superintendent, in the midst of praising the team, added that the Indians "still need a white man to coach, and to manage their finances." Later in the evening, team captain Bemus Pierce, Carlisle's star lineman, publicly rebuked Standing for his unfounded pessimism as to Indian ability. If the Indians' skill on the gridiron proved anything, Pierce offered, it proved that the race could "do most anything." Indeed, in 1906, Pierce was hired as temporary head coach, a position he wanted permanently, only to lose it to a returning Glenn Warner. Particularly revealing is the fact that after Warner was removed in 1914, at least three former players—Frank Cayou, Frank Hudson, and Bemus Pierce—scrambled to replace him. Pierce saw fit to remind superintendent Lipps that he, Pierce, had deserved the position instead of Warner back in 1907, but Major Mercer "was strongly in favor of placing a white man where an Indian could do as good work . . . I feel that Carlisle owe me the favor for I help make her fame in the football world." Moreover, sentiment was growing among students and alumni that the Carlisle Indians should be coached by one of their own. Writing on behalf of the Carlisle Alumni Association, Charles Dagenett wrote Superintendent Lipps, "I think I am voicing the . . . sentiment of the very large majority, if not all of the Carlisle alumni, when I say that they prefer to have the Carlisle team handled by Carlisle graduates." While in the end all the Carlisle applicants were passed over, the episode reveals players' belief in their capacity to perform at all levels of the football hierarchy.

So at what level did players view their contests with white teams as opportunities for gaining symbolic revenge? "All play means something," writes historian Johan Huizinga. Moreover, "The contrast between play and seriousness is always fluid. . . . Play turns to seriousness and seriousness to play." It follows that there are times in a contest when "a player can abandon himself body and soul to the game, and the consciousness of its being 'merely' a game can be thrust into the background." Similarly, anthropologists Brian Sutton-Smith and John Roberts observe, "Games exist to render conflict malleable. They do not merely socialize by mirroring. They socialize by mirroring and inventing. They are radical as well as conservative." The point here is that players, like spectators, were fully capable of reading multiple meanings into Indian-white football contests, and one of those meanings was symbolic revenge. Certainly the atmosphere surrounding such games—the fact that sportswriters and cartoonists were so quick to link the struggle on the gridiron to frontier conflict—did little to dispel such association. Another contributing factor was the presence of the Carlisle band, but especially the cheering section of "Indian maidens," which Carlisle sent to many of the eastern games. Consider the remarks of James Philips, who chose for his topic at the 1902 football banquet "Our Indian Girls." After references to the school's "medicine man" and how the team had "lost our tomahawk" in the game with the University of Virginia, Philips turned to the happier occasion when Carlisle had whipped their arch rival, the University of Pennsylvania. The victory, he suggested, belonged in part to the cheering section of Carlisle women who had come by train to support the Indian effort. The chant emanating from the grandstand was simply too much for the opposition: "Now, then, Pennsy, we will scalp you! /Guards-back formation will not go/ Wheelock and Johnson swift are rushing! To the front to fight the foe."

Glenn Warner certainly thought his players were after more than a football victory. "They did not manifest a school spirit, but they did have a racial spirit," Warner later recalled. "They seemed to recognize the fact that it was upon the athletic field that the Indians had an even chance against their white brothers, and they wanted to show that given an even chance they were the equal of their paleface brothers." Warner noticed, for instance, that his players never displayed the same spirit playing other Indian schools as when it was strictly "Indians against the White man." In keeping with this spirit, "if there was one team that the Indians liked to beat more than another, that team was the Army." Gus Welsh, quarterback in the 1912 game against Army, one of the best football teams of the era, confirmed Warner's contention. Still, as Welsh remembered it, Warner did his best to exploit players' embittered memories of Indian-white struggles on a much deadlier plain: "Warner had no trouble getting the boys keyed up for the game. He reminded the boys that it was the fathers and grandfathers of these Army players who fought the Indians. That was enough!"

On several occasions—and in some of the most unlikely of circumstances— players were known to make pointed historical and cultural references. In 1895, *Red Man* reported that when Pennsylvania's center, William Bull, was knocked flat, a Carlisle player pointed at the prostrate player and quipped to a nearby Indian, "Sitting Bull." According to Glenn Warner, in the midst of another game, when Indian fullback Pete Hauser was unfairly kneed by the opposition, he responded, "Who's the savage now?" And then there is this intriguing incident reported in 1907, when the Indians were in Chicago to play the University of Chicago: The day before the game, owing to the heavy rain, Carlisle prepared by playing an indoor basketball game at Lake Forest College. According to the reporter, during halftime the Indians "spotted a student whom they thought should belong to their race. They immediately grabbed him and proceeded to initiate him into the secrets of the various tribes. The Indians all came on the floor clad in blankets and made this youngster run the gauntlet and subject himself to an initiation of scalping, after which they danced their famous war dance." When the ceremony was over, the news item concluded, the initiate was presented to the crowd of onlookers with his new name—Blossom Berkheiser. What is one to make of this episode? There is much to doubt about the account. Was the subject of the team's attention part Indian, or simply an unsuspecting spectator? The comment that this "captive" was "initiated into the secrets of the various tribes," is nothing short of ludicrous. More than likely, the players were simply having a little fun, Still, as an impromptu ceremony, the performance also suggests that Carlisle players were not adverse to reminding spectators of their not-so-distant Indian past.

And then there are the comments of Dennison Wheelock, Carlisle's Oneida bandmaster. Speaking at the 1897 football banquet, Wheelock addressed what he thought was at stake in Carlisle's performance on the gridiron:

> At this school, we are trying to bring the Indian up to the position that the white men occupy. Long ago, it was said that the Indian could not understand civilization. It is repeated even at the present time. I deny it, I assert that what the Indian could not understand was the greed, the grasping selfishness of the white man in this country and when the Indian learned that his habitation and the hills he so dearly loved were being invaded, he justly cried, "There is eternal war between me and thee." And when he resisted, who will say that he did not do right? Who will say that he would not have done the same? He resisted with a thousand warriors, but he had to retreat westward like a hunted fox. . . . Today the Indian is beyond the Mississippi. The only way I see how he may reoccupy the lands that once were his, is through football, and as football takes brains, takes energy, proves whether civilization can be understood by the Indian or not, we are willing to perpetuate it.

Pratt always remained convinced that his experiment to use football as a mechanism for advancing his image of the "new Indian"—notwithstanding sportswriters' references to Indian savagery—was a thorough success. "During the past eighteen years we have been demonstrating that the Indian is not lazy, that he is industrious, and proved it beyond all peradventure," he told the audience at the 1898 football banquet. "We have talked about it, and published it everywhere, but it had little effect. Nothing has helped us into public notice so much as football." Four years later, at a similar gathering, Pratt announced that a cursory investigation of former players' lives confirmed that football had proved to be solid preparation for life's struggles after Carlisle; only a handful had failed to live up to the school's expectations. While Pratt probably exaggerated, the evidence suggests that many players did put their Carlisle experience to good use. For some, football was a stepping stone to further educational and athletic opportunities at the college level. Either as players or coaches; former members of the football squad would at various times appear on the rosters of the Universities of Illinois, Minnesota and Wisconsin, Georgia Tech, Dickinson College, Washington University, West Virginia Wesleyan, and Ohio University. Along the way, a select few became Indian school superintendents, lawyers, and in at least one instance, a dentist. Several players—among them Jim Thorpe, Joe Guyon, and Pete Calac—returned to the gridiron in the early years of professional football. Most, however, returned to their reservation homes to take up allotments, entered the Indian service, or took their chances in the labor market as semi-skilled laborers.

But once away from the cheering crowds many returnees found that the struggle for existence in the "real" game of life was difficult. In 1910, Superintendent Moses Friedman received this letter from David McFarland, a Nez Perce veteran of the football wars of the 1890s. He wrote in broken English from Lapwai, Idaho:

> Dear Friend: Thank you, of all you, as the school; as one of you many successful graduates who had done many good things towards the school, but if I done nothing good towards the school I done this much. I live up the school discipline and all what I've learned. I have many failures but I'll try to be true, trustful, in all my duties what ever I do. It does me good deal of good that the never forget me, but if I don't anythng wrong towards this school, or when I was as a student, I regret. At present I am clerking one of our stores on our reservation. Thank you for all may Happy New Year and successful 1911. I am your friend. David McFarland. '98.

From other correspondence it is clear that McFarland's strong identification with his alma mater was partly connected to his football experience. In another letter he paid his regards to "my friend 'Pop' Warner," thanking him for a school sweater. On another occasion he closed a letter to Superintendent Friedman with the words that he wished "to be remembered by my friends all that know me at Carlisle, as one of the old member of the foot player."

In the process of reporting on the course of their lives, former players frequently commented on the football team. Peter Gaddy, a Delaware blacksmith living in Shawnee, Oklahoma, recounted:

> I am getting along fine since I left Carlisle. I can never regret going to Carlisle. The period of time I spented at Carlisle has enabled me to start out in the world and I am making the best of it I can. I am interested in the school, because it is not only civilizing the redmen, but is developing him physically as well as moral and ennabled him to become a true citizen of America. I am also interested in the Famous Indian Football team. Glad to know they done so fine this last fall, and my wishes is always for Carlisle.

William Hodge, a Klamath, after reporting in 1914, "I am logging on the Klamath River and getting along fine," followed up with, "Will the football team have good season this year?"

If many former players took to heart Carlisle's uncompromising message of assimilation, not all did so. A case in point is Delos K. Lone Wolf, a full-blood Kiowa who played on Carlisle's earliest teams. In at least two respects Lone Wolf seemed to epitomize the model Carlisle graduate. Immediately upon his return to Kiowa country, he married, took up his allotment, and within a couple of years, secured the coveted position of agency farmer. Lone Wolf was also a life-long advocate of Indian education, and as a prominent tribal leader, continually pressed for increased funding for Rainy Mountain Boarding School. In his advocacy of both agriculture and education, then, the Carlisle-trained returnee appeared to be playing the role of the classic culture broker, helping his fellow Kiowas adjust to the cultural forces swirling around them. But in two other respects Lone Wolf deviated from the Carlisle assimilationist vision. In 1900, on the heels of Congress's ratification of the legally suspect Jerome Agreement, which for all practical purposes liquidated the Kiowa landbase, Lone Wolf assisted his uncle (also named Lone Wolf) and other traditionalists to launch a legal assault designed to forestall the dissolution of the tribal estate. While the litigation would eventually meet with disastrous consequences in the form of the 1903 Supreme Court ruling *Lone Wolf v. Hitchcock*, the episode reveals the former lineman's willingness to transfer his legendary skill at defending Indian turf on the gridiron to the real contest for Kiowa land on the Southern Plains. Indeed, in 1910, when Delos failed to fill out Carlisle's returned student survey, the agent responded for him: "Delos Lone Wolf is not up with the times; he has ambitions to be head of his tribe and lead them in the old tribal ways, which is a thing of the past in Oklahoma." By now, Lone Wolf was also a known user of peyote. In 1916, at a meeting of the Pan-Indian Society of American Indians in Cedar Rapids, Iowa, he was to ardently defend the new religion in open debate against his old school superintendent, Richard Pratt. Two years later, Lone Wolf was listed as one of two trustees of the Kiowa branch of the Oklahoma Native American Church. But Lone Wolf was still remaking himself. By 1923, he had joined the Methodist church, and by 1934, he was protesting John Collier's "Indian New Deal" as being anathema to Indian progress. If the course of Lone Wolf's life reveals anything it is this: Carlisle students in general, and footballers in particular, were more than passive victims in the acculturation drama.

As Lone Wolf's long-time association with the Native American Church suggests, Pratt wasn't always pleased with his former students' life choices. Consider the responses given by Benjamin American Horse on the 1911 returned student survey. A Sioux from Pine Ridge agency, and a member of Carlisle's first football team, American Horse reported that after returning home in 1895 he had married a Lower Brule girl, and over the course of several years had worked as both an agency interpreter and laborer. Moreover, in spite of accumulating little money, he possessed 960 acres of land, a good solid house with three rooms, a bath, 38 head of cattle, 17 horses, two farm wagons, and two plows. All of this would have pleased his former school master. What would have disappointed, even angered, Pratt was the former player's admission that one of his occupations was performing in Buffalo Bill's Wild West Show. The irony of it all. One of Pratt's reasons for allowing Carlisle Indians to play football in the first place was to offer the nation "show Indians" altogether different from those seen in the Wild West Show arena. And here American Horse was playing the part of the savage Indian. Interestingly, the supposed contradiction seems not to have bothered American Horse. Indeed, he indicated on the survey form that the next time Buffalo Bill's show was in the area he would come down and see his "old Carlisle friends." He added: "I had lots time thanks for Carlisle school had done me some goods. I never forget Carlisle school yet. Lots of time I wish I would be at school now. I am getting along O.K." American Horse offers further testimony to the proposition that Carlisle football players were capable of weaving, dodging, and running interference in their post-gridiron lives just as they had in their oftentimes heroic performances on the athletic field.

The various meanings that Pratt, sports journalists, cheering fans, and the Indians themselves read into the drama of Indian-white football were intriguingly complex. Pratt's motives are clear enough: to win public support for his ideas on Indian education and assimilation. But as we have seen, in the wake of recent frontier Indian wars, Pratt could not control the meaning that press and spectators ascribed to the spectacle of Indians and whites locked in a violent territorial struggle. For many onlookers, the gridiron in an Indian-white football contest, like the arena of the Wild West Show, became a mythic space where one of the defining chapters of the nation's history could be revisited anew. And if for some reporters the temptation to construct game narratives around the theme of the savage Indian war was simply too great to resist, others found reason to praise Carlisle players as symbols of the "new Indian." Meanwhile, white crowds cheered enthusiastically for the Indians. And why not? What was America without the Frontier Myth? What was the Frontier Myth without Indians? So much to win, so little to lose.

As for the players themselves, the rewards of the game were also substantial. At various times, football offered Indian players opportunities for testing their athletic ability, attaining status, seeing the country, advancing the cause of Indian reform, acquiring further education, working out issues of personal and cultural identity, and finally, for metaphorically settling old scores. The meanings that Carlisle players read into their gridiron battles were at once imposed and constructed, derived from their individual efforts to find firm footing on uncertain terrain, to make sense of a changing world where both Indian survival and identity were contingent on the ability to simultaneously resist and adapt, sometimes defending, always reconstructing the boundaries of their cultural selves. Carlisle Indians were forging identities—Pan-Indian identities at that—defying the simplistic and dichotomous categories of cultural essence in which Pratt or others might wish to consign them.

In the last analysis, both the degrees and kinds of symbolic weight that Carlisle players attached to their football experience can never be fully known. One wonders, for instance, what John Flinchum was thinking in 1918 when he traded his football jersey for a United States Army uniform. (Whether he enlisted or was drafted isn't clear.) Perhaps his thoughts were on winning military honors on a real field of battle. Or, perhaps Flinchum, who was by blood quantum just one quarter Choctaw, accepted gladly a patriotic duty as an American to "make the world safe for democracy." On the other hand, his thoughts just may have been closer to home—to make America safe for universal Indian citizenship. In any event, just before departing for France, the former football captain wrote to Carlisle with this request. He wanted to order a school sweater, a letter "C" that he planned to stitch on the sweater, and a subscription to the *Arrow*. "I wish you would send me two of those football seals and colors, one to put on my football certificate and one for my commission as Lieutenant." Precisely what significance Flinchum attached to these articles is not revealed, but it is evident that they mattered to him. The gridiron warrior-turned-soldier, it appears, was getting his symbolic ducks in order.

Suggested Reading

David Wallace Adams, *Education for Extinction: American Indians and the Boarding School Experience, 1875–1928* (Lawrence: University Press of Kansas, 1995), is the broadest treatment of the boarding school movement. For the view of the man who founded the Carlisle Indian School, see Richard Henry Pratt, *Battlefield and Classroom: Four Decades With the American Indian, 1867–1904*, ed. Robert M. Utley (New Haven: Yale University Press, 1964). Brenda J. Child, *Boarding School Seasons: American Indian Families, 1900–1940* (Lincoln: University of Nebraska Press, 1988), examines family responses to having children away at school. For a case study of another boarding school, see Robert A. Trennert Jr., *The Phoenix Indian School: Forced Assimilation in Arizona, 1891–1935* (Norman: University of Oklahoma Press, 1988).

CHAPTER SIXTEEN

Alcohol and the Anishinaabeg of Minnesota in the Early Twentieth Century

Kathryn A. Abbott

In the earliest contacts between Europeans and Indians during the colonial era, white observers such as traders, diplomats, and clergy commented on how badly the tribal people abused alcohol. Reports of Native hunters cheated out of their bounty for the year by whiskey peddlers, or of tribal negotiators being duped into signing one-sided treaties while drunk, were common. These accounts spread and reinforced the image of Indians as unwilling or unable to deal with alcohol effectively.

Because such stories appeared so often and over such a long time, their repetition fostered the stereotype of the drunken Indian in American history. Bigots in the frontier population cited examples of intoxication near western reservations as proof of the Indians' moral and physical inferiority and as a justification to discriminate against them. Missionaries and educators supported efforts by federal authorities to keep liquor away from Native groups. While some scholars pointed to alcohol abuse as a sign of personal and community social collapse, this essay places Anishinaabeg drinking in a regional, early twentieth century context.

Sociologist Joseph R. Gusfield posed the question in a 1996 essay, "Why are there so few studies of drinking in America?" Admitting that he was "playing on ambiguities and diversities in the meanings and understandings of the word *drinking*," Gusfield argued that the vast majority of studies of American drinking are concerned with "pathological drinking" dictated by a framework of all drinking as a "social problem." Alcohol researcher Robin Room concurs that in the United

States there has been a "systematic tendency to dramatize the results" of alcohol research in a way that magnifies the problems. In the case of studies on American Indian peoples and drinking, these contentions could not be more true. Indeed, embedded in the discourse about alcohol and Native Americans is the assumption that drinking is a "special" problem for Native peoples. Certainly, the current statistics on American Indians and alcohol seem staggering: a death rate from alcoholism seven times higher than the national average, alarmingly high incidences of alcohol-related deaths, and the suggestion by some that because Fetal Alcohol Syndrome has become "endemic" in American Indian cultures, pregnant Indian women should be jailed to prevent their drinking.

As early as the seventeenth century, long before the idea of alcohol pathology had been clearly articulated, European observers described Indian peoples as "passionately attached," even "addicted" to drinking. From such observations sprang the "firewater" myth, the idea that genetic weaknesses resulted in Indians' innate inability to drink temperately. By the mid nineteenth century, ethnographer and Indian agent Henry Rowe Schoolcraft articulated this myth in the broadest of terms: "All the Indian nations, and almost every person among them, male and female, are infatuated with the love of strong drink. They know no bounds to their desire." This generalized view that drinking is a particular problem for American Indians has limited historical inquiry into alcohol use in individual Native groups.

Scholars have now begun to question both the generalizations and the statistical basis for assessing Indians' alcohol consumption. Sociologist Philip May, for instance, suggests that "an analysis of current mortality data" reveals that many of the assumptions about Indian drinking "are either false or, at best, half-truths." May maintains that alleged "alcohol-related problems . . . may well be found in demographic, geographic, political, and cultural variables that are not necessarily uniquely Indian."

Stephen Kunitz's and Jerrold Levy's two studies of Navajo drinking provide some further conceptual tools for examining Native drinking in cultural and historical context. In the first study, published in 1967, the authors concluded that drinking behavior varied among the Navajo, depending upon geographic location and the cultural parameters of the drinking population. In a 1992 follow-up, the authors found that as the Navajo men aged, most were able to "stop or severely curtail their drinking," an observation that was especially true for those in the "traditional" sample. Further, Kunitz and Levy found "striking similarities" between the Navajo and non-Navajo residents of Arizona's border towns, suggesting that "multiracial regional cultures" exhibit drinking patterns that make them "more similar to one another than either may be to people of the same race elsewhere in the country."

Believing that close analysis of Indian drinking in context is the key to understanding actual drinking behavior, I propose in this essay to apply a regional approach to assess whether or not Anishiniaabe drinking habits in early twentieth-century Minnesota reflected a multiracial, regional pattern and whether some Anishinaabeg consumed alcohol in a manner that was not necessarily destructive to either the individual drinker or to the culture as a whole. I am not attempting to prove that drinking was not problematic for some Anishinaabeg. In fact, the evidence suggests that dispossession during that period, particularly at the White Earth and Leech Lake reservations, increased alcohol-related problems. However, I maintain that any study that focuses solely on problem drinking is incomplete, and that a broader historical approach places drinking along a continuum. There were, in fact, several consumption patterns among the Anishinaabeg, a diversity that was culturally based and historically contingent upon the circumstances facing Minnesota's Native population in the early twentieth century. And this variety was not unique to the Anishinaabeg. Indeed, there was a wide range of non-Indian responses to drinking in northern Minnesota, and comments of concern about non-Indians' alcohol consumption were broadly similar to those expressed about the Anishinaabeg.

In the seventeenth century the Anishinaabeg, composed of several distinct but related bands centered at the Straits of Mackinac, were early participants in the French trade, which included alcohol. Anishinaabe women controlled the exchange of alcohol to French, British, and then American traders, for which they provided items such as maple sugar and corn. In this exchange, both Anishinaabe and Euro-American traders equated alcohol with food. The Anishinaabe term for alcohol, interestingly, means mother's milk, and in the important gift-giving ritual, which sealed the mutual obligation and good faith between the two groups of traders, alcohol played a major role. By the late seventeenth century, a significant number of Anishinaabeg had migrated from Mackinac to the southwestern shores of Lake Superior. Settling at Chequamegon Bay, the Anishinaabeg pursued subsistence strategies based around fishing, farming, hunting, and trading. At Chequamegon, intermarriage between French *coureurs de bois* and Anishinaabe women led to a new, distinct people who would become known as the Métis.

Beginning in the early eighteenth century and increasing after the end of French colonial presence in North America in the 1760s, many Anishinaabeg gradually migrated from the Great Lakes to the area that is now Minnesota. Anishinaabe bands and villages operated independently of each other, and, although alliances formed for military purposes or to negotiate treaties, the daily existence of the Anishinaabe settlements varied widely. The amount of contact each village had with non-Indians also differed greatly.

Given this variation, Anishinaabe people, not surprisingly, developed different styles of drinking. As Jack Waddell explained in his analysis of French trader Francois Malhiot's journal, those Anishinaabeg living near or traveling to trading villages and posts had significantly more access to alcohol than did those in the interior, away from the trading networks. Alcohol arrived in interior villages occasionally but in limited supply. In these isolated settlements, Anishinaabeg sometimes ritualized their alcohol consumption. "It was customary to pour it out into a large kettle and place it over a fire," reported one trader to Henry Rowe Schoolcraft in the early nineteenth century. "A hand of tobacco was then put in. After being heated and stirred about for a time, the mixture was drank [*sic*]." In Anishinaabe tradition, tobacco served the ceremonial offerings of giving thanks and seeking protection. For this particular village of Anishinaabeg, tobacco, when combined with alcohol, served to ritualize and incorporate the "hot toddy" into their lives.

Between 1820 and 1867, U.S. Indian agents increasingly pressured the Anishinaabeg to alter their lifeways and to cede valuable lands. During that period, a series of treaties with the federal government codified their tribal identity as the "Chippewa Nation," but U.S. agents induced the Anishinaabeg to cede the greatest portions of their lands only after 1854. As pressure for lands mounted, conditions for the Anishinaabeg deteriorated.

It was in this context that several Anishinaabe bands in central Minnesota signed treaties agreeing to move to White Earth Reservation, established in 1867. Heralding the potential for Anishinaabe people to adopt white American values by becoming yeoman farmers, federal policymakers at White Earth began in the 1880s to break up the tribal land-base by awarding plots of land to Anishinaabe heads of households while simultaneously granting U.S. citizenship to allottees. Once allotment was underway, Indian agents encouraged—indeed, often compelled—Anishinaabe bands to migrate to White Earth.

Many White Earth residents initially adapted successfully to allotment, the Anishinaabeg settling in bands on those areas of the reservations that suited their lifeways. According to historian Melissa Meyer, "by 1900, those who had migrated to White Earth . . . had evolved a society based on band ties and residence patterns." Despite their early successes, by 1910 rapidly changing circumstances had caused most Anishinaabeg at the White Earth and Leech Lake reservations to lose their lands. Dispossession—and the subsequent destruction of the woodland ecosystems at White Earth and Leech Lake through logging—helped create severe material and physical deprivation for many.

Coinciding with this dispossession was an increasing concern with citizen-Indians' access to alcohol, and a series of Supreme Court decisions attempted to resolve the legal anomaly of Indian peoples who were both citizens and wards of the United States. A 1905 decision, known as *Matter of Heff,* ruled that federal laws prohibiting the sale of alcohol to Indian citizens violated their Fourteenth Amendment rights. The *Heff* ruling led to the passage of the 1906 Burke Act, which allowed for the delay of citizenship for Indian allottees who were "not fitted for its duties or able to take advantage of its benefits

The *Heff* decision also led to the establishment of the Special Office for the Suppression of Liquor among the Indians, part of the Bureau of Indian Affairs that operated from 1906 to 1917; The Bureau of Indian Affairs invested considerable money, time, and manpower into the special office and, for reasons

that reveal as much about the Prohibition struggle among whites as about Anishinaabe drinking habits, the Indian Bureau focused an immense amount of
attention on northern Minnesota. Invoking treaties that were one half century
old, the special office sought to eradicate liquor sales, first for Indian people and
later, as the push for national prohibition intensified, for everyone throughout
the entire "Indian territory" of northern Minnesota.

The available evidence for studying alcohol in Anishinaabe society is problematic. Indian Bureau correspondence and reports and contemporary newspaper accounts constitute the bulk of the written evidence. It is important to
remember several things about observations of Native drinking: first, observers
brought with them particular cultural biases and their own understandings of
alcohol, not only for Indians but for non-Indians as well; non-Indians varied in
their attitudes towards both alcohol and Native peoples. In addition, the social
spaces in which non-Indians observed Native peoples were generally limited.
In the case of drinking behavior, this is particularly true; non-Indians observed
Indian drinking at specific domains, such as the public streets and the semi-
public saloons in and around the reservations. And, if there were places on the
reservations where Anishinaabeg did not drink, reporters and Indian Bureau
agents were unlikely to venture there—they were not looking to scrutinize non-
drinking Anishinaabeg. Thus, the evidence itself necessarily highlights drinking
as opposed to non-drinking.

In the early 1900s, numerous opportunities existed for reservation-based
Anishinaabeg to visit off-reservation towns and villages where they could consume alcohol. Annuity payments in particular brought Anishinaabe people into
towns where they not only purchased goods and supplies, but also socialized
with friends and relatives whom they had not seen in a while. The social atmosphere of these pay towns echoed that of nineteenth-century trading towns.
The annuity payments, which most often occurred in October after the fall harvest, brought together more Anishinaabeg than any other event. Jacob Munnell
(aka Mis-qua-dais), a Leech Lake–born Indian agent, recalled that in the town
of Bena, annuity payments were "a chance for almost every man, woman, and
child" to congregate, making paydays "big and elaborate affairs."

In Minnesota's non-Indian pay towns Anishinaabe people renewed old ties
and caught up on tribal news, often while imbibing alcohol. Saloons played an
important social role for the Anishinaabeg as they did for many non-Indian sa-
loon-goers in the early twentieth century—they were centers of community gos-
sip and conviviality. Some Anishinaabeg entering the saloons at Walker, Detroit,
Park Rapids, or Bena drank too much, and others got drunk, but not everyone
drank to excess at these social activities.

Indeed, Indian agent William Johnson suggested in at least one report that the
Anishinaabeg understood that there were times when drinking was simply not
desired. In 1909, Johnson described a trip of some 80 Leech Lake residents to the
Minnesota State Fair in St. Paul: only a "few" Indians drank and all "came back

sober." The state fair excursion contrasted starkly with his account of activities in the town of Walker where, Johnson claimed, "an average of twenty-five drunken Indians" could be seen daily. Most of the Leech Lake Anishinaabeg doubtless understood that attending the state fair was not an occasion for drinking, whereas socializing in nearby reservation towns was. Such an understanding suggests that the Anishinaabeg were not indiscriminate and uncontrolled inebriates, as they were so often depicted. At the same time, it is also possible that the close supervision of the Indian agents made alcohol consumption less desirable on both a practical and a social level.

Minnesota's towns served a variety of other important commercial functions for the Anishinaabeg. In the early twentieth century, Anishinaabeg traded furs, berries, rice, and maple syrup for dry goods, cloth, blankets, and household items. Such a pattern was a continuation of earlier nineteenth-century customs in trading towns. In 1910, "hundreds" of Anishinaabeg arrived in Walker with "sleigh-loads of furs," which they traded for "supplies" and "whiskey." Others brought in freshly picked berries, which they traded for goods and sometimes alcohol,

One Leech Lake resident recounted that, when Anishinaabe men returned to camp after drinking in town, spousal abuse was a possible result. According to this account, Anishinaabe women would "take off for the woods," sleeping there all night while their fathers and husbands drank. Yet, the available evidence highlights the varied relationship that Anishinaabe women had with drinking. Women were at times the victims of male violence when their husbands, fathers, or brothers became drunk, but some women also drank and fought. They were also at times subjected to the abuse of non-Indian men. And, at all times, observers considered women's drinking a particular problem. Thus, Anishinaabe women fell into a different but sometimes overlapping continuum from Anishinaabe men.

Certainly, non-Indian observers often commented on the impact of men's drinking on Anishinaabe women. One Walker resident claimed that when the saloons there closed in 1910, it was "the first winter their women, children and ponies have been cared for," while a Brager woman claimed that "Indian women come to me for bread for their children barefooted and almost starving" because of their husbands' drinking. Yet the same woman also stated that, when the Native women got hold of some money, there was "some Blood Sucker after them to sell them a bottle of whiskey."

U.S. Indian agents also worried that white men subjected drunken Anishinaabe women to sexual abuse. In 1909, Special Officer William Johnson wrote:

> I have been informed by traveling men, by Indian officials who have visited the place [Mahnomen], and by United States Attorney General Haupt of St. Paul, that it has been the practice of the liquor dealers at Mahnomen to get squaws drunk in their saloons and strip them naked for the edification of the crowds of drunken toughs.

Johnson repeated this story in a 1910 report, and three and one-half years later, U.S. Attorney C. C. Daniels recounted a strikingly similar story about the town of Ogema. Were these stories true? Perhaps, but it is also possible that such discourse provided the justification for the legally questionable activities of the Special Office for the Suppression of Liquor among the Indians. Once the story itself became part of the rhetorical landscape, it held the power to attract the attention of the Bureau of Indian Affairs and its agents.

The perceived danger of women in bars extended far beyond the boundaries of the White Earth Reservation. Indeed, the discourse around Anishinaabe women and saloons echoes that which surrounded non-Indian women in the United States. Increasingly in the 1910s, as urban working women began to frequent saloons both to drink and to partake in the free lunch offered by many establishments, the national press and prohibitionists professed deep concern that the saloons were corrupting "decent and self-respecting girls." At White Earth, Indian agent Alf Oftedal reported in 1913 that behind the saloons on White Earth Reservation "Indian harlots . . . pl[ied] their trade." The connection between alcohol and sexual impropriety permeated the discourse of Victorian and Progressive-era observers. The potential moral dangers made saloons and other public venues unacceptable for virtuous women.

One White Earth resident worried about the potentially damaging influence that an off-reservation education held for Anishinaabe girls. George Michael suggested that Anishinaabe women who learned English were especially susceptible to corruption, averring that a young woman's "ability to talk good English" gained her entree into conversation and eventual "ruin" with "the lumberjack" in the saloon. As a result, Michael maintained that "no Indian girl who goes away from home to attend school is safe after she returns home." Michael's letter and the comments of various Indian agents are remarkably similar in tone to those expressing concern over white women nationwide. No less than their non-Indian counterparts, Anishinaabe women's virtue had to be protected from the certain corruption associated by some with saloons. Although the stereotype of the harlot stood in obvious contrast to women needing protection, the gap between those who viewed Anishinaabe women as degraded and demoralized and those who viewed them as needing protection was not that great—both views justified continued policing of Anishinaabe women.

Observers also often commented on women's participation in the annuity-related saloon visits in northern Minnesota. One newspaper noted that, after the annuity payment, "squaws and bucks alike shared in the exuberance of the occasion." In 1905, Red Lake Reservation's superintendent, G. L. Scott, bemoaned alcohol sales to Indian people, "extending as it does to the women." And a teacher at a White Earth school wrote that she had observed drunken Anishinaabe "men and women, fighting among themselves, [and] with the whites." Accounts of Indian women and drinking were particularly potent because of the assumption that women generally were more susceptible to the effects of alcohol than were men. The seeming acceptance of drinking among women often was used to discredit Indian people as a whole, because what hope is there for a culture in which women drink openly and often to excess?

Some Anishinaabeg also occasionally consumed alcohol while engaged in subsistence activities such as wild ricing and berrying, traditionally female activities until the 1900s. Remains left at a ricing and berrying camp at the Bois Forte Reservation indicate that bringing along bottles of whiskey was an accepted part of the process and that both men and women consumed the beverage. One man claimed:

> [a] lot of Indians come there and camp and drink and I suppose that the Indians emptied the bottles . . . they must have picked the bottles up at the place where [they] camped to scorch their rice.

These subsistence activities began in the summer and continued into the fall, with rice-scorching beginning after the September harvest.

Drinking by Anishinaabeg engaged in berrying and ricing may indicate that alcohol consumption was somewhat commonplace and accepted by the Bois Forte Anishinaabeg. Indeed, as anthropologist Marianna Adler shows in her study of nineteenth-century British Islanders, such communal activities "served to reaffirm principles . . . of social relations of exchange in a precapitalist economy." Similarly, many historians of pre-industrial America note the centrality of alcohol to work and play, activities that were not mutually exclusive. For the Anishinaabeg at Bois Forte, drinking while berrying and ricing may have served to separate these activities from paid labor or farming on isolated homesteads.

Yet some subsistence activities were not compatible with alcohol. Success as a hunter or medicine man depended on keeping to a rigorous and demanding regimen, including days of fasting. One Mille Lacs resident recalled a medicine man who had lost his power because he "got to drinking too much." At the same time, the Anishinaabe campsite became a venue for drinking and storytelling when the hunt was completed. There, after supper, said the informant, they "would start the story telling," reciting a "different one every night." Thus, although the evidence is sketchy, alcohol may have served as part of the oral transmission of Anishinaabe tradition and culture.

A 1912 exchange between Acting Commissioner of Indian Affairs Frederick Abbott and James Draper of Bowstring, Minnesota, highlights yet another style of drinking. This incident raises several issues concerning the Native people in early twentieth-century Minnesota, including assimilation, economic self-sufficiency, and intercultural sociability. On 19 July 1912, Draper sent a letter to the United States Secretary of the Interior, writing:

> I have always made my own living payed [sic] for my own schooling, and drank whiskey bought with my own hard earned money in doing so I didn't harm any body else. I now have a Homestead and doing some locating [surveying]

and it often happens that I meet some of my costumers [sic] in town and natu-
raly [sic] they will want to buy a drink or a cigar, in some cases they tell me
they can't give me a drink. Now that is harrising [sic], and it is not right.

James Draper could not purchase whiskey at the local saloon because he had, in
his words, "some Indian blood in me."

If assimilation into the mainstream of northern Minnesota's culture was in
fact the goal of the Indian Bureau, Draper should have been free to mingle with
his customers in Bowstring's saloons. Draper did not maintain that he was an
Indian, just that he had "Indian blood." Indeed, for the Anishinaabeg, racially
determined categories held little meaning—an "Indian" was someone who lived
with and adopted the habits of Indians. The more "traditional" Anishinaabeg
occasionally referred to the Métis residents of White Earth as "white Indians,"
indicating that, although they had ties to the Anishinaabeg, their lifestyle defined
them as something other than Indian. Yet, just as non-Indian definitions of "Indians" were in flux in the early twentieth century, so too were Native definitions
of their identity. In the early 1900s, as factionalism and resentment over the allotment process grew, White Earth traditionals frequently invoked the mixed-
blood status of their opposition as reason for their corruption. In one case, those
who opposed the Métis businessmen at White Earth sought their removal from
the reservation, referring to the Métis businessmen in testimony as the "Lake Superior mixed-bloods." Although the reasons for these disputes go far beyond the
question of racial mixing, it is significant that the Anishinaabeg themselves were
adapting at least their rhetoric about Native identity to fit into the framework of
the Bureau of Indian Affairs.

People such as James Draper fell even further outside the Anishinaabe definition of Indianness. The 1887 General Allotment Act stated that those who had
"adopted the habits of civilized life" would automatically become U.S. citizens.
This position is reflected in the 1890 U.S. census, where the 58,806 "civilized
Indians" not living in "Indian territory or on Indian reservations," were enu-
merated in the general census. However, non-Indians' definition of an "Indian"
were in flux in the early twentieth century, as U.S. policymakers abandoned the
belief that individual Indian people could achieve civilization, citizenship, and
equality. As social evolution melded into strongly articulated views of scientific
racism, many non-Indians argued that even assimilated Indians were incapable
of achieving complete civilization.

Draper's self-description places him in the ranks of working homesteaders,
many of whom probably counted on the connections solidified at the local saloon to bolster their "locating" or other businesses. Several recent histories have
explored the importance of saloons and saloon culture in the early twentieth
century. Saloons in Chicago's neighborhoods, for instance, served as important
centers for ethnic mixing. In saloons in Worcester, Massachusetts, the practice of
"treating" was a particularly significant custom for establishing and maintaining

social ties. And, outside of Indian America, these predominately male bastions of communication, informal politics, and socioeconomic relations were under attack in the early twentieth century as much for the culture of the saloon as for the alcohol consumed there.

In the 1910s, northern Minnesota's saloons reflected a regional culture of drinking. By accepting a drink or a cigar from his customers, Draper was participating in a common social ritual of saloon culture in northern Minnesota. But increasing legal restrictions placed both Draper and his non-Indian peers in an awkward position. Barred from drinking with his business customers, Draper was cut off from the socially lubricating potential of alcohol, from the possibility of his incorporation into the regional drinking culture of northern Minnesota, and from the larger socioeconomic functions of the saloon. One point seems obvious—U.S. policymakers' definition of assimilation for Native peoples did not include saloon culture, no matter how assimilative participation in northern Minnesota's saloon life might have been.

Prior to the Indian Office's crackdown on Indian alcohol sales, the regional drinking culture in northern Minnesota was multiracial. One Leech Lake resident recalled that, as a boy, the town of Bena was a "mixed settlement" with "saloons and all those other kind of buildings" at which "lumber jacks" and Indians alike drank and socialized. Indian agent Harry Larson described Bena, listed as having 179 people in the 1910 census, as "a small town with an exceptionally large Indian population in and surrounding it." He described other towns near Leech Lake (including the villages of Cass Lake, Federal Dam, and Deer River) in similar terms. Assistant Attorney General E. H. Long wrote that Mahnomen, within the boundaries of White Earth Reservation, had "quite a population of half breed Indians and a number of Whites," noting that on the allotments surrounding Mahnomen were Indians "ranging from Full blood to nearly of White blood." And, Indian agent William Johnson described Deer River's saloons as "dens of thieves," containing a mixture of "Indians and 'rolling' lumber jacks." "The man who does not use liquor here in Northern Minnesota is decidedly the exception," wrote Bois Forte agent Thomas Jackson in 1909. The Anishinaabeg there, said Jackson, "take on the 'polish' of civilization," learned from non-Indians at the saloon.

Between 1890 and 1900, the U.S. Census Bureau dramatically altered their method of identifying Indians, making it difficult to determine the racial composition of northern Minnesota's off-reservation towns in the early 1900s. Between 1900 and 1910, the census approach shifted again. However, it is clear that in the early twentieth century, many Anishinaabeg moved into villages composed of both Indians and whites. Conversely, many non-Indians also moved into newly established towns within reservation borders. It was here that some Anishinaabeg intermingled with non-Indians in the local saloons and in the community. Enforcing regulations against selling alcohol to Indians in this multiracial society, where some Indians were "nearly of White blood," was difficult at best.

With increasing pressure from the Indian Bureau during 1909 and 1910 to refrain from selling liquor to Indians or to close down and face financial ruin, James Draper's customers understandably demurred from buying him a drink at the Bowstring Saloon. Laws preventing liquor sales to people like Draper hampered the economic independence and social interdependence that might have provided Minnesota's Indian people with the tools to integrate successfully into non-Indian society. In the end, the policing efforts of the Special Office for the Suppression of Liquor among the Indians bolstered the conviction among non-Indians that American Indians were racially inferior, unable even to drink alcohol responsibly.

With the heterogeneous social context for drinking removed, the visibility of Indian drinkers increased. Local non-Indians bombarded the Indian Bureau with complaints about Anishinaabeg drinking on the streets, in railroad yards, and in lumber yards. Alcohol consumption for the Anishinaabeg had moved out of the accepted semi-public saloon into unacceptable public spaces. Moving Anishinaabe drinking to the public arena increased arrests and inflamed the debate over the so-called problem of Indian drinking.

Attempts to enforce Indian prohibition in northern Minnesota achieved limited success. Leech Lake resident William Morrell recalled the process. Before the special office's prohibition efforts, Morrell reported, he bought liquor "right in the saloon"; afterwards, though he still bought whiskey in the saloon, he consumed it elsewhere. "The Indian gets all the whiskey he wants," James Draper maintained, "by getting someone to buy it," paying a dollar for the whiskey and dollar to the person obtaining the liquor. Restrictive liquor policies thus penalized Native peoples while simultaneously rewarding bootleggers and middle men. While some saloons openly defied Indian prohibition, most that sold alcohol to Indians did so surreptitiously.

"Blind pig" operations both off and on the reservations, were more common as the 1910s progressed. A Cass Lake bartender sold liquor to Leech Lake Anishinaabeg in his spare time, meeting his customers by the fence outside his house and passing them a brown package containing the contraband. Indian agent John Hinton reported that most of the blind pigs at White Earth were run by non-Indians, but Hinton worried that, with Indian prohibition in full force, the number of Anishinaabe bootleggers was rising.

One of the most elaborate methods of procuring alcohol occurred at the remote Bois Forte (Nett Lake) Reservation, where some Anishinaabeg used their skills and their knowledge of northern Minnesota's terrain to negotiate the tricky boundary waters and procure liquor from Anishinaabeg living on the Canadian side of the border. Indian agent J. P. Brandt reported that the Bois Forte Anishinaabeg would canoe to Canada, obtain alcohol, then drop the contraband in the woods on the American side. The canoeists would then return home. Later, one of them would go on foot to pick up the liquor. Although Canada also had an active prohibition movement (with the North-West Mounted Police establishing a reputation with their success in eradicating liquor sales to American Indians there) Bois Forte's isolation, combined with its proximity to Ontario, contributed to the availability of liquor from Canada—enforcement for a vast geographical area fell to the North-West Mounted Police whose activities in Ontario were minimal.

Some Anishinaabeg, of course, did not drink, and among White Earth Anishinaabeg an active faction opposed alcohol use on the reservation. In 1909, nine White Earth women petitioned the commissioner of Indian Affairs to stop illegal liquor sales at White Earth Village. Claiming that no degree of vigilance would prevent alcohol's devastating effects, the only answer was to drive the liquor sellers from the White Earth Reservation and confiscate their property, thus removing a "hellish menace" from the reservation. The signers of this petition included several members of prominent Métis families; including the Warren and Johnson families, descendants of early fur-trading families. At least two of the women were related to local Protestant ministers. These women, considered part of White Earth's "progressive" faction, likely received an education at Euro-American schools, where they were instructed on the evils of alcohol. At White Earth Reservation, some Anishinaabeg often fueled factional tensions with accusations of alcohol abuse and liquor selling. This petition may have been designed with at least a dual purpose—that of eradicating both the liquor and its sellers.

The White Earth women's petition is similar to those circulated by members of the United States' women's temperance movements in the late nineteenth and early twentieth centuries. Indeed these women may have been active in a local WCTU or other temperance organization. Along with the Prohibition Party, the Anti-Saloon League, and other radical dry advocates, in the early 1900s, the WCTU lobbied against high saloon license fees and local option laws and for a constitutional amendment prohibiting alcohol.

A group of Anishinaabe men also actively opposed the "liquor interests" at White Earth. When, in 1913, the Mahnomen town council refused to revoke the liquor license of a saloon keeper convicted of selling to the Anishinaabeg, Indian agent Alf Oftedal indicated that the "Indians living in the Village of Mahnomen" were "threatening to vote out the saloons at the next primary election." "White people," one Anishinaabe man complained to the commissioner of Indian Affairs, "told one great big lie" when they promised that "no whiskey would be sold to the Indians." The men's activities also reflect the larger pattern of anti-alcohol activity in northern Minnesota. In a drive called the "Campaign of 1909 and 1910," Minnesota's Prohibition State Committee played a central role in trying to persuade the Indian Bureau to use Indian treaties to force Prohibition on all northern Minnesotans, Indian or not.

At several reservations in Minnesota, Anishinaabe men and women in the early twentieth century signed temperance pledges, which promised that they would never drink alcohol. These pledges were a popular form of temperance activity nationwide in the late nineteenth and early twentieth centuries. At White

Earth Reservation, the temperance pledges seem to have been a popular practice among the relatively small number of Episcopalians there. At Bois Forte, however, the temperance pledges were a reservation-wide phenomenon. Temperance pledges were a technique that had a long history in the larger temperance movement. Much of the Anishinaabeg's anti-alcohol activities fit into the larger regional culture's anti-alcohol activity, suggesting yet another dimension of the multiracial regional culture of alcohol. Further, this temperance agitation also points to the active role that Anishinaabe people were willing to take in opposing alcohol in their communities. Indeed, it is important to note that Native peoples have long been in the forefront of defining alcohol not only as a liability for their cultures but a liability in general.

Finally, the evidence, though limited, indicates that U.S. Indian agents in northern Minnesota recognized the futility of absolute prohibition of alcohol. At Leech Lake Reservation in 1913, a tourist informed the Indian Bureau about a powwow he attended at Norway Beach on Leech Lake. The specific incident concerned an Anishinaabe mother who, according to the tourist, had drunk to excess, thus endangering her baby. The resultant investigation refuted the tourist's claim. However, the numerous letters concerning the investigation make it clear that both Leech Lake's superintendent and its doctor knew that the Anishinaabeg had been consuming alcohol at the powwow. This case suggests that, despite its official antipathy to drinking by American Indians, Indian agents may have tolerated a degree of alcohol use among Leech Lake Reservation's Anishinaabeg. Such sanctioned consumption, with the approval of Leech Lake's agents, appears to have been a semi-official "time-out" from prohibitions against alcohol on the reservation. Agents may have felt that by allowing for cultural remission, the day-to-day problems of drinking might even be lessened. While at most reservations, Indians agents pursued a policy of prohibition at Indian festivities, enforcement was difficult. Perhaps Leech Lake's agents viewed limited consumption of alcohol on special occasions as an acceptable compromise.

In conclusion, the evidence presented here suggests that, in the early twentieth century, the Anishinaabeg created and maintained their own styles of drinking. There was a depth and complexity in the Anishinaabeg's relationship to alcohol; some Anishinaabeg used saloons as social centers for intra-tribal socializing while others assimilated into the multiracial saloon "frontier." Still others drank informally while camping and engaged in subsistence activities. And some Anishinaabeg were active opponents of alcohol. In short, the range of responses to drinking varied for Anishinaabe men and women. These drinking and anti-drinking activities were distinctive yet also reflected the unique circumstances of early twentieth-century northern Minnesota.

In the future, historians examining American Indian drinking must place it in clear cultural and historical context, by examining tribal patterns of alcohol consumption while also exploring the larger regional context. This essay has proposed that understanding both the literal and the symbolic meaning of alcohol, as it was understood by the historical subjects themselves, will help create a model for future studies of drinking.

Suggested Reading

Stereotypes of Indians' inability to deal effectively with alcohol have been widespread throughout much of American history. For the colonial era, see Peter C. Mancall, *Deadly Medicine: Indians and Alcohol in Early America* (Ithaca: Cornell University Press, 1995). Margaret Anne Kennedy, *The Whiskey Trade on the Northwest Plains: A Multidisciplinary Study* (New York: P. Lang, 1993), examines related issues in the nineteenth-century West. For a more extensive look at related events in Minnesota, see Melissa L. Meyer, *The White Earth Tragedy: Ethnicity and Dispossession at a Minnesota Anishinaabe Reservation* (Lincoln: University of Nebraska Press, 1994).

CHAPTER SEVENTEEN

"The Old System is No Success"

The Blackfeet Nation's Decision to Adopt the Indian Reorganization Act of 1934

PAUL C. ROSIER

National policies toward the Indians since American independence appear at best confused, even contradictory. Over the generations these policies included military conquest, involuntary land cessions, removal, segregation, voluntary and forced acculturation, and assimilation into the general society. As federal officials implemented these conflicting approaches, they often ignored the desires of the tribal peoples. Indeed, they rarely bothered to ask what might be useful, even acceptable. Predictably, the outcome failed to live up to the goals of the policy makers. Rather than creating literate and skilled people, educational programs disrupted reservation cultures, destroyed family ties and Native languages, and brought disease and death to Indian children. Tribes did not gain economic self-sufficiency but instead became wards of the government.

In 1928 the Meriam Report provided a devastating critique of tribal circumstances. Five years later, recently appointed Commissioner of Indian Affairs John Collier proposed a new system meant to overcome past mistakes and injuries. The Indian Reorganization Act of 1934 offered reservation dwellers an opportunity to create new tribal governments and gave them increased authority over their local circumstances. The contentious program divided many tribal communities. This essay considers how and why the Blackfeet Nation chose to implement the new program.

"'The Old System is No Success'" appeared in *American Indian Culture and Research Journal* 23, no. 1 (1999): 1–37.

If the condition of the Blackfeet Indians at this time is to
be taken as an index of the character of trusteeship which
the Government imposes upon other Indians, the work has
been a failure. The spectacle is a depressing one and calls not
only for immediate relief but for an entire and permanent
change in the manner of handling their affairs.

SENATOR HARRY LANE, 1914

Give us a fair and new deal as we know ourselves the old
system is no success.

BLACKFEET COUNCILMAN RIDES AT THE DOOR, 1933

The Indian Reorganization Act (IRA), the cornerstone of the Indian New Deal,
is the most important piece of legislation in twentieth-century American Indian policy-making. Earl Old Person, the great full-blooded Blackfeet leader,
discussed the IRA's role in twentieth-century Indian progress in his speech to
the 1966 convention of the National Congress of American Indians. "The first
breakthrough came with the Indian Reorganization Act of 1934. This permitted
a Government policy of organization by allowing tribes to adopt constitutions
which provided terms for managing their own affairs." The IRA represented the
start of a long-sought and much-needed dialogue between Indian leaders and
federal officials, whose organizing principle under Commissioner of Indian Affairs John Collier rested on "the revolutionary proposition that Indians were not
obstacles, but peoples." The IRA became an attenuated version of Collier's vision
of Native political economy—a syncretic economy managed by empowered tribal governments that would adopt white business practices and, Collier hoped,
encourage a renewal of Indian culture.

Most studies of the IRA naturally have focused on its impact on tribal eco-
nomic and political organizations. The judgment of most historians is that the
IRA, and the Indian New Deal in general, failed to solve the problems of Indian
America largely because it was the product of white bureaucrats. Thomas Biolsi
argues in *Organizing the Lakota: The Political Economy of the New Deal on the
Pine Ridge and the Rosebud Reservations*—the best case study of the Indian New
Deal to date—that "[t]he Indian New Deal in general and the IRA in particular
were clearly not Indian ideas." Graham Taylor concludes in *The New Deal and
American Indian Tribalism: The Administration of the Indian Reorganization Act,
1934–35*—the best general study of the Indian New Deal to date—that the "reforms of the Indian New Deal failed to endure because, in the last analysis, they
were imposed upon the Indians, who did not see these elaborate proposals as

answers to their own wants and needs." This interpretation of the adoption and administration of the IRA is not entirely mistaken, but the impact of the IRA on Native American communities is too variegated to justify sweeping statements that deny Indians the acuity and agency to adopt the legislation and to use intelligently its various provisions for political and economic change.

The case of the Blackfeet Nation revises this prevailing notion of Indian passivity and white imposition; the tribe's decision-making process was more interactive than coercive. This essay does not study the impact of the IRA on the Blackfeet Reservation, but rather the impact of the idea and the promise of it. The focus is the impetus of the Blackfeet Nation's decision to adopt the IRA: why, given the historical and historiographical opposition to the IRA, did 83 percent of the Blackfeet electorate that voted on October 27, 1934, brave a snowstorm to support it? The essential argument is that Collier's vision and the legislative form it took in the IRA mirrored the Blackfeet Nation's own reform agenda, a mixture of wants and needs and assumptions about its past and its future that had formed during two decades of government supervision. At the same time, the Blackfeet's active participation in the IRA debate influenced the outcome of the bill by helping important policymakers—like John Collier and Senator Burton Wheeler of Montana, who, as chairman of the powerful Senate Indian Affairs committee, was both the act's cosponsor *and* its most vocal critic—understand the viability and desirability of its key provisions. The Blackfeet Nation presents a good case study for several reasons. First, the Blackfeet had a tradition of political activity; thus their debate on the IRA was relatively advanced and thoughtful. Second, Senator Wheeler's relationship with the Blackfeet affected the final shape of the IRA because *his* conception of it was based largely on his decade-long experience with the tribe. Third, the tribe was resource-rich but underdeveloped; the essay will thus help answer Marjane Ambler's question whether oil resources played a part in certain tribes' decision to adopt the IRA.

An understanding of the Blackfeet's decision-making process would be incomplete without some background on the tribe's political and economic development. The first part summarizes twenty years of such development in what is hoped is a felicitous fashion. The second part examines the IRA debate on the Blackfeet Reservation and in Congress during the winter and spring of 1934. The Blackfeet, where appropriate, speak for themselves. Their voices emerge from tribal meetings, council minutes, congressional testimony, and personal letters. If interviews with Blackfeet voters were available, dissenting voices, particularly those of full-bloods unable to speak the English language, would have been more accessible. But the essay is, in the final analysis, about the emergence of a tribal political action which developed as a result of the Blackfeet speaking among themselves, asserting their interests through elected officials and community leaders, and collectively making the decision to adopt "terms for managing their own affairs."

The Battle over the Tribal Estate

Scores of federal allotting agents began swarming like locusts through the American West after Congress passed the 1887 General Allotment Act to start the engines of progress designed to remake the physical domain and cultural character of the American Indian in the image of the yeoman farmer. Allotment came relatively late to the Blackfeet Indians of northwestern Montana. It was not until Congress passed the act of March 1, 1907, that authorization was granted to begin the allotment of the Blackfeet Reservation. One of the most debilitating aspects of the 1887 act was the provision that required tribes to sell their "surplus" land to white homesteaders; the 1903 Supreme Court decision in *Lone Wolf v. Hitchcock* prohibited any legal challenge to Congress' right to abrogate treaties and thus its authority to order the sale of surplus land. The mandated sale of the Blackfeet's 156,000 "surplus" acres divided the tribe during the 1910s. Between 1913 and 1916, open conflict between two factions manifested itself both on the reservation and during congressional hearings held to determine the fate of the Blackfeet land base. Class politics and attendant conceptions of land use emerged as the tribe debated the best way to utilize the reservation's resources from which it hoped to become "self-supporting." The dissension in the tribe was not simply between mixed-bloods and full-bloods, though this was a principal division, but between large stockowners and small stockowners; in 1885 only eighteen mixed-bloods lived among roughly 2,000 full-bloods, while in 1914 there were 1,189 full-bloods and 1,452 mixed-bloods. The Blackfeet allotting agent reported in 1910 that the tribe suffered from an unequal distribution of agricultural wealth: "[Twenty-nine] families, all but one being mixed bloods, own practically one half the number [of livestock], while many full bloods have but one or two if any." In 1915, fifty of the fifty-six owners of more than one hundred head of stock on the reservation were either mixed-blood or white.

The predominately mixed-blood faction comprised large stockowners acting in congress with white business leaders who supported the sale. Faction leaders appeared before congressional committees in 1914 and 1916 to argue that the proceeds of the surplus land sale should be spent to expand the Blackfeet livestock industry. Robert Hamilton, a mixed-blood who represented the interests of the mostly full-blood faction, testified in 1914 that "it looks as though the white man, in many instances, was the beneficiary of the reservation." Hamilton's opposition to the land sale centered on three issues. One, he opposed the unilateral nature of the sale, asking a joint congressional commission in 1914 that Blackfeet "consent be first obtained before any lands are again arbitrarily taken from US." Two, he believed that the government's intent to sell the land to homesteaders was misguided, given the vicissitudes of northwestern Montana weather; government agents had been arguing for decades that farming was a tenuous proposition in Blackfeet country. Three, and most important, Hamilton wanted to use the land as a means to further the tribe's management of its economic affairs, offering a three-point plan that involved the leasing of the surplus acreage to cattlemen, farmers, and mining companies. The Blackfeet have been suffering, he told Congress in 1916, "while the lands lie idle. . . . Lands have been sought by persons willing to pay for the use of them. The development of mines, the development of beet raising, and grazing would give many Indians employment who can not now get anything to do." He also argued that the land contained large deposits of oil and gas that could make the Blackfeet "self-supporting" and called for the protection of the tribe's mineral rights. The Blackfeet were ready to work, Hamilton told Congress. "The blame lies with the governmental supervision." BIA administrators had failed to listen to Blackfeet voices about what would work in their part of the world; policies conceived in Washington would not necessarily take root in Blackfeet soil.

Congress decided the fate of the 156,000 acres when it passed the act of June 30, 1919, which included many of the provisions proposed in a 1916 bill. But it did not order the sale of the land; as a result, each enrolled Blackfeet received an additional eighty-acre allotment. After a long struggle against an "iron triangle" of interests, to use Theodore Lowi's phrase, Hamilton and his full-blood supporters succeeded in preserving the territorial integrity of the Blackfeet Reservation. Although the land was no longer capable of being used for economic development *in toto,* the tribe's mineral rights to the land were protected and it remained in Blackfeet hands. The question for the Blackfeet in the coming decade was whether they would be given sufficient opportunity to construct a political economy that was predicated on the cultural and geographical realities of Blackfeet life rather than the pedagogy of its "guardian."

Oil and Agriculture Don't Mix

Robert Hamilton had been the *de facto* political leader of the Blackfeet since 1915, when he assumed control of the Blackfeet Tribal Business Council (BTBC) and began campaigning to secure exploration of the tribe's putative oil reserves and to expand tribal management of reservation businesses and resources. He told Interior Secretary Franklin K. Lane in 1916 that "we have every reason to believe that our tribe will develope [*sic*] into a self-supporting condition if the natural resources upon this reservation are developed." Congress and the Office of Indian Affairs (OIA) refused to grant the council any authority to lease its lands or even acknowledge its modest attempts to further tribal economic control; for example, the OIA ignored Hamilton's reasonable proposal to manage a tribal commissary. After summer drought and harsh winters in 1919 and 1920 wiped out the economic gains created by the demands of war, the discovery of oil in neighboring Cut Bank and on the Crow Reservation in 1921 created an "oil excitement" among the Blackfeet that lasted for most of the decade. Full-bloods and mixed-bloods alike viewed oil leasing as the best means to produce an economic future for the tribe. By 1921, however, the government had failed to approve a single tribal lease, and thus no oil money had been pumped into the Blackfeet treasury. The OIA, using the Osage Indian phenomenon as its model, gambled that the Blackfeet would achieve a higher return on their oil assets if the region could be determined to contain oil rather than just the possibility of oil. The restrictive policy angered both the tribal council, which was focused on developing its putative oil resources, and individual Blackfeet who were denied a chance to generate an annual rental income.

The BTBC also blamed new superintendent Frank C. Campbell, who assumed office in 1921, for the lack of progress on oil development. Campbell's passion lay in agriculture, not in natural resource development. Campbell sought to insti- tute a formal program of agricultural production, directing it to the reservation's full-bloods, who had been dependent on government rations for the most part since the end of World War I. Campbell's Five Year Industrial Program (FYIP), which became the OIA's prevailing agricultural policy, emphasized the cultiva- tion of small gardens and plots of wheat, the construction of a flour mill and a sawmill, and sheep grazing. Its institutional framework comprised twenty-nine chapters of the Piegan Farming and Livestock Association (PFLA); each chapter elected a president, vice president, and secretary to help manage its operations. For full-bloods, Campbell's program represented a comprehensive approach to community living and an opportunity to participate in the management of their domestic affairs. The object of the program, as full-bloods wrote in their charter, was to create a sense of pride in the Blackfeet Reservation that would put it "first among reservations in a united effort towards Good Homes, Good Citizenship, Self-support and Loyalty."

Campbell's assiduous promotion of the FYIP on and off the reservation alien- ated influential mixed-bloods who had little interest or confidence in subsistence farming. The entrepreneurs of the tribe wanted to expand the reservation econ- omy to include the creation of cash surpluses or profits; they were interested in more than just survival. Campbell's organization of the full- bloods resulted in a polarized reservation: mixed-bloods and the business council they dominated against the full-bloods and their agricultural chapters. The two factions went on the "war path," as one chapter officer put it, when Hamilton and his supporters called for Campbell's termination and for the abolition of the OIA. In pursuing with great zeal the expansion of his "industrial" program, Campbell neglected other issues that mixed-bloods and some full-bloods believed he should have addressed; his inability to facilitate oil leasing and his failure to assist the BTBC's efforts to renegotiate grazing fees proved especially damaging to their relation- ship. Campbell had succeeded in managing well only one part of the reservation, though investigators disputed his claims that the FYIP deserved commendation. He certainly failed to provide competent administration to the tribe as a whole, particularly in the important area of natural resource development.

Frustrated by the constraints of the OIA's leasing system and Campbell's ne- glect of its agenda, the BTBC looked for new ways to expand oil development on tribal land. The tribe received only $2,729.68 from oil leasing between 1921 and 1926, the product of five lease bonuses ranging from $500 to $719; oil leasing on restricted allotted lands netted $11,740.16 from forty-five leases, most of which the OIA eventually "disapproved." In February 1927, the council considered a plan devised by Jack Galbraith, whose own tribal lease had been voided due to the inaction of his development partner. Galbraith proposed that the council mortgage the tribe's timber reserves to raise capital, arguing that the Blackfeet should form their own corporation to develop oil rather than rely upon a diminishing number of white oil prospectors; he explained that "if we operate our own well here we will know what is wrong with our money, and our well and why we quit and what is wrong with our resources." BTBC members expressed interest in the idea of forming a tribal corporation. Full-blood councilman George Starr told his colleagues: "The oil is here, it is all around us. . . . You half breeds are just as smart as any white man and some are smarter and we can do our own drilling, form a company and do our own work and you can do it if you just get it into your neck that you can do it." The council voted to prohibit the use of tribal timber as collateral, but it formed a new oil committee to explore other ways in which the tribe might raise funds to expand its role in developing its own resources.

By late 1928 most Blackfeet had lost confidence in Campbell, who was absent from the reservation for more than eight months each year, and "had apparently changed their minds and were giving a great deal of credence to the theory that they were being very much abused by the government, and that the various investigators were going to correct many of these things and see that their alleged rights were protected." For many mixed-bloods and an increasing number of full-bloods, the Blackfeet Nation had reached a point of diminishing returns from federal supervision.

The Meriam Report and a Congressional Investigation

The congressional investigations that the 1928 Meriam Report helped spawn contributed further to the Blackfeet's perception that reservation management needed a literal and figurative facelift. The report focused on, among other issues, the lack of economic progress in Indian communities, blaming this condition in part on the lack of business education and organization on reservations. The report recommended "using the corporate form of organization for tribal property that consists of great natural resources which cannot be economically administered or developed in small allotments," and thus laid out a "vision," previously lacking in federal policy, for the Indian Office to foster the economic advancement of American Indians. The Indian Reorganization Act of 1934 would embody this vision.

A subcommittee of the Senate Committee on Indian Affairs—comprising Senators Lynn Frazier of North Dakota, Burton K. Wheeler of Montana, and W. B. Pine of Oklahoma—subsequently visited many of the nation's larger reservations to get a firsthand look at the problems of Indian administration and Indian poverty. The subcommittee spent July 24, 1929, on the Blackfeet Reservation and lay bare two decades of agency mismanagement. It charged that Campbell and his predecessors failed to protect Indian property from encroachment by whites, fostered discrimination against Indians in favor of white labor and businesses, failed to assure adequate health conditions, and neglected to keep accurate records of land and business transactions. Walter Liggett, a Senate investigator, reserved most of his criticism for the agency's handling of the tribe's resources, concluding that Blackfeet lands

> do not bring in the revenue they should. They are entitled to a bigger return and they could get it if the agency officials acted with the same zeal that they would display if employed by private interests. But, instead of attempting to get every possible penny for their Indian wards, in many cases they appear to be acting as though they represented the white lessees.

If the Meriam Report was to be used as a guide to bring Indian economies into the twentieth century, then the place to begin, judging from the administration of Blackfeet resources, was with the OIA itself. If the Indian Service was to emphasize economic education, as the report recommended, then it would need new teachers. Assistant Superintendent Forrest Stone would replace Campbell after the hearing, which represented a victory of sorts for the tribe and symbolized the importance of BIA leaders addressing the needs of diverse tribal constituencies.

Both BTBC and PFLA officers pressed for expanded control of tribal finances and expeditious oil development after the 1929 hearing. In May 1931 PFLA members voted to extend the FYIP for another five-year term; attending the annual meeting were influential mixed-bloods Robert Hamilton and Joseph Brown, who were intent on sustaining the tribal unity engendered by the 1929 congressional inquiry. Two resolutions passed at the meeting reinforced the basis of this unity: common frustration with BIA administration and common interest in developing tribal oil reserves. Resolution #1 requested that any tribal money in the United States Treasury be divided equally among members of the tribe and paid out in per capita payments. Resolution #3 promoted the "development of oil and gas on the Blackfeet Indian reservation" and sanctioned the BTBC's role in leasing allotted land as well as tribal land to developers. Chapter officers wanted to minimize the OIA's management of tribal finances and economic development; full-bloods were as frustrated as mixed-bloods about the centralized control of Blackfeet policy. If oil leasing succeeded, then PFLA leaders did not want that money held in Washington or used by the OIA for programs like irrigation without the tribe's consent. In addition, the United States Court of Claims was due to render a decision on a suit filed by the Blackfeet and other Montana tribes to win compensation from the government for failing to honor treaty obligations; the Blackfeet called it the "Big Claim." The "Big Claim" and oil leasing also dominated business council meetings. John G. Carter, the tribe's attorney in Washington, told the council in July 1932 that he believed Congress would reach a decision on the claim within six months and award the tribe two million dollars. Council members asked him to protect from government meddling whatever judgment the tribe received. James White Calf told Carter, "I am asking you to see to this, that instead of putting it in banks or in Washington, I want to see this money given out to us in cash." Rides at the Door was equally concerned with the slow pace of tribal oil development. He asked Carter and the council, "Why is it that these wells on the outside of the reservation are developed and completed, and ours are not? Why is it that the Blackfeet reservation can't be developed?" Natural resource development, he argued, "will help set us on our feet." The Blackfeet were hoping for two windfalls and desperately wanted to ensure that they could control the distribution of any newfound wealth.

By the end of 1932 the "oil excitement" was again at a high pitch. In late December, the *Cut Bank Pioneer Press* reported that "Stone sees prosperous days ahead for Blackfeet Indians through oil development." Stone did not think the Blackfeet would get as rich as the Osage, but did say "the outlook at the present time appears exceptionally bright." The Blackfeet finally saw oil flow on their reservation in April 1933 when wildcatter Tip O'Neil's well produced roughly seventy-five barrels of oil. On April 28, 1933, a group of Blackfeet, including several "Chiefs in full regalia" and the tribe's famous band, visited the tribe's first producing well to celebrate mother earth's new offering. The first oil strike and the per capita distribution that resulted were not large by any means, but after so many years of promises unfulfilled, they were tangible.

Collier, Congress, and a Consensus

The John Collier era in Washington began the same week that the Blackfeet finally achieved a measure of success in oil production, two equally propitious events. The Blackfeet were familiar with Collier from previous visits, and from his defense of Indian rights during the 1920s; as executive director of the American Indian Defense Association, Collier battled the OIA and Congress over Pueblo land rights, Indian oil rights, and an Indian's right to due process. Collier also accompanied the Senate subcommittee to Browning in 1929 for its investigation of Blackfeet affairs. He sent Assistant Commissioner William Zimmerman on a similar journey in 1933 to see firsthand the problems of Blackfeet administration.

When the subcommittee returned to the reservation in October 1933 the two factions were restless and united in their desire for organizational change. The 1933 hearing differed in content and character from the one held four years earlier, in part because the well-traveled Senate subcommittee was familiar with the problems facing the Blackfeet, and because Stone's superintendency had not generated controversy as Campbell's had. Despite little progress in oil production and arguably no progress in grazing resource management, the tribe did not point to Stone as the principal source of failure but to the OIA or, more generally, the guardian relationship of the federal government to the Blackfeet Indians.

Two weeks before the committee arrived, the venerable full-blood Mountain Chief, the Blackfeet's oldest "hereditary chief," organized a meeting to discuss the tribe's need for better representation in Washington. He told the gathering that he believed a delegation should travel to Washington to outline the tribe's demand for better management of its natural resources. "We are tired of the leasing of our grazing lands and tired of outside sheep companies. We want to utilize our own resources and develop our oil lands," he said. Rides at the Door, active in pursuing economic development for many years, called for a "'new deal' as we want to be treated the same as the white people. Give us a fair and new deal as we know ourselves the old system is no success." The tribe's full-bloods had had enough of government supervision and became increasingly outspoken about the "mismanagement" of the tribe's funds and property, joining the chorus of mixed-bloods who had been pushing for more control of the tribal estate since the early 1920s. Those hardened views found expression in other tribal meetings and in the October 19 subcommittee hearing.

The subcommittee first discussed the tribe's dormant irrigation projects, a particularly sore subject for most Blackfeet. The principal question facing the OIA and Congress was whether to abandon several unfinished projects that had been successful only in draining valuable funds from the tribal treasury. Joe Brown, the fifty-eight-year-old BTBC chairman, explained that the council opposed abandonment of the irrigation projects but wanted the tribe and the agency superintendent to take control of them. He told Senator Burton Wheeler that the Blackfeet "can handle them more economically and to the better satisfaction of the Indian than the Reclamation Service." Brown urged the senators to facilitate the replacement of white workers with Indian workers when possible, expressing the desire of his people to assume more responsibility for their affairs, the dominant theme of the hearing; of the seventy-three agency employees only thirty-six were Blackfeet. He also requested that Wheeler find government funding to help the Blackfeet develop a tribal oil company and buy a tribal livestock herd. Brown told Wheeler that if the government would provide seed money for a tribal drilling operation then "why not the Blackfeet themselves as a company borrow money and drill these oil wells themselves and get 100 percent of the oil rather than get the 12 1/2 percent that they get now." If white stockmen could turn a profit after paying taxes and grazing fees, he explained, "why can not we, the Indians who own the land and who do not pay these taxes nor do not have to pay for the grazing, make a success of the stock industry."

While Wheeler opposed tribal control of oil development, he did support Brown's plan to expand the Blackfeet livestock industry. Wheeler continued to champion the allotment policy and a variation of Campbell's Industrial Program, but he also sanctioned greater Blackfeet control of reservation business affairs. "We ought to push as much responsibility onto them as we possibly can," he told Superintendent Stone. Stone answered that if the tribe's competent members were given a chance to manage the livestock industry, tribal irrigation, and a proposed creamery plant, then within ten years "you would find the Blackfeet Indians very largely in control of their own industries." He ended the hearing with an admonishment to the committee: "We cannot afford to lose the interest that they have right now to handle their own affairs."

Tribal, congressional, and Indian Office leaders reached a consensus during the 1933 hearing that the Blackfeet were able and willing to manage their business affairs. Senator Wheeler remarked at the end of the hearing that "the Indians on this reservation are capable of taking care of themselves." Four years earlier, Senate investigator Walter Liggett had concluded that "there has been a tragic failure to teach these Indians the true fundamentals of education. After many years in leading strings they are not equipped to cope with the conditions they are facing." The truth lay somewhere between those opposing sentiments. The prevailing perception, however, was that the Blackfeet could do no worse than the OIA in managing their natural, financial, and human resources; their interest in improving tribal affairs was, to understate it, greater than that of their Indian agents. If the Meriam Report recommended eventually "winding up the National administration of Indian life," then the Blackfeet wanted it sooner rather than later, given the state of affairs on their reservation.

The Idea of the IRA and the First Blackfeet Debate

It was John Collier's sense of mission and passion for Indian reform that led Secretary of the Interior Harold Ickes to appoint him commissioner of Indian Affairs. Ickes defended his selection and Collier's philosophy by saying: "The whites can take care of themselves, but the Indians need some one to protect them from exploitation. I want a man who will respect their customs and have a sympathetic point of view with reference to their culture. I want the Indians to be helped to help themselves." The Collier administration was thus poised to produce a "new day" for the American Indian rather than the "false dawn" of Hoover's New Era. In the reform-minded atmosphere of depression America, Collier and his dedicated staff assiduously promoted a vision of organizational change in Indian administration that would be codified as the Indian Reorganization Act. The incorporation of Indian America became the cornerstone of his reform package.

While Collier and his staff prepared a legislative agenda and an attendant public relations campaign, in early 1934, the Blackfeet considered the changes that were brewing in Washington. The 1933 Senate subcommittee hearing had created an expectation of reform among interested Blackfeet, and they were eager to see what the new administration had to offer them. Their first exposure to the new regime was Collier's circular letter of January 20, which was sent to all tribes and their superintendents to introduce the philosophy of the Indian New Deal. Collier's twelve-page letter, simply entitled "Indian Self-government," first emphasized his hope that Indians would themselves contribute to the process of improving their affairs. The establishment of Indian self-government and the concomitant expansion of economic opportunity were the program's twin goals, Collier wrote, emphasizing that each tribe should be given "the maximum measure of control over its economic life and, in particular, over expenditures of its own funds." He delineated the basic architecture of an organized Indian community, providing a sketchy blueprint for the gradual termination of federal supervision. Collier recommended that state governments assume the responsibilities of education and health matters and ultimately that a reconstituted Indian community, if properly organized, be given "complete supervision over its internal affairs."

On February 5 the business council convened to discuss the letter and Collier's reorganization plan; nearly seven hundred Blackfeet attended the meeting, the largest gathering ever assembled for a discussion of political matters. Superintendent Forrest Stone opened the meeting with a short summary of Collier's letter and legislative agenda, which he called "an opportunity that will never be presented again." He reminded the Blackfeet that the tribe had lost 2.5 million acres of land in the last fifty years and argued that Collier's land policy would end the diminution of the tribal estate and give them "something to hand to your children." Stone raised the controversial issue of communal ownership, saying that the "matter of pooling your lands will equalize things, even though it does take a sacrifice on the part of some of you to do this." Collier's proposal for Indians to remise their allotted lands to tribal ownership sparked a fierce debate. Few Blackfeet expressed a willingness to make the "sacrifice." James Perrine, a supporter of Collier's self-government provisions, expressed skepticism about his land policy, declaring: "We are not Menonites [sic] yet." Owen Heavybreast spoke for many of his fellow full-bloods when he criticized mixed-bloods who would benefit from the pooling of Blackfeet lands, saying that many of them had "squandered" a "share of the reservation" when they sold their allotments; many full-bloods had retained their allotments. Hugh Jackson was the most outspoken, arguing that "it looks as if we want to be governed under a communistic form of government like in Russia I don't believe we should try any changes." The Blackfeet, Jackson said, "are living in the United States, and the system is that you have to own property by title. We are not in a foreign country, and we got to travel along with the people in the state of Montana. We got to live like the rest of them." Speakers did agree that the tribe's best economic policy continued to be the development of its oil reserves. Despite some initial success the previous year, the reservation was not being developed in contrast to neighboring Cut Bank; three wells were in operation compared with seventy in the Cut Bank fields. Collier's proposal failed to mention resource development, Perrine noted, and told the council that it should convince the Interior Department that "this resource should be developed as quickly as possible so that the Indians here will receive the ultimate benefit. Then our reasons for assembling here to ask or beg the government for this and that would be eliminated, because we will then have our own subsistence." Perrine's call for renewed attention to oil development found solid support from both mixed-bloods and full-bloods.

Stone wrote Collier several days later to tell him that despite "doing some pretty strenuous work" explaining Collier's intentions to the tribe, "the feeling is running quite strongly against the plan." The threat of mandatory land consolidation in particular did not appeal to the Blackfeet. There was great confusion about what Collier intended, on the Blackfeet Reservation and elsewhere in the country, especially regarding the idea of communal ownership. Collier wrote Stone three weeks later to encourage him to continue discussing the proposed legislation and explain that "it is not the purpose of the bill to take land away from those who have it and give it to those who have not." The kind of confusion and anger that Collier faced from tribes like the Blackfeet was a principal reason he initiated a series of conferences with Indian leaders the following month.

The Great Plains Congress

The debate on the Wheeler-Howard Bill—Collier's forty-eight-page "plan" that was sponsored by Burton Wheeler and Edgar Howard of Nebraska, chairmen of the Senate and House Committees on Indian Affairs, respectively—began in the House on February 22, and in the Senate on the 27th. Collier announced during the House hearings that he would be taking his reform program to the people it would affect by organizing a series of Indian congresses, the first time the OIA had given its charges an opportunity to consider important legislation before it was imprinted upon their reservations.

Eighteen members of the Blackfeet Nation joined tribal representatives of nearly sixty thousand Plains Indians in Rapid City, South Dakota on March 2, 1934, to hear Collier himself delineate the important facets of his vision of modern Indian administration. In his general remarks to start the conference, Collier emphasized that the OIA and Congress had the authority to unilaterally pass legislation affecting Indians. But they would not do so in 1934, he told the crowd. "We intend to act in partnership with the Indians, and we are not going to act unless the Indians are willing to go with us." This pronouncement of faith elicited applause from those in attendance, who were as excited by Collier's words as by his presence in front of such a disparate collection of Indian leaders.

Collier spoke at length about his plan for tribal reorganization. The basis of the modern world, he said, was organization, which took form in corporations, associations, cooperatives, and municipal governments. Collier explained that "what is almost the heart of our plan" is the organization of the American Indian for "mutual benefit, for local self-government and for doing business in the modern, organized way." Reconstituted tribal organizations would still enjoy the "protective guardianship" of the federal government and the "privilege" of tax exemption, he promised, but they would also enjoy increased responsibility for the internal affairs of the tribe, access to the Indian Office's proposed "credit system," and eligibility for the type of federal assistance contained in Franklin Roosevelt's New Deal legislation. No Indian group would be forced to organize, but if it did,

Collier said to loud applause, it could "take over many of the things that are now being done by the Indian Bureau, and the money being spent on those things would be transferred to the organized body of Indians and they would spend the money and they would hire their own employees." Collier forcefully stressed the need for organization, telling his audience of Indian leaders and entrepreneurs

> that in the United States, if you are going to do business and make money and protect yourself, you have got to do it in an organized way. Otherwise you are just out of luck. You don't make any money, you are not protected, and the other fellow eats you alive. You can't govern yourselves, you can't do business, you can't protect yourself, unless you organize. That is true regarding everybody in the United States.

The American Indian, Collier told the crowd, was an example of Roosevelt's "forgotten man," who had been "carrying a privileged class" and "big business" on his back. The Indian had an opportunity to benefit from New Deal reforms designed to protect the "common man." Sounding like a cross between Henry Luce and Dwight Macdonald, Collier thus presented the philosophical "heart of the plan": the need for Indian America to form countervailing or complementary organizations to those of white America. For Collier, the Indian New Deal was as much about class as it was about race.

After Collier reviewed his vision and the legislative version of it, tribal delegates were given a chance to ask questions and ten minutes with which to offer an "unofficial expression of opinion." Joe Brown opened this segment with a short speech on March 4, telling Collier and his associates that his delegation had tried to be a "good listener" so that its decision would be based on facts. "In the most part of this bill we are in favor of it, and I believe that if we can get together with some of the Bureau officials to work over the objectionable features that we have we are not far apart. Our Reservation is getting so . . . checkerboarded with white settlers that it looks like a man with the small pox." The opinions expressed after Brown were decidedly mixed. The Crow and the Northern Cheyenne delegations, for example, expressed their belief that their tribes could not operate successfully under the self-government provisions. Several delegations remained convinced that the bill would principally benefit landless mixed-bloods who would take advantage of full-blood assets through the vehicle of communal ownership. Elderly delegates were given a chance to speak in their native tongue. Rides at the Door spoke for the Blackfeet, telling the assembly that the Blackfeet tribe needed the IRA to protect its resources from white predators: "My people now own a large area of oil land and we have now on our reservation three producing wells, and that is the reason I came here, and I want some law or protection whereby I can always hold that property intact—so that no white man can take it away from me," he said, eliciting applause from the audience. Referring to the Collier delegation, Rides at the Door expressed hope that "with their protection and support, their guidance, we are not going to let any white man do like that to *us*."

The Blackfeet delegation was, perhaps, the most supportive and unified of those that attended the four-day conference. It certainly gave Collier the most solid endorsement, both by offering a positive opinion of the bill during its allotted ten minutes and by adopting him into the tribe. During the last session, a Blackfeet delegate generated enthusiastic applause by announcing from the stage that the delegation was going to "adopt" Collier into the tribe and make him a "leader in this community plan"; as a result the Blackfeet "expect him to do more for us." The delegates gave Collier the name Spotted Eagle because, the delegate said, it "represents the Indian Reservations, the way they are checkerboarded. We hope that those spots will be rubbed off so that every Indian Reservation will be all in one spot." The Blackfeet closed their unique presentation by singing a Blackfeet song and presenting Collier with a tribal headdress.

Collier ended the conference as he had started it, reminding the delegates of the emphasis he placed on voluntary participation and the need for Indians to organize effectively to "assert their rights" in protecting their assets and their future livelihood. He warned them not to listen to the "local interests," who would call the bill "communism." "Your interests," he said, "are, of necessity, in opposition to many local interests around you. You want to have the capital to put stock on your own lands and yourself enjoy the profits of the cattle business, and, of course, there are white cattle men and banks that don't want you to do it." More important than the conference and the legislation, Collier told the delegates, was the idea that "Indians shall take the responsibility, here and now, of thinking out their own problems and arriving at their own conclusions, and determining their own future." Self-determination through self-government was, Collier concluded, the means to the end of federal supervision as Indians knew it in 1934.

The Second Blackfeet Debate

The Blackfeet Tribal Business Council had tried to assume additional responsibility for the welfare of the tribe for two decades but had faced agency prejudice, favoritism, and in some cases informed opinion. The judgment of tribal, congressional, and agency personnel in late 1933 was that the Blackfeet were, in Senator Burton Wheeler's words, "capable of taking care of themselves." The council now had an opportunity to act upon that judgment. Rides at the Door had said in 1933 that the Blackfeet wanted a "new deal" because "the old system is no success." The Blackfeet Nation now had the option of choosing Collier's new system of political economy to reach its long-standing goal of self-support and self-governance. Collier's speeches at the Great Plains Congress appealed to the Blackfeet because they addressed several important issues besides the rather amorphous notion of self-government, delineating a new system of tribal economic organization that promised a credit-starved tribe access to a revolving loan fund. Collier's pronouncement that his legislation would enable an Indian nation to "take over many of the things that are now being done by the Indian Bureau," spend the money allocated for those activities, and "hire their own employees," mirrored the testimony of Blackfeet leaders during the October 1933 Senate hearing. The Blackfeet had had more practice with representational decision-making than most tribes. The tribe's business council had been in operation since 1915 and its constitution in place since 1922; the election process, however flawed, reminded the Blackfeet of their ability to foster change every two years. The type of centralized government that Collier proposed was not foreign to most Blackfeet, though it was not always acceptable to them. The internecine conflict between the business council and officers of the FYIP had died down, but the legacy of that conflict was a distrust of centralized control of tribal decision-making. Yet the experience that many FYIP leaders had with the opposite model, the disparate collection of chapter organizations, led many of them to oppose any alternative to centralized government. The debate over which form of self-government the Blackfeet should adopt dominated the BTBC meeting of March 31 and three similar meetings held in the reservation's other voting districts.

Council Chairman Joe Brown conceded at the outset of the March 31 meeting that many Blackfeet, particularly full-bloods, were "mixed up" about the Wheeler-Howard Bill and thus had invited Great Falls attorney Cleve Hall to help explain the amendments proposed by the business council. The principal question was whether the Blackfeet should sanction the charter of one central government or numerous self-governing "communities." The question, as Hall put it to the council and more than one hundred Blackfeet in attendance, was "whether you would want a number of communities on the one reservation, bearing in mind that these communities take over the tribal funds and lands, or whether you would want one large community for the reservation." The issue had been debated during the mid-1920s, as the "North" community, the mostly mixed-blood districts and the council they dominated, and the "South" community, which found political expression in the chapter organizations, struggled for political legitimacy. The Blackfeet now were faced with the need to define their community, to formalize the structure of governing within the physical boundaries of the reservation. Joe Brown predicted that confusion would reign if the tribe elected to charter more than one community government. "The whole bill means to gradually take over the range of government on your reservation," he told the crowd, and recommended that the Blackfeet "control our government right here from this office."

It would be quite natural to suppose that Chairman Brown and other mixed-blood councilmen would prefer the central government of the business council, but a consensus emerged that centralized decision-making was the only option to consider. Several influential full-bloods weighed in with support for one government. Bird Rattler, Many Hides, Weaselhead, and John Ground all testified to the need for one community government. Rides at the Door told the assemblage: "You all now realize the experience of that division of the reservation, known as chapter districts. You all know that you never got along good. There was nothing but continuous disagreement all the way through." Hugh Jackson also criticized the experiment of chapter organizations, saying that the Blackfeet "should call it one corporation—the Blackfeet Reservation." There were detractors of the idea of "one corporation." Twenty-four Blackfeet opposed the "one community plan," while eighty-eight sanctioned it. A few holdover opponents believed that "one community" meant the sacrifice of individual property, while some simply did not trust the mixed-blood leadership. Dick Kipp wanted a government like the one the Blackfeet had "in the old times," complaining that full-bloods were generally shut out of tribal decision-making because they did not understand English. Kipp was the exception, however, as most full-bloods, particularly those who were or who had been active in the FYIP, voted to adopt one central government. John Old Chief spoke after Kipp, telling the meeting, "You know I was president of a chapter. Today, I will throw that away. I am going to join this community self-government." Those Blackfeet active in the chapter organizations were both disillusioned with the FYIP and probably wary of seceding from a government controlled by the cohort of mixed-bloods that was active in pursuing oil development; the confusion that Joe Brown described would have made it particularly difficult for full-bloods to monitor the per capita distribution of funds from Court of Claims awards and tribal oil production. While full-bloods in particular held the idea of tribal unity in high regard, they also understood that it was better to work with the principals of any newly formed Blackfeet "corporation" as a member of that corporation than as leaders of competing communities which lacked the requisite business skills for managing the kind of businesses that the Blackfeet needed to expand their economic horizons.

The council also proposed eliminating the secretary of the interior as a policing entity with the authority to affect changes in Blackfeet politics, fearing that a new Republican administration would exercise greater control over any new government. This amendment alarmed Superintendent Stone, who contributed his opinion after a long silence by telling the council that "[i]n every community, every county or state, there is some place a power over it [*sic*]. You could hardly leave that in the hands of the community itself." Stone argued that any government needed checks and balances to guard against corrupt or simply incompetent administration. Hall answered that an autocratic interior secretary was the worse option and that if the Blackfeet government did fail to function, then it would "blow up" on its own. The amendment passed over Stone's objections. Passing the amendment symbolized the Blackfeet's recognition of the need to control the operation of any new government and thus prevent the federal government from making wholesale changes without the tribe's consent, the common denominator of the amendments; in several places the council simply replaced "secretary of the interior" with "three-fourths of the adult members of the tribe." Brown was particularly insistent that any future changes be made "with the consent of the Indian." The consensus among Blackfeet leaders was that the tribe needed a statutory mechanism to "terminate" various supervisory functions of the Interior Department. Not every administration would be as supportive of tribal sovereignty as Collier's. At the end of a long day spent debating the tribe's future, the council endorsed the amendments presented and the Wheeler-Howard Bill that was then circulating in Congress. Brown and three other delegates were chosen to travel to Washington in late April to present the amendments to the House and Senate committees on Indian Affairs in the hopes that Congress would be as attentive as John Collier was to the wants and needs of the Blackfeet people.

The Senate Debate and the Blackfeet

Collier resumed his campaign for comprehensive Indian reform after touring Indian America, testifying before the Senate Committee on Indian Affairs on April 26. The controversial issue of mandatory land transfers and the scope of self-government were the principal points debated. Collier conceded to Senator Wheeler, the committee chairman, that the compulsory nature of Title III remained a barrier, citing the Blackfeet's protest as an example of the concern that had been "persistently raised" by many Indian leaders; the Blackfeet, Collier told Wheeler, wanted land recombination to be "voluntary." Collier now had a "very strong leaning" toward making Title III a voluntary provision. Wheeler had been an initial supporter of Collier's regime and a sponsor of his original bill, but by April he had lost faith in Collier's vision and resolved to weaken it. On several occasions Wheeler asked Collier to clarify his intentions with regard to Montana's Indians. Collier's proposal to offer self-government to Montana Indians represented, Wheeler believed, "a step backward for them rather than a step forward." The Indians of the Blackfeet and Fort Peck reservations already exercised the form of government Collier was proposing and were "becoming more or less assimilated," he argued. If the government of the Blackfeet and other Montana tribes were to evolve toward the form of a "complete town government," he told Collier, then "it would bring about all kinds of conflicts between *your* [author's italics] Indians and the white people and . . . it would set back the Indians."

Joe Brown appeared before the committee two days later to address Wheeler's contention that the Wheeler-Howard Bill would "set back the Indians." Brown testified that the tribe had studied the bill after the Rapid City conference and agreed to accept it if the voluntary nature of land transfer in Title III was codified; the tribe would then "think it is a good bill," he said. He reviewed the tribe's experience with the FYIP, telling the committee that had government representatives "done their part it would have been a success, but as it was, why, it was mostly a failure." Brown expressed excitement about the proposed credit fund, which would provide Blackfeet with the money to buy enough stock and feed to help the chapter organizations expand; the Blackfeet, he said, "are aching to get a chance at that $10,000,000 that is in that bill." Wheeler expressed approval of Brown's enthusiasm for the program and for advocating self-reliance to full-bloods. Senator Lynn Frazier affectionately told him, "I believe you will make good too, Brown." Brown rejoined that "if we just had another chance we are going to make good. The older people have all received an experience and have learned something." Wheeler and Frazier seemed to have great confidence in Joe Brown's abilities. Responding to Brown's request for more Indian employment in the Bureau of Indian Affairs, Wheeler asked him: "You could take over the superintendency, more than likely?" Brown thought that the job was too difficult for him and instead offered support for Forrest Stone, who was a "mighty good man."

Wheeler quickly moved to his critique of the bill, telling Brown that he disagreed with his assertion that the self-government provision of the bill would help the Blackfeet achieve economic and political progress. Wheeler argued that the Blackfeet already controlled most of Glacier County: Indians like Brown were on the school board, were able to run for state senate as Joe Brown had done, and "practically run that community up there now." The Blackfeet were successfully assimilating into white society and white institutions, and if they were to create an Indian community "separate and distinct from the white community" then there would be "trouble between them." When Senator Elmer Thomas asked Brown if he intended to "surrender" involvement in the county government, Brown answered that the bill allowed the Blackfeet to participate in both the community and county government. He provoked laughter when he said that the Blackfeet would "take chances on what laws would be under the community government, because we would make them." Brown's response, however, was precisely what made Wheeler "fearful" of an indigenous form of Indian community government. If the Blackfeet Nation passed its own laws, he told Brown, the result would be "a great deal of confusion and a great deal of bitterness and strife between two classes of people, which would be to the detriment" of the Blackfeet. Brown offered to accept an amendment proscribing such a situation. Wheeler exclaimed, "We *will* [author's italics] amend it." Frazier followed Wheeler's lead by telling Brown shortly before the session ended that "it seems to me that the best thing to do to handle a group like the Blackfeet is to assist them to take part in county government there, the regular county government, give them fair representation, and I believe they will get along all right." Brown responded that "the bill gives us that privilege. We do not have to go into this unless we want to." Despite the handicap of blindness in one eye and only an eighth-grade education, Brown acquitted himself very well in front of congressional committees.

Joe Brown and the Blackfeet did not want to be "handled" by Congress. The pending legislation appealed to Brown and his people because it gave them options for economic growth and the "privilege" to choose their own path based on their own reading of those options. The Blackfeet had been successful in Glacier County, but they remained the poor citizens of the county. The Blackfeet may have been "dominating" public life in Glacier County, as Wheeler contended, but they were not dominating economic life. Without credit they never would. Without the right to negotiate with their white tenants they never would. Collier's plan gave the Blackfeet more political power to negotiate with the state and the federal government, and it gave them greater access to credit, the essential elements of a political economy that the Blackfeet had been requesting for nearly twenty years.

Wheeler, for his part, ran the hearings using the Blackfeet Nation as his model tribe. He was very familiar with conditions on the Blackfeet Reservation, having made official visits to Browning on at least three occasions during the previous five years; in addition, he vacationed in nearby Glacier Park, where delegations of Blackfeet would often visit him, and he had once tried to invest in reservation oil leases in the early 1920s. His conception of Indian-white relations and *his* vision of organizational change were predicated, then, on these specific experiences with the Blackfeet Indians and, to a lesser extent, the other tribes of Montana. Though he clearly understood the variegated nature of the country's Indian population, the sheer variety of the nations within the nation, Wheeler viewed the Blackfeet in many ways as a model for assimilation and acculturation. In his mind, as he told Collier and Brown on separate occasions, Indians were moving in the right direction within the institutional world of white America. Joe Brown's seemingly cavalier assertion of the Blackfeet's right to pass laws supra or contra county laws alarmed Wheeler, who in the end did not have that much confidence in Brown or his people to "do the right thing."

The House Debate and the Blackfeet

Brown told the House Committee on Indian Affairs several days later that the Blackfeet Nation had been "very much opposed to" Collier's plan in February, principally because it "had not had a chance to study it." The tribe had spent considerable time since the Great Plains Congress discussing the bill in a series of meetings that had given all tribal members an opportunity to participate, with the result, Brown testified, that most now supported it; Collier's decision to make land transfers voluntary rather than mandatory also had had an impact on voters' support of the legislation. "There are features in this bill that are very acceptable," Brown testified. "They are extraordinary." He was particularly pleased with provisions advancing Indian education and Indian labor within the Indian Service, changes that he had been requesting for many years; he explained that the Blackfeet could fill every agency position except chief clerk and superintendent, but if the bill passed then the tribe could quickly "develop men that would take those places." The committee allotted only fifteen minutes to each tribe, but Brown pressed his case for the legislation, telling the committee, "We do not know when we will get a chance of this kind, we do not know when we will ever get a man again in the chair of the Commissioner of Indian Affairs whose heart and sympathies are with the Indian." Brown's endorsement of Collier provided an opening for Representatives Theodore Werner of South Carolina and Thomas O'Malley of Wisconsin, members of a contingent of pro-assimilation congressmen, who used it to continue their attacks on Collier and his conception of Indian self-government. Brown's request for more time turned into an interrogation.

Werner tried to chip away at Brown's support of Collier by asking him if he thought Collier had either created "false hopes" or blamed Congress for the Indian's problems during the Great Plains Congress. Brown answered that Collier had done neither. O'Malley implied that Brown and his people did not fully understand the legislation, despite attending the congress and holding several meetings on the bill. He asked Brown, "after what you say was a study of the bill and a discussion of it with members of your tribe, you are in favor of it?" Brown simply answered, "Yes, sir." Representative Werner also questioned Brown's cognitive abilities, asking him, "You say that you have given very careful study to this bill?" Brown simply answered: "Careful in my humble way. I am not a lawyer." After facing Werner and O'Malley's lengthy contumely, Brown reemphasized the importance of the bill's protection of the Blackfeet's land base and its educational and financial provisions, in particular the revolving credit fund. This "wonderful system," Brown said, is "something that has been needed, because our credit system—we have none"; banks would not give Indians credit because the federal government held in trust the title to their land. Frustrated by the committee's lack of faith in his judgment and his ability to decide what was best for his people, he finished his testimony by saying, "I think we could get together if we just all lower our sights a bit and cooperate. I believe we can put a bill through here that will satisfy the Indians."

Wheeler's Re-Vision of the IRA

On June 5 Brown and BTBC secretary Leo Kennerly telegraphed to the Indian Office the council's unanimous approval of the pending Wheeler-Howard Indian Bill. Congress passed the bill on June 16, and President Roosevelt signed it two days later. While the final version of the bill—which became known as the Indian Reorganization Act—contained enough important elements to "satisfy the Blackfeet," Wheeler wielded his power in the Senate to ensure that Collier's vision of cultural pluralism and Indian self-determination devolved into Wheeler's defense of assimilation. After the formal hearings ended in early May, Collier negotiated an acceptable compromise with Howard and Wheeler, but by this time Collier had lost his leverage. It was Wheeler who dictated what the final bill would look like, going so far as to introduce a new bill, S 3645, to replace S 2755. Collier called the IRA a "very much modified, shortened and amended version" of his original bill in his analysis of the act; Wheeler and his colleagues reduced Collier's forty-eight-page bill to five pages and succeeded in deleting Collier's language of self-determination. The IRA improved Collier's original bill in the area of economic development, but weakened or eliminated key provisions for cultural development and self-government. The bill was imperfect, the result of a struggle between two competing visions of Indian America: one sought to protect the Indians' right to construct their own version of the American community; the other fought to sustain the Indians' gradual adoption of white mores and institutions to "fit them as American citizens," as Wheeler put it. Congress wanted to assist Indians in making economic progress, but it did not want to create nations within the nation that held powers in conflict with the dominant society it wanted Indian citizens to eventually adopt. Joe Brown's assertion of his tribe's right to pass laws symbolized for Wheeler, and other influential lawmakers, the danger inherent in Collier's vision of Indian self-determination. As a result, Wheeler had significantly weakened Collier's provision for Indian home rule.

The IRA would not affect any tribe whose majority of eligible voters rejected the legislation, but once a tribe did so it could not claim any benefits provided under the law. Given that Wheeler and other congressmen had successfully weakened Collier's reforms, the OIA leadership struggled to secure tribal votes on the IRA before an even more hostile Congress assumed office the following fall. Felix Cohen, the chairman of the OIA's Organization Committee, wrote in July 1934 that "it is important that a number of tribes strategically located be actually organized before the next session of Congress, since the failure to do this will subject the Indian Office to considerable criticism." The committee decided in September that thirty-three tribes should vote on the IRA by October 27, 1934. The Blackfeet Nation, given its size and its relatively consistent support of the bill's major provisions, was among the thirty-three slated for an early vote.

The Blackfeet Vote

The BTBC's June 5 approval of the Wheeler-Howard legislation would have been rendered meaningless if a majority of the tribe's voting members did not support the IRA. The council organized a series of meetings to inform Blackfeet citizens of the IRA's advantages and enlisted the aid of Hall and McCabe, a local law firm, to analyze the bill to help the council justify its vote for it. Cleve Hall simply recommended that the Blackfeet vote for the IRA, adopt a constitution, and secure a charter of incorporation to gain access to the $10 million credit fund; in addition, the charter would give the tribe the legal means to terminate the Interior Department's supervision of its natural resources, provided that a majority of eligible voters supported the termination. Forrest Stone submitted Hall's analysis to the OIA with the business council's request that the OIA determine the report's veracity before the council distributed it to Blackfeet voters. The OIA called Hall's analysis "very creditable," though not as comprehensive as the CIA's, and recommended that the council distribute it to their constituents for consideration. The OIA tried to avoid coercing tribes or tribal leaders into adopting the IRA, choosing to support when possible the efforts of tribes like the Blackfeet to secure an independent opinion of the act's merits.

The BTBC took the initiative for deciding the IRA's fate on the Blackfeet Reservation on September 11. Stone encouraged council members to support the act, telling them that the Wheeler-Howard Bill "is very important to the Blackfeet Indians We have discussed it from every angle. The time has come for you to decide whether you want it or not. "Twelve of the thirteen councilmen decided that they wanted it, and voted to petition the secretary of the interior to approve October 20 as the date for the tribe's referendum. Stone told Collier two days later that "the Blackfeet are pretty well informed at present as to the provisions of this act. They have spent a good deal of time on it and have listened pretty carefully to the explanations that have been offered them by members of the council, employees, and leaders of the tribe aside from council members." Although the Blackfeet did not agree with all the IRA's provisions, Stone believed that they were going to "accept it with the idea in mind that the good contained in the bill far exceeds the objectionable features."

The Blackfeet proved Stone correct on October 27. Nearly 83 percent of participating voters supported the IRA; 823 Blackfeet voted for it while 171 voted against it. Although a winter storm made it difficult for some Blackfeet to get to the polls, 994 of 1,785 eligible voters turned out to cast their secret ballots; 114 of the 148 Blackfeet who mailed their ballots also voted for the act. It is important to note that the act received support from both mixed-bloods and full-bloods, though it is difficult to determine with any precision either the breakdown of voting by blood quantum or the reason nearly eight hundred Blackfeet did not vote; the tribe's rate of participation fell just under the national average of 58 percent. Some mixed-bloods objected that the IRA granted certain sovereign powers to the BTBC and thus expanded its role in the tribal economy; some full-bloods, largely because of demographic circumstances favoring mixed-bloods by a ratio of four to one, objected for the same reason. In most political communities, an unfortunately high number of voters elects not to participate in the democratic process because of cynicism, despair, or laziness. It was likely no different on the Blackfeet Reservation, particularly when one considers the history of Blackfeet-white relations of the preceding decades. This history, however, compelled more than one thousand Blackfeet to embrace the opportunity to alter the trajectory of those relations. For whatever reason, a large number of voters did not have the same urgency. Snow-swept roads probably kept some older voters home. Some Blackfeet were probably unfamiliar with or uninterested in the issues that day and simply chose to ignore the referendum. But they did not stay home because no one bothered to tell them of this opportunity. The agency staff and leaders of both factions held a series of meetings in mixed-blood and full-blood communities, made themselves available to answer questions, and distributed appropriate information to inform the Blackfeet body politic of its voting options. The 1929 and 1933 Senate subcommittee hearings and the 1934 IRA debates on the reservation and in Washington politicized Blackfeet citizens at a time when they as well as most Americans were looking for answers to a crisis of confidence and comfort. It was a good time to be political.

Conclusion

A year after a Senate subcommittee judged the Blackfeet Indians to be "capable" of running their own affairs, the Blackfeet Nation expressed agreement by overwhelmingly adopting the Indian Reorganization Act and thus grasped the tools of a modern political economy to realize its long-standing goal of "self-support." The business council, under the steady and pragmatic leadership of Joe Brown, had created an environment in which debate and discussion could take place among the reservation's various factions and communities. The Blackfeet participated in an exercise of tribal democracy, electing to "take the responsibility," as Collier told them they should, "of thinking out their own problems and arriving at their own conclusions, and determining their own future." The Blackfeet's widespread acceptance of the IRA resulted from an open and organized debate about the tribe's future and remembrance of a past largely influenced by the vagaries of OIA management. Blackfeet factions agreed during the IRA debate that in order to "decrease Federal overlordship," as Harold Ickes called the OIA's heavy-handed management of tribal affairs, the tribe had to assume greater economic and political control over the development of the reservation's natural and human resources by securing the tools of modern administration offered in the IRA. The IRA would give a reconstituted tribal council the authority to negotiate with other political bodies and conduct "business in the modern, organized way," as John Collier had said they must do to survive in twentieth-century America.

Recent historiography generally does not regard the IRA as a success, or else it focuses on Native communities that rejected it. But it is important to remember the excitement the IRA engendered among the tribes that adopted it, as well as the spirited debate it created among those that did not. Many Indian leaders, like Joe Brown and Rides at the Door, considered the IRA to be the best legislative or political means to further their independence from federal supervision that had stifled economic progress and exacerbated tribal dissension. The OIA had failed for twenty years to provide the Blackfeet with a coordinated economic policy: it debilitated the tribe's search for oil, neglected the tribe's grazing resources, and usurped tribal funds for costly irrigation projects in its zeal to turn the Blackfeet into farmers in one of the country's poorest agricultural regions. The Blackfeet, like their Flathead neighbors to the southwest, embraced the IRA because it gave them access to credit and the statutory power to stage elections to reduce or eliminate federal control of the tribe's financial and natural resources. Unlike their Crow neighbors to the southeast, Blackfeet of all degrees of blood had developed among themselves a confidence that they were capable of self-government. Adopting the IRA's machinery of political economy was a logical first step for tribal members committed to "determining their own future."

The Indian New Deal and the IRA both expanded economic horizons and exacerbated political divisions on the Blackfeet Reservation. Credit programs facilitated the creation of an inchoate Blackfeet middle class by providing livestock, farming, and rehabilitation loans to Indians hungry for economic development. By 1950, 603 individual Blackfeet and four cooperatives had borrowed more than one million dollars from the IRA's Revolving Credit Fund at affordable rates, paid back the money to a high degree, and prospered to an extent greater than that possible without such access to credit, the lifeblood of any business or individual enterprise. The average income for Blackfeet families in 1950 was $2,639, one of the highest among the nation's Indian communities. Opposition to the IRA came mainly from the tribe's full-bloods, whose political power had declined due to demographic circumstances that in 1940 favored mixed-bloods by a ratio of five to one. While some younger full-bloods took advantage of IRA and tribal economic programs, an inability or a disinclination on the part of older full-bloods to do so impelled their campaign to repeal the IRA and abolish the business council. Yet even Blackfeet elders were ambivalent about the IRA. Juniper Old Person, Earl Old Person's father, testified during the tribe's 1945 Constitutional Convention, "my children got a start under the [IRA] and I feel proud of them and they will feed me." For some economically marginalized and increasingly class-conscious Blackfeet, the IRA became a scapegoat for problems created more from cultural resistance, demographic decline, and generational differences than from ethnic or racial discrimination. Labeling the IRA "a nuisance," the leader of the tribe's "minority group" told a congressional subcommittee in 1944 that "each year we just cannot understand it. I want to get rid of the [IRA]." The council attempted to be solicitous of the full-bloods' demands for political and financial dispensation, spending money on a tribal welfare program and earmarking tribal funds for cultural, medical, and credit programs for older full-bloods; the BTBC funded full-blood celebrations like the annual sun dance and encampment, paid for chiropractic and rheumatism treatment for elderly full-bloods, and established a separate credit fund called "Special Loans for Aged Indians." Full-bloods and other Blackfeet dissidents did have legitimate complaints about the IRA and the BTBC. The council's authority to expend tribal oil revenues under IRA provisions enlarged its role in the tribal economy. This it did to mixed results: councilmen practiced favoritism, extravagance, and, in some cases, outright corruption. A cohort of wealthy mixed-bloods exploited the charter's provision for Indian "preference rights" to enlarge their private domains. In addition, pressure from both mixed-bloods and full-bloods for per capita payments created political instability and retarded long-term investment, limiting the council's effectiveness as a vehicle for economic development. Social conflict developed principally from different cultural responses to the distribution of revenues earned from development of community-owned oil reserves. Full-bloods in particular demanded per capita distributions and opposed investment in "rehabilitation" programs that chiefly benefited younger Blackfeet couples of low blood quantum. Yet the very people who sought the IRA's repeal in the 1940s used its provisions for democratic reform in the 1950s to reclaim influence and status by creating a dissenting coalition that crossed class and ethnic lines. Full-blood elders used the IRA's constitutional mechanism for establishing referenda to foster changes in income distribution patterns. In the process, elders became acculturated to democratic practices under IRA administration while retaining what they called their "ancient customs." They also helped to fashion a syncretic Blackfeet political culture based on both "traditional" consensus-oriented decision-making and modern democratic decision-making that rested upon the notion of majority rule.

Regardless of what happened after October 1934 the Blackfeet made the right decision to adopt the IRA. In October 1934 the act made sense to a majority of tribal voters. Hindsight should not preclude a broader understanding of the place where these voters stood as they debated a historic opportunity to take a measure of control over their future. Despite Burton Wheeler's claim that the Blackfeet dominated life in Glacier County, there remained an infrastructure of white interests that had dug its heels into the soil of Blackfeet land. The Blackfeet needed to take the responsibility of managing and protecting tribal assets to ensure that "the wolves," as full-blood leader Oscar Boy called white ranchers and developers, did not "devour" any more of the tribe's natural resources and economic future.

Suggested Reading

Rosier provides a solid context for the ideas presented in this essay in his *Rebirth of the Blackfeet Nation, 1912–1954* (Lincoln: University of Nebraska Press, 2001). Much general scholarship about the 1934 Indian Reorganization Act now appears dated, but the best early studies include Donald L. Parman, *The Navajos and the New Deal* (New Haven: Yale University Press, 1976), and Lawrence C. Kelly, *The Assault on Indian Assimilation: John Collier and the Origins of Indian Policy Reform* (Albuquerque: University of New Mexico Press, 1983). Among the many studies of individual tribal experiences with the IRA, see Thomas Biolsi, *Organizing the Lakota: The Political Economy of the New Deal on the Pine Ridge and Rosebud Reservations* (Tucson: University of Arizona Press, 1992), and Harry A. Kersey Jr., *The Florida Seminoles and the New Deal, 1933–1942* (Boca Raton: Florida Atlantic University Press, 1989).

PART SIX

Changing Lives and Federal Policies

The exodus from reservation life continued. Most relocations grew out of the search for employment and other economic or social opportunities. Leaving home proved difficult for some, obviously, but basic needs overcame reluctance to move away from family and friends. Colleen O'Neil analyzes how Navajo workers who voluntarily sought off-reservation work dealt with this issue. By the 1950s the Bureau of Indian Affairs attempted to lure laborers to the cities through a relocation program that included attractive posters and appealing slogans. The initiative certainly increased the number of Indians living in cities, but many newcomers lacked the clerical or industrial skills needed for urban success.

In the post–World War II era the government revisited earlier efforts to bring Indians into the general society. New legislation not only encouraged movement into the cities but also established a termination program. Drawing support from reformers and those who wanted to destroy Indian tribes, termination worked to end the legal relationship between the federal government and individual tribes as well as its treaty obligations to them. Federal support for reservation programs of all kinds ended under this policy. Even worse, tribes found themselves at the mercy of state and local officials without the federal protections they had enjoyed for decades. John Finger provides one example of the disputes surrounding this new direction. After inflicting immense damage on many tribes, and having failed to provide to them with even basic necessities, by 1970 the government ended the termination program.

The influx of Indians into the cities near major reservations and the dismantling of some tribal communities brought continued social and economic difficulties to many groups. This led to an era of public protest by Indians that paralleled the civil rights and anti-Vietnam demonstrations. By 1968 the militant American Indian Movement appeared in Minneapolis. Dean J. Kotlowski examines the federal response to a variety of Indian sit-ins and public protests ranging from the seizure of Alcatraz Island in San Francisco to an armed confrontation in the spring of 1973 between activists and tribal, local, state, and federal authorities at Wounded Knee, South Dakota. These protests represented the height of Indian public protests. The series of confrontations led to several unexpected results. By the late 1970s the federal government had come to realize that some tribal groups had gone unrecognized for decades, even generations. This provided part of the impetus behind the Federal Acknowledgment Program that authors McCulloch and Wilkins analyze in the final essay.

CHAPTER EIGHTEEN

The "Making" of the Navajo Worker

Navajo Households, the Bureau of Indian Affairs, and Off-Reservation Wage Work, 1948–1960

COLLEEN O'NEILL

By the end of World War II, bureaucrats and reformers alike pushed for a final effort to assimilate Indians into American society. This led to a Bureau of Indian Affairs–funded Relocation Program designed to encourage reservation dwellers to move away from home and seek permanent jobs elsewhere. What some federal officials failed to realize was that movement from reservation communities to nearby towns and cities was nothing new. It had been occurring for decades. During the 1990s scholars focused considerable attention on the motivations and experiences of Indian laborers entering the American workforce.

This essay focuses on how and why Navajo people took part in the ongoing efforts to secure jobs outside their reservation. The author notes that federal livestock reduction programs of the 1930s left many Navajos with only small herds and little choice but to seek work elsewhere. Others worked in defense industries during the war and remained in the cities. The author identifies the migratory and economic patterns Navajo wageworkers developed and ties them to the evolving patterns of labor negotiations and relations with the Bureau of Indian Affairs.

First published as Colleen O'Neill, "The 'Making' of the Navajo Worker: Navajo Households, the Bureau of Indian Affairs, and Off-Reservation Wage Work," *New Mexico Historical Review* 74, no. 4 (October 1999): 375–405. Copyright © University of New Mexico Board of Regents. All rights reserved.

> Arizona employers each year spend many thousands of
> dollars importing foreign and domestic workers, when in
> fact, we have within our backyard a very substantial number
> of resident Indian workers who should be used. The problem
> of getting the Indian to accept the White Man's way of living
> will be most difficult, but in several instances, it has been
> proven in agriculture, mining and lumbering, that over a
> period of a few years' time a transformation can be effected
> which is beneficial to both employer and the Indian.
>
> ARIZONA STATE EMPLOYMENT SERVICE, 1948

In 1939, thirteen-year-old Clarence Kee boarded a truck bound for the carrot fields near Phoenix, Arizona, nearly 350 miles southwest of his home on the Navajo Reservation. Even so young, the Navajo teenager sensed that hardships lay before him. After his father's death, his mother and seven siblings had supported the family by raising sheep, selling wool at the trading post, weaving what was left into rugs, and working at any odd jobs they could find. Even attendance at a school near Fort Defiance fell by the wayside. With his father gone, Kee's mother needed her seven-year-old son at home. As Kee recalled, "she wanted me to take care of the sheep, all my life."

As history would have it, Kee's mother got her wish, but not in the way that she might have imagined. When Kee climbed into the back of that pickup truck six years later, the full-time task of herding sheep would be over. After those carrot fields, Kee worked on a railroad section gang, a job that took him far from his mother's flocks to California, Oregon, and Nebraska for six weeks at a time. Yet familial responsibilities, such as caring for his mother's sheep and tending to some of her other needs, always pulled him back to the reservation. Employed by the railroad until 1948, Kee returned to work in a coal mine near his family's home, ending his days as a migrant worker. Other family members, however, including his wife and children, would continue to work at seasonal jobs into the 1960s. As Kee's mother had wished, they continued to raise sheep. But it was wage work that provided the family with the resources they needed to maintain their small flock and resist permanent migration off the reservation.

Historians and anthropologists have long assumed that federal stock reduction policies and World War II transformed Navajos into wage workers. The federal government's actions and the lure of defense jobs provided compelling external influences that drew Navajos away from the reservation, at least temporarily. Focusing on those variables alone, however, tells us little about why so many people stayed and how they managed to resist such powerful forces. A closer look at the dynamic negotiations between Navajos, the federal government, and Southwestern employers reveals a much more complicated story.

Beginning in the 1930s, partly as a result of declining wool prices and federally enforced livestock reduction, Navajos became increasingly dependent on wages to survive. At that time, Navajos relied on wages for 30 percent of their income. By the 1960s, they were drawing 60 percent of their household income from wages. The federal government played an important role ushering in this transition. In the 1930s, officials from the Bureau of Indian Affairs (BIA) and the Soil Conservation Service decided to reduce Navajo livestock herds by 50 percent. They believed overgrazing had depleted the range to such an extent that the future of livestock on the reservation was in question. One consequence of that program was a sharpening of class lines on the reservation. Navajos with the largest flocks could maintain their sheep-centered households, while those who drew their subsistence from smaller flocks had to find other ways to survive.

For those with fewer head, like the Kee family, Great Depression–era conditions, drought, and federal stock reduction policies made it nearly impossible to make a living raising sheep and working the land. Only those reservation households located in nearly inaccessible areas, cut off by difficult terrain and poor roads, could resist the lure of the capitalist market. Navajo families like the Kees survived by selectively engaging in the capitalist market as wage earners, producers, and consumers. Most pooled their income from a variety of sources, including the wages they earned working on the railroad, herding others' sheep, or selling rugs and other craft items.

Following World War II, BIA officials set their sights on Navajo labor-market behavior. They were still concerned about the carrying capacity of the reservation, but rather than further limit the number of sheep, the agency instead decided to reduce the people living on the land. Federal Indian policy was shifting in the postwar era. Policies that favored termination of Indian reservations were now the rule in Congress, and for Navajos that meant a variety of voluntary relocation programs. BIA representatives were particularly interested in stopping the return migration of many Navajos who had left the reservation to find wage work. Officials attempted to create off-reservation settlements that would function as labor colonies, providing commercial growers with a permanent, year-round workforce. The BIA hoped Navajos would be drawn to these communities, leaving behind, once and for all, the homes and responsibilities that had once brought them back to the reservation.

Wage work did not remake Navajo culture in the way that the BIA and Southwestern employers imagined. Many Navajos withstood BIA efforts to relocate them permanently in off-reservation labor colonies. They insisted on keeping their homes on the reservation and adjusting their wage-work practices so they could continue to meet their household obligations. While the labor market may have pulled Navajo men and, in some cases, their families away from the reservation, they nevertheless continued to contribute to a household economy. Instead of laboring in their wives' fields and tending their flocks, men working off the reservation contributed their wages to the household, returning home sporadically to fulfill kin-based obligations. Thus, wage work did not make Navajos into white-defined workers, but rather it required them to negotiate between often conflicting culturally defined perceptions of work, gender roles, household responsibility and options created by the global market.

For Southwestern employers, the Navajos appeared to offer an attractive labor pool. To pull them successfully into the labor market, commercial farmers, mining companies, and other Western industrialists had to adjust to Navajos' demands and figure out ways to accommodate their culturally defined work practices. BIA officials, reduced to little more than labor contractors, failed to reshape Navajo migratory behavior in the ways they had intended. As they navigated the pull of the market and the push of the state, Navajos located new ways to make a living; they found work consistent with their values of communalism and kinship and endeavored to contribute to the survival of the reservation household in whatever form it might take in the post-stock-reduction era.

The Navajo case suggests economic development in the American Southwest between the 1930s and 1960 was a fluid process, one that shaped and was shaped by local systems of power and culture specific to the region. This story counters the classic modernization tale, which assumes that as soon as indigenous peoples encounter the capitalist market, their cultural traditions erode and subsistence economies decay. The Navajos negotiated the encroaching world market selectively, participating in it when it suited their purposes, but refusing to allow capitalist cultural and economic logic to significantly undermine the basic premises upon which they had shaped these new economic strategies.

Certainly American Indians suffered tremendously as they were drawn into the market economy. The Navajos were no exception. The U.S. government attacked Navajo subsistence as a military strategy in 1863. The military destroyed reservation crops and livestock and subsequently attempted to remake Navajos into sedentary farmers while they were being held in captivity at the Bosque Redondo. Seventy years later and well within the living memory of the "Long Walk," the BIA enforced draconian measures to reduce the Navajo livestock herds, a policy that helped to undermine their mixed subsistence household economies.

Despite—or perhaps because of—these direct assaults on their livelihoods, the Navajos consistently created new ways of making a living within the expanding U.S. economy that were distinctly their own. They participated in the "reworking of modernity" in their region, strategically weaving an alternative history of capitalist development that was as culturally specific as the patterns in a Navajo rug. That process, while painful and difficult, involved, to use William Roseberry and Jay O'Brien's words, "new expressions of cultural difference as well as fundamental redefinitions of old ones."

The Reservation Labor System

Navajos worked for wages long before World War II. Some served as scouts for the U.S. Army in the campaign against the Apaches in the 1870s. Many Navajos were common laborers on Soil Conservation Service projects, as miners in agency-operated coal mines, and as interpreters at other BIA administrative facilities. From the turn of the century onward, those Navajos with few sheep to tend became extra-gang track laborers for the Santa Fe Railroad or traveled to Colorado to find employment in the sugar beet fields.

Before 1948, Navajos found jobs through a variety of networks. Culturally defined internal hierarchies on the reservation had emerged in response to the encroaching U.S. economy. Traders played a central role in this unfolding process. Since the turn of the century, they had acted as the frontline arbitrators of the capitalist market for the Navajos, buying wool, advancing credit, and supplying them with consumer goods. As it became more difficult for Navajos to produce for the market, the traders assumed the role of quasi-labor contractors for the railroads and other off-reservation employers who were recruiting Navajo laborers.

The trading post offered railroad officials a central place to distribute information about job openings. Recruiters valued the traders' knowledge of Navajo culture and relied on their recommendations to fill their job orders. Traders eagerly promoted railroad work because it was seasonal and Navajos would usually bring their wages back to the reservation to spend on goods at the trading posts. The railroads also offered unemployment benefits to Navajo workers in the winter, assuring them a continued cash income during the months when they had previously depended on credit from the trader.

Other industries sought out Navajo elites to act as go-betweens. In fact, leading Navajos began to challenge the prominence of the trader in negotiating their kinsmen's experience in the wage labor market. For example, during World War II, the Phelps Dodge Corporation approached Howard Gorman, a prominent Navajo leader from Ganado, to bring two hundred men to work in the copper mines in Morenci, Arizona. Another tribal council member from Crownpoint recruited workers from his area to work in the notorious farm labor camps in Bluewater, New Mexico.

After World War II, returning veterans and defense workers became an additional layer of cultural brokers. According to one observer, they were "up to date men who knew their way around the white world." They were part of a new generation of Navajo men and women who, in the 1950s, would challenge the "old guard" of Navajo politics by questioning the authority of an elite who derived power from large livestock holdings, relationships with the traders, and an ability to exploit the labor of their extended families.

World War II brought relief from the suffering associated with stock reduction, drawing thousands of Navajo men and women off the reservation to serve in the armed forces and to work in defense-related industries. Like other minority groups, they took advantage of the wartime labor shortage and migrated to reservation border towns and cities like Los Angeles, Phoenix, Albuquerque, and Denver, where they found jobs that would have been closed to them before the war. Navajos were not the only Native Americans to take advantage of the weakening color line in the industrial labor market. American Indians throughout the United States wanted good jobs and livable wages and traveled great distances to get them. As a result, the war inspired the first massive migration of American Indians off the reservations in the twentieth century. According to Alison Bernstein, in 1944 alone, more than forty-four thousand Native Americans left home in search of off-reservation employment. Out of that number, twenty-four thousand found work in non-agricultural jobs. Approximately 25 percent of that total were Navajos.

Some Navajos found new opportunities serving in the armed forces. The military provided a kind of occupational training ground where Navajo soldiers gained skills they found useful in the postwar labor market. For example, in 1942 Myrtle Waybenais left her position as an instructional aid at a BIA day school in Shiprock to join the Women's Army Corps. In a medical course, she learned, "about food and diets" and at a hospital technical school she studied "the fields of being a nurse."

After 1948, the BIA set out to undermine the reservation labor system, determined to challenge the role of the traders, the railroads, and informal recruitment practices initiated by a few Navajo elites. Such strategies had allowed Navajo workers to dip into the wage market for a limited time and then return to maintain their reservation households. Similar to the way they had attempted to rationalize sheep production, BIA officials were hoping to gain control of Navajo wage-labor practices as well.

Stabilizing the Navajo Work Force

BIA officials worried that veterans and war workers would place an unbearable strain on already limited reservation resources when they returned home after the war. In an alarmist tone, they concluded that the land simply could not support them. The officials predicted that "30,000 Navajos need to find a way to live outside the reservation or by some other means than sheep raising and the meager farming available." Congress commissioned a study, later known as "the Krug Report," in an effort to find solutions to these problems and assess the reservation's potential for economic development.

The 1950 Navajo-Hopi Rehabilitation Act, the bill designed to implement the study's findings, was supposed to offer solutions. Sponsors of that legislation allocated $88,570,000 towards this effort and hoped federally financed improvements would boost the reservation economy. Indeed, that investment laid the groundwork for a developing infrastructure. Paved roads, electricity, and telephone lines were essential to attract large-scale industry. This type of development, however, would not necessarily create a dynamic internal economy on

Variety of Navajo Labor

Employer	Number of Jobs
Railroads	7,500
Agriculture	3,500
Military Depots	625
Mining	350
Logging and Sawmills	175
Construction	250
Miscellaneous–Border Towns	850
Total	3,250

the reservation. It connected the Navajo reservation to external markets, but it did not provide Navajos with the capital they needed to create their own local enterprises.

The program embodied contradictory goals. On the one hand it was supposed to improve the reservation economy and provide relief to the Navajo people who lived in terrible poverty. On the other, instead of helping to create a vital reservation working class to participate in the development of an internal economy, the program encouraged workers who were at the height of their productive years to leave the reservation for good. BIA officials set out to transform reservation labor practices because they were convinced that Navajo migratory behavior reinforced the Indians' connection to the reservation, a problem that undermined their eventual assimilation into the white world. Encouraging permanent off-reservation relocation would ease the demand on reservation resources and facilitate Navajo incorporation into the mainstream American economy.

According to BIA estimates, demand for Navajo labor exceeded supply. In 1948, Indian Service officials reported that approximately ten thousand Navajos were available for off-reservation wage work, a number that barely met the demand for their labor the year before. Their relatively large numbers, access to regional commercial agriculture, and availability suggested an alternative source of cheap labor to replace Mexican nationals and other migrant laborers. The BIA, members of the Navajo Tribal Council, and representatives of Western industries now had to figure out how to bring Navajo workers to that market, and, most important, how to make them stay.

Part of that plan meant imposing gender roles that were the norm in the surrounding U.S. economy. An in-depth analysis of the gendered implications of the BIA's relocation plan is beyond the scope of this article. However, the criteria they used to define potential workers offers a revealing glimpse of the significant role gender played in the BIA's attempts to shape the Navajo working class. The BIA estimated that there was a total of sixteen thousand men between the ages of fifteen and sixty-five living on the reservation, 6,350 of whom were not available for work because they were either attending school, physically incapacitated, employed, or self-supporting. Fewer women could be considered potential workers because of their "family ties." BIA officials did not list "family ties" to explain why men might not be prepared to join the wage labor market. In addition, "self-supporting" was a category they only applied to men, although we know that women significantly contributed to the household economy by weaving rugs and selling sheep and wool as well as working for wages on and off the reservation. Since most Navajos at this time pooled their resources and valued women's work as crucial for household survival, it appears that the BIA's criteria were less an actual assessment of the Navajo labor market than a prescription for what they hoped it would become.

In January 1948, James M. Stewart, the general superintendent of the Navajo Reservation outlined a philosophy consistent with federal assimilationist goals, offering a proposal that would guide the BIA's efforts to shape the Navajo labor market. He modeled his plan on how he imagined immigrant communities coped with an unfamiliar and often hostile American cultural environment. In Stewart's eyes, European and Asian immigrants had established neighborhoods that cushioned their arrival with familiar cultural surroundings and simultaneously offered them an avenue for assimilation into the American mainstream. Chinatowns and little Italys, "offered points of departure from which the individual and his children could learn the language and customs of America and ultimately assume his place in our national life." Ethnic neighborhoods drew immigrants to them and provided "training grounds for the new arrivals from the old country." He hoped that the new Navajo "colonies" would serve the same purpose. They would supply employers with labor and, in Stewart's words, "rehabilitate" the Navajo people.

Unlike the Navajos, the Chinese and the Europeans lived "too far away to permit them to return as an escape from nostalgia or frustration." As a result, "they were faced with [the] necessity of creating a familiar environment in the midst of the unfamiliar." Because Navajos could return home at any time, the challenge, according to BIA officials, was to make these off-reservation communities an attractive alternative to life on the reservation. Thus, colonization would break the connection that pulled so many back to the reservation and create a reliable work force for Western employers. Such a plan resonated well with the federal termination agenda.

For BIA officials and some Western employers, Navajo culture was a *problem* that needed to be solved. Stewart noted that the Navajos "subscribe to a way of life, a pattern of thinking, and a system of values which are highly divergent from our own." He knew that transforming those cultural ideas would not be an easy task. He noted that the "customs, institutions, and other characteristics which serve to distinguish one way of life from another are not things which can be shed and replaced at will." Thus, Stewart concluded, any program that the BIA implemented had to address Navajo cultural practices that tended to draw them back to the reservation. He assumed that a continued connection to the reservation household interfered with Navajos' eventual assimilation into the white world of permanent wage labor. Severing those connections was the only answer for insuring the success of the colonization project. Hence, BIA officials launched an all-out battle to transform Navajo ideas and expectations about work and household responsibilities. With stock reduction, the BIA had intruded into Navajo households and undermined their subsistence base. Now, BIA officials were attempting to control how the Navajos engaged the wage labor market.

The BIA did not wait long to implement Stewart's plan. On 30 January 1948, two days after Stewart released his report, William H. Zeh, director of the BIA's District IV, convened a meeting to discuss off-reservation employment for the Navajo and Hopi people. Attending the meeting were representatives from railroad and lumber companies, commercial agriculture, and traders with operations on the Navajo and Hopi reservations. Placement officials from the Arizona and New Mexico employment services represented the state governments. Also in attendance were various federal bureaucrats from the Department of the Interior, the Navajo and Hopi agencies, and the Veterans Administration. Thirteen Navajo leaders attended to comment on working conditions in industries that employed Indian labor.

Six days later, at a meeting of the Farm Labor Advisory Committee in Arizona, Zeh explained to commercial growers what had transpired at the Phoenix conference. He summarized the conclusions, reporting that the participants confirmed the need for a stabilized Navajo labor force. The challenge they faced was how to "keep them on the job longer." He invited employers and BIA officials to "encourage [the Navajo worker] to become an established workman, established in the community and available to work in whatever type of work his capacities, his limitations, or his strength qualifies him for." He laid out the problems that he thought would face all parties involved in off-reservation colonization. Stressing that Navajos were willing to seek off-reservation employment, he acknowledged to his audience that it would be a challenge for the employers and the Indian Service to encourage permanent migration. The problem, according to Zeh, was that for Navajos, "[t]here is a very strong tie to the reservation. The Navajo is in general a primitive sort of individual, the wide world is a foreign world to him, he doesn't feel any happier than we would feel in the Navajo world." In rather paternalistic terms, Zeh encouraged the growers to empathize with the Navajo workers' situation, reassuring them that, in time, the Indians would adjust.

> You can see what a difficult situation the Indian has to meet off-hand to adjust to white man's civilization. It will take a period of time under certain conditions, and the primary condition will be right treatment, and then he will respond quite well. . . . In general, the Navajo has been found to be a desirable employee. The comments made which were adverse to the Navajo were primarily directed to his habit of leaving the job and going back to the reserva-

tion. That is something that education will take care of. Sixty to eighty years ago, the Navajo was a primitive savage. He has come a very long way in a short time. According to our standards, he will have to learn about work habits before he becomes a first class employee of any kind.

According to Zeh, Navajos had to adapt to "modern" workplace practices. Employers, too, had some lessons to learn. They could improve their success with Navajo workers if they made an effort to understand their culture. He noted:

> problems created by language and tribal customs . . . [would] be solvable through sympathetic understanding and education of the Indian and the white employer. It is not only necessary for the Navajo to learn, but the white employer must learn about the Navajo.

After holding a series of meetings with interested employers and consulting officials from state employment agencies, the bureau enacted a pilot project to facilitate the creation of off-reservation communities. The BIA established the Navajo Placement Service in the spring of 1948 to secure off-reservation employment, primarily in agricultural and extra-gang railroad work. The employers or state employment officers would file job orders with the Navajo Placement Service, and it would send them suitable employees. The success of the program, according to BIA representatives, required both educating the employers about Navajo cultural values and teaching Navajos how to behave on the job. The BIA, in conjunction with state employment services in Arizona, Colorado, Utah, and California, would coordinate this exchange, protecting the Navajos from exploitation and at the same time offering to industry workers who were reliable and suited to the task.

Agency officials circulated a calendar that outlined what they understood as the important events that marked the Navajo year in an effort to educate potential employers about the types of cultural and familial commitments that might lure Navajo workers back to the reservation. They explained that from June through September, Navajos would be preoccupied with cultivating their fields and from mid-September through mid-October, they would be leaving work periodically to harvest them. March, April, and May would find many Navajos working on spring planting, tending to new lambs, and shearing mature sheep. Herding, of course, was a responsibility that would draw Navajos home year-round when they were needed. The brochure warned employers that the demands of the reservation household would draw employees back home, particularly in the fall, when the piñon crop was ready for harvesting.

Additionally, the Colorado Department of Economic Security informed employers of spiritual and other cultural events in the Navajo calendar. The Shiprock fair, held at the end of September, the Pow Wow in Flagstaff on July 4th, and the Gallup Ceremonial in late summer were specific events that encouraged Navajos to gravitate away from their jobs. The *Yeibichi* was held in October, November, and December and other Navajo ceremonies, such as "squaw" dances, took place in August and September. In the winter, other household demands limited the availability of Navajos to take jobs off the reservation. Those who had children in school on the reservation were reluctant to leave. Men returned home in the fall to make sure their families had enough firewood to get them through the coldest months. According to the employment service, understanding these rituals and responsibilities would improve the employers' relationship with their Navajo employees.

Representatives of the BIA's Navajo Service suggested that employers designate English-speaking Navajo men as work group leaders. They could interpret the terms of employment and explain the requirements of the job to their fellow Navajo workers. At the Phoenix conference, employers had offered their experience of how successful such a setup could be. John C. Church, a vegetable grower near Phoenix, testified that he always hired Navajos who were bilingual in English and Navajo. As a result, he did not "find the language problem too serious." He explained that he would "pick out leaders from different districts and make them road bosses. All these road bosses speak very good English and they convey our messages."

Some farmers were not as lucky as Church and found out that an interpreter's loyalty did not always favor management. In November 1948, on the Harmon Crismon Farms in Queen Creek, Arizona, a Navajo man named Earl Johnson used his leverage as a go-between to bargain for higher wages and better living conditions for the other seventy Navajos employed to tie carrots. He demanded mattresses for all workers to sleep on, a wage increase from twenty-two to twenty-four cents per crate, and a paid police officer to patrol the camp to "insure that if any of them got drunk they would not wander into town and be arrested." Finally, he insisted on nine dollars a day as compensation for his role as foreman. When the farmers initially refused to grant the pay increase, Johnson and the rest of the Navajo workers ceased work. Disturbed, the farmer called the Navajo Service placement officer to intervene. But Johnson stood his ground. He insisted that the increase "was necessary in order for them to make a living wage." Despite his attempt to intervene, the placement officer reported, "Mr. Johnson was very adamant in his demands that the employer would have to pay the higher rate or he would take all of the workers back to the reservation." Much to the chagrin of other growers in the area, the farmer gave in to Johnson's demands after less than a twenty-four-hour standoff.

That same month, another group of Navajo agricultural workers in Cucamonga, California, staged a similar collective protest. On 20 November, Navajos who had been employed to pick lemons walked off the job because the farmers refused to employ one member of their group, a man the farmers characterized as "hard of hearing and absentminded." Once again, the farmer called in the Navajo Service representative to "reason" with the workers. Unlike the Queen Creek incident, however, the Navajos carried out their threat and returned to the reservation. Either the farmers hired everyone in the group, or nobody would work.

The BIA as Labor Contractor

While some employers applauded the BIA's efforts to control and stabilize the Navajo labor supply and attempted to comply with its suggestions, others were less than enthusiastic. Employers' support for the BIA's policies depended largely on whether they benefited from Navajo migratory strategies. Some commercial growers balked at the BIA's suggestion that they build permanent communities near their farms. Unwilling to assume the expense or responsibility, these farmers objected to establishing communities where Navajo workers would live year-round. One Phoenix grower complained,

> Our particular business is seasonal and we have not been able to figure out a uniform job for this group over the entire year. We bring them in November and the season runs until June, but fluctuates during that period. . . . We don't know how we can cushion over an entire year, because these people, when the time comes, always want to go back to the reservation.

John M. Jacobs, representing general farming and vegetable growers in Phoenix, raised the problem of establishing schools for Navajo children if permanent communities were developed. He argued that the local schools were resisting enrolling Navajo students. He pointed out that:

> [O]ne of the greatest problems of our camp is trying to work with the schools in order to get the children into school. Facilities simply are not set up to take care of these children in school. That is a problem that will be basic in your overall plan of trying to locate these people.

The growers did support a system that would establish off-reservation communities (at government expense) from which they could draw their labor supply. They urged the BIA to create a centralized "pooling" station where they could hire employees according to their labor needs. This, they argued, would solve the problems they had in recruiting enough laborers.

BIA officials may have had the *bracero* program in mind when developing their scheme to relocate Navajos to agricultural labor camps. The Navajo proposal followed the development of the bracero system by six years, and in some ways the two programs were similar. Both programs involved U.S. federal agencies as labor contractors, supplying agricultural workers to the commercial growers in the West. But the aim of the BIA's program differed considerably from the bracero system. BIA officials hoped to encourage Navajos to leave their homes for good. The bracero program, at least officially, expected workers to return to Mexico after staying in the United States for a limited time. It sought to benefit Western agricultural interests, while the BIA's program aimed, at least in theory, to relieve poverty by easing the stress on reservation resources and to encourage Navajo assimilation into mainstream American society.

It is unclear whether the BIA was working in tandem with the Immigration and Naturalization Service and the Labor Department, the two agencies responsible for administering the bracero program. Whether or not these two programs were officially connected, there is evidence that farmers entertained the idea of replacing Mexican contract workers with Navajos. Yet Navajos' numbers could not possibly have met the demand for labor supplied by Mexican workers.

Faced with opposition from the farmers, Zeh offered a compromise proposal that abandoned the BIA's ideal of stable, off-reservation colonies for centralized and less-than-permanent labor camps. He argued that it was inefficient for individual growers to venture out onto the reservation to do their own recruiting. Instead, the BIA would hire five Navajo recruiters to canvas the reservation for available workers. When they found enough candidates to fill the growers' labor orders, the Navajo recruiters would bring them to a central place to be picked up. One of the merits of this plan, Zeh asserted, was that, for farmers, it would "eliminate the necessity of going out and beating the bush for labor." The BIA would not change the labor system that had been in place since the beginning of the century. Its officials would simply attempt to take control of it.

The BIA's relationship with railroad recruiters was not as amiable. Given the choice between placing Navajo workers in commercial agriculture or in jobs working for the railroad, the BIA clearly advocated the former. The agency favored agriculture because railroad employment usually only took men on a seasonal basis, encouraging them to leave their wives and children at home on the reservation. Agricultural work was seasonal as well, but since commercial growers hired whole families, the BIA saw the potential for encouraging entire households to leave the reservation for good. The railroad recruiters were also closely affiliated with the reservation trading posts, an institution that some BIA officials saw as corrupt and exploitative.

Railroad employers were quite satisfied with the system they had in place. Like some of the growers, they opposed creating permanent off-reservation settlements. They preferred recruiting their workers when they needed them, primarily in the spring, summer, and fall, and laying them off in the winter when bad weather slowed track maintenance. Working through the trader allowed them an insider's access to the available work force and a way to identify and keep track of the most reliable workers. Railroad representatives resented the BIA's bias toward agriculture and argued that their system offered the Navajos more economic benefits, including unemployment insurance, sick pay, and retirement.

Railroad employers presented one of the largest stumbling blocks for the BIA. After discussing the Navajo labor situation with Atchison, Topeka, & Santa Fe officials in Winslow, Arizona, Lucy Adams, Director of Welfare and Placement for the Navajo Service, reported:

> It is very difficult to make this individual or any other official of the Santa Fe realize that they should not have a monopoly on Navajo labor. They are firmly convinced that since they pioneered in using Navajo labor that henceforth all Navajos should be directed to their uses. They also believe that the Indians should be kept as a pool on the reservation during the winter months so that they will be available for their uses commencing in the Spring.

It is not surprising that Western mining companies expressed the most interest in what the BIA was proposing. Unlike the agricultural industry and the railroads, mining depended on a stable, permanent labor force. Some mining companies even offered a number of incentives to married Navajo men and their families to encourage them to settle down. For example, the superintendent of the Bingham Canyon mine planned to remodel two old apartment buildings "which, when completed, will provide modern living quarters to between six and eight families." As long as the BIA provided the Navajos with trailers, he was even willing "to provide a camp area, level it off with bull-dozers, and provide water, sewage disposal and electricity." In another example, Phelps Dodge offered to bring a medicine man to Morenci as a way to stem the tide of workers returning to the reservation. That effort failed, however, since the medicine men they approached refused to perform Navajo rituals on land that lay outside the four sacred mountains.

Despite the efforts of BIA officials, tribal leaders, and Western industrialists, Navajo workers continued to view wages as a resource to be pooled for the maintenance of the reservation household. In his 1948 investigation of off-reservation wage work, Robert Young reported that Navajos working and living in Bingham Canyon were not committed to settling there on a permanent basis. Even men who had their wives and families with them set their sights on returning to the reservation. For example, Young reported that Ab Harris, a Navajo man from Marble Canyon, was saving fifty dollars from every paycheck, which would soon amount to two thousand dollars. Despite the good wages, he, his wife, and three children were living in part of a small, dilapidated house in the ruins of an abandoned underground copper mine near the Bingham Canyon operation. Instead of using his savings to move into more comfortable quarters, Harris planned to use the money to build his family a stone house on the reservation, a project that he estimated would require twenty days in the upcoming year to complete. When the house was finished, he expected to continue working at Bingham Canyon to raise more money so that he could build a filling station on the highway nearby. For BIA officials, the small mining community in Rico, Colorado, seemed to provide an ideal model for off-reservation Navajo colonies. Rico was a typical company town that experienced cycles of boom and bust from the 1920s through the 1950s. At its height in 1954, the community reached a population of seven hundred people, 35 percent of whom were Navajos. Located 93 miles north of Shiprock and connected to the reservation by U.S. Highway 666 and Colorado State Highway 145, it was within easy reach of Navajo workers. Unlike railroad work and commercial agriculture, mining offered year-round work for wages that would support a standard of living above the poverty line for families residing off the reservation. Ralph Luebben, an anthropologist who conducted a participant-observer study of the Rico Navajos, noted that the mining company paid relatively high wages. He reported that between July 1953 and June 1954, seventy-five Navajo miners employed by the Argentine Mining company in Rico earned $116,209.08, or an average of $1,549.46 per man, just above the minimum government officials had determined would allow a Navajo man to support himself and his immediate family.

In addition to offering relatively high wages and employment year-round, the mining company offered better housing than other Southwestern industries that employed Navajos. Company housing was by no means luxurious, but in comparison to the migrant agricultural camps where workers would be lucky if the growers provided them with tents and cooking stoves, the Rico facilities were an improvement.

Housing was better than what Navajos would find on commercial farms, but it was worse than what the mining company provided Anglo miners and their families. The Navajo homes were clustered around a common sanitary facility that included central washing places, toilets, and showers. Families living in houses without inside cold water taps had to rely on wells, a fire hydrant, and the water overflow of the nearby Atlantic Cable mine. In contrast, Anglos living in company housing enjoyed hot water and indoor, private toilets and bathing facilities. To make matters worse, the mining company paid Navajo workers less than Anglo miners performing the same work. Such racial discrimination was an all-too-familiar pattern. Rico was just like any other reservation border town.

Despite these difficulties, the high wages Navajos could earn in Rico made it one of the best options available to them off the reservation. Jobs at Rico paid better than what a man could earn working in the reservation mines, on the railroad, or in commercial agriculture. It was also one of the few places where workers could bring their wives and children.

The Draw of the Reservation Household

Much to the chagrin of BIA officials, Navajo workers treated working in the mines like any other off-reservation job. Navajo miners did not view their jobs as permanent. On the average, they worked about four months at a time and returned to the reservation to check on their families, tend to household responsibilities, or participate in Navajo ceremonials or curing sings. Despite the possibility of earning as much as five thousand dollars a year, most Navajos refused to work for more than a few months at a time. Family and ritual obligations consistently drew them back home.

Despite frequent warnings from mining company officials, Navajo mine workers would leave work when pressing matters on the reservation needed their attention. Luebben calculated that Navajos missed twice as many shifts as Anglo workers, the highest rate of absenteeism occurring in the month of the Shiprock fair and during the Gallup ceremonial. They also missed a high percentage of shifts in April to return to the reservation to prepare their farm plots for spring planting. One Navajo miner explained to Luebben in a matter-of-fact way, "I'll go down on weekends and farm. Once a month I'll have to take off on Friday evening to get two days of farming."

Navajo absenteeism was so bad that mining company officials complained that it undermined their operation. But despite efforts to carry out disciplinary actions, Navajo workers refused to change their priorities. The company geologist explained to Luebben:

> I fired a few [for failing to make the shift]. I did it before, but it didn't do any good. They're not on the job as much as I'd like to have them. . . . What I need is a crew of about 55, with half off and half on. I don't know what would happen if they all showed up.

Luebben argued that this behavior indicated "that Navahos [were] interested primarily in short terms of employment and a subsequent temporary monetary income." Interpreting high absenteeism and turnover as their reluctance to identify as permanent wage workers, he concluded that "[t]o most Navahos mining is just another job and their occupational position does not mean economic security nor does it define their status." With the type of discrimination they faced in Rico, it is no surprise that Navajos did not want to make it their permanent home.

The wages they brought home from their off-reservation jobs allowed Navajo workers to maintain their household-centered survival strategies and to navigate the changing political and economic climate on the reservation with increasing flexibility. With the money they earned working on the railroads, in commercial agriculture, or in mining operations, many Navajos achieved relative autonomy from the traders and developed the means to maintain migratory strategies on their own terms. By the early 1950s, with the federal government building roads with money allocated from the Navajo-Hopi Rehabilitation Act, consumer and wage markets were becoming more accessible to reservation households. With the new roads, wages, and an increased demand for goods that could be acquired off the reservation, trucks and cars quickly replaced the horse and wagon as the main means of transportation. Owning a truck allowed Navajos to bypass the trader and purchase food and consumer goods in grocery and department stores located in places like Gallup and Flagstaff.

By purchasing trucks with the very wages they were earning from working in the fields, agricultural workers established a stronger bargaining position for themselves with farm labor recruiters. Driving to the fields in their own vehicles allowed them more freedom to come and go as they pleased, and easier access to return to the reservation at a moment's notice. While growers were relieved to some extent by the reduced cost of transporting Navajo workers back and forth to the reservation, they lamented the problem that increased mobility caused for maintaining a stable work force and for controlling the Navajos' behavior in the labor camps. A Navajo Service representative complained,

> To the grower, this increase of cars is a mixed blessing. Though he is not responsible for transportation, the worker is more likely to leave without notice or go into town and get drunk. It has also meant this summer that workers are

arriving a week or more before the jobs start, and have to apply to local merchants for credit which they are reluctant to extend.

Clarence and Margaret Kee might have been among those Navajo workers who worried Western employers. They traced the lineage of their cars and trucks, like their sheep, back to the first two vehicles they purchased with the wages they earned working on the railroad and in the fields. The wages that Clarence Kee sent home from his job on the railroad bought his mother her first truck. A few years later, Margaret Kee and her adolescent son went to work picking potatoes and sugar beets in Idaho. When they had enough money, they purchased a small car and returned to their reservation home near Window Rock, Arizona. Wage work provided the resources that brought them back to the reservation; it did not encourage them to move away for good.

As much as the Navajo Service hated to admit it, the bureaucrats had not been successful in stemming the tide of return migration. Some Navajos did permanently leave the reservation, but many more came back. In 1953, approximately 375 people left the reservation for long-term employment and relocation purposes. In 1955, 415 people moved to Chicago, Denver, Los Angeles, and San Francisco, where the BIA had field offices to assist those relocating. In January 1956, five hundred more applications were on file. However, approximately 30 percent of those who left with the aim of relocating on a permanent basis returned to the reservation. Compilers of the report detailing the progress of the 1950 Navajo-Hopi Rehabilitation Act noted that the Indians returned because they were "unable to adjust to changing living conditions" and because of "family ties on the Reservation."

In contrast, by 1953 the Railroad-Retirement Board, the BIA's Branch of Placement and Relocation in Window Rock, and state employment services in Arizona and New Mexico reported 23,500 seasonal, off-reservation placements. The difference between the number of placements and the number of people relocating in 1953 suggests that Navajo seasonal migratory strategies persisted. In 1962, responding to a Congressional inquiry on Indian unemployment, Glen R. Landbloom, General Superintendent of the Navajo Service, admitted, "in spite of the interest of the Navajo people toward economic life, the effects of Indian culture still exist." Landbloom confirmed what commercial growers and railroad employers already knew, that Navajos "still prefer to work at employment which enables them to take part in the numerous tribal ceremonies."

Conclusion

The struggle over relocation amounted to a battle over what would constitute the Navajo household in the postwar era. BIA officials wanted to transform extended, kin-based residential groups into nuclear households off the reservation. They hoped Navajos would leave their hogans and become village dwellers and limit their kin obligations to what was customary for an Anglo-style nuclear family. Navajo men and women participated in those BIA programs but did not accept the ultimate goals of colonization. Instead, in an effort to keep their reservation households intact, they treated those "opportunities"—even jobs that offered them more money and permanent year-round employment—as one more source of income that would allow them to maintain a broader, kinship-centered lifestyle on the reservation. The reservation household provided Navajos with a cultural buffer, offering them relief from the hostile racial environment that many Navajos experienced in reservation border towns like Rico, Colorado. When Navajos refused to relinquish that space, the BIA's plan failed. What had begun as a grand plan to reconstitute the Navajo household off the reservation provided, in the end, a way for the BIA to assume the role of glorified labor contractor for Southwestern agricultural interests.

The Navajo experience is similar to what some historians have found in parts of Latin America and Africa. Florencia Mallon's effort to "put flesh on the bones of that skeleton historians call the 'development of capitalism'" reveals that Andean peasants used "traditional relationships" to shape the transition of their villages to a capitalist economy. In the process, those "weapons of the weak" transformed the villagers and their communities. Like members of the Navajo Tribal Council or other Navajo elites who utilized kinship networks and connections with traders to become labor contractors, wealthier peasants in the Yanamarca Valley drew on their influence at the village level to fashion a system of wage-based, commercial agriculture from a kinship-based system.

Navajo wage-work strategies also parallel what Keletso Atkins found in South Africa. From their experience performing agricultural labor in their own village communities, the Natal Africans defined a fair day's work as beginning at sunup and ending at sundown, and kept track of their wages and work days on a lunar cycle. British officials who attempted to impose rationalized time regimes were dismayed when the workers appeared before them and demanded: "The moon is dead! Give us our money!" Those officials who did not conform or at least adjust to the Zulu work ethic were subject to labor shortages.

Working for wages in the Navajo way was a form of contestation over the labor process itself. The Navajo workers defined the terms of employment when they refused to work longer than four months at a time and left their jobs for ceremonials and to tend to familial obligations. Holding on to the land and maintaining the reservation household, however symbolic, gave them a means to negotiate the terms of work. Like the British colonial officials who wanted to ensure their supply of laborers in South Africa, Southwestern entrepreneurs who planned to employ Navajos had to learn their workers' ways of doing things. Shrewd employers did just that. The BIA failed to implement the Navajo colonization program because farmers and railroad officials refused to endorse the plan. Those employers favored the system they had in place because it was in their economic interest to exploit the household-centered cultural practices that the Navajo had developed in the post-stock-reduction period. Resisting permanent relocation and refusing to conform to the BIA's expectations, Navajos made a place for themselves in the Southwestern labor market. They participated in that market but did not embrace the assimilationist goals that BIA officials and some employers promoted.

Navajos did leave the reservation to find jobs. But, for many like the Kees, that work provided them with the resources they needed to preserve, rather than replace their reservation households. Margaret Kee now lives in St. Michaels, Arizona, in a house equipped with all the modern conveniences: Her daughters' mobile homes surround her comfortable home like hogans clustered around the family settlement in the days of her youth. She spends most of her time weaving rugs and tending her sheep while Clarence works at the Pittsburgh and Midway strip mine a few miles east, near Window Rock.

Even though Margaret Kee no longer relies on the sheep for her living, they remain central to her sense of well-being. As her daughter Juanita Brown explains, "[I]f the sheep are not around her, she feels empty . . . so she has to have some kind of sheep around her . . . they're holding that gift from their dad and their mom to this day." For Margaret, sheep were (and are) more than a source of income. They embody a sense of connection with past and future generations, a way to pass on the lessons her father taught her. Translating her mother's story from Navajo to English, Brown explained, "He constantly . . . remind[ed] these two to take care of [the] sheep. . . . Take good care of them. In the future . . . when you guys have kids . . . tell them about the sheep. . . . Let them go on with the sheep."

Like the Kees, Burton Yazzie, a coworker of Clarence Kee's at the P&M Mine and fifteen years his junior, learned that the sheep represented security for the future. "We had to take care of them, and they would take care of you. Vice versa." Even today, when sheep contribute little in terms of household income, Navajos still invest them with deep emotional and spiritual significance. As one daughter of a miner employed at Peabody Coal Company on Black Mesa explained, "the sheep are our culture."

The Navajo case demonstrates that the development of capitalism includes, as Kathy Le Mons Walker suggests, "multiple constructions with different and even conflicting principles and histories." Those stories certainly promise to complicate the master narrative of U.S. economic development, a positivist tale that continues to dominate western historical thinking. As that myth unravels, perhaps the reign of U.S. exceptionalism, a fable that features "the West" as its central drama, will fade as well. The significance of the Navajo example thus becomes more than filling in the gaps in the historical record. Writing about capitalist development in a way that includes Native Americans as historical agents requires pushing past the discourse of development to incorporate alternative visions. Understanding the multiple strands of economic development in the past may help us imagine alternative models for the present and the future. The values and cultural ethics developed by Navajos and other indigenous cultures might offer creative possibilities.

Suggested Readings

Colleen O'Neill's *Working the Navajo Way: Labor and Culture in the Twentieth Century* (Lawrence: University Press of Kansas, 2005), gives her ideas even more space than here in this essay. Brian Hosmer and Colleen O'Neill, *Native Pathways: American Indian Culture and Economic Development in the Twentieth Century* (Boulder: University Press of Colorado, 2004), discuss a variety of Indian labor issues. In his article "The Tohono O'odham, Wage Labor, and Resistant Adaptation, 1900–1930," Western Historical Quarterly 34, no.4 (Winter 2003): 469–89, Eric V. Meeks discusses similar issues for the early decades of the twentieth century. Peter Iverson, *When Indians Became Cowboys: Native Peoples and Cattle Ranching in the American West* (Norman: University of Oklahoma Press, 1994), presents the story of another variety of Indian agricultural labor.

CHAPTER NINETEEN

Termination and the Eastern Band of Cherokees

JOHN R. FINGER

The postwar campaign to "free" Native groups from domination by BIA officials by encouraging the voluntary relocation of Indians to help them secure off-reservation jobs also led to other, more negative, results. In 1946 Congress established the Indian Claims Commission to investigate and settle existing tribal claims against the federal government. A few years later the government developed the termination program to end federal responsibilities to the Indians. This directed the BIA to group tribes into categories based on their degree of acculturation and economic strength. Groups considered most economically successful became the first to be terminated.

The Eastern Band of Cherokees, at least to outsiders, appeared ready to be placed into this category. Like many Indian groups, the Cherokees split sharply over termination. Some tribal members saw opportunities for quick personal gain if they could gain the title to their land and sell it. Others feared that the tribe would dissolve and face economic ruin. Knowledgeable tribal leaders joined prominent local businessmen to pressure state and federal officials to end the plans for termination. This essay analyzes the roles various groups played in helping the Cherokees to escape termination.

Immediately following World War II, political pressures mounted to get the federal government "out of the Indian business" by terminating trust responsibilities to tribes and "emancipating" them from the stifling paternalism of the Bureau of Indian Affairs (BIA). The call for termination was both a repudiation of former Indian Commissioner John Collier's New Deal programs and a reaffirmation of earlier assimilationist assumptions and policies regarding Native Americans. As many terminationists noted, Indians had served well in the war and deserved something better than second-class citizenship. Surely people who had adjusted

"Termination and the Eastern Band of Cherokees" appeared in *American Indian Quarterly* 15, no. 2 (Spring 1991): 153–70.

to military service and a world war were capable of looking after themselves. Surely they would want to enjoy that freedom and share its prerogatives. It was time for Indians to become part of mainstream American society.

Indian policy also reflected some of the postwar paranoia concerning the Soviet Union and the specter of communism. Critics had long decried Collier's programs as socialistic and even communistic and now, amid the tensions of the Cold War, many Americans idealized an individualistic society standing in dramatic counterpoint to the collectivism of our perceived enemies. Tribalism and the maintenance of a number of separate cultures within American society seemed unpatriotic as well as expensive. Many saw the BIA as a collection of entrenched bureaucrats wedded to un-American programs and determined to protect their own jobs.

At one time or another during the postwar period, almost every tribe had to confront the possibility of termination. The Eastern Band of Cherokee Indians, with more than 4,000 members, was no exception. Occupying a reservation of some 56,000 acres scattered over several counties in the mountains of western North Carolina, the Eastern Cherokees claimed descent from a small number of Indians who, through curious and complicated circumstances, remained in the Southeast after the Cherokee Nation was removed to present-day Oklahoma in 1838. They enjoyed federal recognition as a tribe and also operated under an 1889 state charter of incorporation. The Band's precise legal status had been a source of endless dispute, with both the state and federal governments exercising an undefined mixed (or concurrent) jurisdiction. Isolated from most Native Americans, the Eastern Cherokees suffered from a sometimes inattentive BIA and a state government with little knowledge of Indian problems. Thus the Band's experiences amid the termination controversy, while similar in some respects to those of other tribes, more often reflected its unique historical, physical, and economic circumstances. Especially important were the tribe's location next to the Great Smoky Mountains National Park and the remarkable growth of tourism, which gave both Cherokees and many local whites a vested interest in maintaining an Indian identity.

For the Eastern Cherokees, the battle over termination began in January 1947, following a call by Senator Dennis Chavez of New Mexico for abolition of the BIA. A small faction of acculturated tribal members immediately echoed Chavez's sentiments. Their leader was Fred Bauer, former vice chief of the Band, who during the 1930s had been active in the American Indian Federation, a rabidly anti-Collier and pro-assimilationist organization. Bauer had moved to the reservation too late to prevent Cherokee ratification of Collier's Indian Reorganization Act (IRA) in December 1934, but the following year he successfully blocked efforts at drawing up a new tribal constitution under that act. And early in 1939, while at the height of his influence, he even persuaded the council to ask for a reconsideration of the Reorganization Act as it applied to the Eastern Band. In a scenario worthy of a Greek tragedy, Bauer's cousin and adoptive brother,

Principal Chief Jarrett Blythe, staunchly supported both John Collier and the Indian Reorganization Act.

By 1940 Bauer had lost his influence, and the House of Representatives failed to pass a Senate-approved bill which would have ended the IRA's application to the Eastern Band and several other tribes. But Bauer was not to remain silent, and he heard the postwar clamor for termination as a clarion call to renew his holy war against the BIA and tribalism. His wife, Catherine, a former teacher on the reservation, was equally vehement as was W. P. ("Pearson") McCoy, a former member of the tribal council. McCoy was a "white Indian" whose family had been included on the tribal roll—the Baker Roll—despite having only minimal Cherokee ancestry. As proprietor of a gift shop and other tourist-related enterprises on the reservation, he viewed the BIA as an obstacle to his pursuit of private enterprise. Without its meddling, he believed, the Cherokee reservation would be able to compete successfully for tourists with the town of Gatlinburg, Tennessee, on the opposite side of the national park. He succinctly expressed his sentiments in a letter to North Carolina's Senator Clyde R. Hoey:

> We wish the Indian Beaureau Abolished as far as the Cherokee Indians of N.C. are concerned. We wish to injoy our oppertunities that our fine roads, and the Great Smokey Mt. National Park, has made possible for us[.] We wish to lease and develop our Tourist Trade, we want Tourist Courts, Hotels, and everything a free interprise[.] We in other words Senator would like for Congress to transfer the Indian Bureau over to Gatlinburg, Tenn. And keep it there till we could catch up with those people.

McCoy said the Cherokees were not wards but citizens, and he believed the BIA was denying them their constitutional rights. He also reiterated a view developed by Fred Bauer that the Eastern Band was not a tribe but a corporation and that its lands were not a reservation because the Indians themselves had purchased them during the preceding century. In 1925 the Band, acting as a corporation, had transferred those properties in trust to the United States so the government could distribute them as individual allotments to each member. But distribution never occurred—first, because the Cherokees resisted it as long as the Baker Roll, compiled during the late 1920s, included so many white Indians; and second, because Congress finally discontinued all allotments with passage of the IRA in 1934. In the eyes of the Bauers and McCoys, the federal government exercised illegal control over the Band, and its failure to proceed with allotment constituted a breach of contract. (Indeed, Bauer forcefully argued these views right up to his death in 1971, despite numerous court decisions refuting his contentions.)

In February 1947, soon after Senator Chavez's call for abolishing the BIA, Acting Commissioner of Indian Affairs William Zimmerman issued a report assessing the readiness of various tribes for termination. In it he cited four major criteria for making such a decision: the tribe's degree of acculturation; its economic resources and condition; the tribe's willingness to be relieved of federal control; and the willingness of the state government to assume responsibility. His report listed three categories, the first being those tribes ready for immediate termination, the second including those which should be ready within two to ten years, and the third consisting of tribes that would not be prepared until some indefinite time in the future.

Zimmerman placed the Eastern Band in group two—mostly, it appears, on the basis of its acculturation. Using questionable tables based on census data from 1930, the Indian Bureau, in its magisterial wisdom, concluded that the Band retained 31.28 percent of its Indian culture. Each state with federal Indian populations was listed in this acculturation index. North Carolina, with only the Eastern Cherokees, ranked tenth out of 23 in terms of acculturation levels of its Indians. Kansas ranked first, with its several small groups supposedly retaining only 16.22 percent of their Indian culture. New Mexico ranked last, with its Indians retaining 69.30 percent of their traditional ways. It appears from the listing of various tribes in the three categories of readiness that if the North Carolina Cherokees had retained a few percentage points less of their Indian culture they might well have been placed in group one, those supposedly ready for immediate termination.

Despite Zimmerman's assessment of Cherokee readiness, the Bauer-McCoy faction had already convinced some North Carolina politicians that the Eastern Cherokees were indeed prepared for emancipation. In January 1947 Dan Tompkins, the state representative for Jackson County, which included much of the reservation, introduced a bill to memorialize Congress to abolish Indian Bureau control over the Eastern Band. He argued that such a step was "simple justice to a great people" and denounced the BIA's "dictatorship." About the only Cherokee political leader echoing those sentiments was councilman John C. McCoy, Pearson McCoy's kinsman. Tompkins's bill passed the North Carolina House unanimously, prompting officials to invite Cherokees to hearings in Raleigh before the senate education committee, which was considering the bill. Some hardliners like the McCoys refused because they already denied any jurisdiction by the BIA and expressed confidence in their state representatives.

Ten defenders of the Indian Bureau, including Principal Chief Jarrett Blythe, had no such qualms about attending. Wisely avoiding an ideological stance, the wily chief first thanked Tompkins for his interest in the tribe but then pointed out that the federal government spent about $300,000 a year to provide health care and education for the Eastern Cherokees. His tribe would have no objection to Tompkins's bill if North Carolina was willing to provide the same quality of services. In testimony that must have made federal officials blink with surprise, another Cherokee praised the United States government and claimed that without its protection local discrimination against Indians would become even worse. The hearings in Raleigh appear to have been orchestrated by senate committee member Frank Parker of Ashbville who had already performed legal services for the Band and would later become its full-time attorney. Parker was primarily responsible for killing Tompkins's bill in committee.

This setback merely encouraged Fred Bauer to redouble his attacks on the BIA and its connections with the Eastern Band. Early in March 1947 he protested to the chairman of the U.S. House Appropriations Committee about the BIA's alleged wrongdoings. Shrewdly, he also introduced a little cold war rhetoric:

> Bureau policies for the past thirteen years have been communistic, and their schemes have seriously curtailed private enterprise, and will eventually make it non-existent at Cherokee. We are denied hundreds of thousands of dollars annual revenue through the Bureau's refusal to permit enterprises that are begging to be allowed here at the Park entrance.

Bauer also attacked the Band's plans to create, with BIA backing, a tribally-owned complex of tourist facilities on the Boundary Tree tract adjacent to the national park. He labeled it "a Government controlled cooperative" and then returned to the Cold War by claiming that it was inconsistent to spend millions of dollars under the Truman Doctrine to fight communism abroad while spending money at home to promote communism "among a helpless minority of First Americans." He called for an end to all appropriations for the Cherokees' BIA agency.

This letter no doubt was the main reason work on Boundary Tree was held up that spring while Joe Jennings, the superintendent of the BIA's Cherokee Agency, attempted to explain the situation to acting Indian commissioner Zimmerman. After attacking Bauer and Pearson McCoy by name, Jennings noted that most opponents of Boundary Tree were white Indians who had gained inclusion on the Baker Roll over tribal protests. Under the Band's unique system of landholding, which permitted nearly unlimited acquisition of possessory claims on tribal lands, these relatively acculturated individuals had gained control of some of the most attractive tourist sites. Jennings said the white Indians felt insecure and favored abolition of the Indian Bureau because they hoped to receive titles in fee simple. He also pointed to a residue of ill will among local whites who favored termination so they could tax Indian lands. Predatory real estate speculators were likewise lurking about, eager to pounce on choice Cherokee business sites when government trusteeship ended.

When told that Cherokees had signed petitions against the BIA, Jennings replied that the names of some had been used without their knowledge. Others, he alleged, had been swayed by promises of receiving $3,000 each if the reservation were divided following federal withdrawal, while a few had been told they would be deported to Oklahoma or lose certain business rights on the reservation if they did not sign. Although work on the Boundary Tree facilities soon resumed, Jennings was clearly on the defensive.

The Cherokee council was not a passive spectator to these maneuverings. The most striking evidence of how threatening it found any radical alteration of federal ties came in October 1947 at its first regular meeting following the latest Bauer-McCoy crusade against the Indian Bureau. Although Bauer's Cherokee ancestry was sufficient for enrollment, the council noted the disputed status of many of his followers, who were "continually stirring up trouble," denouncing federal actions, and asserting their desire for "freedom" from the BIA. The council therefore resolved to ask Congress to enact legislation allowing the Band to revise its roll in order to eliminate such individuals and asked the government to use non-tribal funds to pay each challenged person a sum equal to the value of one share of tribal assets. The council agreed to pay each for any improvements on reservation lands. A major proviso was that no challenged member would receive such compensation if he had not recently lived on tribal property.

The council was even more forthright a little more than a week later when it resolved that a majority of the Eastern Band wanted "to continue under the bureau." It asked Congress to pass legislation allowing any bona fide members of the Band with less than one-fourth Eastern Cherokee blood to withdraw and sever their relationship with the Band any time they wished. Clearly the council preferred to maintain a tribal identity within the existing federal network and to encourage discontented members of minimal Cherokee ancestry to withdraw. That was probably the major consideration, but no doubt some councilmen also perceived the status quo as a means of retaining political influence and jobs within the BIA. To this extent, at least, Bauer and other critics were probably correct. Whatever the reasons, by the end of 1947 it was apparent that at least two of acting Indian commissioner Zimmerman's four criteria for termination were lacking in the case of the Eastern Band: consent of both the tribe and its state of residence.

Another facet of Indian "emancipation" was the creation by Congress in 1946 of the Indian Claims Commission. For many years various tribes had been arguing that the United States should compensate them for past injustices, but the only way they could obtain redress was through direct congressional intervention. Under the new legislation, a three-person claims commission would review legal briefs and other evidence presented by tribes and make binding judgment on the merits of each case. Congressional sponsors believed the claims commission would streamline tribal litigation, payoff federal obligations in an honorable fashion, and, perhaps, "financially liberate Native Americans from dependency on federal programs implemented during the Collier years." The Indian Claims Commission was thus seen as a necessary step by those politicians who favored termination of federal services to tribes. In effect, supporters believed creation of the commission meant the final reckoning of federal responsibilities to American Indians. Judgment Day was at hand.

Like many tribes, the Eastern Cherokees saw establishment of the claims commission not as a prelude to termination but as a long-needed means of satisfying old grievances. In 1951 the Band filed three claims seeking compensation for some 40 million acres taken from the Cherokees by the United States. These claims were in addition to similar ones filed by the Oklahoma Cherokees. Both groups also argued that various subsequent accounting and procedural errors by the government had cost the Indians millions of dollars. The Band found that dealing with the claims commission was an exasperating, time-consuming process. The volume of tribal claims was so great that Congress several times extended the life of the commission and expanded its membership to five. Not until 1972, long after the threat of termination had passed, did the United States finally award the Band more than $1.8 million.

Prospects for termination brightened considerably in 1950 with President Harry S. Truman's appointment of Dillon S. Myer as Commissioner of Indian Affairs. By the time of his appointment, there was a general consensus among policy makers in favor of Indian "self-determination" which, for Myer at least, meant ending wardship and regulation of Indian lives by the federal government. He had been given a "free hand to put the Indian Bureau 'out of business as quickly as possible'" and wanted to integrate Native Americans into the cultural mainstream. Many Indian leaders also supported self-determination but, it soon became apparent, defined this as greater Indian freedom of action without complete withdrawal of federal assistance.

One of Myer's most ambitious termination-related programs was the voluntary relocation of young Indians into urban centers as a means of offering more opportunities for employment than were available on reservations. The government would provide transportation for Indian families, their first month's living expenses, counseling, and even training. Later the program also included job placement. While many Indians saw relocation as a means of escaping tribal poverty, others viewed it as simply another effort to break up the reservations, abrogate federal responsibilities, and destroy Native American culture. Relocation among the Eastern Cherokees is difficult to assess, Anthropologists pronounced it a failure, while the tribal relocation officer called it a success. This disagreement may reflect different outcomes for those relocated under the aegis of the federal government and those who left the reservation on their own. Certainly by the 1950s more and more Eastern Cherokees were taking outside jobs or entering military service; many periodically returned to the reservation or chose to retire there after satisfying careers elsewhere.

Besides advocating relocation, Commissioner Myer was systematically taking other steps toward termination. In 1952, at the request of the House of Representatives, he collected voluminous information pertaining to the functions of the BIA and tribal readiness for withdrawal of federal services. Joe Jennings reported that many Eastern Cherokees were fearful of being left to the mercy of local whites. Resentment against Indians was especially high in Swain County, he said, because Cherokee lands had been withdrawn from the tax rolls when the federal government assumed trusteeship in 1925, and thousands more acres had been withdrawn when the national park was created a few years later. Cherokees had additional objections to termination, including distribution of tribal assets on the basis of the hated Baker Roll and loss of federal funding for education and health care.

Education was a particularly troublesome issue. Both Swain and Jackson counties, where most Indians resided, were among the poorest in the state, and public schools there did not offer the same opportunities that Cherokees enjoyed on the reservation. Because of federal support, the expenditure per Cherokee student in 1951–52 was almost three times that for students enrolled in North Carolina public schools. Likewise, health services for Cherokees were "at a far higher standard in terms of quantity and probably of quality than those available to the general population of the area." State officials had already informed Joe Jennings that even under the best of circumstances it would be at least six years before North Carolina could assume educational responsibilities for the Indians. But first the federal government would have to agree to construct modern school facilities on the reservation so the counties would not have to incur added financial burdens.

Jennings also said that individual Cherokees held possessory rights to all but about 8,000 of the more than 56,000 acres on the reservation. In his opinion at least 80 percent of the entire reservation should be left in forest, and this obviously required considerable advance planning and cooperation among both Indians and federal agencies. After noting the lack of good agricultural land, Jennings sounded what was to be a recurrent theme in arguments against precipitous termination: "If the tourist business is properly exploited the possibilities are such that it should provide nearly all of the Cherokees with a good living. These same possibilities make the Cherokees very vulnerable if withdrawal should come without proper safeguards set up by the State and Federal Governments." Many whites realized the reservation was a major economic attraction and were therefore interested "in working out a plan whereby the Indian can retain the reservation intact in Indian ownership," but in the meantime federal services should continue while Cherokees developed an ability to handle their own affairs.

Jennings' assessment figured prominently in the subsequent recommendations of the BIA's Minneapolis Area Office, which supervised the Cherokee agency. It placed each tribe in its jurisdiction in one of four groups, the first being those most prepared for termination. The Eastern Cherokee, along with the Menominee of Wisconsin and the Red Lake Chippewa of Minnesota, were in group four, the least prepared. These were not final assessments, however, and the Menominee were soon adjudged ready for termination. As for the Cherokees, the opinion was that their valuable timber resources, complicated system of landholding, and valuable tourist-related real estate necessitated special precautions before ending trust responsibilities. The office believed the Cherokees were still unable to administer their resources because they lacked tribal leadership and the necessary infrastructure. The report concluded with a call for a thorough study by specialists of the "entire complicated and complex Cherokee situation."

For those Indians fearing termination, the change of national administrations early in 1953 offered little solace. There seemed to be a groundswell of political sentiment to "emancipate" as many tribes as possible. President Dwight D. Eisenhower's Commissioner of Indian Affairs, Glenn L. Emmons, was a prominent businessman who intended to continue Myer's policies. Congress was similarly inclined and in July 1953 passed House Concurrent Resolution 108, calling for abolition of several Indian offices and termination of trust responsibilities for certain specified tribes. Emmons enthusiastically supported HCR 108 and suggested a number of additional suitable tribes. During the next decade Indian Office cooperation with politicians like Senator Arthur V. Watkins (Utah) led Congress to pass termination laws for more than 100 Indian groups, ranging from small communities and rancherias to large tribes. For several, notably the Klamath of Oregon and Menominees of Wisconsin, termination proved disastrous.

The North Carolina Cherokees, while not included among tribes listed in HCR 108, were also affected by the rising terminationist sentiment. In August 1953 Congress passed Public Law 280, which transferred civil and criminal jurisdiction over most tribes in five states to the respective local governments and allowed any other states to assume similar jurisdiction over their own Indian reservations. Assistant Secretary of Interior Orme Lewis sent a copy of PL 280 to North Carolina's Governor William B. Umstead and noted the provision allowing state assumption of jurisdiction. When Umstead requested a legal opinion, state Assistant Attorney General Ralph Moody argued that North Carolina did not need to follow up on PL 280 because it already exercised such authority over the Eastern Band. While the Band had received federal recognition as a tribe, Moody said its otherwise unique status had resulted in North Carolina's criminal laws applying "to all offenses committed within the Indian Reservation"—a statement inaccurate both in law and historical experience.

Perhaps the foremost factor working against termination of the Eastern Band was the burgeoning tourist Industry, which both whites and Indians saw as the most viable cure for western North Carolina's economic ills. Amid the postwar prosperity, millions of Americans were buying new automobiles and taking to the highways, many to visit the Great Smoky Mountains National Park. The opportunity to see a "real" Indian on the nearby Cherokee reservation was a bonus. By the late 1940s Western North Carolina Associated Communities (WNCAC), a consortium of eleven counties, had created the Cherokee Historical Association (CHA), a non-profit organization ostensibly dedicated to preserving and promoting Cherokee history and culture. Though established in cooperation with the tribal council and including some Cherokee members, it was clearly a white-dominated organization hoping to attract tourists to the region. In 1950 the CHA first staged its outdoor drama "Unto These Hills," an instant success which became a fixture of every subsequent tourist season and has drawn more than four and a half million paid spectators. The drama and other new tourist attractions on the reservation gave local whites as well as Indians a vested interest in preserving the Cherokee tribal identity—or at least generic "Indian" identity—and the CHA, with Joe Jenning's enthusiastic support, became a powerful force to that end. Tourism had mixed effects. On the one hand, it brought sorely needed revenue to the reservation; on the other, it created antagonisms between tribal haves and have-nots and brought a dependency on the CHA's business expertise. In the opinion of many whites and the BIA, the Indians themselves lacked sufficient skills to manage their tourist industry or tribal resources.

This pessimism regarding Cherokee competency did not prevent the BIA from beginning negotiations with state, local, and even tribal officials about assuming responsibility for providing specific services to the Eastern Band. The government promised to continue federal operation of the reservation hospital while current Principal Chief Osley Saunooke attempted to find a private, nonprofit sponsor to take it over. Saunooke was also instrumental in establishing a three-percent tribal sales tax, enabling the Band to assume more responsibility for sanitation and police and fire protection. Officials of the Cherokee Historical Association also participated in the planning and suggested a 25-year program of tourist-related development, which, much to the disgust of Fred Bauer, would attempt to preserve the "unique quality" of Cherokee life.

Despite these modest gains in tribal self-sufficiency, there remained the troublesome matter of Cherokee education. In July 1954 the BIA reduced the status of the main reservation school from a boarding to a day facility and then attempted to persuade state and local authorities to assume total responsibility for Indian education. The major problem was access to public schools in Swain County. Officials in Bryson City, the county seat, admitted that a few Indian children were already enrolled, but these were predominantly white individuals from acculturated families. There was considerable opposition to accepting phenotypical Cherokees because of racism, past frictions, and resentment over the recent landmark Supreme Court decision of *Brown v. Board of Education,* which declared segregated public schools unconstitutional. State officials were even more nervous about Brown because of widespread southern opposition to integration of blacks. Federal efforts to get Indians into the schools appeared to be one more case of outside meddling in racial matters. Another concern over the Cherokee situation was its possible implication for the state's Lumbee Indians, a heterogeneous group of uncertain origins who had long been segregated from white society.

Hildegard Thompson, Chief of the BIA's Education Branch, thought the volatile racial atmosphere in North Carolina dictated that the government proceed gingerly with efforts to integrate Cherokees into public schools. The BIA should continue to provide education on the reservation and meanwhile work on public relations to change white attitudes in Bryson City, emphasizing the economic benefits of the Band to the area, directing as much business as possible to the town, and also quietly attempting to enroll more Indians there.

Thompson's recommendations basically determined the course of action taken, and the BIA tiptoed diplomatically around the school desegregation issue.

Southern race relations and the simmering impact of the Brown decision, while perhaps not decisive, certainly delayed prospects for full termination of federal services. Meanwhile, without undue publicity, Cherokee enrollment in public schools began to climb. During fiscal year 1955 Indian enrollment in Swain County schools totaled 54, half of whom had at least three-fourths Cherokee blood, while 38 attended school in Jackson County. Four more were enrolled in Graham County. However, the overwhelming majority of Cherokee children— 798—still attended federal day schools. The state of North Carolina, moreover, failed to allot enough money for about 50 Cherokees to attend the Whittier public school because it argued they were strictly a federal responsibility.

The BIA's caution on the educational front was offset by an administrative blunder that attracted considerable negative publicity. On November 12, 1954, the *Asheville Citizen* announced in a front-page headline that the government had notified Joe Jennings that, effective December 1, his office would be eliminated and he would be transferred. In an editorial entitled "Another Trail of Tears," the paper attacked the removal, which came "in the midst of an orderly and well-timed liquidation of the Indian agency's responsibilities at Cherokee." Certainly the paper did not quarrel with an eventual transfer of responsibilities to the state, but argued that it should be done slowly and rationally. The editorial stated Swain County was unable to bear the costs associated with termination and pronounced the situation to be "unalterably dark."

A storm of protest followed Jennings's removal. Editorial comment from other cities echoed that of the Asheville newspaper, while tribal councilmen, choosing their words carefully, denounced the action. Harry Buchanan, chairman of the Cherokee Historical Association, and Bill Sharpe, publisher of a Raleigh magazine, expressed outrage and lobbied with politicians and BIA officials alike. Sharpe complained to Senator W. Kerr Scott that the action would harm the Indians, western Northern Carolina, and the entire state. He made it clear he feared economic dislocations attending a likely reduction in the role of the Cherokee Historical Association and believed the Indians were incapable of managing "Unto These Hills" themselves. The whites of western North Carolina and the historical association, he believed, "have done more for the Indians' independence than all the efforts of the federal government in 100 years." He concluded by saying:

> Realizing that sooner or later the Cherokees must be cut loose and must stand on their feet, yet I believe this move now is like towing a drowning man half way to the bank and then going off and leaving him in deep water. The move should be delayed, and study given to a situation which I am sure is unique among the tribes. All of North Carolina has a deep interest in and stake in the Indians, both economically and morally.

This barrage of criticism forced Indian commissioner Glenn Emmons into a partial retreat. Joe Jennings would still be transferred, but Emmons insisted the

BIA never intended to abolish the Cherokee agency. It was merely withdrawing the agency from the Minneapolis area office and bringing it directly under supervision from Washington. The commissioner agreed that any termination of the agency must be "on a gradual, planned and orderly basis," and insisted that for the present no such program was envisioned. Richard D. Butts, the new Cherokee agent appointed in March 1955, likewise reassured the tribe on this point.

In the meantime the Cherokee Historical Association was mending its fences with certain disgruntled Indians, including Chief Saunooke, and late in December 1954 announced a comprehensive program of protecting Cherokee lands, health benefits, and educational facilities. Chairman Harry Buchanan said his association's objective was "to represent the thinking of the Cherokee and to help the Cherokee get all that they deserve. If federal policies are to be put into effect that the Cherokee don't want," he continued, "we will go to bat for the Cherokee and fight for you." The CHA's program called for continued corporate land ownership by the Indians; an effort to find a suitable non-profit organization to operate the hospital; federal construction and state operation of a consolidated regional school; continued maintenance of reservation roads by the state after the federal government brought them up to standards; assistance in maintaining extension, soil conservation, and forestry services after transferring those responsibilities to state agencies; and continued cooperation in working toward Cherokee community objectives. The tribal council's own program, adopted in March 1955, incorporated most of the CHA's objectives. In addition, it stressed revision of the tribal roll, registration of all possessory claims, and improvement of tribal housing

Revising the roll was a crucial part of the tribal blueprint for confronting possible termination because of the large number of contested white Indians on the old Baker Roll. Frank W. Swan, a white and longtime Cherokee friend, said that practically everyone except white Indians wanted a new roll requiring at least one-sixteenth Cherokee blood. Dewey Tahquette, an acculturated full-blood who favored termination, also insisted on eliminating many of the contested names or else "our 'real Indians' as before would be *losers again.*"

In September 1955 Representative James A. Haley (Florida), chairman of the House Subcommittee on Indian Affairs, held a congressional hearing in Cherokee which probed Indian attitudes toward tribal affairs and, especially, termination. Fred Bauer and a few others predictably called for ending the federal relationship and granting fee simple titles, but many other Cherokees at all levels of acculturation, including Chief Saunooke, were opposed. Haley's call for a show of hands revealed that 45 to 50 Indians wanted to maintain the present trust status while nine favored its abrogation. A few Bryson City whites were also present and testified that Swain County could not afford to take over Cherokee education without considerable federal assistance.

Termination gradually assumed less urgency during the next few years as the BIA, facing mounting national opposition, began to emphasize Indian economic development on and off the reservations as a necessary prelude to *voluntary* termination in the *indefinite* future. Thanks to a continuing expansion of tourism and success in attracting small year-round businesses to its reservation, the Eastern Band was increasingly able to steer a middle course between dependency and tribal autonomy. Indeed, the Eastern Band anticipated future official policy by embarking on a program of self-determination without abrogation of federal trust responsibilities. It had already gone a long ways in that direction by 1962, when Representative Wayne N. Aspinall (Colorado), chair of the House Committee on Interior and Insular Affairs, formally laid to rest the threat of Cherokee termination. Speaking on the reservation at the annual convention of the National Congress of American Indians, Aspinall prompted cheers from delegates by declaring, "As long as I am chairman of the committee no Indian tribe in the United States will be terminated until it is ready for termination."

And so the threat passed. Like Indians elsewhere, many Eastern Cherokees had opposed termination simply because it meant the loss of benefits supposedly guaranteed by treaties and federal guardianship. Local circumstances, however, were even more decisive in safeguarding the Band against possible termination. While tourist-oriented Indians took both sides of the issue, most believed tourism required preservation of their reservation and a Cherokee tribal identity. They had powerful allies among concerned whites, especially those in the Cherokee Historical Association, who also saw a continuing Indian identity as essential for developing the regional economy. Other factors included the inability of Swain and Jackson counties to provide required services to the Indians, the Band's complex legal status and system of possessory landholdings, the unwillingness of most Cherokees to include white Indians in any dissolution of tribal assets, and the volatile racial atmosphere of the mid-1950s. These local considerations merged with a growing national opposition to termination and a conviction that it was possible to be both a modern American and a tribal Indian.

Suggested Reading

Finger gives a more complete discussion of the debates among the Eastern Cherokees over termination in *Cherokee Americans: The Eastern Band of Cherokees in the Twentieth Century* (Lincoln: University of Nebraska Press, 1991). For the experiences of another tribe, see Nicholas Peroff, *Menominee Drums: Tribal Termination and Restoration, 1954–1975* (Norman: University of Oklahoma Press, 1982). Donald L. Fixico, *Termination and Relocation, 1945-1960* (Albuquerque: University of New Mexico Press, 1986), is the standard work on this topic. For a more recent account, see Kenneth R. Philp, *Termination Revisited: American Indians on the Road to Self-Determination* (Lincoln: University of Nebraska Press, 1999).

CHAPTER TWENTY

The Indian Health Service and the Sterilization of Native American Women

JANE LAWRENCE

Throughout American history bad things have been done to Indians. Sometimes the actions resulted from poorly thought-out federal policies. At other times local officials implementing governmental goals used their positions of power unjustly. Nineteenth-century pioneers frequently cheated, robbed, or killed their tribal neighbors. Such raw violence gradually faded so that by the twentieth century openly anti-Indian actions became much less common.

Although the termination program had failed, in the 1960s and 1970s BIA actions and staff continued to represent a federal presence and influence on most reservations. Some mid-nineteenth century treaties had promised medical care to the tribes, and out of those early agreements an Indian Health Division emerged. Before 1900 the first government-built Indian hospital primarily treated tuberculosis and eye diseases. By the 1950s Indian health care shifted to the Public Health Service to offer a wider range of health care for reservation dwellers. As this essay notes, however, racist ideas about Indian intelligence and competence led some Health Service physicians to sterilize large numbers of young Native American women without their consent. This selection explains how and why this happened.

A young Indian woman entered Dr. Connie Pinkerton-Uri's Los Angeles office on a November day in 1972. The twenty-six-year-old woman asked Dr. Pinkerton-Uri for a "womb transplant" because she and her husband wished to start a family. An Indian Health Service (IHS) physician had given the woman a complete hysterectomy when she was having problems with alcoholism six years earlier. Dr. Pinkerton-Uri had to tell the young woman that there was no such

"The Indian Health Service and the Sterilization of Native American Women" appeared in *American Indian Quarterly* 24, no. 3 (Summer 2000): 400–19.

thing as a "womb transplant" despite the IHS physician having told her that the surgery was reversible. The woman left Dr. Pinkerton-Uri's office in tears.

Two young women entered an IHS hospital in Montana to undergo appendectomies and received tubal ligations, a form of sterilization, as an added benefit. Bertha Medicine Bull, a member of the Northern Cheyenne tribe, related how the "two girls had been sterilized at age fifteen before they had any children. Both were having appendectomies when the doctors sterilized them without their knowledge or consent." Their parents were not informed either. Two fifteen-year-old girls would never be able to have children of their own.

What happened to these three females was a common occurrence during the 1960s and 1970s. Native Americans accused the Indian Health Service of sterilizing at least 25 percent of Native American women who were between the ages of fifteen and forty-four during the 1970s. The allegations included: failure to provide women with necessary information regarding sterilization; use of coercion to get signatures on the consent forms; improper consent forms; and lack of an appropriate waiting period (at least seventy-two hours) between the signing of a consent form and the surgical procedure. This paper investigates the historical relationship between the IHS and Indian tribes; the right of the United States government to sterilize women; the government regulations pertaining to sterilization; the efforts of the IHS to sterilize American Indian women; physicians' reasons for sterilizing American Indian women; and the consequences the sterilizations had on the lives of a few of those women and their families.

The IHS evolved out of various government programs designed to address the health care issues of American Indians. Under the auspices of the War Department in the early 1800s, "Army physicians took steps to curb smallpox and other contagious diseases of Indian Tribes living in the vicinity of military posts." Army physicians used vaccinations and other medical procedures to prevent both military men and the Indians they came in contact with from being infected with diseases. The first treaty that included medical services was signed between the United States and the Winnebago Indians in 1832. In 1832 Congress provided funding for Indian health care in the amount of twelve thousand dollars.

In 1849 Congress transferred the Bureau of Indian Affairs (BIA) from the War Department to the Department of the Interior, including all health care responsibilities for American Indians. By 1875 half of the federal Indian agencies had physicians, and the BIA built the first federal hospital for Indians in Oklahoma during the late 1880s. After the turn of the century, the BIA created a separate health division and appointed district medical directors. The health division started special programs to combat tuberculosis and other diseases and established health education classes to support these programs. The Snyder Act of 1921 included congressional authorization for the BIA to provide Indian health care "for the benefit, care, and assistance of the Indians throughout the United States." The BIA contracted with the Public Health Service (PHS) in 1928 to provide sanitation engineers to investigate water and sewage problems at BIA facilities and renewed and expanded that contract through the early 1950s.

In 1955 Congress transferred total responsibility for Indian health from the Department of the Interior to the Public Health Service. The legislation stated that "all facilities transferred shall be available to meet the health needs of the Indians and that such health needs shall be given priority over that of the non-Indian population." The PHS, a division of the Department of Health, Education, and Welfare (HEW), formed the Division of Indian Health, which was renamed the Indian Health Service in 1958. At the time of the transfer, there were not enough physicians or medical facilities available to provide the proper medical care for American Indians. Congress believed that the PHS would be able to recruit a greater number of physicians by offering more attractive salaries and fringe benefits and to increase and improve medical facilities with higher Congressional appropriations for the HEW.

The PHS has greatly improved the health of Native Americans and the governmental medical facilities in the years since it became responsible for American Indian health. The PHS received better funding for Indian health services because Congress appropriated more money for health concerns to the HEW than it ever did to the BIA. Alan Sorkin in *Public Policy Impacts on American Indian Economic Development* reveals that "congressional appropriations increased nearly twelvefold on a per-Indian basis between 1955 and 1983." Deaths from diseases, such as tuberculosis, have dropped significantly, and infant mortality has also declined dramatically. The majority of Indians living on reservations are using the medical services of the IHS as their primary caregiver. The number of IHS doctors increased from 125 in 1965 to 600 in 1980. Even though there have been increases in the number of medical personnel, statistics show that the number of doctors and nurses in relation to the number of Indians seeking service from the IHS has actually decreased since 1966. The actual number of patients per physician rose from 1,220 in 1966 to 1,500 in 1980 because of the increase in the Native American population. Despite the low ratio of medical personnel to Native American patients, it must be remembered that the IHS improved the overall health of Native Americans following its inception in 1958.

The IHS began providing family planning services for Native Americans in 1965 under the authority of the HEW and the PHS. Family planning services provide women with information on the different methods of birth control, how the methods work, and how to use them. They are supposed to provide patients with assistance in determining which form of contraceptive is right for them. Family planning methods include the birth control pill, the intrauterine device, spermicidal jellies and creams, and sterilization. Unless there is a medical problem that a specific form of contraception can either alleviate or aggravate, a woman is supposed to choose whether or not she wishes to participate in the program and what type of birth control she wishes to use, since only she can know how the usage of a specific contraceptive measure will affect her life overall.

The United States government agency personnel, including the IHS, targeted

American Indians for family planning because of their high birth rate. The 1970 census revealed that the average Indian woman bore 3.79 children, whereas the median for all groups in the United States was 1.79 children. The 1970 and 1980 censuses included specific information on Indian tribes, including family size and fertility rates for women in the childbearing years (fifteen to forty-four). The data show that the average number of children per woman in specific tribes were as follows:

Average Number of Children per Woman by Tribe, 1970 and 1980

	1970	1980
Navajo	3.72	2.52
Apache	4.01	1.78
Zuni	3.35	1.90
Sioux (combined)	3.41	1.94
Cherokee (Oklahoma)	2.52	1.68
Ponca/Omaha	2.73	1.51
Average for all tribes	3.29	1.30

The average for white women was 2.42 children in 1970 and that number lowered to 2.14 in 1980; a difference of .28 children in the ten-year span compared to 1.99 for the Native American community. Cheryl Howard, Russell Thornton, and Veronica Tiller, in their separate studies on Navajo, Cherokee, and Apache tribal demographics, contend that higher levels of education among American Indian women, along with the availability of family planning programs, may have contributed to the lower birthrates in 1980. They do not specify sterilization as a partial cause of the decline, but sterilization must be considered as a factor.

Court rulings have played an important role in federal family planning policies that have an influence on IHS family planning programs. The Supreme Court, and lesser courts, set legal precedents regarding informed consent, family planning, and sterilization between 1914 and 1973. *Schloendorff v. Society of New York Hospital* in 1914 concerned a surgeon who performed an operation that left a man partially paralyzed. The court stated that any person who physically touches another individual without that person's consent commits battery. Justice Benjamin Cardoza spoke for the court when he stated that "every human being of adult years' and sound mind has a right to determine what shall be done with his own body; and a surgeon who performs an operation without his patient's consent commits an assault."

In 1942 the Supreme Court heard the case of *Skinner v. Oklahoma*. Jack Skinner was incarcerated in an Oklahoma prison following his third offense of armed robbery. Oklahoma had passed legislation that allowed habitual criminals to be sterilized. During this time period many states believed that sterilization laws were valid because the eugenics movement advocated sterilization for those deemed "unfit." The Court recognized "the right to have offspring as a fundamental right but did not declare compulsory sterilization laws totally invalid." Justice William Douglas wrote the majority ruling stating that Skinner's crime did not merit sterilization, declared that the Oklahoma sterilization law was unconstitutional under the Fourteenth Amendment, and expressed concern over the possibility of sterilization abuse arising from such legislation. He stated that "the power to sterilize, if exercised, may have far-reaching and devastating effects . . . [and in] evil hands it can cause races or types which are inimical to the dominant group to wither and disappear."

In 1965 the Supreme Court heard the case of *Griswold v. Connecticut*. In 1879 the state of Connecticut had passed a law forbidding the distribution and usage of drugs, articles, or instruments used to prevent contraception, including information on birth control. The law was not vigorously enforced, but in 1963 state officials arrested the executive director and the medical director of the Planned Parenthood League of Connecticut. Family planning and free speech advocates then challenged the law in court. Associate Justice William O. Douglas wrote that a state could not "consistently with the spirit of the First Amendment, constrict the spectrum of available knowledge" in the majority decision. The most important factor of the ruling, however, was that it defined the right to privacy as part of the First Amendment, thereby providing citizens with a constitutional right to select birth control as a method to control their family size and to receive information on the various methods of birth control.

In 1969 a federal court of appeals heard the case of *Jessin v. County of Shasta* that alleviated the fears of many physicians who were wary of performing sterilization procedures and encouraged doctors to perform more of the operations during the 1970s. The case involved a woman who sued her county hospital for performing a sterilization operation on her after she had signed a consent form. The judge ruled that "voluntary sterilization is legal when informed consent has been given, that sterilization is an acceptable method of family planning, and that sterilization may be a fundamental right requiring constitutional protection." Prior to this case, many physicians had assumed that sterilization as a birth control method was illegal.

In March 1974, the district court in the District of Columbia combined two cases that directly concerned the Department of Health, Education and Welfare's sterilization regulations. The two cases were *Relf et al. v. Weinberger et al.* and *National Welfare Rights Organization v. Weinberger et al.* Judge Gerhart Gesell declared that "Regulations of Department of Health, Education and Welfare governing human sterilizations are arbitrary and unreasonable" because "they fail to implement congressional command that federal family planning funds not be used to coerce indigent patients into submitting to sterilization." He continued with the statement that "federally assisted family planning sterilizations are permissible only with the voluntary, knowing, and uncoerced consent of individuals competent to give such consent." Judge Gesell then explained that the legislation providing funds for low-income family planning services did not mention sterilization, but that the secretary of the HEW, Casper Weinberger, considered sterilization to be covered by the statute. The judge ordered that "the regulations must also be amended to require that individuals seeking sterilization be orally informed at the very outset that no federal benefits can be withdrawn because of a failure to accept sterilization. This guarantee must also appear prominently at the top of the consent document already required by the regulations."

All of the above cases dealt with the issue of informed consent and the patient's right to make an informed decision about what could be done to his or her body. For informed consent to be given, a doctor must fully impart the nature and purpose of the procedure to the patient along with the possibility of success, the risks involved, and any alternative treatments. It is then up to the patient to decide if the procedure is the right treatment for his or her own personal well-being. Marc Basson and Eli Bernzweig, specialists in medical law and ethics, both argue that it is the physician's obligation to reveal all necessary information to the patient and that the failure to provide such information is a violation of the doctor-patient relationship and, therefore, a form of malpractice. Marc Hiller, another expert on medical law and ethics, asserts that "informed consent reflects one of our highest ethical values—individual autonomy; it implicates strong emotional needs both for control over our own lives and for dependence upon others; and it deals with a subject of fundamental importance, our health." Accurate information is a vital component of informed consent, and although there were court decisions that proclaimed the necessity of providing informed consent before 1973, the HEW did not publish any guidelines for providing family planning services or any directives protecting an individual's right to receive informed consent for family planning or sterilization procedures until that year.

The HEW publishes its regulations in the *Federal Register* and, as subsidiaries of the HEW, the PHS and IHS are required to follow those regulations. On 3 August 1973 the HEW published regulations establishing a moratorium on the sterilization of anyone under the age of twenty-one and on anyone doctors had declared mentally incompetent. Another HEW notice, published on 21 September 1973, announced that the secretary had approved the proposed regulations with minor amendments to the original guidelines. The regulations stated that competent individuals must grant their informed consent, that there must be a signed consent form in the possession of the agency performing the sterilization showing that the patient knew the benefits and costs of sterilizations, and that a seventy-two-hour waiting period must occur between the time of consent and the surgical procedure.

Judge Gesell's ruling in *Relf et al. v. Weinberger et al.* required the HEW to correct deficiencies in the guidelines, including the need for a definition of the term "voluntary," the lack of safeguards to ensure that sterilizations were voluntary, and the absence of prohibitions against the use of coercion in obtaining consents. The HEW published revised regulations on 18 April 1974. The new requirements included the changes that Judge Gesell required in *Relf et al. v. Weinberger et al.* The amended regulations define informed consent as "the voluntary, knowing assent" of any person undergoing sterilization procedures verified with a consent form that includes information on the actual procedure, any possible risks or discomforts, any benefits of the operation, information on alternative methods of birth control along with an explanation that sterilization is an irreversible procedure, and a statement "that the individual is free to withhold or withdraw his or her consent to the procedure at any time prior to the sterilization without prejudicing his or her future care and without loss of other project or program benefits to which the patient might otherwise be entitled." The revised regulations also dictated that every sterilization consent form exhibit prominently at the top of the form the legend, "NOTICE: Your decision at any time not to be sterilized will not result in the withdrawal or withholding of any benefits provided by programs or projects." The HEW restricted the performance of any sterilization unless the patient voluntarily requested the operation and unless agency personnel advised the patient verbally, as well as in writing, that no benefits would be denied if he or she refused to be sterilized.

Congress and the general public believed that the revised regulations would help protect women from involuntary sterilizations but accusations soon arose that the IHS was sterilizing women without their informed consent and was not following the HEW regulations. Native American doctors and hospital personnel from Oklahoma and New Mexico sent letters to Senator James Abourezk of South Dakota, chairman of the Senate Interior Subcommittee on Indian Affairs about sterilization abuses. After his staff conducted an initial investigation the senator requested the Government Accounting Office (GAO) to conduct an investigation on both Indian sterilization and the experimental use of drugs on reservations on 30 April 1975.

On 6 November 1976, the Government Accounting Office released its report (hereinafter referred to as the GAO Report). The GAO Report did not verify that the IHS had performed coerced sterilizations, but it did state that the IHS had not followed the necessary regulations and that the informed consent forms did not adhere to the standards set by HEW.

The GAO conducted its investigation of IHS sterilization practices in four of the twelve IHS program areas: Aberdeen, Albuquerque, Oklahoma City, and Phoenix. The GAO investigators examined IHS records and found that the IHS performed 3,406 sterilizations during the fiscal years 1973 through 1976. These numbers did not include those conducted in the Albuquerque area because contract physicians performed all sterilizations in that IHS region. GAO personnel did not interview any Native American women who had been sterilized during this period, because they said they "believe[d] that such an effort would not have been productive." The foreword of the GAO Report revealed that the IHS performed twenty-three sterilizations of women under the age of twenty-one between 1 July 1973 and 30 April 1974, despite the HEW moratorium on such sterilizations. It was also reported that thirteen more underage sterilizations occurred between 30 April 1974, when the HEW published new regulations in the *Federal Register,* and 30 March 1976, when the actual GAO study ended. The report stated that the violations occurred because "(1) some Indian Health Service physicians did not completely understand the regulations and (2) contract physicians were not required to adhere to the regulations." The GAO discovered that the sterilization consent forms used did not comply with HEW regulations and that IHS medical providers used several different forms. The majority of the forms "did not (1) indicate that the basic elements of informed consent had been presented orally to the patient, (2) contain written summaries of the oral presentation, and (3) contain a statement at the top of the form notifying the subjects of their right to withdraw consent." The GAO Report then proceeded to add detail to the initial overview.

The IHS records did not specify whether the sterilizations that had taken place were voluntary or therapeutic. The HEW defined voluntary, or nontherapeutic, sterilizations as "any procedure or operation, the purpose of which is to render an individual permanently incapable of reproducing." When the purpose of a sterilization is to treat a woman for a medical ailment, such as uterine cancer, it is a therapeutic sterilization. The GAO Report revealed that "as of August 1976, however, IHS was unable to supply us with complete and statistically reliable data on whether or not the sterilizations were voluntary or therapeutic."

The HEW regulations required that a waiting period of at least seventy-two hours elapse between the signing of the consent form for a voluntary sterilization and the actual operation. The investigators found thirteen infractions of the regulations applying to the required seventy-two-hour waiting period. Medical records reveal that "several" consent forms were dated the day the woman had given birth, usually by Cesarean section, while she was under the influence of a sedative and in an unfamiliar environment. Medical documents also disclose that a "few" women signed consent forms on the day following their sterilization operation.

Despite the claims that some physicians did not understand the regulations, the notice sent to the area directors on 2 August 1973 stated clearly that "there is, effective immediately, a temporary halt in the IHS sterilization procedures performed on an individual who is under the age of twenty-one or who is legally incapable of consenting to sterilization. This policy does not apply when the operation is performed for the surgical treatment of specific pathology of the reproductive organs." A memorandum to the area directors reconfirmed the moratorium on 16 October 1973 and again on 29 April 1974. The IHS sent all of these notices by telegram so that there was no delay in receiving them.

On 12 August 1974, the IHS sent a memorandum directly to the IHS physicians stressing the importance of the HEW regulations, along with a copy of the regulations and copies of the director's telegrams to the area directors. On 15 December 1975, the IHS director again notified the area directors and hospital and health center personnel that the HEW regulations must be followed and that the sterilization of women under the age of twenty-one or women judged mentally incompetent, "is permissible only when 'the procedure is carried out for medical reasons related to the primary intent to sterilize the individual.'" The IHS justified the exceptions to the sterilization moratorium reported to the GAO in several ways: IHS doctors continued to believe that they could perform these sterilizations until they received the notice dated 29 April 1974; they misunderstood the policy; they performed the sterilizations for medical reasons but intended to render the patients incapable of having children; or the patients would be turning twenty-one in a few weeks time. Two cases were not included in these numbers, increasing the total sterilizations in violation of the moratorium to thirty-eight. The deputy director of program operations reported to the investigators that, while the IHS had established surveillance over the sterilizations of women under the age of twenty-one, physicians may not have reported these cases knowing that there was a moratorium against them.

The GAO investigators examined 113 of the 3,406 consent forms for sterilization procedures. They discovered that IHS medical facilities used three different versions of the form and that all three forms were variations of the short form. Two of these forms did not provide all of the necessary information required by the HEW regulations. The consent forms did not record whether or not medical personnel orally informed the patient of the risks, dangers, and alternatives to the procedure; they did not include written summaries of any oral information that may have been given; and they did not incorporate the required statement alerting patients to their rights if they decided to forego sterilization. IHS personnel used the third form, Form HSA-83, in twelve cases, and this form appeared to the GAO to comply with most of the HEW regulations; although the GAO revealed that Form HSA-83 was also inadequate because it did not contain enough detail to ascertain whether the patients received all of the necessary information. The form also did not have a written disclosure of all of the elements of informed consent and did not include a section where medical personnel could add a summary of the oral presentation.

In order to assess the justification for the surgeries, the GAO investigating committee reviewed fifty-four sterilizations performed at the Phoenix Indian Medical Center between 1 April and 30 September 1975. While the GAO Report stated that most of the cases revealed valid cause, the reasons behind nineteen were questionable. The GAO Report recounted that investigators discussed these sterilizations with the chief of obstetrics and gynecology at the center and that the reasons for the nineteen sterilizations remained unresolved. The GAO did not explain why the nineteen cases were questionable.

The GAO Report gave two causes for deficiencies found in the sterilization practices of the Indian Health Service. First, the IHS area offices failed to follow the HEW regulations pertaining to sterilization procedures. Second, IHS headquarters did not provide specific directions to the area offices, neglected to create a standard consent form for all of its facilities, failed to revise its manual to reflect the new HEW regulations, and did not provide guidelines for the area offices to use in implementing the procedures. The GAO Report also stated that IHS headquarter officials attributed the above deficiencies to the HEW'S "inability to develop specific sterilization guidelines and a standardized consent form for all its agencies to use."

The weaknesses in the sterilization consent forms included the failure to divulge fully the required information on the risks involved in the procedure and the alternative methods of birth control that the individual could use. The GAO Report declared that "The forms also failed to include the required statement 'Your decision at anytime not to be sterilized will not result in the withdrawal or withholding of any benefits provided by programs or projects.'" The IHS officials in the areas examined did not monitor the sterilization practices of contract care facilities. The contracts they signed with outside doctors did not stipulate that those doctors had to follow the HEW regulations. Yet the regulations declared that "the provisions of this subpart are applicable to programs or projects for health services which are supported in whole or in part by federal financial assistance, whether by grant or contract, administered by the Public Health Service." The regulations required that the IHS monitor the sterilization activities of the doctors with whom they had contracts.

Why did these sterilizations take place? In order to understand the reasons behind the sterilizations it is necessary to remember that physicians were performing large numbers of sterilizations not only on American Indian women, but also on Mexican American and Hispanic women. The number of women on welfare had also increased dramatically since the mid-1960s with Lyndon Johnson's War on Poverty. The main reasons doctors gave for performing these procedures were economic and social in nature. According to a study that the Health Research Group conducted in 1973 and interviews that Doctor Bernard Rosenfeld performed in 1974 and 1975, the majority of physicians were white, Euro-American males who believed that they were helping society by limiting the number of births in low-income, minority families. They assumed that they were enabling the government to cut funding for Medicaid and welfare programs while lessening their own personal tax burden to support the programs. Physicians also increased their own personal income by performing hysterectomies and tubal ligations instead of prescribing alternative methods of birth control. Some of them did not believe that American Indian and other minority women had the intelligence to use other methods of birth control effectively and that there were already too many minority individuals causing problems in the nation, including the Black Panthers and the American Indian Movement. Others wanted to gain experience to specialize in obstetrics and gynecology and used minority women as the means to get that experience at government expense. Medical personnel also believed they were helping these women because limiting the number of children they could have would help minority families to become more financially secure in their own right while also lessening the welfare burden.

Various studies revealed that the Indian Health Service sterilized between 25 and 50 percent of Native American women between 1970 and 1976. Dr. Connie Pinkerton-Uri conducted a study that revealed that IHS physicians sterilized at least 25 percent of American Indian women between the ages of fifteen and forty-four. Cheyenne tribal judge Marie Sanchez questioned fifty Cheyenne women and discovered that IHS doctors had sterilized twenty-six of them. She announced her belief that the number of women the GAO reported sterilized was too low and that the percentage was much higher than 25 percent. Mary Ann Bear Comes Out, a member of the Northern Cheyenne tribe, conducted a survey on the Northern Cheyenne Reservation and Labre Mission grounds. She found that in a three year period, the IHS sterilized fifty-six out of 165 women between the ages of thirty and forty-four in the survey area. She wrote that "the data indicate that the same rate of sterilizations would reduce births among this group by more than half over a five-year period." The sterilization of Indian women affected the families and friends; many marriages ended in divorce, and numerous friendships became estranged or dissolved completely. The women had to deal with higher rates of marital problems, alcoholism, drug abuse, psychological difficulties, shame, and guilt. Sterilization abuse affected the entire Indian community in the United States.

In September 1977, the National Council of Church's Interreligious Foundation for Community Organization (IFCO) held a conference in Washington DC to plan strategies for a "fight for survival" against sterilization abuse. Over sixty delegates from Native American, African American, Hispanic, civil rights, religious, and other groups attended the conference. While the conference addressed the abuses that all minority groups faced, it focused on those that Native American and Hispanic women underwent.

The IHS damaged tribal communities in several ways. Tribal communities lost much of their ability to reproduce, the respect of other tribal entities, and political power in the tribal councils. Tribal communities represent sections of the entire tribe, much as counties represent specific areas within a state. The population of a community reflects the number of representatives it can elect to the tribal council and to national pan-Indian organizations. Therefore, a community's level of power within the tribal government is affected by the number of people in the community. A lowered census number might also affect federal services a tribal community receives. Finally, a tribal community that suffers a great number of sterilizations can lose the respect of other tribal communities because of its inability to protect its women.

Some Indian leaders believe that the sterilization of Native American women also affects the tribe's economic base and sovereignty. Lee Brightman, president of United Native Americans Inc., argues that "the sterilization campaign is nothing but an insidious scheme to get the Indians' land once and for all." Everett Rhoades, past president of the Association of American Indian Physicians, argues that there is a non-Indian backlash that "seems to have arisen from the recent gains made by Indians in the sale of natural resources." The Women of All Red Nations state that "the real issue behind sterilization is how we are losing our personal sovereignty" as Native Americans. Members of the organization assert that communities having large numbers of sterilizations lost the respect of other tribal communities because of their inability to protect Native American women.

In 1974, Choctaw-Cherokee physician Dr. Connie Pinkerton-Uri conducted a study that indicated that twenty-five thousand Native American women would be sterilized by the end of 1975. The information she gathered revealed that IHS facilities singled out full-blood Indian women for sterilization procedures. Based on her findings, Pinkerton-Uri stated that "we have only 100,000 women of child-bearing age total—that's not per anything. The Indian population of this country is dwindling no matter what government statistics say to the contrary." Pinkerton-Uri's study also discovered that Indian women generally agreed to sterilization when they were threatened with the loss of their children and/or their welfare benefits, that most of them gave their consent when they were heavily sedated during a Cesarean section or when they were in a great deal of pain during labor, and that the women could not understand consent forms because they were written in English at the twelfth-grade level. Dr. Pinkerton-Uri related that she did not believe the sterilizations occurred from "any plan to exterminate American Indians," but rather from "the warped thinking of doctors who think the solution to poverty is not to allow people to be born." At a meeting held with IRS officials in Claremore, Oklahoma, Pinkerton-Uri criticized the argument that "a poor woman with children was 'better off' sterilized." She maintained that "She's still going to be poor. She just won't be able to have children."

Children are very important to Native American women for economic reasons, tribal survival, and to secure their place in the tribe. Marie Sanchez, a Cheyenne tribal judge, declared that "the Native American woman is the carrier of our nation." Mary Crow Dog, a Lakota member of the American Indian Movement (AIM), claimed that most of the women of AIM did not accept the use of birth control because they did not believe that there were enough Indians left in the United States. She stated that "like many other Native American women . . . I had an urge to procreate, as if driven by a feeling that I, personally, had to make up for the genocide suffered by our people in the past." Emily Moore and Ann Clark, in their separate studies of numerous Native American cultures and family structures, found that children were important not only for the joy they gave the parents but also because group survival was an important aspect of tribal culture. At a conference on birth control in 1979, Katsi Cook, of the Mohawk

Nation, declared that "women are the base of the generations. Our reproductive power is sacred to us."

Family planning personnel who believe that American Indian women are incapable of adhering to the instructions for contraceptive methods such as the birth control pill do not recognize that Native American women have centuries of experience using various natural methods to prevent conception. Some Indian tribes recognized that a woman's menstrual cycle related to fertility and the women in these tribes did not have intercourse during their fertile period. Other tribes used the dried and crushed roots of the red cedar and juniper plants in a tea or concoctions prepared from other plants such as deer's tongue to prevent births. Henry de Laszlo and Paul Henshaw reported in 1954 that Indians used oral contraceptives including the boiled roots of dogbane or wild ginger, beverages made from milkweed, arum, Indian paintbrush, or rosemary, and the dried roots of thistle, squaw root, and the Mexican wild yam. The basic material that pharmaceutical companies use in birth control pills is diosgenin from the Mexican wild yam. Indians also used derivatives from plants to induce abortions and cause sterility. Native Americans used a variety of birth control methods, and they understood how to use the methods that were available in their homeland. Even in the late 1970s, in the Southwest and other regions, Indian women used herbal teas and brews to prevent pregnancies.

Native Americans' use of commercial contraceptives depends, in large part, on tribal attitudes and personal beliefs. Many Indian women either do not believe in contraception themselves or their husbands or extended family do not believe in it. In general, tribal traditions and beliefs work against the use of commercial contraceptives. A woman's age and number of children also helps to determine whether she will use birth control. For example, Navajo women tend to use contraceptives when they are in their latter childbearing years and already have four or five children. Fertility studies conducted on Indian women from the Hopi tribe in Arizona, the Seminole tribe in Florida, the Sells Reservation Papago in Arizona, the Blackfeet in Montana, and Alaskan Natives reveal the same tendencies.

Native American women do not often reveal their feelings about family planning or sterilization, but one author conducted several interviews with women whom IHS practitioners had sterilized. The interviews reveal the ways in which these women believe the procedure directly affected their lives and what their responses to the IHS have been following the sterilizations.

Employees from a nearby IHS hospital approached Janet about sterilization in 1973. Janet [pseudonyms are used to protect the identity of the interviewees] was twenty-nine and had three children. The social workers came to Janet's home six times when her husband was at work. "They told me that I should be sterilized because I didn't want any more babies right then, so I said yes and signed a consent form. My tubes were tied the next day." Janet found out that the sterilization was irreversible during an American Indian Movement demonstration against

IHS sterilizations at Claremore, Oklahoma, in 1974. For the next fifteen years a psychiatrist treated Janet for severe depression. Her youngest daughter still refuses to use the IHS for any type of medical care.

In February 1974, physicians at Claremore Indian hospital in Oklahoma performed a hysterectomy on Diane right after she gave birth to her son by Cesarean section. Diane does not remember signing a consent form, but believes she must have signed one since they performed the surgery on her. When she found out three days later that the doctors had sterilized her, Diane "told them they had to fix it. They told me they couldn't, that they'd done a hysterectomy." Diane saw a psychologist for ten years following the sterilization because she had problems with depression. "I still get really depressed about it when I think about it. But now I get angry, too." The sterilization caused Diane to fear that something "deadly" would happen to her two sons. That summer she refused to take her nine-year-old's bicycle out of the garage because she "was afraid he'd get hit by a car or something." She described how she "was really protective of the baby and now he's having problems adjusting to being an adult. I didn't let him learn to make decisions on his own. And it's all my fault. I was never like that before they did this to me." Diane has never returned to the IHS facility in Claremore and sees a private physician in Tulsa.

In 1974 an IHS facility in Minnesota sterilized Julie when she was twenty-eight. While she was in labor, she signed a form that she thought was for a painkiller. Julie stated that she does not remember exactly what she signed because she "was in pain at the time and wasn't paying too much attention to [the forms]." She revealed that the nurses told her about sterilization throughout her pregnancy and while she was in labor. While Julie had a second healthy daughter in the hospital, she revealed that she and her husband wanted three children. Her husband left her shortly after he found out about the sterilization because he "wanted a real woman. He didn't think I was a woman anymore without my uterus. What was I? An it?" Julie no longer trusts the IHS and goes there only for routine health problems such as the flu or strep throat.

Debra is from Montana, and an IHS physician sterilized her in the spring of 1975. At the age of twenty-six she underwent a hysterectomy immediately following a Cesarean section. She related that "they came in the next day and said they needed me to sign some forms that hadn't been signed before the c-section. And they wanted me to date it the day before, but I put the right date on it." Debra believes that hospital personnel did not inform her about the sterilization, or about other methods of birth control, because she had already completed several years of college and was better informed than the majority of Indian women. She stated that the sterilization "made me change my life in important ways. I didn't become an alcoholic or go berserk like some women did. I changed my major at college and went on to become a lawyer. I specialize in medical cases and family law." Debra claimed that the sterilization made her more aware of the problems that Native Americans face, especially in the breakup of Indian families: "I try to keep families together. Not so much from divorce, but from the social services trying to separate children from their parents. I know I've made a difference in some lives, but I wish could do that for more of them."

The experiences of these four women, along with other evidence provided earlier in the paper, reveal that the IHS sterilization procedures drastically affected all aspects of Native American life. IHS practices harmed the relationships between Native Americans and the government and between tribal communities, husbands and wives, and mothers and their children. The operations also caused an inordinate amount of harm to the individual Native American women whom the Indian Health Service physicians sterilized.

In 1976, Congress passed the Indian Health Care Improvement Act. This measure gave tribes the right to manage or control Indian Health Service programs. Native American tribes have taken over many IHS facilities and have started their own health services. While the sterilizations that occurred in the 1960s and 1970s harmed Native Americans, Indian participation in their own health care since 1976 has strengthened their tribal communities. Sterilization abuse has not been reported recently on the scale that occurred during the 1970s, but the possibility still exists for it to occur. The Department of Health, Education, and Welfare does not audit Indian Health Service programs; it only audits the computer records on reported sterilizations that do not meet the guideline's requirements. Until the department conducts full audits on all sterilizations that the federal government funds, sterilization abuse will continue to concern Native Americans.

Suggested Reading

Readings related to Indian health issues are scattered and often not readily available. For a brief discussion of the subject, see John L. Schultz, *White Medicine, Indian Lives: As Long as the Grass Shall Grow* (Denver: Colorado State University Press, 1983). For a government-sponsored study of these issues, see U.S. Department of Health, Education, and Welfare, U.S. Public Health Service, *The Indian Health Program of the Indian Health Service* (Washington, D.C.: Government Printing Office, 1978). Nancy Shoemaker, *American Indian Population Recovery in the Twentieth Century* (Albuquerque: University of New Mexico Press, 1999), brings demographic and health issues up to date.

CHAPTER TWENTY-ONE

Alcatraz, Wounded Knee, and Beyond

The Nixon and Ford Administrations Respond to Native American Protest

Dean J. Kotlowski

Many of the essays in this collection give only modest attention to federal Indian policies and the political contexts within which officials formulated their approaches to Native people. This Indian-centered approach allows the reader to focus more on the tribal perspectives of events than merely the formal policies as done years ago. Yet policy and legal issues remain at the heart of any full analysis of federal-tribal relations. As tribes gathered data to support their cases before the Indian Claims Commission, or to slow or even overturn termination, they accumulated the contacts and skills necessary to attract public attention. Although a few modest public protests occurred during the mid-1960s, most Indian activism occurred late in the civil rights and anti–Viet Nam War eras.

This essay examines the federal responses to the American Indian Movement's Red Power activism in the middle of the Richard Nixon and Gerald Ford administrations. It depicts President Nixon with a view of Indians as a "safe" minority in an era of massive social conflict. It also shows how Nixon changed his views because of the violence and negative attention the Red Power movement attracted through its protests. The author shows how closely the implementation of federal policies followed public opinion and evolved with the ever-changing national political situation.

Before Richard M. Nixon entered the White House, federal Indian policy had swung from reform to reaction and back to reform. In the 1930s President Franklin D. Roosevelt enhanced tribal autonomy and self-government under the "Indian New Deal." During the 1940s and 1950s the government reverted to a

"Alcatraz, Wounded Knee, and Beyond" appeared in *Pacific Historical Review* 72, no. 2 (May 2003): 201–27.

policy of assimilating Indians into Anglo society. In 1953 the House of Representatives passed House Concurrent Resolution 108, which listed the tribes to be freed "from federal supervision and control and from all the disabilities and limitations applicable to Indians." Under this policy, called "termination," tribes would lose all privileges related to treaties with the federal government. Tribal lands, once held in trust by the government, would be opened for sale to non-Indians, and Indians would become subject to the same laws as Anglos. Many Native Americans clung to their unique status and resisted termination. Accordingly, Presidents John F. Kennedy and Lyndon B. Johnson modified the policy by vowing not to terminate any tribe without its consent. Both Presidents, however, stressed development and economic self-sufficiency for reservations. In 1968 Johnson vaguely pledged to end the "old debate" about termination and begin an era of "self-help, self-development, and self-determination." The slogan "self-determination without termination" would not come into fashion until the next administration.

The reversal in Native American policy that President Nixon implemented proved dramatic. Under the banner of "self-determination without termination," he and his staff repudiated the policy of termination, protected tribal rights, and encouraged reservation Indians to run many federal programs themselves. These "Nixonians" also settled land claims with the Taos Pueblo and Yakima tribes and with Alaska's Native peoples. While they neither reorganized the Bureau of Indian Affairs nor ended the poverty of urban Indians, Nixon administration officials were practical reformers, not ambivalent onlookers, with regard to Native American rights. More importantly, they accomplished all these changes while simultaneously defusing heated protests by Indians at Alcatraz Island, the BIA headquarters, and Wounded Knee, South Dakota.

During the 1970s the Nixon administration's Indian policy drew mixed responses: Elected tribal leaders, who represented reservation Indians and enjoyed support from the BIA, applauded the administration. Navajo leader Peter MacDonald even hailed Nixon as "the Abraham Lincoln of the Indian people." Yet non-elected urban radicals, not tied to the BIA were skeptical of Nixon's intentions and at times hostile to his administration. Russell C. Means, a leader of the American Indian Movement (AIM), complained that the policy of self-determination "was designed and intended to bolster rather than dismantle the whole structure of BIA colonialism." LaNada Means, one of the leaders of the Alcatraz occupation, more bluntly opined that "anything Nixon says is shit."

While scholars are beginning to examine Nixon's legacy in federal Indian policy, the policies of President Gerald R. Ford, Nixon's handpicked successor, are still largely unexplored. Likewise, while some studies of Red Power have been published, scholars have paid scant attention to the nexus between Native American protest and federal policy. Additionally, Native American unrest under Ford remains to be covered.

This article argues that grassroots protest shaped federal Indian policy by first placing and then keeping Native American concerns on the national agenda. The Nixon and Ford White Houses both endorsed tribal self-determination and responded patiently to unrest, allowing Congress to enact presidential initiatives. Since the confrontations that Nixon faced drew national publicity, they had greater influence over national policy than those that erupted on Ford's watch. Nonetheless, some of Ford's aides seemed haunted by the prospect of another Wounded Knee-like standoff. Interestingly, by the end of Ford's presidency, Native American activists had exchanged civil disobedience for timely litigation, setting the stage for further legislation during the presidency of Jimmy Carter. Alcatraz and Wounded Knee cast long shadows indeed.

At the start of the first Nixon administration, American Indians were demanding "self-determination," an elastic concept that suggested many things. To rural, tribal-based organizations, self-determination meant an end to termination and greater tribal control over BIA programs. The National Congress of American Indians (NCAI), a pan-Indian advocacy group formed in 1944, vigorously opposed termination and assimilation and urged Indians to defend their special status. The NCAI insisted that the federal government fulfill its treaty commitments, respect the authority of elected tribal officials, and consult Indian leaders before drafting legislation concerning tribes. Native Americans, the NCAI leaders asserted, refused to "swim in a mainstream they largely regarded as polluted." Economic development for reservations, a goal advanced by liberal policymakers during the 1960s, remained a lesser concern for NCAI. To achieve its aims, the organization worked within "the system" by recruiting young and old members on reservations and by lobbying the federal government to change its Indian policies. As late as 1967 the NCAI proudly proclaimed: "Indians Don't Demonstrate."

Meanwhile, young urban Indians, imbued with the rights-conscious spirit that had inspired African Americans, attacked the entire federal system by espousing "Red Power" and founded the American Indian Movement in 1968. Red Power advocates distrusted federal officials, elected tribal leaders, and the NCAI, which had long dismissed the concerns of urban Indians as "dangerous diversions" from the political agendas of reservations. Along with terminationists, some urban radicals sought to abolish the BIA. The former wanted to free Indians from reservations and the BIA's special benefits, while the latter despised the BIA as a symbol of Anglo wardship. To urban radicals, self-determination meant using direct action to promote cultural awareness for all Indians, not new legislation to enhance tribal authority. In urban areas, AIM dispensed financial and legal assistance and built centers to showcase Native American culture. The leaders of AIM, which seemed "less a political movement than a force of nature," would visit a reservation, where their support was slight, stage a sit-in or an armed takeover, and then bargain with federal government officials before moving on to other targets. Unlike the NCAI, AIM encouraged civil disobedience.

Whatever their differences, Native Americans rejected the integrationist goals of the black civil rights movement. "In the past," historian Vine Deloria, Jr., has argued, "they had experienced so many betrayals through policies which purported to give them legal and social 'equality'" that they distrusted "anyone who spoke of either equality or helping them to get into 'the mainstream.'" By the late 1960s self-determination, however defined, was a concept whose time had arrived.

Nixon showed sympathy for Native Americans, whom he considered a "safe" minority to help. Because the Indian movement was just getting under way during the late 1960s, Native Americans proved responsive to presidential gestures. Since they numbered fewer than one million, their problems seemed more manageable than those of blacks. Popular sympathy favored Indian rights, at least at first, and, unlike liberal African Americans who favored integration, Native Americans welcomed Nixon's anti-assimilationist message. "Our overriding aim, as I see it," Nixon had declared in 1960, "should not be to separate the Indians from the richness of their past or force them into some preconceived mold of human behavior. Such words resembled his later argument against "forced integration" of blacks and whites. Running for President in 1968, Nixon backed self-determination for Indian tribes and blasted current federal policy as "unfair," "confused," and "tragic."

Nixon supported Indian rights for many reasons. Here was a way, he reasoned, to appease younger Americans—who leaned Democratic—as well as appeal to the public at large. "He feels very strongly," White House chief of staff H. R. Haldeman noted in 1969, "that we need to show more heart, and that we care about people, and thinks the Indian problem is a good area." Nixon also acted out of principle. "There are very few votes involved," the President privately conceded, but "a grave injustice has been worked against [Indians] for a century and a half and the nation at large will appreciate our having a more active policy of concern for their plight." Such sentiments partly reflected Nixon's fond memories of his Whittier College football coach, Chief Wallace Newman, a Cherokee. At any rate, by 1969 the subject of Native American rights was ripe for statesmanship.

Change in federal policy came slowly. Nixon initially entrusted domestic policy to White House Counselor Arthur F. Burns, a friend and a former economist at Columbia University, who proved cautious and systematic. Moreover, Interior Secretary Walter J. Hickel remained ambivalent on Indian rights. The emergence of John D. Ehrlichman as Nixon's top domestic adviser, coupled with the seizure of Alcatraz Island by Indian activists, strengthened the hand of reform-minded advisers such as Barbara Greene Kilberg, a White House fellow, White House Consultant Leonard Garment, and his deputy Bradley H. Patterson Jr. The most surprising defender of Native American rights was Spiro T. Agnew who, as vice president, chaired the National Council on Indian Opportunity (NCIO), a panel of federal officials and Native American leaders established in 1968. For the most part, Nixon allowed his subordinates to handle Native American policy, except when a new initiative or unforeseen crisis demanded his attention.

Nixon's team faced its first challenge when Indians seized Alcatraz Island in San Francisco Bay. The dispute had actually begun in 1964, when five Sioux Indians briefly occupied Alcatraz and claimed the one-time federal prison under the Fort Laramie Treaty of 1868. The controversy resurfaced in 1969, after fire destroyed an Indian center in San Francisco. When Hickel offered to turn Alcatraz into a national park, Native Americans took action. On November 20, 1969, fifty Indians occupied Alcatraz and vowed to stay put until Hickel ceded the island to them. This "invasion" was more than an isolated stunt. Indian activists, mostly urban, had organized similar protests on federal lands to highlight treaty violations and to assert Red Power. By the end of 1969 more than 100 Indians had made "the Rock" their home. Some of them commuted between Alcatraz and the mainland on the boat *Clearwater*, purchased with money donated by the rock band Credence Clearwater Revival.

In responding to these events, Nixon's moderate advisers first fumed and then sought compromise. Garment decried the seizure as "confrontation politics" by "an irresponsible, but PR-conscious group." To calm the waters, he and Patterson sent Robert Robertson, director of the NCIO, to Alcatraz to bargain with the occupiers. When Robertson promised to build a park for the Indians on the island, the occupiers, calling themselves the "Indians of all Tribes, Inc.," refused. They insisted upon possession of Alcatraz, where they hoped to build a cultural center. The White House would not cave in to the protesters, but it would not forcibly remove them either. As the seizure's first anniversary neared, Garment warned that Alcatraz could become "the biggest political sideshow of 1971" if a single Indian or federal marshal died. Coming after the shootings at Kent State University in 1970, Ehrlichman and Nixon agreed to remain patient. The public eventually lost interest in the escapade, the Indians squabbled among themselves, and most abandoned the island. Federal marshals removed the last band, numbering fifteen, on June 11, 1971.

Nixon's moderate advisers used the occupation to plead for change in Indian policy. "The Alcatraz episode is symbolic," read one unsigned memorandum, "to the Indians and to us it is a *symbol* of the lack of attention to [their] unmet needs." Agnew assumed command by convening the NCIO on January 26, 1970. "Rather than 'termination,'" he told the participants, "our policy objective is that the right of choice of the Indian people will be respected." The vice president next urged Nixon to disavow termination "in the most forceful way possible" and to allow tribes, by majority vote, "to assume complete control" over any federal Indian program. He advised replacing area offices with centers to ease the "transition from Federal to tribal control." Agnew argued that his proposals would advance the "New Federalism," the President's policy to transfer power from federal to local authorities, and Patterson and Gannent agreed. They then composed a statement explaining Nixon's policy.

Patterson and Gannent had more say in drafting the Indian message than either Agnew or Hickel. Nixon's Indian message of July 8, 1970, renounced termination as "morally and legally unacceptable" and asserted that "self-determination among Indian people can and must be encouraged without the threat of eventual termination." The President asked Congress to pass eight bills to advance tribal autonomy, as well as a resolution repealing termination. Under Nixon's legislation, federal agencies would "contract out" educational and health care services to tribes. His statement won wide acclaim among Native American tribal leaders.

In 1970 and 1971 two issues moved to the top of Nixon's Native American agenda: the Taos Pueblo's claim to the area surrounding Blue Lake, in New Mexico, and the land claims of Alaskan Natives. Blue Lake had symbolic appeal, while the ongoing Alaskan dispute delayed construction of an oil pipeline. The White House settled these matters through new legislation, with the Alaskan Native Claims Settlement Act of 1971 marking the most noteworthy Indian policy enacted during Nixon's watch. The act transferred 40 million acres, a record amount of land, and $1 billion to Alaskan aboriginals. The measure proved so sweeping that Ehrlichman had to secure the President's personal support before pushing it through Congress. But Nixon's other reforms languished on Capitol Hill, in what one scholar called a "congressional sitzkreig." Accordingly, the President addressed Indian concerns through administrative actions, by establishing new offices to protect Indian rights. He also increased federal expenditures for Native American programs and the BIA, and, through an executive order signed in 1972, returned the land around Mount Adams in Washington state to the Yakima.

Such actions underscored the strengths and weaknesses of Nixon's Native American policy through 1972. By settling land claims, disavowing termination, and courting duly elected tribal leaders, Nixon took a rigid, legalistic approach to Indian affairs. The administration insisted that urban Indians from federally recognized tribes use regular social services from state and local agencies, not the BIA, which remained unchanged. Moreover, it disappointed radicals by refusing to renegotiate the government's treaties with Native Americans. This issue, raised by the occupiers of Alcatraz, resurfaced during later protests. "Urban Indians," one unsigned memorandum predicted in 1971, "will most likely be creating more confrontations with federal, state, and city authorities over the next two years." Such unrest forced the White House to revisit Native American concerns.

Rising Indian protest derived partly from Nixon's failure to reform the BIA. From the outset, Nixon wanted to change the agency's operations. At a meeting of the Council on Urban Affairs in 1969, Nixon condemned the BIA's "routine bureaucratic mentality" and directed Interior Secretary Hickel to recruit fresh personnel. Hickel assured the President that Louis R. Bruce, the new Indian commissioner, was "not part of the establishment." Nevertheless, intramural feuding impeded change. The new Interior Secretary, Rogers C. B. Morton, who replaced

Hickel in 1971, considered Bruce's staff to be long on zeal and short on managerial competence. Morton named standpat, career bureaucrats to oversee policy: John Crow became deputy commissioner, and Wilma Victor served as special assistant to the secretary for Indian affairs. He then tried to shift authority from Bruce to Crow, only to retreat when tribal leaders opposed the change.

The wrangling at the BIA coincided with rising Indian militancy. During 1971, AIM, led by Russell C. Means (Oglala Sioux) and Dennis J. Banks (Chippewa), staged protests at Fort Snelling, Minnesota, and in the Black Hills of South Dakota. Objecting to federal control of the Black Hills, a site sacred to the Sioux, Means openly urinated atop Mount Rushmore. AIM also sought to protect Native American culture while it attacked elected, moderate tribal leaders perceived as being "too establishment" or as locked into the BIA. Additionally, AIM followers incited violence in Topeka, Kansas, when they protested white Boy Scouts attempting to perform Indian dances in 1972. What AIM lacked in size, having just 4,500 members, it made up for in daring.

The faction-ridden, inert BIA emerged as AIM's next target. Late in 1972 Russell Means and Banks led the "Trail of Broken Treaties," a caravan of militant Indians, to Washington to present a list of twenty grievances, several of which dealt with Indian treaties. On November 2, the Indians refused to leave the headquarters until the government promised to help them find housing. They overturned desks and file cabinets, barricaded doors, and smuggled in firearms and cans of gasoline. The White House, applying the lessons of Alcatraz, responded to the occupation with restraint. After Nixon indicated that he did not want bloodshed to mar his reelection, the Justice Department sought a court injunction to evict the trespassers. Garment and Frank C. Carlucci, deputy director of the Office of Management and Budget, then opened talks to entice the Indians to leave. Garment and Carlucci formed a panel to study their demands, including review of treaties, religious freedom, restoration of Indian lands, and increased funds for education and health care. They then paid $66,000 to transport the Indians home. Such appeasement ended the seizure at the BIA after one week, not nineteen months, as had been the case with Alcatraz.

In the short run, the occupation of the BIA weakened Nixon's support for Indian rights. The President "took it very hard," recalled Ehrlichman, because he thought he had been responsive to Indian concerns. Seeing Native Americans, like African Americans, as ungrateful, Nixon vowed that "he was through doing things to help Indians." When Agnew, a week after the occupation, asked permission to continue his work on Indian matters, Nixon labeled the issue a "loser," adding that the vice president "should not be tied to a loser." He dismissed the BIA as a "classic mess." Nevertheless, Nixon did not reverse his Indian policy.

In the long run, the trashing of the BIA further divided moderate tribal officials from urban radicals. Knowing that they could not compete with elected tribal leaders for support on reservations, AIM leaders denounced "established" tribal leaders as "Uncle Tomahawks" or "apples" who were "red on the outside, white on the inside." Other Indians, resentful of the national attention lavished on AIM, began chiding the organization as "Assholes in Moccasins." Tribal leaders, such as President Richard Wilson of the Oglala Sioux, assailed AIM's "destructive actions" and distanced themselves from the organization. Wilson would personally observe the widening gap between Indians when AIM occupied Wounded Knee on the Oglala Sioux reservation.

Red Power protest crested during the "Second Battle of Wounded Knee." In February 1973, 200 members of AIM converged at the hamlet of Wounded Knee, on the Pine Ridge Indian Reservation. Means and Banks, backed by traditional Sioux leaders, sought to replace the elected tribal government, headed by Wilson, with a hereditary, hierarchical one. AIM's leaders disliked the existing government because it had been established under the Indian Reorganization Act of 1934, the centerpiece of President Roosevelt's Indian New Deal. AIM also demanded revision of the Oglala Sioux's 105-year-old treaty with the federal government. To achieve their goals, AIM followers took over Wounded Knee at gunpoint and proclaimed an independent Sioux nation. After Wilson threatened to invade Wounded Knee to eject the outsiders, U.S. marshals, Federal Bureau of Investigation (FBI) agents, and BIA police cordoned off the town with armored personnel carriers supplied by the U.S. Army. AIM members, armed mainly with hunting rifles, dug fox-holes and fashioned explosives. Over the next three months, the two sides traded gunfire on the South Dakota plain. "Some morning we will wake up to see 8–10 people dead," Patterson warned Garment.

Why the standoff at Wounded Knee? Indian militants wished to settle scores with moderates, such as Wilson, who seemed closely tied to the BIA. They also sought national attention. Although the White House formed a task force to answer the Trail of Broken Treaties, it had refused to confer with the AIM followers who were charged with plundering the BIA headquarters. Moreover, the administration rejected many radical demands, especially the Trail of Broken Treaties' call for new treaties with the U.S. government. Most importantly, Wounded Knee, like Alcatraz, exemplified white mistreatment of Indians. In 1890 U.S. troops had slaughtered over 100 Sioux, including forty-four women and eighteen children, at Wounded Knee. Eighty years later, Dee Brown's bestseller, *Bury My Heart at Wounded Knee*, reminded Americans of this calamity. Patterson remarked that "when those guys picked Wounded Knee—what a place!"

In responding to "Wounded Knee II," some administration officials ignored history. In March 1973 Nixon cryptically told aides that he was "for action, even in long run." At Wounded Knee, the FBI's special agents in charge were eager to act; on March 2 they "unanimously agreed" that "something must be done and done today." Staring at so many armed Indians, however, Nixon's moderate aides again urged restraint. "Satisfying law enforcement requirements simply doesn't justify the potential loss of life," warned Col. Volney F. Warner, the military liaison for Wounded Knee. Garment described the "options involving real force" as "just about unthinkable." Nixon himself ruled out using tear gas to evict the occupiers. "There are going to be no dead babies at Wounded Knee," he resolved. "Just lay off the gas." Upon hearing this command, Assistant Attorney General J. Stanley Pottinger breathed easier, confident that "something crazy was not going to happen."

The administration found itself in an ongoing struggle to keep its "hawks" in check. On March 2 the FBI special agents in charge, speaking through an intermediary, urged Attorney General Richard Kleindienst to "call out the National Guard" to reinforce Wounded Knee. At that point, Acting FBI Director L. Patrick Gray informed the attorney general that "there will be no frontal attack" by the FBI on the Indians and ordered his agents to refrain from launching an assault. Although Gray and Kleindienst permitted FBI personnel to defend themselves, the attorney general instructed them to concentrate on "intelligence work" rather than probe for evidence against the Indians. The attitude of the U.S. military—and its Commander-in-chief—diminished the chance for bloodshed. Maj. Gen. Roland M. Glezer, director of military support, knowing that his aim "was not to kill or injure the Indians" and that any loss of life "would reflect badly on the Army," approved a plan to "wait out" the occupiers. Throughout the crisis, the Department of Defense furnished the FBI with logistical support but refused to send army troops into Wounded Knee "unless the President directs their participation." Nixon never did.

Officials outside of both the White House and AIM eventually signed a settlement. Assistant Attorney General D. Kent Frizzell and his deputy, Richard Hallstern, bargained with Sioux leaders. On May 6, 1973, the occupiers surrendered their arms in exchange for an investigation of Wilson's management of the Pine Ridge reservation. Garment then sent Patterson to Wounded Knee to discuss the Sioux Treaty. Nixon's staff, using some well-worn patience, had avoided a second massacre at that site, and the President was pleased. "It was important to do it right," Nixon privately said of his aides' handling of Wounded Knee, and "it was well done." But he added, referring to Watergate, "we didn't get much credit . . . because other things were happening that [were] bigger news."

Wounded Knee spurred some tactical second-guessing. AIM leaders, stung by mounting press skepticism of their sensational occupations, offered a truce with the White House. Banks bade Patterson a happy New Year and thanks for "all of your assistance and quick response to our calls . . . a job well done." "Brad," Garment joked, "this is one for the memory book. Point to it with pride and astonishment." AIM's flattery proved short-lived. In 1974 Means and Banks denounced the National Tribal Chairmen's Association (NTCA), which had been fashioned at White House instigation, as a "hoax." AIM also organized a sit-in at a BIA area office in Aberdeen, South Dakota, and requested a meeting with federal officials. The U.S. government refused.

Nixon's staff became harsher toward AIM. Following the occupation of the headquarters, the Department of Justice ordered the FBI to "intensify its efforts in identifying violence-prone individuals" within AIM. Although such intelligence efforts did not prevent the occupation of Wounded Knee, the government's surveillance continued. Acting FBI Director Gray ordered the bureau's San Francisco office to monitor financial contributions from "subversive and illegal groups" to AIM's bank account in Berkeley in April 1973. In the aftermath of Wounded Knee, the intelligence gathering widened, with the FBI's Minneapolis office requesting two "hippie-type Special Agents" for use in undercover work near Wounded Knee. The Office of Management and Budget audited federal agencies suspected of channeling money to AIM, and Deputy Attorney General Joseph T. Sneed asked his Community Relations Service to report "any indications of future militant action." Although such tactics resembled Nixon's repression of the Black Panthers, another group willing to use violence against existing authority, the Community Relations Service and FBI uncovered only minor Indian unrest and trivial information on AIM leaders.

In the aftermath of Wounded Knee, federal officials affirmed their commitment to Indian self-determination. Nixon, in fact, wanted more publicity for his "remarkably progressive record on Indians." White House moderates used the seizure to move his Indian bills. Wounded Knee, Patterson contended, was "wrapped up in the larger question of how well we've followed up on the effectiveness of our Indian program." John C. Whitaker, another aide, resubmitted Nixon's legislative package and then rebuked Congress for failing to act sooner. Between 1973 and 1975, Congress approved a spate of Indian reforms. It restored the Menominee, a Wisconsin tribe terminated in 1961, to federal trust responsibility, all but repealing termination, as Nixon had asked. It approved the Indian Financing Act of 1974, the President's proposal to lend tribes money via a revolving fund. In 1975 Congress passed the Indian Self-Determination Act, which allowed federal agencies to contract out services to tribes and expanded Indian control over their schools. The head of the Association on American Indian Affairs, an advocacy group, lauded the ninety-third Congress as "perhaps the most constructive Congress in the field of Indian affairs in our history."

Credit for these advances belongs to many people. Tribal leaders and White House staff members conceived the reforms, and Congress passed them. Special praise must go to Senators Henry "Scoop" Jackson, Democrat of Washington and chair of the Interior Committee, and James Abourezk, Democrat of South Dakota and chair of the Subcommittee on Indian Affairs, who, following Wounded Knee, sponsored legislation to advance Native American rights. Either Jackson or his staff saw Indian policy moving toward self-determination, leading the powerful senator to repudiate his past support of termination. Grass-roots protest played a major role as well. In June 1973, following the standoff at Wounded Knee, Senator Dewey F. Bartlett, Republican of Oklahoma and a member of the Subcommittee on Indian Affairs, foresaw no trouble passing Nixon's Indian legislation, even though he privately admitted that his committee had ignored most of the President's agenda for two and a half years. The President, after Alcatraz, issued his message on Indian rights; Congress, following Wounded Knee, began implementing it. Those were the bookends of Nixon's Native American reforms.

The shift in federal Indian policy did not end with Nixon's resignation; President Gerald R. Ford also stressed tribal self-determination. The new President seemed less interested in Indian affairs than his predecessor, partly because Indian protest never again reached the level of Alcatraz or Wounded Knee. Unlike Nixon, Ford issued no sweeping statement on Native American concerns, and he won few symbolic breakthroughs along the lines of Blue Lake. Nevertheless, legislation to enhance Indian rights passed during Ford's administration, and there were enough hints of unrest to keep the new President's team on the track of self-determination. Moreover, following Wounded Knee, Indian activists changed tactics, filing lawsuits to win redress of long-standing grievances.

At first, President Ford displayed scant interest in Indian rights. As a congressman from western Michigan between 1949 and 1973, Ford represented few Native Americans and compiled almost no record on Indian rights. Like Agnew, he became acquainted with federal policy during his brief tenure as vice president, while chairing the NCIO. Unlike Agnew, however, Vice President Ford treated the NCIO, the sole agency for which he was responsible, with indifference. Swayed by aides, he declined to back legislation to extend the panel's life, a move that disappointed both tribal organizations and former Vice President Hubert H. Humphrey, the NCIO's first chair.

But as President, Ford could not ignore tribal concerns, especially since the Pine Ridge Reservation remained a tinderbox. After the reservation suffered thirty-seven murders between January 1974 and July 1975, Senator Abourezk called for an investigation and additional law enforcement agents. The administration, in turn, dispatched a dozen extra police officers to Pine Ridge. Hopes for peace rose in 1976, when Albert Trimble defeated Wilson to win the presidency of the Oglala Sioux. Trimble pledged to dismantle Wilson's security forces, which had terrorized Wilson's critics. But days after Trimble's triumph, Wilson's supporters allegedly fired shots into the house of a Pine Ridge resident before killing another man during a high-speed automobile chase. A month later a rancher found the corpse of Anna Mae Aquash, a Canadian Indian with ties to AIM, alongside Highway 73. After the FBI failed to report the bullet wound in Aquash's head, many Native Americans suspected the agency of complicity in her murder. "The sentiment prevails," John A. Buggs of the U.S. Commission on Civil Rights correctly observed, "that life is cheap on the Pine Ridge Reservation."

By the mid-1970s Red Power protest began to fade, but not to vanish. Wounded Knee had diminished AIM's standing among tribal leaders and Anglos, and the press paid scant attention to the trials following the standoff. "I don't know where AIM is going to end up," Navajo Chairman Peter MacDonald opined, "but if their methods don't change, they are not going to last very long." Following their acquittals at the Wounded Knee trials, Dennis Banks and Russell Means never regained the limelight, and Means left the movement in 1975. Accordingly, Governor Richard F. Kneip of South Dakota noted that AIM's "more militant confrontations" had "subsided," and its capacity for violence had been "minimized." And yet AIM's belief that cultural identity could cure Native American ills endured. By 1976 the *Seattle Times* observed that the message of "Indian militants" had reached "the most isolated reservations of [Washington] state." The political heirs of Banks and Means still caused headaches for the Ford White House.

The administration's first challenge was a bizarre escapade, a cross between the sort of "guerrilla theater" practiced by the Youth International Party ("Yippies") during the 1960s and the novel *The Mouse That Roared;* in that book, the puny Duchy of Grand Fenwick declared war on the United States to gain postwar reconstruction aid. In 1855 the Kootenai had lost 1.6 million acres in northern Idaho during a conference at which they had no delegates. To make amends, Congress in 1974 considered granting the sixty-seven member tribe a parcel of land for use as a reservation. But when the federal government refused to send envoys to Idaho, the Kootenai declared war on the United States and assembled roadblocks around Bonners Ferry, Idaho, a town thirty miles south of the U.S.-Canadian border. The tribe requested outside assistance, a veiled plea for AIM volunteers, and charged motorists a dime to cross their ancestral lands. When Idaho's governor dispatched seventy state troopers, armed with mace and sawed-off shotguns, the Kootenai rescinded their ten-cent toll, although not their declaration of war. Ford's team, stocked with holdovers from the Nixon years, used patience and legislation to soothe the Kootenai protesters. The matter was serious enough to draw the attention of Ford's cabinet, which discussed "how to prevent another Wounded Knee-take-over." After warning that AIM might seize this opportunity, Patterson backed a "positive response" to "keep the situation cool." Both Patterson and BIA chief Morris R. Thompson refused to travel to Idaho. Instead, on the advice of aides, the President signed a bill transferring 12.5 acres of federal land into trust status for the Kootenai. The government then placated the tribe by building a road to its new reservation, awarding the Kootenai $100,000 for a community center, and spending $7,000 per tribal member over a twelve-month period. One official attributed such generosity to the so-called war, making the Kootenai, not the Duchy of Grand Fenwick, the true mouse that roared. Bonners Ferry was never in danger of becoming another Wounded Knee. Amy Trice, the Kootenai's chair, later conceded: "[T]he closest thing we had to a weapon in our tribal office was a flyswatter."

The next confrontation stirred memories of Wounded Knee but little violence. In May 1974 seventy-five Mohawks occupied an abandoned girls' camp near Eagle Bay, in New York's Adirondack State Park. The Mohawks demanded the return of land lost under an agreement signed in 1797 between Joseph Brant, a Mohawk, and the state of New York; Brant had sold 5.5 million acres to the state for just $1000. The occupiers sought to reestablish the Mohawk Nation of Ganienkeh, the "Land of Flint," with sufficient acreage for hunting, fishing, and farming. They also planned to form their own nation, open to all peace-loving North American Indians. The Mohawks posted guards and denied non-Indians access to their camp, leading the BIA's law enforcement chief to groan about "militant" Indians "armed with long guns" occupying Eagle Bay. "New York fears another Wounded Knee," the *Chicago Tribune* reported. Yet there was little exchange of gunfire, and one visitor sensed a "Walden II," not a "Wounded Knee II," atmosphere at the site. After the take-over, Mohawks and non-Indians aired their differences publicly, and the local press offered mixed editorials on native demands. In a preview of later Indian tactics, the Mohawks hired a lawyer to assert their claim to this parcel of land. Violence surfaced only in October 1974, when a nine-year-old girl and a twenty-two-year-old man suffered injuries in shootings near Eagle Bay.

Ford turned aside appeals from Mohawks and state officials to become involved in this dispute. Norman E. Ross, a White House aide, argued that recent congressional legislation had transferred jurisdiction over the Iroquois or Six Nations, of which Mohawks were a part, from the federal government to the state of New York. The White House from afar simply monitored the standoff that, like Alcatraz, dragged on for two years but with little national publicity. The task of settling the controversy fell to Mario Cuomo, New York's secretary of state, who in 1976 offered to resettle the Mohawks on a temporary, 900-acre reservation while their claims received consideration.

In a general sense, incidents like Eagle Bay, coming a year and half after Wounded Knee, reminded the Ford administration that it needed to remain sensitive to Native American rights. By approving the Indian Self-Determination Act of 1975, Ford reaffirmed Nixon's policy. With the White House and Department of the Interior behind the bill, a presidential signature was inevitable. Ford called the act a "milestone" that gave "permanence" to the goal of allowing tribes to run many federal programs themselves. Between 1974 and 1975, he also approved laws granting parcels of land to such tribes as the Hualapai of Arizona, the Cheyenne-Arapaho of Oklahoma, and the Sisseton-Wahpeton Sioux of the Dakotas. He also signed acts giving the U.S. government authority to hold submarginal lands in trust for tribes and to transfer excess federal property to reservations.

Ford resolved a significant claim when he approved a bill to enlarge Grand Canyon National Park and add 185,000 acres to the Havasupai Indian Reservation in Arizona. While Nixon in 1974 had endorsed expanding the tribe's domain, Ford's signature was not assured. The Department of Agriculture and Office of Management and Budget opposed the bill as setting "an undesirable precedent" of giving public lands to particular groups for "their exclusive use." But the Interior Department, the NCAI, and Senator Barry M. Goldwater, Republican of Arizona and the act's principal sponsor, disagreed. The President sided with the bill's proponents and signed it in January 1975. William Byler, executive director of the Association on American Indian Affairs, hailed the Havasupai's "stunning victory," which, he said, had come "against all odds."

Since Red Power radicals opposed federal initiatives to strengthen tribes, such legislation would never satisfy them. The specter of another armed occupation haunted the Ford White House. Patterson, who had joined the first lady's staff in November 1974, advised Theodore Marrs, Ford's assistant for Indian policy, that Indian "militancy" must be met with patience, not force. "Garment's and my experience with five years of that crap," he explained, "indicated that the 'setting of a deadline' tends to play very much into Indian hands." After reading that a group called the "Trail of Self-Determination" planned to descend upon the U.S. capital, Patterson warned of "another 'Trail of Broken Treaties'" and moved to alert intelligence and law enforcement personnel. Such concerns seemed justified when, in October 1976, 100 armed Puyallups occupied the Cascadia Juvenile Diagnostic Center in Tacoma. They wanted the BIA to purchase the state of Washington's interest in that hospital and then turn it over to them for use as a counseling center. With a Native American caravan preparing to march on Washington, D.C., and with Indians seizing property at gunpoint, the events of 1972–73 seemed about to replay themselves.

But these protests were not on the scale of Wounded Knee. Marrs and R. Dennis Ickes, an Interior Department official, pledged to remain "open-minded" in addressing native concerns while reminding the Trail of Self-Determination group that elected tribal governments "will have the greatest influence" on administration policies. The Tacoma showdown ended when the Puyallups agreed to end their occupation in exchange for an administration promise to consider transferring the hospital to the tribe. Patterson's formula—restraint plus discussion equals peaceful settlement—had held true once again.

The U.S. government had learned to master Native American protest just when such unrest was becoming passé. By 1976 a new generation of college-educated Indians was filing lawsuits to reclaim land, fishing, and water rights. Columnist Sterling Noel noted: "[T]he trend among most of the Western tribes seems to be toward organizing for court action and away from violent protest." A similar story prevailed in the Northeast where nonviolent resistance had given way to litigation. For instance, in Maine, 100 members of the Passamaquoddy tribe occupied two state forestry buildings in 1975. An Indian-staffed legal team, the tribe's governor asserted, had shown that the buildings belonged to the tribe. The Passamaquoddy and Penobscot tribes, in fact, soon claimed title to over 12 million acres, two-thirds of the state's area. The tribes argued that the transfer of their land to the state was invalid since it had occurred without the consent of the U.S. government, a violation of the Trade and Intercourse Act of 1790. In 1975 two federal courts ruled in favor of the tribes, suggesting that well-prepared lawsuits might shake the moorings of Anglo society more than armed takeovers.

Ford gladly passed the Maine imbroglio on to his successor. Patterson, who in October 1976 had returned to coordinate Indian policy, warned his colleagues to say nothing about this case. He understood that if the government fulfilled its duty and defended native claims, Maine's tribes stood to gain most of the state's land. The White House feared that an Indian court victory would trigger lawsuits by tribes in Massachusetts, New York, and North Carolina. When Ford requested a set of options, Patterson advised the President to leave the "problem for the Carter administration." Interestingly, one of the scenarios that Patterson sketched out, a Maine native claims settlement act modeled after the Alaskan Native Claims Settlement Act of 1971, was passed by Congress during Jimmy Carter's presidency.

Ford bequeathed another problem to Carter: rising Anglo backlash against Native American rights. In addition to vying for land, fish, and water, Indians and whites clashed over the degree of tribal sovereignty. Ford fed the dispute in July 1976 when he remarked that tribes should be able to decide for themselves whether they would fall under state or federal jurisdiction. The proposal was not new, since both the NCAI and Senator Jackson had endorsed it. But the Associated Press (AP) mistakenly reported that the President wanted to grant reservations jurisdiction over all residents, whether Indian or Anglo. Although the White House denied that Ford favored such authority for tribal governments, the AP's misstep energized two recently formed, western-based Anglo "rights" organizations, the Interstate Congress for Equal Rights and Responsibilities and Montanans Opposing Discrimination (MOD). Both groups flooded the White House with letters and telegrams denouncing sovereignty for Indian tribes. The protests of the Interstate Congress and MOD underscored how much Native American policy had shifted under Nixon and Ford, away from termination and assimilation and toward empowerment and tribal self-determination. According to a correspondent for the American Indian Press Association, "The Nixon administration . . . has been in the eyes of even the most critical observers one of the most active in Indian affairs since that of . . . President Franklin D. Roosevelt." During the presidential campaign of 1976, Jimmy Carter also endorsed "self-determination without termination," promising that "the majority of decisions affecting Indian tribes will be made in the Tribal Council and not in Washington, D.C." "Existing tribal governments," historian Roger L. Nichols argued in 1988, "exercise more direct and a wider variety of authority than at any other time in this century." Without question, the Nixon and Ford administrations initiated this change in policy.

Nixon and Ford proved remarkably enlightened and tolerant in Indian affairs, even under difficult circumstances. Officials in both administrations, along with a Democratic Congress, secured legislation to implement a policy of self-determination. They resolved numerous land claims, from Blue Lake to the Grand Canyon, and the Alaskan Native Claims Settlement Act inspired later legislation for Maine and Rhode Island. Both White Houses were solicitous of elected tribal leaders; in settling the Maine dispute, Patterson urged Carter's White House to confer with the tribes involved, although such advice often went unheeded. Some Native American leaders, such as LaDonna Harris (Comanche), president of Americans for Indian Opportunity, even expressed nostalgia for the days of Republican rule. Slights by the Carter administration, Harris complained, had led her allies within the Indian community "to say that the Nixon Administration was much more accessible. This is very disconcerting for a dyed-in-the-wool Democrat." Indeed, Garment later boasted about the Nixon White House "having an 'open door' in American Indian policy-making."

Nixon's interest in and influence over Indian policy did not end with his resignation. In 1989 the former President privately urged members of the Senate Select Committee on Indian Affairs to back further legislation on Native American rights. Nixon hoped that any renewed interest in civil rights would not leave "American Indians high and dry as it had in the 1960s." "As President," he reflected, "I took special pride in supporting the policy of 'Self-Determination Without Termination,' whereby my Administration endorsed Indian control and responsibility over government service programs." It remains unclear how closely the recipients of this missive—Senators Dennis DeConcini and John McCain of Arizona and Thomas A. Daschle of South Dakota—heeded his advice. Suffice it to say, the committee interviewed former Nixon administration officials, including Garment and Patterson. Its recommendations, which promised each tribe "the freedom to assess its own needs, set priorities, and design budgets," were in tune with the policy of self-determination. Even the title of the committee's report, "A New Federalism for American Indians," sounded strangely Nixonian.

For the most part, Presidents Nixon and Ford responded with considerable tact and skill to Native American unrest. Any of the take-overs they faced, particularly Wounded Knee, might have ended in tragedy. Even leaders of the opposition party had to give them their due; in 1981, Abourezk privately praised the "humane way" in which Nixon had "made decisions" with respect to Wounded Knee. Following centuries of confrontation and decades of fruitless assimilation efforts, the U.S. government and American Indians, by the close of the Nixon-Ford years, were beginning resolve their differences peacefully, albeit litigiously. Wounded Knee was receding into history.

Suggested Reading

Stephen Cornell, *The Return of the Native: American Indian Political Resurgence* (New York: Oxford University Press, 1988), looks at the 1970s. For an account of the beginnings of Red Power, see Paul Chaat Smith and Robert Allen Warrior, *Like a Hurricane: The Indian Movement from Alcatraz to Wounded Knee* (New York: The New Press, 1999). Larry Nesper analyzes one issue in *The Walleye War: The Struggle for Ojibwe Spearfishing and Treaty Rights* (Lincoln: University of Nebraska Press, 2002). Alvin Josephy Jr., Joane Nagel, and Troy Johnson, *Red Power: The American Indians' Fight for Freedom,* 2nd ed. (Lincoln: University of Nebraska Press, 1999) is a documentary history of 1970s activism. Russell Means with Marvin J. Wolf, *Where White Men Fear to Tread: The Autobiography of Russell Means* (New York: General Publishing Group, 1995) gives a major participant's view of what happened.

CHAPTER TWENTY-TWO

"Constructing" Nations within States

The Quest for Federal Recognition by the Catawba and Lumbee Tribes

Anne Merline McCulloch and David E. Wilkins

In 1946 Congress established the Indian Claims Commission in part to assess claims against the federal government for past wrongs. Envisioned to function for only ten years, it remained in operation for thirty-two years until 1978. By then the process had drawn claims from hundreds of tribal groups across the country, many of them awarded sizeable settlements. A number of small Native groups found themselves excluded or lacking the contacts, leadership, or funds necessary to present their claims. Other groups, not always so small, discovered that they were ineligible to participate in the claims process because they had no legal relationship with the federal government. They had signed no distant treaties with federal officials, lacked reservations, or could not prove they were Indians.

To deal with these groups, the BIA established the Federal Acknowledgement Program in 1978 to identify "real" Indians who had been overlooked. At least two hundred groups applied to enter the process by the early twenty first century, and to date about thirty have been decided. The program moves slowly; about half of the applicants have failed to gain recognition. This essay examines the experiences of two Native groups and analyzes the bases for the decisions they received.

Creating and in some cases re-creating viable tribal political communities within the construct of the modern nation-state has proven to be a troublesome task for indigenous populations worldwide. The task for indigenous governments in the United States has been further complicated by federalism's divisions of power between the states and the national government. Native American tribes often find themselves waging a two-front battle in which they must resist state

"'Constructing' Nations within States" appeared in *American Indian Quarterly* 19, no. 3 (Summer 1995): 361–88.

encroachments over their lands and their inherent governing authority; while at the same time they must lobby the federal government for protection of those same lands and powers.

History is replete with attempts by the federal government to forcibly remove tribes from their ancestral and treaty-recognized homelands, to facilitate assimilation using acts of cultural genocide, and to sever the federal trust relationship with tribes. These often well-intentioned, but highly destructive policies have taken their toll on tribes' political status, economic resources, and cultural integrity. This is particularly true for many Eastern tribes, especially those in the mid-Atlantic region, that generally were not accorded federal recognition in the form of treaties and thus did not benefit from the accompanying "protection" of the federal trust relationship. In addition, many Eastern tribes never had reservations set aside for them, a major source of geographic security that many Western tribes have enjoyed. Federal recognition is the primary method used by tribes to affirm their existence as distinct political communities within the American system. Federal recognition buffers tribal existence from most jurisdictional encroachments by state and local governments and, ideally, should shield the tribes from federal encroachments as well. It also provides tribes and their members with certain political, legal, and economic benefits. Tribes have been marginalized and have experienced great difficulty sustaining themselves as viable political and cultural entities without federal recognition.

This paper will analyze the campaigns for federal recognition of the Catawba Indian Tribe of South Carolina and the Lumbee Indian Tribe of North Carolina. The Catawba were successful in their battle to re-establish a federal relationship when Congress passed legislation in 1993 finalizing the settlement between the Catawba tribe and South Carolina. The settlement transferred responsibility for the tribe and its reservation from South Carolina to the federal government and also settled a treaty land claim that had been outstanding since 1840. The Lumbee Tribe, on the other hand, has been unsuccessful in its quest for complete federal recognition despite efforts dating to the 1880s.

Our analysis of these campaigns for federal recognition is based on the thesis that federal recognition is dependent on the tribes' externally and internally constructed social identities. The model we have chosen in analyzing this thesis is the policy formulation model recently proposed by Anne Schneider and Helen Ingram. This model uses the socially constructed identity of a target group or population to analyze and predict the types of federal policies that will be directed toward that group. Schneider and Ingram argue that the "dynamic interaction of power and social constructions leads to a distinctive pattern in the allocation of benefits and burdens to the different types of target groups." Those groups with positive social constructions and with strong levels of power, as defined by the ability to mobilize resources for action, will be overcompensated and are termed "advantaged groups." "Contenders" are those groups that are negatively constructed but have sufficient power to affect policymakers. In the case of the latter group, public officials "will prefer policy that grants benefits noticed only by members of the target groups and largely hidden from everyone else." "Dependent groups" are positively constructed but lack sufficient power to direct political benefits. Finally, "deviants" are both negatively constructed and are lacking in power, making them susceptible to policy constraints or even punishments. It is our argument that Native American tribes constructed by the "Anglo" community as "advantaged" or "dependent," i.e., as having a positive image, will have a greater probability of becoming federally recognized than those constructed as "contenders" or "deviant."

By examining two Southeastern tribes, each with extensive historical relations with the United States, we hope to illuminate the factors inherent in the construction of the tribes' social identity and to determine which factors seem most critical to federal recognition. Analysis of these factors may benefit the more than one hundred other tribal groups that are petitioning the federal government for the establishment of diplomatic relations.

Federal Recognition

Federal recognition historically has had two distinctive meanings. Before the 1870s, "recognize" or "recognition" was used in the cognitive sense. In other words, federal officials simply acknowledged that a tribe existed. During the 1880s, however, "recognition" or, more accurately, "acknowledgment," began to be used in a formal jurisdictional sense. Today the federal government's acknowledgment is a formal act that establishes a political relationship between a tribe and the United States. Federal acknowledgment affirms a tribe's sovereign status. Simultaneously, it outlines the federal government's responsibilities to the tribe.

Federal acknowledgment means that a tribe is not only entitled to the immunities and privileges available to other tribes, but is also subject to the same federal powers, limitations, and other obligations of recognized tribes. What this means, particularly the "limitations" term, is that "acknowledgment shall subject the Indian tribe to the same authority of Congress and the United States to which other federal acknowledged tribes are subjected." In short, tribes are informed that they are now subject to federal, particularly congressional, plenary power. The doctrine of "plenary power" is one of the central, yet most problematic, concepts in federal Indian policy and law. Since Indian nations were not and have not been included in the constitutional structure of the United States, the doctrine of federal "plenary power" has been derived through Supreme Court interpretation of the Indian Commerce Clause to give to the United States Congress the right to exercise all but unbridled power over tribal governments, lands, and resources. Because the power is not within the construct of the Constitution, it is not limited by it. Constitutional protections (federalism, equal protection, Bill of Rights) against governmental intrusion into the lives of people do not apply to Indian governments.

Although Congress traditionally has had recognition authority, in 1978 the Bureau of Indian Affairs developed an administrative process which unacknowledged tribes were to follow when seeking recognition. This set of guidelines was based mainly on confirmation by individuals and groups outside the tribe that members of the group were Indians. The mandatory criteria were as follows: the identification of the petitioners "from historical times until the present on a substantially continuous basis, as 'American Indian' or 'Aboriginal'" by the federal government, state or local governments, scholars, or other Indian tribes; the habitation of the tribe on land identified as Indian; a functioning government that had authority over its members; a constitution; a roll of members based on criteria acceptable to the Secretary of the Interior; not being a terminated tribe; and members not belonging to other tribes. These criteria largely were designed to fit the aboriginal image of the existing and recognized western tribes and were problematic for many eastern tribes that sought recognition. As M. Annette Jaimes has complained, some of these requirements presented a catch-22: "An Indian is a member of any federally recognized Indian Tribe. . . . To gain federal recognition, an Indian Tribe must have a land base. To secure a land base, an Indian Tribe must be federally recognized."

Because of the problematic nature of many of these criteria, and Congress's impatience with a process that seemed interminable, unfair, and ponderous, the BIA was forced on February 25, 1994, to issue revised criteria. The new criteria, it is alleged, are more in keeping with the contemporary condition of tribes seeking federal recognition. For instance, instead of requiring that the tribe be continuously identified as a distinctive Indian entity since "historical times," the criteria require only that there has existed an "American Indian entity on a substantially continuous basis since 1900." Also, the land requirement has been changed to require evidence of a "distinct community," a broader term that has in its meaning social as well as geographic ties. It is too early to ascertain the effect of these rules on the remaining petitioners.

The significance of recognition is two-fold: First, federally recognized tribes are eligible for a number of federal benefits. These benefits include educational and medical services and exemption from many state taxes. Second, by recognizing an Indian tribe the federal government is affirming the legal position of its members as Indians. Without such recognition, an ethnically identified "Indian" may not be able to benefit from federal programs tailored for "legally-recognized" Indians. Monroe E. Price and Robert N. Clinton note that according to the 1982 amended regulations of the Indian Reorganization Act of 1934 an Indian is defined as: (1) a member of a federally recognized tribe, (2) descendants of members of recognized tribes who were residing on an Indian reservation on June 1, 1934, or (3) a person who has one half or more Indian blood." This definition entails both an ethnological and a political/legal meaning. As Felix S. Cohen observed in his classic *Handbook* of *Federal Indian Law,* ethnologically, the Indian race may be distinguished from the Caucasian, Negro, Mongoloid, and other races. If a person is three-fourths Caucasian and one-fourth Indian, it is absurd, from the ethnological standpoint, to assign him to the Indian race. Yet legally such a person may be an Indian. From a legal standpoint, then, the biological question of race is generally pertinent, but not conclusive. Legal status depends not only upon biological, but also upon social factors, such as the relation of the individual concerned to a white or Indian community.

Equally pertinent to our discussion is that when the United States deals with tribes in an intergovernmental way it has done so not on the basis of race, but on a political basis. This is to say, the United States treats with tribes as social-political groups towards which it has unique legal/political responsibilities because of the inherent sovereignty of each party.

While Cohen's categorization of four racial groups has a number of problems scientifically, it remains a pertinent fact that for the purposes of federal Indian policy and law *race* coexists uneasily alongside the *political basis* (as exemplified in the hundreds of ratified treaties negotiated between tribes and the European nations and later the United States) as the defining factors in the tribal-Western relationship. Price and Clinton and Cohen's definitions of "Indian" actually raise more questions than they answer. And since the term "tribe" has similar racial/political connotations, it also is problematic. For example, to what extent is the federal government's relationship with tribes based on race? On politics? Does this vary from tribe to tribe? From administration to administration? Does the United States have a legal and moral obligation to *all* indigenous groups, or only to those with whom it has maintained long-standing political (read: treaty) relations? Does the issue of "domicile" (geographic location) have any legitimate bearing on the tribal-federal relationship? Finally, should the issue of "federal recognition" be used to distinguish tribes apart from "state-recognition"? And if so, to what degree?

We argue that the social construction of "Indianness" created by Euroamericans is among the most critical elements in determining which tribes will be recognized. What a person or group is perceived to be is just as much a function of subjective phenomena as of objective phenomena. Therefore, as we will demonstrate, the concepts of race, rights, obligations, and even domicile are as much dependent on the social construction put upon them as on their objective existence. The ability of an Indian tribe to become and remain a federally recognized tribe is dependent on how well that tribe "fits" the social construction of "Indian tribe" as perceived by federal officials.

Social Construction of Groups and Federal Indian Policy

The literature on interest groups and public policy is extensive. Factors such as size and cohesiveness, resources, social status, and incentives have all been analyzed in attempts to explain the differential success rates of interest groups in policy formulation and implementation. But until recently the concept of the social construction of group identity has been overlooked as a factor in public policy analysis. The concept of group identity may be of little importance in a homogeneous society, in that everyone in the population has a similar racial, religious, or cultural identity. In a heterogeneous, pluralistic society, particularly one in which discrimination based on racial or ethnic identity has been relatively common, group identity can be critical to the benefits or burdens levied on the group. The difficulty in addressing the impact of socially constructed identities of groups in the United States derives from the regime's commitment to liberalism. Lockean liberalism, upon which the United States Constitution is based, argues that governments are created to protect the individual natural rights of "life, liberty and property." Liberalism has been an attractive and successful political philosophy worldwide because it rejects the political legitimacy of most socially constructed group identities such as class and race. Yet despite philosophical and constitutional denial of group differences, in practical politics they remain firmly entrenched. Behavioral scientists often use group identity (e.g. race, religion, gender, etc.) as explanatory factors in social analysis. The high explanatory power of these "identity" factors demonstrates their significance for study and discourse about political issues and theory.

Identity politics is critical to understanding the background and intent of federal Indian policies. The term "Indian" itself is a social construction. Historians Robert F. Berkhofer Jr. and Brian W. Dippie both argue that "Indian" is a social construction created by the European immigrants to America. According to Berkhofer, "The initial image of the Indian, like the word itself, came from the pen of Columbus." The Arawak people were described by Columbus as "well built and of handsome stature," "marvellously timorous," "so guileless and so generous," and having a "very acute intelligence," in other words, he crafted the image of the "noble savage," the innocents of nature extolled by the later Romantic poets and philosophers. Columbus also originated the concept of the hostile and depraved "red devil" when he described the ferocious and cannibalistic Caribs. That image was permanently embedded in the European immigrants' impressions as well. The frontier stories of Indian "massacres" are but later examples of this same social construction of the indigenous inhabitants of the Americas.

Dippie maintains that these images served to reflect the moral dichotomy of Euroamericans' lives. On the one hand, these settlers championed the moral superiority of the civilization they were bringing to the wilderness and, on the other hand, they mourned the loss of innocence and virtue that civilization meant. Since the Indian represented the innocence of the lost wilderness to the white man, the Indian, by definition, could not continue to exist. So the myth of the "Vanishing American" was born. Books like *The Last of the Mohicans* by James Fenimore Cooper and artistic depictions like *The End of the Trail* by James E. Fraser helped to cement this myth into the American culture.

A curious aspect of these constructions was their timelessness. "In spite of centuries of contact and the changed conditions of Native American lives, whites picture the 'real' Indian as the one before contact or during the early period of that contact." By creating an image that was "uncivilized" by European standards, the immigrant Americans were able to define away any Native Americans who adopted white culture. Federal Indian policy in the nineteenth century reflected these myths. Indians were removed to reservations where they were illegally confined until they had become suitably acculturated so that they could begin "productive" lives in the Euroamerican political/economic culture.

In the attitudes of federal policymakers of the time, it was thought impossible for Indians to lead "productive lives" in their homelands. Reservations were considered little more than temporary detention colonies where tribal members languished until such time as the communal land could be individually allotted. The 1887 General Allotment Act was the inaugurating policy which eventually culminated in the allotment of 118 of 213 reservations by 1934, a gross reduction in indigenous land control from 138 million acres to 52 million acres. Importantly, most of the land loss was a result of subsequent amendments to the allotment measure and in the specific congressional acts which subdivided reservations.

Alongside allotment, a number of devastating assimilation measures—i.e., federally funded Christian missionaries, exertions of criminal jurisdiction over reservation lands and residents, boarding school policies, among others—were introduced to Americanize indigenous peoples. As long as Indians maintained ties to their tribe or tribal homeland, they were denied status as "Americans," entitled to the full panoply of federal benefits and protections. Federal citizenship prior to the 1924 Indian citizenship law was conferred only upon those who accepted an allotment (or who, preferably, left the reservation altogether). With citizenship, Indians became subject to state law. But even in cases where Indians voluntarily left the reservations or where they had received individual land allotments, they were still denied full citizenship rights and benefits because, according to the Supreme Court, they "remained Indians by race." Although Indians were unilaterally extended federal citizenship in 1924 and have since World War II been at least nominally integrated into the general Euroamerican political culture, the myth persists that the only "real Indian" is the "aborigine he once was, or as they imagine he once was."

It is important to note that the social construction of indigenous Americans, involving more than 540 distinctive groups, as "Indians" has persisted without input from the Native Americans themselves who traditionally, and in many cases still today, regard themselves primarily in terms of their tribal affiliation rather than in terms of "Indianness" or political allegiance to the United States or the states. Early European explorers and settlers homogenized the vastly heterogeneous tribes under the misnomer "Indians" despite their knowledge of the myriad languages and customs of the tribes. The rise of the nation-state in Europe made Europeans sensitive to differences among themselves. This sensitivity, however, was not extended to non-Western peoples.

Only in the last two decades has there been serious reevaluation of the concepts of race and ethnicity by the Census Bureau, anthropologists, and others. For much of the twentieth century, schools taught that there were three races: Caucasoid, Mongoloid, and Negroid. The category Mongoloid was then divided into two racial groups, Asians and Native Americans. Recent scientific scholarship categorically demonstrates that physiognomy and skin color are useless measures of race, and that the concept of race itself is more a process of self identification and social construction than physical characteristics. Nevertheless, the ongoing tendency by a number of federal agencies to treat Indian tribes monolithically is based on the obsolete and, more importantly, fictitious concept of "the" mythic, aboriginal Indian. However, by socially constructing a mythic Indian and then measuring demands for recognition against it, federal recognition seems more often to depend on how many Aboriginal traits the petitioning tribe retains in common with the mythic notion of "Indian" or "tribe."

The social construction of the Aboriginal Indian has "benefited" Western tribes more than the Eastern tribes. The western tribes (excepting the Southwestern groups, and their long history of interactions with the Spanish) had later contact with European culture; thus they have been able to retain more of their pre-Columbian cultures and much of their ancestral lands. The Northwest tribes who treated with Great Britain over trade developed quite different intergovernmental relations than those that evolved between the British, the colonies, and the Eastern tribes. By the time the United States treated with the Western tribes, the policy of removal (1830s–40s) was being replaced by the reservation system. While reserved land had been used by the British Crown during colonial times, it was not until the 1850s, when the policy of removal became impossible because of the westward migration of Americans to Oregon, California, and other Western regions, that the United States began as a general policy to set aside or "reserve" lands for its indigenous inhabitants. Many eastern Indian communities were biologically, materially, and culturally transformed by the British and American experience to the point where they no longer fit the "image" of the "Indian"—that is, the western Indian—which by the twentieth century was well ingrained in the minds of federal policymakers.

Hence, eastern tribes have often had a difficult time convincing the federal government (and their neighbors) that they remained "indigenous" and were entitled to comparable recognition and benefits as their western cousins. In fact, there is evidence that the intention of certain federal lawmakers in the 1930s for narrowing the "blood quantum" requirement from one-half to one-quarter during Indian reorganization was to reduce the number of Indians eligible for federal services, while maintaining a policy that the more "primitive" and "ancient" tribes like the Hopi, Navajo, and Tohono-O'odham needed ongoing federal tutelage in the form of education, cultural activities, and technical support, to facilitate their gradual assimilation into the American mainstream.

Two additional factors are particularly salient when examining the persistence of the federal government's efforts in attempting to assimilate Indians by destroying their cultures and religions. The first is land ownership. The tribes held lands coveted by the United States and her citizens for settlement or for their natural resources. In order to legally acquire title to the land and its attendant resources, federal policymakers, the press, state governments, railroad interests, and others had to eliminate the Indian title. It was easier, less expensive, and more moral to do this by allotting reservations and forcibly assimilating Indians rather than attempting an extermination policy that would have violated the very principles on which the United States was founded. Other racial minorities held no comparable economic leverage/burden to the budding hegemony of Euroamericans. African-Americans, Asian-Americans, and Hispanics were often segregated or simply denied any chance to assimilate.

The second factor to be considered is the level of group solidarity exhibited by the Native American tribes. Most tribes were quite cohesive social, economic, and political units. The national or tribal ties to ancestral lands and culture of other minority groups within the United States were generally broken by the immigration process or, in the case of African-Americans, by slavery. Since Native Americans still had some physical power over their traditional lands, as well as a functioning social and political unit, the only way to overcome Native Americans' collective resistance was to eliminate the tribal unit and disperse the individuals. The General Allotment Act of 1887 and House Concurrent Resolution 108—the Termination Resolution—were both attempts by the federal government to accomplish this.

Factors of Social Construction Important for Recognition

The above discussion leads us to suggest that the following four factors are of particular importance in affecting the success or failure of a tribe to gain federal recognition.

1. How well the tribe and its members meet the social construction of the image of an Indian. The model of social construction proposed by Scheider and Ingram lends weight to earlier suggestions that the image policymakers have of a group will have a profound impact on the policies that are directed toward the group. Since social constructions continually evolve, we believe the time period in which recognition is sought will affect both the characteristics of the social construction and the ability of the tribe to meet that image. We hypothesize that tribes whose members exhibit the most cultural and physical attributes of the mythic, aboriginal "Indian" will have the greatest likelihood of being acknowledged with federal recognition.

2. How cohesive is the self-identity of the tribes' members? Self-identification is a crucial element in the construction of an image by others. If the tribe has

a well-defined social image, it will have a better chance of projecting that image effectively to others. The more ambiguity there is in the tribe's self-image, the more room there will be for projection of traits onto that group by others. We suggest tribes at are internally cohesive with a well-developed tribal image will be more successful in pressing their demands for recognition than those that are not.

3. The general public's perception of the legitimacy of the benefits or burdens directed toward a target population. The moral value of the perceived rewards or punishments are important here. The more the general public perceives a tribe as legitimately "Indian" and morally due its benefits, the greater the likelihood of success. An established record of broken treaties and historically harsh treatment of tribal citizens lends greater legitimacy to claims against the system. As Schneider and Ingram note, "Social constructions become part of the reelection calculus when public officials anticipate the reaction of the target population itself to the policy and also anticipate the reaction of others to whether the target group *should* be the beneficiary (or loser) for a particular policy proposal." Since federal recognition provides significant benefits to the tribe and tribal members, we hypothesize that the tribe's demands for acknowledgment *must* be considered legitimate by the general public, including other Indian tribes, if the tribe is to be successful.

4. What are the tribes resources that can be used in support of its recognition efforts? Interest group theory would lead us to predict that factors such as size, wealth, and social status are positively associated with successful efforts. For tribes that are alienated from the system, or have been negatively constructed, then the use of threats is the most likely lobbying tactic. Tribes constructed as "dependent" have fewer resources to bring to bear in lobbying efforts but have a positive climate in which to use those resources. In keeping with interest group theory and Scheider and Ingram's model, we hypothesize that those tribes with greater resources, i.e., population, wealth, land, etc., will be more likely to be recognized by the federal government because they can bring more resources to the effort of lobbying the Congress.

In the next two sections we will use these factors to analyze the history of the Catawba and Lumbee campaigns for federal recognition.

Catawba Tribe

On November 10, 1763, King George III of England ceded the Catawba Tribe of South Carolina a tract of land "fifteen miles square" comprising about 144,000 acres in the Treaty of Augusta (Georgia). The Catawba were treated well because they had had a long-term friendship with the English that included sending men to fight alongside Colonel George Washington in the French and Indian War and alongside the English in the Cherokee War. Though the Catawba were not completely satisfied with the Treaty of Augusta, it was accepted and became the basis for the Catawba land claims and recognition demands 230 years later.

European settlers began moving onto the Catawba Reservation sometime before the Revolutionary War. One of the first European settlers among the Catawba was Thomas "Kanawha" Spratt II who settled on the land near present-day Fort Mill about 1761. Though Spratt got along well with his Catawba neighbors, he soon began selling parcels of the land the Catawbas had leased him to other non-Indians. Within a few years almost all of the most fertile tracts within the reservation had been leased to English colonists. In 1782, after boundary disputes arose, the leaseholders agreed to have all the lands surveyed, platted, and recorded. That same year, the Catawba petitioned Congress to secure their land so it would not be "Intruded into by force, nor alienated even with their own consent." Not wanting to deal with the tribe, Congress the following year passed a resolution stating that the British title over the Catawba Nation had passed into the hands of South Carolina. Congress recommended that South Carolina "take such measures for the satisfaction and security of the said tribe as the said legislature shall, in their wisdom, think fit." Thus the Catawba nation became beneficiaries of a trust relationship with South Carolina rather than the United States. Ironically, the Cherokee, who had sided with the British during the Revolutionary War, were federally recognized and taxes from Fort Mill on the Catawba Reservation were sent to support them while the Catawba were left to their own resources.

Settlers continued to invade Catawba lands and by the early 1800s most of their remaining land had been leased. The non-Indian leaseholders worried about the permanence of their leases, so in 1838 South Carolina Governor Patrick Noble authorized commissioners to enter into negotiations with the Catawbas for the sale of their land. The Catawbas were willing to part with full title if the state provided enough money for land acquisition near the Cherokee in North Carolina. In 1840 the Catawba Nation and the State of South Carolina entered into the Treaty of Nation Ford. The treaty provided that the Catawbas would cede the land granted to them under the Treaty of Augusta in 1763 in return for

> a tract of land of the value of $5,000, 300 acres of which is to be good arable lands fit for cultivation, to be purchased in Haywood County, North Carolina, or in some other mountainous or thinly populated region, where the said Indians may desire, and if no such tract can be procured to their satisfaction, they shall be entitled to receive the foregoing amount in cash from the state.
>
> The Commissioners further engage that the State shall pay the said Catawba Indians $2,500 at or immediately after the time of their removal, and $1,500 each year thereafter, for the space of nine years.

Unfortunately, in its haste to remove the Catawba, South Carolina had neglected to secure North Carolina's permission to have the Catawba moved to the Cherokee reservation. When the permission was belatedly requested, North Carolina refused. Some Catawba journeyed to the Cherokee reservation and did live there for a time but old tribal jealousies and the stress suffered by the remaining Cherokee as a result of the "Trail of Tears" tragedy prevented them from making a permanent home with the Cherokee. Eventually, most of the Catawbas found themselves back on their former soil but without land or money. The settlement of $2,500 and the annual payment of $1,500 promised them under the 1840 Treaty were withheld by the state because the Catawba had returned to the land. The plight of the Catawbas led South Carolina Indian Agent Joseph White to secure for them in 1843 a tract of 630 acres near the center of the "Old Reservation."

South Carolina and the United States continued to try to rid themselves of the "Catawba problem." During the Removal, Congress appropriated money in 1848 and again in 1854 in an effort to remove the Catawba west of the Mississippi. In the meantime, Governor Seabrook of South Carolina was trying to get the Commissioner of Indian Affairs to underwrite the outstanding debt of $18,000 owed by South Carolina to the Catawba. As early as the 1840s the Catawba realized that they had been defrauded but it was not until the 1880s that the tribe retained lawyers to investigate their claims against South Carolina. In 1905 the Catawba launched their legal battle to recover their lands, arguing that the 1840 Treaty of Nation Ford was null and void because it violated the Indian Nonintercourse Acts, which required submission of all land transactions involving tribal lands to Congress.

The tribe had been able to maintain its internal cohesiveness and social identity throughout the nineteenth century despite the lack of federal or state protection because of several factors acknowledged by BIA Special Indian Agent Charles Davis in a report to the agency dated January 5, 1911. These factors included, among others, size, tribal organization, religion, and character. At the time he was writing, ninety-seven individuals lived on or near the Catawba reservation who were recognized by South Carolina as being members of the Catawba Tribe. One-hundred and ten individuals were recognized as members by the tribe, the discrepancy hinging on a matrilineal descent requirement by the state. Davis noted that the small tribe had not intermarried much with their white neighbors and not at all with their black neighbors, thus "[t]he large majority are so nearly full blood as to retain the Indian characteristics, and by reason thereof they have retained their tribal life and organization. . . . This tribe has maintained a tribal organization for all time, so far as can be ascertained now. And the State [*sic*] has seemingly always recognized their tribal character." Religion was another factor he discussed as having some impact on the tribe's internal cohesion. Most Catawba tribal members had converted to the Mormon religion twenty to thirty years earlier and had continued in that religion during a time when there were violent activities against Mormons in South Carolina. Despite poverty, lack of schooling, and general neglect by the State, the Catawba tribe was still regarded by Davis as ranking very high in regard to integrity. The tribe's solidarity, acknowledged both internally and externally, helped to support the perseverance needed to pursue its legal claims against South Carolina.

The tribe persisted in its campaign in the courts and in Congress until 1934 when the South Carolina Legislature passed a resolution recommending that the care and maintenance of the Catawba Indians should be transferred to the United States. It was not until 1943 that a Memorandum of Understanding was signed between the tribe, the state, and the Department of Interior. South Carolina acquired 3,434 acres of farmland for a federal reservation. The tribe adopted a constitution under the Indian Reorganization Act, and the federal government assumed its trust responsibility over tribal affairs.

The Catawba's federal recognition was short-lived. In keeping with the federal government's termination philosophy instituted in 1953, the Catawba tribe was approached in 1958 by both the BIA and South Carolina with a proposal for termination. The BIA agent at the time assured the Catawba that their long-standing land claim against the state based on the Treaty of Augusta and the Treaty of Nation Ford (which still had not been resolved) would be unaffected by the termination. Thus, in 1962 the federal trust relationship between the United States and the Catawba tribe was terminated. The 3,434 acre federal reservation was divided up and distributed to tribal members. South Carolina continued to hold the 640 acre tract from the 1840 treaty in trust for the tribe. At the time of termination, there were 631 enrolled members.

The activism of the American Indian Movement in the early 1970s served to reignite the determination of the Catawbas—and many other tribes—to reinstitute claims. The tribe contacted the Native American Rights Fund, and in 1976 papers were filed with the Department of Interior to recover the land recognized under the 1763 Treaty of Augusta. Negotiations were proceeding between the tribe, South Carolina, and the United States when two events in December 1977 dashed all hopes of resolution. First, the local paper obtained and published tribal maps identifying specific parcels of land the tribe and state were considering for a reservation. Threatened non-Indian landowners quickly organized the Tri-County Landowners Association with the intention of stopping any settlement by asking Congress to extinguish the land claim in return for a monetary payment. Second, the increased publicity of the pending land claims led to demands by nonresident tribal members to join in the action in hopes of securing land, benefits, or both. Negotiations stalled. The impasse continued until 1980 when the tribe filed suit in federal district court to recover possession of the 1763 treaty reservation.

In 1982, Senior Judge Joseph P. Wilson dismissed the Catawba's case on the basis that the ten-year state statute of limitations for claims had expired—it being twenty years since the Catawbas' 1962 termination. The Fourth Circuit, however, reversed the decision arguing that termination did not affect the 1763 reservation. The State appealed to the United States Supreme Court. In the meantime the Solicitor for the United States Department of Justice under the Reagan Administration switched sides and filed an *amicus curiae* brief in support of South Carolina. The Supreme Court reversed the Fourth Circuit by ruling that termination did make the land claim subject to state law and then remanded the case to the Fourth Circuit to determine what the impact would be on the tribe's claim.

The Fourth Circuit Court in 1989 found that there was still some standing for the claim. South Carolina law concerning adverse possession of real property limits claims to ten years when there has been continuous occupancy of the land by the trespasser, and to twenty years if the land has changed hands during that period. The twenty-year limit (1962–82) meant that a substantial amount of the land claimed would still be subject to litigation since the clock had stopped running on the claim when the tribe filed suit in 1980. It was estimated that sixty percent of the original 27,000 land owners were still subject to litigation by the tribe. Most real estate transactions in York County, home of the Catawba claims, were held up because of the unwillingness of mortgage companies to provide title insurance.

At this point Congressman John Spratt (a descendent of Thomas "Kanawha" Spratt), Governor Carroll Campbell, and Secretary of the Interior Manuel Lujan expressed their interest in a settlement. Negotiations began again in 1990 and continued through 1991, until South Carolina's interest faded after both the Federal District and Appeals Court denied the Catawba's petition for a class-action suit. It seems South Carolina and the landowners believed they could win the case by outlasting the tribe. With the clock running on the twenty-year statute of limitations (the clock had been restarted in 1991 when Judge Wilson refused the class-action petition), the tribe decided to proceed with its claim, and NARF attorneys began preparations to serve papers on 61,767 individual occupants of the disputed claim area.

This action prompted immediate interest on the part of South Carolina and land holders in renewed negotiations. To facilitate negotiations, Congress enacted legislation extending the statute of limitation for an additional year to October 1, 1993. The tribe established the date of September 2, 1993 as the deadline. If agreement had not been reached by that date, they argued, the summons would be mailed. On January 5, 1993, H. R. 399, the Catawba Indian Tribe of South Carolina Land Claims Settlement Act of 1993, was introduced into Congress by Congressman John Spratt. Negotiations were resumed in good faith and on February 20, 1993 the tribe voted 289 to 42 to accept the settlement. Congress passed the act that summer and the final agreement was signed by South Carolina Governor Carroll Campbell on November 29, 1994 at the Catawba Reservation.

The settlement provided for the following: The trust relationship between the Catawba Indian Tribe and the United States would be restored, the tribe would become a federally recognized tribe, and its members would be eligible for federal benefits. The United States and South Carolina would contribute $50 million dollars over a period of five years to be put into five trust funds: Land Acquisition Trust, Economic Development Trust, Social Services and Elderly Assistance Trust, Education Trust, and a Per Capita Payment Trust to be managed by the

Secretary of the Interior. The tribe was given ten years to expand the existing reservation to 3,000 acres, plus 600 acres of wetlands or undeveloped land. Tribal jurisdiction was recognized over basic governmental powers, including zoning, misdemeanors, business regulation, taxation, and membership. Tribal membership would be based on direct descendency from the 1961 Federal Catawba Roll. South Carolina, however, reserved the right to continue to exercise criminal jurisdiction over Indians and non-Indians on the reservation. Finally, the tribe was exempted from the Indian Gaming Regulatory Act.

The victory for the Catawbas was as welcomed as it was incomplete. Some tribes complained that the Catawbas gave too much of their sovereign powers to the state. However, after 153 years of negotiation, legislation, and litigation (the final litigation process having been continuously in the federal courts for seventeen years), it appeared that the settlement was at least sufficient. The Catawbas were able to recover their status as a federally recognized tribe and their land base was expanded and confirmed. The fact that both issues were so clearly drawn by the long-standing claim and the cohesiveness of the tribe in pressing that claim helped to cement the perception that the Catawbas were still a tribe. Conversely, the fact that they were so acculturated into the Euroamerican system and had lived so long under South Carolina law negatively affected their ability to reclaim criminal and regulatory powers from the state. In the areas that the Catawbas managed to fit the image of the "real" Indian, they were successful; in areas where they seemed too "westernized" and assimilated, they lost. The losses were sustained because the claims were not considered legitimate.

Lumbee Tribe

The Lumbee Nation, numbering about 39,000, are a majority of Robeson County's indigenous population. According to Robert K. Thomas, the noted Cherokee anthropologist, genetically the Lumbee people (the term Lumbee, we shall see shortly, is of recent vintage) are the descendants of remnants of several small Southeastern tribes: the Hatteras, Saponi, and Cheraw, who from the 1780s through the 1840s worked their way into Robeson County where they intermarried and gradually developed a distinctive tribal identity. This account of Lumbee origins, however, directly contradicts the most prominent theory of Lumbee roots that posits that the Hatteras Indians living on the Outer Banks of North Carolina intermarried with John White's "Lost Colony" of Roanoke Island sometime in the late 1500s. The latest Lumbee "origin" theory asserts that the Lumbees are primarily descended from the Cheraw Tribe of South Carolina and related Siouan speakers who were said to have inhabited the area now known as Robeson County since the later eighteenth century. These conflicting origin theories have contributed in no small part to some of the identity questions Lumbees have confronted internally. Since we are focusing, in part, on how important the federal government's social construction of "Indian identity" is, we will see that these social-cultural questions have clearly discernible political manifestations.

Interestingly, there are six other groups in Robeson County that insist they also are distinctive political-cultural tribal polities. This tribal differentiation—the separation of Robeson County's indigenous population into several politically, though not genetically, disparate groups—and the ramifications of this segmentation for internal tribal dynamics and intergovernmental relations is a powerful dynamic affecting the Lumbee's quest for federal acknowledgment. This is arguably the most persistent conundrum confronting the county's indigenous population, especially as it pertains to the tribe's efforts to project a common tribal identity that might facilitate federal recognition. The Lumbee's leadership understands, in other words, that it is crucially important for recognition purposes that they be able to meet, or at least give the appearance of having met, the extant Anglo social construction of what a "tribe" should appear to be like: that is a tight, fairly cohesive unit lacking any disruption to their common identity.

The non-Lumbee indigenous population of the county, however, is less concerned about satisfying the federal government's social construction, and seems more intent on satisfying the perception of other tribes, particularly established Northeastern tribes like those constituting the Iroquois Confederacy. This has contributed to the proliferation of disparate organizations—six in all, besides the Lumbee Tribe. Most of these groups have adopted the name Tuscarora as part of their tribal designation, because the Tuscarora Tribe for several centuries inhabited portions of eastern North Carolina before they were defeated in battles with North Carolina colonists. The bulk of the tribe departed for New York in the early 1700s.

Each of these six other groups is pursuing an independent path toward federal recognition. This is not the forum, however, to detail the controversial developments leading to this recent proliferation of groups. This splintering and the lack of consensus among the competing political, yet biologically related, groups have made it much more difficult for the Lumbees or the other groups to secure federal acknowledgment.

This has been most evident since the latest administrative and legislative recognition began in the late 1980s. Before then, the Lumbee tribe generally understood itself internally and presented itself externally as a relatively cohesive people. However, since the formation of the first splinter group, the Eastern Carolina Tuscarora Organization in 1970, this cohesion has been shattered. Thus, when the early versions of the Lumbee recognition bill were introduced in Congress during the 1980s, the measures were vigorously opposed not only by some other tribes and BIA officials, but also by the non-Lumbee indigenous groups. The general fear of these tribal fragments was that they would be subsumed under the Lumbee tribe and would not be allowed to petition the federal government separately.

This indigenous segmentation also creates uncertainty and confusion among outsiders about Lumbee Identity. For instance, the federally recognized Eastern Band of Cherokee has been a stalwart opponent of Lumbee recognition. In part, its resistance results from the historical fact that the Lumbees were misnamed Cherokees of Robeson County by non-Indians and that at least one segment of contemporary Robeson County Indians still identifies itself as "Cherokee." Jonathan Taylor, a former Eastern Cherokee chief, said in testimony against the Lumbee recognition bill in 1988 that "there are only two Cherokee Tribes; one of them is in North Carolina [the Eastern Band] and the other one is in Oklahoma [the Cherokee Nation of Oklahoma]."

Notwithstanding the importance of tribal segmentation, we concentrate on the Lumbee for several reasons: first, the Lumbee tribe dwarfs the other factions and all other non-recognized Indian tribes; second, the Lumbees are one of a handful of tribal groups that was informed by the associate solicitor of Indian affairs of the Department of Interior that they were precluded from using the administrative process for recognition established by the BIA in 1978; and third, a focus on the Lumbees is warranted because their original (1956) acknowledgment legislation arose during the termination era when the United States unilaterally severed its political relationship with a number of tribes. The termination years have since been replaced by self-determination and a majority of the tribes and Indian groups that were terminated in the 1950s and 1960s have since been restored to federal status. The Lumbee Tribe remains, politically speaking, frozen in time—connected to an aberrant federal policy that has since been forcefully repudiated by the Congress and the executive branch.

The Lumbee Nation, unlike the Catawba Nation, which has had bilateral political dealings with European nations, the colony (later state) of South Carolina, and the federal government since the 1700s, has been in active pursuit of either federal acknowledgment or federal aid for a little more than 100 years. The Lumbee's initial contact with the federal government was in 1888 when the tribe's leadership petitioned Congress for education aid. The Commissioner of Indian Affairs denied the tribe's request on the grounds that North Carolina already was providing some money for the Indians' education and because the BIA maintained that it did not have enough money to meet the "recognized" tribes' needs.

And unlike the Catawba, who had long-standing dealings with South Carolina from the colonial period, the Lumbees relations with North Carolina were of a more recent vintage. This is the result of several factors. The Lumbees were a relatively small and powerless tribe during the formative years when the colonial, later state government, was evolving. The Lumbees' predecessors settled in an area of North Carolina that enabled them to avoid prolonged contact with colonial/state government. They largely were ignored by the federal government because they posed no military threat to the United States or American settlers, they did not inhabit lands deemed desirable, and they were perceived to have been an incorporated tribe in relation to the state's political and economic infrastructure.

Collectively, the Lumbee tribe had few formal political dealings with the state before the 1860s. This era of nonpolitical relations began to change after the Civil War when the legislature enacted a law that provided for separate white and Negro schools. The Lumbees then sought political redress from the state because they were denied admittance to white schools and refused to send their children to Negro schools.

Gradually, the county's Democratic leadership became aware of the tribe's growing voting potential. North Carolina's response was enactment of a law in 1885 which acknowledged the Lumbee as the Croatan Indians of Robeson County. What this law did was establish a separate school system for tribal members. The Lumbees (Croatans) were able to parlay their growing political clout into additional state legislation that established the Croatan Normal School, which was under exclusive Indian control.

By the early 1900s, the term Croatan had attained a pejorative connotation, with local whites often shortening it to "Cro," short for "Jim Crow," the vernacular term for institutionalized racial segregation. The Croatans perceived this as a racial slur and requested a different tribal name. In 1911 the legislature enacted a law that deleted the now-despised word "Croatan" and simply inserted the generic term "Indian." They were henceforth to be known as "Indians of Robeson County."

This terminology proved unsatisfactory as well and, in 1913, anxious to be defined culturally and socially as distinct from others, they were given yet another name. This time they were designated as "Cherokee Indians of Robeson County." This resulted from the contention of some historians and anthropologists who argued that some western North Carolina Cherokees had intermarried with the Indians of Robeson County during the Revolutionary War.

Officially, the "Cherokee" designation remained on the state's statute books, and over the Eastern band of Cherokees' strenuous objections, until the 1950s, when the name Lumbee was adopted. In the early 1930s, there had been another legislative push, this one on the federal level, to rename the Robeson County Indians. The term bandied about was "Cheraw," an historical tribe inhabiting north-central South Carolina. Research on the Cheraw connection was conducted by the noted anthropologist Dr. John P. Swanton of the Smithsonian Institution. At the time it was the most historically accurate and detailed to date. Swanton argued that the Indians of Robeson County were "descended mainly from certain Siouan Tribes of which the most prominent were the Cheraw and Keyauwee." He proposed the name "Siouan Indians of Lumber River," This measure, however, was opposed by the BIA who argued that it would entitle the tribe's fairly substantial membership to federal services. Ultimately the measure was tabled.

In the early 1950s, a campaign was begun by several prominent local Indians to have the tribe's name changed again. The Reverend Doctor F. Lowry, the leader of this movement, argued that because the tribe was comprised of members from various tribes, no single historical name was appropriate. He suggested that the tribe adopt a more geographically based name. The name chosen was "Lumbee," which was derived from the Lumber River that flows through the county. In 1953 North Carolina enacted a law designating the people as the "Lumbee Indians of North Carolina." This law often is interpreted as an extension of "recognition," but a credible case can be made that the state still had not explicitly defined the services to which the tribe was entitled, the immunities to which recognition entitled the tribe, and the aspects of self-government the state was willing to acknowledge.

After the Lumbees were acknowledged by North Carolina, they then launched their drive for federal recognition. Three years later, on June 7, 1956, Congress passed "An Act Relating to the Lumbee Indians of North Carolina." The federal law used language nearly identical to that of the state law. However, at the request of the Department of Interior—the agency spearheading the national termination policy—an exclusionary clause was inserted providing that "nothing in this Act shall make such Indians eligible for any services performed by the United States for Indians because of their status as Indians, and none of the statutes of the United States which affect Indians because of their status as Indians shall be applicable to the Lumbee Indians."

Ironically, then, the 1956 federal law acknowledged the Lumbees as a distinctive tribe, yet simultaneously precluded them from the federal services and protection generally provided to other acknowledged tribes. In other words, the tribe was recognized and terminated in the same legislation. The Lumbees made several sporadic efforts to have the restrictive language excised in the 1970s, all to no avail. It was not, however, until 1988 that the tribe decided to go full speed for the establishment of diplomatic relations. Bills have been introduced in every Congress since then to extend the full range of federal benefits and sanctions to the Lumbee tribe. To date, each bill has been defeated.

While the end to the Lumbee's quest is closer than ever (the House in 1993 passed the measure), there are no guarantees that it will be enacted anytime soon with the Republicans steering Congress toward less government and lower federal expenditures. The overwhelming preponderance of evidence suggests that the Lumbee tribe meets most of the ethnological and legal-political criteria that the federal government uses to determine the Indian groups to which it has obligations. Yet it retains a nebulous status as a quasi-recognized tribe.

Analysis of Recognition Factors

In this last section we return to our social construction model and comparatively assess the political "success" of the Catawbas, in contrast to the political "defeats" of the Lumbees.

Social Construction of the Tribe

There have been nearly 300 years of relations between the Catawba Tribe, South Carolina and the United States. Since before the French and Indian Wars,

South Carolina has had formal government-to-government relations with the Catawbas. Although the state had tried several times to terminate the relationship, the social construction was one of an established Indian tribe.

On the other hand, the major argument used by Lumbee opponents is their contention that the Lumbee "lack" certain "genetic" and "cultural" features which other recognized tribes are said to possess. Thomas noted this in his 1980 study and said that many local whites and some other tribes express the opinion that Lumbees are not "real" Indians. In other words, they are perceived as not being a "pure genetic race, they do not have a distinctive aboriginal language, and they lack a 'distinct tribal religion.'" This is a perception that dates back to the nineteenth century and continues today even when contradicted by solid historical, anthropological, and political evidence. The matter is further complicated by the fact that the Lumbees "present themselves as members of different tribes [i.e. the six other Indian groups in the county], which causes some confusion on the part of many Indians of other tribes."

Karen Blu's 1980 study, *The Lumbee Problem: The Making of an American Indian People,* which focused on the political and legal history of the Lumbees, essentially argued that Lumbee political activities have been affected by the "interplay between their own and others' conceptions of who they are." More importantly, her work posited that Lumbee ethnic identity—which is a blend of several tribes with an unquantifiable but discernible amount of Euroamerican and African-American ancestry—by "lacking what are thought to be 'traditional' Indian customs and traits, that Indianness is based in an orientation toward life, a sense of the past, 'a state of mind.' It is a *way* of doing and being that is 'Indian,' not what is done or the blood quantum of the doer." This unique brand of indigenous identity is a central factor that has precluded the Lumbee people from securing federal acknowledgment.

Additionally, because the Lumbees did not sign treaties with colonial, state, or federal powers (political recognition), and since they have never inhabited a reservation (territorial dimension), these factors are sometimes weighed against them as further evidence that the Lumbees are not a legitimate tribe.

Social Cohesiveness

There are at least three factors contributing to the maintenance of the continued social cohesion of the Catawba tribe. First, outsiders accord the tribe legitimacy. Second, importance has been placed on continuing the traditional cultural arts of the tribe, particularly pottery from the clay of the Catawba River bottoms, despite having lost title to most of the land wherein the clay is found. The Catawba are the only Eastern tribe to have continued, uninterrupted, pottery making using the traditional designs and the same clay used by their ancestors. One tribal member credited the survival of the tribe during the Great Depression to pottery, as it was the only income-producing activity the tribal members had during that period. The third factor was religion. Although the Catawba were exposed to Christian missionaries since the early 1700s, it was not until Mormon missionaries approached the tribe in the 1880s that many Catawba converted to Christianity. A report from 1934 noted that ninety-five percent of the 300 tribal members participated in Mormon services. The Mormon affiliation contributed to social cohesion through church participation, a banding together for protection, and a sense of uniqueness.

The fact that the Lumbees are a melange of several tribes appears to be an inherent weakness in their social cohesion from the federal government's perspective. The recognition process seems to prefer tribes with a long historical track record, even though it was European colonization that scattered the original tribes and destroyed their internal governing structures. Nevertheless, the Lumbees have developed, over a relatively short period of time, a fairly strong internal cohesion. However, the contemporary fragmentation which has erupted within the tribe has caused severe intertribal and intergovernmental problems.

Perception of the Legitimacy of Tribal Benefits

The United States history of severed treaties and broken promises with American Indian tribes has generated a reservoir of sympathy toward Indians. In the case of the Catawbas, the failure by South Carolina to live up to its treaty obligations was well-documented and contributed to public empathy for the Catawbas. The major roadblock toward resolution of the claim was the time that had elapsed and the number of people involved in the claim as a result of the centuries of inequitable treatment. But as Justice Blackmun stated in his dissent in *South Carolina* v. *Catawba Indian Tribe*:

> When an Indian Tribe has been assimilated and dispersed to this extent—and when, as the majority points out, thousands of people now claim interest in the Tribe's ancestral homeland . . . the Tribe's claim to that land may seem ethereal, and the manner of the Tribe's dispossession may seem of no more than historical interest. But the demands of justice do not cease simply because a wronged people grow less distinctive, or because the rights of innocent third parties must be taken into account . . . I agree with Justice Black that "[g]reat nations, like great men, should keep their word."

The perception of the legitimacy of the Lumbee claim for benefits, on the other hand, is problematic for the reasons listed above. Although the tribe has garnered a great deal of support over the years, there is still the perception that the Lumbees simply have not fared as poorly as tribes with whom the United States negotiated and then subsequently broke treaties. In other words, while the Catawba have been seen as weak and dependent, the Lumbee are often perceived as strong contenders. Their large population size, relative to other tribes, also makes it more difficult for the Lumbees to gain the sympathy of non-Indians and western tribes who believe that the Lumbees' needs are not as legitimate as those of other tribes because they have not suffered the historical humiliations of tribes like the Catawbas.

Economic Resources

The Catawbas are a small and relatively poor tribe. In 1980 there were only 953 enrolled members. The tribe had no other resources than its 640 acre reservation. Yet it had an unresolved land claim stemming from the Augusta Treaty in 1763. Ultimately, it was that claim that provided the leverage to obtain federal recognition, as well as a substantial cash settlement.

The Lumbee, by contrast, are the largest non-federally recognized tribe, and they are in the top five among all tribes in population. The elements of large population and the estimated costs of serving the tribe's membership have been used as evidence by the BIA on many occasions to oppose the Lumbees' legislative attempts at recognition. In 1890, Indian Commissioner Thomas J. Morgan responded to the Lumbee request with the following statement:

> While I regret exceedingly that the provisions made by the State of North Carolina are entirely inadequate, I find it quite impractical to render any assistance at this time. . . . So long as the immediate wards of the government (some 36,000 Indian children) are so insufficiently provided for, I do not see how I can consistently render any assistance to the Croatans or any other civilized tribes.

Testifying in 1988, Assistant Secretary of Indian Affairs Ross Swimmer (Cherokee), said a major reason for the administration's opposition to Lumbee recognition was "the sheer [financial] impact, which is estimated to be $30 to $100 million per year." BIA officials have been quoted as saying that if it had not been for the size of the tribe, the Lumbees would have been recognized long ago."

On the first three factors our original hypotheses hold. It is only on the last factor the hypothesis was contradicted. It was the very size and wealth of the Lumbee tribe that in the end helped defeat its demand for recognition. The findings have import for interest group theory and the newly emerging work in identity politics, in that the factors surrounding how tribes are socially constructed have in this area of public policy at least as much and perhaps more significance than traditional measures of power such as size, wealth, and economic resources.

Conclusion

This preliminary research and the social construction theory applied within it is intuitively understandable to indigenous nations, their citizens, and their political representatives. Tribal groups have known for the better part of nearly two centuries that Americans, particularly Anglo-Americans, harbor well-defined, if inherently contradictory ideas about who is an "Indian," and what constitutes a "tribe." In fact, indigenous groups have sometimes been able to manipulate the competing social constructions to gain tangible benefits (i.e., the Hopi in their long-standing battle with the Navajo Nation over disputed territory in Northern Arizona, effectively parlayed the image many Anglos have of them as a small, surrounded, and still largely "traditional" people in the grips of the Navajo, a numerically superior and somewhat less "traditional" people, to wrest substantial congressional victories *vis-a-vis* the Navajo Nation.)

Thus, the core political question of "Who gets what, when, and how?" is a reciprocal process in which tribes are far from passive recipients of power-driven policymakers. Of course, federal lawmakers control not only the purse strings, but the recognition string as well. Therefore, their decisions have greater weight in terms of the benefits to be dispensed or withheld. Moreover, federal policymakers are not above manipulating their constructs of Indian tribes though the motivations and goals vary from person to person and agency to agency. And while tribes today are in a better position to respond practically and quickly to such image orchestrations, they remain tenuously situated and are overly dependent on the good will of Washington lawmakers to make sound policy decisions since they lack lobbying clout.

By adding the concept of social construction to interest group theory we have been able to more completely analyze the factors associated with federal recognition. We are not suggesting that interest group theory is unimportant. On the contrary, the ability of the Catawba Tribe to use economic resources in the form of a land claim to apply pressure to the system was the catalyst that eventually led to their success in Congress. The sheer size of the Lumbee Tribe, and the implications of that size for the federal budget, has been a critical factor in the denial of their petition. Nevertheless the social construction of each tribe presents the image and framework within which those factors are addressed and at least in these cases is the more powerful determinant. The social construction of the Catawbas as a historic Indian tribe with an outstanding claim against South Carolina lent legitimacy to their petition. On the other hand, the petitions of the Lumbees, despite more resources, have been denied because the social construction of the tribe has not as yet been seen by either the federal government, or for that matter enough other recognized Indian tribes, as legitimate.

Social constructions of tribes—particularly of so-called non-recognized tribal groups—which are overtly prejudicial, based on archaic understandings, or simply steeped in wrong-headed and pseudo-scientific language, must be counteracted with balanced, historically based, accurate information so that intertribal and intergovernmental decisions as important as the extension of diplomatic relations are made in full view of the facts and not in the shadows of lingering stereotypes.

Suggested Reading

The most effective general discussion of acknowledgment is Mark E. Miller, *Forgotten Tribes: Unrecognized Indians and the Federal Acknowledgment Process* (Lincoln: University of Nebraska Press, 2004). For an in-depth look at a single group, see Gerald M. Sider,

Lumbee Indian Histories: Race, Ethnicity, and Indian Identity in the Southern United States (New York: Cambridge University Press, 1993). Two briefer treatments are Bruce Miller, "After the F. A. P.: Tribal Reorganization after Federal Recognition," *Journal of Ethnic Studies* 17, no. 2 (1989): 89–100; and Frank W. Porter III, "In Search of Recognition: Federal Indian Policy and the Landless Tribes of Western Washington," *American Indian Quarterly* 14, no. 2 (1990): 113–32.

Conclusion

This volume's introduction posed the question, "Why do Indians, who comprise such a small part of American society, continue to receive so much more attention than their numbers seem to warrant?" These readings provide a variety of possible answers. At least three broad reasons may explain the attention and popularity Native people continue to engender. First, American Indians acted in ways that differed substantially from other American minority groups. They held the land and its resources. Occasionally they represented a tangible, physical threat to other Americans. They expressed little desire to join the dominant society. Second, since the era of James Fennimore Cooper and George Catlin in the early nineteenth century, the identity of American Indians was hopelessly tied to images presented by the nation's literature, arts, and the entertainment industry. Third, the success of American territorial expansion came as a result of Native loss and near destruction, and this may have engendered a sense of guilt among some Americans.

Whatever the reasons for their continuing popular appeal, scholars find that certain aspects of the present American Indian experience do not promote an understanding of national social issues. Indian gaming, for example, which has grown into a multi-billion dollar industry since its 1988 inception, has drawn attention throughout the country. Some Americans believe that this business gives Native people an unfair economic advantage over non-Indians. At the same time, some tribal members worry about the potential difficulties posed by organized crime and that social problems related to gambling addiction will merely add to existing reservation issues. Thus far scholars have written little about gaming, but to date they have no choice. Few casino records, if any, are available, so research on the topic remains limited.

Increased enforcement of tribal treaty rights raises similar concerns. In many states between the Great Lakes and the Rocky Mountains, white hunters and fishermen living near tribal reservations complain repeatedly that Indians get special or favored treatment. Indians can, at times, avoid state game restrictions on when and how they can hunt or fish. Despite numerous court decisions in support of Indian treaty rights disputes continue over a variety of similar issues.

Since the Red Power movement of the 1960s and 1970s, tribal groups have objected to the use of Indian names, likenesses, and logos by professional, college, and university athletic teams. In some cases—Stanford University, for example—the institution changed its team mascot. Others declined. Florida State University actually obtained public support for its mascot from groups of Florida Seminoles. At the University of Illinois upper-level administrators continue to support the school's team mascot. Using Indian symbols for mascots has become so contentious that in 2005 the governing body for college sports, the National Collegiate Athletic Association, threatened to prevent teams refusing to change or drop their Indian symbols from playing in national tournaments.

In 1996, the discovery of skeletal remains (the Kennewick Man) along the Columbia River, drew national headlines and created legal controversy. Based on the provisions of the Native American Grave Protection and Repatriation Act of 1990, it seemed clear that the remains had to be given to a Native group for reburial. This did not occur, but the lingering dispute caused great frustration and bitterness between Indian leaders on one side and anthropologists and museum personnel on the other. Issues related to the returning of funerary objects, sacred artifacts, and human remains continue to draw the attention of scholars and newscasters alike.

Indian self-determination and local sovereignty likewise continue to be topics of debate for both the federal government and tribal authorities. Beginning with the idea that reservation governments should exercise local powers much like those of a city or county, this concept has moved beyond those original jurisdictions. Today tribal governments quarrel with other local or state officials as they seek to expand their authority. These disputes have yet to receive much scholarly attention, but the related topic of tribal acknowledgement has caught the interest of many researchers. The final essay by McCulloch and Wilkins offers an example of what may lie ahead as Native groups strive to gain tribal status and begin to put self-determination into practice.

For generations Indian education has drawn a great deal of attention from officials, reformers, Indian communities, and scholars. Much of that writing examined the operations of the boarding schools, but by the early twenty-first century the focus shifted. The development of over thirty Indian tribal colleges has attracted the interest of researchers. Located mostly in the northern states, from Michigan west to Washington, the colleges represent major tribal investments and attempts to help educate reservation dwellers. They also became sources of immense local pride. This educational movement succeeded to the point where it has generated a quasi-scholarly quarterly publication, the *Tribal College Journal*, that has been published for the last eighteen years. These institutions and the increasing numbers of young Indians funded by casino revenue now at state colleges and universities mark some of the distinct changes that education is bringing to Indian country. Can scholars be far behind in examining the new and increasing opportunities in Indian education?

Study Questions

Chapter 1. Shoemaker, "How Indians Got Red"

1. What colors did English and French colonists use to describe American Indians?
2. When and why did Eastern tribes begin to identify themselves as red?
3. What connections does the author make between the use of color labels for Native people and developing racial attitudes toward them?

Chapter 2. Bowden, "Spanish Missions, Cultural Conflict, and the Pueblo Revolt of 1680"

1. What similarities did Spanish missionaries see between their religious beliefs and those of the Pueblo people?
2. What were the basic differences between the two religious worldviews?
3. How does the author explain the focus of the attacks on the missionaries during the revolt?

Chapter 3. Anderson, "King Philip's Herds"

1. In what ways did the colonists' livestock cause changes in everyday life for the Indians?
2. How did tribal people respond to those changes?
3. Is the author successful in connecting disputes over livestock to the growing antagonism between the tribes and the colonists?

Chapter 4. Hämäläinen, "The Rise and Fall of Plains Indian Horse Cultures"

1. What were the positive results of obtaining horses for the people of the Southern Plains?
2. What negative impact did the horse culture have for the Indians?
3. In the long run, does the author see horses as more positive or more negative for plains groups? Why?

Chapter 5. Merrell, "The Indians' New World"

1. Which elements in colonial life does the author present as destructive to Catawba life and society?
2. What tactics did the Indians use to deal with these elements? How successful were they?
3. How does the author explain Catawba survival?

Chapter 6. Cave, "The Delaware Prophet Neolin"

1. Why does the author say that Indian prophets begin to offer new teachings?
2. To what extent were Neolin's teachings new to the Indians? How much and in what ways did he adapt Christian ideas into his teachings?
3. In what ways were Neolin's ideas important at the time? Why?

Chapter 7. Calloway, "'We Have Always Been the Frontier'"

1. Why does the author say that one cannot understand the impact of the American Revolution on the Shawnees without looking beyond the 1776–83 period?
2. How did the major tribal divisions attempt to use the war to their own benefit? Were any of them successful? Why?
3. What did this tribe gain because of the disruptions caused by the war? What did it lose?

Chapter 8. Akers, "Removing the Heart of the Choctaw People"

1. What sources does the author claim that most historians ignore when they write Indian history? Why is her point important?
2. Which Choctaw ideas does she present as being of central importance for gaining a thorough understanding of the Removal experience?
3. Is her evidence persuasive? Why?

Chapter 9. Nichols, "Backdrop for Disaster"

1. Who were the Arikara Indians? Why was this war important?
2. Which groups of whites and Indians played central roles in events leading to the fighting? Which person or group was most important? Explain.
3. How did the actions of the U.S. government fit into the story?

Chapter 10. Lansing, "Plains Indian Women and Interracial Marriage in the Upper Missouri Trade, 1804–1868"

1. In what ways did Native women have a direct part in the upper Missouri Valley fur trade?
2. Did the trade change their situations in their home villages? Why?
3. How important were mixed marriages for individual traders? Why?

Chapter 11. DeMallie, "Touching the Pen"

1. Does the author consider the minutes of treaty negotiations to be reasonably accurate? Why?
2. In what ways did Indians try to control treaty negotiations? Were they often successful?
3. What may be learned about tribal leadership from the treaty councils?

Chapter 12. Fisher, "'They Mean to be Indians Always'"

1. Why was the Warm Springs agent angry with some Indians on his reservation?
2. What did the so-called Columbia Indians expect to achieve when they refuse to stay on the reservation?
3. How successful were they? Why was the agent unable to retain control of the local situation?

Chapter 13. Andrews, "Turning the Tables on Assimilation"

1. What did white teachers at the Pine Ridge day schools expect to accomplish? What did the Lakota want the schools to do?
2. What methods did the teachers use? How successful were they? Why?
3. How did the schools come to be used as local cultural centers?

Chapter 14. James, "The Allotment Period on the Nez Perce Reservation"

1. What was allotment? How was it supposed to work?
2. What did local ranchers and farmers expect to get from allotment?
3. Does the author consider allotment among the Nez Perce to have been a success or a failure?

Chapter 15. Adams, "More than a Game"

1. What were the central goals of the Carlisle Indian School? How did school leaders see athletics as a way of achieving those goals?
2. How did football players view their competition against major eastern colleges? How did the press depict their games?
3. What does the author suggest was the major result of the Carlisle football program? Did it achieve school goals? Why?

Chapter 16. Abbott, "Alcohol and the Anishinaabeg of Minnesota in the Early Twentieth Century"

1. What stereotypes about Indian alcohol abuse does the author identify?
2. What range of Indian drinking patterns does the author examine?
3. In what ways are those patterns similar to or different from present stereotypes? Explain.

Chapter 17. Rosier, "The Old System is No Success"

1. What does the author present as the standard view of how the Indian Reorganization Act (IRA) worked among many tribes?
2. In what ways did the experiences of the Blackfeet differ from the general view?
3. Did the Blackfeet see this program as a positive experience? Why?

Chapter 18. O'Neill, "The 'Making' of the Navajo Worker"

1. What roles does the author say the federal government played in creating an off-reservation labor force?
2. In what ways did Navajos control and direct their efforts to find wage labor from 1948 to the 1960s?
3. What were the major benefits the author says Indians received by working away from home? What were the social costs resulting from their jobs?

Chapter 19. Finger, "Termination and the Eastern Band of Cherokees"

1. What motivated the federal government to establish its termination program during the 1950s?
2. Explain the divisions within the Eastern Cherokee Band over this issue.
3. How and why did the Cherokees successfully avoid termination?

Chapter 20. Lawrence, "The Indian Health Service and the Sterilization of Native American Women"

1. How widespread was the practice of uninformed sterilization of young women at Indian Health Service facilities? How does the author explain this?
2. What were the long-term results of this practice?
3. How and why did the practice come to an end?

Chapter 21. Kotlowski, "Alcatraz, Wounded Knee, and Beyond"

1. What motivated Indians to launch public protests in the 1960s and 1970s?
2. How does the author explain the usually mild federal response to the early protests? When and why did this change?
3. How effective was the federal government in its dealings with Indian protesters. How does the author explain this?

Chapter 22. McCulloch and Wilkins, "'Constructing' Nations Within States"

1. What is the Federal Acknowledgment Program and how does it work?
2. What roles do Indians from other tribes and those in the Bureau of Indian Affairs play in this process?
3. Why do the authors think that the Catawba Tribe succeeded while the nearby Lumbee Tribe failed to achieve federal recognition?

Contributors

Kathryn A. Abbott is a developmental editor in history for Bedford/St. Martin's Press.

David Wallace Adams is Professor Emeritus of History at Cleveland State University.

Donna L. Akers is Assistant Professor of History at the University of Nebraska.

Virginia DeJohn Anderson is Professor of History at the University of Colorado.

Thomas G. Andrews is Assistant Professor of History at California State University at Northridge.

Henry Warner Bowden is Professor of Religion at Rutgers University.

Colin G. Calloway is Professor of History at Dartmouth College.

Alfred A. Cave is Professor of History at the University of Toledo.

Raymond J. DeMallie is Professor of Anthropology at Indiana University.

John R. Finger is Professor Emeritus of History at the University of Tennessee.

Andrew H. Fisher is Assistant Professor of History at the College of William and Mary.

Pekka Hämäläinen is Assistant Professor of History at the University of California, Santa Barbara.

Elizabeth James is Assistant Professor of History at the University of Alaska-Anchorage.

Dean J. Kotlowski is Associate Professor of History at Salisbury University.

Michael Lansing is Assistant Professor of History at Augsburg College.

Jane Lawrence is deceased.

Anne Merline McCulloch is Professor of American Government at Columbia College.

James H. Merrell is Professor of History at Vassar College.

Roger L. Nichols is Professor of History at the University of Arizona.

Colleen O'Neill is Associate Professor of History at Utah State University.

Paul C. Rosier is Assistant Professor of History at Villanova University.

Nancy Shoemaker is Professor of History at the University of Connecticut.

David E. Wilkins is Associate Professor of American Indian Studies at the University of Minnesota.